Aging and Diversity

2nd Edition

Aging and Diversity

2nd Edition

An Active Learning Experience

Chandra M. Mehrotra • Lisa S. Wagner

Routledge
Taylor & Francis Group
New York   London

Routledge
Taylor & Francis Group
711 Third Avenue,
New York, NY, 10017, USA

Routledge
Taylor & Francis Group
2 Park Square
Milton Park, Abingdon
Oxon OX14 4RN

International Standard Book Number-13: 978-0-415-95214-9 (Softcover) 978-0-415-95213-2 (Hardcover)

Library of Congress Cataloging-in-Publication Data

Mehrotra, Chandra.
  Aging and diversity : an active learning experience / by Chandra M. Mehrotra and Lisa Wagner. -- 2nd ed.
    p. cm.
  Originally published: Aging and diversity : an active learning experience / by Stephen B. Fried, Chandra M. Mehrotra. Washington, D.C. : Taylor & Francis, c1998.
  Includes bibliographical references and index.
  ISBN 978-0-415-95213-2 (hardbound : alk. paper) -- ISBN 978-0-415-95214-9 (pbk. : alk. paper)
  1. Older people--United States. 2. Minority older people—United States. 3. Pluralism (Social sciences) 4. Intercultural communication. I. Wagner, Lisa (Lisa Smith) II. Fried, Stephen. Aging and diversity. III. Title.

HQ1061.F725 2008
305.26089'00973--dc22   2008021690

Visit the Taylor & Francis Web site at
http://www.taylorandfrancis.com

and the Routledge Web site at
http://www.routledge.com

To Stephen B. Fried
who was a wonderful colleague, teacher,
collaborator and scholar. He played a key role in
preparation of the first edition of the book. We are
saddened by the unexpected loss of this great colleague.
His emphasis on active learning will continue to
influence our thinking, writing and teaching.

Contents

Acknowledgments

To work on a book about aging, as we ourselves age, is an interesting experience. To share this experience as co-authors who are from different ethnic and cultural backgrounds, of different genders, and from different age groups enriched both our writing and our appreciation for life. Writing a book, as is true with many things in life, takes much longer than one expects. This book would not have been completed without the assistance and support of many people.

We are particularly indebted to the National Institute on Aging whose funding to Chandra Mehrotra for the Research Training Institutes at the College of St. Scholastica (R13–AG14120) provided the venue for us to meet, and whose subsequent funding to Lisa Wagner for research on stereotype threat and older adults (R03-AG20777-01) was due in no small part to these institutes. In particular, we are grateful to NIA staff members Richard Suzman, Robin Barr, Sidney Stahl, and Jared Jobe (now of National Heart, Lung, and Blood Institute), for their dedication to issues around aging and diversity and for their continuing support to help bring new researchers into this field.

Our families provided support in so many ways throughout the length of this project. Chandra Mehrotra expresses deep appreciation to Indra Mehrotra, his wife and best friend, for her enduring support. He also recognizes their two adult children, Vijay and Gita, whose personal and career development brings increased enrichment to their family. Whether it be the addition of a wonderful daughter-in-law, Jennifer Black, or the fulfilling way in which their academic lives now intersect, life's transitions are enhanced through family. Lisa Wagner gives both her gratitude and love to Todd Wagner, her husband and true life-partner, who provided both emotional support and hard work as a very involved dad and spouse spending time with their children and preparing meals as she worked on this project. Without his support, she would not have started, let alone been able to finish this book. As our writing progressed, our families also grew with Lisa Wagner welcoming a new daughter, Jessica Rae, to join son Cameron in their family and Chandra Mehrotra becoming a grandfather to Eden Lillian. These life changes helped us appreciate the importance of family in every aspect of life.

Chandra Mehrotra would like to express his gratitude to Larry Goodwin, President of the College of St. Scholastica (CSS) for his continuing interest and support in all of his activities related to aging. Lisa Wagner would like to recognize three faculty members at the University of Washington who provided the interest, skills, and courage to pursue her initial interests in aging: Naomi Gottlieb, Edwina Uehara, and Ana Mari Cauce. This support was continued at the University of

San Francisco (USF) where she thanks her colleagues in the USF department of psychology and the university administration for their amazing mentoring and support. We give our gratitude to the library staff at both CSS and USF for responding to our many requests throughout the preparation of this book. Without their ongoing work and collections, we could not have written this book.

We offer our tremendous thanks to Beth Helfont whose timely entrance into the midst of this project and her incredible hard work allowed us to complete our long-distance collaboration. We also appreciate the work of our undergraduate students, Katie Ek, Heather Kuhn, Alejandro Nuno, Kimberly Schultz, and Roberta Sutton, who assisted in all stages from creating the initial reference database to indexing the page proofs.

We thank George Zimmar at Routledge whose unflagging support for providing a complete examination of aging and diversity through this revision was so important. We appreciate Fred Coppersmith's shepherding us through the review process, and finally, we offer our gratitude to Marta Moldvai and Sylvia Wood; without their editorial assistance, the different parts of each chapter would have blurred together without distinction. Truly this text is the result of many people's hard work.

About the Authors

Chandra M. Mehrotra is professor of psychology and dean of special projects at the College of St. Scholastica in Duluth, Minnesota. He received his Ph.D. in psychology from Ohio State University. He is a fellow of the American Psychological Association and the Gerontological Society of America. He received his college's Distinguished Teaching Award in 1979 and the APA Division 20 Mentor Award in 2003. He directs faculty training programs in aging research with support provided by the National Institute on Aging, National Institutes of Health, and the Hartford Foundation. His books include *Teaching and Aging* (Jossey-Bass, 1984), *Distance Learning: Principles for Effective Design, Delivery and Evaluation* (Sage, 2001), and *Measuring Up: Educational Assessment Challenges and Practices for Psychology* (APA Books, 2004). He has guest-edited two special issues of the journal *Educational Gerontology*: (a) *Strengthening Gerontology and Geriatrics Education*; and (b) *Fostering Aging Research in Undergraduate Psychology Programs*. His activities with Native American communities include civic engagement among elders, culturally appropriate program evaluation, intergenerational relationships, and improvement of teaching and learning in tribal colleges. He currently serves as a member of American Psychological Association's Committee on Aging and the Minnesota Board of Examiners for Nursing Home Administrators.

Lisa Wagner is associate professor in the Department of Psychology at the University of San Francisco (USF). She completed her B.A. in honors English language and literature at the University of Michigan, and her Ph.D. in social and personality psychology at the University of Washington. As Chair of the USF Interdisciplinary Committee on Aging, she helps create opportunities for positive, mutually beneficial interactions between younger and older people on campus. She has conducted research funded by the National Institute on Aging on stereotype threat and older adults, she has designed and offered a course entitled *Communication between Generations* that enrolled both younger and older adult students, and she currently teaches courses on the social psychology of aging and the psychology of prejudice. She has published on issues related to stereotyping and older adults and serves as a reviewer for *Psychology and Aging*.

Introduction to the Second Edition

Since the publication of the first edition of *Aging and Diversity* in 1998, we have witnessed an explosion of new knowledge and a dramatic increase in the number of conference presentations, journal articles, monographs, and Internet sites related to aging in populations from different ethnic and cultural groups. A number of federal agencies, such as the National Institutes of Health, the Administration on Aging, and the Health Resources and Services Administration have given high priority to ethnic and cultural diversity in their agendas for research and training related to aging. Why? This increased attention by both researchers and funding agencies is being given because, within the rapidly increasing population of older Americans as a whole, elders from different ethnic and cultural groups are growing at a much faster rate than those from European American backgrounds. Despite the continuing increase in this segment of the population, and the ongoing support for research on aging and diversity, limited attention has been given to make new research and scholarship accessible to current students and service providers. We have, therefore, prepared this revised edition. Our hope is that making new research available to those who work with or are planning to work with diverse elders will help reduce the gap between the generation of new knowledge and its utilization in addressing the needs of this population. This, in turn, will improve the lives of elders from diverse ethnic and cultural groups.

Although there has been a dramatic increase in research and scholarship on aging, there is an unevenness in the quality and amount of data currently available on key aspects of diversity. For example, there is a huge literature on Blacks and religion and spirituality and extremely limited information on religion and spirituality in Gay and Lesbian populations. So, this is an emerging field and availability of research varies across diverse groups. However, as noted earlier, new research continues to become available at a rapid pace and indications are that this pace is likely to continue.

To make these advances accessible to you on a continuing basis, the revised edition includes a new feature called Aging and Diversity Online. These Internet sources interspersed throughout the book will allow you to look at new research and publications and thus keep yourself abreast of recent developments in your area of interest. As you read the chapters and use these Internet sites, you will note that the study of aging is multidisciplinary in nature. It draws upon knowledge and methodology from disciplines such as psychology, sociology, social work, medicine, nursing, occupational therapy, physical therapy, public health, epidemiology, humanities, and economics. Professionals who contribute to aging research represent a wide range of disciplines and work in a variety of institutions, academic departments, programs, and settings.

ACTIVE LEARNING EMPHASIS

As with the first edition, our overreaching goal for the revised edition remains the same: to present up-to-date knowledge and scholarship in a way that engages students in active learning. Active learning is, therefore, an integral part of this text. We are cognizant of the fact that students who are learning about diversity and aging are themselves from diverse groups in terms of ethnicity or race, national origin, gender, age, language, social class, rural/urban community location, and sexual orientation. Since different "people learn in different ways" (Meyers & Jones, 1993, p. 10), active learning strategies can be extremely helpful in strengthening their education in diversity and aging. We have tried to include the following important characteristics of active learning in the text: (a) placing more emphasis on developing learners' skills rather than on simply transmitting information; (b) engaging students in higher order thinking (analysis, synthesis, and evaluation); and (c) encouraging them to explore their personal values and attitudes. We hope that by engaging learners in this way, they will be able to understand and apply the concepts presented here in ways that will improve both the lives of older people and their own aging experience.

ELEMENTS OF DIVERSITY

Unlike texts that focus on one aspect of diversity, we discuss the following elements of diversity and how they relate to aging:

- Gender
- Race or ethnicity
- Religious affiliation and spirituality
- Social class
- Rural/urban community location
- Sexual orientation

Consideration of only one element of diversity conveys a limited view of diversity and makes it difficult to piece together a comprehensive understanding of aging in the United States. We hope that by focusing on these different elements of diversity, we will convey some of the rich complexities of our diverse culture—complexities that provide both challenges to meet the needs of diverse people and opportunities to learn better ways of living as we age.

DISTINCTIVE FEATURES

There are several features of this text that we hope will increase learners' understanding of the material presented here. Our opening vignettes use short stories to present a sampling of how the issues in the chapter apply to diverse elders. Although these vignettes are fictional, they are also realistic portrayals of diverse elders and issues they face. Throughout each chapter, we also present several active learning experiences, such as interviewing diverse elders, conducting Internet research, and giving an in-depth analysis of a specific case study. Instructors may ask students to complete these exercises for a specific class assignment or discussion, or students may choose to do them independently simply to enhance their own learning. These activities require that students actively work with the concepts being presented in the chapter. We hope that students will find these activities interesting and engaging. This, in turn, will increase their understanding of aging and diversity. Instructors may find that certain active learning experiences are not suitable for some classes or for particular students, and they need to be sensitive to the fact that some students may be uncomfortable engaging in activities related to various topics (e.g., death and dying, family customs). Students' values and need for privacy should be respected. Also, some of the activities ask students to interview community or family members. Principles of confidentiality and informed consent should be shared with students before they initiate these activities. Instructors may wish to submit selected learning activities to their institutional review boards if doing so conforms with institutional policy.

Following each chapter summary, we have provided a quiz to help learners ascertain whether they have truly learned the material; the key for the quiz includes details about correct and incorrect responses so that additional learning can occur. The glossary gives definitions for key concepts covered in the chapter. The suggested readings and audiovisual resources also serve as a guide to additional information on the chapter's topics. Again, information on diverse elders can be difficult to find. With this text, we have provided many "next step" sources of information in case readers would like more information about a particular group or issue for their work, for their own personal growth and development, or even for an advanced term paper assignment.

WHY DID WE CHOOSE TO FOCUS ON THE TOPICS WE HAVE INCLUDED IN THE TEXT?

First, we selected content areas that are influenced by diversity and have a body of knowledge currently available. Second, the topic areas we have selected will also provide readers with opportunities to learn about concepts, research designs, measures, and analytic approaches useful in conducting research with diverse racial, ethnic, and cultural groups. Third, we also selected topics that convey useful knowledge. We present information that has implications for designing and delivering culturally sensitive programs and services. In other words, we selected topics that have a knowledge base useful for those who are working with or plan to work with older adults and their families.

A BRIEF OVERVIEW OF THE BOOK

With the goal of making up-to-date information accessible to learners, the book has been completely rewritten. The new edition devotes an entire chapter to research methods rather than to present them as a part of the chapter on psychological aging. In addition, this edition includes two new chapters on health—one focusing on health beliefs and behaviors and the other focusing on illness and health inequalities. Also, within each chapter, we have expanded the content to address key elements of diversity. In addition, at the end of each chapter, we have provided recommendations for related readings and audiovisual resources. A brief overview of what is included in the book is presented below.

In Chapter 1, "Aging and Diversity," we provide an in-depth discussion of diversity and how it applies to aging. Because traditional research methods and measures may or may not work well for different minority groups, "Research Methods," Chapter 2, examines areas of the research process that have particular relevance for conducting research with minority communities. This chapter also includes sections on research methods that are gaining increased use with diverse communities. Other chapters also include discussions of methodological issues that one should consider in conducting research with diverse populations. In "Psychology and Aging," Chapter 3, we examine how race and ethnicity influence basic psychological processes of sensation, perception, cognition, and memory. We also present social psychological concepts of attitudes, stereotyping, and prejudice and discuss how attitudes toward ethnicity/race, aging, and older people can intersect to affect both our treatment of older people and our own aging processes. Chapter 4, "Health Beliefs, Behaviors, and Services" considers the role of diversity in how older people define health and in how they maintain health as they age. It also examines how health-related services are structured and paid for in the United States. Chapter 5, "Inequalities in Health" examines common health issues for older people from diverse backgrounds and discusses disparities in health status across ethnic groups.

In "Informal and Formal Care for Older Persons," Chapter 6, we outline the living arrangements of older people, and discuss both informal and formal caregiving among Blacks, Hispanics, Asian Americans, Native Americans, and Lesbians, Gays, and Bisexuals. We discuss the barriers that hinder the use of available services, present how to overcome these obstacles, and also describe examples of programs and services that have been successful in addressing health and social service needs of ethnically diverse elders and their caregivers.

The work and retirement experiences of older persons (Chapter 7) represent another area that is significantly affected by their gender, race, and class. The concepts of "retirement" and "leisure" can and do have different meanings for persons from different socioeconomic backgrounds. Affluent retirees enjoy the greatest discretion in choosing among productive and leisure activities. Many of them continue to play leadership roles through volunteer positions in the community and have the financial resources to pursue their leisure activities. On the other hand, there are others who have spent their lives struggling to make ends meet and can't afford to retire completely. They need to supplement their economic resources with part-time work (Calasanti & Bonanno, 1992).

Throughout the book we introduce examples from varied perspectives that lead to new insights related to aging processes and experiences. We will see, for example, in Chapter 8, "Religious Affiliation and Spirituality," that Muslims (followers of the religion of Islam) believe that both health and illness come from God and healing comes from supplications, prayers, and fasting. Similarly, religiously committed Buddhists, Hindus, and Native Americans have other theological doctrines and behavioral customs that influence their attitudes and beliefs related to the role of spirituality in old age as well as toward therapeutic interventions. We also present research regarding the high prevalence of religious activity among older Blacks and outline its implications for the well-being of this population. Finally, "Death, Dying and Bereavement," Chapter 9, explores the role that diversity plays in conceptualizations of death and bereavement.

In short, this text will introduce you to a wide variety of topics that are central to an understanding of the many ways in which elements of diversity such as ethnicity, gender, rural/urban community location, religious affiliation, class, and sexual orientation affect the aging experience. As noted earlier, increased attention is now being given to conducting research in diversity and aging and providing culturally sensitive services. Consider this book a starter kit toward reaching the goal of developing a broader and deeper understanding of the full spectrum of the aging experience.

REFERENCES

Calasanti, T. M., & Bonanno, A. (1992). Working overtime: Economic restructuring and retirement of a class. *Sociological Quarterly*, 33(1), 135–152.

Meyers, C., & Jones, T. B. (1993). *Promoting active learning*. San Francisco: Jossey-Bass.

1

Aging and Diversity

- What do we mean by diversity? What does it include?
- Why should we focus on diversity and aging?
- What are the demographics of American elders in terms of each element of diversity?
- Why is it important to distinguish between (a) heterogeneity *within* a group, and (b) differences *across* several groups?

When you hear the words "senior citizen," what picture pops into your head? An older White man? Although our stereotypes and even our research on aging have historically focused on White males, in reality, the older adult population reflects the colorful diversity of the U.S. society. Differences in ethnicity, culture, gender, sexual orientation, social class, and even rural or urban community location create unique circumstances for these different groups as they age. Consider, for example, the following vignettes:

Vignette 1

Lucinda Williams has always worked throughout her life. Her parents moved their family to the city during WWII when African Americans could find work in the wartime factories. She worked as a waitress to pay for her schooling, she worked as a nurse for 30 years, and even when she retired from nursing due to health reasons, she took care of her grandchildren during the day while their parents worked. Now she is done working and she celebrates this fact. Her children and grandchildren gently tease her about her "van" in which she travels around visiting her family and taking the occasional trip to Reno to gamble. When they see her pulling up to their house for a visit, they know that they are in for an exciting and fun time. But if any of them asks her to babysit, she'll say, "No thanks, I've done all of that already. Now is my time to live."

Vignette 2

Freda Santos immigrated to the United States with her husband from the Philippines when she was 20. She has had a variety of jobs in the United States, most recently running a convalescent home out of her house. When her husband became ill with Hepatitis C, Freda took care of him in her home until he recently died. But when her children grew up, they all migrated to another area of the country and Freda missed them. So, she sold her home and joined her family. She now lives with one of her daughters and several nieces and nephews in a large house. They have frequent family gatherings at the house and Freda is pleased to be able to see all of her children on a regular basis.

Vignette 3

Michael Nelson has spent his adult life making close friends who live around him—he calls them "chosen family" as opposed to his biological family, who cut off relations with him when he told them that he was gay 30 years ago. Michael and his partner Samuel recently celebrated their 25th anniversary by getting married. It had been a lifelong dream for both of them and they are glad to have lived long enough to see it as a reality. Even though they are now married, they both worry about what will happen when they become ill. They worry that biological family may take over and prevent them from honoring their health care wishes and from being together in their old age. Even if their families do leave them alone, if one of them needs care in a long-term-care facility, they aren't sure that the other partner will be allowed to comfort him there.

Vignette 4

Ruth Levy's husband had always been the driver in their family, but when he became ill 10 years ago, she started driving again at 82 years of age. She relished the freedom that driving gave her and often drove her friends to the local shopping mall or grocery store. Recently, she started having traffic accidents. Her children, who live several hours away, enlisted the help of Ruth's physician and her rabbi to convince Ruth to stop driving. After many difficult conversations, Ruth finally agreed to sell her car. Her retirement community offers frequent shuttles to stores, but Ruth now feels stifled by her lack of freedom. Since giving up her car a year ago, she has withdrawn from her friends and spends most of her time alone in her apartment. At 92, she feels that there isn't much more left for her to do.

WHAT DO WE MEAN BY DIVERSITY?

As you can see from these vignettes, diversity is more than just the color of someone's skin. Instead of assuming that all people are the same and that they all have the same experiences, when we talk about diversity we often focus on the vast range of human experience that is created by differences between people. There are many things that people can differ on, for example, gender, age, community location, etc. When a group of people share the same difference (for example, they are all women, or they are all the same age), this difference creates social categories. When we talk about *diversity,* we are looking at differences shared by a group of people that may affect the experiences that the person from this group has in life as well as how he or she is viewed and treated by others. In this text, we will be using the term diversity to refer to these social category differences between groups of people. Of course, even though people are grouped together by a shared social category, people within a group can be very different from one another. These within-group differences refer to their heterogeneity. Recognizing the importance of both diversity between groups and heterogeneity within groups is essential for understanding the full spectrum of aging. Historically, aging research has focused on the mainstream population or on what was perceived to be the majority or dominant group. We will examine the aging experience of diverse or different groups.

WHY SHOULD WE FOCUS ON DIVERSITY AND AGING?

Whether you are a traditional student enrolled in a gerontology program, a service provider engaged in working with older people, or just someone interested in the aging process, you may be wondering why it is important to focus on aging and diversity. Isn't it true that all older people have the same basic needs that must be met? Isn't it also true that we use the same concepts and principles in the study of aging regardless of which ethnic groups we focus on? Isn't it also true that we maintain the same standards in conducting research with all segments of the older population? Why, then, should we devote our attention to their ethnic and cultural backgrounds, socioeconomic status, gender, sexual orientation, religion and spirituality, and even work and retirement experiences? Furthermore, how will research be more useful, your services be more effective, and your understanding be affected if you become knowledgeable about the life course of members from different groups? In this section we address such questions and discuss why a focus on diversity and aging should be an essential component of your study of aging processes.

Examining the aging experience from multiple perspectives assists us in developing an understanding of human development and aging that is truly universal. The scientific study of aging implies that basic processes and mechanisms should be investigated in populations that include participants from different genders, ethnic groups, and social classes, not just those conveniently available to investigators. Why? Race, gender, culture, and ethnicity are not merely independent variables defining group membership and structural position, but instead more fundamentally may influence basic psychological processes of perception, cognition, intellectual functioning, health beliefs, health behaviors, and social interaction. Given this perspective, aging research should be pluralistic in its orientation; should consider the important contribution diversity may make in expanding our conceptualizations, constructs, and methods; and should assist in the evolution of a science of human development and aging that is truly universal (Jackson, 1989). Universalism assumes that although people have surface differences, at a deep level we all share common core characteristics (for example, what we drink differs by culture, but we all must drink to survive). Although you may argue that the assumption of universality is questionable, remember that inattention to ethnic and cultural factors in the vast majority of current research represents a tacit statement of universality. Furthermore, failure to ensure adequate representation of all segments of the population in aging research results in limited generalizability and applicability of findings.

What you learn from working with people of different genders, races, ethnic groups, and social classes will deepen your understanding of aging and old age and perhaps will influence the research you undertake, the programs you design, and the services you provide. We believe that interacting with diverse populations, listening to their voices, and developing an understanding and appreciation of their aging experience are likely to yield new insights, create the fusion of horizons, and provide new lenses through which to view the multiple social worlds that exist in the same community. Trying on different lenses can help you see significant aspects of social reality that you may have overlooked in the past (Stoller & Gibson, 2000). The new attitudes and insights that you develop may, in turn, shape what research questions you ask, what data you collect, how you collect these data, and how you interpret your observations. For example, by observing how adult daughters in different ethnic groups provide care to older relatives while at the same time meeting the demands of other roles, you may design creative research to explore the burden and rewards of providing care to frail elders from multiple perspectives— perspectives you may not have considered earlier. In addition, what you learn from working with ethnic and cultural minorities may be useful in designing new programs and services for the mainstream population. For example, the knowledge of how religion and spirituality help African American elders in coping with stress and losses may be useful as you work with members of other groups who are experiencing difficulty in coping with recent losses. Similarly, drawing upon what you learn from the grandparenting role played by elders in Native American, African American, and Asian American families, you can design effective training programs for grandparents from the mainstream population. In short, being knowledgeable about the experiences, traditions, and values of different genders, races, ethnic groups, and social classes will enrich your understanding of aging and old age and will prepare you to live and work in a pluralistic society.

Aging and Diversity Online: Major Websites on Aging

The Internet provides a vast array of information on aging, diversity, and even some information on aging *and* diversity. One difficulty of the Internet is wading through the multitude of hits to find relevant sites with up-to-date, trustworthy information. Throughout the text, we will list websites that are related to the points we discuss. In addition to providing relevant background information, these websites will help you find areas of interest that are beyond the scope of this text. Major websites that provide information on aging in general are listed below:

National Institute on Aging (NIA). NIA is a part of the National Institutes of Health (NIH), and "leads a broad scientific effort to understand the nature of aging and to extend the healthy, active years of life." http://www.nia.nih.gov/

The Gerontological Society of America (GSA). GSA is a professional organization that provides researchers, educators, and service providers with opportunities to improve the quality of life as people age. http://geron.org/

The American Society on Aging (ASA). ASA is a diverse, multidisciplinary association whose goal is to "to support the commitment and enhance the knowledge and skills of those who seek to improve the quality of life of older adults and their families." http://www.asaging.org/index.cfm

American Psychological Association (APA). APA is an excellent resource for researchers, service providers, educators, and students interested in psychology. APA has 53 divisions that focus on different areas within psychology. At least six of these have particular relevance to aging and diversity: Division 9, Society for the Psychological Study of Social Issues (SPSSI); Division 12, Society of Clinical Psychology; Division 20, Adulthood and Aging; Division 35, Society for the Psychology of Women; Division 44, Society for the Psychological Study of Gay, Lesbian, and Bisexual issues; and Division 45, Society of the Psychological Study of Ethnic Minority Issues. http://www.apa.org

American Association of Retired Persons (AARP). AARP is a nonprofit organization dedicated to helping older Americans achieve lives of independence, dignity, and purpose. The association has an extensive array of publications and reports on issues of significance to older minorities. http://www.aarp.org

---

WHAT ELEMENTS OF DIVERSITY WILL WE INCLUDE IN THIS BOOK?

Clearly, some differences or social categories are more relevant than others. We could categorize everyone in terms of eye color, but this characteristic by itself is not particularly relevant to aging. Instead, we will focus on elements of diversity that do have an important impact on aging. Throughout this book, we will focus on the following elements of diversity:

- gender
- race or ethnicity
- religious affiliation and spirituality
- social class
- rural/urban community location
- sexual orientation

Some elements of diversity in which we are interested are, at least on the surface, more clear cut and biologically determined. For example, gender is one primary category on which people differ. Early research focused on what was considered the primary or mainstream group—men—and then assumed that any important findings would generalize to women as well. One look at the demographics of aging shows that this focus omits more than half of the picture, as 58% of people over age 65 in the United States are women and women make up 69% of people over age 85 (Federal Interagency Forum on Aging-Related Statistics, 2004). Although biology determines whether one is a man or a woman, many psychological and social consequences of one's gender are determined by our culture. For example, biology may determine that women bear children, but it is our culture that influences whether a woman continues to work after her child's birth. Women are more likely than men to step out of the workforce to care for children or aging family members, and this has a direct impact on their retirement income in later life.

WHAT DO WE MEAN BY RACE OR ETHNICITY?

In comparison with gender, race and ethnicity are much more difficult concepts to define. Race is often defined "in terms of physical characteristics like skin color, facial features, hair type that are common to an inbred, geographically isolated population" (Betancourt & Lopez, 1993, p. 630). But researchers have found that classifying people according to race is very difficult, as there are greater differences within racial categories than there are between them, thus making the usefulness of the categories suspect. On the other hand, people *are* treated in certain ways due to factors such as skin color, so race is an important concept. Thus, we often say that race is a *social construct,* a categorization system with strong physical, psychological, and social consequences, but without the clear biological determination of something like gender.

Take, for example, how racial classifications have changed over time in the United States. Although they are now considered "White," in 1911 people of Irish, Polish, and Italian descent were considered to be separate "races" from people who were of English descent (Cruz & Berson, 2001). Laws preventing marriage between people from different racial groups date back to 1661 and were common in the United States until 1967. These laws typically forbade marriage between Blacks and Whites, but as immigrant populations from Italy, for example, were not considered "White" when they entered the United States, marriage between Blacks and people from these immigrant groups was often not prohibited. To be categorized as Black took only one drop of Black African blood, even if one's parents were from several racial groups (Cruz & Berson, 2001). In the past, people of mixed racial heritage had to choose one group with which to identify and were often identified by others based on which group it "looked" like they belonged to. Many current older adults grew up in the era where there were more sharp delineations between racial groups and people were identified with one racial group. Now, in many areas of the country, racial identification is changing. As interracial marriage becomes more common, many younger people are multiracial and are personally identifying as such. Increasingly, ties to multiple racial groups are being recognized. As of the year 2000 census, it is possible to select more than one racial category on the U.S. Census. The fact that our categorization of race is changing supports the idea that race is a social construct that is actively created (and now changed) by society (see the concluding section of this chapter for more details on changing terminology).

Ethnicity

Given the difficulties defining race and our past experiences with race, many people turn to the concept of ethnicity. Ethnicity is often defined as one's feeling of membership toward a group with which one shares a common religion, national origin, culture, or language. Ethnicity's broad definition gives it flexibility to apply to many different groups, but can also lead to confusion. For example, people who may identify with the Latino or Hispanic ethnic group can be classified racially as Black, White, Asian, or American Indian.

Other Categorizations

Often related to race and ethnicity, we can also categorize people according to their national origin, the country in which they were born, their immigration status, and their religious affiliation. We will use the concepts of race or ethnicity, national origin and religious affiliation throughout the book. Sometimes these categories are important because a categorization has been imposed on a group of people and it affects how they are treated and the resources to which they are given access. Other times these categories are important because people self-identify with these groups and are provided with community, culture, and life-meaning through membership in them.

The last three elements of diversity on which we will focus are social class, community location, and sexual orientation. Social class or the financial resources and status that a person has certainly impact the available choices as one ages. Wealthy elders' experience of retirement is different from that of working-class elders who may have to continue working well into old age. Given that many of our nation's elders live in rural areas, it is important to understand the role that community location plays in access to health care, technology, and recreational facilities. Sexual orientation adds another layer of complexity to aging, as much of our society is not designed to accommodate anything other than heterosexual orientation. Lifelong gay or lesbian partners face unique problems as they make decisions regarding retirement, nursing home care, and social security. Although limited research has been conducted on sexual orientation's impact on aging, we will present research that has been done and point out areas where more research is needed. When we talk about aging and diversity, we have chosen areas of diversity that are particularly relevant to aging. If one did not pay attention to these areas of diversity and actively seek out information from people who differ on these characteristics, one would receive an incomplete and fragmented view of aging.

INTERACTIONAL NATURE OF ELEMENTS OF DIVERSITY AND AGING

These elements of diversity—gender, race or ethnicity, religious affiliation, social class, community location, and sexual orientation—are not independent of one another. Religious affiliation is often related to race or ethnicity, with certain religions predominating in certain ethnic groups. Similarly, ethnicity is related to social class, with some ethnic groups having greater financial resources than others. Each of these elements interacts with the others to add to the complexity of our society.

Focusing on just one element of diversity in isolation may give an incomplete picture. Thanh Tran's (1990) research on Vietnamese immigrants' English-language acculturation provides an excellent example of the interactional nature of these elements.

Tran analyzed data from a national survey of more than 2,000 Vietnamese immigrants. Many older immigrants experienced English language difficulties so profound that they were not able "to shop for food, to apply for aid, and to contact the police or fire department when needed" (Tran, 1990, p. 99). Degree of language proficiency was associated with age, gender, health, education, and length of time in the United States. Younger Vietnamese immigrants had fewer problems acquiring a second language, whereas older Vietnamese women had more difficulties learning and using English than did Vietnamese men. This latter finding may be due to the fact that in traditional Vietnamese society, women occupy roles with less status and education than their male peers. Simply looking at age, gender, or social class would not have uncovered the complex relationship between age, gender, and language acquisition. Similarly, examining any category in isolation may create inaccurate perceptions. If we focus solely on gender, for example, women who are White might be considered oppressed, but we then ignore the advantages or privileges accorded to them due to their race. Clearly, the intersections between these social categories create a complex and dynamic situation (Stoller & Gibson, 2000).

ACTIVE LEARNING EXPERIENCE: ELEMENTS OF DIVERSITY

The Case of Mrs. Osaki

The purpose of this experience is to illustrate the interaction of elements of diversity and aging. Upon completion of this activity, you will be able to:

1. List and discuss elements pertaining to the diversity of older adults.
2. Understand how these elements interact.
3. Apply this knowledge in conducting a case analysis.

This activity will require 30 minutes (15 minutes to answer the questions in groups and 15 minutes for class discussion).

Instructions:

1. Your instructor divides the class into groups of three to five people.
2. Each group answers the questions following the case.
3. Each group selects one person to record and present the group's findings to the entire class.
4. After the groups have answered the questions, the group recorders share responses with the entire class.
5. The instructor leads a class discussion on group responses.

Case Study

Read the following case study. With your group, read and analyze the case and answer the questions that follow it.

When Mrs. Osaki's only child, her daughter, moved from Japan to the United States to marry, she was happy for her. After Mrs. Osaki's husband died suddenly, her daughter brought her to the States to live with her, her husband, and their new baby. Mrs. Osaki was able to take care of the baby during the day while her daughter and son-in-law were at work. Everyone was pleased with the situation. But when Mrs. Osaki's health became increasingly frail 10 years later, there wasn't anyone at home to help her and they could not afford a full-time nurse's aide. Her daughter found a local adult daycare center and that worked for a while, but Mrs. Osaki had never really learned English well and she was isolated all day and couldn't communicate with the staff. As her health continued to decline, even the daycare center could not care for her and Mrs. Osaki was moved into a nursing home. No one is happy with this situation, but they do not know what else to do.

Discussion Questions:

1. With which groups (e.g., women, immigrants, Japanese Americans) might Mrs. Osaki identify?
2. What are some ways in which the following elements of Mrs. Osaki's diversity could interact with one another: gender, national origin, language, social class, culture, and size and location of community?
3. List three elements of diversity of one of your older adult family members.

CHANGING NATURE OF GROUPS

Within-Group and Between-Group Differences.

While there are important differences in the aging experience between groups from different ethnic, cultural, and religious backgrounds and the mainstream population, there is tremendous variability within each group as well as across different groups. For example, not all older Asian elders live in poverty, have limited education, are female, are spouseless, or are disabled. Similarly, there is substantial variability across different minority groups in their education level, economic well-being, health status, and life expectancy. This means that you cannot infer the characteristics of one minority group to another, or the characteristics of some members of a given group to all members of that group. The writings of Fernando Torres-Gil demonstrate, for example, that treating Hispanics as a monolithic group obscures major differences in the health, education, and poverty status of Cubans, Puerto Ricans, and Mexican Americans. Older people from each of these groups may have specific needs for health and social services that may not be addressed if we treat all Hispanics as a member of the same group.

Acculturation

Ethnicity is not a fixed entity. It changes in response to the experiences and interactions in the life of the individual or the group. Why? When individuals come in contact with another culture they change both culturally and psychologically in numerous and various ways. To help describe these changes, anthropologists and psychologists have coined the term acculturation, literally meaning "to move toward a culture." Acculturation is defined as culture change resulting from contact between two autonomous cultural groups. In principle, the contact results in changes to both groups. However, in practice, more change occurs in the nondominant than in the dominant group (Berry, 1994). Even within one ethnic group, acculturation can differ across individuals. For example, working with immigrants from Latin America or Asia requires not only an understanding of their ethnicity but also such factors as their age when they came to the United States.

The life course of the individuals who immigrated from another country when they were young is potentially very different from the life course of individuals who came to the United States at the age of 65 to join their adult children. The young immigrants had the opportunity to obtain education; develop language fluency; interact with people from different ethnic and cultural groups; and be exposed to a wide range of cultural beliefs, traditions, and values. Over time, these influences may have made a significant impact upon them regarding their own ethnicity, way of thinking, and adherence to traditional norms and values. Compare these young people with their parents who came to join them in the United States at the age of 65. People who immigrated when they were older may have limited familiarity with the language, religion, health care system, and cultural norms of the host society. They may achieve a functional level of adaptation to the American culture but may be much more comfortable within the ethnic communities, where they are able to maintain a traditional way of life. Because the immigrant population from Asia and Latin America is continuing to increase (He, 2002), the knowledge of their language, their religious background, their social customs, their beliefs, their values, and their cultural traditions has immediate relevance for those who currently provide or plan to provide health care and social services.

In sum, when working with members of immigrant populations, it is important to take into account (a) at what age they immigrated to the United States; (b) to what extent they consider it to be of value to maintain cultural identity and characteristics; and (c) to what extent they consider it important to interact with members of the larger society. Because their language, religious backgrounds, cultural traditions, and values may be markedly different from those of the host society, it is essential to be knowledgeable about these differences and take them into consideration when working with members of these diverse populations. The Active Learning Experience on acculturation examines these issues further.

ACTIVE LEARNING EXPERIENCE: ACCULTURATION

The purpose of this experience is to help you understand what happens to individuals when they come in contact with another culture and what are the implications for those who provide or plan to provide services to this population. Upon completion of this activity you will be able to:

1. Identify the characteristics of foreign-born individuals who differ from each other in terms of (a) maintaining their cultural and ethnic identity; and (b) interacting with members of a larger society.
2. Outline the implications of working with older immigrants with varying levels of acculturation.

   This activity will require 30 minutes (15 minutes to answer the questions in groups and 15 minutes for class discussion).

Instructions:

As we have discussed, two issues predominate in the daily lives of most individuals from different ethnic and cultural backgrounds. The first pertains to the extent to which one values maintaining one's own cultural identity, characteristics, and customs. In Figure 1.1 we have labeled this dimension Cultural Maintenance and Development. The other issue involves the extent to which one considers it desirable to seek and maintain relationships with other groups in the larger society (Contact and Participation dimension in Figure 1.1). These two issues are essentially questions of values and can be examined on a continuous scale. However, as suggested by Berry (1994), we can treat them as dichotomous ("yes" and "no") preferences, thereby creating the fourfold model presented in Figure 1.1.

   In this figure, Cell A represents foreign-born individuals who retain a strong ethnic or cultural identity and also show a high proportion of contacts with members of the host society. Their friendship patterns, membership in organizations and interests show a strong bicultural perspective; they move easily in and out of both cultures. Further, they are knowledgeable about

		Contact and Participation with Mainstream Society	
		YES	**NO**
Cultural Maintenance and Development	**YES**	Cell A	Cell B
	NO	Cell C	Cell D

Figure 1.1   Patterns in the adaptation of foreign-born individuals in the United States. Adapted from Berry, (1994).

their ethnicity and ethnic culture and feel comfortable with this identity. This category represents bicultural individuals. Some examples of bicultural individuals may be college students whose parents immigrated to the United States when their children were very young, some college and university professors, and some older adults brought up with a multicultural perspective.

Now examine carefully the remaining three cells from Figure 1.1 and then answer the following questions. After completing your responses, discuss them with another person.

1. Fill in the following blank: Cell B represents newly arrived immigrants who do not initiate much interaction with members of the host society but _____ ethnic and cultural identity.
2. Outline three characteristics of the members of this group and identify the implications of these characteristics for health care providers and social service personnel.
3. Cell C represents foreign-born individuals whose friendships and social patterns show a high proportion of contacts with members of the host society. What is their status in maintaining their ethnic identity?
4. Outline key characteristics of older individuals from Cell C and give examples of challenges they face in living in the United States.
5. What is the status of individuals in Cell D on (a) acquiring American culture and (b) maintaining their ethnic identity?
6. Which of the four groups represented in Figure 1.1 would especially require culture-specific knowledge and skills from providers of health care? Why?

DEMOGRAPHICS OF AMERICAN ELDERS

The population of the United States is growing older. In 1900, people aged 65 and older numbered 3.1 million. By 2000, this group encompassed 35 million, 11 times as large. Projections indicate that this trend is likely to continue. By the year 2010, the older population is projected to be 40 million. The first Baby Boomers (people born between 1946 and 1964) will turn 65 in 2011, inaugurating a rapid increase in the older population during the 2010 to 2030 period. The older population in 2030 is projected to be double that of 2000, growing from 35 million to 72 million. During the subsequent two decades, the older population will grow by another 15 million, from 72 million in 2030 to 87 million in 2050. In terms of the proportion of all Americans, the population aged 65 and older increased steadily from 4.1% in 1900 to 12.4% in 2000. It is projected that this population will grow to 17.7% in 2020 and to 22.9% in 2050. In other words, by 2030, one in every five Americans could be over age 65 (He, Sengupta, Velkoff & DeBarros, 2005).

Recognizing the differences between a healthy 65-year-old and a frail 90-year-old, researchers often focus on subgroups within the 65-and-older population. The oldest, those 85 years and older, compose a small but rapidly growing segment of the older population. In 1900, only 122,000 people were 85 years or older. By 2000, this group reached 4.2 million, 34 times as large. In contrast, the population aged 65 to 84 was 10 times as large, having increased from 3.0 million to 30.8 million (He, Sengupta, Velkoff & DeBarros, 2005).

What Is the Race or Ethnicity of These Older Adults?

We are about to give you a great deal of demographic information about groups of people, and when doing so we tend to use shorthand terms such as "Asians," "Blacks," or "Whites," and as we do this repeatedly, it can be easy to think of these groups as faceless entities from which we are separate, and within which everyone is all the same. Nothing could be further from the truth when considering racial and ethnic groups in the United States. Within each of these groups, tremendous diversity exists. As we present data about these groups in this chapter and throughout the text, we would like you to remember the heterogeneity within each group even though we will use shorthand terms. We hope that the following brief examination of the different ethnic groups will help facilitate this understanding.

Blacks or African Americans People of African descent who reside in the United States are categorized as Black or African American and they come from varied backgrounds. Most African Americans are descendants of peoples who were enslaved and brought to the United States from Africa. But there are also Black immigrants in the United States who migrated here from the Caribbean (e.g., Haiti, Jamaica) or more recently directly from Africa (e.g., Ethiopia, Somalia). Little is known about the health and well-being of these more recent Black immigrants (Williams, 2004). Knowing the cultural background and remembering the life experiences of current African American elders is very important to understanding their current situation. Black elders who were born in the United States have experienced a tremendous change in the nation's overt treatment of people of color from the 1930s when they were born to now. They have experienced racial segregation, educational segregation, low socioeconomic status (SES), and limited access to the health care system (Rooks & Whitfield, 2004). When they were young, they were denied access to hospitals, schools, and housing. This, then legal, institutional racism certainly had an impact on their health and well-being (Williams, 2004). Although their children and grandchildren experienced a different United States as much of this discrimination became illegal, the lives of these younger generations have also been affected, both from the aftermath of the overt institutional racism and from more covert racism that continues to result in neighborhoods and schools that are segregated by race and social class. These neighborhoods also tend to have poor quality schools and limited access to health care. Thus, African Americans of all ages continue to face tremendous adversity due to the color of their skin.

Hispanics or Latinos Hispanic groups are extremely diverse in a number of areas and this diversity affects their behavior in different ways. Hispanic groups include people of different racial backgrounds (American Indian, Black, White) and include people of Mexican, Cuban, Puerto Rican, Spanish, and Central or

South American origin (Angel & Hogan, 2004). Each of these different cultural groups share a common language and some core values that result in their being classified together, yet each group also carries its own unique culture, traditions, and perspective. People from these different groups also have different immigration histories that further contribute to the diversity within the Latino group. The health of Latinos is affected by their culture of origin and the length of time they have been in the United States. For example, a current Hispanic elder could have lived his entire life in the southwestern United States as his family lived there before it was acquired by the United States in 1848. Thus, his dietary and health practices could be very similar to mainstream Americans and his facility with the English language very good. In contrast, a Hispanic elder could have immigrated from Cuba in the 1960s when Castro came into power, in which case he may have significant language issues and his health may be affected by cultural practices from his culture of origin, by the stress of immigration, and by his access to health care once in the United States. In further contrast, a Hispanic elder could have immigrated from Mexico during the Bracero movement (1942–1966) when Mexican laborers were brought to the United States to address agricultural labor shortages. This Hispanic elder's health will also be affected by his cultural background, his immigration, his legal status, and even his work history once in the United States (for example, exposure to harmful pesticides). Although each of these Hispanic elders will speak Spanish, their educational levels, income, family wealth, and even their cultural beliefs and health practices are likely to be very different. As we talk about Hispanic or Latino elders, and in the future as you work with members of this population, it will be important to consider how the heterogeneity within this group may result in different issues of aging for individual group members.

Asian and Pacific Islanders   Asian elders in the United States also have tremendous diversity within their group. They include people of many different nationalities. In the United States, the three largest groups of Asian elders are of Chinese (29%), Filipino (21%), and Japanese (20%) origin. Vietnamese, Cambodians, and Hmong were 9% of Asian elderly population in 2000 (Angel & Hogan, 2004). Understanding the influence of culture on Asian elders can be even more complicated than with other racial or ethnic groups. First, people of Asian heritage do not share a common language as do Hispanics or Latinos. Second, the different nationalities that form Asia have not been geographically isolated. For example, over time, people of Chinese ethnicity immigrated to other countries in the South Pacific and then more recently to the United States. Thus, a person's cultural background may be much more complicated than simply identifying a country of origin. To understand the influence of culture, one must thus know the person's ethnicity (e.g., Chinese), their country of origin before the United States (e.g., Vietnam), and their length of U.S. residence or the number of generations the family has been in the United States (Yee-Melichar, 2004). The health and well-being of an Asian elder can vary depending on these factors. For example, an Asian elder who describes herself as "Chinese" may be someone who was born in the United States and is thus fairly acculturated with the U.S. health care system, or may be someone who was born in Vietnam and came to the United States as a refugee after the Vietnam War with all of the health issues facing a refugee, or may be a very recent immigrant from China whose child immigrated to the United States for education and stayed for career options. Pacific Islanders are often included within the Asian category, which further increases the diversity within the Asian group. Beginning with the 2000 census, a separate category was created for Native Hawaiian and Pacific Islanders and thus more recent research categorizes them separately. Pacific Islanders include people whose origin was the "islands and atolls in Polynesia, Micronesia and Melanesia" (Braun, Yee, Browne, & Mokuau, 2004, p.55). These islands were colonized and thus the indigenous people's experiences are similar to other colonized people such as American Indian and Alaska Natives (Braun, Yee, Browne, & Mokuau, 2004). In the United States, Native Hawaiians and Pacific Islanders make up less than 1% of the entire population. Again, simply determining that an elder is "Asian" is not enough to be able to ascertain the elder's beliefs and behaviors.

American Indians or Native Americans

American Indians reflect a diversity similar to "Asian" Americans in that although American Indians may share a common racial background, they come from numerous cultural groups who speak different languages, have different beliefs and practices, and who live in vastly different geographic areas. There are more than 550 federally recognized Indian tribes in the United States. Grouping them all together as "American Indians" is problematic given this diversity. On the other hand, all American Indians do have a shared experience of adversity through the generations as their varied cultures, languages, and ways of life were decimated by colonization by Whites. Current American Indian elders were born during a time in which many of them were forced away from their families on reservations into boarding schools in which the maintenance of their Indian culture was not allowed. This shared history has resulted in a population that has substantial risk factors for poor health such as low socioeconomic status, low educational levels, and limited access to health care for both rural and urban American Indian elders, with many elders speaking English as a second language, if at all (Dwyer, 2000) and yet diversity within and between tribes depending on individual circumstances. For example, the Lakota Sioux live in South Dakota, where the climate allows for family garden plots and thus promoting family gardening can be a valuable tool to promote healthy eating. The desert climate in Arizona makes such a project unrealistic for many Navajo tribes.

Recognizing the role that racial and ethnic group differences play in the lives of elders and yet being alert for variations within each group is a delicate balancing act that service providers, researchers, and indeed anyone who is interested in aging and diversity must do. We hope this brief description of the major racial or ethnic groups has given you an appreciation for the varied life experiences of these elders. We would like you to keep these experiences in mind as we now turn to examine the "numbers" behind each of these ethnic groups.

The racial and ethnic diversity of older adults is currently quite high. Furthermore, because of different fertility, mortality, and migration rates among minority Americans in previous years, the racial and ethnic diversity among the aged will grow more quickly during the coming decades. By the middle of the century, the minority elderly population will include one in almost four older persons. In 2050, the minority elderly population will include 530,000 Native Americans,

5 million Asian and Pacific Islanders, 10 million Blacks, and about 14 million Hispanics. Thus, while at the present time the number of aged Blacks is significantly higher than that of other ethnic groups (Figure 1.2), by 2030 the number of Hispanic elders will be larger than that of Black elders and by 2050 there will be almost four million more elderly Hispanics than Blacks (Hayward & Zhang, 2001). Remember that the United States' Hispanic population itself is quite heterogeneous. Of the total Hispanic elderly population, Mexican Americans make up the largest fraction and Cuban Americans represent the next larger subgroup.

The main reason for the great heterogeneity in the United States' Hispanic elderly population is their varied immigration histories (Angel & Angel, 1998). Some Mexican Americans have been residents of the southwestern United States since colonial times. Others arrived when the use of temporary Mexican agricultural labor was encouraged in the United States. More recently, the substantial growth in the number of immigrants from Mexico has increased the size of this population. While the first two groups include persons who are now reaching old age, the more recent immigrants represent a much younger population. The aging of these adults will contribute significantly to the growth of the Hispanic elderly population.

As shown in Figure 1.2, by the year 2030 the population of Black elders is projected to reach over 7 million and 20 years later it will be over 10 million. Note that we have used the Census Bureau's term "Black" rather than African American, to include older persons from the Caribbean, Africa, and Europe.

In addition to the Hispanic population, the Asian elderly population will also become increasingly important during the coming decades. As shown in Figure 1.2, the Asian elderly population is expected to reach over 5 million in 2050. This population is also quite diverse. More than 30 Asian groups are now represented in the United States including Chinese, Koreans, Indians, Pakistanis, Filipinos, Afghans,

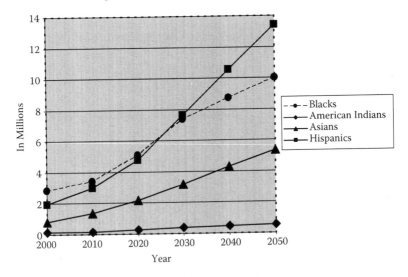

Figure 1.2 Growth of Minority Elderly Population: 2000–2050. U.S. Census Bureau (2000).

Hmong, Cambodians, Laotians, Vietnamese, Thais, and Japanese. The Asians of Chinese, Filipino, and Japanese origin represent about 75% of the Asian elderly population. The elderly Asian population comprises three major groups: (a) those who came to the United States as young persons early in the 20th century; (b) children who were born to these adult immigrants; and (c) middle aged and older persons who came to the United States after changes in U.S. immigration laws were instituted in 1965 (Takaki, 1998). In addition, more than 800,000 refugees from Vietnam and from other southeastern Asian countries have come to the United States since 1975. As a group, Asian Americans do not resemble other racial or ethnic minorities. In addition, they vary widely in their characteristics according to their cultural origins and when they arrived in the United States (Gardner, Robey, & Smith, 1985).

Of the four groups included in Figure 1.2, the Native American elderly population is relatively small in size. Overall, less than 1% of the minority aged identified themselves as American Indian or Native American in the 2000 census. However, this population has grown from 80,000 in 1980 to 187,000 in 2000 (Angel & Hogan, 2004). One factor in this apparent increase is the renewed sense of ethnic awareness that has developed among Native Americans in recent years (Passel, 1997), rather than an actual increase in cohort size or improved survivorship. Although nationally the percentage of elderly Native Americans is expected to remain relatively small in comparison with other minority groups, the diversity and heterogeneity of the American Indian community cannot be overstated. At the present time there are 558 different federally recognized tribes or nations and 126 tribes or nations applying for recognition. In addition, more than 100 Indian languages are spoken in this population. Data from the 2000 census indicates that the Native American population 65 years and older will continue to concentrate in certain parts of the country and will persist in preserving its cultural heritage.

Aging and Diversity Online: Demographics

Federal Interagency Forum on Aging. This forum was created in 1986 to bring together federal agencies that have an interest in improving aging-related data and to facilitate dissemination of that data. This site is an excellent source for demographic summary information. http://www. agingstats.gov

U.S. Census Bureau. The Census Bureau collects information on the nation's people and economy. Its statistical abstract is a collection of data that also serves as a guide to additional data sources. http://www.census.gov/compendia/stat/abl

Administration on Aging. Provides latest statistics on older Americans in key subject areas, presents narrative and statistical charts, and includes links to a large variety of resources related to diversity. http://www.aoa.gov/prof/statistics/profile/profiles.aspx

What Is the Gender Distribution Among Older Adults?

In 2000, there were 14.4 million men and 20.6 million women aged 65 and over, yielding a male to female ratio (the number of males per 100 females) of 70. As Table 1.1 reveals, the male to female ratio drops steadily with age group. In the 65–74 age group the male to female ratio was 78 in 1990 and 82 in 2000; in the 75–84 age group the ratio was 60 in 1990 and 65 in 2000; and in the 85 and over age group the ratio was 39 in 1990 and 41 in 2000. Thus, the male to female ratio for each age group in the older population has risen since 1990. In fact, the Census Bureau projects the male to female ratio for those 65 or older to rise to 79 by the year 2050. Furthermore, a male to female ratio of 62 is anticipated for those age 85 and over.

Despite these continuing improvements, the fact remains that a very large proportion of older women today will outlive their spouses and face the challenges of later life alone. It is, however, important to note that in comparison with White and Black women the percentage of Asian and Hispanic women living alone is significantly lower. Research indicates that minorities have a greater propensity to live with others. One-third of Black, Asian, and Hispanic women live with other individuals, whereas the proportion is much lower (16.4%) for White women (Federal Interagency Forum on Aging-Related Statistics, 2004).

What Is the Socioeconomic Status of Older Adults?

As Table 1.2 reveals, there is considerable variation among older persons in years of formal education and poverty, two widely used measures of socioeconomic status (SES). A substantial proportion of older adults of all racial groups have fewer than 9 years of formal education. Furthermore, more than 10% of Blacks and Hispanics have not completed high school. Interestingly, Asian Americans are overrepresented at both ends of the educational distribution. In comparison with their White counterparts they are more likely to not have completed high school and to have a bachelor's degree or higher. In addition, this group has the highest percentage of individuals (29%) who have obtained a bachelor's degree or higher.

The lower panel of Table 1.2 shows poverty rates by race at age 65 and older. As these data indicate, the rates of poverty are significantly higher for Blacks and Hispanics. Other data reveal that the levels of poverty for American Indian elders resemble that of Blacks (John, 1996). Across all racial groups, women are more

TABLE 1.1   Population 65 years and Over by Age and Sex: 1990 and 2000 (Numbers in Thousands)

Age	1990			2000		
	Women	Men	Ratio	Women	Men	Ratio
65–74	10,165	7,942	78	10,088	8,303	82
75–84	6,289	3,766	60	7,482	4,879	65
85 and over	2,222	858	39	3,013	1,227	41
TOTAL	18,676	12,566	67	20,583	14,409	70

Source: U.S. Census Bureau (1990, 2000).

TABLE 1.2   Selected Socioeconomic Characteristics by Race at Age 65 and Older

Socioeconomic Characteristics	Whites (%)	Blacks (%)	Hispanics (%)	Asian and Pacific Islanders (%)
1. **Education**				
Less than 9th grade	11.3	25.5	52.4	22.2
9th to 11th grade	11.3	20.2	9.4	5.8
12th grade no diploma	1.2	2.7	1.9	1.6
High School graduate	38.6	27.4	21.5	25.8
Some college/ Associate's degree	18.9	13.9	8.7	15.5
Bachelor's degree or more	18.6	10.2	6.1	29.1
2. **Poverty**				
Percent below poverty level	8.0	23.7	19.5	14.1

Source: Adapted from He, Sengupta, Velkoff and DeBarros (2005).

likely than men to be poor (Proctor and Dalaker, 2002). In 2003, 12.5% of older women were in poverty compared with 7.3% of older men (He, Sengupta, Velkoff, and DeBarros, 2005). However, data on poverty tell only a part of the story of economic vulnerability, given the large number of older persons who are only slightly above the poverty level. Combining the poor and the near-poor, 35% of non-Hispanic Whites, 56% of older Blacks, and 56% of Hispanics are economically vulnerable. (United States Census Bureau, 2001).

It is important to remember that race and socioeconomic position are related but nonequivalent concepts. For example, although the rate of poverty is three times as high for Black compared with White elders, two-thirds of Blacks are not poor. Furthermore, there are important variabilities within the Hispanic and Asian population.

What Proportion of Older People Live in Rural Settings?

The population 65 and older living in non-metro areas numbered just under 7.5 million in 2004, with rural areas composed of a higher proportion of older persons than urban areas. At the present time, older adults make up 20% of the rural population, compared with only 15% of the urban population. This difference in the composition is due to the out-migration of younger people to urban areas with more job opportunities and the immigration of retired people to rural areas that occur alongside the aging-in-place of rural older people.

Rural older adults are predominantly non-Hispanic Whites, but certain regions have high percentages of American Indians (e.g., northwest and southwest), Hispanics (e.g., southwest), or African Americans (e.g., south) and the composition of the population continues to change. Overall, however, only 7% of rural older adults are African Americans, versus 12% of metropolitan older adults. American Indians are the most rural of all ethnic older adults, with about half living in rural areas (often reservation communities). Other characteristics of the rural population include:

- Aging in place and net migration affect older non-metropolitan populations differently. On average, older Americans are less well-off in non-metro areas than in metro areas. However, non-metro counties are becoming increasingly heterogeneous for two main reasons: (1) population growth from aging in place and net migration happens at varying rates in rural communities; and (2) the non-metro, aging-in-place population is less well-off socioeconomically than are recent retirees moving to rural areas. Thus, there are counties with a large proportion of older adults who have aged in place and there are others that are retirement-destination counties with a high net relocation of retirees who tend to be better educated, wealthier, and more likely to be married than living alone than the aging-in-place population.
- For the aging-in-place population, the range of available health care services is narrower, less accessible and more costly to deliver, and fewer health care providers offer specialized services. These location disadvantages are hard to address in areas that are still losing younger working-age people and experiencing declining tax bases. On the other hand, retirement areas often benefit from growth as relocating retirees boost the tax base and help sustain local businesses. Taking into account these differences across rural communities could enhance the effectiveness of policies and programs for the older population.
- Rural areas generally have a limited supply of community-based services such as adult day care, hospice care, and respite care (Bellamy, Goins, & Ham, 2003).
- Lack of public transportation in rural communities inhibits access to health care services offered in metro areas. Nearly 80% of rural counties have no public bus service and 57% of rural poor do not own a car (Bellamy, Goins, & Ham, 2003).
- Many older adults in rural areas do not have family nearby to provide care. This is mainly because they age in place, while younger people tend to migrate out of rural areas. This results in fewer sources of informal care. Given the limited availability of community-based services and lack of informal care providers, rural older adults have few choices other than nursing homes.

Aging and Diversity Online: Elements of Diversity

The Resource Centers for Minority Aging Research (RCMAR). These centers were created by the National Institute on Aging and National Institutes of Health "to reduce health disparities between minority and non-minority older adults." This site provides information on recent research findings, funding opportunities, conferences, and publications on aging and diversity. http://www.rcmar.ucla.edu

The Older Women's League (OWL). A nonprofit organization that focuses on issues that are particularly unique to women and strives to improve the lives of women as they age. http://www.owl-national.org/welcome.html

Services and Advocacy for Gay, Lesbian, Bisexual, and Transgender Elders (SAGE). SAGE is the nation's oldest and largest social services agency dedicated to senior lesbians and gay men. http://www.sageusa.orgmen/index.cfm

The National Rural Development Partnership (NRDP). NDRP promotes coordination and collaboration among government, private for-profit, and non-profit organizations to address the needs of rural America. http://www.rurdev.usda.gov/nrdp

---

How Many Elders Are Lesbian, Gay, Bisexual, or Transgender?

Accurate assessment of the demographics of the older lesbian, gay, bisexual, or transgender (LGBT) population is extremely difficult. Most of the published studies about LGBT elders contain samples that are small and not generalizable to the LGBT population as a whole (Kimmel, Rose, Orel, & Greene, 2006). These studies typically interview individuals who have already publicly disclosed their sexual orientation and are typically educated White men and women from urban areas. A few studies have included ethnic minority samples or samples from rural communities but these samples are also not generalizable to their groups. Part of the problem with measuring the number of LGBT elders is that there is no accurate count of LGBT individuals at any age. Few national surveys ask the sexual orientation of the respondent (Cahill, South, & Spade, 2000). Even for the few surveys that do ask questions about sexual orientation, the accuracy of the data is suspect, as participants may be reluctant to answer such questions truthfully for fear of being exposed and targeted given the anti-LGBT attitudes prevalent in much of U.S. society. Estimates of the LGBT elder population hinge on estimates of the overall LGBT population within the United States. Cahill, South & Spade (2000) estimated that there were between 1 and 3 million Americans over age 65 who were LGBT; they based this number on an estimate that the overall LGBT population was between 3% and 8% of the total population. By the year 2030, they estimate that there will be 4 million LGBT elders (Cahill et al., 2000).

A recurrent theme in our discussion of aging and diversity is to emphasize the heterogeneity *within* each element of diversity. Elders who are LGBT are no exception. They are as diverse as the general aging population and come from every combination of gender, ethnicity, class, and rural or urban location (Cahill et al., 2000; Kimmel et al., 2006). Kimmel et al. (2006) reminds us that, "What is often called the LGBT community is, in fact, many smaller populations that have in common only their minority sexual orientation. Issues such as age, race, ethnicity, religion, class and gender often are more relevant to a person's sense of self and sense of community than is sexual orientation" (p. 10). Although the LGBT population is also diverse, images of people of color who are lesbians, bisexuals, and gay men are missing from most portrayals of people of minority sexual orientation.

If you haven't been impressed by the demographic realities of our aging nation and are still uncertain why you should be interested in aging, consider another reality of aging: barring early death, every one of us will become old. If we hope to fully understand the breadth of the human aging experience, to design services that truly make a difference for elders, and to have a positive aging experience ourselves, then it will be critical to explore aging and diversity to its fullest.

A NOTE ON TERMINOLOGY FOR DIVERSE GROUPS

As stated earlier, the elements of diversity on which we will focus include gender, race or ethnicity, religious affiliation or spirituality, social class, community location, and sexual orientation. Within some of these elements, there is no consensus about the specific labels used to describe different groups. For example, are indigenous peoples of North America called Native Americans or American Indians? A large national survey found differences within ethnic groups as to their preferred label, with 50% of American Indians preferring "American Indian" (37% prefer Native American), 58% of Hispanics preferring "Hispanic" (12% prefer Latino), 44% of Blacks prefer "Black" (28% prefer African American), and 62% of Whites preferring "White" (17% prefer "Caucasian") (Tucker et al., 1996). Even we, the authors of this text, use different labels for some groups. To refer to people of Hispanic or Latino heritage, the first author typically uses the term "Hispanics," the principal term used in the research literature and the one that most Hispanics prefer, whereas the second author typically uses the term "Latino," reflecting her residence in California where the term Latino is preferred over Hispanic (Talamantes, Lindeman, & Mouton, 2000). We will follow David Williams' example (Williams, 2004), which he describes as an effort to recognize individual dignity, and will use the most preferred terms for each ethnic group interchangeably throughout the text. Similarly, there are differences in appropriate labels for sexual orientation with the term "homosexual" currently in disfavor. Accordingly, we will refer to elders who are not heterosexual by the preferred labels of lesbian, gay, bisexual or transgender.

In addition to group members' preferences for a particular name or label, the federal government determines how a particular group is categorized. For example, in the past, Pacific Islanders were included in the Asian American group, which was sometimes denoted as API or AAPI (Asian American and Pacific Islanders). Given the differences between Pacific Islanders and other Asian groups, many argued that Pacific Islanders should have a separate category. In 1997, the Office of Management and Budget (OMB) revised the statistical directive that guides the collection of information regarding ethnicity and race by federal agencies (Ross, 2000). In response, the 2000 U.S. census collected information on race and ethnicity in the following manner. There were five categories for race: American Indian or Alaska Native, Asian, Black or African American, Native Hawaiian or other Pacific Islander, and White. There were two categories for ethnicity: Hispanic or Latino and Not Hispanic or Latino. Thus, research prior to 2000 often groups Asians and Pacific Islanders together, whereas later research does not. In contrast, some consider that the Native American label includes Alaska Natives, whereas the American Indian label does not. Sometimes this is clarified in writing by describing the population as American Indian or Alaska Native, other times when using the American Indian label, it may be unclear whether the Alaska Natives are included in the group. In sum, the names or labels that we use to describe different groups of people are in flux and we, both as authors of this text and as members of our diverse society, do our best to accurately and respectfully identify and recognize different groups.

Aging and Diversity Online: Films and Videos on Aging

Educational Videos in Adult Development and Aging. Presents a list of more than 200 videos related to adult development and aging, including cultural diversity. http://apadiv20.phhp.ufl.edu/idlist.htm

The Great Circle of Life: A Resource Guide to Films and Videos on Aging. Provides an annotated bibliography of educational videos. http://www.tc.umn.edu/~ryahnke/greatcircle/index.htm

Aging and the Cinema. Lists feature-length films related to aging and human development. http://apadiv20.phhp.ufl.edu/cinema.doc

---

SUMMARY

This chapter has provided a general overview of diversity and aging. We first defined what we mean by "diversity." In answering the question, "Why should we focus on diversity and aging?" we presented two key points: (1) examining the aging perspective from multiple perspectives helps us develop an understanding of human development that is truly universal; and (2) this deeper understanding will impact the choices that we make in research on, service to, and work with elders as well as in our own lives as we age. We then turned to the elements of diversity. We described the six elements of diversity on which we focus (gender, race or ethnicity, religious affiliation and spirituality, social class, rural/urban community location, sexual orientation) and we highlighted the interactional nature of the elements of diversity and aging. We also noted that when looking at the different elements of diversity, differences *within* groups can be quite large and often overlooked, resulting in stereotyping of those group members. Also, some of the labels that we use to differentiate groups (e.g., Hispanic American, Asian American) actually correspond to many different nationalities and cultural groups within that one label. Another area in which group members can differ is acculturation. We described acculturation and discussed the role that age can play in acculturation. In our examination of the demographics of American elders, we described the growth of the American elder population, examined the U.S. population characteristics for each element of diversity and emphasized the increasing numbers of female and ethnic minority elders. The following quiz addresses some of the key points presented in chapter 1.

ACTIVE LEARNING EXPERIENCE: CHAPTER 1 QUIZ

The purpose of this experience is to gauge your present knowledge of issues related to aging and diversity. Upon completion of this activity, you will be able to:

1. Assess your knowledge of diverse elders.
2. Gain feedback on your knowledge of important issues related to aging and diversity.

Complete the following quiz. Your instructor may lead an in-class review of the answers to the quiz. This activity should take 30 minutes (10 minutes to complete the quiz and 20 minutes to discuss your answers with another person or in a classroom setting). Check the appropriate column to indicate whether each of the following statements is true or false.

Instructions:

Quiz Items	True	False
1. The ethnic makeup of elderly Americans is changing mainly because of the rapidly increasing number of older people who are moving to the United States from Africa to join their children.	___	___
2. Men outnumber women at every age among the older adults.	___	___
3. Those aged 65–74 represent the fastest growing segment of the elderly population.	___	___
4. The racial composition of the centenarian population is similar to that of all other older ages.	___	___
5. Elderly Black women are more likely than women in other minority groups to be living in married-couple households.	___	___
6. As compared with the mainstream population, a larger proportion of minorities live with others.	___	___
7. Older lesbians freely disclose their sexual identity.	___	___
8. Older minorities, as a group, experience higher poverty rates than other older populations.	___	___
9. Diversity includes a number of factors such as religion, language, social class, and gender.	___	___
10. Race is primarily a social construct.	___	___

11. The degree of acculturation may be different for
     foreign-born persons than for their second- or
     third-generation children and grandchildren.   _____ _____

12. Rural older adults have access to programs and
     services similar to their urban counterparts.   _____ _____

13. There are more older people and fewer younger
     people among Native Americans.   _____ _____

14. The greatest growth in the older minority
     population will be seen among Hispanic
     Americans.   _____ _____

15. Poverty rates among Asian Americans were higher
     than Blacks.   _____ _____

GLOSSARY

acculturation: The level at which one functions as a member of the host society, speaks the primary language (e.g., English in the United States), participates in the political process, and integrates oneself into social and civic life.

cohort: An aggregation of people having a common characteristic. The term generally refers to the time period in which persons were born.

culture: A relatively organized system of shared meanings, including beliefs and symbols that guide but do not determine individual behaviors.

diversity: While heterogeneity refers to individual-level variation, diversity refers to group-level variation within a society. For example, cultural diversity can refer to a group's ethnic background, its country of origin, and the language and heritage it brings to the society.

ethnicity: A shared sense of identity that includes a set of cultural meanings.

race: A social distinction based in part on observable physical differences such as skin color. A social construct used to classify and separate people.

SUGGESTED READINGS

Angel, R. J., & Angel, J. L. (2006). Diversity and aging in the United States. In R. H. Binstock & L. K. George (Eds.), *Handbook of aging and the social sciences (6th ed.)* (pp. 94–106). Burlington, MA: Elsevier Academic Press.

This chapter focuses primarily on the demographic, socioeconomic, and cultural characteristics of Latinos and African Americans. It also includes a thought-provoking discussion regarding the demands that minority elders will place on the health care system and on other formal and informal sources of support.

Bengtson, V.L., Kim, K.D., Myers, G.C., & Eun, K.S. (Eds.) (2000). *Aging in East and West: Families, states, and the elderly.* New York: Springer.

This book examines comparatively recent developments among Eastern and Western nations concerning population aging. It focuses on social, cultural, political, and economic consequences of population aging and discusses the implications for policy formulations and reforms. The analyses primarily focus on demographic trends, sociocultural contexts, and policy implications in each of the six countries selected as case studies. These countries include China, Korea, Japan, Germany, the United Kingdom, and the United States.

Gelfand, D.E. (2003). *Aging and Ethnicity: Knowledge and Services* (2nd ed.). New York: Springer.

One of the leading researchers in the area of ethnicity and aging discusses specific issues and themes important to understanding and addressing the needs of older people from diverse backgrounds. The author devotes considerable attention to the impact of immigration on the United States and offers a useful model to those who provide services to older persons from diverse ethnic backgrounds. References at the end of each chapter include some excellent source material.

Goins, R. T., & Krout, J.A. (2003). *Service Delivery to Rural Older Adults: Research, Policy, and Practice*. New York: Springer.

This edited volume provides a comprehensive discussion of contemporary challenges experienced by older rural residents and their communities in accessing and providing services. The editors present in-depth analysis of important components of rural systems including nutrition, health service delivery, long-term care, caregiving, housing, and transportation.

Herdt, G., & deVries, B. (Eds.) (2004). *Gay and Lesbian aging: Research and future directions*. New York: Springer.

The authors in this interdisciplinary book have considered major theoretical and methodological questions bearing on the emergence of well-being at midlife and beyond for gay and lesbian seniors. The book is organized into three sections. The first section is designed to set the stage by addressing broadly and somewhat selectively issues of aging for lesbians and gay men. The second section presents accounts of empirical research into the myriad issues of aging for lesbians and gay men. The concluding section reconsiders some of the issues of aging among gay men and lesbians and suggests future directions in the study of midlife and older sexual minorities.

Stoller, E.P. & Gibson, R.C. (Eds.) (2000). *Worlds of difference: Inequalities in the aging experience*. (3rd ed.). Thousand Oaks, CA: Pine Forge Press.

This book of readings emphasizes the use of a life-course framework in the study of aging and focuses on topics such as cultural images of aging; expanding the definition of productivity in old age; the diversity of American families; and gender, race, and social class differences in disease, disability, and mortality in old age. The major issues of the book are explored in an introductory chapter written by the editors. The readings cover numerous groups based on ethnicity, gender, sexual orientation, and socioeconomic class.

AUDIOVISUAL RESOURCES

Aging in America: The Years Ahead. This video project began as an award-winning story published by the *New York Times Magazine.* Julie Winokur and photographer Ed Kashi then traveled the country covering a broad range of topics ranging from the increase in immigrant elders to the devastation a tornado caused to a rural older adult community. 60 minutes. http://www.talkingeyesmedia.org/aging_film.php.

Silent Pioneers: Gay and Lesbian Elders. This documentary about lesbian and gay aging is widely distributed and frequently shown in college classrooms and on public television. The video includes interviews with eight older people who are lesbian or gay, including two men who have been in a relationship for 55 years and an African American great-grandmother. 42 minutes. Available from Water Bearer Films.

The Open Road: America Looks at Aging. This documentary examines what lies ahead for individuals and society as 77 million Baby Boomers near retirement age. 60 minutes. Available from http://theopenroadfilm.com.

KEY: CHAPTER 1 QUIZ

1. False. In addition to Africa, a large number of older adults have also moved from Asia and Latin America. The ethnic makeup is changing because of these older immigrants plus the aging of immigrants who came to the United States as young adults (Himes, 2001).
2. False. Women outnumber men at every age among older adults. In 2000, there were an estimated three women for every two men aged 65 or older, and the sex ratio is even more skewed among the oldest old. The preponderance of women in the older population reflects the higher death rates for men than women at every age. In recent years, male mortality has improved faster than female mortality, primarily because of a marked decline in deaths from heart disease. The gender gap at older ages has narrowed and is expected to narrow further.
3. False. Those age 85 or older, the "oldest old," are the fastest growing segment of the elderly population in the United States. More than 4 million people were 85 or older in the 2000 census and by 2050 a projected 19 million will be in this age group (20% of the total older population). This group is of special interest to planners because it may require health services.

4. True. Data from 2000 census indicates that the racial composition for centenarians is similar to that for all older Americans—78% of centenarians were non-Hispanic White and the remaining 22% included Hispanic, Blacks, Asian, Pacific Islanders, and American Indians. However, the Census Bureau projects that, by 2050, non-Hispanic Whites may account for only 55% of the total centenarian population, with Hispanic and Asian and Pacific Islander populations accounting for a greater share of the population aged 100 years and above (Krach & Velkoff, 1999).

5. False. Data from the Federal Interagency Forum on Aging-Related Statistics show that elderly Black women (24.3%) are *less* likely than women in other minority groups (37% of Hispanics and 41% of Asian and Pacific Islanders) to be living in married-couple households. This pattern reflects the relatively high rate of marital disruption early in the life course and much lower age specific rates of marriage for Black women.

6. True. Minorities have a greater propensity to live with others. While 16.4% of White women live with others, about one third of Black (35%), Asian (38%), and Hispanic (36%) women live with other individuals.

7. False. Reluctance to disclose sexual identity remains common in older age (Quam, 1997, p.2). It has been a major factor responsible for their low rate of participation in research and has, thus, limited what is currently known about lesbian aging.

8. True. As indicated in Table 1.2, only 8% of Whites aged 65 and over live below the official poverty level, compared with 23.7% of Blacks, 19.5% of Hispanics, and 14.1% of Asian and Pacific Islanders.

9. True. Among the many elements of human diversity are age, ethnicity, language, health status, religion, gender, sexual orientation, and social class (Kavanaugh & Kennedy, 1992).

10. True. Race is a social and political category, not a biological category. Within the United States we use skin color as a defining characteristic of race, despite the fact that the world's population cannot be divided into categories of "white" and "black."

11. True. People who come to America later in life are less likely to become as fully acculturated as their children and grandchildren who have spent all or most of their lives in the United States (Angel & Angel, 2006).

12. False. Rural older adults are disadvantaged relative to their metropolitan and urban counterparts by being on average poor, more functionally impaired, and less educated, and having less access to, and a more limited range of, health care services (Olson, 2001).

13. False. There are more younger people and fewer older people among Native Americans. This is for two main reasons: (1) birth rate in this population has been higher than it has been for the overall

population; and (2) life expectancy at birth is shorter for Native Americans than for the mainstream populations.

14. True. The percentage of the elderly population of Hispanic origin is expected to almost double from 6.0% in 2000 to 11.2% in 2030. By 2050 this population could increase to 13.7%.

15. False. As shown in Table 1.2, poverty rates among Asian Americans were higher than Whites and lower than those of Blacks and Hispanics.

REFERENCES

Angel, J.L., & Angel, R.J. (1998). Aging trends: Mexican Americans in the southwest. *Journal of Cross-Cultural Gerontology*, 13, 281–290.

Angel, R. J., & Angel, J. L. (2006). Diversity and aging in the United States. In R. H. Binstock & L. K. George (Eds.), *Handbook of aging and the social sciences* (6th ed.) (pp. 94–106). Burlington, MA: Elsevier Academic Press .

Angel, J.L., & Hogan, D.P. (2004). Population aging and diversity in a new era. In K. E. Whitfield (Ed.). *Closing the gap: Improving the health of minority elders in the new millennium*. Washington, DC: The Gerontological Society of America.

Barrow, G.M. (1992). *Aging, the individual, and society* (5th ed.) St. Paul, MN: West.

Bellamy, G. R., Goins, R. T., & Ham, R. J. (2003). Overview: Definitions, clinical issues, demographics, health care, and long-term care. In R. J. Ham, R. T. Goins & D. K. Brown (Eds.), *Best practices in service delivery to the rural elderly: A report to the administration on aging* (pp. 1–19). Morgantown, WV: West Virginia University, Center on Aging.

Berry, J.W. (1994). Acculturative Stress. In W.J. Lonner & R.S. Malpass (Eds.), *Psychology and Culture* (pp. 211–215). Needham Heights, MA: Allyn and Bacon.

Betancourt, H., & Lopez, S. R. (1993). The study of culture, ethnicity, and race in American psychology. *American Psychologist*, 48, 629–637.

Braun, K. L., Yee, B. W. K., Browne, C. V., & Mokuau, N. (2004). Native Hawaiian and Pacific Islander elders. In K. E. Whitfield (Ed.), *Closing the gap: Improving the health of minority elders in the new millennium* (pp. 55–67). Washington, DC: The Gerontological Society of America.

Butler, R.N., Lewis, M.I., & Sunderland, T. (1991). *Aging and mental health: Positive psychosocial and biomedical approaches* (4th ed.). New York: Merrill.

Cahill, S., South, K., & Spade, J. (2000). *Outing age: Public policy issues affecting gay, lesbian, bisexual and transgender elders*. Washington, DC: National Gay and Lesbian Task Force Policy Institute.

Cruz, B. C., & Berson, M. J. (2001). The American melting pot? Miscegenation laws in the United States. *Organization of American Historians: Magazine of History, 15*(4).

Dannefer, D. (1988). The neglect of variability in the study of aging. In J.E. Birren & V.L. Bengtson (Eds.), *Emergent theories of aging* (pp. 356–384). New York: Springer.

Dwyer, K. (2000). Culturally appropriate consumer-directed care: The American Indian choices project. *Generations, 24*(3), 91–93.

Federal Interagency Forum on Aging-Related Statistics (2004). *Older Americans 2000: Key indicators of well-being*. Washington, DC: United States Government Printing Office.

Gardner, R., Robey, B., & Smith, P. (1985). *Asian Americans: Growth, change and diversity*. Washington, DC: Population Reference Bureau.

Hayward, M.D., & Zhang, Z. (2001). Demography of aging: A century of global change, 1950–2050. In R.H. Binstock & L.K. George (Eds.), *Handbook of aging and the social sciences* (5th ed.) (pp. 69–85). San Diego: Academic Press.

He, W. (2002). The older born foreign-born population in the United States: 2000. *Current Population Reports*, Series P23-211. United States Census Bureau. Washington, DC: United States Government Printing Office.

He, W., Sengupta, M., Velkoff, V. A., & DeBarros, K. A. (2005, December). *65+ in the United States: 2005* (P23-209). Washington, DC: U.S. Government Printing Office.

Himes, C. L. (2001). Elderly Americans. *Population Bulletin* 56(4). Washington, DC: Population Reference Bureau. Boston: Allyn & Bacon.

Jackson, J. S. (1989). Race, ethnicity, and psychological theory and research. *Journal of Gerontology: Psychological Sciences*, 44(1), 1–2.

John, R. (1996). Demography of American Indian elders: Social, economic, and health status. In G.D. Sandefur, R.R. Rindfuss, & B. Cohen (Eds.), *Changing numbers, changing needs: American Indian demography and public health* (pp. 218–231). Washington, DC: National Academy Press.

Kavanaugh, K. H. & Kennedy, P. H. (1992). *Promoting cultural diversity: Strategies for health care professionals*. Newbury Park, CA: Sage.

Kimmel, D., Rose, T., Orel, N., & Greene, B. (2006). Historical context for research on lesbian, gay, bisexual and transgender aging. In D. Kimmel, T. Rose & S. David (Eds.), *Lesbian, gay, bisexual, and transgender aging: Research and clinical perspectives* (pp. 1–19). New York: Columbia University Press.

Krach, C.A., & Velkoff, V.A. (1999). Centenarians in the United States. *Current Population Reports P23-199RV*. Washington, DC: United States Government Printing Office.

Olson, L.K. (2001). *Age through Ethnic Lenses: Caring for the elderly in a multicultural society*. Lanham, MD: Rowman & Littlefield Publishers.

Passel, J. S. (1997). The growing American Indian population, 1960–1990: Beyond demography. *Population Research and Policy Review*, 16, 11–31.

Proctor, B.D., & Dalaker, J. (2002). *Poverty in the United States: 2001*. Current Population Reports, (pp. 60–219). United States Bureau of the Census. Washington, DC: United States Government Printing Office. Retrieved from http://www.census.gov/prod/2002pubs/p60-219.pdf.

Quam, J.K. (Ed.) (1997). *Social services for senior gay men and lesbians*. Binghamton, NY: Harrington Park Press.

Rawls, T.W. (2004). Disclosure and depression among older gay and homosexual men: Findings from the Urban Men's Health Study. In G. Herdt & B. deVries (Eds.), *Gay and lesbian aging: Research and future directions* (pp. 117–141). New York: Springer.

Rooks, R. N., & Whitfield, K. E. (2004). Health disparities among older African Americans: Past, present and future perspectives. In K. E. Whitfield (Ed.), *Closing the gap: Improving the health of minority elders in the new millennium* (pp. 45–54). Washington, DC: The Gerontological Society of America.

Ross, H. (2000). *New federal standards recognize Native Hawaiians and other Pacific Islanders as distinct group*: Office of Minority Health Resource Center, United States Department of Health and Human Services.

Speas, K., & Obenshain, B. (1995). *AARP Images: Aging in America: Final Report*. Washington, DC: American Association of Retired Persons.

Stoller, E. P., & Gibson, R. C. (2000). *Worlds of difference: Inequality in the aging experience* (third ed.). Thousand Oaks, CA: Pine Forge Press.

Takaki, R. (1998). *Strangers from a different shore: A history of Asian Americans*. New York: Penguin.

Talamantes, M., Lindeman, R., & Mouton, C. (2000). Health and health care of Hispanic/Latino American elders. In G. Yeo (Ed.), *Core curriculum in ethnogeriatrics: Ethnic specific modules* (pp. 2–62). Stanford, CA: Stanford Ethnogeriatric Education Center.

Tran, T. V. (1990). Language acculturation among older Vietnamese refugee adults. *The Gerontologist, 30*, 94–99.

Tucker, C., McKay, R., Kojetin, B., Harrison, R., de la Puente, M., & Stinson, L. (1996). Testing methods of collecting racial and ethnic information: Results of the current population survey supplement on race and ethnicity. *Bureau of Labor Statistical Notes, 40*, 1–149.

United States Census Bureau (2000) Census Summary File 4 (NP-T4) *Projections of the Total Resident Populations by 5-Year Age Groups, Race, and Hispanic Origin with Special Age Categories: Middle Series, 1999-2100.* Washington, DC: Author.

Williams, D. R. (2004). Racism and health. In K. E. Whitfield (Ed.), *Closing the gap: Improving the health of minority elders in the new millennium* (pp. 69–80). Washington, DC: The Gerontological Society of America.

Williams, D. R., & Wilson, C. M. (2001). Race, ethnicity, and aging. In R.H. Binstock & L.K. George (Eds.), *Handbook of aging and the social sciences* (5th ed.) (pp. 160–178). San Diego, CA: Academic Press.

Yee-Melichar, D. (2004). Aging Asian Americans and health disparities. In K. E. Whitfield (Ed.), *Closing the gap: Improving the health of minority elders in the new millennium* (pp. 13–25). Washington, DC: The Gerontological Society of America.

2

Research Methods

- Why discuss research methods in a book about diverse elders?
- How is the research process affected when studying different groups?
- What can we do to improve research with diverse elders?
- Why is it important for researchers to give back to the community? How can we make this process culturally sensitive?

Research helps us understand human behavior and this understanding, in turn, suggests ways to improve people's lives. In this chapter, we explain the importance of research methods, describe different disciplines that typically conduct research on aging, and briefly review the history of research on aging and diversity. We also examine the research process as a whole and present areas in which studying elders from diverse groups can differ from studying mainstream populations. Finally, we highlight ways to conduct culturally appropriate research. For a taste of the kinds of issues that can arise in research on minority elders, please consider the following vignettes:

Vignette 1

Yolanda Estrada is beginning to plan research for her master's degree. Her program requires that she conduct both basic research and an applied intervention. As an undergraduate, she became interested in the local Vietnamese immigrant community and has done a great deal of reading about their experiences. She would like to investigate social isolation among Vietnamese elders and then see whether a program to increase interaction between Vietnamese grandparents and grandchildren would decrease their social isolation. Yolanda lacks contacts within the Vietnamese community as well as skills with the language. Although she wants to pursue her interests in diversity, she feels overwhelmed by the problems of studying a culture so different from her own. She wonders whether she should just do something easier for her thesis.

Vignette 2

Leroy Anderson, an African American man in his eighties, sees his doctor regularly for his high blood pressure and hypertension. At a recent visit, his doctor suggested that he participate in a research study to improve the health of African Americans being conducted by a local university. Leroy agreed to participate and the researchers called him and scheduled a visit to his apartment. Leroy's apartment has been broken into several times and he's learned the hard way to never open his door to strangers. When the researchers arrived, Leroy wasn't sure whether they were really legitimate, so he refused to let them inside.

Vignette 3

May Thomas, age 75, *loves* research and volunteers for every study that she sees advertised in her neighborhood paper or at the local senior center. She fills out surveys by mail and has even had researchers come to her house three different times. Her daughter asks her why she commits so much time to this and May responds that she believes she is helping to make other people's lives better and that she truly enjoys seeing the questions they ask and meeting the researchers. Her only complaint is that she rarely gets to hear what these studies found—only one study of the many that she's participated in has ever sent her the results.

Vignette 4

Mrs. Chiu has been experiencing troubling memory problems for the past several years. Her daughter Shari noticed that it wasn't just forgetting where the house keys were, but she would find household objects in strange places, like the waffle iron in the bathroom closet. Fortunately, Mrs. Chiu lives in a large city with a state-of-the-art memory center. Shari was impressed with the different types of tests that were conducted to determine her mother's problem: she had a complete physical with blood tests to rule out other conditions, she was asked different kinds of questions to assess her thinking skills, and she also had magnetic resonance imaging (MRI) to take an image of her brain. Although Shari was born and raised in the United States, her mother came to the United States from China. Through the Internet, Shari was able to find lots of information about memory loss and dementia, but little information for people of Chinese heritage. At the memory center, they told her about a study being conducted with elders of Chinese heritage. To participate in this study, Mrs. Chiu would have the entire memory assessment (including the MRI) done every year to chart the course of her dementia. Mrs. Chiu decided to participate even though she knew this observational study did not offer her any new treatment for her condition. She hoped that a better understanding of how dementia affects different groups of people might help people of Shari's generation when they get older.

WHY FOCUS ON RESEARCH METHODS?

How Do We Understand People and Their Behavior?

How do we determine what people are like, what problems they may have, and how to help improve their lives? In the social sciences, we value systematic observation as a way to figure this out. This empirical focus means that we base our knowledge of people on these observations. Sometimes researchers serve as observers as they record behavior they see, but other times researchers ask people to serve as their own observer and describe their experiences, or give a "self-report" to us. If someone is unable to report or someone else may give a more accurate report, we may then turn to physicians or family members to help us learn more about the subject. We can also use special equipment to give us observations of things we cannot see, like the inside of someone's brain through functional magnetic resonance imaging (fMRI). Through these different types of observations, we are able to figure out people's characteristics and the causes of their problems and their joys, and thus identify potential ways to help improve their lives. We then again use research to conduct interventions to ameliorate the problems people are having or to promote changes that we think will help people live happier, healthier lives. Without systematic research, we would not have an accurate picture of people and important issues might go unnoticed. Problems might be left unsolved or effective coping strategies might be overlooked, and others who could benefit from them would suffer needlessly. Thus, we use research methods to help us understand people, and more specifically for this text, to understand older people.

What Disciplines Study Aging?

Although many different disciplines have subfields that are interested in aging and older people (for example, biology, psychology, nursing), the field of gerontology focuses solely on advanced aging. Gerontology is the scientific study of aging from adulthood, or maturity, to old age (Cavanaugh & Blanchard-Fields, 2006). Given that advanced aging processes affect all people who live to adulthood, the field of gerontology necessarily includes many different disciplines. Gerontology has a strong interdisciplinary nature, including disciplines such as biology, psychology, sociology, medicine, nursing, social work, epidemiology, economics, communications, anthropology, humanities, demography, public health, and exercise and sports science. Although there is some theoretical debate over whether gerontology is a discipline in its own right or whether it is an interdisciplinary field of study (Alkema & Alley, 2006; Ferraro, 2006b), readers should note that researchers of aging could have been trained in gerontology with its interdisciplinary focus, or could have been trained in a specific discipline (e.g., biology or psychology) and conduct research from within that discipline (e.g., the biology of aging or the social psychology of aging). Alkema and Alley (2006) argue that biology, sociology, and psychology are the three primary disciplines that have historically anchored gerontology and that a gerontologist needs to have some understanding of each of these disciplines. In working to further advance the field of gerontology, Ferraro coined the term "gerontological imagination," which he defined as "an awareness of the

TABLE 2.1   Tenets of a Gerontological Imagination

	Tenet	Description
1.	Aging and causality	Aging is not a cause of all age-related phenomena. Thus, gerontologists maintain a healthy skepticism for what is attributed to be *age* effects.
2.	Aging as multifaceted change	Aging involves biological, psychological, and social changes in individuals at varying rates. The transitions associated with growing older are probably not linearly related to chronological age, and the process of aging itself is also multidimensional in nature.
3.	Genetic influences on aging	The imprint of genetics on development and aging is substantial. Genetics influence not only longevity but also biological and behavioral processes across the life course.
4.	Aging and heterogeneity	Age is positively associated with heterogeneity in a population.
5.	Aging and life-course analysis	Aging is a lifelong process, and using a life-course perspective helps advance the scientific study of aging.
6.	Aging and cumulative disadvantage	Disadvantage accumulates over the life course, thereby differentiating a cohort over time.
7.	Aging and ageism	There is a propensity toward ageism in modern societies; ageism may also exist among elderly people or those who work with or for elderly people. Even scholars interested in aging may manifest ageism.

Source: Ferraro, (2006b).

process of human aging that enables one to understand the scientific contributions of a variety of researchers studying aging" (Ferraro, 2006a, p. 327). With the term gerontological imagination, Ferraro outlined seven tenets of how gerontologists think about aging (see Table 2.1).

These tenets articulate the way many gerontologists approach the study of aging. For them, the true focus is to examine age *changes* and not age *differences* (Ferraro, 2006b). When a researcher finds that older adults have higher vocabulary scores than younger adults, this is an age difference. Age differences do not distinguish between the particular time period during which an individual was raised (their cohort) and between developmental changes that occur as people age (age changes). Many gerontologists are interested in the developmental processes that occur as we age, not in the fact that one age group may have had more focused vocabulary training (or access to computers) than another. To study age changes, many gerontologists use longitudinal research designs to follow people over time to determine what stays the same and what changes with age instead of the more common cross-sectional methods in which different groups of people are compared at one time. Indeed, as gerontology has developed as a discipline, more complex sequential design models have been developed that combine both longitudinal and cross-sectional research designs (Schaie & Willis, 2002) to be able to separate effects of age, cohort, and time of measurement.

ACTIVE LEARNING EXPERIENCE: UNDERSTANDING THE SEVEN TENETS OF GERONTOLOGY

This experience will provide you with an opportunity to think in detail about Ferraro's seven tenets of gerontology and what they mean. Upon completion of this activity, you will be able to:

1. List Ferraro's seven tenets of gerontology.
2. Give an explanation of each one's meaning.
3. Give an example from the real world that illustrates one of the seven tenets.

This activity will require 45 minutes (30 minutes answering questions and 15 minutes of discussion).

Instructions:

Follow the instructions below and write out your responses to the questions given.

1. Go to Table 2.1 to find the seven tenets of gerontology.
2. Read each tenet and its corresponding description.
3. What does each tenet mean to you? Write your response to this question for each tenet.
4. Find an example from the real world that you think illustrates one of the seven tenets.
5. Share your example with another student. Your teacher may lead a discussion of these tenets and of your examples.

What Disciplines Study Issues of Diversity?

As we discuss throughout the text, most research examining human behavior has been conducted with participants from mainstream groups (that is, White, middle-class, and male) and thus has ignored the elements of diversity we spotlight in this book (gender, race or ethnicity, social class, religion, sexual orientation, and rural or urban community location). Some disciplines, such as cultural anthropology, have long studied different cultural groups of people, whereas other disciplines, such as sociology and social work, have studied the experiences of people from oppressed groups for some time. More recently, subfields that specialize in understanding particular areas of diversity (e.g., race or ethnicity) have developed. For example, in psychology there is a relatively new subfield of racial and ethnic minority psychology that focuses on understanding issues that develop for people from different racial and ethnic groups (see suggested readings at the end of the chapter). Thus, although there are researchers investigating issues in specific areas of diversity (like ethnicity or race), no single field examines issues of all of the different levels of diversity that we discuss in this book.

Are There Disciplines That Study Both Aging and Diversity?

Given the relatively recent move to studying issues of people from diverse groups, it may not be surprising that there are not specific disciplines that focus on the intersection of aging and diversity in general. To conduct this research, one would have educational training in aging *and* in diversity. While there are no disciplines that have this general focus, we are beginning to see subfields develop that, similar to the research examining diversity, focus on one particular element of diversity and examine aging within that area. For example, ethnogeriatrics is a field that is at the intersection of aging, health, and race or ethnicity. Geriatrics is a branch of medicine that focuses on the health of older people. Ethnogeriatrics focuses on the health of older people from diverse ethnic and racial groups (Yeo, 2000). It is exciting to see the research that comes from these subfields because they truly enrich our understanding of aging and how the different elements of diversity can affect the aging process in both positive and negative ways. Unfortunately, it is difficult to get a comprehensive picture of the different elements of diversity and aging because no discipline studies them in a comprehensive manner.

Aging and Diversity Online: Professional Organizations

Gerontological Society of America (GSA). GSA is an organization committed to the multi- and interdisciplinary study of aging. Thus members of GSA include biologists, economists, social workers, nurses, physicians and psychologists, just to name a few. http://www.geron.org/default.asp

Division 20 of the American Psychological Association. Division 20 is dedicated to studying the psychology of adult development and aging. Its website provides useful links for students, researchers, and clinicians, including the latest news on aging issues. http://apadiv20.phhp.ufl.edu/index.htm

National Association of Social Workers (NASW). This website includes information about aging and cultural diversity that is relevant for students, clinicians, and researchers in social work and other helping disciplines. http://www.socialworkers.org/

A BRIEF HISTORY OF RESEARCH ON AGING AND DIVERSITY

To understand the current state of research with diverse elders, it is important to examine key pieces of the past. Originally, most research on aging focused on mainstream populations or the dominant group in society (Liang, 2002). For example, one of the longest running American studies on aging is the Baltimore Longitudinal Study on Aging (BLSA) that started in 1958. The original participants in this study came from convenience samples recruited by friends and family members who were White, male, and upper middle class. Women did not join the BLSA as participants until 1978. Even more recently, additional diverse populations have been recruited to join the BLSA, but the majority of the participants are still White and upper middle class.

In addition to ignoring women and minority elders, there is also a notorious example of inclusion of African Americans in a study that began in 1932. The Tuskegee Syphilis Study examined the life course of syphilis among a sample of African American men. Once a cure for syphilis was found, instead of giving that treatment to the sample, the researchers continued to watch the progression of the disease in the sample and, in some instances, actively prevented the participants from getting treatment. Many of these men unknowingly infected their wives and children and ended up dying from syphilis. The reverberations from this study can still be felt within the African American community as trust in research and in researchers must be regained.

The BLSA and Tuskegee studies aside, most early research on aging was "cross-sectional" in that it compared two different age groups (for example, college students and older adults). As the research community began to recognize that some groups did carry characteristics that differed from the mainstream, women and African Americans began to be included in research studies. These studies primarily focused on finding differences between Whites and African Americans or between men and women (Liang, 2002). Few studies examined other ethnic groups and even fewer studies focused solely on one diverse group to understand their experience from within, without referencing the comparison to the mainstream group (Kurasaki, Sue, Chun, & Gee, 2000). Now we know that people from different groups often have different characteristics and that it is important to include diverse groups in our research in order to get a complete and accurate picture of the aging process. Fortunately, the research world is changing.

ACTIVE LEARNING EXPERIENCE: THE INTERNET AS A SOURCE OF INFORMATION ABOUT PEOPLE*

This experience will provide you with an opportunity to gather information about diverse elders from the Internet and then evaluate the quality of that information. You will also compare that information with websites we have provided.

This activity will take 45 minutes (30 minutes on the computer and 15 minutes of discussion).

Instructions:

Find a computer that has a search engine on the Internet (for example, Google or Yahoo), follow the instructions below and write out your responses to the questions given.

1. Choose a group that represents an element of diversity from our text (for example, Japanese elders or older women in poverty).
2. Enter that group name into the search engine and locate at least three websites related to that group.

---

* Adapted from Dr. Shirley McGuire.

3. What type of information is contained in each website? For example, is it academic or social in nature?

4. What criteria would you use to evaluate the quality of the information on each website? Do you think that you could use the information for a research paper? Why or why not?

5. Do any of the websites contain assurances about accuracy or provide disclaimers?

6. Look at any of the following websites:
   http://www.aoa.gov/prof/Statistics/profile/profiles2002.aspx
   http://nihseniorhealth.gov/
   http://apadiv20.phhp.ufl.edu/
   http://geron.org/
   http://www.aarp.org/

7. Compare the information you see about older adults on these sites with the sites you found for this exercise. Are there any differences?

8. Look at the following recommendations for making a senior-friendly website: http://www.nlm.nih.gov/pubs/checklist.pdf

9. Would it be easy for older adults to use the websites that you visited? Why or why not?

10. Discuss your findings with another person.

As you can see from the above Internet activity, it can be difficult to find information about diverse groups and, when we do find information, it can be difficult to assess its accuracy and quality. Through the "Aging and Diversity Online" sections in this textbook, we point out web resources that we have found to be particularly useful with regard to aging and diversity.

We are now in the midst of a gradual shift from a focus on *age deficits* (from simply comparing younger and older adults) and on *ethnic differences* (from showing only African American and White differences) to showing how we can achieve accurate and rich descriptions of diverse populations, design interventions to aid specific populations, and monitor the effects of interventions over time to find those that are effective and include diverse elders. As we turn to examine the research process, we hope that it will become clear that aging research is now moving away from using single methods to using multiple methods to get at the problem being addressed. As researchers began to be interested in diverse groups, it became clear that adaptations to the research process would need to be made; not only are diverse groups different from mainstream groups, but the diversity of the research participants can affect every aspect of the research process and the conclusions that we draw.

OVERVIEW OF THE RESEARCH PROCESS

As we briefly review the basic research process, think about how the diversity of groups might affect the process. Researchers typically start with a research question they want to answer or a problem they want to solve. For example, it may be clear that immigrant elders are experiencing high levels of stress and a researcher wants to first document the levels of stress, determine what are the causes of that stress, and how can it be alleviated. The researchers then need to determine how they will measure the concepts such as stress (e.g., by survey, by taking saliva samples and measuring cortisol levels) and how they will collect these measurements (e.g., in person, by mail). The researchers also need to find people to participate in the study and then help ensure that the participants are able to complete it. The researchers will then need to examine the information collected, come up with any conclusions from the data and then communicate those conclusions to the world. Finally, sometimes researchers try to change people's behavior. Perhaps they have gained information from previous studies that suggests exercise or support groups might alleviate stress, or perhaps a new drug to combat stress has been developed. In these cases, intervention studies are conducted to try to change people's behavior.

The traditional research process is often presented as being composed of the following steps:

1. Identify a research question or problem.
2. Construct a conceptual model based on theory.
3. Develop hypotheses.
4. Conduct research.
5. Analyze and interpret the data.
6. Report the findings.

In this traditional presentation of the process (readers may have even seen a schematic like this in an introductory research methods text), researchers start with a research question they want to answer or a problem they would like to solve. They then find an existing theory or develop a new theory that answers the question or explains why this problem occurs. From that theory, they define the concepts they will examine and develop hypotheses to test. They then conduct the research study, analyze the data they have collected and report their findings. Often, these results lead to additional questions and the research process begins again. Thus, the research process follows prescribed steps and is iterative as new research questions and problems continually come up and the process is started again. It is also possible to begin this process midstream, for example beginning at step 5, when one reviews the results of someone else's research and new questions stem from those results. But even when starting at a different step, the subsequent steps are followed and the process continues in this iterative way.

HOW DIVERSITY CAN AFFECT THE RESEARCH PROCESS

As mentioned previously, conducting research with diverse elders can affect all aspects of the research process. If one does not pay attention to or is not aware of these effects, it may be very difficult to obtain any information from the group of interest, or the information that is obtained may not be accurate or representative of all members of that group. In other words, the information will not be very useful in helping to describe the characteristics of the group and their problems, and in suggesting any solutions to those problems. Similarly, it will not be clear whether the results from any intervention studies will generalize to the population as a whole.

It may seem very daunting to consider how much participants' diversity can affect the research process. One may start to wonder whether one can do this research as our character in the first vignette, Yolanda Estrada, did. Fortunately, each researcher does not have to start from scratch. Instead, we can learn from the previous experiences that researchers have had with diverse groups. We will now examine different aspects of the research process and briefly describe how the diversity of the participants can affect the research. Lessons learned from intervention studies enrolling diverse groups will be especially important in conducting culturally sensitive research (Arean, Alvidrez, Nery, Estes, & Linkins, 2003; Gallagher-Thompson et al., 2003a; Gallagher-Thompson, Solano, Coon, & Arean, 2003b; Gilliss et al., 2001; Levkoff & Sanchez, 2003; Williams, Tappen, Buscemi, Rivera, & Lezcano, 2001).

Identifying the Research Question or Problem

Often, one of the first steps in conducting research is to identify the research question or problem one wants to examine. When working with diverse groups, determining the research question or focus can be difficult. Researchers may have a perspective of the problem that may or may not match the community's perspective. Thus, even this initial step can be affected by diversity, if, for example, the researchers do not fully understand the characteristics of the population they are studying. Caregiver burden is a problem that has been examined with mainstream populations. If one wants to examine this topic with diverse elders, simply applying knowledge from the mainstream research would lead to several problems. For example, in research with Latino caregivers, Gallagher-Thompson, Solano, Coon, & Arean (2003b) concur that these caregivers do experience stressors and difficulties related to caregiving, but they do not characterize them as a "burden" because taking care of one's family is such a strong cultural value. Researchers who approach a Latino cultural group and conceptualize their research question as "caregiver burden" may alienate the participants as the question framed this way is not relevant to them.

Conducting Focus Groups To avoid imposing inappropriate cultural values on a particular group, conducting focus groups within the community prior to determining the research question can be extremely helpful. Focus groups are relatively small groups of people (eight to ten) who are asked their opinion or perspective about a particular issue (Krueger, 2000). This is typically done in an interactive session in which a trained leader asks a series of probing questions designed to elicit discussion and opinions from the group members. Instead of a researcher's assuming that he or she knows the problems faced in a community, it is a good idea to ascertain whether the community views the situation as a problem. For example, members of an immigrant elder population may be experiencing high levels of psychological distress, and the researcher's task is to figure out (1) causes for the distress to then (2) be able to help alleviate it. One researcher might assume that it was the immigrants' traumatic exit from their country that is causing the distress and that researcher might construct a survey that focuses on those experiences. But perhaps the biggest stressor for the immigrant elders may be the poverty they are now experiencing in the United States. To avoid focusing on the wrong issue, assessing the current situation is important.

Focus groups of American Indian participants from the southwestern United States helped identify some unique cultural perceptions of caregiving difficulties for their group (Hennessy & John, 1996). Similar to mainstream populations, American Indian caregivers experienced stress and difficulties while trying to fulfill both outside work and home caregiving roles. One might assume that caregivers are frustrated that the caregiving role prevents them from accomplishing things they need to do at work. This assumption might lead researchers to consider providing families with institutional care for the elder so the caregiver will be free to continue his or her work. Hennessy and John (1996) report that some experts believe that, given the decrease in family size and the increase in the numbers of both spouses working, people will need to relinquish their caregiving roles to outside institutions. From the American Indian focus group participants, it became clear that they would not do this. They repeatedly stated that institutional care was simply unacceptable. Instead, they would prefer to have outside care that can supplement their caregiving roles instead of supplant them. Information from the American Indian focus groups also suggested that caregiver stress was actually from having to do things outside the home in addition to caring for the elder. American Indian caregivers did experience stress in their caregiving, but it was expressed as a job burden rather than a caregiving burden: they were stressed that their outside responsibilities (job) did not allow them to be as good a caregiver as they wanted to be. They wished that they could just stay with the elder all of the time. If this is indeed the cause of their caregiving stress, then easing work roles (perhaps along the lines of allowing family medical leave from work) might be a better solution rather than institutional care for the elder. Without a clear understanding of different groups, determining an appropriate research question is very difficult. Focus groups can be used to better understand a cultural group so that services that they really need, want, and will use can be provided.

Aging and Diversity Online: Program Evaluation

American Evaluation Association. This is "an international professional association of evaluators devoted to the application and exploration of program evaluation, personnel evaluation, technology, and many other forms of evaluation." Focus groups are but one example of methods used in program evaluation. The association is currently working to make their Program Evaluation Standards more culturally appropriate. http://www.eval.org

The Importance of Culture in Evaluation: A practical guide for evaluators. This publication offers thoughtful guidelines and important questions for people conducting program evaluation with different cultural groups. http://www.thecoloradotrust.org/repository/publications/pdfs/EVALUATION/CrossCulturalGuide.r3.pdf

Learning From Elders Representing Diverse Groups   In addition to promoting better understanding of different cultural groups, conducting culturally appropriate research may also allow more mainstream groups to learn from diverse groups. White elders, for example, use long-term institutional care at higher rates than other ethnic groups, but it may be that in some cases this is not the best option for them, or it may be that they would ultimately prefer other arrangements if available. The insights gained from American Indian focus groups suggests that building outside supports for the family caregiving situation (caregiver training and education, caregiver family consensus building and education, respite care) would ease the difficulties of the caregiving situation (Hennessy & John, 1996). Building similar supports for White caregivers may allow elders to stay out of institutions.

Finding the keys to longevity is another area from which research with elders of different ethnic groups could help all elders. In the United States, both people of Asian heritage and people of Hispanic heritage live, on average, longer than White and African American elders (Angel & Angel, 2006). Determining what factors contribute to this increased longevity could help all of us live longer, healthier lives.

Although conducting focus groups can help increase understanding about diverse groups, conducting focus groups also requires cultural sensitivity. For example, the group may respond differently depending on who is facilitating the group. Is the facilitator someone of their own gender, of their own group? What language is the focus group facilitator using? The type of questions that one asks during a focus group may also be impacted by culture. For some cultures, merely asking about what services they *might* use implies that those services will be available in the future. When the services do not materialize (perhaps due to a lack of funding or even due to low interest) it can represent a breach of faith or trust for that community and could damage future relationships.

Thus, step 1 of the traditional research process, identifying the research question or problem, can be a complex one. A researcher's perspective on a particular issue may not reflect community members' perspectives. If researchers are interested in having their study represent the perspective of the community in which members are doing the research, then including the community (by conducting focus groups, for example) when defining the research question is important. Linking it with the theory is the next step in the traditional research process.

Aging and Diversity Online: Sources of Research Conducted With Diverse Elders

Databases of research publications can be an excellent source to find both information about how to conduct research with people from diverse backgrounds and research that has been conducted with elders from diverse groups. Some of these databases, such as Pubmed (formerly Medline), are provided free to the public by the federal government; others may have a subscription fee. Often universities or colleges pay these subscriptions and make the database available to their students and faculty at no charge. Two of the databases that we frequently use are described below.

PubMed. PubMed is a service of the United States National Library of Medicine that includes over 17 million citations from MEDLINE and other life science journals for biomedical articles back to the 1950s. PubMed includes links to full text articles and other related resources. www.pubmed.gov

PsycINFO. PsycINFO is an abstract (not full-text) database of psychological literature from the 1800s to the present. It is an important tool for researchers and students who are interested in literature related to the field of psychology. PsycINFO is typically accessed through a university library, but for those who may be interested in details about the database or in purchasing an individual subscription, see the website below. http://www.apa.org/psycinfo/

Theory and Conceptual Models

A theory is an explanation of the relationship among different concepts or variables. Often this theoretical perspective is operationalized through a conceptual model that pictorially presents the variables and their interrelationships as well as describing the population to be studied and the research design to be used. For example, different theories can explain risk factors for complications from diabetes. One theory may focus on socioeconomic status (SES) as an important variable because people of low SES often cannot afford to live in areas where there is access to healthy foods. Another theory might focus on the lay explanations different groups may have for diabetes and how their folk constructions affect adherence to doctors' instructions. The research conducted will be very different depending on the theory being used to investigate the research question. Hypothesis development, the next step in the research process, is driven by the theories one is using. A detailed examination of the inclusion of theories, conceptual models, and hypothesis development in research is beyond the focus of this book, but we do want to stress the importance of using theories and conceptual models to conduct research. Two commonly used conceptual models include the Andersen Behavioral Model of Health Services Utilization (Andersen, Lewis, Giachello, Aday, & Chiu, 1981; Gelberg, Andersen, & Leake, 2000) and the Proceed-Precede Model of Health Programming, Planning and Evaluation (Green & Kreuter, 2005). These models are commonly used in research with diverse populations. The Andersen model, with its predisposing, enabling, and need constructs, attempts to explain why people obtain health care. The Proceed-Precede model, developed by Green and Kreuter, has been used predominantly in health program planning and health behavior research. See Aging and Diversity Online section for additional information about conceptual models, theory, and measurement.

Theory application and conceptual model development is often a step that new researchers gloss over (even though it is required by funding agencies). Theories may also differ depending on the group one is studying, as one theory may explain behavior in one group, but may not explain the same behavior in another group. This is particularly relevant when conducting research with people from different groups within the elements of diversity. For example, SES may be a strong predictor of diabetes complications for White women, but not for Asian women. Both the research question and the theory used determine the concepts or variables that one studies and the hypotheses that one tests. Thus, these are important steps in the research process. Once the research question has been identified, and the theory, hypotheses, and the conceptual model are determined, the method that one will use needs to be determined before one can conduct the research study.

Aging and Diversity Online: Theory and Measurement

Proceed-Precede Model of Health Programming, Planning and Evaluation. This website summarizes the Green-Kreuter Proceed-Precede conceptual model. http://www.lgreen.net/precede.htm

Health Behavior Constructs. Theory, Measurement and Research. Created by the Division for Cancer Control and Population Sciences (DCCPS) at the National Cancer Institute (NCI), this website gives a basic overview of theory and constructs, and then provides definitions of 12 major theoretical constructs used in health behavior research and information about the best measures of these constructs. http://dccps.cancer.gov/brp/constructs

Conducting the Research

The next step in the research process is to conduct the research. For most research studies, this means preparation for gathering the data. But for some research studies, this step has already been completed.

Secondary Data Analysis   Sometimes, we do not need to collect data ourselves to be able to answer our research question because another researcher or organization has already done so. Analyzing data that has already been collected is typically referred to as secondary data analysis. For example, researchers at the University of Michigan were interested in determining whether socioeconomic status was related to pain experienced during the last year of life. Specifically, they wanted to know: Do poor people experience more pain at the end of their lives than wealthy people?

Silveira, Kabeto and Langa (2005) conducted secondary data analysis using data from the Health and Retirement Study (HRS), which is conducted by the University of Michigan's Institute for Social Research and is funded by the NIA. This study involves interviews with a nationally representative sample of 22,000 Americans over the age of 50 every two years. Using data already collected for the HRS, Silveira et al. (2005) examined the experience of pain in the last year of life and found that wealthier elders were significantly less likely than poorer elders to suffer from pain at the end of their lives, even after controlling for age, gender, ethnicity, education, and diagnosis. Please note that the HRS is not the only dataset suitable for secondary data analysis.

Unfortunately, many of the large longitudinal studies on aging, such as the Baltimore Longitudinal Study mentioned earlier, did not include adequate representation of diverse populations when they were started. The Established Populations for the Epidemiologic Studies of the Elderly (EPESE) is another example of a large-scale study with limited diversity. Data were collected from four sites in Boston; two counties in Iowa; New Haven, Connecticut; and Duke University, North Carolina. At the New Haven site, the EPESE sample included an African American and White sample, but otherwise the samples were predominantly White. To expand the generalizability of the EPESE, additional samples are being collected from other ethnic groups. For example, the Hispanic EPESE (H-EPESE) collects data on the same variables from the EPESE study, but its sample includes "3,050 Mexican-origin individuals aged 65 and older who reside in Texas, California, New Mexico, Arizona, and Colorado" (Hill, Burdette, Angel, & Angel, 2006, p. 4).

For researchers who are going to collect their own data, there are many details to be addressed. As they prepare to conduct the actual research study, they must choose a particular method and a study design and must decide how to measure or assess the concepts in which they are interested. Once these details are determined, the entire study must be submitted to an Institutional Review Board (IRB) that determines whether the proposed research study adheres to ethical standards. After obtaining approval from the IRB, researchers can then begin to ask people to participate in their study (to recruit participants) and to conduct the actual research. Each of these steps can be affected when conducting research with diverse populations.

Method and Design Issues

The research method one uses is determined by several factors, but the primary determinant is the research question. If the research question involves gaining an initial understanding of an existing situation or problem, then *observational or descriptive research* is the appropriate method. In observational research, researchers study a particular issue (e.g., a social problem, a disease, a social group) but they do not try to make changes or intervene while they are conducting the research. For example, they do not try to improve participants' diets or suggest medications or solutions until after their observations are complete. With observational research, researchers are trying to understand the problem better, often with the goal that through better understanding, good solutions can be found.

In contrast to observational research, *experimental research* does make changes in the normal course of a participant's life. In applied settings, experimental research is often called intervention research as the researchers are changing or intervening in participants' lives. Clinical trials are an example of intervention research in that they test the safety and effectiveness of new treatments ranging from new drugs to exercise programs. Clinical trials often follow strict protocols to both ensure the safety of their participants and to maintain control over the study so that outside factors do not affect its results. They must be able to determine whether it was the treatment that actually made the difference. Most clinical trials maintain control over the study by randomly assigning participants to the different treatment conditions. This random assignment allows individual differences in the participants to be randomly distributed across the different treatment conditions and thus any effects can be attributed to the treatment and not to individual differences. For additional information on clinical trials, see the Aging and Diversity Online section.

Aging and Diversity Online: Clinical Trials

Clinical Trials. The National Institutes of Health provides a website that gives basic information regarding clinical trials and also provides regularly updated information about federally and privately supported clinical research. This website contains information about a trial's purpose, eligibility requirements, locations, and phone numbers for more details. http://www.clinicaltrials.gov/ct

In addition to determining whether one will conduct observational or experimental (also called intervention) research, the study design also will be determined by the research question. As we discussed earlier in the chapter, most research was originally cross-sectional in nature. Researchers would study different groups of people (for example, older and younger adults) at one point in time. If researchers are interested in differences between groups, cross-sectional designs are appropriate. But these cross-sectional designs do not examine how people change over time as they age and mature and they cannot separate age and cohort effects, so longitudinal designs have been developed. In longitudinal designs the same people are studied at two or more points in time to determine how they have changed (or not changed) over time. More recently, complex sequential designs that combine both longitudinal and cross-sectional research designs have been developed (Schaie & Willis, 2002). Thus, the study design depends on whether one is looking for differences across groups or for changes over time.

How are these method and design issues affected by diversity? As we mentioned during our review of historical issues around research on diversity, some groups have had extremely negative experiences with research and others have been virtually ignored. These previous experiences set up attitudes toward research that may affect people's interest in allowing research in their community and in participating in such research. Thus, researchers need to take into account their participant population's attitude toward research when developing the study method and design. Although ideally one's method and design are determined by the research question, if the community in which one is interested has been virtually ignored by the mainstream research community, then potential participants may be resistant to having an intervention created for and tested on other groups in their community. Under these conditions, beginning with an observational study may be more appropriate. In other communities where research has been conducted but the results have never been conveyed back to the community, observational research may be viewed with disdain, as the community members may wonder what they can gain from such research. An understanding of the community interest and good communication about the purpose of a study will help members of the community better understand the choice of method and design.

Measurement of Concepts   Culture can also affect the concepts studied and how the researcher measures them (Teresi, Stewart, Morales, & Stahl, 2006). As mentioned earlier, studying caregiver difficulties using the concept of caregiver "burden" would not be culturally appropriate for certain ethnic minority groups. How a researcher assesses or measures the concepts of interest also has

cultural implications. Concepts could be measured using anonymous survey questionnaires, individual face-to-face interviews or even in focus group settings. For example, if we were interested in determining how stressed immigrant elders are, we could measure this quantitatively by asking immigrant elders to give us a rating of their stress level on a scale from 1 (not at all stressed) to 10 (extremely stressed). The numbers obtained from these responses can then be analyzed using statistical techniques. Using qualitative methods, we would ask immigrant elders to describe in their own words (and often in their own language) the stress they are experiencing. These descriptions would then be analyzed using qualitative methods in which the actual words of the participants would be systematically examined for themes or topics that would help explain immigrant elders' stress.

Computer-based surveys give yet another example of how researchers can collect information *and* how different elements of diversity affect its use. For example, with computer-based surveys, it may be easier to obtain certain groups of participants and to get accurate answers to sensitive questions as some elders might be more comfortable filling out an anonymous computer-based survey than participating in a face-to-face interview or focus group. Indeed, one of the first large-scale studies of lesbian and gay Baby Boomers used a computer-based approach (MetLife Mature Market Institute, 2006). Zogby International, a research company that maintains a nationally representative selection of people to whom web-based surveys are given, sent email invitations to 34,829 individuals who had agreed to participate in online surveys. Of these, 1000 people, 157 of whom had not previously identified themselves as gay or lesbian, identified themselves as LGBT and agreed to participate in the survey. It is hard to imagine a more cost-effective way to contact more than 34,000 people to (1) determine their eligibility, and (2) to ask them to volunteer for research.

Computer-based surveys have the potential of reaching many populations, such as rural populations, who otherwise would not have the opportunity to participate in research, but they also have the problem that the sample gained from computer-based research often differs from the general population. Many groups of elders—rural, low-income, and new immigrant elders—do not currently use computers, so this method, if used exclusively, would also miss many segments of the population. Thus, computers become yet another method that researchers can use but they have both benefits and drawbacks.

The amount of contact that a participant has with a researcher varies across different methods of collecting data. When data are collected from a medical file or when a survey is mailed or given over the Internet, a participant may never see the researcher, or a participant may spend several hours with researchers in a face-to-face interview. Cultural influences will be different depending on the amount and type of interaction the participants have with the researcher.

Which type of measurement is better: having participants put numbers to concepts or respond in their own words? This question has plagued research for a long time with many researchers feeling forced to choose one measurement approach over the other. Fortunately, researchers are beginning to recognize the strengths and weaknesses of both qualitative and quantitative methods and to then use each to their appropriate advantage. These mixed-method models take advantage of the strengths of both methods by using the flexibility and rich description gained from a qualitative study to help describe and understand the circumstances and problems that a particular group faces. The information gained from the qualitative study can then be used to construct a survey with appropriate questions to assess whether the information gleaned from the qualitative study generalizes to a larger group. A special supplement to the journal *Medical Care* describes these measurement issues in more detail (see suggested readings at the end of the chapter). Resources are also available to help researchers determine how to focus their evaluation research to get the most use from it (Patton, 2008).

Levkoff and Sanchez (2003) report that a combination of quantitative and qualitative (or ethnographic) research has been most effective in their research with people from diverse ethnic groups. Qualitative research methods helped "create an environment in which participants, family members, and agency administrators felt comfortable sharing information" (Levkoff & Sanchez, 2003, p. 25). It was also easier to convey sensitivity to the diverse group when doing qualitative work. They also found that some quantitative scales may be inappropriate for the population and that the length may be burdensome. On the other hand, the cultural affiliation of the interviewer may differentially impact qualitative responses more than a mailed quantitative survey. The match (or mismatch) of researcher with participant in terms of gender, ethnic background, socioeconomic status, sexual orientation, or religion may impact the participants' responses more strongly in qualitative studies than in an anonymous quantitative survey. There is also some evidence that different ethnic groups may have preferences for qualitative or quantitative research (Yeo, 2000). For example, Asian groups may prefer Likert-scale-based measurement, where they can select a number on a scale, whereas other groups may prefer giving qualitative open-ended responses. Thus, preferences for how a question is asked (e.g., through an interview, on a questionnaire) and how it is answered (e.g., in a participant's own words, through a numerical rating) vary depending on the participant's cultural background.

Multiple Methods   In recent years, researchers have turned to using multiple methods and measures to understand human behavior in all of its complexity. These methods can be used in a range of studies from observational studies to understand complex conditions like dementia to behavioral clinical trials designed to increase people's physical activity. To better understand dementia, instead of relying on one measure of an elder's thinking abilities (or cognitive status) at one point in time, several different measures of cognitive status and different methods of assessing thinking abilities are used and are then administered at later dates. The Memory and Aging Clinic (MAC) at the University of California at San Francisco uses many of these methods and measures. One study entitled *Characterization of Dementia in Asian-Pacific Islanders* is directed by Bruce Miller and sponsored by the NIH. This descriptive or observational study is designed to understand dementia in Chinese individuals and involves multiple methods including neurological and physical exams, magnetic resonance images of the brain (MRI), cognitive testing, and neuropsychiatric assessments. The stated goal of this study is to increase the knowledge of dementia among people of Asian-Pacific Islander heritage.

Intervention research also uses multiple methods and measures. To test the effectiveness of the Community Healthy Activities Model Program for Seniors

(CHAMPS), a behavioral clinical trial was conducted (Stewart et al., 2001). This was a randomized controlled trial in which participants were randomly assigned either to receive the physical activity intervention or to be in a wait-listed control group (who would receive the activity intervention after the study was over). Researchers used both physiological measures and self-report measures of physical activity collected before and after the intervention and found that the program increased older adults' physical activity over that of a control group (Stewart et al., 2001). In addition to the different types of measures used during the main part of the study, participants completed a survey to determine which parts of the program they found most helpful and a small subset of the sample also attended a focus group to further evaluate the program. Thus, the researchers were able to get quantitative survey data from a relatively large number of participants and qualitative responses from a subset of them and provide an excellent example of how these methods can work together.

From the quantitative survey data, it was clear that the telephone call component of the study (program staff checking in with participants) was rated as very helpful. This information in itself is useful, but the survey data did not tell *how* the telephone calls were helpful. Through the focus group discussions, it became clear that, in addition to serving as a reminder to be physically active, the telephone calls "created a bond between participant and counselor, fostering continued commitment to the activity program" (Gillis, Grossman, McLellan, King, & Stewart, 2002, p. 348). Thus, both the qualitative and quantitative measures worked together with the main study measures (physical activity and weight) to help fully evaluate the program.

Aging and Diversity Online: Research Resources

Medical Effectiveness Research Center for Diverse Populations (MERC) at the University of California at San Francisco. This center was established in 1993 to (1) discover mechanisms that explain health disparities, to (2) develop and evaluate interventions to eliminate disparities, and (3) train investigators to conduct research on health disparities. Associated with this center is the Center for Aging in Diverse Communities (CADC), one of the six national Resource Centers for Minority Aging Research (RCMAR). http://dgim.ucsf.edu/diversity

Instructional Strategies for Interviewing Elders from Diverse Ethnic Backgrounds. Developed by the Stanford Geriatric Education Center as a part of the Curriculum in Ethnogeriatrics (listed as a suggested reading in Chapter 4), this document provides concrete suggestions for interviewing elders from diverse groups. http://www.stanford.edu/group/ethnoger/AppC.pdf

The Centers for Disease Control (CDC). The CDC provides a website with information on healthy aging and links to additional relevant areas such as health statistics and research. http://www.cdc.gov/aging

Institutional Review Boards and Culture Before the researchers approach people asking them to participate in their studies, the researchers have to receive approval from an Institutional Review Board (IRB). To get this approval, the researchers prepare an IRB application that summarizes their research and includes all of their research materials. This includes the manner in which they will obtain people's agreement to participate (informed consent) and the procedures in the study. The IRB committee often comprises individuals from the researchers' university, but does not include any member of the research team. Thus, IRB committees are designed to give objective and fair evaluations of the ethical nature of the research. Although this IRB approval procedure is used with almost all research involving human participants, it is not problem-free. When conducting research with diverse populations, it may be difficult for an IRB committee to evaluate whether a proposed research study will be deemed ethical within that particular community. Unless members of the IRB committee have expertise with the population being studied, it will assess whether the proposed study is ethical from the research community's perspective, but not necessarily from the participant community's perspective. Thus, IRB committees may not always have the cultural competence to evaluate research with diverse elders and could potentially miss some important or sensitive issues in proposed research.

Recruitment, Retention, and Diversity   Recruiting a representative sample of participants from the community in which one is interested is essential to be able to generalize one's findings from the sample to the community population as a whole. For example, if one is interested in Vietnamese elders' experiences, then having Vietnamese college students ask their grandparents to be in the study is unlikely to result in a very representative Vietnamese elder sample. This sample would likely include only the Vietnamese elders who had experienced sufficient economic success to enable their grandchildren to attend college and it would fail to represent more impoverished elders. Similarly, keeping participants in the study through its completion (that is, the retention of participants) affects the validity or accuracy of the conclusions drawn. For example, if a subset of participants fail to complete the study due to transportation difficulties, then the findings from the study will be unlikely to generalize to the more impoverished members of that group (as they are the most likely to have transportation difficulties). Some researchers have found that recruitment and retention of minority elders was much more successful when both the ethnic minority community and the research community shared the same goals in the research (Levkoff & Sanchez, 2003). Holding focus groups with community members can help determine community goals and then overlap between the community and the researchers' goals can be found.

Even if one's research goals do overlap with community goals, finding diverse elder participants can be a big challenge in itself. Having a good understanding of the cultural group can help in this regard. Different cultural groups frequent different places (e.g., churches, community centers, gyms). Knowing the characteristics of a culture will help one to know, for example, if contacting local churches or inviting family members to participate in the program will help one find research participants (Gallagher-Thompson et al., 2003b).

Once researchers have found people from their population of interest who are interested in participating in their research study, they want to ensure that the participants actually complete the study. Issues of retention are important for any research study, but can be especially important when conducting research with participants from diverse groups. Some retention strategies may seem obvious when pointed out, yet they can be easily overlooked if one is focused on the mechanics of getting and keeping a study running or if one does not know or understand the participant population very well. For example, the study location, where one will actually collect the information from the participants, may affect whether they are able to complete the study. Relatively simple suggestions such as collecting data in locations where the participants feel comfortable, rather than in research offices that may be hard to find, may have stairs to climb, and may not have easy parking, can help improve retention. Making reminder phone calls and sending thank-you notes for each completed assessment are examples of ways that researchers improve retention in longitudinal studies (Gallagher-Thompson et al., 2003b). Other suggestions for retention may be tailored to the specific group with which you are working. For example, sending out birthday, holiday, and sympathy cards (as appropriate for the participant's religious practices) can be a way to personalize a research study and enhance retention (Gallagher-Thompson et al., 2003a). The effectiveness of both recruitment and retention strategies rely on how well the researchers know the participant group and can tailor their study or program to fit that particular group.

Informed Consent and Diversity

Once researchers have located potential participants, they need to describe the research to be conducted and obtain informed consent. Previous research has demonstrated the importance of being sensitive to the degree of acculturation of the participant and being flexible in the consent process. Williams, Tappen, Buscemi, Rivera & Lezcano (2001) describe significant barriers in getting Cuban-Americans to participate in research because members of this group did not want to disturb the *tranquilidad* (comfort) and *soledad* (solitude, be left alone) of the elders with dementia. They also did not see that the research would be beneficial and thus had *futilidad* (futility) and misperceptions about dementia in elders. Williams and colleagues realized that their assumptions about how to "sell" the research as researchers did not match this cultural group. When the researchers focused on the fact that their intervention was going to improve the life of the elder, some family members thought this implied that they should have been doing more for their elder. This negative implication did not settle well with the families and did not make them interested in participating in the study. The researchers found increased participation when they instead *de-emphasized* that the intervention was so much better than the current care the elder was getting, and instead focused on the idea that visits from research staff were appreciated by the elder and when they used Spanish language forms to describe the research and obtain consent. Again, the issue of using culturally appropriate concepts arose as the word "exercise" was counter to the word *tranquilidad*, so a focus on the "activities" of the study seemed more culturally appropriate. When these changes were made to the recruitment process, more people volunteered to participate in the study.

Giving informed consent is usually thought of as a process where the researcher(s) describes the research to a person, the person can then ask questions about the research, and, if still interested, will agree to participate (or give consent) often by signing a consent form. In the case of dementia, the person who is the guardian for the elder would be legally able to give consent for the elder. Even in these cases, informed consent is treated as a process between the researcher and the guardian who is approached and asked to consent for the elder. For some cultures, however, informed consent is actually a process that involves not just the individual participant or guardian, but other people as well. Family members must be involved in the decision-making process and thus, for some families, giving consent involves discussion of the research among the family members and then the family decides whether to give consent for participation. Cultures also vary on who within the family can officially speak for the family. This may not be the person who is listed as "next of kin" on an institutional form. In their research with Cuban Americans, next of kin usually meant the caregiving daughter and that was the individual who was approached, but usually she consulted with the family and a decision was made with them (Williams et al., 2001). Similar experiences have occurred in different ethnic groups. In trying to obtain consent from the Chinese American caregiver of an elder, the caregiver declined to give her consent until she had talked with her uncle in a distant state who was the eldest male in her family (Levkoff & Sanchez, 2003). Clearly, giving consent is affected by the participant's culture and traditions.

Language Issues   Throughout the research study process, language issues can arise when participant groups speak a language different from the researcher's or when standard measures were developed in one language but needed to be used in a different language. Initially, researchers focused on simply translating all study materials (recruitment advertisements, informed consent forms, questionnaires) into the participant's language. This translation was made more accurate with a process called "back translation." In this process, a bilingual person first translates the material from English into the participant's language. Then, a different bilingual person translates the translated material back into English. Finally, both English versions are compared to see whether the translation process maintained the integrity of the information. Researchers are now finding that simple translation and even a one-time forward-and-back translation is not enough. At the very least, there often need to be many iterations of this process, but many times this translation process does not result in equivalent meaning (Li, McCardle, Clark, Kinsella, & Berch, 2001).

One difficulty in translating occurs with idioms, or short phrases that have meaning beyond the actual literal meaning of the words. Great care with idioms needs to be taken so that information is conveyed clearly in all languages. For example, on the Mini-Mental State Exam (Folstein, Folstein, & McHugh, 1975), one item asks individuals to read the phrase "close your eyes" and then perform the action. But in Shanghai, the translation of "close your eyes" has a death connotation (Katzman et al., 1988). Thus, if an individual from Shanghai had difficulty or hesitated with this item, one would not be able to tell whether it was a result of confusion regarding the item or whether it was that he or she had diminished mental capacity. Although careful back translation is important, it does not ensure that the meaning of the original measure is still intact. Thus, people who have expertise with the culture and the language need to be consulted whenever one is working with translated measures.

Instead of focusing solely on language translation, researchers also need to realize that it is not only the language, but also the content that needs to be made appropriate for the culture (Li et al., 2001). Instead of translating a particular measure, question, or test, the focus should be on adapting the test rather than on translating it. For example, digit-span tests, where individuals repeat a series of numbers or tasks that involve naming the months of the year, vary in difficulty depending on the complexity of each language for numbers and for months. In Japan, the months are simply named in their order (Month 1, Month 2, etc.) as opposed to in the United States (January, February, etc.) (Wolfe, 2002). Thus, the simple task "name the months of the year" has a significant difference in difficulty depending on the language one is using. Clearly, scores on a month-naming task could not be compared across different languages. Even something as seemingly innocuous as a phrase such as "immediate family members" can be difficult to translate. Daughters-in-law, who are often the primary caregivers of elders in Chinese cultures, have been traditionally considered part of their husbands' families and *not* part of their families of origin. Even though the daughter-in-law may provide all the care for an elder, the elder's son is viewed as the "official" caregiver and he is the person who must provide consent and be present for the interview (Levkoff & Sanchez, 2003).

One alternative to translation is to develop measures of important concepts in several languages simultaneously. Thus, instead of developing and validating a measure in one language (and often in one culture) and then working to translate that measure into different languages, development of the initial measure can be made in several different languages from the start. Stewart and Napoles-Springer (2000) present an example of how this worked in developing an international Quality of Life (QOL) measure. Qualitative pilot work (including focus groups) was conducted in 15 field centers worldwide to identify concepts and generate items that were important across cultures. Cultural, language, and research experts from different cultures were brought together to develop this measure. This resulted in a measure that had already been developed and validated in many different languages and cultures. Of course, simultaneous development of a measure into different languages can be very expensive (Li et al., 2001). While praising this work for the international QOL measure, Stewart and Napoles-Springer (2000) point out that this rarely happens with development of different measures within the United States even though many of the same language and cultural differences exist. They argue that researchers need to assess the equivalence of measures for ethnic and cultural groups within the United States as well.

Aging and Diversity Online: Language

Diverse Voices. Inclusion of Language-Minority Populations in National Studies: Challenges and Opportunities. This publication from the National Institute of Child and Human Development and the National Institute on Aging discusses both the challenges and benefits of including language-minority (non-English speakers) in research. http://www.nichd.nih.gov/publications/pubs/upload/Diverse_Voices.pdf

Match Between the Researcher and the Participants   Whether the research staff "matches" the study participants in terms of gender, ethnicity, language of origin, SES, religion, sexual orientation, or age can also affect the research study. At first glance, this issue may seem relatively unimportant, but it may be more obvious in some settings than in others. If a White male professor who speaks only English was interested in conducting research on older women's depression in a Middle Eastern culture where no one spoke English, one of the first recommendations might be that he find good translators and interpreters. But to conduct meaningful research on this topic, he will need to do much more than have excellently translated questionnaires. He will need to have cultural brokers, people who understand both the culture in which he is interested and his own culture. It is easy to recognize the barrier of language differences, but culture conveys more than just language. Similarly, when there is a mismatch between researchers and potential study participants in terms of key elements of diversity, cultural differences may arise that can have just as big an impact as language differences.

ACTIVE LEARNING EXPERIENCE: ANALYZING A RESEARCH STUDY ON ELDERS FROM DIVERSE GROUPS

This purpose of this experience is to give you an opportunity to read and evaluate an example of research on elders from diverse groups. This activity will take approximately 3–3.5 hours (2.5–3 hours of learner preparation and 30 minutes of class discussion).

Instructions:

1. Find and read an article that describes research on diverse elders. Often articles like this appear in such journals as *The Gerontologist*, the *Journal of Gerontology: Social Sciences*, *Research on Aging*, and *Psychology and Aging*.
2. Check with your instructor that the article you have chosen meets the following criteria: (a) It is relevant to aging and diversity; (b) it comes from an appropriate academic journal; and (c) it contains original research (i.e., it is not simply a review of previous studies).
3. Read the article you found and that your instructor approved.
4. Provide a complete citation of the article.
5. Prepare a written answer to the following items:
    a. Note the research method(s) used, a description of the participants, and the results (what the researchers found).
    b. Describe what aspects of the research process may have been affected by the diversity of the participants. Did the researchers make any adjustment to standard research methods to accommodate this diversity?
    c. Describe any personal reactions to the study you may have.
6. Turn in your response to the above questions to your instructor.
7. Your instructor will lead a discussion of student critiques.

In the preceding sections, we have shown how the research process can be affected when doing research with diverse groups. From the initial stage of problem definition throughout the research study, the cultural background of the people in the study can affect the study process. The challenges that we have discussed are large, but the potential benefits of conducting research that will aid in our understanding of all people are also huge. In this next section, we will examine recommendations for conducting meaningful research with elders from diverse groups.

HOW TO IMPROVE RESEARCH WITH ELDERS FROM DIVERSE GROUPS

Although much research on aging and diversity is in its infancy and, for some groups, the research is very limited, there are researchers who are working with elders from diverse groups. This research is happening primarily with ethnic minority elders around issues of health. We can learn from these researchers' experiences and extend their recommendations for research on ethnic minority elders to research with elders from other groups as well. In summarizing research on diverse ethnic minority elders, Curry and Jackson (2003) found several themes that emerged. They listed the following issues as critical for the success of a project (Curry & Jackson, 2003, p. 4):

- Trust and connection with the community
- Involvement of ethnic and racial minority researchers at all levels (from lead investigator to data collector)
- Communication regarding potential benefits of participation
- Cultural sensitivity on the part of researchers and research institutions

These global themes will anchor our discussion below. We will conclude this section with more specific recommendations for researchers.

Issues of Trust

When a researcher approaches a community to ask members to participate in research, perceptions of that researcher (and of the research) can be affected by the institution with which the researcher is affiliated. Universities can be seen as huge elite entities interested only in research for its own sake and having no genuine concern for communities outside of the mainstream. This perception may have been exacerbated by interactions with prior research studies in which the researchers imposed their ideas on the community, failed to communicate effectively with the community, and gave no research findings back to the community.

Thus, one big stumbling block for some researchers may be something over which they have no control—the population's experience with previous researchers. Did they have a good experience? Did the researchers keep their promise to the community? Did they return to the community with their results? If people have had negative experiences with other research, then they will be much less likely to participate this time (Levkoff & Sanchez, 2003). Remember May Thomas in our earlier vignette. She was very interested in research and had participated in several studies, but she was very disappointed that she never learned what the studies' findings were. Perhaps in the future, she may be less willing to participate in research.

Members of groups that have been marginalized in U.S. society may have an extra layer of concern when asked to participate in research. Not only are they interested in knowing the potential risks and benefits of the research to themselves personally, but they are also concerned about the risks and benefits to their group as a whole. Mainstream research participants do not consider, "Will White people be discriminated against as the result of this research? Will they be denied insurance coverage as a result of these findings?" but groups that have experienced mistreatment due to their group membership may have those worries. For example, with differential treatment of same-sex couples still legal discrimination in most of the United States (for example, in most states, same-sex couples cannot marry and do not have access to the same retirement income rights as married couples), a participant from the LGBT community must trust that the researcher is not going to use the results to his or her own political end. Even if the participant has trust in the researcher's goals, he or she may wonder if others may twist the results to support their own agenda. This example highlights the added issues that members of minority groups can face when asked to participate in research.

Although researchers cannot control participants' *prior* experiences, researchers can recognize the potential impact *they* are having on their participants and work to make that impact a positive one so that the participants believe their participation was worthwhile and they will be positively predisposed when approached by a future researcher. Previous researchers have found steps researchers can take to assist the development of a positive relationship: become a familiar face in the community, have researchers (not just research assistants) who are members of the minority community being studied, and develop a regular community newsletter that updates the community on the research and provides relevant helpful information (e.g., health tips) for the community (Levkoff & Sanchez, 2003). We will address some of these suggestions in more detail below.

Include Cultural Brokers or Stakeholders in the Research Process   As we mentioned earlier, to conduct effective research in diverse communities, researchers need to ensure that they have culturally appropriate research questions, research methods, measures, and procedures to communicate with the community as they work to recruit and retain participants. To develop these culturally appropriate studies, the research team needs to have expertise in the culture. Cultural brokers or stakeholders can help in this process. These people are typically members of the group being studied who possess intimate knowledge of the culture and can help remove barriers to research participation and facilitate accurate, reliable collection of information about the group. The importance of including this cultural expertise in every aspect of the research process cannot be overstated.

The selection of cultural brokers needs to be done carefully. Differences within groups are often quite large, and simply because a researcher might think someone is of a particular group and thus could easily serve as a broker, that may not mean the person actually is an expert in the specific group the researcher wants to study (Li et al., 2001). Depending on the culture being studied, potential problems can arise. If the potential broker's age or gender is different from that of the group being studied, this may affect his or her ability to serve as an effective broker. Similarly, if the broker immigrated to the United States during a different time frame, is from a different ethnic group within that culture, or even is from a different socioeconomic status from the group of interest, this also may affect his or her ability to be a broker.

When researchers first realized the importance of having cultural expertise on their research team, they started by hiring support staff (e.g., outreach workers, site coordinators, secretaries) from the cultural group of interest. This can result in a research study where the people designing the research are from one culture and the people communicating with the participants are from a different one. Although it is an improvement to include some cultural brokers on the research team, researchers have since found that it is much more effective to have members of the group of interest at all levels of the research team—lead researchers, project coordinators, and support staff. With a diverse team that has cultural competence at all levels, all aspects from the formation of the research question through the completion of the study will have the best likelihood of finding accurate information about the community and of creating a positive research experience for its participants.

In addition to helping with the research, cultural brokers can help match all aspects of the research to the participant culture. For example, in research there are often people who do not actually participate in the research but who facilitate access to the participants. This may be the director of a community center, the receptionist at a community mental health office, or even the religious leader at a church. These people take on added work for the project but often receive little or no compensation for doing so. Cultural brokers can help to match reinforcement for people who are involved in the research with their culture. Levkoff & Sanchez (2003) found that, for some cultural groups, special snacks are appreciated, for others giving money to the office is better, whereas others value individual financial incentives. Other groups want to see the researchers and their staff members at community social events. Determining appropriate ways to encourage and thank all of the community members who help in the research process is an important and complex task.

Morano and Bravo (2002) describe the lessons they learned during their intervention research that included a week-long caregiving workshop for Latino caregivers. Accepting and respecting the cultural values from the group were very important. For example, participants wanted to bring homemade treats to share at the workshop and felt a real need to give something back to the educators before they could accept the information given to them. This can require a shift in roles for the researchers as they may have been focused on easing these caregivers' difficulties, not on accepting something from them. Time also had cultural implications, such that the start time for the workshop was often pushed back as socializing was very important (and some participants found it even more important than the content of the workshop). Including other family members in some parts of the workshop taught different generations the cultural understanding that they were missing from the caregiving experience.

Giving Back to the Community   Throughout this chapter, we have stressed that when conducting research with diverse groups (and probably with any group), connections and communication with the community are important to obtaining meaningful information about the group. Thus, instead of researchers' swooping in, gathering data, and then swooping out, it is important to give something back to the community. Levkoff and Sanchez (2003) describe this as promoting a long-term positive relationship instead of a one-shot "take the data and run" experience. To promote this positive, long-term relationship, it is imperative that researchers:

- Keep the commitments they may have made to the community.
- Return with their findings and ask community members for their interpretation of findings.
- Stay with the community throughout the study and become a part of the community.

How do researchers report back to the community? This also depends on the community. For research conducted with highly educated elders, mailing a written report of the findings might suffice. A more formal talk by the researchers followed by a question and answer period might even be appropriate. But for other cultural groups, this type of presentation might be viewed as useless at best and offensive at worst. Determining a culturally appropriate way to convey the information gained is important. For an evaluation conducted with an American Indian group in New Mexico, the information gained was conveyed through a "give-back" ceremony that included storytelling and visuals and not written material (The Colorado Trust, 2002). Clearly, researchers need to take into account the cultural background of the people to whom they are reporting. We should ask communities when we first start working with them, "How would you like us to give you the findings? How do you want us to report back to you?"

Another way of giving research back to the community is to ensure that research findings are actually translated into needed services and programs. Traditionally, research is conducted, the findings and recommendations are published, and then the research sits on the shelf. How can we translate research findings into services and programs? How do research findings inform programs and services to improve people's lives? The term "translational research" refers to the process of applying findings that were discovered through basic research (e.g., research that has found evidence that a particular activity works to reduce cardiovascular disease) and then developing needed programs and services from that research. Translational research focuses on applying basic science research results to the practical, everyday world. Recently, federal agencies have become concerned about the tendency for basic research findings to languish in research publications and not being applied to practical situations. To address this problem, federal agencies have created initiatives to offer grants to people to take others' research findings and then develop programs based on that research. One such initiative is called the Evidence-Based Prevention Programs Initiative funded by the Administration on Aging. This initiative represents a 3-year interdisciplinary effort to translate evidence-based practices (research findings) into aging network programs (Alkema & Alley, 2006). Research findings need to be reported both to the community members who participated in the research and to the broader society as a whole. In addition, the findings also need to be translated into useful programs to actually improve peoples' lives.

The process by which Dolores Gallagher-Thompson and her colleagues (2003b) developed the national behavioral clinical trial entitled Resources to Enhance Alzheimer Caregivers Health (REACH) (the intervention itself is described in detail in the chapter on caregiving) is a good example of how to go about conducting culturally appropriate research. They began by developing community partnerships with agencies that served the older Hispanic population (their population of interest). With the help from these agencies, focus groups were conducted to understand issues of caregiving stress in this population. From the information gained from the focus groups, a multicultural advisory group helped develop a pilot project to determine the appropriateness of specific psychoeducational techniques in this population. Using these experiences as a base, the researchers then developed a nationwide project to determine whether this program is effective for different ethnic groups across the country. Based on their 5 years of experience conducting this research, Gallagher-Thompson and colleagues (2003b) make specific recommendations for conducting research with people from a Latino heritage, but many of their recommendations are appropriate for research with elders of different groups. They stress that the research process must be built on a foundation of a strong ongoing relationship between community and the researchers. Their concrete guidelines serve as an excellent summary of this section on improving research with elders from diverse groups. They make the following recommendations:

1. Hire bilingual/bicultural staff in key positions.
2. Use a conceptual rather than literal translation of study materials.
3. Develop culturally appropriate outreach and advertisement materials.
4. Develop or tailor interventions to be culturally relevant and appropriate.
5. Improve accessibility by addressing and resolving practical barriers.
6. Use specific strategies to maximize retention.
7. Provide feedback to community.

ACTIVE LEARNING EXPERIENCE: CONDUCTING RESEARCH WITH DIVERSE GROUPS OTHER THAN YOUR OWN

This experience gives you the opportunity to reflect on the different ways diversity affects research and apply the suggestions that have been made in this chapter. This activity will take approximately 1 hour to answer the questions and 15 minutes for discussion with a classmate.

Instructions:

Choose a group from key elements of diversity (e.g., gender, ethnicity, social class), but make it a group to which you do not belong (for example, if you are of Asian heritage, you can choose any ethnic group other than Asian). Think about the different steps in the research process and how those steps might be affected by the characteristics of the group you selected. Write your responses to the questions below.

1. Write the name of the group you have chosen (e.g., elder Japanese women).
2. List the steps of the research process.
3. Describe which steps you think will be affected by conducting research with this particular group.
4. Given the recommendations in this chapter, describe what steps you would take to conduct research with this particular cultural group.
5. What accommodation would you make that would be most important?
6. Discuss your response to the above items with a classmate.
7. Turn in your written responses to your instructor.

BRIGHT LIGHTS FOR AGING AND DIVERSITY RESEARCH

At the beginning of this chapter, we mentioned that there are several bright lights on the horizon helping to promote high-quality research on minority aging. One of these bright lights comes from efforts to make the research process include the diverse perspectives of communities that have been marginalized and ignored in the past. Community-Based Participatory Research (CBPR) is one example of such an approach. Another encouraging factor comes from new initiatives designed to promote research on diversity and aging. The Resource Centers for Minority Aging Research (RCMARs) were created as the result of such an initiative. Both of these bright lights will be discussed below.

Community-Based Participatory Research

Earlier in the chapter, we presented the traditional research model with six steps. If you have ever tried to conduct research in a community setting, you may have quickly realized that several critical steps are missing from this model. These steps have to do with engaging the participation of the researchers' target population. Most likely, this omission is because traditional research is often done within a specific academic setting for which populations are readily available. For example, if researchers want to determine the effects of exercise on cognitive status, they can often turn to their undergraduate students and ask them, either through course requirements or through financial incentives, to participate in their study. The generalizability of the findings from such research then becomes limited because of the characteristics of that participant population—age, ethnic background, socioeconomic status, rural or urban community location, etc.

When we examine issues around aging and diversity, we are especially interested in research that includes populations of different ages, ethnic backgrounds, gender, SES, rural or urban community location, and sexual orientation. When conducting research with groups from outside the mainstream population, the traditional research model does not address some key aspects of the research process. For example, the traditional research model begins with identification of a question or problem and neglects to consider input from the community being studied and the work that must be done to make meaningful community ties. Alternative research models address these steps that the traditional model neglects. We present Community-Based Participatory Research (CBPR) as an example of an alternative research approach that works toward "partnerships between academic, health services and community-based organizations" (Isreal, Schulz, Parker, & Becker, 2000, p. 16). Through greater community involvement in the research process, CBPR "emphasizes the participation, influence and control of non-academic researchers in the process of creating knowledge and change" (Isreal et al., 2000, p. 17). Many researchers do not specifically conduct CBPR, but do follow many of the steps listed in Table 2.2.

Similarities between the traditional and the CBPR research process can be seen, especially in steps 3–6 of CBPR. The primary differences in these approaches occur in the additional steps at the beginning and end that transform the research process from one in which all steps of the process are determined by the researchers to one in which the partnership determines the trajectory of the research. In the traditional research process, the problem or question is typically chosen by the researcher and is often described as beginning the process. With CBPR, developing (and then maintaining) partnerships among the different entities (research academics, health services, community-based organizations) comes first in the process.

TABLE 2.2 Comparison of Research Process Models

Traditional Research Process Model		Community-Based Participatory Research Process Model	
1.	Identify a research question or problem	1.	Develop and maintain partnership with community members
2.	Construct a conceptual model based on theory	2.	Conduct community assessment
		3.	Define the problem
3.	Develop hypotheses	4.	Develop research methodology
4.	Conduct research	5.	Collect and analyze data
5.	Analyze and interpret the data	6.	Interpret data
6.	Report the findings	7.	Determine intervention and policy implications
		8.	Disseminate results
		9.	Conduct interventions (as appropriate)
		10.	Outline what has been learned
		11.	Establish mechanisms for program sustainability

Source: Community-Based Participatory Research Process Model adapted from Israel, Schulz, Parker, & Becker, (2000).

Instead of the researchers' determining the problem to be solved, a community assessment is conducted (a process to determine what problems are perceived by the community) and then the partnership determines how the problem should be defined. Research approaches like CBPR result in research that reflects the unique perspective of the population participating in the research instead of the researchers' perspective.

The additional steps at the end of the CBPR research process further connect the academic and community organizations. In more traditional approaches, the results of the research are often published solely in academic journals with little or no communication with the community from which the results were found and for whom the results may have important implications. In contrast, researchers using approaches like CBPR often share their results with the participant community before publishing them in academic journals. In this way they can share the information learned with the community, and they can also hear the community's interpretation of the results and perhaps learn even more from that interpretation. Results often suggest potential avenues for solving a problem. These solutions (or *interventions*) can again be proposed in partnership with the community instead of imposed from an outside perspective. The final summary of what has been learned is also jointly determined by researchers and the community and finally, how to sustain any interventions that have been proposed and the relationship that has been established between the research and community. In this model, instead of the researcher's coming into the community from outside, gathering data and then leaving, the researcher becomes a part of the community and the community is an integral part of the research process. Key principles of this research approach include (Israel et al., 1998, 2000):

1. Recognize community as a unit of identity.
2. Build on strengths and resources within the community.
3. Facilitate collaborative, equitable involvement of all partners in all phases of the research.
4. Integrate knowledge and intervention for mutual benefit of all partners.
5. Promote a co-learning and empowering process that attends to social inequalities.
6. Understand that this research is a cyclical and iterative process.
7. Address health from both positive and ecological perspectives.
8. Disseminate findings and knowledge gained to all partners.
9. Ensure a long-term commitment by all partners.

Note that we have included an example of a published study using CBPR in the suggested readings section at the end of this chapter. We will now turn to another positive element in research on aging and diversity: initiatives designed to increase quality research.

Resource Centers for Minority Aging Research

Another bright light in aging research comes from new initiatives to promote research on diversity and aging. The National Institute on Aging's Resource

Centers for Minority Aging Research (RCMARs) is an example of one such program. The Resource Centers are in six different locations in the United States. Each center has an interdisciplinary focus to reduce health disparities among the largest minority groups throughout the country. To help support a research infrastructure that promotes research on minority aging, the RCMARs address the following objectives:

1. Establish mechanisms for mentoring researchers for careers in research relevant to the health of minority elders.
2. Enhance the diversity of the professional research workforce conducting research on the health of minority elders.
3. Develop and deploy strategies for recruiting and retaining older minority group members for epidemiological, psychosocial, and/or biomedical research.
4. Develop and deploy racially/ethnically sensitive and standardized measures for use in diverse populations (Stahl, 2002).

In addition to conducting research with diverse elders, the RCMARs work to create a solid foundation on which future researchers can build (Stahl, 2002). And, true to the "lessons learned" in the earlier sections of this chapter, the RCMARs follow the guidelines for culturally competent research. Each RCMAR works to promote positive relationships with its local community. They all communicate their research findings so that community members are not left wondering, as was May Thomas in our third vignette. They also offer community education and service to their communities, thus further developing trust and ongoing relationships. In recruiting and training researchers who are themselves from diverse groups, they ensure that the principal investigators of future studies will be minority group members. Finally, the culturally appropriate research they conduct helps build a foundation of knowledge regarding diverse elders.

CHAPTER SUMMARY

This chapter has focused on how we study issues of aging in people from different groups. We began by describing the different disciplines that study issues of aging, diversity, and both aging *and* diversity. We also provided a brief history of the experiences of different groups in research. Given the historical neglect and mistreatment of certain groups in research and the importance of including people from diverse groups to fully understand issues of aging, we argue that it is important to consider how the traditional research process must be changed in order to conduct meaningful research with people from diverse groups. Including meaningful input from the community being studied is important at all stages of the research process, from identifying the research question through reporting the results of the study.

Language differences are one obvious way difficulties can arise when conducting research with different ethnic and cultural groups, but equally important difficulties can come up over cultural differences that may affect recruitment and retention in research. Modifying the traditional research process to include the voices of elders from diverse groups will enrich our understanding of aging so that we can learn new ideas from these diverse groups as well as identify areas in which they may be experiencing difficulties. Fortunately, many researchers who have conducted research with elders from diverse groups have shared their experiences and recommendations, such as the importance of considering people from the community in key positions in the research team, in recognizing issues of trust between researchers and the community, and in the importance of reporting the results to the community in a way that is meaningful to them.

As we find that more traditional models of conducting research do not work well with diverse groups, alternative models of conducting research are being developed. Community-Based Participatory Research develops partnerships between researchers and communities to conduct research that is relevant and meaningful to both groups. The federal government can also help promote research on elders from diverse groups by creating initiatives to train researchers and then fund such research. The six RCMARs around the country train researchers from different ethnic minority groups to conduct research on aging and diversity.

ACTIVE LEARNING EXPERIENCE: CHAPTER 2 QUIZ

The purpose of this experience is to gauge your present knowledge of issues related to diversity and research on elders. Upon completion of this activity, you will be able to:

1. Assess your knowledge of diversity and research on elders.
2. Gain feedback on your knowledge of important issues related to research on aging and diversity.

Complete the quiz below. Your instructor may lead an in-class review of the answers to the quiz. This activity should take 30 minutes (10 minutes to complete the quiz and 20 minutes to discuss your answers with another person or in a classroom setting). Indicate whether each of the following statements is true or false, and explain your reason for selecting that response.

Instructions:

Quiz Items	True	False
1. The research process always begins with a research question and is concluded when one find the answer to that question.	___	___
2. Translational research involves maintaining language equivalence when translating questionnaire measures from one language to another.	___	___

3. Traditionally, mainstream psychological research did not include women and people from different ethnic groups. _____ _____

4. Recruitment and retention of research participants from different ethnic groups is one of the primary challenges facing researchers. _____ _____

5. Gerontology is the scientific study of aging from adulthood, or maturity, to old age. _____ _____

6. In gerontology and developmental psychology, the research focus is often on discovering age differences rather than age changes. _____ _____

7. Research findings from carefully conducted studies will be applicable to all groups of people. _____ _____

8. All research measures are subject to cultural influences. _____ _____

9. Quantitative research methods yield substantially more accurate research results than qualitative measures. _____ _____

10. Whether researchers and participants are of the same gender, ethnicity, or cultural background does not affect the research process. _____ _____

11. Institutional Review Boards for the Protection of Human Subjects are used only in biomedical research where the participants' health could be affected. _____ _____

12. One advantage of being a bilingual researcher is that one can conduct back translation of all measures into another language without having to find another bilingual person to assist with the process. _____ _____

13. Secondary data analysis occurs when a researcher examines data from an existing dataset to answer his or her research question. _____ _____

14. Retention refers to when a researcher uses (or retains) measures developed for a different study in his or her new study. _____ _____

15. The federal government has little impact on the research that is conducted in the United States. _____ _____

GLOSSARY

age changes: Aspects of people that develop (or change) over time through the process of aging. Age changes are typically studied through longitudinal research.

age differences: Aspects or characteristics on which two or more age groups differ. Age differences are typically studied through cross-sectional research.

back translation: The process by which a questionnaire measure is translated from its original language into a second language by a person who is fluent in both. A separate bilingual individual, looking only at the translated material, translates the measure back into its original language. The original and back-translated measures are then compared to determine equivalence of the measures.

clinical trials: Health-related studies in which participants are randomly assigned to different treatment groups and the effects of the treatment (the outcomes) are then measured.

cohort effects: The historical time period in which one lives can create unique experiences and circumstances for people from that cohort. These cohort effects can sometimes be mistaken as being due to one's age (or age effects), rather than being due to the historical time period during which one grew up.

community-based participatory research: a research approach that creates a partnership between researchers and the communities that they study. This partnership results in a research process that takes into account the community perspective in almost all stages of the research.

cross-sectional research: When some characteristic of different groups of people is observed at the same time and then compared (e.g., younger adults', middle-aged adults' and older adults' interest in politics).

cultural broker: A person who is a member of a particular cultural group and who possesses intimate knowledge of the culture, who can help remove barriers to research participation, and who can facilitate accurate, reliable collection of information about the group.

ethnogeriatrics: A field of study that focuses on the health of older people from diverse ethnic and racial groups.

focus group: A relatively small group of people (eight to ten) who are asked their opinion or perspective about a particular issue. This is typically done in an interactive session in which a trained leader asks a series of probing questions designed to elicit discussion and opinions from the group members.

gerontology: The scientific study of aging from adulthood, or maturity, to old age (Cavanaugh & Blanchard-Fields, 2006).

institutional review board: A review panel that examines proposed research to determine whether the treatment of the research participants is ethical.

longitudinal study: A research design in which a group of people are studied over two or more times to see how they change. For example, younger adults' interest in voting is measured at age 18 and then again at age 28 to see whether this interest has changed over time.

measurement: The process of assessing or measuring a particular concept of interest be it very concrete (e.g., body weight) or much more abstract (e.g., self-esteem). Although often interpreted as applying to quantitative research with numbers, any study that seeks to understand humans uses measurements of concepts, even if that measurement is in words.

physiological measures: Assessments of the physical, biochemical, or mechanical functions of a person. Examples: blood pressure, cortisol levels, and fMRI.

qualitative research: An approach to understanding people that involves allowing participants to respond in their own words, or observers to describe what they see in words. This approach often conveys a rich description with much depth and detail.

quantitative research: An approach to research that involves quantifying or assigning numbers to the characteristic in which one is interested.

RCMAR: This acronym stands for the Resource Centers for Minority Aging Research. There are six of these centers across the nation and each has an interdisciplinary focus with the goal to reduce health disparities among the largest minority groups of older adults in the United States

secondary data analysis: The analysis of data that were collected by someone else (perhaps for some other purpose).

self-report: Responses in a research study that are given by the participant about himself or herself.

sequential designs: Research designs that involve combinations of cross-sectional and longitudinal designs in order to separate effects of age, time of measurement, and cohort.

theory: An explanation of the relationship between different concepts or variables.

translational research: Research that takes research findings (e.g., research that has found evidence that a particular activity works to reduce cardiovascular disease) and then uses them to develop needed programs and services.

SUGGESTED READINGS

Burlew, A. K. (2003). Research with ethnic minorities: Conceptual, methodological, and analysis issues. In G. Bernal, Trimble, J.E., Burlew, A.K., & Leong, F.T.L. (Ed.), *Handbook of racial and ethnic minority psychology*. Thousand Oaks, CA: Sage.

This chapter presents very pertinent issues regarding conceptual, methodological, and analysis issues when conducting research with ethnic minorities. However, neither the chapter nor the handbook focuses specifically on research with older people.

Chadiha, L. A., Morrow-Howell, N., Proctor, E. K., Picot, S. J., Gillespie, D. C., Pandey, P., et al. (2004). Involving rural, older African Americans and their female informal caregivers in research. *Journal of Aging and Health, 16*(5 Suppl), 18S-38S.

This research is unique in that it examines *rural* African American elders. The article is worthwhile reading for insights gained in research with rural elders and with ethnic minority elders.

Curry, L., & Jackson, J. (Eds.). (2003). *The science of inclusion: Recruiting and retaining racial and ethnic elders in health research*. Washington, DC.: The Gerontological Society of America.

This special publication of GSA comprises a series of articles (some of which were previously published elsewhere) describing recommendations for conducting research with diverse groups. The articles by Curry and Jackson (Curry & Jackson, 2003), Gallagher-Thompson and colleagues (2003b), and Levkoff and Sanchez (2003) are particularly useful.

Ethnicity and Disease, Vol. 17, No. 1, Supplement 1.

This journal is dedicated to research on ethnicity and health. The articles represent some of the scientific knowledge available on CBPR at the RCMARs.

Kimmel, D., Rose, T., & David, S. (2006). Lesbian, gay, bisexual, and transgender aging: Research and clinical perspectives. New York: Columbia University Press.

This book details issues related to LGBT aging. Chapter 1 specifically gives a historical perspective and outlines factors that affect research with LGBT elders.

Krueger, R. A. (2000). *Focus groups: A practical guide for applied research* (3rd ed.). Thousand Oaks, CA: Sage.

A very readable and practical guide to conducting focus groups. Some readers find the 2nd edition conveys more of the importance of conducting focus groups as a systematic research tool, whereas the 3rd edition omits this and thus might leave the reader conducting focus groups in a less systematic (and thus less useful) way.

Manson, S. M., Garroutte, E., Goins, R. T., & Henderson, P. N. (2004). Access, relevance, and control in the research process: Lessons from Indian country. *Journal of Aging Health, 16*(5 Suppl), 58S–77S.

This article addresses the challenges in conducting health research in American Indian communities. The authors examine the community-based participatory research in this setting and how successful collaboration can help improve research and speed the translation of research findings into practical application.

Teresi, J. A., Steward, A. L., Morales, L. S., & Stahl, S. M. (2006). Measurement in a multi-ethnic society, overview to the special issue. *Medical Care 44*, Issue 11, Suppl 3.

The articles in this supplement describe the quantitative and qualitative measurement issues that occur when conducting research with elders from diverse ethnic groups. This research also comes from the knowledge gained from the research conducted at RCMARs.

Morgan, D. L., & Krueger, R. A. (Eds.). (1997). *Focus Group Kit*. Thousand Oaks, CA: Sage.

A highly rated kit that contains a six-volume set of "how-to" books that describe all aspects of how to conduct focus groups.

Patton, M. Q. (2008). *Utilization focused evaluation* (4th ed.). Thousand Oaks, CA: Sage.

This highly regarded book helps both novices and professionals develop their evaluation skills. It is easy to read and includes activities and other tools to help improve the reader's skills. It also contains a section summarizing the philosophy behind evaluation.

Stahl, S. M., & Vasquez, L. (2004). Approaches to improving recruitment and retention of minority elders participating in research: Examples from selected research groups including the National Institute on Aging's Resource Centers for Minority Aging Research. *Journal of Aging and Health, 16*(5 Suppl), 9S-17S.

This introduction to the special journal supplement "addresses the importance of recruiting and retaining racial and ethnic minority elders in biopsychosocial research. It highlights developments by scholars, many associated with the National Institute on Aging's Resource Centers for Minority Aging Research, to develop and reinforce a research infrastructure intended to minimize the minority/nonminority differential in health and its social sequelae for older people."

AUDIOVISUAL RESOURCES

Gay and Gray in New York City. This film includes personal stories about older gay men in New York. The directors include facts related to LGBT aging. One of the main themes of the film is the older generation of LGBT individuals "making a path" for future generations. 22 min. Available from www.fanlight.com or info@fanlight.com.

The Grand Generation. Looks at aging from the perspective of people with varied ethnic backgrounds and experiences. There is no narrative, only the stories of the individuals told in their own words. It has a strong folklore element. These individuals are examples of older adults who have aged successfully. The focus is not only on their past experiences, but who they are now as older adults. 28 min. Available from www.filmakers.com or info@filmakers.com.

Grandparents Raising Grandchildren. This film focuses on the difficulties and responsibilities placed on grandparents who are raising their grandchildren. It looks at how the grandparents deal with this unexpected change in their lifestyle when most had anticipated a different aging experience. The film highlights the emotions related to their role as parents, as well as the problems they face, and also generalizes to the wider social issues to consider. One of the main goals is to put an emphasis on the need for social policy change and some sort of financial and community support for these families. 22 min. Available from Fanlight productions (www.fanlight.com).

Qualitative Research: Methods in the Social Sciences. This video presents an overview of qualitative research methods including the types of questions addressed, problems of validity and analysis of qualitative data. It includes qualitative textual analysis, conversation analysis, and content analysis. 20 min. Available from Insight Media (insight-media.com).

Survey Savvy: Planning and Conducting a Successful Survey. This video describes a framework for preparing, conducting, and reporting the results of a survey. 24 min. Available from Insight Media (insight-media.com).

KEY: CHAPTER 2 QUIZ

1. False. The research process can be started at almost any point in the process outlined in the chapter. We typically think of the research question as the starting point, but a very puzzling result might lead us to ask new questions, or we might instead begin with a theory that leads to interesting predictions, etc. Thus, the research process is almost never finished by finding *the* answer. Instead, it is an iterative process that we use to help discover some answers, rule out others and point us in the direction of new questions.

2. False. Translational research is concerned with having basic science research results applied in the practical everyday world.

3. True. In the United States and Western Europe, the belief was that researchers were discovering universal psychological principles that would apply equally to all humans. Thus, the fact that White males were primarily participants in the research was not considered to be a problem. In the past 40 years (and particularly in the past 10), steps have been taken to ensure the participation of women and people from different ethnic groups in research.

4. True. As this chapter details, locating and encouraging participation in research from people of different ethnic groups is a real challenge. Understanding one's participant population and having members from that group as a part of the research team can help facilitate recruitment (Gallagher-Thompson et al., 2003b).

5. True. Gerontologists study aging and issues around aging.

6. False. Age differences is the term used to describe characteristics that are found to differ between two age groups, for example, 20-year-olds tend to be more computer savvy than 80-year-olds. Age differences are often confounded with cohort effects. Gerontologists and developmental psychologists are much more interested in age changes, or characteristics in people that change or develop as they mature and age.

7. False. Although conducting research in a scientific manner helps ensure the quality of the results, it does not necessarily determine whether the results will generalize to groups of people other than the group that participated in the research. For example, research evaluating the effectiveness of a physical activity program for older adults, CHAMPS, was conducted in a scientific manner (Stewart et al., 2001). It was a randomized controlled trial in which participants were randomly assigned to receive their activity intervention. It was found that the program increased older adults' physical activity compared with a control group. But this research was conducted with primarily White participants (over 90%). Thus, it is not clear from this research whether these results would be the same for a different group of people (e.g., for a different ethnic group) or in a different setting (e.g., in a rural setting). Either research needs to include different groups of people or additional research needs to be done to determine whether results generalize to other groups of people. The above researchers did conduct additional research to determine whether their results would generalize to more diverse populations (Stewart et al., 2006). This research is discussed in chapter 4 on health beliefs and behaviors.

8. False. Some measures, such as measures of blood cortisol or fMRI brain images are not subject to cultural bias. On the other hand, although these measures are not subject to cultural influences, what they are measuring—cortisol levels or brain function—may differ due to cultural influences as different cultures may interpret stressful events differently (hence changing cortisol levels) or culture may affect our thinking patterns (hence the areas of our brain that are used in different tasks).

9. False. One cannot judge the accuracy of results simply by the method used. One's research method depends on one's research question and goals. Some methods work better in some settings and worse in others. Qualitative methods are preferred, for example, when doing community-needs assessment because they allow community members to determine the issues that are important to them, rather than the researcher's imposing his or her beliefs about the problem. On the other hand, when conducting a large nationally representative survey, qualitative methods can be difficult to manage and can lead to difficulties in interpreting the data.

10. False. Many researchers have found that having a match between participants and researchers (in gender, ethnicity, or cultural background) can improve the recruitment and retention of research participants (Gallagher-Thompson et al., 2003b; Levkoff & Sanchez, 2003). This match does not guarantee the success of a research study, but it can help.

11. False. Institutional Review Boards for the Protection of Human Subjects review all research conducted with human populations in both academic and medical settings. This includes research in the social sciences.

12. False. Although bilingual researchers can translate a measure from its original language into a second language, back translation must be done by a different bilingual person to ensure equivalence of the translation.

13. True. Secondary data analysis is currently receiving favor with federal granting agencies as it is a cost effective way to make use of already collected datasets to answer new questions.

14. False. Retention refers to keeping or retaining participants in a research study through the study's completion.

15. False. The federal government can create programs or other incentives to promote research in a particular area. These may include offering funding for studies that examine a particular research topic or creating centers that provide training for people who are interested in learning how to conduct research. The RCMARS are an example of the kind of influence that the federal government can have on research.

REFERENCES

Alkema, G. E., & Alley, D. E. (2006). Gerontology's future: An integrative model for disciplinary advancement. *Gerontologist, 46*(5), 574–582.

Andersen, R., Lewis, S. Z., Giachello, A. L., Aday, L. A., & Chiu, G. (1981). Access to medical care among the Hispanic population of the southwestern United States. *Journal of Health and Social Behavior, 22*(1), 78–89.

Angel, R. J., & Angel, J. L. (2006). Diversity and aging in the United States. In R. H. Binstock & L. K. George (Eds.), *Handbook of aging and the social sciences* (6th ed.) (pp. 94–106). Burlington, MA: Elsevier Academic Press.

Arean, P. A., Alvidrez, J., Nery, R., Estes, C., & Linkins, K. (2003). Recruitment and retention of older minorities in mental health services research. *Gerontologist, 43*, 36–44.

Cavanaugh, J. C., & Blanchard-Fields, F. (2006). *Adult development and aging* (5th ed.). Belmont, CA: Thomson Wadsworth.

Colorado Trust. (2002). Guidelines and best practices for culturally competent interventions. Denver, CO: The Colorado Trust.

Curry, L., & Jackson, J. (2003). Recruitment and retention of diverse ethnic and racial groups in health research: An evolving science. In L. Curry & J. Jackson (Eds.), *The science of inclusion: Recruiting and retaining racial and ethnic elders in health research* (pp. 1–7). Washington, DC: Gerontological Society of America.

Ferraro, K. F. (2006a). The gerontological imagination. In J. M. Wilmoth & K. F. Ferraro (Eds.), *Gerontology: Perspectives and issues* (3rd ed.) (pp. 325–342). New York: Springer.

Ferraro, K. F. (2006b). Imagining the disciplinary advancement of gerontology: Whither the tipping point? *Gerontologist, 46*(5), 571–573.

Folstein, M. F., Folstein, S. E., & McHugh, P. R. (1975). "Mini–mental state": A practical method for grading the cognitive state of patients for the clinician. *Journal of Psychiatric Research, 12*(3), 189–198.

Gallagher-Thompson, D., Haley, W., Guy, D., Rupert, M., Arguelles, T., Zeiss, L. M., et al. (2003a). Tailoring psychological interventions for ethnically diverse dementia caregivers. *Clinical Psychology: Science and Practice, 10*(4), 423–438.

Gallagher-Thompson, D., Solano, N., Coon, D., & Arean, P. (2003b). Recruitment and retention of Latino dementia family caregivers in intervention research: Issues to face, lessons to learn. *Gerontologist, 43*(1), 45–51.

Gelberg, L., Andersen, R. M., & Leake, B. D. (2000). The behavioral model for vulnerable populations: Application to medical care use and outcomes for homeless people. *Health Services Research, 34*(6), 1273–1302.

Gillis, D., Grossman, M., McLellan, B., King, A. C., & Stewart, A. L. (2002). Participants' evaluations of components of a physical-activity-promotion program for seniors (champs ii). *Journal of Aging and Physical Activity, 10*, 336–353.

Gilliss, C. L., Lee, K. A., Gutierrez, Y., Taylor, D., Beyene, Y., Neuhaus, J., et al. (2001). Recruitment and retention of healthy minority women into community-based longitudinal research. *Journal of Women's Health & Gender-Based Medicine, 10*(1), 77–85.

Green, L. W., & Kreuter, M. W. (2005). *Health program planning: An educational and ecological approach, 4th ed.* New York: McGraw-Hill.

Hennessy, C. H., & John, R. (1996). American Indian family caregivers' perceptions of burden and needed support services. *Journal of Applied Gerontology, 15*(3), 275.

Hill, T. D., Burdette, A. M., Angel, J. L., & Angel, R. J. (2006). Religious attendance and cognitive functioning among older Mexican Americans. *Journals of Gerontology: Series B: Psychological Sciences and Social Sciences, 61*(1), P3.

Israel, B. A., Schulz, A. J., Parker, E. A., & Becker, A. B. (1998). Review of community-based research: Assessing partnership approaches to improve public health. *Annual Review of Public Health, 19*, 173–202.

Israel, B. A., Schulz, A. J., Parker, E. A., & Becker, A. B. (2000). *Community-based participatory research: Principles, rationale and policy recommendations.* Washington, DC: National Institute of Environmental Health Services.

Katzman, R., Zhang, M., Orang-Ya-Qu, Wang, S., Liu, W. R., Wong, S., et al. (1988). A Chinese version of the mini-mental state examination: Impact of illiteracy in a Shanghai dementia survey. *Journal of Clinical Epidemiology, 41*, 971–978.

Krueger, R. A. (2000). *Focus groups: A practical guide for applied research* (3rd ed.). Thousand Oaks, CA: Sage.

Kurasaki, K. S., Sue, S., Chun, C.-A., & Gee, K. (2000). Ethnic minority intervention and treatment research. In J. F. Aponte & J. Wohl (Eds.), *Psychological intervention and cultural diversity* (2nd ed.) (pp. 234–249). Needham Heights, MA: Allyn & Bacon.

Levkoff, S., & Sanchez, H. (2003). Lessons learned about minority recruitment and retention from the centers on minority aging and health promotion. *Gerontologist, 43*(1), 18–26.

Li, R. M., McCardle, P., Clark, R. I., Kinsella, K., & Berch, D. (Eds.). (2001). *Diverse voices: Inclusion of language-minority populations in national studies: Challenges and opportunities.* Bethesda, MD: National Institute on Aging and National Institute of Child Health and Human Development.

Liang, J. (2002). Assessing cross-cultural comparability in mental health among older adults. In J. H. Skinner, J. A. Teresi, D. Holmes, S. M. Stahl & A. L. Stewart (Eds.), *Multicultural measurement in older populations* (pp. 11–21). New York: Springer.

MetLife Mature Market Institute. (2006). Out and aging: The Metlife study of lesbian and gay baby boomers. Westport, CT: MetLife Mature Market Institute.

Morano, C. L., & Bravo, M. (2002). A psychoeducational model for Hispanic Alzheimer's disease caregivers. *Gerontologist, 42*(1), 122–126.

Patton, M. Q. (2008). *Utilization focused evaluation* (4th ed.). Thousand Oaks, CA: Sage.

Schaie, K. W., & Willis, S. L. (2002). *Adult development and aging* (5th ed.). New York: Prentice-Hall.

Silveira, M. J., Kabeto, M. U., & Langa, K. M. (2005). Net worth predicts symptom burden at the end of life. *J Palliat Med, 8*(4), 827–837.

Stahl, S. M. (2002). A long-range innovative approach to reducing health disparities: The National Institute on Aging's resource centers for minority aging research. In J. H. Skinner, Teresi, J.A., Holmes, D., Stahl, S.M., Stewart, A.L. (Ed.), *Multicultural measurement in older populations*. New York: Springer, 221–223.

Stewart, A. L., Gillis, D., Grossman, M., Castrillo, M., Pruitt, L., McLellan, B., et al. (2006). Diffusing a research-based physical activity promotion program for seniors into diverse communities: CHAMPS III. *Preventing Chronic Disease: Public Health Research, Practice and Policy, 3*(2), A51.

Stewart, A. L., & Napoles-Springer, A. (2000). Health-related quality-of-life assessments in diverse population groups in the United States. *Medical Care, 38*(Suppl 9), II102–II124.

Stewart, A. L., Verboncoeur, C. J., McLellan, B. Y., Gillis, D. E., Rush, S., Mills, K. M., et al. (2001). Physical activity outcomes of CHAMPS II: A physical activity promotion program for older adults. *The Journals of Gerontology, 56A*(8), M465–470.

Teresi, J. A., Stewart, A. L., Morales, L. S., & Stahl, S. M. (2006). Measurement in a multiethnic society. Overview to the special issue. *Med Care, 44*(11 Suppl 3), S3–4.

Williams, C. L., Tappen, R., Buscemi, C., Rivera, R., & Lezcano, J. (2001). Obtaining family consent for participation in Alzheimer's research in a Cuban-American population: Strategies to overcome the barriers. *American Journal of Alzheimer's Disease, 16*(3), 183–187.

Wolfe, N. (2002). Cross-cultural neuropsychology of aging and dementia: An update. In *Minority and cross-cultural aspects of neuropsychological assessment.* R. F. Ferraro (Ed.) (pp. 285–297). Lisse, The Netherlands: Swets & Zeitlinger.

Yeo, G. (Ed.). (2000). *Core curriculum in ethnogeriatrics,* (2nd ed). Stanford, CA: Stanford Geriatric Education Center.

3

Psychology and Aging

- How is psychology relevant to aging and diversity?
- What are the practical ramifications of age-related changes in sensation and perception?
- How does diversity affect ways of thinking?
- How do people, especially those from diverse ethnic and cultural groups, view older adults and the aging process?

Psychology is the scientific study of mental processes and behavior. Many argue that psychology is one of the core areas in the study of older people (Alkema & Alley, 2006) as it considers the relationship between aging and mental processes and behavior. This chapter focuses on how the psychological experiences of the aging individual can be affected by changes in sensory processes and perception, by changes in thinking processes, by elders' own beliefs about the aging process, and by beliefs that others may have about older adults. It also discusses how the psychological experiences of the aging individual may be affected by elements of diversity. Considerable research has examined the relationship between aging and mental processes (the psychology of aging) and recently researchers have turned to examining how cognitive processes may differ across diverse groups of people. Unfortunately, few areas of research in the psychology of aging have focused specifically on the intersection of aging and diversity. We highlight areas in which research has been conducted and then draw inferences to suggest how knowledge from these two fields, the psychology of aging and cultural diversity, might apply to diverse groups of elders.

To see how aging and diversity relate to the psychological experiences of individuals, please consider the following vignettes:

Vignette 1

Marjorie Miller is an 84-year-old former school teacher who lives in a small rural community in Eastern Pennsylvania. Although she lives on a very modest income provided almost solely by Social Security, she finds ways to enjoy her life's passions: theatre, opera, and museums. She can tell that her reflexes aren't what they used to be, so she has stopped driving at night and takes local roads rather than the interstate. Getting to evening events can require some creativity. Last week, she was given opera tickets to a performance in New York City. She and a friend took a Greyhound bus into the city and then took local buses to and from the theater. She was very pleased that the entire experience cost her only $45 and yet she still got to see a fantastic performance.

Vignette 2

Clair Yoon, age 22, gets to see two very different examples of aging in her own family. Her parents, in their 60s, are older than most of her friends' parents, and they each have very different attitudes toward aging. Clair's mother moans about every year that she ages, does not exercise regularly, and generally dreads aging. Clair's father seems to enjoy each new stage in his life, is actively hinting for grandchildren, and stays very physically active. Both Clair's parents moved to the United States from Korea when they were in their 20s and Clair wonders how they could each develop such different perspectives about aging and what would have happened had they both stayed in Korea. She worries that her mother's negative outlook will ultimately make her age in a more negative fashion.

AGING, SENSATION, PERCEPTION, AND COGNITION

Considerable research has examined the effects of aging on cognitive processes and behavior. One area that has received particular attention is sensation and perception, specifically how these change as we age. We can make a distinction between them. Sensation is the reception of environmental stimuli, for example, the ear receiving sound waves. Perception is the meaning that we give to those sound waves, as one might interpret that the loud sound indicates a car's backfiring. Aging processes can affect both sensation (e.g., input of sound) and perception (e.g., giving meaning to the sounds). Culture, on the other hand, affects only perception. For example, aging affects sensation because of changes in the visual and auditory systems that in turn affect perception. For some things, such as hearing, we have corrective steps to improve sensory input (i.e., amplifying sound using a hearing aid), but not for perception. Sensory input does not vary by culture and thus is the same across different cultural groups. But perception is giving meaning to those sensations, so perception is affected more by culture and early upbringing. It is in the perceptual arena that we may encounter cultural differences.

Indeed, cross-cultural research on optical illusions has demonstrated clear cultural differences in how two-dimensional figures are perceived. People raised in nonindustrial societies perceive two-dimensional optical illusions differently from people raised in industrial societies. However, the practical ramifications of these perceptual differences are not clear. Whether these two-dimensional perceptual differences translate into real-world practical differences is not known.

There are also intriguing age differences in the susceptibility to some optical illusions. Segall and colleagues (1966) found that older adults showed less illusion effect than younger adults. They theorized that age-related changes in visual acuity may cause these aging effects, but it may also indicate a cohort effect. Clearly, perception is very complex, with both culture and age affecting one's perception, at least in research settings. We now turn to focus on how sensation and perception change with age.

Sensory and Perceptual Changes

Although we, the authors of this text, struggle against the U.S. mainstream culture's tendency to portray aging as a period marked by physical, mental, and social declines, we also do not want to paint an inaccurate view of aging. The fact is that there *are* losses that occur with aging. For example, as we age, changes occur in our sensory systems such that our sensation or reception of external stimuli (for example, light, sound, odor, touch) significantly degenerates (Kausler, 1991). Perception, or the "ability to integrate, organize, and interpret the stimuli registered by the senses" also tends to be compromised with aging (p. 72). An in-depth examination of all age-related changes in sensation and perception is beyond the scope of our text. Instead, we will focus on areas of sensation and perception that have particular practical relevance for the day-to-day lives of older people.

Decreases in sensory function have been found for the visual, auditory, taste, and olfactory systems. For example, as we age, structural changes in the eye result in decreases in the amount of light that enters the eye and in the ability to adjust to changes in light. This decreased sensory ability means that as we age we need more light to read, we do not see as well at night, and that it takes longer for our eyes to adjust to a darkened theater or recover from the glare of oncoming headlights (Cavanaugh & Blanchard-Fields, 2006). Similarly, the eye's ability to adjust and focus declines and it becomes more difficult to see objects up close. Day-to-day activities can be affected as reading a menu or the correct dosage on a pill bottle may become impossible without a magnifying glass. Research has also found age-related declines in the sensitivity to some tastes (salt, bitterness) but not to others (sweet, sourness) (Kausler, 1991). Similarly, age deficits have also been found in sensitivity to odors, and in sensitivity to high-pitched sounds.

Age-related decreases in perceptual abilities have been found, with those that occur in vision and hearing having the most immediate practical importance. Perceptual differences in vision result in elders' decreased color perception and depth perception and may contribute to older adults' increased likelihood to have accidents. Age differences in speech perception have tremendous practical importance. When speech occurs at a normal conversational rate with little background noise, older adults' speech perception differs little from younger adults'. But when speech is altered (e.g., by background noise), then significant age deficits are found, with older adults being less able to comprehend the speech than younger adults (Kausler, 1991). Similar difficulties in comprehension can occur when trying to understand someone who speaks with an accent. Older adults may have much more difficulty in comprehending this speech than younger adults.

These changes in sensation and perception that occur with aging, although often small in scope, can have surprisingly large impacts on one's quality of life. For example, one may think that the sense of smell is relatively unimportant and so age-related decreases in this ability may not be so important. But one's sense of smell is very important for safety, social, and quality of life reasons. The ability to smell leaking gas or smoke can be critical for warning us of imminent danger. Socially, if one's sense of smell decreases, then the ability to determine whether one has an appropriate odor (not too much cologne, no offensive body odor, etc.) will also decrease and may affect one's ability to have positive social contacts with others. For one's quality of life, given that smell plays a large role in taste, when our ability to smell decreases, so does our ability to taste (think of how nothing tastes good when one has a head cold), and thus we may experience decreased enjoyment in eating. If we don't enjoy eating, it will not only affect quality of life, it may also affect health.

Hearing is another area where age-related changes can have a big impact. Hearing loss can impact one's ability to converse with others and this can in turn lead to social isolation. Social isolation is associated with poor health outcomes and mortality (Fratiglioni, Wang, Ericsson, Maytan, & Winblad, 2000; House, Landis, & Umberson, 1988). Gender differences in hearing loss show that men are more likely than women to experience hearing impairment (Cavanaugh & Blanchard-Fields, 2006). This may be a cohort effect as today's older men may have been exposed to damaging sounds in their work (e.g., in a factory or while operating farm machinery) when they were younger, whereas elderly women of today were less likely to have had jobs where they were exposed to high levels of noise. Thus, as a cohort effect, we might expect to see a different pattern of hearing impairment as the middle-aged adults become old themselves. Indeed, today's younger adults also need to be aware that headphones used at even a moderate volume level, in particular the newer style that fits inside one's ear, can cause significant irreversible hearing damage. We may find a cohort effect with a future generation of elders' experiencing substantial hearing loss if the current younger generation does not reduce exposure to this kind of sound input.

Sensory and perceptual age-related declines also occur in combination. For example, our sense of balance is actually a complex combination of senses. As we age, changes in the vestibular and visual systems result in increased dizziness and vertigo and more frequent falls. Even a small fall can have a significant impact on an elder's health. As we will discuss in more detail in the chapter on health, beliefs, and behaviors, people can be trained to improve their balance and posture to help prevent falls. Marjorie (in the first vignette) is responding to multiple age-related sensory and perceptual changes by adjusting her driving behavior. Though this adjustment may keep her and others safe, her reduced driving may affect her ability to see family and friends and may also affect her ability to get access to health care. Most of the changes in sensation and perception that we have discussed here are considered a part of "normal" aging (Cavanaugh & Blanchard-Fields, 2006) as they occur in varying degrees in most adults as they grow older. Of course, "normal" aging includes a broad range of individual experiences with some older adults' experiencing minimal changes in one or more sensory areas (e.g., continuing to have excellent vision), even though most elders experience some decline.

Age-related changes in sensation and perception do not suddenly appear overnight when one turns age 65, but begin much earlier, with the cumulative effects being felt in older age. For example, changes in the visual system begin in one's 40s and, as we have already mentioned, hearing loss may occur at even younger ages.

Given the gradual declines in sensory processes, one may not even be aware that they are occurring, until the decrements get so big as to be noticeable. In contrast, most of us have experienced temporary hearing loss after a plane flight or a bad cold, when our ears do not adjust properly. We notice this loss because it happened relatively suddenly and we know that just yesterday (or perhaps even 1 hour ago), we could hear voices and other sounds that now are muffled. But age-related hearing loss occurs much more slowly and one may not be aware that one's hearing has decreased dramatically—one would have to notice that one is no longer hearing things, and noticing the absence of something is much harder than noticing something newly added. Instead of becoming aware that one's ability to hear has been diminished, we are more likely to simply adjust things (such as television and radio volumes) and wonder why everyone else mumbles and why restaurants are so noisy that we cannot hear people talk. The idea that we are not aware of the severity of our loss is supported by research that shows that many older people who have relatively severe hearing loss consider that their hearing has been only mildly affected (Dancer, Pryor, & Rozema, 1989). Similar delays in recognizing declines can also happen with vision. As with a windshield that slowly becomes dirty over time and goes unnoticed until suddenly one realizes how difficult it is to see in sunlight, so do changes in the ability to see things creep in. For elders who lose their ability to see things up close, very slow changes occur. Hand-washing dishes or even putting on one's makeup will slowly be affected as one's vision gets more blurry up close. Seeing small food particles on a glass will not be possible and reading the correct dosage and important instructions on a medicine bottle will become increasingly difficult.

Adaptations and Accomodations   How can we assist elders (and ourselves) in recognizing and then adapting to these age-related declines before they become a problem? One way is to find adaptive strategies to deal with problem objects as they are. For example, keeping a magnifying glass or reading glasses strategically placed near medication bottles would facilitate correct reading of dosages. Another strategy is to *design* objects (e.g., medication bottles, cell phones) to enable accurate use by older people. For example, Target stores have begun using prescription bottles with flat sides so that dosage and warnings are easier to read (instead of having to read around the bottle) and so that they are easier to open (the flat sides give leverage to arthritic hands). Similarly, a new cell phone plan (http://www.jitterbug.com/) is being marketed that includes a phone with larger buttons and print size that is reportedly easier for older people to use.

The field of human factors (also known as ergonomics) works to understand how people behave in relation to environments, products, or services. With products, for example a medication bottle, the goal of human factors is to adapt existing products and plan new products so that people use them more effectively and accurately. Using a larger font size and colored warning labels are examples of adapting an existing product whereas making a bottle with a flat side is an example of planning a new product. Alphonse Chapanis (considered by many to be the "father" of human factors) and others have argued that we need to create environments, design products, and use type size so that older adults can use them effectively and safely. In addition to considering age when designing environments, products, and services, Chapanis reminds us that we also must consider culture.

Human factors and ergonomics have been focused mainly on the United States and western Europe and thus have not fully considered the impact that different languages, customs, and practices have on behavior (Chapanis, 2004).

Accommodations can be made for all of the losses we have discussed. Hearing aids, smoke and carbon monoxide detectors, specific exercises to improve balance, and limiting driving at night are all examples of ways to accommodate to these changes. Although these adaptations do not fix the actual impairment, they can ameliorate some of the detrimental effects. But neither making accommodations to one's existing environment and products nor creating better, new environments and products can happen overnight. Determining that one needs a magnifying glass or a flat prescription bottle in the middle of the night when one is ill or is trying to get medication for a loved one is not ideal. Advance awareness that accommodations may be needed and knowledge of the accommodations are important.

Unfortunately, many elders are reluctant and even resistant to making accommodations. Some may not be fully aware that they have a problem or that there are accommodations available to deal with the problem. For others, this reluctance may be due to their own or mainstream society's negative attitudes toward aging and the aged and their interest in avoiding becoming one of "them." For diverse groups of elders, there may be important cultural differences in how to convey information about accommodations (e.g., hearing aids, reading glasses) in an effective manner. Successful promotion of the use of these accommodations depends on a clear understanding of the barriers, often psychological, to their use. Unfortunately, we do not yet have a good understanding of the resistance to accommodation for either mainstream or diverse groups of elders.

Aging and Diversity Online: Seniors and Technology

How to make your website senior friendly. This online pamphlet was created to make websites more accessible to all older adults. It lists research-based, concrete suggestions for making websites more easily used and navigated by older people. http://www.nlm.nih.gov/pubs/checklist.pdf

NIH Senior Health. The National Institute on Aging and the National Library of Medicine collaborated to design a website on senior health using "senior-friendly" guidelines. http://nihseniorhealth.gov

CREATE. CREATE is the Center for Research and Education on Aging and Technology Enhancement. A consortium of three universities, CREATE conducts projects that focus on how humans (often older people specifically) interact with technology with the goal of expanding the usefulness and usability of technology. http://www.create-center.org

Sensory Changes and Diversity

As in many areas of aging and diversity, little research has examined how different groups of elders might experience these age-related changes in their senses differently or how their different life experiences and resources might affect their experience of these losses. In general, changes that are generally thought to be a part of "normal" aging are also thought to be the same across different ethnic and socioeconomic groups. But we can certainly infer how different groups of elders may be impacted in different ways by these age-related changes. For example, the ability to drive may be much more critical for rural elderly as alternative transportation is often nonexistent. Without an alternative, elders may drive longer than is safe in order to meet their daily needs (e.g., get groceries, go to the doctor, etc.). Similarly, some groups of elders are more likely to have been exposed to hearing-damaging noise than other elders. Elders who operated farm machinery or who worked in factories may suffer more hearing impairment than others. Interventions to make elders aware of how to compensate for these age-related declines, whether it be reading glasses, changing one's driving behavior, checking smoke alarms, or getting a hearing aid, would certainly need to be made culturally appropriate by asking questions such as:

- Who is the best person to approach (e.g., the elder person herself or her son)?
- What is the best message route (e.g., radio public service announcement or church bulletin)?
- How should the content of the message be focused (e.g., focus on one's family or on maintaining autonomy)?

Answers to these questions are likely to differ according to the elder's ethnic and cultural group. We also must remember that the age-related losses we are describing are based on averages of groups of older people. Not every older person has the same degree of loss; for example, some elders are able to hear better than younger adults. Some elders' vision is just fine. On average, though, many elders experience varying degrees and types of sensory and perceptual losses. Our challenge is to determine how to facilitate recognition of and accommodation for these losses in culturally appropriate ways.

ACTIVE LEARNING EXPERIENCE: PROMOTING ACCOMMODATIONS TO AGING

The purpose of this experience is to provide you with experience in proposing accommodations to age-related changes. Upon completion of this activity, you will be able to:

1. Recognize age-related changes in perception.
2. Suggest ways to accommodate to those changes.

Time Required: 45 minutes (30 minutes to complete the questions and 15 minutes to discuss the answers with another person).

Instructions:

1. Read the following case study, either as a homework assignment or in a class setting.
2. Prepare written responses to the questions at the end of the case study on your own or as a part of the class discussion designed for this activity.
3. Discuss your responses with another person.

Case Study

Lidia Sanchez moved to the United States from Guatemala when she was 20 years old. She and her husband have two children who are in high school. As a child in Guatemala, Lidia's grandmother raised her. In the United States, when Lidia needed to work outside of the home, her grandmother came to live with Lidia to help with the children. Lidia loves and respects her grandmother tremendously and she has been a wonderful help with the children. Recently, Lidia has noticed some small changes around the house. Dishes that used to be washed spotless are sometimes now placed back in the cupboard dirty. Her grandmother sometimes wears clothing that is stained. At their large family dinners, her grandmother often sits quietly and sometimes even leaves dinner early. Last weekend, when Lidia's son had a bad cough, Lidia's grandmother almost gave him an amount of cough syrup that was twice the required dose. Lidia is worried about her grandmother and isn't sure what to do about these things.

Discussion Questions:

1. Which sensory systems may be affected by age-related changes for Lidia's grandmother?
2. What accommodations may be available for her?
3. What suggestions do you have for Lidia?
4. How would your suggestions change if Lidia's grandmother were from a different cultural group?
5. What cultural characteristics (e.g., family structure, rural or urban, religious beliefs, gender roles, financial resources) do you need to take into account when making these suggestions?

Cognitive Changes

Greeting cards often present older adults as slow-thinking and incompetent, but is this stereotype accurate? Do older adults actually think differently from younger adults? In psychology, the study of cognitive aging examines how the mind functions and whether this changes as we age. As with sensation and perception, research on cognitive aging has documented declines that occur in some cognitive capacities as we age. Although a detailed examination of cognitive aging is beyond the scope of this book, in general, speed of mental processing, working memory, and ability to inhibit irrelevant information have all been shown to decline as we age (e.g., Park, 1998; Salthouse, 2004). What does this mean? The decreased processing speed means that older adults are slower at processing information and completing tasks than younger adults. The effect of reduced working memory means that older adults have less capacity to simultaneously manipulate different types of information (i.e., less working memory) than do younger adults. Finally, poorer inhibition means that elders have a decreased ability to eliminate distractions and focus on specific information than younger adults. Thus, research on cognitive aging demonstrates that some cognitive abilities decrease as we age, but this does not mean that the older adults' thinking processes are severely compromised or that all cognitive abilities decline with age. Semantic memory is often described as the "storehouse of our world knowledge" (Howard & Howard, 1991, p. 11). Semantic memory is what allows us to remember the meaning of words and to use language. Research has found that age declines are rare with semantic memory (Bowles, 1993; Light, 1992). Thus, knowledge is maintained into old age and life experience can give elders a strong knowledge base to solve problems. In sum, older adults maintain their lifelong experiential and knowledge base, but the speed with which they access that knowledge base slows with age (Park & Gutchess, 2000).

Why is it important to know about aging-related changes in cognitive processes? This knowledge gives us a much more precise understanding of thinking processes in older adults. Although experimental research shows declines in basic thinking processes as we age (e.g., decreased processing speed), in general many older adults' thinking skills continue to function quite well until very old (Schaie, 1995, 1996). For example, Ybarra and Park (2002) asked older and younger adults to process information about a person for whom they had been given either a positive or negative impression. Even though older adults performed worse on specific processing speed and working memory measures (unrelated to the impression formation task), when older adults were allowed to process the information about the person in a self-paced, unlimited time context, their memory of the information did not differ from that of younger adults (Ybarra & Park, 2002). Importantly, in a second experiment, researchers limited the amount of time the younger and older adults had to process the information. In this condition, unlike younger adults, older adults failed to change their initial positive impressions about the person when later given information about his negative characteristics (Ybarra & Park, 2002). Although this research was done in an experimental setting, there are relevant practical applications. Elders are often the target of financial scams that exploit them, and reports in the popular press suggest that elders are more susceptible to these scams than younger adults. Ybarra and Park's research suggest that indeed, in certain situations (e.g., where the older adult is being rushed), older adults may be more susceptible to scams than younger adults. Alerting elders to conditions under which their judgment might be impaired may aid them in avoiding these scams. For example, recommendations to avoid making decisions under time pressure may help them avoid situations in which advantage might be taken of them.

In sum, older adults do tend to think more slowly than younger adults, but this decline in speed does not necessarily come with a decline in the quality of problem solving. Thus, instead of incorrectly generalizing the stereotype from slow-thinking to incompetent, one can instead recognize the cognitive declines that do occur and create situations that allow older adults to make high-quality decisions by not rushing them and by limiting distracting information

Aging and Diversity Online: An Application of Cognitive Aging

How Seniors Learn. The Center for Medicare Education was funded to provide information on how to develop programs to educate seniors and their families about Medicare. The following newsletter takes knowledge gained from cognitive aging research and applies it to explain "How Seniors Learn." Tips for written educational materials and for oral presentations are given. http://www.mathematica-mpr.com/pdfs/howseniors.pdf

Maintaining Mental Abilities Given that aging does seem to result in a slowing of some thinking processes, is there anything elders can do to reverse or even prevent these declines? Some people follow the "use it or lose it" perspective of aging: if people don't use their abilities (mental or physical), then they will eventually lose them. This perspective argues for keeping both mind and body active. Can people improve their cognitive processes and physical health by keeping their minds and bodies active?

Cognitive Training Cognitive training has blossomed in recent years as people work to find ways to keep the brain healthy and active at all ages. Cognitive training typically consists of different mental exercises that are designed to improve functioning in specific cognitive areas. For example, cognitive training is done with children and adults with attention deficit hyperactivity disorder (ADHD) to help improve attention span. For older adults, cognitive training can be either preventive, working to prevent the cognitive declines associated with aging, or rehabilitative, working to restore cognitive abilities that may have been harmed by a stroke, for example. New companies have been founded with the primary purpose of promoting "brain health" through their specific cognitive training programs. This training can be delivered in a classroom setting, online, or even through a handheld gaming device (e.g., the Nintendo Wii).

Does cognitive training work? Until recently, most studies examining the effects of cognitive training had small homogeneous samples and lacked random assignment to training and control conditions. Thus, it was not clear whether results from these studies would generalize to older adults and whether the cognitive training itself was effective. Fortunately, Sherry Willis and colleagues (2006) conducted the first multisite, randomized controlled clinical trial to examine the long-term effects of cognitive training on daily functioning for a relatively diverse sample of independently living older people. This study was called the Advanced Cognitive Training for Independent and Vital Elderly (ACTIVE) study. The study included a "ten-session training for memory (verbal episodic memory), reasoning (inductive reasoning), or speed of processing (visual search and identification), and four-session booster training at 11 and 35 months after training in a random sample of those who completed training" (Willis et al., 2006, p. 2805). The study sample was fairly diverse: 26% of the sample was Black (73% was White, <1% of any other ethnic group) and 76% was female. Participants were recruited from communities in and around Birmingham, Alabama; Detroit, Michigan; Boston, Massachusetts; Baltimore, Maryland; Indianapolis, Indiana; and State College, Pennsylvania.

Was the ACTIVE program effective? The cognitive training conducted in the ACTIVE program did result in specific improved abilities in the targeted areas: memory, reasoning, and speed of processing. These specific improvements were maintained through 5 years. But one of the main goals behind ACTIVE was to determine whether cognitive training targeting a specific area of cognitive functioning (e.g., speed of processing) would result in improved everyday function. In other words, would specific training generalize to more everyday abilities? In general, the answer is no. At least at the 5-year mark, only limited generalization to everyday function was found in the reasoning condition and no generalization was found in the memory and speed of processing conditions (Willis et al., 2006). Thus, cognitive training that targets areas of aging-related decline does improve cognitive performance in those areas, but this improved performance does not seem to generalize to other activities of daily living and thus does not prevent aging-related declines in cognition.

Although the results from ACTIVE were not as transferable as had been hoped, there still are positive outcomes from ACTIVE and hope for cognitive training in general. Perhaps beyond the 5-year study measurement, as the ACTIVE participants age, the training will provide them with a protective buffer from the effects of aging-related cognitive declines. Alternatively, the lack of generalization from the ACTIVE study may suggest that researchers should look to different kinds of training to prevent cognitive decline. Perhaps instead of focusing on training areas of cognition that decline with age, researchers should focus on training other areas of the brain to compensate for those declines. Park and colleagues (2007) examine research demonstrating that older adults show "compensatory frontal recruitment compared to younger persons while performing both working memory and long-term memory tasks" (p. 45), suggesting flexibility in the brain as we age. Park and colleagues suggest that nontraditional approaches to improve cognitive function, such as broad-based intervention strategies that provide general intellectual stimulation (for example, participating in theater productions), might result in a more generalized increase in cognitive function. Cognitive training is an area currently receiving a great deal of focus by both academic researchers and for-profit companies.

Aging and Diversity Online: Cognitive Training

Please note: We include these websites as examples of the recent creation of businesses that provide cognitive training to older people. We do not vouch for the effectiveness of these cognitive training programs.

PositScience. This company sells a brain fitness program developed by company founder neuroscientist Michael Merzenich. http://www.positscience.com/

Happy Neuron. This company provides scientifically based, quick and entertaining ways to exercise the brain. http://happy-neuron.com

SharpBrains. This company provides information about many different programs for "brain health" and fitness. http://www.sharpbrains.com

---

Physical Exercise   Although mental exercise can improve older adults' cognitive functioning and, counter to the adage about old dogs and new tricks, it is possible to teach older adults new cognitive skills, mental exercise does not slow the *rate* of their cognitive decline (Salthouse, 2006). But what about physical exercise? Does keeping your body active allow you to keep your physical abilities? Research suggests it does, *and*, even more important, *physical* exercise may actually improve one's *cognitive* function. In mainstream U.S. culture, one may connect cognitive training with maintaining one's thought processes and physical exercise with maintaining one's physical abilities. But research suggests that physical exercise can also help maintain cognitive vitality. Colcombe and Kramer (2003) conducted a meta-analysis examining research on the effects of fitness training on cognitive function of older adults. They found that fitness training had a positive influence on cognition. In particular, fitness training effects were larger when aerobic training programs were combined with strength and flexibility training, and fitness training effects were larger for women than for men. They also found that short bouts of exercise (fewer than 30 minutes) had very little effect on cognition. In a more recent study, Colcombe and colleagues (2006) found that moderate aerobic exercise such as brisk walking resulted in increased *brain* volume in older adults. Clearly, research shows that doing moderate physical exercise (using one's body) improves cognitive functioning (improves one's mind). Exercise the body and the mind benefits.

Adapting Interventions for Diverse Groups   How do key elements of diversity relate to aging-related cognitive decline, cognitive training, and physical exercise? Aging-related cognitive decline does occur in groups of diverse elders just as it does in mainstream elders. Research has found ethnic differences in cognitive function of older adults with the greatest cognitive function differences observed between Blacks and Whites. Hispanic and "other race" cognitive function levels were in between Whites and Blacks (Sloan & Wang, 2005). As with Whites, research has found that both level of education and physical health are related to cognitive functioning in Black older adults (Whitfield et al., 1997), but the causes of the racial differences in cognitive functioning are not well understood. Some differences may be due to differences in the quality of education that different ethnic and racial groups received, other differences may be due to the lack of adequate health care in certain groups, and other differences may be due to the fact that some of the cognitive measures may be less culturally appropriate for some groups (Whitfield et al., 2000).

Religious involvement has also been found to be related to cognitive functioning. Researchers analyzed data collected for the Hispanic Established Populations for Epidemiologic Studies of the Elderly (H-EPESE) in which 3,050 Mexican-origin older adults were surveyed beginning in 1993 with repeated measurement every 2–3 years. They found that attendance at religious events was related to decreased cognitive decline in older adults compared with those who did not attend religious events (Hill, Burdette, Angel, & Angel, 2006). Thus, we have evidence for cognitive decline in elders from diverse groups as well as evidence for potential protective factors (such as religious participation), although the full complexity of diversity and cognitive decline is not completely understood. In addition, it is unclear how cognitive training and physical exercise interventions will work with elders from different cultural groups.

Although the results from cognitive training and physical exercise interventions show improvements in cognitive functioning, these interventions were developed for use with mainstream groups of elders. It may be that different groups of elders (e.g., low income, immigrant, or ethnic minority) may respond differently to interventions. For some groups, training that is delivered as a class and couched in crossword puzzles and other mind "games" might be engaging and fun. For others, this interaction might be strange, isolating, and seemingly irrelevant.

Similarly, attitudes toward exercise differ by cultural group. Although we know that cardiovascular exercise can improve the health of most elders, people differ in their interest and willingness to do certain kinds of exercise and even to label them as exercise. Focus groups conducted with different ethnic groups in Seattle found similarities and differences across the cultural groups (Belza et al., 2004). Just as activities that promote cultural dances might be more effective than providing treadmills for some elders, cognitive training that reflects the group's cultural values and practices might also be more effective. Elders from different groups might have different interests in and attitudes toward certain activities that might increase their likelihood of living a long and healthy life. Wisdom Steps is an example of a health promotion program developed and run by the American Indian community in Minnesota. One of their programs, "We Walk, Many Together" is being developed to help increase participation in walking and exercise programs. Following the cultural value of "Our elders are our teachers," this program encourages older people to take a younger person with them to do the elder's exercise of choice and help teach the younger person the importance of exercise. These culture-specific programs may work better for certain cultures than programs designed for mainstream older adults. It may also be that programs developed within specific cultural groups may also be more effective for mainstream elders. New strategies for promoting cognitive well-being may come from elders from diverse groups.

Aging and Diversity Online: Culture-Specific Interventions

Wisdom Steps. This health promotion program is developed and run by the American Indian community in Minnesota. They use cultural values from within the community to help promote healthy behaviors such as exercise. http://www.wisdomsteps.org/home.htm

Culture and Cognition

Although many cultural anthropologists have focused on the differences that occur between cultural groups, mainstream psychology has long assumed that basic psychological processes, such as the way we think, were the same across cultures. Recent research has suggested that mainstream psychology was incorrect and that some basic thinking processes may be different across cultural groups. For example, consider the thinking process that psychologists call the "correspondence bias" or the "fundamental attribution error." According to this principle, when explaining why someone behaved in a certain way, people tend to make personality-based or dispositional explanations. If someone was late to a meeting, some people would tend to explain this tardiness as being due to that individual's personality, that he was a lazy or uncaring person. But more recent research has found that the fundamental attribution error is not quite so "fundamental." People from more collectivistic cultures that put a higher priority on group harmony, for example Asian cultures, tend to make explanations for others' behavior that are based on the situation, rather than on the individual's personality. In explaining the late behavior, people from collectivistic cultures would tend to look for a situational explanation such as there must have been bad traffic that delayed the person. Explanations for these cultural differences have often focused on cultural differences in individualism and collectivism. In cultures that value individualism and the autonomy of the individual, the focus is often on the person. In cultures where in-group harmony is valued, the situation or the interconnection between the individual and the context is the focus. Similar cultural differences in self-definition also occur. In individualistic Western cultures (e.g., the United States), the self is defined as separate from the context and one is encouraged to "be all that you can be," whereas in more collectivistic Eastern Cultures (e.g., Japan), the self is defined by one's connection to and membership in different groups and one is encouraged to "fit in" (Markus & Kitayama, 1991).

Nisbett and colleagues (2003) have conducted research that suggests that the very basics of what we pay attention to differs depending on the culture in which one was raised. This research has found that people from different cultural groups "perceive the world and think about it differently" (p. 11163). People from Western cultures favor a feature-based, analytic style that puts attention on a focal object in a situation. People from East Asian cultures instead use a more holistic focus in which they attend to the situation or context in which a focal object is placed. For example, when asked to take a photo of a person, American students tended to take photos that literally contained only the person, like a school yearbook photo, whereas Japanese students' photos included the environment by stepping back from the person and thus including the surrounding room in the photo (Nisbett & Masuda, 2003). When asked to report what they had seen in animated underwater scenes that contained both focal objects (e.g., brightly colored moving fish) and background or field information (e.g., inert objects, the floor of the scene), American participants were more likely than Japanese participants to start their statements by mentioning focal objects and the Japanese made more observations about the field than did the Americans (see Figure 3.1). Japanese participants also described more relations between focal objects and the field than did American participants. Thus, in addition to attending to both focal objects and the field in

Figure 3.1   An example of animated vignettes. The arrows refer to the directions of the figures' movements (Masuda & Nisbett, 2001).

which these objects are located, people from East Asian cultures make connections between the field and the focal objects, making explanations based on the environment (much like the explanations for late behavior described above), whereas the Americans' attention on the focal object results in missing the connections between the object and its environment. These differences in the focus of attention result in different strengths. When trying to determine whether two versions of the same scene were the same, American participants were better able to detect changes in the focal objects and Japanese participants were better able to detect changes in the background features (Nisbett & Masuda, 2003).

In addition to this focus on the surrounding context, evidence suggests that people from East Asia favor different strategies when solving problems with conflicting pieces of information. For example, in a disagreement between a mother and daughter, resolution could be achieved by deciding that one person was right and the other person was wrong, or by finding a middle ground in which each one is a little bit right and a little bit wrong. Peng and Nisbett (1999) found that people in the United States and Europe have a tendency to determine which person is "correct," ending up with one decision in which each side is either right or wrong, but not allowing both to be a little right and a little wrong. In contrast, people from East Asia tend to seek a middle ground, finding that each side may have areas in which they are right and other areas in which they are wrong, thus working for a more harmonious solution. In the above mother–daughter example, people from Asian cultures determined ways in which the mother was right and ways in which the daughter was right, whereas people from the United States tended to side either with the mother or the daughter. We can extend this research to imagine that when resolving complex issues or solving complicated problems, the need to find the "correct" answer might result in ignoring the benefits of the rejected option. Similarly, when it is impossible to find a "right" answer, frustration may be greater among people who value that type of decision.

Culture, Aging, and Cognition

Research examining cultural differences in cognition and age differences in cognition are not often considered jointly, as the role that age plays in cultural differences in thinking (and the role that culture plays in age-related cognitive changes) are not well understood. There are a couple of notable exceptions as research has begun to examine the intertwining roles of aging, culture, and cognition (Park, Nisbett & Hedden, 1999). Given the analytical, feature-based thinking style of people from Western cultures, their performance on tasks that require categorization into logical categories may be better than the performance of people from Eastern cultures. In contrast, on tasks that require a focus on context, people from Eastern cultures should perform better. But how will elders from each culture perform? Park and colleagues hypothesize that, to the extent that the task uses cognitive processes that have been shown to decline with age (e.g., processing speed), cultural differences found in younger adults should be much smaller in older adults as the decreased processing speed that comes with age should reduce cultural differences in the elders' performance. To the extent the task calls for strategies that have a cultural basis, then differences found among elders in different cultures should be as big as differences found among younger adults in different cultures. Some research has found that the cross-cultural differences in cognitive performance between Chinese and American participants were much smaller in older adults than in younger adults (Hedden et al., 2002). These researchers argue that the effects of aging on thinking decreases the strategies that older adults use and can result in more similar cognitive performance in older adults from different cultures than in younger adults. What are the practical ramifications of cultural differences in cognition?

Although the practical ramifications of these cross-cultural thinking differences have not been fully examined, there are important implications. In working with diverse groups of people, information may be processed differently depending on the cultural thinking style. Elders who were raised in Asian cultures may process information more holistically, paying attention to both focal points and their context and accepting conflicting information by working to find a middle-ground decision that acknowledges the good and the bad of the individual options. If, in a search for the one "right" answer, a service provider forces a cut-and-dried solution that ignores the complexities of the situation, this message may not be positively received by the Asian elders. On the other hand, if one is working with elders who process information in a more analytic fashion who want to find the one correct solution, acceptance of conflicting information may be difficult. They may desperately seek one "right" answer instead of looking for the more complex nuances and may be frustrated by a provider who does not facilitate that resolution. Similar difficulties can occur in families that contain different generations with different cultural thinking styles (e.g., some members raised in East Asia and others raised in the United States) as this difference could create communication difficulties. Interestingly, these differences do not seem to be genetically hardwired, as some evidence suggests that U.S.-born and -raised East Asians show the same thinking pattern as Euro-Americans (Park, Nisbett, & Hedden, 1999), with other evidence suggesting that Asian Americans are actually in between Euro-Americans and East Asians (Nisbett & Norenzayan, 2002).

Throughout the first half of this chapter, we focused on how the psychological processes of sensation, perception, and cognition are affected by aging. We also examined how cognitive and physical activity can improve both cognitive and physical health. But what do people think about aging? What beliefs do they have about older adults? We now turn to examine attitudes toward aging and older people.

ATTITUDES TOWARD AGING AND OLDER PEOPLE

As discussed in Chapter 2, gerontology can be defined as the intersection among three related concepts: age, aging, and aged. The following sections will explore psychological aspects of two of these concepts in more depth: attitudes toward aging and attitudes toward the aged. Attitudes toward the aging process (aging) and older people (the aged) are important components of our understanding of old age. Significant differences can exist between different cultural groups in their attitudes toward the aging process and in their attitudes toward older people. These attitudes can, in turn, affect behaviors related to the aging process and toward older people.

Defining Terms

Attitudes can be thought of as evaluative judgments that we make about a person, object, or idea. Attitudes (or evaluative judgments) include our affective, cognitive, and behavioral responses to the attitude object. Our feelings about the aging process and about older people reflect the affective or emotional part of our attitude. Similarly, thoughts, beliefs, and expectations about aging and about elders reflect the cognitive part of our attitude. Stereotypes of older people are examples of the cognitive part of our attitude. Finally, our treatment of older people is the behavioral part. This treatment includes a full range of behaviors from deference and respect to discrimination. Prejudice is often defined as an attitude one has toward a group of people simply because of their group membership. Butler (1969) coined the term *ageism* to reflect attitudes held about older people simply because of their advanced age. When these attitudes are collectively held by a society, they create a system of disadvantage based on one's advanced age. Ageism is often conceptualized as prejudice against older people. This chapter discusses attitudes in general, but an in-depth discussion of ageism and the workplace occurs in Chapter 7, Work, Retirement, and Leisure. We are interested in people's attitudes about aging and about older people because such attitudes affect how we treat older people and because these attitudes (toward both aging and older people) may affect our own behavior as we age.

Attitudes About the Aging Process Across Cultures

Mainstream U.S. Attitudes   We need only look at birthday cards or open a magazine to find anecdotal lay constructions of attitudes toward the aging process. Jokes about being "over the hill," magazine advertisements for "anti-aging" creams, or black, funereal birthday cards imply that the aging process is negative and something to be avoided at any cost. These comments on aging are framed within a humorous context and can help us make light of acknowledged shortcomings that occur with age, but they may have negative effects as well. Some of these effects may depend on who is making the joke. It is qualitatively different for members of a group to joke about themselves than it is for someone from one group to make a joke about a different group. For example, members of a particular cultural group (e.g., African Americans, people with disabilities, gay men, or lesbians), sometimes do make jokes about their own group, even referring to group members using derogatory names. But when members of a particular group make the same jokes or use the same names for members of a *different* cultural group, this behavior is deemed offensive and unacceptable. For example, women may make reference to the "girls" in the office, whereas the same comment by men has a much more pejorative connotation. And yet greeting cards, advertisements, and jokes often make "fun" of aging and older people. Does the same standard hold that elders can make jokes about their own group, but that younger people should not? If so, why are these "jokes" about aging so ubiquitous?

"Successful" Aging   Recently, the view of aging in mainstream U.S. culture has broadened to include some positive expectations about aging. These are typically associated with retirement and leisure, portraying active, healthy, and relatively young elders enjoying later life doing things such as playing golf or traveling. Another example of the increasing positivity in U.S. attitudes toward aging is reflected in the successful aging movement. Although the term "successful aging" was coined more than 50 years ago, Rowe and Kahn (1987, 1997, 1998) popularized it both in scientific research and in the mainstream press, and supported it with evidence from the MacArthur Study of Successful Aging. By appreciating the positive aspects of aging, they worked to develop a conceptual basis for a "new gerontology" that did not focus on aging as the inevitable decline to death. Their model of successful aging includes three components:

1. Avoidance of disease and disease-related disability.
2. Maintenance of high physical and cognitive functional capacity
3. Active engagement in life

Rowe and Kahn acknowledge that individuals do not completely control their vulnerability to disease and disability, but they suggest that "successful aging is dependent upon individual choices and behaviors. It can be attained through individual choice and effort" (p. 37). With the demographic shift toward more older adults both in overall number and in proportion to the younger age groups of the U.S. population, many view successful aging as a way to change negative attitudes toward aging and to promote positive behaviors (such as healthy eating and exercise) that will increase the likelihood of having a healthy old age. Many baby boomers actively support the successful aging movement, as it seems to offer a way to age that gives control over aging to the individual instead of being an inevitable decline that simply happens to everyone. There are many predictions in the popular press that the image of aging will change as the baby boomers grow older, and that they will redefine aging as they remain healthy and active well into their advanced years. From this perspective, the desired norm for aging becomes an active, attractive, older person bicycling or cross-country skiing as the season dictates.

Unfortunately, these positive expectations cannot apply to all elders in that they portray elders with economic prosperity and physical health and thus include only high socioeconomic groups and healthy young-older adults, ignoring frail, rural, or poor older people. Certainly the successful aging focus on active, health-promoting behaviors is very positive, but the focus on individual control (and thus responsibility) over the aging process may end up with a backlash on those elders who do not match this image of successful aging. Minkler and colleagues (Holstein & Minkler, 2003; Minkler & Fadem, 2002) argue that when an older person does not meet the components of successful aging, then society (and perhaps even the older person him or herself) will consider the person to be aging unsuccessfully. Due to the successful aging focus on individual choices and behavior, people who age unsuccessfully may be considered at fault because they did not make the right choices. This is particularly likely for older people with disabilities. As the first component in the successful aging model is the avoidance of disability, then older people with disabilities would not be considered to be aging successfully and, even worse, people might think that had they made better individual choices they too might be bicycling or cross-country skiing (Minkler & Fadem, 2002). Of course, many possible causes for disability are unrelated to individual choice (for example, car accident, genetic predisposition to certain diseases, lifelong inaccessibility to health care) but these potential causes are not salient when one sees an older person in a wheelchair or using a walker. The successful aging movement may make people *more* likely to judge disabled elders negatively.

As presented earlier in this chapter, aging is associated with declines and, although these declines are not all inevitable and do not occur in every person at the same rate, these declines do occur, especially as people reach very advanced age. If people are supposed to be able to age "successfully" by eating right and exercising, then those people who experience the declines and frailty that can come with aging may be criticized for not having successfully aged. Disability may then be viewed as a failure of the individual and that the person did something wrong. So, trends such as successful aging may create more positive images of aging, but the negative attitudes will still be there. For some groups of elders, those who are poor or disabled, these positive images may actually harm them, as they are seen much more negatively in contrast to the new "standard" of what successful aging looks like.

To accept the prescriptions of successful aging uncritically would be to ignore the broader societal factors that lead to differential outcomes for people from minority ethnic groups, for the poor, for those from a rural location, and for those with disabilities. These external and environmental factors affect the likelihood that the person was able to receive a quality education, to have stable employment, to be paid a living wage in that employment, to have easy access to fresh fruits and vegetables, to have a safe neighborhood in which to exercise, and to have access to preventive health care. All of these external factors influence the likelihood that one will be able to avoid disease and disability, maintain high physical and cognitive functioning, and have an active engagement in life.

In addition to ignoring the role diversity plays in aging, the successful aging model also presents a polarized view of aging (it is either positive or negative) instead of a dialectical acceptance of both the positives and negatives of aging. This polarized view is typical of much of mainstream Western thought (see earlier section on cognition and diversity). Instead of aging either successfully or unsuccessfully, a person can be experiencing both declines related to aging and positive aspects of aging. Aging can bring both frailty and strength to the same person at the same time. This more complex perspective on aging advocated by Thomas Cole and others (Cole, 1988, 1992; Minkler & Fadem, 2002) recognizes the roles that both individual choice and external factors play in aging. It allows for understanding and compassion for elders who are experiencing declines in aging and yet also recognizes the positives that can come with aging. It acknowledges that personal choice can affect how we age, but does not ignore the external factors that also have an effect. It also opens us up to be able to learn from elders from diverse groups about different ways to age.

In spite of the successful aging movement, in general the aging process in mainstream U.S. groups is not viewed positively. It is viewed as the end of life, with each additional year bringing one closer to a dreaded negative, dependent end. We will examine attitudes toward elders later in this chapter, but negative attitudes toward the aging process in general affect our own expectations about aging. Additional research-based examinations of attitudes toward aging concur that attitudes toward aging, in the form of our expectations about aging, are often negative. Research by Heckhausen and colleagues (1989) has shown that adults of all ages expect that losses are much more common than gains as one ages. Similarly, regardless of type of memory examined, participants in this research expected that memory declines as we age (Ryan, 1992; Ryan & See, 1993), and that beliefs about one's control over one's memory will also decline as we age (Hertzog, Lineweaver, & McGuire, 1999).

Aging and Diversity Online: Different Portrayals of Aging

AARP Travel. The American Association for Retired Persons (AARP) website includes information that reflects the more positive view of aging in the United States. Their pages on travel for seniors are good examples of this. http://www.aarp.org/travel

"Humor" on Aging. This website is sponsored by a company that provides assistance with finding elder care (P&M Homecare Services). The company argues that "humor is the best medicine." Your instructor may want to facilitate a more critical discussion about this topic. http://pmcaregivers.com/GreetingCards.htm

Examination of the aging process from other research perspectives includes Erikson's theory of the psychosocial stages of development. In this theoretical model, development is divided into eight stages, the first five (infancy, early childhood, play age, school age, adolescence) all occurring before age 18. Three stages (young adulthood, adulthood, and old age) describe the rest of life (Cavanaugh

& Blanchard-Fields, 2006). For readers from Western cultures, these stages may seem intuitive and "correct," but they also reflect the idea that aging (development) is a linear process that proceeds in stages starting from birth and ending at death. Also, note the focus and attention on the beginning stages of the life process (five stages) and the one global stage that encompasses decades of life at the older-adult end of the spectrum. One may interpret this as reflecting the cultural attitudes that privilege youth and stereotype old age. Instead of viewing older age in a nuanced, complex way, these decades of life are lumped together into one category.

One of the problems of living in a culture that has negative attitudes toward the aging process means that we may derogate the aging process and try to deny applying the characteristics of aging to ourselves. This means that we do not learn from the aging-related processes what losses to be aware of and, when we do experience age-related losses, we hesitate to take corrective steps (e.g., getting a hearing aid or wearing reading glasses) in order to avoid being stereotyped as elderly. If instead we were all aware of the common declines that occur with aging as well as of the physical and cognitive abilities that tend to experience little change, people would be better equipped to ameliorate anticipated changes and respond quickly to other changes that might indicate a more serious problem.

Of course, it is important to remember that not all older people experience age-related declines in the same way or in the same degree. Some elders may experience very minimal declines in any area, others may experience declines in just one area. But if we were aware of age-related changes in hearing and we were having an event with multiple generations, then we would want to take into account the environment for the event. Will the setting allow the conversations that we would like to happen? If not, what steps can we take to ensure a positive experience for all? Similarly, in the earlier vignette about the grandmother's vision, accommodations could be easily made. Attractive and stylish eyeglasses with magnifying capabilities are easily available at pharmacies. Putting a pair of these glasses in the kitchen where dishes are washed and another pair in the medicine cabinet so that a senior is not squinting to try to see a dose or medicine name on a label would be easy fixes. How might this knowledge help younger adults? Knowing that these age-related changes are likely to happen will allow for an accurate understanding of the aging process. This understanding allows one to differentiate "normal" aging from problems that are not typically related to aging and may indicate a different health-related condition. In addition to allowing younger adults to better understand and help older people, this understanding may also allow for advance preparation and knowledge as younger adults themselves age.

ACTIVE LEARNING EXPERIENCE: CREATING ENVIRONMENTS THAT ACCOMMODATE ELDERS

The purpose of this experience is to provide you with empathy for age-related hearing loss and with experience in developing solutions. Upon completion of this activity, you will be able to:

1. Recognize effects of diminished hearing.
2. Suggest ways to accommodate to those changes.

Time Required: 45 minutes (15 minutes to do the experiment, 20 minutes to respond to the questions, and 10 minutes to discuss the answers with another person).

Instructions:

1. Take ear plugs (available at any local drugstore) and surreptitiously insert them in your ears the next time you are at a large gathering. Then rejoin the group and mentally note what your experience is like.
2. Respond in writing to the following questions:
   a. Were you able to participate in the conversations?
   b. What did you do to try to understand others? (e.g., did you ask them to speak up?)
   c. After a while, did you start checking out of the conversation? Did you start daydreaming?
   d. How do you think you looked to others—engaged or absent, at ease, or having difficulties? How might this be similar to situations that older people with hearing impairments might experience?
   e. What steps could you take to ameliorate this problem for others? Where might you do this? At your next family gathering? At a community meeting? In your local library?
3. Discuss your responses with another person.

Attitudes Toward Aging in Diverse Groups   Compared with the U.S. mainstream view, other ethnic, racial, and cultural groups have substantially different views of aging. Sometimes it can be difficult to truly recognize the influence of culture on one's beliefs, especially if one was raised in that culture. Examining artifacts from different cultures can help bring into stark contrast beliefs that may have seemed to be a "given." A portrayal of the stages of life in a temple in Thailand provides such a contrast. In Figure 3.2, examine the stages of life portrayed there. Note that there are also similarities with Western culture in that the temple monument portrays several stages moving from infant through young adulthood (and also privileges male development by portraying only a male figure), but there are also significant differences. Note the number of stages that reflect the older stages of life. Also note that life does not seem to end at death, but rather continues into another phase. This contrasts sharply with the Western notion of old age as being close to the end of life.

Figure 3.2 A Buddhist image of the life cycle as inscribed in a wall of a Thai temple (National Research Council, 2000).

ACTIVE LEARNING EXPERIENCE: THAI TEMPLE PORTRAYAL OF LIFE CYCLE

The purpose of this experience is to provide an opportunity to examine a different cultural portrayal of the life cycle and to reflect on your own beliefs about the aging process. Upon completion of this activity, you will be able to:

1. Identify different stages of life from both the Thai temple and from your own culture.
2. Find similarities and differences in these portrayals of the aging process.
3. Recognize the implications of these portrayals.

Time Required: 80 minutes (30 minutes to answer the questions, 30 minutes to construct your representation, and 20 minutes to discuss your answers and share your representation with another person).

Instructions:

1. Carefully examine the Thai Temple photo.
2. Respond in writing to the following questions:
   a. What stages of life does your culture typically consider important?
   b. What stages of life do you see in the Thai Temple photo?
   c. Are there similar stages from your culture that correspond to the Thai Temple stages? Identify any similar stages you find.
   d. Are there different stages? Describe any different stages (including stages in the Thai Temple photo that are not considered in your culture and vice versa). Why do you think that these differences exist? What might be the effect of considering different stages important?
3. Construct your own representation of the life cycle. This representation can be from your own cultural beliefs, or an idealized version that you wish reflected societal beliefs.
4. Share your life cycle representation with another person (or with your class) and discuss your responses to the above questions.

Although attitudes toward the aging process have not been well studied in different ethnic and cultural groups, there is evidence that different ethnic groups have more positive beliefs about the aging process. For example, for the Inuit in the Canadian north, successful aging depends not on having good health, but on the ability to respond to and manage declining health (Collings, 2001), thus, their approach to aging reflects an understanding of the challenges that occur in aging. As a part of a study on rural mental health, interviews with members of five southwestern American Indian tribes were conducted. When asked how they felt about getting old, both positive and negative factors were mentioned. Echoing the Inuit, concerns about poor health were important, but caring for family (children, grandchildren, and great-grandchildren) and helping others in the community were positive aspects of aging (Polacca, 2001). For Latino elders, family is also very important. In a study that interviewed 83 Latino elders in the United States, more than two thirds reported positive attitudes toward aging. For many of them, their well-being was related to the pleasure that comes from having a culturally defined place within the family (Beyene, Becker, & Mayen, 2002). In traditional Latino cultures there is a concept called "*respeto*," which gives respect to people based on their age, experience, or service. Having a valued and respected place within the family may be related to the Latino elders' positive attitudes toward aging.

Respect and family are also present when considering Native Hawaiians and Pacific Islanders (NHPI) (Braun, Yee, Browne, & Mokuau, 2004). Infused in many NHPI cultures are values of connections and relationships. In Chamorro culture in the Mariana Islands and Guam, elders (*manamko*) are respected and families honor the tradition of *setbe*, meaning to "serve one's parents." Reciprocity can even extend beyond one's currently living relatives to one's relationship with ancestral spirits. "People worship their ancestral spirits, and in turn believe that the spirits guard the land" (Braun et al., 2004, p. 60). For Asian Americans, dependency tends to be viewed in a more positive light when compared with the mainstream U.S. culture (Olson, 2001). One can infer then that the increased dependency that can occur in advanced age is also not as feared. Of course, acculturation can affect these cultural attitudes toward aging. For example, Kim and Kim (2001) report that growing numbers of Korean immigrant elders who traditionally live with their adult children and look forward to doing so when they first come to the States, often choose their autonomy and move out when they are faced with the difficulties that can occur in their Americanized Korean family. Similarly, in traditional Vietnamese culture, the older a person gets, the higher that person's social status. "Children were taught to respect their elders so that they too could live a long life" (Tran, Ngo, & Sung, 2001, p. 64). Vietnamese immigrants brought these cultural values with them to the United States, but for many Vietnamese Americans, the values have been affected through the acculturation process (Tran et al., 2001).

In gay communities, the aging process has typically been viewed very negatively as something to be avoided. The reasons for this are complex (as any explanations for why a particular group has a particular belief often are). Physical health and beauty are valued and revered, and aging is often seen as the antithesis to this. For some, this negative attitude toward aging can have a useful side effect, in that it motivates them to avoid stereotypical aspects of aging by exercising regularly and maintaining a fit body, behaviors that will likely result in a healthier advanced age. But this negative attitude can also result in a derogation of the aging process and of older people in general. We will discuss attitudes toward older people later in this chapter, but a negative attitude toward the aging process can result in negative feelings toward oneself when one becomes older. Minority communities often serve to buffer the minority group from experiencing the mainstream culture's prejudice against the group. When one has spent years being part of a minority community, to find oneself suddenly viewed negatively by that same community (due to one's advanced age) can be very painful and can make the aging process particularly difficult for some LGBT people. The documentary film *Beauty Before Age* (referenced in the audiovisual resources section at the end of this chapter), presents an excellent portrayal of attitudes toward aging in the gay community.

As further evidence that differences *within* a group can be quite substantial, Claes and Moore (2001) describe a different perspective on aging for some LGBT elders. A lifetime of "feeling different" and having to make their own way in a culture that was often extremely hostile to them has allowed some LGBT elders to approach aging in their own way with flexibility and creativity. As a result of having lived for decades outside of the mainstream culture as a person with a minority sexual orientation, these elders became used to doing things their own way and learned to ignore mainstream society's expectations and judgments. Thus, becoming an older adult was not a big transition for them.

Our attitudes toward the aging process are important because they can affect how we approach the experiences that elder relatives and friends have, and they can also affect our own thoughts and behaviors as we age. Attitudes toward older adults are similarly important. These attitudes affect how we treat older people as well as how we might look forward to being treated when we become older adults.

Older People: Attitudes Toward Elders Across Cultures

Mainstream United States   For much of the 20th century, it was commonly thought that older adults were viewed negatively in the U.S., whereas they were viewed much more positively in many Asian cultures (e.g., Japanese and Chinese cultures). Classic work by Brewer and colleagues (1981, 1984) and by Hummert and colleagues (1994) examined the beliefs about older adults held by young, middle-aged, and older adults in the United States. Their research indicated that there is no single global stereotype about older adults in the United States and that the stereotypes we do have are not uniformly negative. Instead, the term *older adult* functions as a superordinate category that encompasses many specific subcategories or subtypes. Mainstream U.S. beliefs include several different subtypes of elders, some of which are positive and some negative (see Table 3.1). Hummert and colleagues (1994) found that younger, middle-aged, and older adults show substantial similarities in their beliefs about older adults and that the different subtypes of beliefs about elders do match the negative stereotypes many consider to be pervasive in U.S. mainstream culture. For example, the "severely impaired" type includes characteristics such as slow-thinking, incompetent, and senile. Yet other types are viewed as extremely positive, as with the "golden-ager" that includes many characteristics that are counter to the negative stereotypes: active, capable, independent, and interesting. Elders do view members of their own age group in more complex ways than do younger adults as they create more subcategories of older adults and have more positive beliefs about elders' ability to

TABLE 3.1   Traits Associated with Stereotypes of Older Adults

Stereotype	Traits
Negative	
Severely impaired ·	Slow thinking, incompetent, feeble, incoherent, senile
Despondent	Depressed, sad, hopeless, afraid, neglected, lonely
Shrew/curmudgeon	Complaining, ill-tempered, demanding, stubborn, bitter, prejudiced
Recluse	Quiet, timid, naive
Positive	
Golden ager	Active, capable, sociable, independent, happy, interesting
Perfect grandparent	Loving, supportive, understanding, wise, generous, kind
John Wayne conservative	Patriotic, conservative, determined, proud, religious, nostalgic

Source: Hummert, Garstka, Shaner, & Strahm (1994).

change (Heckhausen et al., 1989). In general, however, mainstream adults (young, middle-aged, and older) in the United States share the same kinds of beliefs about older adults.

ACTIVE LEARNING EXPERIENCE: POSITIVE BELIEFS ABOUT OLDER PEOPLE

The purpose of this experience is to recognize positive beliefs that one has about older people. Upon completion of this activity, you will be able to:

1. Recognize positive beliefs toward older people.
2. Be aware of differences between people's beliefs.

Time Required: 45 minutes (15 minutes to do the experiment, 20 minutes to respond to the questions, and 10 minutes to discuss the answers with another person).

Instructions:

1. Make a list of positive beliefs you have about older people.
2. Respond in writing to the following questions:
   a. Was it easy or difficult to come up with positive beliefs?
   b. What is the source of these positive beliefs? (e.g., family, media, etc.)
   c. Would you like people to have these beliefs about you when you become old?
   d. Do you think that people from different ethnic or cultural groups have different beliefs about older adults? How do you think they differ?
   e. Compare your list with Table 3.1. Do any of your beliefs match these stereotypes? Which of your beliefs are not represented in this table?
3. Compare your list and your responses to the above questions with another person. Be prepared to present any similarities and/or differences to the class.

In spite of the positive beliefs about some types of older adults, in their meta-analysis of over 100 studies that included evaluations of older adults, Kite and colleagues (2005), found that attitudes were more negative toward older adults than younger adults. This negative evaluation bias decreased significantly when elders were evaluated on their own (instead of being compared with younger adults) and often when contextual information about the elder was given to the evaluator, for example, describing the elder as a "working older adult" instead of just an "older adult." Often, younger and middle-aged adults' attributions about older adults' experiences are wrong. For example, middle-aged and younger adults significantly overestimated the percentage of older adults who were lonely, felt they were not needed, and were suffering from ill health (Speas & Obenshain, 1995). Similarly, although there are commonly held beliefs about a generation gap between older and younger adults, a survey conducted by the National Council on Aging (NCOA) found that older and younger people showed substantial agreement about where tax dollars should be spent (The National Council on Aging, 2002). In sum, we can conclude that although the mainstream American attitude toward older adults includes both positive and negative images, there is also evidence of an overall negative bias toward older people and evidence of misunderstandings between different generations.

Often when people express their thoughts and beliefs about older adults (that is, they stereotype them), they refer to stereotypical older adult characteristics as if these were due to aging. This may be true for some characteristics and for some older people, but this stereotyping inappropriately simplifies a complex situation. As discussed earlier in the chapter, decreases in speed of processing, vision, and hearing, among others, are associated with aging, but not every older adult experiences decrements in each of these areas. On average, older adults may be slower than younger adults, but there is large variability within the older adult population and the results depend on the context of the testing (such as the type of instructions given) and the knowledge area (new area versus an expertise area) in which the testing is being conducted (Howard & Howard, 1991). Also, this stereotyping sometimes confuses age changes with cohort differences. As discussed in Chapter 2, age changes are those that occur as people age and thus everyone who ages will experience those changes. Cohort differences refer to those that are due to the varying life experiences of two groups, or cohorts, of people. Often we attribute a stereotypic characteristic to old age and fail to pay attention to how that difference between generations may have occurred. For example, a common stereotype is that older adults are overly careful with their money. For the current cohort of people aged 75 and older, this may have nothing to do with being old and everything to do with being raised during the Great Depression when money was extremely tight. Future cohorts of older people (e.g., the baby boomers) may be much less careful with their money.

Why does it matter that we fail to differentiate cohort and age differences? It matters because this misattribution can affect our treatment of older people. Understanding the life experiences of a person and how those life experiences combine to make him or her the person that we see today helps us treat the person accurately rather than stereotyping and placing him or her into a box that may not fit. This understanding is especially important when working with older people from diverse groups because their life experiences are often different from those of the mainstream population and so are not reflected in our common societal knowledge. For example, hoarding (gathering and collecting piles of things like newspapers) by an older person from a mainstream group may be a psychological issue related to aging, whereas hoarding done by an elder who had a traumatic immigration experience may be caused by different factors entirely. Understanding the role of different life experiences in the aging process not only allows us to value and respect individual differences but also to treat problems more accurately.

ACTIVE LEARNING EXPERIENCE: EFFECTS OF ELEMENTS OF DIVERSITY AND LIFE EXPERIENCES ON THE BEHAVIOR OF YOUR PARENT OR GRANDPARENT

The purpose of this experience is to provide you with an opportunity to examine how the various elements of diversity relate to an elder in your family. Upon completing this activity, you will be able to:

1. Describe some of the influences of race or ethnicity, gender, religion, education, occupation, rural versus urban community location on adult behavior.
2. Examine what effect, if any, large-scale societal events may have had on your parent or grandparent.

Time Required: 1.5 hours (45 minutes to talk with a parent or grandparent, 30 minutes to complete the questions, and 15 minutes to discuss the answers with another person).

Instructions:

1. Contact one of your parents or grandparents (or any other adult who is older than you).
2. Through your conversation, find answers to the questions provided below.
3. Prepare written responses to the questions.
4. Discuss your responses with another person.

Questions:

1. Who is the person being described (your parent, grandparent, other person)?
2. How old is this person and what is this person's racial or ethnic background and gender?
3. Is this person affiliated with a specific religious group, and, if so, which one?
4. Give examples of how this person's gender, ethnic, and religious background and his community location affect his or her behavior (e.g., daily or weekly rituals, eating habits, attitudes, membership in community groups, etc.)
5. What is the person's educational background? What is or was the person's occupation? Give examples of how the person's education and occupation may have affected his or her behavior.

6. Go to the events from the cohort graph in Figure 3.3. Find events that would have happened when the person was 5, 10, and 15 years old. Mention each event and ask whether the event had any impact on his or her life. Ask whether there were other events that happened when the person was young and what impact those events had on his or her life.

How Different Cultural Groups Look at Older People

Do different ethnic groups have different beliefs about older adults? Initial research seems to show both substantial differences and similarities in beliefs about older adults. In terms of differences, there is a general sense that elders are more valued and respected in different ethnic groups than they are in White Americans. For example, for American Indians, the term "elder" does not just delineate age, it refers to a position of leadership that is "based on experience, spirituality, and community service rather than on chronological age. There are elders in their 40s and 50s, and many Indian grandparents in their late 30s" (Hendrix, 2000, p. 10). One must make a distinction between "old Indians" and "elders" in the American Indian community. To further complicate the issue of age, the Indian Health Service (discussed in more detail in Chapter 5,) considers Indians who are 55 years of age and older to be elders, but to be eligible for government programs for older people, one needs to be 65 years of age (Hendrix, 2000). In any case, regardless of their age, American Indian elders "play a significant role in the life of the tribe because they are the keepers of tradition, culture, and spirit" (Dwyer, 2000, p. 92). "Elders are held in high esteem, and most families want to care for their elders in ways that preserve and promote their dignity and honor cultural traditions" (Goins & Spencer, 2005, p. 33).

For Hispanic elders, cultural values promote respect. The concept of *familismo* reflects the importance of the family at all levels, with the family's needs often taking precedence over individual needs and the respect for hierarchy that comes with *jerarquismo* (respect for hierarchy) (Talamantes, Lindeman, & Mouton, 2000).

For Asian Americans and Pacific Islanders, the cultural influence of Confucianism explicitly promotes filial piety, which sets expectations for obeying, respect, support, and care for one's parents throughout their lives including old age (Blanchette, 2000). In many Asian and Latino cultures, multigenerational households are accepted and valued arrangements. In Philippine society, for example, respect and caring for parents and older family members are taught to children. "Caring for aging relatives is integrated over time into these relationships" (McBride, 2001, p. 5).

Within each of the above examples, the implicit comparison suggests more respect and value for older people in different ethnic groups when compared with mainstream U.S. culture. So, is it true that other cultures value elders more than U.S. mainstream culture? The answer to this question is complex. There is much anecdotal evidence that elders in many cultures are revered and valued more than elders in the United States. For example, in some Asian cultures, younger

1941 Cohort	1931 Cohort	1921 Cohort	years	Event
		Born	1921	
		5 years old	1926	
	Born		1929	Stock market crashes
			1931	
	5 years old	15 years old	1935 / 1936	Social Security Act
Born			1941	Pearl Harbor, U.S. enters WWII
5 years old	15 years old	25 years old	1946	Baby Boom begins
			1950 / 1951	U.S. enters Korean War
15 years old	25 years old	35 years old	1955 / 1956 / 1957	Polio vaccine / Women age 62-64 eligible for reduced Social Security benefits / Social Security Disability Insurance Implemented
			1961 / 1962 / 1964 / 1965 / 1966	Men age 62-64 eligible for reduced Social Security benefits / Self-Employed Individual Retirement Act (Keogh Act) / U.S. enters Vietnam War, Civil Rights Act, Baby Boom ends / Medicare and Medicaid established
25 years old	35 years old	45 years old	1969	First man on the moon
			1971 / 1972 / 1973 / 1974 / 1975 / 1976	Formula for Social Security cost-of-living adjustment established / Social Security Supplemental Security Income Implemented / IRAs established / Age Discrimination Act
35 years old	45 years old	55 years old	1978	401 (k)s established
			1981 / 1983 / 1984	Social Security eligibility age increased for full benefits / Widows entitled to pension benefits if spouse was wasted
45 years old	55 years old	65 years old	1986	Mandatory retirement vested eliminated for most workers
			1989 / 1990 / 1991	Berlin Wall falls / Americans with Disabilities Act
55 years old	65 years old	75 years old	1996 / 1997	Medicare payment policies changed by Balanced Budget Act
			2000 / 2001	Social Security earnings test eliminated for full retirement age / September 11
			2003	Medicare prescription drug benefit passed
65 years old	75 years old	85 years old	2006	Medicare coverage of prescription drugs begins for all beneficiaries

Figure 3.3 The Historical Experience of Three Cohorts of Older Americans: A Timeline of Selected Events. Federal Interagency Forum on Aging-Related Statistics (2006).

people greet their elders by kissing their feet and will go to tremendous lengths to ensure that their elders are comfortable. But this respect and value depends on the specific culture, and research evidence suggests that there are also other factors to consider. Although respect for elders is emphasized much more in many cultures with many rituals and special roles for elders, there are also negative attitudes toward older people in many of these cultures. Although there is limited information about beliefs regarding elders of color (either about their own or other ethnic groups), Adams and Hummert found that African Americans have similar stereotypes as those of White Americans described in Table 3.1 (as cited in Hummert, 1999). It seems that older people are often viewed as kind but incompetent both in White communities and in some communities of color (Cuddy & Fiske, 2002; Whitley & Kite, 2006).

Recent cross-cultural work conducted in China suggests that the older and younger generations disagree in their preference for certain culturally based communication styles (Zhang, Harwood, & Hummert, 2005; Zhang & Hummert, 2001). Chinese older adults considered it appropriate for an elder to sharply criticize a younger adult, whereas younger adults showed significantly decreased support for this hierarchically based communication style. These cohort differences may be due to the rapid changes that are happening in parts of the world where there are positive attitudes toward aging and older people (e.g., China), such that for the younger generations, expectations and treatment of elders are changing.

These societal changes may also be reflected in the recent research results that find many similarities between Western and Eastern attitudes toward older adults. Harwood and colleagues (2001) examined the traits that older people associate with younger, middle aged, and older people. The older people were from countries with Western cultural traditions (Australia) and Eastern cultural traditions (People's Republic of China, Hong Kong, Philippines, Thailand). In general, traits such as attractiveness, strength, and flexibility were seen to decrease as one ages, whereas kindness was seen to increase. There is also evidence that intergenerational relationships in Asia are not as positive as many in the United States have portrayed them to be. It may be that industrialization has rapidly changed intergenerational relationships or that there is a difference between knowledge of how one ought to behave and how one does behave. Or it may be a little bit of both.

Consider an international study that examined young adults' perceptions of interactions with family elders, non-family elders, and same-age peers (Giles et al., 2003). Participants were young adults from Western countries (Canada, United States, and New Zealand) and young adults from East Asian countries (Philippines, South Korea, and Japan). Only participants who were from the majority ethnic group in their country were included. A little over 100 participants were included from each cultural group. Contrary to the stereotype of Western countries' having more negative attitudes toward older people, there was considerable overlap in the younger adults' perceptions of the different groups. Both Western and East Asian participants indicated "an obligation to be most deferential" to non-family elders, followed by family elders, followed by same-age peers. Some interesting differences did arise, however. South Koreans were the only group for whom equal levels of deference were required for both older family and non-family elders. The Philippines and South Korea differed in interesting ways with the Philippines often having responses closer to the Western countries. This reminds us of the large differences that exist within the global category of "Asian" and even "East Asian" and thus the important differences that can be lost when these groups are lumped together. Both Western and East Asian groups viewed interactions with same-age peers more positively than with the older groups, and, counter to the stereotypes of culture and attitudes toward older adults, the Western group viewed the older age groups more positively than did East Asians. Young adults from the Western countries found family elders more accommodating than same-age peers. Thus, there is some evidence that our attitudes toward elders are a complex combination of culture and other factors that do not simply follow the stereotypes that we have about each culture. As we mentioned earlier, this may be due to the fact that the East Asian cultures are experiencing a tremendous shift in culture as they become more Westernized and thus problems between younger and older generations may be more apparent there than in Western cultures that have already experienced this shift.

These potentially changing values can create an interesting situation for elders in the United States. Elder immigrants may long for the status and value they remember from their culture of origin when, in actuality, that culture is changing as well. If they returned to their country of origin, they might not be happy with relationships. Also, mainstream U.S. elders may view other cultures with wishful awe, but without understanding the complexity that comprises beliefs about and behaviors toward older people.

Finally, we must be careful that respect and reverence do not actually harm elders. When examining sexism, researchers often describe two types of sexism: hostile and benevolent. Hostile sexism is overt negative treatment of women due simply to their gender. Benevolent sexism is more subtle as people who support it argue that they are actually treating women well by respecting them and taking care of them. The result of benevolent sexism for women can be disenfranchisement from society as they are prevented from doing jobs and pursuing education in fields that might be considered too difficult for a woman to handle. Similarly, benevolent ageism is something to guard against. For example, if people are "taking care" of older people because they respect them, they must make sure they are not preventing them from maintaining their physical and cognitive abilities in their well-meaning treatment of them. Anecdotally, people report wanting to "take care of" their elders and protect them from stress and hard work. Remember the value of *tranquilidad* (comfort) for older people in many Cuban American communities. When trying to increase physical activity levels of elders in this community, the idea of exercise was counter to the value of tranquilidad. Researchers adapted to this difference (and yet still promoted increased physical activity) by using the word "activity" instead of exercise (Williams, Tappen, Buscemi, Rivera, & Lezcano, 2001). If well-meaning benevolent protection removes elders from activity (e.g., don't do anything strenuous) and connections with others (e.g., stay home and rest), elders may stop doing activities that are keeping their bodies and minds healthy. Also, they may begin to believe they are not capable of doing some things. It can be a difficult balancing act to respect someone and yet not prevent them from being an active, engaged person.

How Older Adults View Themselves

In our opening vignette, Clair wondered whether her mother's negative beliefs about aging might actually make her aging experience worse. Of course, it is difficult to determine the direction of causation as it is possible that some elders' negative aging views are caused by their poor health (instead of their views' causing their poor health), but some intriguing research by Levy and colleagues suggests that our views toward aging may indeed affect the way we age. Levy and colleagues have found that when older adults are implicitly primed (unconsciously made aware of) negative beliefs about aging, they "exhibit greater physiological responses to stress (Levy, Hausdorff, Hencke, & Wei, 2000), reduced walking speed (Hausdorff, Levy, & Wei, 1999), and poorer handwriting" (Levy, 2000, as cited in Hess, 2006, p. 396).

In another study, Levy and colleagues (1999) again implicitly primed either positive or negative aging stereotypes and then gave all participants hypothetical medical situations describing potentially fatal illnesses. Older participants who were primed with negative aging stereotypes tended to refuse life-prolonging treatments whereas older participants primed with positive aging stereotypes tended to accept those treatments (Levy, Ashman, & Dror, 1999).

Additional evidence for the effects of positive self-perceptions of aging comes from Levy and colleagues' (2002) secondary analysis of data from the Ohio Longitudinal Study of Aging and Retirement (OLSAR). When compared with older individuals with less positive self-perceptions of aging, older individuals with more positive self-perceptions lived 7.5 years longer (Levy, Slade, Kunkel, & Kasl, 2002). These findings suggest that one's attitudes toward aging can influence our will to live and perhaps even how long we live. Levy's work has been done with the mainstream U.S. elderly, but it certainly has implications for different cultural groups. If we return to our discussion of the cultural differences in beliefs about the aging process, then it would follow that elders with cultural beliefs that support healthy aging and give their elders a valued position in their culture may end up with more positive aging experiences. This is yet another example of how mainstream U.S. culture could benefit from diverse perspectives. Changing the attitude toward aging into a more positive one may ultimately mean a more positive aging experience for all.

Early in this chapter, we presented many areas in which, on average, older adults experience age-related declines (e.g., vision, hearing, working memory, etc.). Focusing on declines may lead one to think that older adults' life satisfaction or morale may be quite low. In fact, research suggests that the opposite is true. Research suggests that, on average, older people are more satisfied with their lives than are younger or middle-aged adults (George, 2006). Measures of happiness, life satisfaction, or even quality of life are often called measures of subjective well-being. In her review of research on subjective well-being (SWB), George summarizes research results showing that older adults' SWB differs between several key elements of diversity. Gender is related to SWB, with older women reporting lower SWB than do older men. Similarly, education and income (both indicators of social class) are related to SWB with people with less education and lower income reporting lower levels of SWB. SWB does not differ between different racial and ethnic groups once socioeconomic status is taken into account. Finally, health, the focus of our next two chapters, is the strongest single predictor of SWB in older people (George, 2006). Although older people often do experience the age-related declines that we have presented in this chapter, they also often report being very happy and satisfied in their lives.

Discrimination and Ageism

In this section on attitudes toward aging and older people, we would be remiss if we did not mention prejudice against people due to their advanced age. Prejudice toward older people is defined as an attitude based on their advanced age. As we discussed earlier, that attitude includes feelings toward older people, thoughts and beliefs about what older people are like (i.e., stereotypes), and behavior toward older people (i.e., discrimination). Ageism is often considered more than just prejudice and as such can be defined as a system of disadvantage that occurs at the societal level in which attitudes toward older people occur simply due to the age of the older person. This can result in stereotypes that may not fit many elders and differential treatment or discrimination that occurs only because they are older. Certain kinds of discrimination against older people are illegal in the United States and these are discussed in more detail in Chapter 7.

As we close this chapter on psychology and diversity, we would like you to consider the ways in which key elements of diversity might intersect with ageism. For elders from ethnic minority groups, racism might also affect the ageism they experience. For women, their lifelong experience with sexism (e.g., lower pay for equal work, limited or no maternity or caregiving leave, etc.) may affect them in their advanced age. How do people who, throughout their lives, have had limited access to education, to job security, and to health care, experience old age?

SUMMARY

This chapter focuses on the intersection between psychology and aging. We began by examining how the psychological experiences of older people can be affected by changes in sensory processes and perception. We discussed age-related changes in vision, hearing, touch, taste, and smell and described ways to adapt to these changes. Cognition is another area in which older people may experience age-related changes, though these changes are in specific areas of mental functioning (e.g., working memory) and do not typically result in global cognitive difficulties. Cultural differences in thinking processes may also be affected by age and we argued that service providers should be aware of these cultural differences in thinking styles when working with elders from diverse groups. As we turned to examine attitudes toward aging and older people, we first defined important concepts: attitude, stereotype, prejudice, and ageism. We then examined both U.S. mainstream and other cultures' attitudes toward aging and argued that different attitudes toward aging may lead to different treatment of older people and to different aging experiences for us all. We also described how stereotypes about older adults are both similar and different across cultures and we ended this section with a discussion of how older people's beliefs about aging might actually affect their own aging process. We concluded the chapter with a brief description of discrimination and age and considered how the different elements of diversity might interact with ageism to produce varied aging experiences for members of diverse groups.

ACTIVE LEARNING EXPERIENCE: CHAPTER QUIZ

The purpose of this experience is to gauge your present knowledge of issues related to psychology and aging. Upon completion of this activity, you will be able to:

1. Assess your knowledge of (a) aging, sensation, perception, and cognition; and (b) attitudes toward aging and older people.
2. Gain feedback on your knowledge of important issues related to psychology and aging.

This activity should take 30 minutes (10 minutes to complete the quiz and 20 minutes to discuss your answers with another person or in a classroom setting).

Instructions:

Complete the quiz below. Your instructor may lead an in-class review of the answers to the quiz. Indicate whether each of the following statements is true or false, and explain your reasons for selecting that response.

Quiz Items	True	False
1. Declines in sensation occur as one ages, but older adults' perception remains the same across the lifespan.	_____	_____
2. Age-related declines in sensation occur in all of the major senses: vision, hearing, taste, touch, and smell.	_____	_____
3. The main difference between younger and older adults' thinking processes is that older adults experience significant losses in their knowledge base as they age.	_____	_____
4. Research has shown that the way people think differs across cultures.	_____	_____
5. Attitudes toward the aging process in cultures outside the United States are uniformly positive.	_____	_____
6. People in the United States have solely negative stereotypes of older adults.	_____	_____
7. People who have positive expectations about old age have better health and tend to live longer.	_____	_____
8. Older adults report greater life satisfaction than do middle-aged adults.	_____	_____

9. Successful aging is a philosophy that focuses on maintaining financial health throughout the lifespan. ___ ___

10. Ageism is prejudice against people due to their age. ___ ___

11. Cognitive training involves exercise for the brain. ___ ___

12. ACTIVE is the acronym used to describe an intervention to increase physical activity among older people. ___ ___

13. Physical exercise improves physical health, but not cognitive function. ___ ___

14. Cognitive training improves physical health. ___ ___

15. A dialectical view of aging acknowledges both the positives and negatives of aging. ___ ___

GLOSSARY

aged: People who have lived for many years. In Western cultures, typically people who have lived at least 65 years or more.

ageism: Prejudice (or attitudes) toward older people due to their advanced age; these attitudes include feelings toward, stereotypes about, and discrimination against older people.

aging: The developmental process that occurs as a person lives over time.

benevolent ageism: A subtle prejudice against older people in which apparently positive beliefs and emotions about caring for older people coexist with beliefs about their incompetence and frailty.

cognitive aging: The study of how the human mind functions and the changes in its functioning as people age.

cognitive training: Mental exercises that are designed to improve functioning in specific cognitive areas.

perception: The process of integrating, organizing, and interpreting stimuli registered by the senses.

prejudice: An attitude toward a group of people due solely to their membership in that group.

psychology: The scientific study of mental processes and behavior.

sensation: The reception of external stimuli (for example, light, sound, odor, touch).

stereotype: The thoughts and beliefs that are held about a person simply because the person is a member of a particular group.

successful aging: A model of aging that defines the desired form of aging as avoidance of disease and disease-related disability, maintenance of high physical and cognitive functional capacity, and active engagement in life (Rowe & Kahn, 1998).

working memory: The capacity that one has to simultaneously hold and work with different concepts in one's mind. This is analogous to the working memory or RAM in a computer.

SUGGESTED READINGS

Beyene, Y., Becker, G., Mayen, N. (2002). Perception of aging and sense of well-being among Latino elderly. *Journal of Cross-Cultural Gerontology, 17*(2), 155–172.

This journal article provides a unique perspective on a group that is often absent from both popular media and academic research: Latino elders. It examines their attitudes toward aging and their subjective well-being.

Cole, T. (1992). *The journey of life: A cultural history of aging in America.* Cambridge, UK: Cambridge University Press.

This book examines the meaning of aging in American Society and how it has developed and changed from the Reformation to post-World War I. Cole argues for a dialectical view of aging that includes both the losses and gains that can come with advanced age.

George, L. K. (2006). Perceived quality of life. In R. H. Binstock & L. K. George (Eds.), *Handbook of aging and the social sciences, 6th ed.* (pp. 320–336). Burlington, MA: Elsevier Academic Press.

This handbook chapter reviews the research literature on perceived quality of life (often referred to as subjective well-being) and older adults. It examines several elements of diversity and how well-being differs between groups.

Hess, T. M. (2006). Attitudes toward aging and their effects on behavior. In J. E. Birren & K. W. Schaie (Eds.), *Handbook of the psychology of aging, 6th edition* (pp. 379-406). Burlington, MA: Elsevier Academic Press.

This handbook chapter provides a thorough review of the psychological research on attitudes toward aging. It is an excellent resource for readers wanting to acquaint themselves with this large body of research.

Iwamasa, G. Y., & Sorocco, K. H. (2007). The psychology of Asian American older adults. In F. T. L. Leong, Inman, A.G., Ebreo, A., Yang, L.H., Kinoshita, L., Fu, M. (Eds.), *Handbook of Asian American psychology.* Thousand Oaks, CA: Sage.

This handbook chapter provides important information regarding Asian American older adults, their beliefs, characteristics, and behaviors.

Minkler, M., & Fadem, P. (2002). "Successful Aging": a disability perspective. *Journal of Disability Policy Studies, 12*(4), 229–235.

This journal article provides a critical reading of the very popular successful aging movement. Given the elements of successful aging, people who have disabilities would be described as aging unsuccessfully. Minkler and Fadem argue for a more holistic view beyond successful and unsuccessful aging that recognizes both the external and internal influences on how we age.

Morrell, R. W. (Ed.). (2002). *Older adults, health information, and the world wide web*. Mahwah, NJ: Lawrence Erlbaum.

This book examines how the Internet can be used as a tool to deliver health information to older adults. It includes information on how age-related changes in vision and cognition might affect processing of information and suggests ways to present information to accommodate for these issues. It also describes actual projects in which older people use the web for health information.

Nisbett, R. E., & Masuda, T. (2003). Culture and point of view. Proceedings of the National Academy of Sciences. 100(19), 11163–11170.

This article contains a succinct yet thorough review of the literature on culture and cognition. It does not discuss age.

Park, D. C., Gutchess, A. H., Meade, M. L., & Stine-Morrow, E. A. (2007). Improving cognitive function in older adults: Nontraditional approaches. *The Journals of Gerontology: Series B, 62 Special Issue No 1*, 45–52.

This article examines nontraditional alternatives to standard cognitive training that might result in more generalized improvements for cognition and more protection against aging-related declines. Although it does not address elements of diversity at all, its approach certainly allows for inclusion of different approaches from diverse perspectives.

Park, D. C., Nisbett, R., & Hedden, T. (1999). Aging, culture, and cognition. *The Journals of Gerontology: Series B: Psychological Sciences and Social Sciences, 54B*(2), 75–84.

This article describes the basics that are known about culture and cognition and then presents a framework for understanding how age-related declines in cognitive abilities will manifest themselves in different cultural groups.

AUDIOVISUAL RESOURCES

Beauty Before Age: Growing older in gay culture. This documentary portrays gay attitudes toward the aging process and older adults. These attitudes are predominantly negative and can lead to a focus on youth and physical beauty and a derogation of signs of aging and of elders in general. 22 min. Available from http://www.newday.com/films/BeautyBeforeAge.html

Lifestyle Choices to Maximize Memory: Healthy brain diet, stress reduction, and other lifestyle strategies. This is a videotape of a lecture given by Gary Small, MD (author of *The Memory Bible*), describing four important areas to keep memory performance strong and brains healthy: mental activity, stress reduction, physical activity and healthy diet. 55 min. Available from http://www.aging.ucla.edu/wintercmeeting2003video.html

Living With Pride: Ruth Ellis @ 100. This documentary portrays the life of Ruth Ellis, an African American lesbian living in Detroit. As viewers learn about this remarkable woman, they also learn about the experiences of lesbian women from this era and can see how three elements of diversity—being African American, being a woman and being lesbian—can affect one's life. 60 min. Available from http://www.sistersinthelife.com/1024index.html

Memory Training Techniques: Never forget names and faces again. This videotaped lecture, given by Gary Small, MD, describes memory training techniques. 60 min. Available from http://www.aging.ucla.edu/fallcmeeting2002video.html

Reimaging America: How America can grow older and prosper. This short video provides several positive examples of aging and couples them with images of elders from diverse ethnic groups. This video can serve as a starting point for discussions of which groups are shown in the video (e.g., different ethnicities, people who have financial means) and which groups are omitted (e.g., the poor). In addition to this video clip, the website also contains a pdf file of an AARP report on this topic and a classroom discussion guide. 6 min. Available from http://www.aarp.org/research/academic/images_of_aging.html

Successful Aging: Images of aging: Stereotypes and ageism in society. This videotaped lecture shows how the media can be a powerful force in shaping our society's attitudes toward aging and older people. Joaquin Anguera reviews these existing images and their impact on society and our own outlook on the aging process. 53 min. Available at http://www.uctv.tv/search-details.asp?showID=9128.

KEY: CHAPTER 3 QUIZ

1. False. Older adults experience both sensory and perceptual ability declines as they age.
2. True. Older adults experience declines in vision, hearing, smell, and some areas of taste as they age (Kausler, 1991). Evidence suggests that one's sense of touch may also decline as one ages.

3. False. Older adults maintain their knowledge base throughout their lifespan. They do experience slower speed of processing, more limited working memory and decreased inhibition than younger adults (Park, 1998; Park & Gutchess, 2000; Salthouse, 2004; Ybarra & Park, 2002).

4. True. Recent research has found systematic differences in the way East Asian and mainstream Americans think. East Asians tend to think more holistically, taking into account the context of the situation, whereas people in the United States tend to think more analytically, focusing more on the focal object in the situation (Nisbett & Masuda, 2003).

5. False. Although attitudes toward the aging process in some cultures may contain more positive aspects than mainstream U.S. attitudes, these cultures also recognize that there are losses or declines that occur with age.

6. False. Hummert and colleagues have shown that instead of one global negative stereotype of older adults, several different stereotypes (or subtypes) of older adults exist and that some of these are quite positive in nature (Hummert et al., 1994).

7. True. Levy and colleagues have found that older people who are implicitly primed with positive aging stereotypes have lower blood pressure, walk faster, and accept life-prolonging treatments, compared with older people who were primed with negative aging stereotypes. Similarly, older people with positive aging self-perceptions lived longer than people with less positive self-perceptions even after they controlled for age, gender, socioeconomic status, loneliness, and functional health (Levy et al., 2002).

8. True. Studies have found that older people are more satisfied with their lives than younger and middle-aged adults (George, 2006).

9. False. In contrast to earlier models of aging that focused on aging-related declines, successful aging posits that it is possible to have more positive or optimal aging and that such aging involves (1) avoidance of disease and disease-related disability, (2) maintenance of high physical and cognitive functional capacity, and (3) active engagement in life (Rowe & Kahn, 1998).

10. False. Butler (1969) coined the term *ageism* to reflect attitudes held about *older* people simply due to their advanced age. When these attitudes are collectively held by a society, they create a system of disadvantage based on one's advanced age. Prejudice against younger people due to their youth is not called ageism.

11. True. Cognitive training involves mental exercises that give the brain "practice" performing certain cognitive tasks.

12. False. ACTIVE is the acronym for a multisite clinical trial entitled Advanced Cognitive Training for Independent and Vital Elderly. As the title implies, this trial involved training in three different

cognitive areas: memory, reasoning, or speed of processing (Willis et al., 2006).

13. False. Physical exercise improves both physical health and cognitive function (Colcombe et al., 2006; Colcombe & Kramer, 2003).

14. False. Cognitive training improves cognitive function in the same area and on tasks similar to those included in training (e.g., cognitive training on working memory improves working memory on tasks similar to the task on which one was trained), but there is not yet any evidence that cognitive training improves physical health.

15. True. Unlike the successful aging movement that tends to view aging as either successful or unsuccessful, the dialectical view of aging advocated by Thomas Cole and others (Cole, 1988, 1992; Minkler & Fadem, 2002) presents a more complex perspective. Instead of being either positive or negative, aging includes both positives and negatives. This more complex view of aging recognizes the roles that both individual choice and external factors play in the aging process.

REFERENCES

Alkema, G. E., & Alley, D. E. (2006). Gerontology's future: An integrative model for disciplinary advancement. *Gerontologist, 46*(5), 574–582.

Belza, B., Walwick, J., Shiu-Thornton, S., Schwartz, S., Taylor, M., & LoGerfo, J. (2004). Older adult perspectives on physical activity and exercise: Voices from multiple cultures. *Preventing Chronic Disease: Public Health Research, Practice and Policy, 1*(4), A09.

Beyene, Y., Becker, G., & Mayen, N. (2002). Perception of aging and sense of well-being among Latino elderly. *Journal of Cross-Cultural Gerontology, 17*(2), 155–172.

Blanchette, P. L. (2000). Health and health care for Asian and Pacific Islander American elders. In G. Yeo (Ed.), *Core curriculum in ethnogeriatrics, 2nd ed.* (pp. 1–5). Stanford, CA: Stanford Geriatric Education Center.

Bowles, N. (1993). Semantic processes that serve picture naming. In J. Cerella, J. Rybash, W. Hoyer & M. L. Commons (Eds.), *Adult information processing: Limits on loss* (pp. 303–326). San Diego, CA: Academic Press.

Braun, K. L., Yee, B. W. K., Browne, C. V., & Mokuau, N. (2004). Native Hawaiian and Pacific Islander elders. In K. E. Whitfield (Ed.), *Closing the gap: Improving the health of minority elders in the new millennium* (pp. 55–67). Washington, DC: The Gerontological Society of America.

Brewer, M. B., Dull, V., & Lui, L. (1981). Perceptions of the elderly: Stereotypes as prototypes. *Journal of Personality and Social Psychology, 41*(4), 656–670.

Brewer, M. B., & Lui, L. (1984). Categorization of the elderly by the elderly: Effects of perceiver's category membership. *Personality and Social Psychology Bulletin, 10*(4), 585–595.

Butler, R. N. (1969). Ageism: Another form of bigotry. *Gerontologist, 9*(4, Pt. 1), 243–246.

Cavanaugh, J. C., & Blanchard-Fields, F. (2006). *Adult development and aging (5th ed.).* Belmont, CA: Thomson Wadsworth.

Chapanis, A. (2004). National and cultural variables in ergonomics. In M. Kaplan (Ed.), *Cultural ergonomics* (Vol. 4, pp. 1–29). Amsterdam, Netherlands: Elsevier Science Publishers.

Claes, J., & Moore, W. R. (2001). Caring for gay and lesbian elderly. In L. K. Olson (Ed.), *Age through ethnic lenses: Caring for the elderly in a multicultural society* (pp. 217–229). Lanhan, MD: Rowman & Littlefield Publishers.

Colcombe, S. J., Erickson, K. I., Scalf, P. E., Kim, J. S., Prakash, R., McAuley, E., et al. (2006). Aerobic exercise training increases brain volume in aging humans. *Journal of Gerontology A: Biological & Medical Sciences, 61*(11), 1166–1170.

Colcombe, S. J., & Kramer, A. F. (2003). Fitness effects on the cognitive function of older adults: A meta-analytic study. *Psychological Science*.

Cole, T. (1988). The specter of old age: History, politics and culture in America. *Tikkun, 3*, 14–18, 93–95.

Cole, T. (1992). *The journey of life: A cultural history of aging in America.* Cambridge, UK: Cambridge University Press.

Collings, P. (2001). 'If you got everything, it's good enough': Perspectives on successful aging in a Canadian Inuit community. *Journal of Cross-Cultural Gerontology, 16*, 127–155.

Cuddy, A. J. C., & Fiske, S. T. (2002). Doddering but dear: Process, content and function in stereotyping of older persons. In T. Nelson (Ed.), *Ageism: Stereotyping and prejudice against older persons* (pp. 3–26). Cambridge, MA: The MIT Press.

Dancer, J., Pryor, B., & Rozema, H. (1989). Hearing screening in a well elderly population: Implications for gerontologists. *Educational Gerontology, 15*, 41–47.

Dwyer, K. (2000). Culturally appropriate consumer-directed care: The American Indian choices project. *Generations, 24*(3), 91–93.

Federal Interagency Forum on Aging-Related Statistics. (2006). *Older Americans update 2006: Key indicators of well-being.* Washington, DC: U.S. Government Printing Office.

Fratiglioni, L., Wang, H.-X., Ericsson, K., Maytan, M., & Winblad, B. (2000). Influence of social network on occurrence of dementia: A community-based longitudinal study. *The Lancet, 355*, 1315–1319.

George, L. K. (2006). Perceived quality of life. In R. H. Binstock & L. K. George (Eds.), *Handbook of aging and the social sciences, 6th ed.* (6 ed., pp. 320–336). Burlington, MA: Elsevier Academic Press.

Giles, H., Noels, K. A., Williams, A., Ota, H., Lim, T., Ng, S. H., et al. (2003). Intergenerational communication across cultures: Young people's perceptions of conversations with family elders, non-family elders and same-age peers. *Journal of Cross-Cultural Gerontology, 18*, 1–32.

Goins, R. T., & Spencer, S. M. (2005). Public health issues among older American Indians and Alaska Natives. *Generations, 29*(2), 30–35.

Harwood, J., Giles, H., McCann, R. M., Cai, D., Somera, L., Ng, S. H., et al. (2001). Older adults' trait ratings of three age-groups around the Pacific Rim. *Journal of Cross-Cultural Gerontology, 16*, 157–171.

Hausdorff, J. M., Levy, B. R., & Wei, J. Y. (1999). The power of ageism on physical function of older persons: Reversibility of age-related gait changes. *Journal of the American Geriatrics Society, 47*(11), 1346.

Heckhausen, J., Dixon, R. A., & Baltes, P. B. (1989). Gains and losses in development throughout adulthood as perceived by different adult age groups. *Developmental Psychology, 25*(1), 109–121.

Hedden, T., Park, D. C., Nisbett, R., Ji, L.-J., Jing, Q., & Jiao, S. (2002). Cultural variation in verbal versus spatial neuropsychological function across the life span. *Neuropsychology*.

Hendrix, L. (2000). Health and health care for American Indian/Alaska Native elders. In G. Yeo (Ed.), *Core curriculum in ethnogeriatrics, 2nd ed.* (pp. 1–57). Stanford, CA: Stanford Geriatric Education Center.

Hertzog, C., Lineweaver, T. T., & McGuire, C. L. (1999). Beliefs about memory and aging. In T. M. Hess & F. Blanchard-Fields (Eds.), *Social cognition and aging* (pp. 43–68). San Diego, CA: Academic Press.

Hess, T. M. (2006). Attitudes toward aging and their effects on behavior. In J. E. Birren & K. W. Schaie (Eds.), *Handbook of the psychology of aging, 6th ed.* (pp. 379–406). Burlington, MA: Elsevier Academic Press.

Hill, T. D., Burdette, A. M., Angel, J. L., & Angel, R. J. (2006). Religious attendance and cognitive functioning among older Mexican Americans. *Journals of Gerontology: Series B: Psychological Sciences and Social Sciences, 61*(1), P3.

Holstein, M. B., & Minkler, M. (2003). Self, society, and the "new gerontology." *Gerontologist, 43*(6), 787–796.

House, J. S., Landis, K. R., & Umberson, D. (1988). Social relationships and health. *Science, 241*(4865), 540–545.

Howard, J. H., & Howard, D. V. (1991). Learning and memory. In D. H. Kausler (Ed.), *Experimental psychology, cognition and human aging* (2nd ed., pp. 7–26). New York: Springer-Verlag.

Hummert, M. L., Garstka, T. A., Shaner, J. L., & Strahm, S. (1994). Stereotypes of the elderly held by young, middle-aged, and elderly adults. *Journals of Gerontology, 49*(5), 240–P249.

Hummert, M. L. (1999) A social cognitive perspective on age stereotypes. In T. M. Hess & F. L. Blanchard-Fields (Eds.), *Social Cognition and Aging* (pp. 175–196). San Diego: Academic Press.

Kausler, D. H. (1991). *Experimental psychology, cognition and human aging, second edition.* New York: Springer-Verlag.

Kim, S., & Kim, K. C. (2001). Intimacy at a distance, Korean American style: Invited Korean elderly and their married children. In L. K. Olson (Ed.), *Age through ethnic lenses: Caring for the elderly in a multicultural society* (pp. 45–58). Lanhan, MD: Rowman & Littlefield Publishers.

Kite, M. E., Stockdale, G. D., Whitley, B. E., Jr., & Johnson, B. T. (2005). Attitudes toward younger and older adults: An updated meta-analytic review. *Journal of Social Issues, 61*(2), 241.

Levy, B. R. (2000). Handwriting as a reflection of aging self-stereotypes. *Journal of Geriatric Psychiatry, 33*(1), 81.

Levy, B. R., Ashman, O., & Dror, I. (1999). To be or not to be: The effects of aging stereotypes on the will to live. *Omega: Journal of Death and Dying, 40*(3), 409.

Levy, B. R., Hausdorff, J. M., Hencke, R., & Wei, J. Y. (2000). Reducing cardiovascular stress with positive self-stereotypes of aging. *Journals of Gerontology: Series B: Psychological Sciences and Social Sciences, 55*(4), P205.

Levy, B. R., Slade, M. D., Kunkel, S. R., & Kasl, S. V. (2002). Longevity increased by positive self-perceptions of aging. *Journal of Personality and Social Psychology, 83*(2), 261–270.

Light. (1992). The organization of memory in old age. In F. I. M. Craik & T. A. Salthouse (Eds.), *The handbook of aging and cognition* (pp. 111–166). Hillsdale, NJ: Erlbaum.

Markus, H. R., & Kitayama, S. (1991). Culture and the self: Implications for cognition, emotion, and motivation. *Psychological Review, 98*(2), 224–253.

Masuda, T., & Nisbett, R. E. (2001). Attending holistically versus analytically: Comparing the context sensitivity of Japanese and Americans. *Journal of Personality and Social Psychology, 81*(5), 922–934.

McBride, M. (2001). Health and health care of Filipino American elders. In G. Yeo (Ed.), *Curriculum in ethnogeriatrics, 2nd ed.* Stanford, CA: Stanford Geriatric Education Center.

Minkler, M., & Fadem, P. (2002). 'successful aging:' A disability perspective. *Journal of Disability Policy Studies, 12*(4), 229–235.

National Council on Aging. (2002). *American perceptions of aging in the 21st century.* Washington, DC: The National Council on Aging, Inc.

Nisbett, R. E., & Masuda, T. (2003). Culture and point of view. *Proceedings of the National Academy of Sciences of the United States of America, 100*(19), 11163–11170.

Nisbett, R. E., & Norenzayan, A. (2002). Culture and cognition. In H. Pashler & D. Medin (Eds.), *Steven's handbook of experimental psychology (3rd ed.), vol. 2: Memory and cognitive processes* (pp. 561–597). Hoboken, NJ: Wiley.

Olson, L. K. (2001). Multiculturalism and long-term care: The aged and their caregivers. In L. K. Olson (Ed.), *Age through ethnic lenses: Caring for the elderly in a multicultural society* (pp. 1–16). Lanhan, MD: Rowman & Littlefield.

Park, D. C. (1998). Cognitive aging, processing resources, and self-report. In N. Schwarz, D. C. Park, B. Knauper & S. Sudman (Eds.), *Aging, cognition and self-report* (pp. 35–68). Philadelphia: Psychology Press.

Park, D. C., & Gutchess, A. H. (2000). Cognitive aging and everyday life. In D. C. Park & N. Schwarz (Eds.), *Cognitive aging: A primer* (pp. 217–232). New York: Psychology Press.

Park, D. C., Gutchess, A. H., Meade, M. L., & Stine-Morrow, E. A. (2007). Improving cognitive function in older adults: Nontraditional approaches. *Journals of Gerontology: Series B, 62 Special Issue No 1*, 45–52.

Park, D. C., Nisbett, R., & Hedden, T. (1999). Aging, culture, and cognition. *Journals of Gerontology: Series B: Psychological Sciences and Social Sciences, 54B*(2), 75–84.

Peng, K., & Nisbett, R. E. (1999). Culture, dialectics, and reasoning about contradiction. *American Psychologist*.

Polacca, M. (2001). American Indian and Alaska Native elderly. In L. K. Olson (Ed.), *Age through ethnic lenses: Caring for the elderly in a multicultural society* (pp. 113–122). Lanhan, MD: Rowman & Littlefield.

Rowe, J. W., & Kahn, R. L. (1987). Human aging: Usual and successful. *Science, 237*(4811), 143.

Rowe, J. W., & Kahn, R. L. (1997). Successful aging. *The Gerontologist, 37*(4), 433.

Rowe, J. W., & Kahn, R. L. (1998). *Successful aging*. New York: Random House.

Ryan, E. B. (1992). Beliefs about memory changes across the adult life span. *Journal of Gerontology, 47*, 41–46.

Ryan, E. B., & See, S. K. (1993). Age-based beliefs about memory changes for self and others across adulthood. *Journals of Gerontology, 48*(4), 199–P201.

Salthouse, T. A. (2004). What and when of cognitive aging. *Current Directions in Psychological Science, 13*(4), 140–142.

Salthouse, T. A. (2006). Mental exercise and mental aging. *Perspectives on Psychological Science*.

Schaie, K. W. (1995). *Intellectual development in adulthood: The Seattle longitudinal study*. New York: Cambridge University Press.

Schaie, K. W. (1996). *Intellectual development in adulthood: The Seattle longitudinal study*. New York: Cambridge University Press.

Segall, M. H., Campbell, D. T., & Hersokovits, J. (1966). *The influence of culture on visual perception*. Indianapolis: Bobbs-Merrill.

Sloan, F. A., & Wang, J. (2005). Disparities among older adults in measures of cognitive function by race or ethnicity. *Journals of Gerontology: Series B: Psychological Sciences and Social Sciences, 60*(5), P242.

Speas, K., & Obenshain, B. (1995). *AARP images: Aging in America: Final report*. Washington, DC: American Association of Retired Persons.

Talamantes, M., Lindeman, R., & Mouton, C. (2000). Health and health care of Hispanic/Latino American elders. In G. Yeo (Ed.), *Core curriculum in ethnogeriatrics: Ethnic specific modules* (pp. 2–62). Stanford, CA: Stanford Ethnogeriatric Education Center.

Tran, T. V., Ngo, D., & Sung, T. H. (2001). Caring for elderly Vietnamese Americans. In L. K. Olson (Ed.), *Age through ethnic lenses: Caring for the elderly in a multicultural society* (pp. 59–70). Lanhan, MD: Rowman & Littlefield.

Whitfield, K. E., Fillenbaum, G. G., Pieper, C., Albert, M. S., Berkman, L. F., Blazer, D. G., et al. (2000). The effect of race and health-related factors on naming and memory. The MacArthur studies of successful aging. *Journal of Aging Health, 12*(1), 69–89.

Whitfield, K. E., Seeman, T. E., Miles, T. P., Albert, M. S., Berkman, L. F., Blazer, D. G., et al. (1997). Health indices as predictors of cognition among older African Americans: Macarthur studies of successful aging. *Ethnicity and Disease, 7*(2), 127–136.

Whitley, B. E., Jr., & Kite, M. E. (2006). *The psychology of prejudice and discrimination,* New York: Thomson/Wadsworth.

Williams, C. L., Tappen, R., Buscemi, C., Rivera, R., & Lezcano, J. (2001). Obtaining family consent for participation in Alzheimer's research in a Cuban-American population: Strategies to overcome the barriers. *American Journal of Alzheimer's Disease, 16*(3), 183–187.

Willis, S. L., Tennstedt, S. L., Marsiske, M., Ball, K., Elias, J., Koepke, K. M., et al. (2006). Long-term effects of cognitive training on everyday functional outcomes in older adults. *Journal of American Medical Association, 296*(23), 2805–2814.

Ybarra, O., & Park, D. C. (2002). Disconfirmation of person expectations by older and younger adults: Implications for social vigilance. *Journals of Gerontology: Series B: Psychological Sciences and Social Sciences.*

Zhang, Y. B., Harwood, J., & Hummert, M. L. (2005). Perceptions of conflict management styles in Chinese intergenerational dyads. *Communication Monographs, 72*(1), 71.

Zhang, Y. B., & Hummert, M. L. (2001). Harmonies and tensions in Chinese intergenerational communication: Younger and older adults' accounts. *Journal of Asian Pacific Communication, 11*(2), 203.

4

Health Beliefs, Behaviors, and Services

- What is health? How do definitions of health differ by culture?
- How does cultural and ethnic diversity affect health-related behaviors?
- How do American elders pay for health care? What are the key components of the health insurance plans available to older persons?
- What do we mean by cultural competence? How does it affect the quality of care?

When examining health beliefs and behaviors for diverse groups, it is critical both to determine the needs of current elders and to look forward to the future for how those needs may change as subsequent generations age. Within each diverse group, one must consider differences in culture, education, language proficiency, and immigration history in order to appropriately support the health of its aging elders. In addition to the challenges associated with learning to understand the role that diversity plays in the health of elders, the diversity of the U.S. population offers a great opportunity to learn how the general population could adapt their own beliefs and behaviors so that we can promote healthy aging among all elders. This chapter considers the role of diversity in the health of older adults. In this chapter we examine definitions of health from different groups, explore ways to promote healthy behavior among diverse elders, describe the services available for older adults, and discuss how these services are experienced by elders from diverse groups. To see a sampling of the issues addressed in this chapter, please consider the following vignettes:

Vignette 1

Mrs. Patel came from India with her husband in the mid 1960s. Her three children have all completed college and are living on their own. She enjoys good health and takes a long walk every day. When she has minor illnesses, she treats them herself with special foods (herbs and spices) that her mother taught her to use when she was growing up in India. If this does not work and her illness continues, then she will see her doctor and follow his prescriptions. Mrs. Patel's doctor is concerned about her family history of diabetes and monitors her carefully, but so far her health is excellent.

Vignette 2

Norma Luger thought she was doing everything right. As an artist and an educator, she was exposed to alternative ways of doing things before they became popular. She'd been eating a low-fat diet and exercising regularly for years. She had tap and folk dancing twice a week and only recently did she give up yoga in favor of the less strenuous Pilates. When her doctor told her that her slight build and small bone structure put her at risk for osteoporosis, she increased her calcium intake but declined to take a new drug designed to rebuild bone strength. Last month she fell in her apartment and broke her hip. Her osteoporosis had accelerated without her knowledge. Perhaps if she had taken the drug earlier, she would not have broken her hip. She has since started taking the new drug and, given her previous active lifestyle, she is making good progress recovering from surgery to repair her hip. She wonders whether her distrust of medication has made her suffer needlessly.

Vignette 3

Mrs. Chiu moved from China to the United States 40 years ago with her husband. They are well-educated and their son recently completed medical school in the United States. Mrs. Chiu suffers from arthritis. She sees her doctor regularly and carefully follows his prescriptions. When her husband returns to China on business, he gets her a supply of herbs and other Chinese remedies for her condition. Mrs. Chiu takes these as well. She does not tell her doctor about these herbs. Her son worries that the herbs have not been tested and that at best they are doing nothing, but at worst, they may interact harmfully with the prescribed medications.

HEALTH BELIEFS AND BEHAVIORS

What Is Health?

How we define health affects our beliefs about what we can do to maintain it and to return to it if we are ill. The many different definitions of health vary by ethnic and cultural group. Historically, mainstream U.S. beliefs about health have been strongly influenced by the biomedical model of health and disease. From this model, disease is seen as the result of a specific, identifiable cause, called a pathogen, originating from inside the body (Matsumoto & Juang, 2004). These pathogens can be viral or bacterial and are viewed as the root of all physical and medical diseases (Matsumoto & Juang, 2004). Given this causal link between pathogens and poor health, removing the pathogen and curing disease has historically been the focus for health professionals in the United States. Health has thus been defined as the absence of illness or disease. Psychology has also been heavily influenced by the biomedical model of health and disease such that abnormal behavior and psychopathology are often viewed as originating from within the person (for example, as due to low levels of a neurotransmitter). One can see how the biomedical model of health impacts how we treat illness. If illness originates from within the individual, then the individual must be the focus of treatment. And if health is defined as the absence of disease, then preventing and treating disease becomes the focus, rather than promoting health.

When one compares the biomedical model with other definitions of health (as we are about to do), the limitations of such a narrow approach become very clear. But it is also important to note that prevention of and treatments for many diseases were developed under this framework, as illnesses that often killed people such as polio, small pox, and even pneumonia are no longer the serious threat to large portions of the population that they once were. More recently in the United States, there has been recognition that additional factors within the individual (personality, health beliefs, coping skills) and also outside the individual (the environment, one's cultural background, and even a mother's nutrition prior to one's birth) can affect health. This biopsychosocial model recognizes that health is the result of multiple factors. These factors are often separated into biological, psychological, and social factors. We will discuss this model in more detail in Chapter 5 to help explain social inequalities in health. Now we turn to considering different ethnic and racial groups' definitions of health.

In many different ethnic and racial groups, the focus of health is much broader than the individual. Many cultures view health as a balance among different components. The Chinese concept of health is based on religion and philosophy. There, the negative energies of yin and the positive energies of yang need to be balanced. If they are balanced, then one has good health; if they are unbalanced, poor health results. Many different things can cause an imbalance: changes in social relationships, supernatural forces, eating too much of one particular type of food, etc. (Matsumoto & Juang, 2004). To regain good health, one must bring the yin and yang back into balance. This classical Chinese approach to health has also influenced Japan, Korea, and southeast Asia. In addition to balancing yin and yang through herbs and diet, there is also the belief that one can "unblock the free flow of qi (chi) or vital energy through meridians in the body by acupuncture, tai chi, moxibustion and cupping" (Levkoff, Kyong Chee, Reynoso-Vallejo, & Mendez, 2000, p. 23).

Although other Asian groups have been influenced by Chinese philosophy, each group brings its own unique beliefs and behaviors to its definitions of health. For example, the Hmong from southeast Asia believe that illness can be a sign from spirits. A spirit may have been wronged and may be seeking revenge, or spirits may even be giving the power to become a shaman healer to the person who is ill (Udesky, 2006). Having a shaman appease this spirit through ritual and animal sacrifice is one way to bring the person back to health. Traditional Hawaiian healers also use various techniques including herbs, massage, conflict resolution, and prayer and they integrate these into daily religious and social routines. They view Western medicine as conflicting with their approach as it is more individualistic and autocratic. Similarly, many cultural groups disagree with the separation of mind and body as followed by mainstream Western medicine and evidenced by differential treatment and health care coverage for mental versus physical ailments.

For many Pacific Islanders, mental and physical health issues are not viewed as distinct. In Native Hawaiian, the general word for trouble (*pilikia*) is used to describe a psychological problem (Braun, Yee, Browne, & Mokuau, 2004). Thus, as with physical health, mental health issues can also be caused by the same imbalances and the same treatments would apply.

American Indian and Alaska native definitions of health vary by tribal group, but also often contain a notion of balance. For many American Indian tribes, being healthy involves living in harmony with oneself and one's environment. If one breaks that harmony, then the result can be ill health (Mulatu & Berry, 2001). Illness thus does not come from within the body, but is due to some discord. Treating an illness can involve ritual ceremonies to return harmony to the system. In everyday practice, American Indian elders do use traditional tribal medicine, but this tends to be used as a complement rather than an alternative to mainstream health care (John, 2004). Some researchers have described American Indian elders as having a "fatalistic" attitude and this may affect their use of services (John, 2004). With a fatalistic attitude, a person does not believe that what he or she does has much effect on one's health. Thus, cancer screenings, for example, are not seen as useful because a diagnosis of cancer may be seen as a death sentence for someone with a fatalistic attitude toward health. In terms of mental health, many American Indian tribes consider mind and body to be one, so the separation of mental and physical health does not fit culturally for them. They also somaticize (convert mental distress into physical symptoms) mental health problems and so when mind and body are out of balance, it is reasonable for symptoms to occur within the body (John, 2004).

African American and Latino definitions of health represent blends of several cultural influences. African American health traditions often incorporate European, American Indian, and Christian traditions. Some research (Becker, Beyene, Newsom, & Rodgers, 1998) suggests that African Americans agree with mainstream U.S. conceptions of health but may also see illness as a result of evil spirits or of some sin the person committed. Healing can involve the power of religion and the use of herbs, sometimes called "root working" (Levkoff et al., 2000, p. 22). Among African American males, there has been described an "ethic of toughness" as a coping mechanism to protect against powerlessness in a racist society. This ethic involves "being emotionally strong and distant, having a high tolerance for physical and emotional pain, being physically strong, and being a provider" (Rooks & Whitfield, 2004, p. 49). Some argue that this ethic might make it difficult for African American men to admit that they are in physical or psychological pain and thus decrease their likelihood of seeking help. "John Henryism" is another coping mechanism that African American men may use to deal with stress. John Henryism is defined as high-effort coping (both cognitive and emotional) in response to stress. This high effort results in increases in heart rate and blood pressure. Thus, in response to stress, people demonstrating John Henryism work harder and exert more effort. This can be a positive coping mechanism when one has sufficient resources to make such added effort productive. But for people with limited educational and financial resources who also face tremendous discrimination, increased and focused effort over many years may not be productive and may actually lead to poor health outcomes. When even Herculean efforts cannot produce the desired outcome, tremendous frustration and disappointment may also occur (Rooks & Whitfield, 2004).

Different Latin American groups have developed complex cultural beliefs that reflect a blend of Native American, European, and African practices, often with religion playing an important role (Levkoff et al., 2000). *Curanderismo*, a type of folk medicine practiced by some Mexican Americans is one example of these complex blends. According to Gafner and Duckett (1992), curanderismo includes (1) a belief that God heals the sick through persons, called *curanderos*, who are blessed with the *don*, a special gift, (2) the reality of a number of conditions that can be cured, (3) the belief in mystical diseases such as *susto*, or soul loss, (4) the belief that both health and illness exist on material, mental, and spiritual levels, and (5) the use of proscribed rituals and herbs for healing. A Mexican American elder might follow curanderismo exclusively or in conjunction with mainstream medical care. For example, a person might take prescriptions from a licensed physician and then also consult a nearby folk healer. This folk healer might suggest that the person also take a particular kind of herbal tea, pass a raw egg over a painful area of the body, or give a massage while applying aromatic oil. Mexican Americans may find curanderos to be attractive alternatives to licensed physicians as they are often conveniently located in the person's neighborhood, do not require insurance or medical history forms, and share the same language, beliefs about illness, and religious traditions (Gafner & Duckett, 1992). Fatalistic attitudes toward health have also been found in some Hispanic groups. Some believe that these attitudes make people from Hispanic groups less likely to participate in health-related screenings because they do not believe that anything can be done once one finds out that he or she has a disease (Berg, 2001).

In the previous cultural definitions of health, we also included strategies that each group may use to manage illness outside of the mainstream health care system. These "alternative" treatments are common and are not restricted to ethnic minority groups. In a study of White elders in upstate New York, a variety of self-care, alternative, or lay strategies were used such as cranberry drinks for urinary problems; heating pads and liniments for joint or muscle pain, and various gargles (water with salt, baking soda, vinegar, or whiskey) for sore throats (Stoller, Forster, & Portugal, 1993). In recent years, there has been increasing medical pluralism in the United States as even mainstream cultural groups have begun to reject the notion of health's being solely the absence of disease and recognize the impact of lifestyle, behavior, and social support on health. This has led many people to embrace alternative conceptions and treatment of health. The acceptance of different ways to improve health such as teas and herbal treatments, acupuncture, yoga, and tai chi are examples of this pluralism. In response to the general population's acceptance and use of these alternative treatments of health, the National Institutes of Health (NIH) has sponsored research to examine the effectiveness of complementary and alternative medicine (CAM).

Aging and Diversity Online: Alternative Medicine

National Center for Complementary and Alternative Medicine. Established in 1998, this center's primary focus is to examine complementary and alternative medical treatments (CAMs) to determine whether they are safe and effective. The center trains researchers to both test CAMs and disseminate the findings. Please visit the website below to find the latest scientific research about many CAM practices. http://nccam.nih.gov

Often it is hard to recognize the role our own culture plays in our beliefs about health. For example, when thinking about "alternative medicine," one may always think of treatments that are very different from the mainstream, such as acupuncture, rather than recognizing one's own use of folk remedies, such as gargling with saltwater or putting honey in tea to ease a sore throat. The next learning activity will allow you explore the roots of your own beliefs about health and illness.

ACTIVE LEARNING EXPERIENCE: DISCOVERING FAMILIAL SOURCES OF HEALTH BELIEFS*

The purpose of this experience is to help you gain insight into the beliefs of family elders regarding health. Upon completion of this activity, you will be able to:

1. Describe and understand the health and illness beliefs of your family elders.
2. Describe and understand health and illness practices of family elders.
3. Understand how current family health and illness beliefs and practices may have been influenced by culture and family history.

Time required: 2.75 hours (1 hour for interview, 1 hour to type up the response and 45 minutes of discussion).

Instructions:

1. Interview the oldest family member that you can. If it is not possible to interview a member of your family, locate an elder outside of your family but from within your ethnic or cultural group.
2. Ask your interviewee to answer the questions given below.
3. Prepare a one- to two-page summary of what you learned from the interview. Compare your own health and illness attitudes and practices with those of the family elder you interviewed.
4. Discuss your findings with another person.

---

* This learning experience was adapted from the first edition of this text. The idea for this experience comes from R.E. Spector (1996). *Cultural diversity in health & illness* (4th ed.) Stamford. CT: Appleton & Lange.

5. Your instructor may wish to lead a class discussion of findings comparing the beliefs and practices of diverse families.

Ask the following questions of your family elder:

1. In what country (or countries) were your parents born?
2. When you were a child, what did your parents teach you about staying healthy?
3. What did your parents do when you or your brothers or sisters became ill? Did you go to a doctor? Did you go to another type of healer?
4. Did your parents use folk remedies when you were sick? For example, were you given herbs, roots, cod liver oil, or other types of home remedies?
5. What special foods were you encouraged to eat in order to stay healthy?
6. What special foods were you given when you were ill?
7. What part did religion play when family members were sick?
8. When your parents experienced physical pain, did they tend to complain about it or tend to keep it to themselves?
9. What health practices have you continued to use as an adult that you learned from your parents or other family members?

Working with elders from diverse groups around issues of health requires knowledge of their cultural definitions of health and any treatment plans associated with them. It also requires recognition of the diversity within each cultural group and varying levels of agreement with the cultural beliefs. One must acknowledge that even when cultural beliefs are strong, individuals may not actually behave in accordance with the beliefs, perhaps due to lack of access to culturally appropriate remedies. We also want to recognize both the positive and negative effects that a particular definition of health can have and then work with the community to maintain the positive effects and try to change the negative. For example, in their native cultures, many groups had healthy diets of whole grain and little red meat before they came to the United States. As part of assimilating to the United States, they may have increased their consumption of meat and high-fat foods, thus negatively impacting their health. It would be much healthier for them to maintain their whole-grain diet after moving to the United States.

Helping diverse elders maintain positive traditional health beliefs and working to add new behaviors that improve health are important tasks for health practitioners (Gelfand, 2003). Similarly, ascertaining when cultural practices might negatively affect health is very important. As with Mrs. Chiu in our second vignette, taking a nontraditional remedy alongside prescribed medications could be very harmful. Many elders use both physician-prescribed medication and alternative remedies simultaneously without letting their physicians know. Depending on the specific medication and remedies, this mixture could be potentially deadly. The

Aging and Diversity Online section on health across cultures gives information about a specific culture's health beliefs and characteristics.

Aging and Diversity Online: Health Across Cultures

Ethnogeriatric Curriculum. Developed by the Stanford Geriatric Education Center, this is a "comprehensive curriculum in the health care of elders from diverse ethnic populations for training in all health care disciplines. It was developed by representatives from over 30 Geriatric Education Centers and includes five Core Curriculum modules and eleven Ethnic Specific Modules to be used in conjunction with the Core Curriculum." http://www.stanford.edu/group/ethnoger/index.html

Ethnomed. This site is designed to be used by health care providers immediately prior to seeing a client from a different culture. The ethnomed site "contains information about cultural beliefs, medical issues and other related issues pertinent to the health care of recent immigrants to Seattle or the US, many of whom are refugees fleeing war-torn parts of the world." http://ethnomed.org

Center for Cross-Cultural Health. The center's goal is to provide materials and resources for health care and service providers who need information about culture and health. http://www.crosshealth.com/index.html

Within this organization is a list of relevant cross-cultural health links. http://www.crosshealth.com/links.htm

NativeWeb. This international nonprofit educational organization uses the Internet to connect indigenous peoples around the world with both non-indigenous and indigenous peoples. The website contains information about indigenous cultures and also information about health and research. http://www.nativeweb.org

---

Thus far we have focused on variations in different ethnic groups' conceptions of or beliefs about health. Ethnic or racial background is much more likely to affect health *beliefs* than the other aspects of diversity (gender, socioeconomic status, residence location, and sexual orientation). But these other factors can and do affect health and health *behaviors*. For example, gender affects people's health behaviors. In the United States, women are more likely than men to have seen a doctor regularly throughout their lives. As soon as girls and young women are at an age to become sexually active, they are instructed to have yearly physical exams. Boys and young men see a doctor only if they are ill or if they need a physical exam to participate in sports. As young women advance further into adulthood, their yearly exams continue and, if they become pregnant, they then receive medical care throughout the pregnancy on a monthly and even weekly basis. Men at this age, on the other hand, see physicians only if they are severely ill or injured. These gender differences mean that women have much more experience and familiarity with the health care system. This regular interaction may make it easier for women to access care as they age. Of course, this gender difference in health behaviors is also affected by other elements of diversity such as socioeconomic status (SES), urban or rural location, and sexual orientation. For example, people with lower

SES are also less likely to have health insurance and thus are also less likely to have access to preventive care such as annual exams.

How Do Behaviors Influence Health?

As you can see, health and wellness can be approached from different cultural perspectives. These perspectives not only influence our definitions of health, but also affect health-related research and interventions. As we mentioned above, the medical model has been the dominant model of health in the United States. This model focuses on treating diseases. Given this focus, much of the federal funding for research has also followed the medical model such that research focused on treating disease and specific conditions is much more prevalent than research focused on promoting health and keeping people healthy. This focus on disease can be very shortsighted, and recently there have been efforts to give health promotion increased attention.

A large portion of the population of older adults is healthy and there are many behaviors that they can and should be doing to keep themselves healthy. Similarly, all of us are aging and the choices we make regarding food, exercise, and other lifestyle behaviors will certainly affect our quality of life as we age. Thus, figuring out ways to maintain and even improve the health and well-being of all adults as we age is very important. There have been interventions that were effective in helping older adults increase their healthy behavior, but these have not been broadly applied (Center for the Advancement of Health, 2006). Also, much of the research that has been done has focused primarily on mainstream elderly populations. Only very recently have some of these interventions been modified and applied to more diverse groups. To increase the translation of research findings into needed programs and services, the Administration on Aging funded the Evidence-Based Prevention Programs Initiative (Alkema & Alley, 2006).

In our discussion of health promotion, we will present some successful health promotion interventions. Many of these have been conducted with mainstream groups and may need to be modified to be culturally appropriate for more diverse groups. Although we highlight several programs below, through initiatives like the one mentioned above new programs are developed and tested each day. The National Council on Aging provides information about effective programs on its Center for Healthy Aging website. See the website for new programs developed after the publication of this text.

Why is behavior now so important to our health? In the past 100 years, life expectancy has experienced a dramatic increase in the United States. Americans who were born in 1900 had a life expectancy of only 47 years, whereas those who were born in 2001 can expect to live to age 77 (National Center for Health Statistics, 2003). The primary reason that we have a greater life expectancy from birth is that medical care and prevention have improved so much. Instead of dying from infectious diseases and acute illnesses such as pneumonia, influenza, and tuberculosis, chronic diseases and degenerative illnesses such as heart disease, cancer, stroke, and diabetes have become the leading causes of death (National Center for Health Statistics, 2002). The interesting thing about these chronic conditions is that, contrary to conventional wisdom, they are often *not* the inevitable result of aging.

Instead, we can prevent these conditions from developing in many people and ameliorate their occurrence in others by promoting simple healthy behaviors. We need to ensure that every person has regular physical activity, eats a healthy diet, and does not smoke. If older adults increase their physical activity, eat more healthily, do not smoke, and take care to minimize their risk of falling, they will live longer and more healthy lives (Center for the Advancement of Health, 2006). Adding regular screenings to catch conditions early and minimize their health impact, and immunizations to prevent influenza and pneumonia would also significantly impact the length and quality of people's lives (Merck Institute of Aging and Health, Centers for Disease Control and Prevention, & The Gerontological Society of America, 2004).

What specific behaviors are important? Several areas of health behavior particularly impact the quality of older adults' lives. Four areas important for younger ages are also important for older adults:

1. Physical activity
2. Nutrition
3. Obesity
4. Not smoking

We cannot overstate how much these four areas affect both the quantity and quality of one's physical, emotional, and even cognitive well-being. Having a physically active lifestyle helps one remain independent. It can help reduce the risk of arthritis, high blood pressure, diabetes, osteoporosis, stroke, depression, and colon cancer. For older adults, the activity does not need to be strenuous or obsessive; daily walking or even activity associated with other pastimes such as gardening can be beneficial. Eating a diet rich in fruits and vegetables may reduce the risk of some cancers and other chronic diseases such as diabetes. Being obese is associated with cardiovascular disease and diabetes and can worsen conditions such as arthritis. Smoking cessation is also important for older adults and even lifetime smokers can improve their health by quitting smoking in old age. Finally, older adults need to engage in immunization and preventive screenings for health conditions. At the present time, immunization rates are significantly lower for Blacks and Hispanics than for Whites. Rates are 69% for flu and 64.8% for pneumonia for Whites whereas they are 50.6% flu and 44.5% pneumonia for Blacks and 54.8% flu and 44.4% pneumonia for Hispanics (Merck Institute of Aging and Health et al., 2004). Alleviating these differences and getting people to make healthy choices is very important. The question thus remains, how do we promote these relatively simple behaviors among all people?

Aging and Diversity Online: Health Promotion

HEALTHY AGING

Healthy Aging for Older Adults. This website from the Centers for Disease Control and Prevention (CDC) provides access to the State of Aging and Health report, as well to basic information regarding health information and health statistics. www.cdc.gov/aging

Healthy People 2010. The Department of Health and Human Services (DHHS) provides a set of health objectives for the United States to achieve.

This site offers information related to these health objectives and ways to achieve a healthier lifestyle. www.healthypeople.gov

Center for Healthy Aging. The National Council on Aging compiles model health programs that have demonstrated evidence-based practices. http://www.healthyagingprograms.org

Elders and Families. Administration on Aging (AOA) has an information section on elders and families that contains good information on health-related issues for seniors and their family members. http://www.aoa.gov/eldfam/eldfam.asp

Physical Activity

National Blueprint: Increasing Physical Activity Among Adults Age 50 and Older. This organization provides information and grants for activity programs for older adults. www.agingblueprint.org

NIA Exercise Guide for Older Adults. This manual and companion video gives older adults safe and effective endurance, strength training, balance, and flexibility exercises. It is also available in Spanish. http://www.nia.nih.gov/HealthInformation/Publications/ExerciseGuide

NCOA Best Practices in Physical Activity Programming. This guide provides the information necessary to create programming for physical activity. It cites evidence for best practices and then makes suggestions for local implementation. http://www.healthyagingprograms.org/resources%2FBP%5FPhysicalActivity%2Epdf

Active for Life is a grant program to learn how to deliver research-based effective physical activity programs to large numbers of seniors in a variety of community settings. http://www.activeforlife.info/default.aspx

Nutrition and Obesity

CDC Obesity Information. http://www.cdc.gov/nccdphp/dnpa/obesity/index.htm

Lifecycle Nutrition. U.S. Department of Agriculture provides nutrition information for seniors. www.nal.usda.gov/fnic/etext/000002.html

Oral Health

The Oral Health of Older Americans. This publication from the CDC and NIA highlights an often overlooked but very important part of health and well-being, oral health. http://www.cdc.gov/nchs/data/ahcd/agingtrends/03oral.pdf

---

Promoting healthy behaviors often involves changing people's behavior. How can we effectively change behavior? Research suggests that if we can (a) provide information about the importance of the behavior, (b) provide information from the right sources, and (c) improve access to the behaviors, then people will change their behavior. For example, studies have shown that older adults often respond to physicians' (and other health care providers') recommendations. Helping physicians provide appropriate information to older adults about how to make healthier behavior choices and then facilitating older peoples' access to needed services (e.g., exercise, healthy food, prevention screenings) in the local community is important. One program that strives to do this is SPARC (Sickness Prevention Achieved through Regional Collaboration). SPARC connects regional providers and then helps implement local interventions to increase access to preventive services. For additional information about SPARC and other health promotion services, see the Aging Online box that follows. Promoting healthy behaviors makes the most sense for everyone. Although there may be some initial cost in these healthy behaviors (e.g., fruits and vegetables can be more expensive than junk food; transportation to exercise programs has a cost), the long-range benefits clearly outweigh these costs. "Healthy choices provide four primary benefits—they extend life, they reduce the likelihood of physical disability, they support good mental health and cognitive function, and they reduce costs" (Center for the Advancement of Health, 2006, p. 1). All of us need to make these changes in our behavior.

How Do Elements of Diversity Affect These Health-Related Behaviors?

Socioeconomic Status   The focus in this section has been on the many ways older adults can positively affect their health, that is, on ways they can thrive in their old age instead of merely surviving. We want to be careful though, that in this focus on individual autonomy and behavior, we don't forget the societal structural forces that can either facilitate or hinder people's health behaviors. For example, in comparison with high-SES people, those living in impoverished neighborhoods are much less likely to have a full-service grocery store nearby. These impoverished elders are also less likely to have safe transport to and from grocery stores. Thus, their ability to access fruits and vegetables is severely hindered by the very neighborhood in which they live. Even if they wanted to eat the recommended five-plus servings of fruits and vegetables each day, they would find it extremely difficult to get them. This is where we, as members of communities, can make a difference. Different community members who work with social service agencies, volunteer groups or churches and other religious organizations, need to recognize that simply instructing people to exercise and eat five or more servings of fruits and vegetables every day is not enough for some groups. We need to think more creatively about how to promote healthy behaviors in different groups.

For example, in Seattle, Washington, a community partnership was formed with the famous Pike Place Market in which fresh fruits and vegetables were delivered to low-income people in the downtown area. Research on the effectiveness of this intervention found that when compared with seniors outside of the delivery area, elders who were a part of the program ate more fruits and vegetables (Johnson, Beaudoin, Smith, Beresford, & LoGerfo, 2004). A similar program funded by the U.S. Department of Agriculture provides coupons for low-income elders to use to purchase fresh fruits and vegetables at local farmers' markets. As service providers, educators, and community members, we need to work together to promote healthy aging among all elders, particularly those who are in high need.

Community-based participatory research (discussed in Chapter 2) provides an entrée into creating programs to help seniors from diverse groups make healthy choices. We will present two recent efforts to increase diverse elders' physical activity. To determine how to promote physical activity among diverse elders, focus groups with older adults from seven cultural or linguistic groups were conducted: American Indian and Alaska Native (AI/AN), African American, Vietnamese, Cantonese-speaking Chinese immigrants from Vietnam, Korean, Tagalog-speaking immigrants from the Philippines, and Spanish-speaking immigrants primarily from Mexico and also from El Salvador, Colombia, Nicaragua, Peru, and Ecuador. These focus groups examined the motivations and barriers to physical activity within each of the groups. The groups were conducted in the primary language of the participants, who were recruited from local community agencies that served that particular group (Belza et al., 2004). Some findings were similar across all groups. Walking was the activity of choice among all elders. Many mentioned both the physical and social benefits of physical activity, often connecting the body and the mind. Family also played an important role in encouragement. There were some culturally specific comments as well. AI/AN and Koreans expressed feelings of isolation from members of their ethnic group and wished to better connect with them. Although all groups mentioned the social nature of physical activity, Latinos and African Americans mentioned religious faith as a component of their exercise. For example, for African Americans, walking was described as a time for meditation and prayer. These cross-cultural similarities should allow creation of an intervention template that can then be used by each group to make culturally appropriate adaptations.

Researchers in the San Francisco Bay area tried to do just this in yet another example of community-based participatory research. Researchers collaborated with community service providers to modify CHAMPS (Community Healthy Activities Model Program for Seniors), a physical activity program that had been shown to be effective in more structured clinical trial settings (described in Chapter 2) to promote physical activity increases in diverse community settings (Stewart et al., 2006). This program was implemented in three very different sites: (1) at a site that provides case management for elders in a predominantly African American community, (2) at a senior center in a Latino community, and (3) at a hospital-affiliated outpatient center in a more affluent yet ethnically diverse community.

The researchers acknowledged both the complexities and benefits of connecting the research and service communities. The methodological control that is normally present in clinical trials was significantly diminished in these community settings. But, although measurement of increases in physical activity was difficult to obtain, related activity programs sprang from this program. In the African American community, a performance group evolved from the line-dancing physical activity sessions. This group now performs at community events. Tai chi was added to the program at the senior center in the Latino neighborhood, and at the outpatient center, it became clear that elders limited their physical activities because they were worried about potential falls, so a program to decrease falls and increase balance among elders was created and then disseminated to local senior centers. These unintended side effects of the intervention continue to grow and benefit these communities.

Yet another program, the EnhanceWellness program (formally the Health Enhancement Program), combines several elements that are important for promoting healthy behaviors. This program involves three steps: Screen, Plan, and Action.

1. Screen: an initial assessment of health
2. Plan: development of a personalized "health action plan"
3. Action: involves encouragement, feedback, and monitoring. Participants are encouraged to enroll in an exercise class and a chronic disease self-management course, and are teamed up with a trained volunteer senior who serves as a health mentor to attend senior center activities and provide peer support. They can also have meetings with a social worker to discuss psychosocial issues that were identified in the initial assessment.

EnhanceWellness has been found to be effective at decreasing depression and increasing physical activity and personal assessments of health (Phelan et al., 2002) and is now being conducted in over 33 sites across the country. Results from these sites should help determine whether this intervention works across diverse groups and what aspects of the program need to be adjusted for each group.

Efforts to improve other health-related behaviors among diverse populations have not progressed as far as the physical activity interventions. For example, there are tremendous racial and ethnic health disparities in immunization rates for elders. The Department of Health and Human Services and the Centers for Disease Control launched a Racial and Ethnic Adult Disparities in Immunization Initiative (READII) in July 2002. READII is being conducted in five sites to understand how to increase immunization rates among diverse elders, particularly African American and Hispanic elders. This demonstration project is currently under way.

Aging and Diversity Online: Programs That Work

PHYSICAL FITNESS

EnhanceFitness (Formerly Lifetime Fitness Program). This exercise program is taught by trained instructors and is designed to be safe and effective for participants with a range of physical abilities. Participants have experienced improvements in physical and social functioning and declines in pain, fatigue, and depression (Wallace et al., 1998). http://www.projectenhance.org

Arthritis Foundation Exercise Programs. These programs have been evaluated for effectiveness and are then disseminated by the Arthritis Foundation. The programs work to counter the often incorrect belief that people with arthritis cannot exercise. http://www.arthritis.org/programs.php

NUTRITION

Seattle Senior Farmers' Market Nutrition Program. This program provides healthy, locally grown fruits and vegetables to low-income seniors. http://nutrition.wsu.edu/markets/sfmnp.html

Senior Farmer's Market Programs. Sponsored by the U.S. Department of Agriculture, these programs exist around the country. http://www.fns.usda.gov/wic/SFMNP-Fact-Sheet.pdf

HEALTH PROMOTION AND SCREENINGS

EnhanceWellness Program. This community-based program targets seniors who are at risk for functional decline. It involves an initial assessment of health and encourages enrollment in effective exercise class, a chronic-disease management class, and can involve regular meetings with a social worker who monitors psychosocial issues. http://www.projectenhance.org/pro/wellness.html

Sickness Prevention Achieved through Regional Collaboration (SPARC). SPARC is a nonprofit health organization serving residents of the four counties at the junction of Connecticut, Massachusetts, and New York. They help people of all ages improve and extend life by encouraging use of basic disease-prevention services. SPARC promotes the use of vaccinations; cancer detection tests including pap smears, mammograms, and colon cancer screening; and cardiovascular tests including cholesterol and blood pressure checks. http://www.sparc-health.org

Sexual Orientation

When promoting health among lesbians and gay elders, it is important to remember the life experiences of the current cohort of LGBT elders. These elders grew up in an era where hiding one's sexuality was often essential for survival. Thus, they have not experienced the "coming out" revolution of the past few years and they may feel very isolated from the younger LGBT community whose experiences around their sexuality are very different. As they age, given that older adults are stereotypically seen as sexless and lesbians and gay men are defined by their sexuality, lesbian and gay elders can experience tremendous discrimination (Claes & Moore, 2001). For some elders, the challenges they have experienced may give them additional strength in old age. They have experienced being "different" most of their lives and thus may have more flexibility and experience than others in adjusting to aging. Youth and beauty have been a big focus in the gay community. As we discussed in the chapter on psychological issues and aging, this can have negative effects in that the attitude toward older people who are gay can be negative. But this also can have a positive effect in that it may make older people who are gay more amenable to health promotion interventions and more likely to exercise, eat healthy diets, and take care of their bodies in ways that the general population does not.

Health Promotion in Rural versus Urban Areas

As with many issues related to urban versus rural aging, *access* can be key to promoting healthy behaviors. In rural areas where homes are spread out and towns may be small, access to basic services such as grocery stores, community centers, and health care is very important. For example, a frail elder living in a rural area may have difficulty getting fresh fruits and vegetables as the nearest grocery store may be far away. Finding a place where age-appropriate exercise is supported or even getting to one's physician to obtain approval to begin a new exercise program can be significant barriers to health promotion. Service providers and community members must continue to think creatively, as the location in which one lives can introduce challenges to aging healthily. Developing programs that build on existing strengths (for example, a sense of community) while recognizing the challenges (large distances between residences and services) is very important.

Disability   Disability rates increase with age. It is estimated that approximately 20% of people in the United States have a disability and approximately 50% of those with a disability are older adults (Kaiser Permanente, 2004). Defining the term "disability" can be difficult, as it includes a wide range of abilities (e.g., visual, physical, mental, emotional) as well as occurring across the full spectrum of people. Different definitions of disability may be used by different communities, organizations, and institutions. Definitions are important because government and health institutions use them to determine who is eligible for services. In 2001, the World Health Organization (WHO) moved toward a new classification of disability that emphasizes functional status or how well one is able to function when completing daily tasks rather than focusing on the mere diagnosis of a condition (World Health Organization, 2001). Thus, WHO defines disability as the impairment of one's ability to complete multiple daily tasks and recognizes that disability is not necessarily a permanent state, as one's ability to function may improve or the environment may be changed (installment of ramps so that one can go to work in a wheelchair) such that one's function may improve. In the United States, definitions of disability often focus on activities of daily living (ADL) which refer to the ability to perform basic personal care tasks (e.g., eating, bathing, dressing, etc.), and instrumental activities of daily living (IADL) which refer to the ability to perform complex, multidimensional activities that require effective interactions with the environment (e.g., grocery shopping) (Hooyman & Kiyak, 2008). Approximately 20% of older people experience disability in their IADLs or ADLs. In 1999, 3% had disability in only IADLs, 6% had disability in 1–2 ADLs, 6% had disability in 3–6 ADLs, and 5% were institutionalized (Federal Interagency Forum on Aging-Related Statistics, 2006).

People with disabilities are a heterogeneous group. They include men and women from diverse racial or ethnic backgrounds, socioeconomic levels, religious groups, rural or urban communities, and sexual orientations. Similar to older people living in rural communities, access can be the biggest barrier to healthy behaviors for older people with disabilities. Accessible (and affordable) transportation for doctor visits, to buy healthy foods, and to exercise is just one of the barriers people with disabilities face when trying to live a healthy life. In addition to difficulties accessing health care, people with vision or hearing-related disabilities may have difficulty communicating with health care providers. Older people with disabilities also face the stereotypes that others have about them. These stereotypes might lead a physician to fail to suggest health-promoting behaviors such as exercise because the physician may think that someone with a disability is not capable of doing such activities, or an employer might assume that an elder will retire when he or she becomes physically disabled. Given that people with disabilities do not fit the model of "successful aging," it may be assumed that they have already failed at aging and may not suggest health-promoting, longevity-enhancing behaviors to them (Minkler & Fadem, 2002). Finally, our attitudes toward disability might also affect elders themselves, as they may think that disability signals the end of their healthy life instead of recognizing that adaptations to the environment exist and that people with disabilities can continue to live healthy, active, meaningful lives. The availability of assistive technologies such as those described by Able Data in the following Aging and Diversity Online section can make a difference for people with disabilities.

Aging and Diversity Online: Disability

Center for Excellence in Disability Education, Research and Service. Part of the national network of programs funded by the Federal Administration on Developmental Disabilities, this center is located at the University of Montana Rural Institute. The center's goal is to support "the independence, productivity, and inclusion of persons with disabilities into the community." http://ruralinstitute.umt.edu/

Able Data. This organization is sponsored by National Institute on Disability and Rehabilitation Research and the U.S. Department of Education. It provides information, publications, and consumer reviews of all types of assistive technologies for persons with disabilities. http://www.abledata.com

WHO International Classification of Functioning, Disability, and Health. Visit this site for more information on the WHO definition of health and its potential ramifications for the way we think about disability worldwide. http://www.who.int/classifications/icf/en

---

Disability and Falls   One of the things that can inhibit older adults from exercising and from getting out and socializing is the fear of falling. Indeed, fear of falling is a valid concern because, in addition to the negative immediate effect on an elder's health (e.g., a broken hip), there are also long-term recovery issues stemming from the fall. The older person will have increased exposure to illness when in the hospital getting treatment for the fall and can become bedridden as a result of the fall or as a result of complications from the fall. Preventing falls in a way that also promotes healthy physical and social activity is key. See the Aging and Diversity Online section for one example of an effective program to reduce falls.

Aging and Diversity Online: Preventing Falls

A Matter of Balance: Managing Concerns about Falls. Funded by a grant from the Administration on Aging, this program was created by Partnership for Healthy Aging, Southern Maine Agency on Aging, Maine Medical Center's Geriatric Center, and the University of Southern Maine. This program is designed to help decrease falls and then promote healthy, safe physical activity. http://www.mmc.org/mh_body.cfm?id=432

Ethnicity   As discussed in the chapter on psychological issues and aging, people's beliefs about what elders should be doing in old age vary by cultural group. For example, in Cuban culture, old age is viewed as a time for comfort (*tranquilidad*) and a vigorous exercise program conflicts with the value of relaxation. Traditional exercise programs may not work well in communities that share this "seniors should take it easy" belief, as the researchers may face some cultural barriers in these beliefs about old age (Hockenson Ryall, Abdulah, Rios, Hausdorff, & Wei, 2003). This does not mean that one should abandon the idea of physical activity in communities that believe elders deserve a break. Instead, one should work within their cultural beliefs to develop culturally appropriate ways to promote physical activity. For example, "exercise" could be reframed into a culturally appropriate activity like dancing. Or the ability to play with one's grandchildren could be mentioned as a reason for improving and maintaining one's physical health. An activity program designed for elders framed this way and made culturally appropriate in both the activity and the setting might be more successful.

Similar to exercise, interventions to promote healthy nutrition need to take culture into account. Different cultures have different relationships with food, particularly specific kinds of food. These relationships are important and can be complex. For example, Latino cultures have been stereotyped in terms of the importance of rice and beans. Yet, within specific Latino cultures, the relationship with different foods changes subtly. Mexican cuisine often involves corn-based items (tacos, enchiladas, tamales) in rich, spicy combinations with meat or beans. In contrast, Puerto Rican cuisine focuses on rice combined with pinto beans, roasted pork, and fried plantains. Cuban cuisine is similar to Puerto Rican, but with black beans and a different way of combining spices and other ingredients (Bermudez & Tucker, 2004). In Chinese culture, maintaining the balance of yin and yang promotes health. Because of their age and frailty, Chinese elders believe that they are "naturally predisposed to yin, or cold energy forces. Therefore, they should avoid eating many "cold foods," such as leafy green vegetables—an avoidance that, by Western standards, is not conducive to good health" (Wong, 2001, p. 29).

One can see how when working to improve nutrition, cultural food values must be considered. For example, reducing one's carbohydrate intake can help prevent the onset of diabetes or ameliorate its problems after it has developed. When trying to change elders' diets to decrease the consumption of carbohydrates, one could say "no rice, no pasta" and for some individuals and groups, this would not be a problem. But for many Asian and Latino cultures, the suggestion of removing rice from one's diet is so radical that it might make individuals from those cultures ignore the rest of the nutrition recommendations as well. If these group members were instead shown an appropriate serving size of rice for a diabetic person (1/3 cup), their responses would be much more positive and indeed their nutrition and adherence to diabetic protocols would improve.

Aging and Diversity Online: Minority Health

Office of Minority Health. The mission of this office within the federal government seeks to improve the health of racial and ethnic minorities through the development of health policies and programs that will eliminate health disparities. http://www.omhrc.gov

ACTIVE LEARNING EXPERIENCE: DESIGN YOUR OWN HEALTH PROMOTION INTERVENTION

The purpose of this experience is to give you practice in designing a program to promote healthy behavior. It allows you to combine knowledge you have gained about a particular group with an intervention program that has been effective in promoting healthy behavior. Time required: 60 minutes.

Instructions:

1. Choose your group representing an element of divesity (e.g., low-income, ethnicity/race, immigration, disabled, sexual orientation).
2. Choose a behavior that you would like to change (e.g., exercise, nutrition, smoking, etc.)
3. Visit one of the programs websites listed under Aging and Diversity Online: programs that work.
4. Design your own intervention taking into account factors related to your group, the behavior you want to change and using features from the successful programs.
5. On paper, describe your proposed program.
6. Discuss your intervention with another person. What challenges does the person see in implementing it? What improvements could you make?
7. Present your intervention to either a small group in your class, or to the class as a whole.

HEALTH CARE SERVICES AND DIVERSE ELDERS

In this section we examine issues that pertain to diverse elders around health care services. We first discuss how health care for older adults is paid for in the United States with explanations of Medicare and Medicaid and a brief discussion of the new prescription drug coverage, Medicare Part D. We then turn to the actual use of these services to explore issues such as cultural and language differences that have particular relevance for diverse elders. As you read the sections that examine health insurance in some detail, please keep specific older adults in your mind—perhaps the elder that you interviewed in an earlier chapter, or even your grandparents or parents. How do they pay for health care and how will any changes in these plans affect them? As they try to choose health care plans, what advice would you give them? Also, as a U.S. taxpayer, how do these programs affect you? And, finally, as someone who plans to age in the United States, what programs do you want to see remain and how do you want them to change as you age?

Health Insurance

Health insurance plays a crucial role in allowing people to access the health care system and have protection against expensive health care costs (Roberts, 2006). In the United States, how we pay for health care (health care financing) has become an important issue both for individuals and for society as a whole. Unlike most younger Americans, a substantial portion of older adults' health care coverage is provided by government programs. But many people do not realize that these programs do not cover all of older adults' health care costs. Unlike many employee-based health care plans, these government programs fund only certain portions of older adults' health care. Often older adults must pay a considerable sum to get the same health care coverage that they may have enjoyed when they were employed. If younger and middle-aged adults do not save adequately during their working years, they may have difficulties being able to afford health care when they are older.

A variety of sometimes overlapping programs provide some coverage for most older adults. To understand the complexities of health care financing for older adults, a bit of background is necessary. In the United States, access to health insurance has been historically tied to one's place of employment. Indeed, even today for people under age 65, one's best chance of getting affordable health insurance is through one's workplace. Prior to 1966, insurance companies often did not offer coverage to people who were over age 65, or if they did, the insurance was too expensive for people to afford (Moon, 2006). Thus, if one retired or needed to stop working to take care of a spouse or simply due to one's own age, then his or her access to health insurance was affected. Up until 1966, getting health insurance was extremely difficult for people over age 65. In 1966, Title XVIII of the Social Security Act went into effect and Medicare and Medicaid were created.

Prior to 1966, only about 50% of people over age 65 had health insurance, but after Medicare was implemented, twice as many older adults gained access to health coverage. Since 1970, Medicare has covered more than 97% of people over age 65 and Medicaid supplements this coverage for about 1 in 7 older adults (Moon, 2006). Medicare was designed to help people with acute care needs and Medicaid helps low-income people fill in the gaps of Medicare to pay for needed services. For example, Medicare does not cover nursing home stays, but Medicaid does. Medicare is broken up into different parts, primarily Part A (hospital insurance) and Part B (Supplementary medical insurance). Part A covers "hospital, skilled nursing and hospice care and is funded by payroll tax contributions from workers and employers that are earmarked for an HI trust fund" (Moon, 2006, p.381). Only people (or their dependent spouses) who are eligible for any type of social security benefit will receive Part A. This is a concern because some older adults came to the United States when they were older and may not have been employed and therefore cannot use this program. Thus, while these programs are available, some people are not eligible for them because they did not pay into them through social security. The only programs that do not require payment into social security are those available through the Older Americans Act (OAA) (Gelfand, 2003). The OAA was enacted in 1965 with 10 titles or objectives that provide for programs such as congregate meals. Gelfand (2006) provides a detailed description of the original 10 titles and an accounting of how the titles have changed in the past 40 years.

When the Medicare program was started, Part A received most of the focus, as people were concerned about the cost of hospital stays. But, over time, the rate of acute illnesses decreased and hospital stays were thus reduced, while the rate of chronic conditions increased and thus other services associated with chronic conditions are now used much more frequently. Part B (Supplementary Medical Insurance) covers the services that are much more common today, such as physician visit, hospital outpatient procedures, and other kinds of walk-in care. Part B is available to people over age 65 on a voluntary basis if they enroll and pay the monthly insurance premiums. Part B is funded by a combination of general revenues and beneficiary premiums (Moon, 2006). Through Medicare, older people have gained access to health insurance that cannot be revoked no matter how old or how sick they become. In a world of rapidly increasing health care costs and denial of coverage due to preexisting conditions, Medicare has provided protection for older adults against these problems.

Because Medicare does not provide comprehensive coverage for older adults, several private and public supplemental programs have been developed:

- Medicaid
- Employer-sponsored plans
- Medigap private policies

For low-income seniors, Medicaid is available. This is a joint state and federal program, with individual states controlling its implementation, and using its own names. Thus, Medicaid coverage can vary and the quality and quantity of services vary tremendously by state (Moon, 2006). Medicaid is often thought of as a health insurance program for low-income people although one third of its spending goes for long-term care.

Employer-sponsored plans are available to some seniors. They may have this supplemental insurance through their previous workplace, as some companies offer retiree insurance to their employees. People who have this benefit tend to be wealthier and their health care needs are covered well. About 33% of current Medicare beneficiaries have this type of supplemental insurance, although it may be much less available in the future. Employers are cutting back these benefits to control costs. They often do this by increasing the employee contribution, sometimes even to 100% of the policy cost.

Medigap policies are offered by private insurers. These individual supplemental coverage policies are touted to cover the "gaps" in Medicare coverage. These policies can be expensive and complicated. For example, premiums may be based either on a "community-rated" plan in which everyone pays the same premium regardless of age, or an "attained age" plan in which premiums increase drastically as a person ages. An older adult at age 65 may choose an attained age plan because it is initially much more affordable than a community-rated plan, but the premiums may rise so quickly that the person cannot afford the premiums just when the insurance is needed most.

Finally, private health plans that contract with Medicare to provide Medicare-covered services sometimes offer an additional supplemental benefit plan. These plans are called "Medicare Advantage" and they were becoming more popular until 1997 when legislative changes made the plans much more expensive for people. The 2003 Medicare Modernization Act has introduced incentives to encourage insurance companies to continue offering coverage through these programs so they may become popular once again. Of course, all of these supplemental programs have a cost and many seniors have difficulty affording the plans and thus go without additional health care coverage. This puts them at tremendous financial risk when they experience health related costs that are not covered by Medicare. About 9% of Medicare beneficiaries do not have any supplemental insurance to cover the gaps in Medicare. These people are "less likely to see a doctor in any given year, less likely to have a usual source of care, and more likely to postpone getting care in a timely fashion" (Moon, 2006, p. 388). These barriers to care can significantly affect health.

Health care costs have skyrocketed in this country and Medicare and Medicaid have not been unaffected. Medicare and Medicaid programs are often criticized for their cost, but actually their costs have not risen at a rate higher than other health care costs and yet they receive much more focus and criticism. To control costs, some states keep Medicaid payments to providers very low or require people to enroll in managed health care plans to ensure that their health care will be covered. These reduced payments for physicians can result in problems with access because service providers decide not to serve Medicaid patients. Also, if an older adult must enroll in a managed care program, he or she may lose access to the regular health care provider with whom they may have developed a long relationship and who may understand their life health history very well. Losing this continuity of care can result in decreased quality of care for these elders. The high cost of mental health care services is also of concern. Under Medicare, mental health services are not covered at the same rate as other forms of health care. This is yet another example of how mental health and physical health are treated as separate entities in U.S. culture. For outpatient mental health services, Medicare will reimburse at a 50% rate compared with the 80% rate for other health care services (Karlin & Humphreys, 2007). When we discuss mental health issues in Chapter 5, consider how the costs of mental health services might affect older people's use of them; a 50% co-pay for psychotherapy is indeed a significant barrier for many older people.

In 2003, Congress passed the Medicare Prescription Drug, Improvement and Modernization Act. This plan started in January 2006 and will result in many changes to Medicare that will likely increase Medicare's spending. Popularly called Medicare Part D, the prescription drug plan has received the most attention. This drug plan is financed by premiums paid by the older adults (about 25%) and by governmental revenues (about 75%). Any older adult who wants to get prescription drug coverage must enroll in a private plan. For most older adults, this will mean that they now have at least three types of health care coverage: (1) Medicare, (2) their supplemental insurance to cover gaps in Medicare, and (3) their prescription drug care plan. The multiple choices of prescription drug plans are confusing at best with many highly educated people unable to determine which program would be best for them.

Thus far, the only diversity issue in our discussion on health insurance has been income—although Medicare covers almost all adults over the age of 65, the gaps in its coverage differentially affect lower-income people who may make too much money (or have too many assets) to qualify for Medicaid and yet may not have enough money to pay for expensive supplemental coverage policies. Medicare provides access to insurance for almost all people over age 65, regardless of their race or ethnicity, but access to health care earlier in life is also critical for health. In addition to the concrete health care provided, health insurance at younger ages provides access to health care that can serve as a template for a lifelong relationship with the health care system. If one does not have health insurance, then one is less likely to see a physician on a regular basis and more likely to postpone needed medical care. Over a lifetime, these delays in care and lack of regular interaction with the health care settings can affect one's health. When one turns 65 and is eligible for Medicare, this lifelong pattern is unlikely to be forgotten.

So, does health insurance vary by race and or ethnicity? Hispanics are the most likely racial or ethnic group to be uninsured (Roberts, 2006) and a report from the Commonwealth Fund found that uninsured rates for Hispanic and African American adults are significantly higher than for White adults. Hispanics and African Americans are also more likely to experience gaps in insurance coverage, to lack access to care and to face medical debt than White Americans (Doty & Holmgren, 2006). Recent immigrant elders may also face difficulties obtaining health care coverage. In 1996, the Personal Responsibility and Work Opportunity Reconciliation Act, a welfare reform bill, imposed eligibility rules for noncitizens in Medicaid and other public assistance programs. This act prohibits states from providing federally funded Medicaid benefits to noncitizen elders for the first 5 years of their stay in the United States. Additional difficulties face elders with limited English language proficiency as navigating these health programs can be extremely difficult for people fluent in English, let alone adding the difficulties of language and cultural barriers. For a description of the major federal programs that support health care and long-term care services for older people, see Table 4.1. The following active learning exercise on health insurance will allow you to learn about how these federal programs are actually experienced by older people.

TABLE 4.1   Major Health-Related Programs for Older People and People with Disabilities

Program	Objectives	Administration	Services
Medicaid/Title XIX of the Social Security Act	Pays for medical assistance for certain low-income persons	Federal: HCFA/HHS State: state Medicaid Agency	Nursing home care, home and community-based health and social services, facilities for persons with mental retardation, chronic care hospitals
Medicare/Title XVIII of the Social Security Act	Pays for acute medical care for the aged and selected disabled	Federal: HCGA/HHS	Home health visits, limited skilled nursing facility care
Older Americans Act	Fosters development of a comprehensive and coordinated service system to serve the elderly	Federal: Administration on Aging/ Office of Human Development State: state agency on aging	Nutrition services, home and community-based social services, protective services, and long-term care ombudsman
Rehabilitation Act	Promotes and supports vocational rehabilitation and independent living services for the disabled	Federal: Office of Special Education and Rehabilitative Services/ Department of Education State: state vocational rehabilitation agencies	Rehabilitation services, attendant and personal care, centers for independent living
Social Services Block Grant/ Title XX of the Social Security Act	Assists families and individuals in maintaining self-sufficiency and independence	Federal: Office of Human Development Services State: state social services or human resources agency; other state agencies may administer part of Title XX funds for certain groups; for example, State Agency on Aging	Services provided at the states' discretion, may include long-term care
Medicare Part D	Adds some prescription drug coverage to Medicare plans	Federal: plans are offered by insurance companies and other private companies approved by Medicare	Prescription drugs

* The information in this table was adapted from (a): U.S. General Accounting Office, Health, and Human Services Division (1995) and (b) U.S. Dept. of Health & Human Services, Medicare.gov

ACTIVE LEARNING EXPERIENCE: HEALTH INSURANCE FOR PEOPLE OVER AGE 65

The purpose of this experience is to give you the opportunity to learn about an older person's experience with health insurance programs like Medicare. It allows you to see how the federal programs that you have read about in this chapter actually work in practice with real people. Time required: 60 minutes.

Instructions:

1. Find a person who is over age 65 and no longer fully employed and who is comfortable answering questions about his or her health insurance coverage.
2. Ask the following questions:
   a. How do you pay for your health care (for example, for doctor visits)? Do you have Medicare? Medicaid?
   b. Do you have any other insurance that covers co-pays or other health expenses that are not covered by Medicare? Do you pay extra for this coverage or was it a benefit from a previous job?
   c. How do you pay for prescriptions? Do you use Medicare Part D, the prescription drug plan? If so, how did you choose which plan to use? If not, why did you not enroll?
   d. What has your experience been with health insurance—positive, negative, or neutral? Please explain.
   e. Did your experience with health insurance change after you became 65? Was it better or worse before you were 65? Please explain.
3. Prepare a summary of your interviewee's responses.
4. After your interview, consider key elements of diversity (e.g., SES, race or ethnicity, etc.). How might an older person's experience with health insurance change depending upon each element of diversity?
5. Based on the knowledge you have gained through this exercise and through this chapter, what recommendations can you make to improve older people's access to affordable health care?
6. Discuss your findings with another person.
7. Your instructor may lead an in-class analysis to determine what issues were shared and what issues were different for different older adults.

Aging and Diversity Online: Medicare and Medicaid

The following three sites provide updated information on Medicare and Medicaid programs and eligibility requirements:

U.S. Department of Health and Human Services Centers for Medicare and Medicaid Services. http://www.cms.hhs.gov/home/medicaid.asp

AARP Medicare Information. Published by the AARP Public Policy Institute. http://www.aarp.org/research/medicare/coverage/aresearch-import-673-FS45r.html

AARP Medicaid Information. Published by the AARP Public Policy Institute. http://www.aarp.org/research/assistance/medicaid/medicaid_facts.html

---

Service Providers

Cultural Competence   Given the differences in health beliefs and behaviors observed across cultural groups, a thorough knowledge of the cultural group with which health care providers work is very important. Having the appropriate knowledge and skill base to work with a particular ethnic or cultural group is called cultural competence. Cultural competence in health care settings includes the delivery of health care services in a manner that acknowledges and understands cultural diversity, respects members' health beliefs and practices, and values cross-cultural communication. Gaining this cultural competence (also referred to as cultural sensitivity), can be difficult for health care service providers who may be already overwhelmed with large patient loads and the challenge of keeping up with new treatments. But an openness to the values and characteristics of different cultural groups can facilitate the development of this competence and numerous resources are available on the web, at special cultural competence workshops, and in texts. To further illustrate the importance of cultural competence, we turn to communication issues that can occur in the health care relationship.

Communication Issues (Health Care Provider–Patient Relationship)   Gaining cultural competence can be challenging for health care providers who have completed rigorous training steeped in the medical model of health. But gaining cultural competence and an understanding of different cultures' beliefs can result in increased trust in health care professionals and thus give those cultures access to needed medical expertise. For example, in Merced, California, there is a large population of Hmong immigrants. Many of the Hmong came to the United States as refugees because they assisted the United States during the war in Vietnam. New refugees continue to arrive in the States. Hmong cultural beliefs and behaviors are very different from mainstream U.S. culture. Hmong culture did not have a written language until the 1950s and many new Hmong immigrants struggle both to learn English and also to learn to read and write. "Healthy House Merced" was created to offer "cultural brokering and mediation" in which to help people from non-Western cultures better understand the U.S. health care system and to help U.S. health care providers understand different cultures' beliefs and behaviors. For example, many Hmong believe they are born with all of the blood they will have in their lifetime, so having blood drawn repeatedly for tests can be very disturbing. Helping Hmong understand why blood draws are necessary, and explaining to health care professionals why Hmong might resist them, promotes mutual understanding and appreciation between the groups.

For the Chinese, communication with a health care provider can be a problem as it is courteous to nod yes to an authority figure even when one means no. Positive head nodding in the presence of a physician might lead the physician to think that the person agrees with what is being said, but actually the patient may not understand but may not wish to embarrass the physician by asking (Wong, 2001). Similarly, in Latino cultures, a nod of the head may be a gesture of respect, not an affirmative response. Because of the strong hierarchical nature of many Latino cultures, doctors are viewed with tremendous respect and are expected to be authoritative and directive, yet also warm and kind (Kaiser Permanente, 2001). Communication differences also occur with many American Indian and Alaska Natives. Often they are very comfortable with silence and just sitting and minimizing eye contact is valued. African American patients may be especially sensitive to a brusque or hurried care provider, given African Americans' experience with both interpersonal and institutional racism. Personalized interactions including a greeting, an introduction, and a handshake are preferred (Kaiser Permanente, 2003). Communication issues are not restricted solely to ethnic or racial minority groups. For older people who are LGBT, health care providers' unthinking questions (e.g., "Are you married?") may send a message that this provider is not sensitive to or aware of the unique circumstances of LGBT individuals. As a result, the patient may not disclose his or her sexual orientation and the provider then misses what may be important health-related information.

In addition to these differing cultural communication styles, actual language barriers between the patient and the health care provider also must be addressed in order to have effective communication. Interpreters are needed for a large range of groups—Mexican, Vietnamese, Hmong, Chinese, Indian—just to name a few, and as immigration patterns change and new groups come to the United States (e.g., Iraqi), interpreters will be needed for the languages from those groups. In some cases, family members who speak English have been called upon to serve as interpreters for their relatives who speak limited English. Although at first this may seem like an expedient solution, it has several drawbacks. Using untrained interpreters such as family members can impede the communication between the health care provider and the patient. Family members often lack the health care knowledge needed to accurately translate medical questions or procedures into their native language. In addition, having a family member interpret may also violate the patient's confidentiality.

The relation of the family member to the patient is also important to consider. In some cultures, having a family member of the opposite sex serve as an interpreter may violate cultural gender norms in addition to confidentiality. School-age children as interpreters raise additional concerns about violating cultural norms. Often the family member who is most fluent in English is a school-age child who has learned English in school. In many cultures, the elder traditionally has the more authoritative role and the child looks to the elder for guidance. As the interpreter, the child assumes a more authoritative position and this may violate cultural norms of hierarchy. To put a young child, who may not even be of the same gender, in the role of knowing intimate details about an elder's health and then asking him or her to be responsible to accurately convey details about health care options is not appropriate. The federal government agrees. By federal law, any health care program that receives federal funding (including Medicare and Medicaid), must provide interpreter services; some states, for example, California, have considered bills to prohibit the use of school-age children as interpreters except in emergencies (Dower, 2003). Many health care providers now comply with these regulations. In areas that have large concentrations of people who speak limited English, health care providers may post multilingual signs that allow a patient to point to his or her language so that staff members know which interpreter to call. Resources have become available to help health care providers navigate language and cultural differences. We describe several of these resources in the next online box.

Aging and Diversity Online: Cultural Competence

National Center for Cultural Competence. The mission of this center is to facilitate the design, implementation, and evaluation of culturally and linguistically competent service health delivery systems. http://www11.georgetown.edu/research/gucchd/nccc

Healthy House Merced. This is a "partners in healing" program in Merced, California. In this program, staff members work to educate Hmong shamans about Western conceptions of health and to educate physicians about Hmong health beliefs. This exchange of knowledge helps both health care providers and the Hmong. Once a Hmong shaman has completed the shaman training from Healthy House, he or she is given identification that gives access to Hmong patients in the hospital. http://www.healthyhousemerced.org/default.aspx

Diversity, Healing and Healthcare. This web-based resource was developed by On Lok Senior Health and the Stanford Geriatric Education Center to provide information for clinicians to work with patients from cultures or religions different from their own. http://gasi-ves.org/diversity.htm

DiversityRx. This site promotes language and cultural competence to improve the quality of health care for minority, immigrant, and ethnically diverse communities. http://www.diversityrx.org

Culturally Competent Care Package. This guidebook and CD-ROM were developed by the American Academy of Orthopedic Surgeons to help promote cultural competence among health care providers. http://www4.aaos.org/product/productpage.cfm?code=02872

Culturally Competent Care Online Resource Center. This center at Harvard University Medical school was developed to share resources and information on cross-cultural education and training from at Harvard Medical School. http://medweb.med.harvard.edu/cccec

Improving the communication among health care providers and their patients is not just important for elders from minority groups. Effective communication can make the difference between accurate and inaccurate adherence to the prescribed behaviors and medications. One side effect of promoting cultural competence and improving communication is that health care providers may become more focused on ensuring that *all* patients understand important information. Medical literacy, or the ability to understand common medical information such as prescription instructions or instructions for preparing for a screening test, can be critical to treating a serious condition. David Baker and colleagues (2007) examined data from 3,260 Medicare enrollees (people over age 65) who completed a shortened version of a health literacy test. They found that 25% of these participants were found to be medically illiterate on the basis of their scores on the health literacy test. Five years later, after controlling for demographics, SES, and baseline health, those participants with inadequate or marginal health literacy had a 50% higher mortality rate than participants with adequate health literacy (Baker et al., 2007). Findings like these suggest that health literacy can have life or death consequences. What can health care providers do to ensure that their patients understand their instructions? One method is using a process called "teach back" (Goldman, 2007). Many patients are reluctant to ask a provider to explain something further if they don't fully understand. This reluctance may stem from cultural communication styles that frown on asking questions of authorities or from embarrassment that one doesn't understand the directions. If a provider then asks, "Do you understand?" these patients may simply nod or say "yes." With teach back, the health care provider asks that patient to repeat back the instructions in his or her own words. If a patient cannot explain it back, then it is likely that he or she does not understand the directions. For additional information on health literacy, see the Aging and Diversity Online section.

Aging and Diversity Online: Health Literacy

Health Literacy Fact Sheets. Created by the Center for Health Care Strategies, Inc., this series of nine fact sheets provides information for service providers who work with people with low-literacy skills. http://www.chcs.org/publications3960/publications_show.htm?doc_id=291711

Health Literacy Improvement. Created by the Office of Disease Prevention and Health Promotion with the DHHS, this site contains links for numerous resources on health literacy. http://www.health.gov/communication/literacy/default.htm

---

Mental Health Care Providers Culture matters for both ethnic minority clients and for the mental health clinicians who treat them. The clinician brings his or her own culture just as the client does. Clinicians' culture has been influenced by their training within the mainstream U.S. medical system with its focus on disease and its principles rooted in empiricism and the power of the experimental method. This disease focus has many strong points and has produced many amazing treatments for disease, but this focus can also miss the role of culture in mental health, which can result in misdiagnosis and incorrect treatment. An additional point is that approximately 40% of physicians currently studying psychiatry are foreign born. These future psychiatrists will need to be culturally competent in both mainstream and other diverse cultures (Vedantam, 2005). In addition to concerns regarding cultural competence of those who provide mental health care, the U.S. health care system has historically neglected wellness and the maintenance of mental health. We also need to promote positive mental health just as we need to promote positive physical health.

Aging Expertise As we've discussed throughout this chapter, an important factor in quality health care services for diverse elders is the cultural competence of the service providers. But service providers need to not only understand the diversity of their clients, but also to be experts in aging. "The average 75 year old has three chronic conditions and uses five different prescription drugs" (Merck Institute of Aging and Health et al., 2004, p. i). Older adults have unique health conditions that are different from people of younger ages. Unfortunately, few service providers have such expertise. Very few physicians have formal training in geriatrics. There are only 2.5 geriatricians for every 10,000 elderly and less than 3% of current medical students take any elective courses in geriatrics (Merck Institute of Aging and Health et al., 2004). Schools of pharmacy, nursing, and social work do not do any better. Only 720 pharmacists (out of 200,000) have geriatric certification, only 23% of nursing schools require even one course in geriatrics, and only 5% of social workers list geriatrics as their primary practice area. Many health care providers consider some conditions such as incontinence, depression, and memory loss to be normal side effects of aging even though effective interventions exist to treat these conditions. Older adults who receive specialized geriatric care tend to do better than those who receive standard care (Kovner, Mezey, & Harrington, 2002). Given that many elders respond to health care providers' recommendations, counseling from physicians promoting healthy behaviors for seniors is very important. Clearly, we are in desperate need of people who are both interested in and competent to work with older adults.

SUMMARY

This chapter focuses on health beliefs, behaviors, and service utilization. We begin by examining how health is defined by different ethnic groups and then discuss the influence of their beliefs on health-related behaviors. Given these differences in beliefs and their potential impact on the health of older adults, health practitioners need to take cultural factors into consideration and at the same time encourage their clients to add new behaviors essential to maintaining and enhancing their health. We note the widespread increase in the acceptance and use of alternative treatments of health by the mainstream population. This has led to the establishment of a National Center for Complementary and Alternative

Medicine as one of the units of the National Institutes of Health. The Center's mission is to sponsor research on alternative medicine and to make its findings widely accessible.

Although culture is much more likely to affect health beliefs and behaviors than other elements of diversity (e.g., gender, SES, and sexual orientation), these other elements can and do affect health beliefs and behaviors. These factors should, therefore, also be taken into consideration when designing interventions aimed at improving participants' health. We have included a discussion of culturally appropriate interventions, their design, their distinctive features, and their outcomes. The next major section examines issues related to health care services. We have discussed how health care for older adults is paid for in the United States, have provided an explanation of Medicare and Medicaid, and have also included a brief discussion of the new prescription drug coverage, Medicare Part D. In the concluding section, we discuss cultural competence in health care settings and explore communication issues that have practical relevance for diverse elders.

ACTIVE LEARNING EXPERIENCE: CHAPTER 4 QUIZ

The purpose of this experience is to gauge your present knowledge of issues related to health beliefs, behaviors, and services for elders from diverse groups. Upon completion of this activity, you will be able to:

1. Assess your knowledge of health beliefs, behaviors, and services for elders.
2. Gain feedback on your knowledge of important issues related to health and diversity.

This activity should take 30 minutes (10 minutes to complete the quiz and 20 minutes to discuss your answers with another person or in a classroom setting).

Instructions:

Complete the quiz below. Your instructor may lead an in-class review of the answers to the quiz. Indicate whether each of the following statements is true or false.

Quiz Items	True	False
1. In the United States, health was historically defined as a lack of illness or disease.	_____	_____
2. Alternative medicine is used primarily by immigrants in the United States.	_____	_____
3. Curanderos are holy healers for the Hmong from Southeast Asia.	_____	_____
4. To change people's behavior, both providing information about the importance of healthy behaviors and removing barriers to those behaviors are necessary.	_____	_____
5. Access is one of the biggest barriers to promoting healthy behaviors among rural and disabled elders.	_____	_____
6. All people in the United States are eligible to receive federally provided health insurance.	_____	_____
7. Medicare pays for nursing home care.	_____	_____
8. Many evidence-based practice programs have been adapted for use with elders from diverse groups.	_____	_____
9. Prescriptions for medications are partially covered under Medicare Part D.	_____	_____
10. Given the increase in the aging population, many medical students choose to specialize in geriatrics.	_____	_____

GLOSSARY

complementary and alternative medicine: Diagnostic and therapeutic techniques considered to be outside mainstream Western medicine. These techniques, often adopted from other cultures, may enhance conventional treatment. Examples include homeopathy, herbal treatments, acupuncture, and massage therapy.

culturally competent care: Refers to the delivery of health care services in a manner that acknowledges and understands cultural diversity, respects members' health beliefs and practices, and values cross-cultural communication.

curanderismo: A form of folk medicine practiced by some Mexican Americans in the Southwest. It includes the belief that God heals the sick through *curanderos*, persons blessed with a special gift (the *don*). This system includes the idea that health and illness exist on material, mental, and spiritual levels.

Medicaid: This nationwide health insurance program is administered by the States, with federal financial participation. Within certain broad federally determined guidelines, States decide who is eligible; the amount, duration, and scope of services; rates of payment for providers; and methods of administering the program. Medicaid pays for health care services, including nursing home care, for certain low-income people.

Medicare: This nationwide program provides health insurance to people age 65 or older, people entitled to Social Security Disability payments for 2 years or more, and people with end-stage renal disease, regardless of income. Medicare covers acute care services and generally does not cover nursing homes.

Medicare Part A: Covers inpatient care in hospitals, critical access hospitals, and skilled nursing facilities (not custodial or long-term care). Also covers hospice and some home health care.

Medicare Part B: Covers doctors' services, outpatient hospital care, and durable medical equipment. It also covers some other medical services not covered by Medicare Part A, such as physical and occupational therapy and some home health care. Also pays for some supplies when they are medically necessary.

Medicare Part D: Medicare offers partial prescription drug coverage, called "Part D," for everyone with Medicare. This coverage may help lower prescription drug costs and help protect against higher costs in the future. These plans are run by insurance companies approved by Medicare. Note that Part D is optional. If you join it, you pay a monthly premium. If you have limited income and resources, you might qualify for extra help paying your Part D costs.

SUGGESTED READINGS

Ferraro, K. F. (2006). Health and aging. In R. H. Binstock & L. K. George (Eds.), *Handbook of aging and the social sciences* (6th ed.) Burlington, MA: Elsevier Academic Press. pp. 238–256.

This handbook chapter focuses on the relationship between health and aging, specifically examining the way research in this area has changed in the past 50 years. Although it does not focus on diversity specifically, it does describe theories and research (e.g., cumulative disadvantage theory, research on race and ethnicity) that have been used to explain the health of disadvantaged groups.

Garroutte, E. M., Kunovich, R. M., Buchwald, D., & Goldberg, J. (2006). Medical communication in older American Indians: Variations by ethnic identity. *Journal of Applied Gerontology, 25*(1), 27S.

This journal article details the different communication styles used by American Indians with differing levels of ethnic identity. The authors suggest that if physicians are unaware of these cultural communication styles, they may underestimate the magnitude of a patient's distress.

Gelfand, D. E. (2006). *Aging network: Programs and services* (6th ed.). New York: Springer.

This book describes the complex system of programs and services provided for older people in the United States. Several chapters are particularly relevant for health-related services. Chapter 2 describes the legislative bases for programs and services, in particular the Older Americans Act (OAA) with its original list of 10 titles or objectives that have changed and been modified throughout the years. Chapter 3 includes a detailed discussion on the distinctions between and eligibility for Social Security and Supplemental Security Income (SSI). These factors affect one's eligibility for Medicare and Medicaid, both of which are discussed in detail in Chapter 4.

Moon, M. (2006). Organization and financing of health care. In R. H. Binstock & L. K. George (Eds.), *Handbook of aging and the social sciences* (6th ed.) Burlington, MA: Elsevier Academic Press. pp. 380–396.

This handbook chapter presents a brief, yet thorough overview of how health care is organized and financed in the United States.

Shankle, M. D. (Ed.). (2006). The handbook of lesbian, gay, bisexual, and transgender public health: A practioner's guide to services. Binghampton, NY: Haworth Press.

This edited book provides information for those who will work with people who are lesbian, gay, bisexual, or transgender. Chapter 11 focuses specifically on the needs of LGBT elders, and Chapters 2 and 3 present basic background information on the field of public health and its relationship with the LGBT community. Barriers to Chapter 8, Health Care Access, is particularly relevant for readers of our textbook.

Sheehan, S. (2004, October 25). Not poor enough: Cassie Stromer's old age. *The New Yorker,* 36-42.

This article presents Cassie Stromer as an example of the difficulties poor, older people face in paying for health care and medications. Her experiences vividly illustrate the problems with our current system of health care.

Working with your older patient: A clinician's handbook. (2004) (NIA Publication No. 04-7187). National Institute on Aging.

This pamphlet provides a brief guide to help clinicians communicate more effectively with their older patients. Although many of the sections are very brief, given the pamphlet format (for example, the section on diversity is two pages), this is an excellent starting resource for clinicians who have limited experience working with elders.

AUDIOVISUAL RESOURCES

Abandoned to Their Fate. A history of social policy toward people with disabilities. Traces the way the people with disabilities have been treated from the Middle Ages through modern times. 30 minutes. Available from http://www.lookiris.com/store/Developmental_Disabilities/Abandoned_to_Their_Fate

Dominick and Margaret: Independent Living for Elderly Disabled. Portrays the lives of two people with bilateral amputations who live independent lives. 56 minutes. Available from http://www.videopress.umaryland.edu/videopress_careelderly/videopress_careelderly_CE625.html#anchor

Exercise: A Guide from the National Institute on Aging. This manual and companion video give older adults safe and effective information about how healthy diet and exercise are important for staying healthy. The video shows safe endurance, strength training, balance, and flexibility exercises. It is also available in Spanish. 48 minutes. Available from http://www.niapublications.org/exercisebook/exercisebook.asp

Fear of Falling: It's a Matter of Balance. This video contains interviews with elders about their thoughts and fears about falling and describes the challenges they face as they work to maintain their independence. It was produced in conjunction with the Boston University's cognitive-behavioral intervention study on fear of falling. 17 minutes. Video and companion facilitator manual is available from http://www.bu.edu/hdr/products/balance/index.html

Miss Nora's Store: Understanding of the Rural Elderly. An award-winning documentary that portrays the lives of elderly individuals living in a rural community. 28 minutes. Available from http://www.videopress.umaryland.edu/videopress_careelderly/videopress_careelderly_CE626.html

The War Against Diabetes: Kings County Hospital Cooking Class. This brief video shows a healthy cooking class for recent immigrants conducted in New York City. The instructors take foods from the immigrants' cultures (e.g., oxtail) and then help the participants cook the dishes in ways that are both healthy and flavorful. 3 minutes. Available at http://link.brightcove.com/services/link/bcpid452319854/bctid1264562785

KEY: CHAPTER 4 QUIZ

1. True. In the past, the biomedical model, which defines health as the absence of illness or disease, was the predominant model in the U.S.
2. False. Research has found that alternative medicine is common in all groups in the United States (Stoller et al., 1993).

3. False. Curanderos are people with a special gift to heal illness using rituals and herbs for healing. Curanderismo is practiced by some Mexican Americans.

4. True. Simply providing people with information about healthy behavior is not enough. The information needs to come from a source that is influential for the group (e.g., often physicians for older adults) and access to the healthy behavior needs to be improved (e.g., by offering coupons to make fresh fruits and vegetables affordable).

5. True. Transportation (for health care visits, for shopping, for exercise) for rural and disabled elders can be very difficult to obtain.

6. False. Medicare is provided only for people who are 65 and older and, who meet federally defined eligibility requirements.

7. False. Medicaid pays for nursing home care and only very low-income elders are eligible for Medicaid. All other older adults must pay for nursing home care themselves or through long-term care insurance that they purchased when they were younger.

8. False. Initiatives are just being created to promote the translation of research findings into practical evidence-based programs, but these programs typically are designed for use with mainstream groups of elders.

9. True. The Medicare Prescription Drug, Improvement and Modernization Act (MMA) that was passed by the Congress in 2003 included a provision for prescription drug plans. It is popularly called Medicare Part D.

10. False. There is a tremendous shortage of service providers with training in aging. This is true in the field of geriatrics, where there are only 2.5 geriatricians for every 10,000 elderly and fewer than 3% of current medical students take any elective courses in geriatrics (Merck Institute of Aging and Health et al., 2004). This lack of aging expertise is also found in nursing, social work and pharmacy—all fields with particular relevance for older people.

REFERENCES

Alkema, G. E., & Alley, D. E. (2006). Gerontology's future: An integrative model for disciplinary advancement. *Gerontologist, 46*(5), 574–582.

Baker, D. W., Wolf, M. S., Feinglass, J., Thompson, J. A., Gazmararian, J. A., & Huang, J. (2007). Health literacy and mortality among elderly persons. *Archives of Internal Medicine, 167*(14), 1503–1509.

Becker, G., Beyene, Y., Newsom, E. M., & Rodgers, D. V. (1998). Knowledge and care of chronic illness in three ethnic minority groups. *Family Medicine, 30*(3), 173–178.

Belza, B., Walwick, J., Shiu-Thornton, S., Schwartz, S., Taylor, M., & LoGerfo, J. (2004). Older adult perspectives on physical activity and exercise: Voices from multiple cultures. *Preventing Chronic Disease: Public Health Research, Practice and Policy, 1*(4), A09.

Berg, B. (2001, October 4, 2001). Culture counts. *Fred Hutchinson Cancer Research Center News Online, 7.*

Bermudez, O., & Tucker, K. (2004). Cultural aspects of food choices in various communities of elders. *Generations, 28*(3), 22–27.

Brady, T., Kruger, J., Helmick, C., Callahan, L., & Boutaugh, M. (2003). Intervention programs for arthritis and other rheumatic diseases. *Health Education and Behavior, 30*(1), 44–63.

Braun, K. L., Yee, B. W. K., Browne, C. V., & Mokuau, N. (2004). Native Hawaiian and Pacific Islander elders. In K. E. Whitfield (Ed.), *Closing the gap: Improving the health of minority elders in the new millennium* (pp. 55–67). Washington, DC: The Gerontological Society of America.

Center for the Advancement of Health. (2006). *A new vision of aging: Helping older adults make healthier choices* (No. Issue Briefing No. 2): Center for the Advancement of Health.

Claes, J., & Moore, W. R. (2001). Caring for gay and lesbian elderly. In L. K. Olson (Ed.), *Age through ethnic lenses: Caring for the elderly in a multicultural society* (pp. 217–229). Lanhan, MD: Rowman & Littlefield.

Doty, M. M., & Holmgren, A. L. (2006). Health care disconnect: Gaps in coverage and care for minority adults. The Commonwealth Fund.

Dower, C. (2003). Health care interpreters in California. UCSF Center for Health Professions.

Federal Interagency Forum on Aging-Related Statistics. (2006). *Older Americans update 2006: Key indicators of well-being.* Washington, DC: U.S. Government Printing Office.

Flowers, L., & Gibson, M. J. (2005). *Six things that you might not know about the Medicaid program.* Washington, DC: AARP Public Policy Institute.

Gafner, G., & Duckett, S. (1992). Treating the sequelae of a curse in elderly Mexican Americans. In T. L. Brink (Ed.), *Hispanic aged mental health* (pp. 145–153). New York: Haworth Press.

Gelfand, D. E. (2003). *Aging and ethnicity: Knowledge and services* (2nd ed.). New York: Springer.

Gelfand, D. E. (2006). *Aging network: Programs and services* (6th ed.). New York: Springer.

Goldman, L. (2007, September 25). Literacy can be a matter of life and death: Millions can't process health data. *Chicago Tribune.*

Hockenson Ryall, A. L., Abdulah, D. R., Rios, D. A., Hausdorff, J. M., & Wei, J. Y. (2003). Recruitment and retention of ethnically diverse elderly research subjects in an exercise intervention study. In L. Curry & J. S. Jackson (Eds.), *The science of inclusion: Recruiting and retaining racial and ethnic elders in health research.* Washington, DC: The Gerontological Society of America.

Hooyman, N., & Kiyak, H. A. (2008). *Social gerontology: A multidisciplinary perspective* (8th ed.). Boston, MA: Allyn and Bacon.

John, R. (2004). Health status and health disparities among American Indian elders. In K. E. Whitfield (Ed.), *Closing the gap: Improving the health of minority elders in the new millennium* (pp. 27–44). Washington, DC: The Gerontological Society of America.

Johnson, D. B., Beaudoin, S., Smith, L. T., Beresford, S. A., & LoGerfo, J. P. (2004). Increasing fruit and vegetable intake in homebound elders: The Seattle senior farmers' market nutrition pilot program. *Preventing Chronic Disease: Public Health Research, Practice and Policy, 1*(1), A03.

Kaiser Permanente. (2001). *A provider's handbook on culturally competent care: Latino population* (2nd ed.). Kaiser Permanente National Diversity Council.

Kaiser Permanente. (2003). *A provider's handbook on culturally competent care: African American populatio n*(2nd ed.). Kaiser Permanente National Diversity Council.

Kaiser Permanente. (2004). *A provider's handbook on culturally competent care: Individuals with disabilities:* Kaiser Permanente National Diversity Council.

Karlin, B. E., & Humphreys, K. (2007). Improving Medicare coverage of psychological services for older Americans. *American Psychologist, 62*(7), 637–649.

Kovner, C. T., Mezey, M., & Harrington, C. (2002). Who cares for older adults? Workforce implications of an aging society. *Health Affairs, 21*(5), 78–89.

Levkoff, S., Kyong Chee, Y., Reynoso-Vallejo, H., & Mendez, J. (2000). Culturally appropriate geriatric care: Fund of knowledge. In G. Yeo (Ed.), *Core curriculum in ethnogeriatrics* (pp. 21–33). Stanford, CA: Stanford Geriatric Education Center.

Matsumoto, D., & Juang, L. (2004). *Culture and psychology* (3rd ed.). Belmont, CA: Thomson Wadsworth.

Merck Institute of Aging and Health, Centers for Disease Control and Prevention, & The Gerontological Society of America. (2004). *The State of Aging and Health in America.* Retrieved July 29, 2006, from http://www.cdc.gov/aging/pdf/State_of_Aging_and_Health_in_America_2004.pdf

Minkler, M., & Fadem, P. (2002). "Successful aging:" a disability perspective. *Journal of Disability Policy Studies, 12*(4), 229–235.

Moon, M. (2006). Organization and financing of health care. In R. H. Binstock & L. K. George (Eds.), *Handbook of aging and the social sciences* (6th ed.). (pp. 380–396). Burlington, MA: Elsevier Academic Press.

Mulatu, M. S., & Berry, J. W. (2001). Health care practice in a multicultural context: Western and non-Western assumptions. In S. S. Kazarian & D. R. Evans (Eds.), *Handbook of cultural health psychology* (pp. 45–61). San Diego: Academic Press.

National Center for Health Statistics. (2002). *Mortality report.* Hyattsville, MD: U.S. Department of Health and Human Services.

National Center for Health Statistics. (2003). *Health, United States, 2003.* Hyattsville, MD: U.S. Department of Health and Human Services, Centers for Disease Control and Prevention.

Phelan, E. A., Williams, B., Leveille, S., Snyder, S., Wagner, E. H., & LoGerfo, J. P. (2002). Outcomes of a community-based dissemination of the health enhancement program. *Journal of the American Geriatric Society, 50*(9), 1519–1524.

Roberts, M. (2006). Racial and ethnic differences in health insurance coverage and usual source of health care, 2002: Rockville, MD: Agency for Healthcare Research and Quality. MEPS Chartbook No. 14. AHRQ Pub. No. 06–0004.

Rooks, R. N., & Whitfield, K. E. (2004). Health disparities among older African Americans: Past, present and future perspectives. In K. E. Whitfield (Ed.), *Closing the gap: Improving the health of minority elders in the new millennium* (pp. 45–54). Washington, DC: The Gerontological Society of America.

Stewart, A. L., Gillis, D., Grossman, M., Castrillo, M., Pruitt, L., McLellan, B., et al. (2006). Diffusing a research-based physical activity promotion program for seniors into diverse communities: CHAMPS III. *Preventing Chronic Disease: Public Health Research, Practice and Policy, 3*(2), A51.

Stoller, E. P., Forster, L., & Portugal, S. (1993). Self-care responses to symptoms by older people: A health diary study of illness behavior. *Medical Care, 30*, 24–42.

Udesky, L. (2006, June 4). A matter of respect: Training Hmong shaman in the ways of Western medicine is saving lives in Merced. *San Francisco Chronicle*, pp. 8–11.

Vedantam, S. (2005, June 26, final edition). Patients' diversity is often discounted: Alternatives to mainstream medical treatment call for recognizing ethnic, social differences. *Washington Post.*

Wallace, J. I., Buchner, D. M., Grothaus, L., Leveille, S., Tyll, L., LaCroix, A. Z., et al. (1998). Implementation and effectiveness of a community-based health promotion program for older adults. *Journal of Gerontology: Medical Sciences, 53a*(4), M301–M306.

Wong, M. G. (2001). The Chinese elderly: Values and issues in receiving adequate care. In L. K. Olson (Ed.), *Age through ethnic lenses: Caring for the elderly in a multicultural society* (pp. 17–32). Lanham, MD: Rowman & Littlefield.

World Health Organization. (2001). *WHO publishes new guidelines to measure health.* Retrieved November 17, 2007, from http://www.who.int/inf-pr-2001/en/pr2001-48.html

5

Inequalities in Health

- What illnesses and conditions typically affect older persons?
- How are the elements of diversity related to physical health and mental health?
- What are the leading causes of death for older persons across different racial/ethnic groups?
- How does longevity differ by gender, ethnicity, and socioeconomic status?

Health inequalities refer to the difference in the rate of morbidity (illness) and mortality between different social groups in the United States. Often this difference mirrors societal inequities experienced by people from ethnic minority groups and those from lower socioeconomic groups; members of these populations often have higher rates of morbidity and mortality than their counterparts who are White or are from higher socioeconomic groups. Health inequalities are also often referred to as health disparities.

In examining how health differs in elders of different ethnic groups, it is important to remember that "minority group status is a risk factor for poor health and not an inevitable sentence to lower class status" (Angel & Hogan, 2004, p. 10). There is a tremendous need both to address the negative health inequalities that occur between elders from diverse and mainstream populations and to learn from diverse groups some ways the general population could change their behaviors so that we can promote healthy aging among all elders. In this chapter, we discuss health inequalities and mental health issues for elders in the United States. To see examples of the interaction between health and diversity, please consider the following vignettes.

Vignette 1

Nina Chen is a research assistant for a project that promotes health among immigrant Chinese with diabetes. The principal investigators for the project carefully developed a research team that includes people of Chinese heritage who speak Cantonese or Mandarin or both. While the research focus was supposed to be improving health around diabetes, participants expressed urgent needs to Nina around many issues unrelated to diabetes such as intense depression, suicidality, and spousal abuse. The participants were so relieved to finally find someone they could talk with in their language about these critical issues. For the participants, adherence to diabetes protocols was of minimal importance compared with the emotional crises that they experience in other areas. Nina was very surprised to discover that her expectation that people of Chinese heritage don't talk with outsiders about family issues and aren't interested in mental health services was strikingly disconfirmed with their particular participant sample.

Vignette 2

Seema Singh has just spent her summer helping her father recover from bypass surgery. Her father and mother came to the United States from India in the mid-1960s and raised Seema, her two brothers, and one sister here. When they discovered that her father would need to have this surgery, the family came together to help him recover. Fortunately, the surgery was scheduled during the summer break so Seema and her siblings were home from college. Seema was relieved that it happened during the summer because she would have felt torn between delaying her education and not being there for her family if it had occurred during the school year.

Vignette 3

As a Lakota Sioux, John Hunter grew up on the Pine Ridge Indian Reservation in South Dakota. There is extreme poverty on the reservation, with estimates of unemployment ranging as high as 80%. Like almost half of the adult population of Pine Ridge, John has diabetes and in the past often had difficulty getting to medical treatment. Sometimes his daughter drove him more than 100 miles to Rapid City to see a specialist. Now there is Porcupine Clinic, an Indian community-controlled health clinic in Pine Ridge. Although it is still a distance from his rural home, he can get dialysis there, and bilingual nurses help him monitor his diabetes more effectively. Porcupine Clinic has also started the Campaign Against Diabetes in which the clinic works with school-age children to help prevent the development of diabetes as they age. Part of this intervention involves Project Grow to help the community return to growing their own food to improve access to healthy fruits and vegetables.

Vignette 4

Esperanza Cruz grew up in Tijuana, Mexico, but she now lives and works in San Jose, California. Her parents and her brothers and sisters all still live in Tijuana, and Esperanza visits them at least once a year. On her last visit, she noticed that her mother was acting somewhat strangely, having difficulty finding things in the house. When Esperanza mentioned something to her sister, she found out that the week before her mother had gotten lost on the way home from the market and one night couldn't seem to wash the dishes, as if she had forgotten how. Esperanza is worried about her mother and wonders if she is developing Alzheimer's disease, but her sister is certain that their mother's forgetfulness is just a normal part of aging. Her sister does not want to see a doctor about their mother because "what good would it do anyway? She's just getting old."

ILLNESS AND AGING

Although we do not want to characterize older adults as being ill, self-reported health does decline with age. Almost half of people aged 65–74 reported very good or excellent health compared with 34% of those aged 75–84 and 28% of those 85 and older. These results vary by race: Only 25% of Blacks report very good or excellent health whereas almost 40% of Whites do (Merck Institute of Aging and Health, Centers for Disease Control and Prevention, & Gerontological Society of America, 2004).

Common Conditions That Affect Older Adults in General

Chronic Conditions   "The average 75-year-old has three chronic conditions and uses five prescription drugs" (Merck Institute of Aging and Health et al., 2004, p. i). When considering physical illness, we often differentiate between two different types of conditions: acute and chronic. Acute conditions like pneumonia occur over a short duration and have severe symptoms. Chronic conditions occur over a much longer period of time than acute conditions (more than three months), are very difficult to resolve, and are often permanent. They may start with more mild symptoms and are usually not an immediate threat to one's life, although they certainly impact the quality of life and ultimately affect longevity. Approximately 80% of American elders have at least one chronic condition, and 50% have at least two. As we discussed in the previous chapter, our increased longevity can be attributed to the fact that we are now able to cure many acute conditions so we live long enough to develop chronic conditions. The bad news is that chronic conditions are prevalent in older age and can negatively impact all areas of one's life. The good news is that healthy behaviors can, in some cases, prevent the development of these conditions and in others can delay the onset of and then can ameliorate the effects of many chronic conditions. Diabetes is an example of a chronic condition affected by health-related behaviors. Diabetes results from one's body being unable to use carbohydrates. When glucose (sugar) levels in the blood get too high, people with diabetes may go into a coma. Approximately 20% of Americans over the age of 65 have diabetes, and it can often be controlled with regular exercise and a careful diet low in fat and carbohydrates. If one's glucose levels can't be controlled by diet and exercise or by medication, high blood glucose levels may lead to serious complications as the disease advances that include stroke, cognitive impairment (vascular dementia), and poor circulation in one's extremities, which can lead to gangrene and amputation (Hooyman & Kiyak, 2008). To the extent that healthy behaviors can prevent or ameliorate the side effects from this disease, the promotion of healthy diets and exercise among all age groups is important.

Other common chronic conditions among older people include cardiovascular (heart) disease, cerebrovascular disease (stroke), arthritis, some types of cancer,

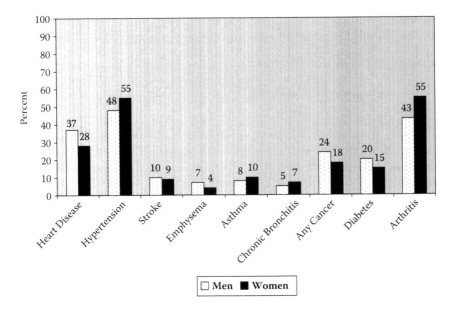

Figure 5.1   Chronic health conditions in men and women. *Source*: Federal Interagency Forum on Aging-Related Statistics (2006).

and osteoporosis. As noted with diabetes, one interesting fact about these chronic conditions is that health-related behaviors like healthy diet, exercise, and not smoking affect the likelihood of developing the condition. This is particularly relevant for younger adults as it is important for them to know that the behaviors that they are choosing to do today (e.g., eating foods high in fat, smoking) may have long-term consequences. Given both the prevalence of chronic conditions and the potential for behavior change to improve the experience of the disease, implementing effective programs that help individuals manage their condition is very important. Developing effective programs for elders from diverse groups (either by taking existing effective programs and then adapting them to fit diverse elders or by creating effective interventions tailored for a specific group) is one of the challenges facing the United States. Figure 5.1 shows the percentage of older people who have selected chronic conditions.

Aging and Diversity Online: Managing Chronic Disease

Chronic Disease Self-Management Program (Living a Healthy Life workshop). Researchers in the School of Medicine at Stanford University have created a program to help individuals manage their chronic conditions. Participants who completed the program showed improvements in both physical and psychological health http://patienteducation.stanford.edu/programs/cdsmp.html

Mental Health Aspects of Diabetes in Elders from Diverse Ethnic Backgrounds. This curriculum was developed to teach "culturally-appropriate care for depression and cognitive loss for elders at high risk for diabetes" http://sgec.stanford.edu/dmh/Curriculum_UserGuide.pdf

Dementia One of the prevailing stereotypes of aging is that older adults are forgetful. Of course, people of all ages forget things, but when an older adult forgets something, people (both the elder and others) attribute it to advanced age, sometimes even calling it a "senior moment." When being forgetful moves beyond the norm, it is classified as a disorder called *dementia*. Dementia is characterized by the loss of cognitive function, especially memory function. In diagnosis, dementia is a "clinical syndrome evidenced by the presence of memory impairment and disturbances in at least one additional cognitive domain (language, visuospatial skills, executive function)" (Longobardi, Cummings, & Anderson-Hanley, 2000, p. 123). Dementia can be found in all ethnic and cultural groups (Larson & Imai, 1996) and may be the result of a large number of conditions that affect brain function. Common dementia-causing conditions include Alzheimer's Disease (AD), vascular dementia, depression, drug-induced dementia, and chronic medical conditions. Note that some of these conditions (e.g., depression and drug-induced dementia) can be reversed, whereas others (e.g., AD, vascular dementia) are irreversible. In mainstream populations, the most common cause of dementia is AD followed by vascular dementia.

Alzheimer's Disease AD is a "common, chronic, disabling, and ultimately fatal disease of the brain that strikes people in the later decades of life" (Allery et al., 2004, p. 81). It is estimated that 1 in 10 people over the age of 65 and 1 in 2 people over the age of 85 has AD. In the last 25 years, tremendous advances have been made in understanding how the brain ages and in trying to determine what occurs in the brain with AD. It seems that the behavioral and clinical problems of AD "center around loss of communication among certain nerve cells and the eventual destruction of these cells" (Allery et al., 2004, p. 81). Although several drug treatments are available for AD, there is no cure. Even though dementias have a biological basis, there is evidence that their prevalence rates vary by ethnicity, race, and gender (Yeo & Gallagher-Thompson, 2006). The drug treatments can sometimes offer a temporary and partial relief from the steady progression of the disease, and advances in methods have also been made for managing behavioral symptoms of AD, but neither drug treatments nor behavioral treatments have been well studied to date in major ethnic and cultural groups, despite the variability in the prevalence rates across groups.

ACTIVE LEARNING EXPERIENCE: CHRONIC CONDITIONS AND DIVERSITY

The purpose of this experience is to give you the opportunity to (1) learn about a chronic condition that an older relative may have (or have had), and (2) consider how the chronic condition may be affected by different elements of diversity. Time required: 60 minutes (45 minutes to research the condition, 15 minutes for discussion).

Instructions:

1. Choose a chronic condition that one of your family members has (or has had).
2. Determine the basic details about the condition: What causes it? What can people do to prevent it?
3. Determine what Web-based information resources are available for that condition.
4. Consider key elements of diversity and determine what resources are available for different groups (e.g., are there resources for non-English speakers, what seems to be the educational level needed to understand the resources).
5. If you develop this chronic condition, are there resources available for you? Do you think that elders from different groups would agree with you?
6. Present your findings to at least one other person. Briefly describe the chronic condition (e.g., what causes it, what can people do to prevent it or ameliorate their symptoms), and state how you think the elements of diversity might affect the chronic condition. Your instructor may want you to do this as part of a small-group exercise or as a class discussion.

Mental Illness and Aging

We have separated our description of mental illness from physical illness because the health care system in the United States has historically treated mental and physical health differently. For people who do have health insurance, only rarely is mental health coverage included. In the instance where it is, often severe limits are placed on the amount of mental health treatment that one can receive both in type of mental health issues that are covered and the length of time allowed to treat an issue (e.g., limiting someone to a small number of sessions). Please note that this distinction between mental and physical health is a cultural one and that many cultures do not make this emotional/physical or mind/body distinction. When we discussed health beliefs from different cultures, we noted that many cultures describe health in terms of balance and that for most, emotional well-being is an integral part of health. So, even though this chapter follows the mainstream U.S. construction of mental health as separate from and perhaps even different from physical health, many cultures do not make this distinction.

Prevalence of Mental Illness
Many major mental disorders such as depression, schizophrenia, bipolar disorder, and panic disorder are found worldwide in all racial and ethnic groups. The prevalence, or the number of cases at any given time, for schizophrenia is about 1% of the U.S. population, and there is the same prevalence worldwide, suggesting that genetics plays a big role in causation of the disease. Depression, on the other hand, may be more influenced by culture and

social context, with its prevalence ranging from 2% to 19% (Weissman et al., 1996). The overall rate of mental disorders in the United States is approximately 2%, but the rates of mental illness in many minority groups have not been sufficiently studied, so comparison of the prevalence of mental illness between ethnic groups is extremely difficult. We discuss the relationship between elements of diversity and mental illness when we discuss mental health inequalities later in this chapter.

Depression   Depression is particularly relevant in old age as there is an incorrect belief that depression is an inevitable part of growing old. This belief has been around for centuries. Depression is a pervasive mood disorder that is associated with illness, mortality, and diminished life quality (Bell et al., 2005). Both older adults and medical professionals often believe that mental health problems like depression and dysphoria are natural occurrences of old age. This belief ignores the following facts (Butcher & McGonigal-Kenney, 2005):

1. Depression can be treated.
2. Depression can coincide with other medical illnesses and then can go unnoticed and untreated.
3. Depression may be caused by medications that were prescribed to treat a different illness.

As older adults are more likely to report physical complaints rather than psychological, detecting depression can be even more difficult. Some evidence even suggests that older adults' symptoms of depression may be different from those of other age groups, further confounding diagnosis (Butcher & McGonigal-Kenney, 2005). Of those older adults who acknowledge mental health problems, only half actually receive any treatment, and less than 3% of those receive treatment from a mental health provider. This rate is lower than for any other age group (Lebowitz et al., 1997). One of the consequences of ignoring depression can be suicide. Older men have the highest suicide rate in the United States (Merck Institute of Aging and Health & Gerontological Society of America, 2002). Primary care physicians need to be trained to recognize mental health issues with older adults. Studies have shown that many older adults who committed suicide had visited a primary care physician close to the time of the suicide: 20% on the same day, 40% in the same week, and 70% within one month of the suicide (Conwell, 1994). If professionals who work with older adults were trained to recognize mental health issues, depression could be diagnosed and treated, and then perhaps some of these suicides could be prevented.

Aging and Diversity Online: Mental Health

The "Get Connected!" Toolkit. A resource kit that gives service providers assistance in linking older adults with medication, alcohol, and mental health resources. The kit discusses health promotion and education and provides screening and referrals for mental health problems and alcohol and medication misuse. It is available in both English and Spanish. http://ncadistore.samhsa.gov/catalog/ProductDetails.aspx?ProductID=16523

Try This: Best Practices in Nursing Care to Older Adults. This site provides links to several geriatric screening tools including the Geriatric Depression Scale, a measure often used to assess depression in older people. http://www.hartfordign.org/resources/education/tryThis.html.

Mental Health and Aging. This website provides assistance in finding mental health services that are specific to the needs of older adults http://www.mhaging.org.

Health Inequalities

Recently, both researchers and the federal agencies that fund research have shifted their focus to examine the differences in health between different social groups. Although the relationship between health and socioeconomic status has been known for some time, this attention has highlighted the health differences for ethnic minority, low income, and rural elders. The term *health inequalities* refers to the difference in the rate of morbidity (illness) and mortality between diverse groups in the United States. Health inequalities are also commonly called *health disparities.* Too often, at least in this early stage of health disparities research, the focus is simply on health outcomes—the final product of health. With this focus, we simply compare rates of illness in different groups and note which groups tend to be different from the "mainstream" group. Given that in this text we focus on many elements of diversity, this "mainstream" comparison group changes depending on the element of diversity being examined. For example, if we are focusing on gender, then we compare women and men; if we are focusing on ethnic or racial background, we often compare to Whites; if we are focusing on lesbian, gay, bisexual, and transgender (LGBT) populations, then heterosexuals become our comparison group. Sometimes this focus on health outcomes can be useful, in particular if the health difference is a fairly simple one. For example, early research on health disparities found that immunization rates were especially low in African American populations. There was widespread publicity about this disparity and initiatives to promote immunizations in this population. Initial evaluation of these initiatives suggests that the disparity in immunization rates by race has decreased dramatically, thus indicating some success from this health outcomes focus. But other times this disparities focus is comparing much more complex health issues. In this case, we are left with statistics showing social group differences and no real explanation for those differences. If we do not work to understand the cause or causes of these disparities, then we do not have much hope of alleviating them.

As we discuss health inequalities in the following sections, we try to move beyond the simple health outcomes focus by first examining the processes by which these disparities could occur. Using a conceptual model, we discuss how the elements of diversity can affect health. We also examine one particular health condition in depth—dementia—to see how the elements of diversity affect various aspects of dementia. We then review the morbidity and mortality rates, giving a more traditional presentation of the health outcomes statistics. We hope that when you read a health inequality statistic (e.g., diabetes is twice as common among women of color than in White women), you will not simply read that statement without critical thought but instead will return to our conceptual model to think about why and how this disparity may have occurred.

Aging and Diversity Online: Health Inequalities

NIH Centers for Population Health and Health Disparities. Established by NIH in 2003, these centers for population health and health disparities are designed to support research to understand and reduce differences in health outcomes, access, and care http://dccps.cancer.gov/populationhealthcenters/cphhd/index.html.

Racial and Ethnic Disparities in U.S. Health Care: A Chartbook. This chartbook was developed to serve as a resource to help a wide range of people understand the health disparities in their communities. One goal of the chartbook is to promote solutions to these disparities rather than simply acknowledging that they exist http://www.commonwealthfund.org/publications/publications_show.htm?doc_id=672908.

Conceptual Model to Explain Social Inequalities in Health   The conceptual model shown in Figure 5.2 is not meant to be used for theory testing, nor is it meant to be a comprehensive model of all of the factors that influence health. Rather, it is a conceptual framework to help us understand how several different factors—primarily gender, race/ethnicity, and socioeconomic status—can affect the intermediate variables (i.e., health behaviors, health care, psychosocial

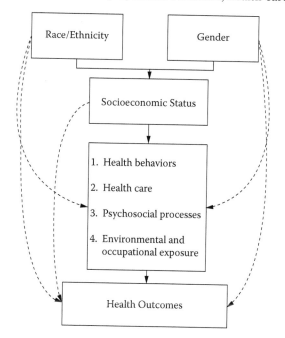

Figure 5.2   Conceptual framework for understanding social inequalities in health. Adapted from: House, Lantz, & Herd (2005).

processes, and environmental/occupational exposure), which in turn affect health outcomes. Certain important variables, like genetics, have been omitted from the model both for simplicity's sake and to maintain the focus on three variables of interest in this text: gender, race/ethnicity, and socioeconomic status (SES). This omission of genetics and other factors is not meant to imply that genetics and other factors do not affect health.

In this conceptual model, gender and race/ethnicity primarily affect SES. Gender and race/ethnicity can also directly affect the intermediate variables like health behaviors (given the differences in health beliefs described in Chapter 4) or exposure to environmental toxins (given that toxic sites are more likely to be located in ethnic minority communities). Note that House, Lantz, and Herd (2005) have argued that gender and race/ethnicity typically work through socioeconomic status. Both race/ethnicity and gender can affect the quality and level of education that one receives, the income that one earns, and the family wealth that might have been passed on. These are just a few examples of measures of SES. In turn, one's SES can affect the intermediate variables. Why do health behaviors differ depending on one's socioeconomic status? Knowledge of appropriate healthy behaviors and then access to those healthy behaviors is one possible explanation. For example, people with lower levels of education may not know the kinds of exercise (cardiovascular) that are important for promoting healthy blood sugar levels. Similarly, people with lower levels of education are less likely to live in areas where it is safe to exercise, or, due to the extended hours they must work to make ends meet, they may not have time to exercise. Similarly, access to and the quality of health care in the United States depends on one's SES. The intermediate variables listed here really serve as categories of variables. For example, health behaviors encompass all behaviors, healthy and unhealthy, that affect health. Health care includes both the quality of and access to care. Psychosocial processes include personality, stress, social support, and coping skills. Environmental and occupational exposure refers to the effects of the environment and of one's occupation on health. Finally, these intermediate variables affect one's health outcomes. Health outcomes encompass positive mental and physical health as well as morbidity (illness) and mortality (death).

To illustrate the use of the model, let us consider the chronic condition described earlier: diabetes. As seen in Figure 5.1, rates of diabetes differ between men and women, and African Americans, Asian Americans, and Pacific Islanders, Latinos, and American Indians are all more likely to die from diabetes than are Whites (Gorina, Hoyert, Lentzner, & Goulding, 2006). Why might these differences occur? Explanations range from racial/ethnic group differences in the biological or genetic predisposition to develop diabetes to differences in health-related behaviors. Given that we know that diabetes is related to people's health behaviors, one might be tempted to conclude that people from ethnic-minority groups should simply change their behavior and their diabetes' rates would decrease. This simplistic explanation ignores other variables that might affect diabetes rates, like SES. Access to the knowledge of appropriate healthy behaviors and access to affordable fruits and vegetables may be much more difficult for people living in low-income neighborhoods. Simply telling them to "eat better and exercise more" may not improve their health outcomes unless the root cause is addressed. For a chance to conduct your own detailed application of this model, complete the active learning experience that follows.

ACTIVE LEARNING EXPERIENCE: UNDERSTANDING HEALTH INEQUALITIES

The purpose of this experience is to help you examine possible routes through which one's socioeconomic status can affect health outcomes. Upon completion of this activity, you will be able to follow a hypothetical elder through our conceptual model and explain in specific ways how gender, ethnicity/race, and SES may influence health. Time required: 45 minutes (30 minutes to answer the questions and 15 minutes for discussion).

Instructions:

Imagine an elder from one of the diverse groups that we cover in this text (choosing the person's race/ethnicity and gender). Using Figure 5.2, complete the tasks listed next, and write your response to the questions.

1. Choose your diverse elder.
2. How do race/ethnicity and gender affect this person's socioeconomic factors?
3. What additional variables would you include in this model? What health outcomes would you see?
4. How does socioeconomic status influence health behaviors, health care, and environmental exposure? Give a specific example for each one of them.
5. How do these intermediate variables affect health outcomes? Give a specific example for each one.
6. Discuss your findings with at least one other person. Your instructor may want you to do this as part of a small-group exercise or as a class discussion.

Dementia as a Case Example   As described earlier, before turning to examine health inequalities in different illnesses, we use dementia as an example to examine how an element of diversity, race, or ethnic background can affect health. Our examination ranges from how beliefs about dementia, assessment, and treatment of dementia, and the services for people with dementia and their families are all affected by the older person's ethnic background.

Dementia Rates by Racial or Ethnic Background   One problem in assessing social inequalities of health is that often we do not have representative data from which to draw conclusions. The data on the risks of dementia for elders from diverse ethnic and racial backgrounds are no different. The studies are often drawn from community-based samples as there are no national data sets, so our ability to generalize to the population as a whole is compromised. Also, the age ranges, the measures, and the methods within each study vary, so comparison is difficult (Yeo, 2006). However, as we mentioned earlier, "existing studies suggest that there are differences in the frequency, causes, clinical phenomenology, treatment responsiveness, and caregiving factors across ethnic groups" (Longobardi et al., 2000, p. 139). By comparing prevalence rates in different countries, we can see whether dementia is likely to vary by racial or ethnic backgrounds. Indeed, prevalence rates between different countries range from 1% to 19%, which suggests that dementia may indeed vary by ethnicity. In comparison, remember the consistent 1% rate of schizophrenia across different cultures, which suggests that rates of schizophrenia do not vary by ethnic background.

When examining studies within the United States, again one must recognize limitations of the data. There are very few large-scale studies, and comparisons between studies are difficult because the types of dementia included in the study (e.g., vascular vs. AD) can differ (and sometimes go unspecified) and because the population included can differ with people from nursing home populations sometimes being omitted from a study (and sometimes because it is unclear whether the nursing home population was included). Given that nursing home rates differ by ethnic background (see Chapter 6 for more details), omission of the nursing home population from a dementia study would underestimate the rate of dementia in White populations. Thus, it would not be clear whether any differences in rates of dementia were true ethnic group differences or were due simply to the undercounting of White people with dementia.

Despite these limitations with the data, the studies that do examine dementia and ethnicity present a very intriguing picture that needs additional study. For example, there is evidence that some ethnic groups are at higher risk for different types of dementia. Many ethnic groups experience characteristics that put them at risk of developing dementia both more severely and at a younger age: lower income, poorer health, less access to health care. One consistent finding is that ethnic minority elderly have a higher rate of dementia caused by two or more conditions (mixed dementia). As cerebrovascular disease is more common in many ethnic minorities, this may result in higher rates of vascular dementia in ethnic minority elders than in White elders and in higher rates of AD in White elders than in ethnic minority elders (Longobardi et al., 2000). Some studies have also shown dramatically higher rates of dementia for African American and Hispanic populations compared with non-Hispanic Whites, but this association seems to be driven by educational differences in the ethnic groups (Gurland et al., 1997). Although potential reasons for why education might affect dementia have been proposed, no definitive answer is yet available (Yeo, 2006).

Research is just beginning to examine whether certain aspects of some cultures might function as a protective resource and which aspects might have more negative effects. For American Indians the prevalence of dementia is not known, but there is anecdotal evidence from clinicians who say it is rare with American Indians. One research study found that as degree of Cherokee ancestry increased, AD decreased, and another study found that AD was rare in the Canadian Cree (Yeo, 2006), although alcohol-related dementias occur at higher rates than in the general elderly population. Another possibility may be that dementia occurs in American Indian populations but that it is not labeled as a problem (John, 2004). Some research has found a lower incidence of Alzheimer's disease among less acculturated Japanese Americans: "Those with traditional Japanese lifestyles and/ or were exposed to the Japanese language as children have lower risks of experiencing cognitive decline" (Shibusawa, Lubben, & Kitano, 2001, p. 35). These limited findings about dementia in different ethnic groups offer an intriguing but incomplete picture.

Beliefs about Dementia   As we discussed in Chapter 4, health beliefs about illness affect one's health behavior. For some Chinese Americans, dementia symptoms may be interpreted as mental illness, which is considered shameful (Elliot, Di Minno, Lam, & Tu, 1996). Families may be reluctant to seek help for a family member who experiences dementia-related symptoms as they do not want to bring shame to the individual and to the family. Dementia symptoms also may be viewed as "normal aging," as an imbalance of yin and yang, or even as retributions for the sins of the family (Yau & Yeo, 2007). If dementia is considered part of normal aging, then no intervention is needed and the family simply must adapt, whereas if it is viewed as an imbalance, then restoring the balance through herbs or certain foods might be the treatment. In Vietnamese populations, dementia symptoms may also be viewed as "normal aging," or they may be viewed as the result of brain shrinkage, stroke, or spirit possession. For Latino Americans, dementia symptoms also have a wide range of both biomedical and folk explanations including stress, scattering of family, punishment from God, and witchcraft. African Americans have a similar range of explanations, with symptoms due to mental illness, God's will, alcohol abuse, and exposure to toxins (Yau & Yeo, 2007). There is some evidence that both physicians for and families of ethnically diverse patients respond differently to the disease. Ethnic minority families do not recognize early symptoms, perhaps attributing them to culturally defined "normal aging," but when they do turn to health-care professionals, physicians more frequently ignore patient and family complaints and less frequently offer evaluations, prescribe medications, and make referrals to services than with mainstream individuals (Allery et al., 2004).

Neuropsychological Assessment of Dementia and Diverse Elders   One of the difficulties associated with dementia has been determining whether an elder has dementia and what kind of dementia (e.g., vascular dementia, AD, drug-induced) the elder may have. There is no definitive test for dementia, but recent developments in the assessment of AD have improved to the extent that the disease can be diagnosed with accuracy, especially at major medical centers and research universities, even in the milder stages. Accurately identifying the type of dementia (e.g., vascular) is important for determining treatment. For example, if one is suffering from dementia induced by depression, then treatment of the depression is likely to improve the dementia. Difficulties abound with assessment of diverse elders. One problem is that education is related to performance on the neuropsychological tests. For example, less educated or illiterate people can score like brain-injured people and thus be incorrectly classified with a neurological disorder (Ardila, 1995). This has been shown to affect people with lower education levels and rural elderly such that their cognitive impairment could be overestimated using existing measures and norms (Longobardi et al., 2000). In addition, items have been found in common cognitive screening measures that are biased for low education and different ethnic groups (e.g., African American, Hispanic) (Teresi, Holmes, Ramirez, Gurland, & Lantigua, 2002). Another problem is that correct assessment often hinges on being able to assess cognitive function using language by asking the elder questions or by asking the elder to follow some simple instructions. For elders who speak little or no English, these language-based assessments may not be valid as they assume language familiarity. Symptoms also can differ by ethnic group. For example, the Geriatric Depression Scale, a commonly used assessment for depression, may be less valid for Latino and Asian American older people as they typically report symptoms (e.g., somatic symptoms) that are not emphasized in this screening tool (Baker & Espino, 1997). Basically, ethnic differences in rates of dementia could have to do with underlying genetic factors, environmental forces, or methodological problems with assessment (Larson & Imai, 1996). Determining the cause of these ethnic differences will be important to improve the treatment and well-being of diverse elders with dementia.

Aging and Diversity Online: Alzheimer's Association

Alzheimer's Association (AA). AA is a private organization dedicated to the treatment, elimination, and cure of AD. AA has been working to improve our knowledge of diverse elders and AD. Links for diverse groups are provided below.

Caring for Diverse Communities. This AA site provides links to the Diversity Toolbox, which contains resources for professionals and researchers who work with diverse communities. http://www.alz.org/professionals_and_researchers_11194.asp

Chinese Communities. These educational and outreach materials are designed to help researchers and professionals who work with the Chinese community. http://www.alz.org/professionals_and_researchers_chinese_communities.asp

Korean Communities. These educational and outreach materials are designed to help researchers and professionals who work with the Korean community. http://www.alz.org/professionals_and_researchers_korean_communities.asp

Latino Resources. This AA site focuses on AD in Latino communities. The information is available in English and Spanish. A slideshow version of the fotonovella is also available by clicking on "What's Happening to Grandpa." http://www.alz.org/espanol_latino_resources.asp

Additional Latino resources are available at http://www.alz.org/professionals_and_researchers_hispanic_latino_communities.asp

African Americans and AD. This AA site focuses on AD in African American communities. It gives details about dementia specific for African Americans and then provides links for pamphlets specially designed for this population. http://www.alz.org/living_with_alzheimers_african_americans.asp

Additional African American resources are available at http://www.alz.org/ professionals_and_researchers_african_american_communities.asp

Treatments for Dementia   The effects of drug treatments for dementia and AD have not been examined in different ethnic groups. There is some evidence for ethnic group differences in effects from some drugs. For example, African Americans, Hispanics, and Asians show adverse side effects from lower dosages of tricyclic antidepressants than do Whites (Silver, Poland, & Lin, 1993). These effects are not well understood and need additional study. Similarly, as noted earlier, the methods for managing behavioral symptoms of AD have not been adequately studied in diverse groups.

Services for People with Dementia and Their Caregivers   We conclude this section of dementia as a case example, by examining how services for people with dementia and their caregivers can be tailored for people from specific ethnic and racial backgrounds. When comparing themselves with people who are White, many people from ethnic minority backgrounds emphasize the essential role that taking care of their aging family members is for them. Putting a family member into a nursing home is unthinkable for them. But dementia can put tremendous strain on caregivers and their families, and providing a safe place for the person with dementia 24 hours a day, 7 days a week can be very difficult. Groups like the Alzheimer's Association (AA) have been working to help provide culturally appropriate services for these families. We briefly describe some different approaches here, and additional programs are discussed in detail in Chapter 6. For Chinese, Korean, and Japanese American communities, partnering with existing community agencies that already have a strong, trusting relationship with the specific ethnic group has been useful. Needed services can then be provided through these community agencies resulting in an effective strategy for reaching these communities (Yau & Yeo, 2007). Although providing any care outside of the family can be a difficult decision for members of these groups, having that care be provided from an agency within the community makes it more acceptable. Although traditionally support groups have not been heavily used by Asian American groups, after offering a series of educational programs, staff members were able to identify a core group of people who kept attending the programs and were able to form both Chinese and Vietnamese support groups (Yau & Yeo, 2007).

To reach Latino Americans, educational levels can be a real barrier. Some organizations simply translate materials into Spanish without paying attention to the educational level of those materials. In some Latino communities, the average number of years of formal education is 7, with many members who have never had any formal education (Yau & Yeo, 2007). Simply translating materials is not going to reach this population. AA has recently created a telenovella modeled after Spanish-language TV soap operas. A fotonovella booklet has also been created, and radio novellas for Spanish-language radio may be tried in the future. These innovative approaches provide information about dementia in an engaging manner that reflects cultural interests (Yau & Yeo, 2007). Given the important role played by churches in many African American communities, connections through pastors are often tried. Pocket-sized pamphlets have been created by the National Alzheimer's

Association with a special pamphlet for pastors to provide them information so that they can help their church members find needed services. For additional information regarding diversity and dementia, see the online sources listed in the Aging and Diversity Online section. We now turn to examine key elements of diversity and how they relate to social inequalities in health.

Socioeconomic Status and Health   One of the most consistent findings regarding health and diversity is that there is a strong relationship between health and SES. People who are poor, have less education, and are in lower-paying jobs tend to have worse health and lower longevity than do people who are wealthy, have higher education, and have more wealth (Stoller & Gibson, 2000). Initial research that examined the relationship between SES and health was cross-sectional. For example, it compared the health of people from different educational levels and found that people who had less education also had poorer health. Given the correlational nature of this research, the cause of this relationship was not clear. It is quite plausible that people with poor health were unable to complete higher levels of education due to their ill health or that a lack of education gave one poor health perhaps through numerous possible routes like having a limited knowledge of healthy behaviors. Identifying the cause of this relationship is key to improving people's health and well-being.

As we discussed in Chapter 2, to disentangle cohort, age, and time effects one needs to do simultaneous longitudinal and cross-sectional research. Cohort-sequential designs in which sequential birth cohorts are followed over time achieve this goal (Schaie & Willis, 2002). The Americans' Changing Lives (ACL) study is a longitudinal study of a nationally representative sample of adults measured in four waves that, so far, span 15 years, from 1986 to 2001. It was funded by the National Institute on Aging to examine the role that different factors, both psychosocial and behavioral, play in maintaining health and functioning from adulthood to later life (House, 2002). Although not initially funded to be a full cohort-sequential design, subsequent funding has allowed the continuation of the study. Initial analysis of cross-sectional data in the study confirms the long-supported view that socioeconomic factors, especially education and income, are related to health. The longitudinal nature of the study also allows examination of the causal path of this relationship. These investigators report that the health disparities found in different educational and income groups are due to SES and that somehow one's socioeconomic position affects one's "exposure to and experience of almost all variables or risk factors that shape health" (House et al., 2005, p. 24).

The ACL study also examines how these health disparities change as people age and over time. The investigators report that health differences are small in early adulthood, grow much larger in middle age and early older adulthood, and then decrease in the very old (House et al., 2005). This is important because one of our goals is to compress morbidity or to put off illness until the very end of life. This compression of morbidity involves maintaining the health and well-being of older adults such that they are healthy and active and can live life fully with declines in health coming only at the very end of life. Thus, the period of one's older adulthood in which one experiences health-related decline is put off into very old age. House and colleagues reported that the compression of morbidity is much greater for

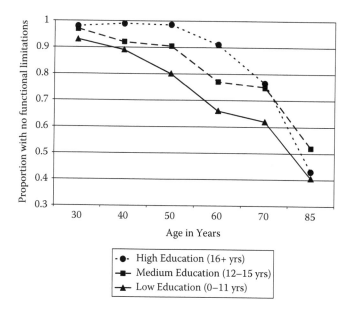

Figure 5.3 Functional limitations by age and education. Adapted from: House, Lantz, & Herd (2005).

people of higher SES. Figure 5.3 shows this relationship. For people with higher levels of education, the proportion with no functional limitations is high, with a slow curve down as people age. If we were to compress morbidity even further with this group, the proportion with no limitations would stay high across old age with a steep decline at the oldest ages. As we move from people with medium education to people with low education, it is evident that the proportion of people with no limitations more sharply decreases as people age, even in the young old. Thus, people with medium and low education demonstrate little compression of morbidity, as their health declines steadily as they age. It is only at the oldest ages that the effect of SES on health declines; the figure shows that the high education line actually crosses down to be between low and middle education. At the oldest ages, some groups that showed worse health than the mainstream group at younger ages sometimes have better health than the mainstream group. This is called the *crossover effect,* and we discuss it in some detail when we examine health inequalities in different racial and ethnic groups.

You may be wondering exactly how SES could affect health. House and colleagues (2005) developed a model to show possible pathways through which one's social class or SES could influence health. The conceptual model presented in Figure 5.2 is a simplification of House's model. House and colleagues argued that one's socioeconomic position is a "fundamental cause" that "shapes people's exposure to and experience of almost all risk factors for health" (p. 17). Although there are small direct effects of race/ethnicity, gender, and SES on health. For example, education and income shape one's access to insurance, utilization of medical care, health behaviors, social support, and stress. Exposure to physical environmental hazards is also affected by education and income as is exposure to more social environmental hazards like lack of safety at work and home.

Although the relationship between SES and health is very strong, it is also important to note that one's economic status does not fully explain the ethnic/racial health disparities presented later in this chapter. For example, as we discuss in more detail in the following section, at almost every level of education Blacks die at a younger age than Whites (Williams, 2004). In statistical terms, we would say that both SES and race are related to health and that one does not fully explain the other.

Gender and Illness   Although women tend to live longer than men, they also suffer from more chronic (or long-term) health conditions than men (Rieker & Bird, 2005). So, women's longer years may be filled with health problems. Gender differences in health are complicated, and the causes for many of these differences are not well understood. For example, on the one hand, men and women have the same three leading age-adjusted causes of death (i.e., heart disease, cancer, and stroke), but there are also substantial gender differences. Men "have more life-threatening chronic diseases at younger ages, including coronary heart disease, cancer, cerebrovascular disease, emphysema, cirrhosis of the liver, kidney disease, and atherosclerosis. In contrast, women face higher rates of chronic debilitating disorders such as autoimmune diseases and rheumatologic disorders as well as less life-threatening diseases such as anemia, thyroid conditions, gall bladder conditions, migraines, arthritis, and eczema" (Rieker & Bird, 2005, p. 40). Cardiovascular disease is often stereotyped to affect men more than women, but more women ultimately die from it "because of their greater life expectancy, the older age at onset, and the range of cardiovascular disease risk factors associated with aging" (Rieker & Bird, 2005, p. 41). So, although we often worry about men having heart attacks (and we should as the prevalence and age-adjusted death rate is greater for men compared with women), we may neglect to consider women's lifelong risk of cardiovascular disease and then fail to promote behaviors that might prevent cardiovascular disease in women.

Within specific ethnic groups, sometimes striking gender differences can exist. For example, the proportion of American Indian male elders who have emphysema is almost three times greater than for American Indian female elders and the proportion of American Indian male elders with cancer is twice that of female elders (John, 2004). We now turn to examine how the race or ethnicity of elders is related to illness.

Race/Ethnicity and Illness

Overview   As we turn to examine health inequalities within each ethnic group, it may be helpful to begin with an overview. In general, Black elders have the worst health of the five major ethnic groups. American Indians and Alaska Natives are also less healthy than other groups (except for Blacks). Given their risk factors, Hispanic or Latino elders are surprisingly healthy—often healthier than Whites—and Asian American elders are healthier than any other ethnic group (Bulatao & Anderson, 2004). These health disparities can help indicate where our society is failing specific groups, can suggest groups and illnesses for which we should target health interventions, and can also provide healthy aging models from which we can glean suggestions for improving the health of all elders.

African Americans As with other ethnic groups, remembering the life experiences of current Black elders is very important to understanding their current health status. They have experienced racial segregation, educational segregation, low SES, and little access to health care (Rooks & Whitfield, 2004). Given our earlier discussion of SES and health, it is important to remember that African Americans in particular have lower SES throughout life and experience barriers to care and problems in the doctor–patient relationship and that African American patient distrust of the medical profession may be high. Chronic disease rates are higher for African Americans than Whites, and African Americans also have higher rates of disability and lower rates of immunizations. When examining specific conditions, African Americans have higher rates of diabetes, cardiovascular disease, and stroke (Land & Yang, 2006); thus, these conditions are of particular importance for African American elders.

Sometimes the lay understanding of health issues can interfere with treatment (Stoller & Gibson, 2000), and this can occur for some Black elders around the issue of hypertension. A study of lay understandings of hypertension among low-income elderly Black women found that the mainstream medical condition that indicates risk of cardiovascular disease, hypertension, was at risk for being confused with two folk illnesses, "high-pertension," and "high blood" (Heurtin-Roberts, 1993, as described in Stoller & Gibson, 2000). "High-pertension" was described as a disease of the nerves, and high blood is said to occur when hot, thick, or rich blood rises up in the body and is thought to be caused by eating salty, highly seasoned, or greasy foods but can be worsened by other things like heat or stress. If an elder is prescribed medication or exercise to improve hypertension but she thinks she is being treated for "high-pertension" or high blood, it is easy to imagine how her trust in the doctor may be affected when her symptoms from those illnesses are unaffected by the medication or exercise—yet her doctor may insist that she continue with the treatment.

Aging and Diversity Online: African American Health

International Society on Hypertension in Blacks (ISHIB). This unique, nonprofit, professional, medical membership society's mission is to improve the health and life expectancy of ethnic minority populations around the world. They target both African Americans and other underserved populations. The journal *Ethnicity and Disease* is the official, peer-reviewed publication of the ISHIB. http://www.ishib.org/index.asp

Black Health Care. This organization provides health and medical information to address health needs of African Americans http://www.blackhealthcare.com.

African American Health Network. This group provides information on health, cultural, and culinary-related issues for African Americans. http://www.aahn.com/old

---

Asian Americans and Pacific Islanders When one aggregates all Asian Americans into one group, elder illness rates are often lower than rates for White Americans. But this aggregate ignores the serious health differences that occur in specific Asian groups, and it overlooks the health problems that occur in all of the Asian American groups. For example, although elder Japanese Americans tend to be educated and middle class and to have many better health outcomes compared with White elders, they still suffer from substantially higher rates of cardiovascular disease than elders in Japan. Researchers think that this may be the result of a more sedentary lifestyle in the United States with a diet higher in animal fat (Shibusawa et al., 2001). Examination of these within-ethnic group differences could help identify health-related behaviors that would promote longevity in all groups.

The "model minority" stereotype that depicts people of Asian heritage as experiencing tremendous success in the United States ignores the fact that many groups within the Asian and Pacific Islander category experience, for example, poverty, high unemployment, and limited educational opportunities. This is especially true for more recent immigrants such as the Vietnamese and Hmong populations and for the Native Hawaiian and other Pacific Islander populations. For Native Hawaiian and other Pacific Islanders, there are significant disparities between their health and that of the mainstream White population. Diabetes is a much larger problem, and a large proportion of the population is overweight. One factor that is especially important for Native Hawaiian and other Pacific Islander elders is language: "English is not the first language of 43.3% of NHPI [Native Hawaiian and other Pacific Islander] elders, compared with 12.6% of elders in general population" (Braun, Yee, Browne, & Mokuau, 2004). As discussed in Chapter 4, effective communication between health-care providers and patients can result in improved understanding for both the provider and the patient. Accurate understanding of the health problem and of the treatment plan is critical for health promotion and treating illness. Thus, to the extent that language differences create a barrier to understanding, these differences could be important.

Aging and Diversity Online: Asian American and Pacific Islander Health

Selected Patient Information Resources in Asian Languages (SPIRAL). This website provides resource information for working with Asian elders with limited English. http://spiral.tufts.edu

Asian American & Pacific Islander Health Forum. This website provides health information that is particularly relevant for this population. http://www.apiahf.org

Association of Asian Pacific Community Health Organizations (AAPCHO). Provides access to information on medically underserved Asian Americans, Native Hawaiians, and Pacific Islanders, their health issues, and the community health centers that serve them. http://www.aapcho.org/site/aapcho

Latino Elders   Given the strong relationship between socioeconomic status and health, one would expect Hispanic elders to be at high risk for poor health: 47% live below or near the poverty level; education rates are lower than other ethnic groups; and although many Latino elders are eligible for federal programs like Medicare and Medicaid, these health-care benefits may come after a lifetime of little to no health insurance. Other Latino elders may not be eligible for federal programs due to their immigration status. Culturally, they may have fatalistic attitudes toward health—in one study, 26% of elderly Mexican Americans thought that "nothing could be done to make heart disease better once a person was diagnosed" (Du Bois, Yavno, & Stanford, 2001, p. 79). But actually, given all of their risk factors, people of Hispanic or Latino heritage are surprisingly healthy and live longer lives than Whites. For Hispanic or Latino elders, primary health concerns are diabetes (twice as frequent as Whites), hypertension and cardiovascular disease, and growing rates of cancer (Du Bois, Yavno, & Stanford, 2001). They are also likely to have conditions that predispose them to cardiovascular disease: diabetes, obesity, and hypertension. They have higher levels of disability compared with other ethnic groups.

Although immigration to the United States can result in some indicators of improved health (e.g., lower rates of adult and infant mortality compared with people who stayed in their country), as one acculturates and adopts the mainstream U.S. lifestyle, the earlier immigrant health advantage declines over time (Williams, 2005). Acculturation can bring increases in a sedentary lifestyle, foods high in saturated fat, smoking, and alcohol consumption, which can in turn result in poor health outcomes and increases in chronic health conditions. Determining ways to maintain the native culture's healthy behaviors when people move to the United States is very important.

Aging and Diversity Online: Latino Health

The Center for the Study of Latino Health and Culture. This center at the University of California–Los Angeles (UCLA) provides expertise regarding the health and well-being of people of Latino heritage. http://www.cesla.med.ucla.edu

---

American Indians   In the past 30 years, American Indians have experienced tremendous improvements in life expectancy at birth as factors that affect mortality in infancy, adolescence, and young adulthood have started to be addressed. Programs to improve maternal and child health have been successful such that death from acute and infectious diseases has decreased whereas death due to chronic and degenerative diseases has increased. American Indian elders represent a very small proportion of the ethnic minority elder population (less than 1% in 2000) (Angel & Hogan, 2004), but they have striking health disparities compared with White Americans in spite of their recent health improvements.

American Indians differ from most other groups in the United States in that they have a separate health-care system, the Indian Health Service (IHS), which is responsible for providing for their health care. The IHS is an agency within the U.S. Department of Health and Human Services that provides free health care for approximately 1.6 million tribally enrolled American Indians. Dwyer (2000) states that the IHS "is considered by many to be the oldest health maintenance organization in the country—and the most overburdened and under funded" (p. 92). The IHS manages "37 hospitals, 64 health centers, fifty health stations, 34 urban Indian health projects, and five school health centers" (Dwyer, 2000, p. 92). In the last 25 years, American Indians have gained some control in the health care that they receive as they are working to develop their own tribe-specific sources of health care. Local control by individual tribes has occurred, and this can result in more culturally appropriate care for the tribe members. Unfortunately, this can also have an unintended side effect as data gathering on the health of the tribal members may not be a high priority for the tribes. Of course, these data are essential for determining the health status of the people and for demonstrating continuing disparities in health and health care for American Indians (John, 2004). Thus, moving to care provided by the tribe may provide more culturally appropriate care but may lead to less tracking of the health status of this population.

American Indians have high rates of diabetes, much higher than among the general U.S. population. They also have high rates of arthritis (Dwyer, 2000). Disability is more of a problem for American Indians, so although the oldest old may live longer than older Whites, they have a lowered *active* life expectancy. It also may be that looking at single factors of health obscures the issue that ethnic elders may have more conditions in one person than do White elders. Comparing the number of American Indian elders with more than one illness or examining "multimorbidity" across ethnic groups would provide a better indication of health inequalities. John (2004) provided some preliminary evidence for health inequalities in multimorbidity: American Indian elders experience increased multimorbidity compared with other ethnic groups.

Some descriptive statistics may aid in understanding the characteristics of American Indian elders. Approximately 25% of American Indian elders live on reservations, 40% receive social security, less than 50% receive Medicare, and less than 40% receive Medicaid (Polacca, 2001). Those who live off reservation find it difficult to get access to health care through the IHS or to obtain their Medicare and Medicaid benefits. From John (2004), we summarize that Native Americans don't have access to the same range of services as the general population and that access is still a problem for both rural and urban American Indians. Second, they don't use services at the same level or in the same way. Third, the quality of care available to the general older population is not available to many American Indian elders. Fourth, American Indian elders may experience discrimination due to ethnicity or social class when outside the IHS.

For American Indians, the top three causes of death are heart disease, cancer, and diabetes. Given that smoking, diet, and alcohol consumption influence these illnesses, death from these causes could be greatly reduced with "culturally appropriate prevention programs and wellness education" (John, 2004, p. 33). Trying to create culturally appropriate interventions to reduce morbidity among American Indians is made more difficult by tribal and regional differences.

Aging and Diversity Online: American Indian Health

Indian Health Service (IHS). This agency within the U.S. Department of Health and Human Services is responsible for providing health services to members of federally recognized American Indian and Alaskan Native tribes. http://www.ihs.gov

National Indian Council on Aging (NICOA). NICOA "was founded in 1976 by members of the National Tribal Chairmen's Association that called for a national organization to advocate for improved, comprehensive health and social services to American Indian and Alaska Native Elders." http://www.nicoa.org

National Resource Center on Native American Aging. This national resource center is housed within the Center for Rural Health at University of North Dakota. Its purpose is to improve quality of life and delivery of related support services for American Indian, Alaska Native, and Native Hawaiian elders. http://ruralhealth.und.edu/projects/nrcnaa

American Indian and Alaska Native Programs (AIANP). The purpose of these programs is to promote the health and well-being of American Indians and Alaska natives of all ages through research training and continuing education. http://www.uchsc.edu/ai/index.htm

Native American Elders Health Care Series. The SHARE Project. Developed in collaboration with Native American nurses and care providers, this online program was developed to promote culturally competent care for Native American elders. This program was designed for nurses and nursing students, but anyone who is interested in providing services for Native American people would benefit from the program. http://learn.sdstate.edu/share

The Center for American Indian/Indigenous Research and Education (CAIIRE). CAIIRE is located in the School of Nursing at UCLA. Its goal is to "improve the status of Native peoples by promoting, developing, and evaluating culturally appropriate health, education, and social programs." http://www.nursing.ucla.edu/CAIRE

Rural Issues in Health and Illness The U.S. Bureau of the Census defines rural residents as people who live outside urban areas in places with a population of less than 2,500. Few elders live on farms (2%). As youth leave the rural areas, things get more difficult for the rural elderly. Krout found that rural elderly have lower education, income, health, housing, and access to services (as cited in Scott, 2001).

When examining research regarding rural elders, it is important that one be aware of how the researcher defined the concept of *rural*. Differing definitions may give rise to seemingly inconsistent findings regarding the health status of rural elders. As mentioned previously, the sparsely populated large distances that define rural areas create the most important rural health issue: access. Rural elders have more difficulty in getting access to health care than do urban elders. Disparities between urban and rural elders can occur at a very basic level in that rural elders may die because they cannot get to a hospital quickly. These basic access issues include access to pharmaceuticals and access to health information technology in rural areas (National Advisory Committee on Rural Health and Human Services, 2006).

Thorson and Powell (1993) studied urban and rural elders in Nebraska. Comparing 196 randomly selected elders from Douglas County (including Omaha) and 200 elders residing in the rural counties in the sand hills of western Nebraska, these researchers found that their rural interview respondents, while on average 5 years older than their urban participants, reported less illness and briefer stays in the hospital. Two thirds of both samples viewed their health as excellent or good, and fewer than 1% indicated delays in securing health-care services. Most of the rural counties included in this study had "no resident physician, hospital, or health department" (Thorson & Powell, 1993, p. 141). There were some important demographic differences between the urban and rural respondents, with the urban respondents being younger (73.8 years vs. 76.6 years) and more likely to be married (55% vs. 47.5%). There was minority representation (7%), but there were no minority rural participants. Additional information on rural health is available in the Aging and Diversity Online Section.

Aging and Diversity Online: Rural Health

American Psychological Association (APA). APA has developed a committee on rural health. http://www.apa.org/rural

Agency for Health Care Research and Quality (AHRQ). AHRQ has a focus on rural health. http://www.ahrq.gov/research/ruralix.htm

National Rural Health Association (NRHA). NRHA has promoted leadership, communication, education, research, and advocacy for rural health since 1978. http://www.ruralhealthweb.org

National Rural Behavioral Health Center at the University of Florida (NRBHC). The NRBHC houses a team of behavioral health scientists, educators, scholars, and practitioners dedicated to improving the health care status of rural Americans." http://www.nrbhc.phhp.ufl.edu/

The University of Montana Rural Institute. This center for excellence in disability education, research, and service was responsible for creating the American Indian Choices project previously described. In addition to its work with Native American populations, the institute promotes the "full participation in community life by rural Americans of all ages." http://ruralinstitute.umt.edu

---

Sexual Orientation and Health Issues   Lesbian and gay elders, although not typically economically deprived, suffer from difficulties with health care, medical neglect, and social services as a result of discrimination due to their sexual orientation. The health-care system is very heterosexist, with the default questions that everyone is asked often pertaining primarily to heterosexuals (e.g., "Are you married? Do you have children?"). Both lesbians and gay men avoid interactions with the health-care system such that they seek care only at later stages of an illness. This means that they miss regular screening and are at risk for many diseases that could be treated if caught early (Claes & Moore, 2001). Most LGBT community groups have focused on the social, political, and health needs of younger people, but recently groups like Rainbow Gardens and Senior Action in a Gay Environment (SAGE) have focused on meeting the needs of LGBT elders (Claes & Moore, 2001).

Aging and Diversity Online: LGBT Health and Well-Being

Senior Action in a Gay Environment (SAGE). This organization works to meet the unique needs of LGBT elders. http://www.sageusa.org/index.cfm
Rainbow Gardens. This group develops assisted living services for older lesbians and gay men and for their families and friends. http://www.rainbow-gardens.com/index.htm

GRIOT Circle. This is an intergenerational and culturally diverse community-based organization that works to improve the lives of older LGBT persons, especially people of color. GRIOT stands for Gay Reunion in Our Time but also is the word for a storyteller in Western Africa who continues the oral tradition and history of a village. http://www.griotcircle.org

The Gay and Lesbian Association of Retired Persons (GLARP). GLARP is a "US-based non-profit corporation dedicated to encourage gay and lesbian individuals and businesses to give financially, and of their time and talent, to enhance the aging experience of all retiring gay men and lesbians in exchange for tax and other benefits." http://www.gaylesbianretiring.org

---

Mental Health Inequalities

As we mentioned earlier in the chapter, comparison of the prevalence of mental illness between different groups is very difficult. Based on smaller studies, the Office of the U.S. Surgeon General tentatively determined that the *prevalence* or occurrence of mental disorders for racial and ethnic minorities living in the community does not differ from that of Whites (U.S. Department of Health & Human Services, 2001). Even though the overall prevalence of mental disorders does not differ by race, there still may be mental health inequalities that occur across diverse groups. Obtaining a clear picture of the mental health status of diverse group members is very difficult for several reasons. The prevalence of mental illness is higher in some high-risk subgroups, such as people who are homeless, incarcerated, or institutionalized. And some minority subgroups are overrepresented in these subgroups. People in these high-risk subgroups are very difficult to include in population-based studies. Thus, although the initial research suggests that prevalence rates are the same across groups, some underlying mental health inequalities may be hidden due to difficulties accessing certain populations. In addition, for minority elders stressful events caused by racism and discrimination can also adversely affect mental and physical health.

There has been limited comprehensive research on mental illness in different racial and ethnic groups. Research that focuses on diverse *elders* is even more limited. The surgeon general found that the following disparities in mental health care occur for racial and ethnic minorities in general (U.S. Department of Health & Human Services, 2001):

- Minorities have less access to, and availability of, mental health services.
- Minorities are less likely to receive needed mental health services.
- Minorities in treatment often receive a poorer quality of mental health care.
- Minorities are underrepresented in mental health research.

Minority group members are less likely to seek mental health help and, if they do seek help, are less likely to seek it from a mental health professional, turning instead to primary care physicians, clergy (especially African Americans), traditional healers (especially American Indian and Native Alaskans), and family and friends (U.S. Department of Health & Human Services, 2001). All Americans face difficulties in access to mental health services due to the "cost, fragmentation of services, lack of availability of services, and societal stigma toward mental illness," but racial and ethnic minorities face additional barriers: "mistrust and fear of treatment, racism and discrimination, and differences in language and communication" (U.S. Department of Health & Human Services, 2001). Communication barriers are especially important for mental health because the diagnosis and treatment of mental health issues depend on the communication that occurs between client and clinician. In addition to these barriers to mental health care, the report found that racial and ethnic minorities also experience greater disability from mental illness than do Whites. This higher disability is likely the result of receiving "less care and poorer quality of care, rather than from their illnesses being inherently more severe or prevalent in the community" (U.S. Department of Health & Human Services, 2001).

There is also evidence of misdiagnosis for disorders like schizophrenia and mood disorders for ethnic or racial minorities (U.S. Department of Health & Human Services, 2001). One study of 134,523 mentally ill patients in the Veterans Affairs (VA) mental health registry determined that Blacks were more than four times as likely and Hispanics were more than three times as likely as Whites to be diagnosed with schizophrenia (Blow et al., 2004). Given that the prevalence for schizophrenia is the same worldwide, this difference in diagnosis suggests that people of color are being incorrectly diagnosed with the disorder. Some researchers and clinicians argue that many incorrect diagnoses are due to misinterpretations of cultural cues. For example, schizophrenia is characterized by social withdrawal; lack of eye contact can signify this in mainstream U.S. cultures, but in Hispanic culture lack of eye contact can be seen as a sign of respect. Training in cultural competence may help reduce these misdiagnoses and then get people the help they need. Clinicians who have competence in a particular culture have often changed patients' incorrect schizophrenia diagnoses to reflect their depression. Correct treatment depends on the correct diagnosis. Similarly, blind adherence to the medical model in treating mental illness solely with medications can ignore the strengths that can come from other cultures. For example, people with schizophrenia in less industrialized, poorer countries are more likely to be socially connected and employed, are less likely to relapse, and have longer healthy periods between relapses than people with schizophrenia in the United States (Vedantam, 2005b).

Asian American and Pacific Islanders

For Asian Americans and Pacific Islanders, barriers due to language, lack of insurance, stigma, and shame deter use of mental health services. The stigma associated with mental illness is present in many cultures, but it may be particularly salient for some ethnic groups. Zhang, Snowden, and Sue (1998) found differences in their willingness to seek help from others between Asian Americans and White Americans living in Los Angeles. Only 12% of Asians would mention their mental health problems to a friend or relative compared with 25% of Whites; 4% would seek help from a psychiatrist or specialist (26% of Whites); and 3% would seek help from a physician (13% of Whites). For Chinese Americans, research suggests that despite rates of depression that are at least as high as Whites (and perhaps higher), they are less likely to be identified as having depression by health providers and so then are less likely to receive treatment (Wong, 2001). Some research has also found that Chinese have higher rates of suicide than Whites, with more elderly Chinese American immigrants committing suicide than native-born Chinese. Chinese American women have 10 times the rate of suicide as White women (Wong, 2001). Japanese Americans are also reluctant to seek mental health services due to the shame associated with mental illness. They postpone service use until there is a crisis and so are more likely to use psychiatric emergency services (Shibusawa et al., 2001). This means that elders who are depressed or who have dementia are prevented from getting early treatment. There are higher rates of suicide among older (over 75) Japanese Americans compared with Whites (Baker, 1994). There is also evidence for somatization of mental health symptoms among Asian Americans. Some sources suggest that somatization is a contextual factor and that in some settings (e.g., with a mental-health-care provider) Asians will express somatic symptoms whereas with close friends or family they may show depressive symptoms (U.S. Department of Health & Human Services, 2001). For Pacific Islanders, there is also very limited mental health information. Similar to American Indians, they do not view the mental and physical health issues as distinct. In Native Hawaiian, the general word for "trouble" (*pilikia*) is used to describe a psychological problem (Braun et al., 2004). The surgeon general's report also cautions about making generalizations based on the limited findings about older Asian Americans' mental health. Often participants for these studies have not been randomly selected and are instead recruited through Asian American senior organizations. It is not clear whether these findings can be generalized to older adults not participating in organizations for seniors (U.S. Department of Health & Human Services, 2001).

Latinos   As with most ethnic groups, few comprehensive studies have examined the mental health status of older Hispanic American adults. The studies that do exist suggest that depression in Hispanics may be related to poor health. Older Hispanic adults who have physical conditions may be at risk for developing depression (U.S. Department of Health & Human Services, 2001). One study of Los Angeles area older Hispanics found that more than 26% had major depression or dysphoria. Depression for these Latinos was related to physical health, with only 5% of those without physical conditions reporting depression (Kemp, Staples, & Lopez-Aqueres, 1987). Additional evidence suggests that more acculturated Latinos are at risk for mental disorders. People of Mexican descent who were born in the United States are at a greater risk of developing depression and anxiety or of abusing drugs than more recent Mexican immigrants (Vedantam, 2005a).

African Americans   Little is known about the prevalence of mental illness and the rates of service use among older African Americans (U.S. Department of Health & Human Services, 2001). Some studies have found that the need for mental health services for community-dwelling African Americans does not differ from Whites, but African Americans have less access to mental health services due to their lack of health insurance. Also, African Americans are overrepresented in noncommunity dwelling groups, and it can be difficult to generalize from community household surveys as they miss African Americans who are in more high-risk settings, for example those who are in shelters, are homeless, or are incarcerated. However, one study found that older African American adults often do not get the care they need. A study of older African American public-housing residents determined that 47% of residents who needed mental health care had not received it (Black et al., 1998).

American Indians and Alaska Natives   For American Indians and Alaska Natives, mind and body are considered to be one, so the separation of mental and physical health does not fit culturally for them. They also somaticize mental health problems, so when one is out of balance, it is reasonable for symptoms to occur within the body (John, 2004). There are poor research data given the heterogeneous groups and small size of the population, but it is clear they have mental health needs, that availability of services is limited by the rural nature of many communities, and that there are fewer mental health providers in rural areas. Depression among American Indians is very prevalent, but its cause and symptoms are not fully understood. Suicide is relatively low for older American Indians (U.S. Department of Health & Human Services, 2001).

SES, Gender, and Sexual Orientation   Thus far, we have discussed mental health issues that face all seniors and have examined how that differs by race or ethnicity, but other aspects of diversity are related to mental illness as well. For example, people with lower SES are two to three times more likely than those of higher SES to have a mental illness. Interestingly, men and women's overall mental health is similar, but there are gender differences in certain conditions. For example, women are more likely than men to experience depression, although once depression develops, the course of depression is similar for men and women (Rieker & Bird, 2005). Women are also more likely to experience anxiety disorders than men. Men, on the other hand, are more likely than women to have substance abuse problems, to exhibit antisocial behavior, and to commit suicide (Kessler, Barker, et al., 2003; Kessler, Berglund, et al., 2003). "The suicide rate is higher for older white men than for any other group, including teenagers" (Gorina et al., 2006, p. 8). For some, health status is also related to mental health. Research indicates that depression is a complication for people with diabetes. To see whether rural elders of different ethnic groups with diabetes also suffered from depression, Bell and colleagues (2005) found that older rural elders were at risk for depression regardless of their ethnicity (African American, Native American, and White). Although there has been relatively limited research on older LGBT persons, research thus far has found that prevalence rates for mental health difficulties do not differ between older LGBT persons and older heterosexual persons (Hunter,

2005). No differences in depression or social isolation have been found, although heterosexual individuals tend to derive more support from family whereas LGBT individuals derive more support from friends (Hunter, 2005).

ACTIVE LEARNING EXPERIENCE: MENTAL HEALTH AND DIVERSE ELDERS

The purpose of this experience is to integrate your knowledge of elders' mental health issues with the inequalities that are faced by elders from diverse groups. You will consider (1) how mental health care services may be affected by elements of diversity, and (2) what steps could be taken to improve access to mental health care for elders from diverse groups. Time required: 45 minutes (30 minutes to answer the questions and 15 minutes for discussion).

Instructions:

1. Consider the mental health of older adults. What are barriers that may prevent them from access to mental health care?
2. Consider key elements of diversity. What are additional barriers that older people from diverse groups may face regarding mental health issues?
3. What concrete steps could be taken to remove (or at least lessen) the barriers that you have described?
4. Discuss your findings with at least one other person.

MORTALITY AND DIVERSITY

At first it may seem strange to focus on mortality in a chapter on health, but one of the primary ways to determine whether health differences (or disparities) exist is to examine "what do people die from?" and "at what age do they die?" We can then group people according to key elements of diversity—by gender, by race/ethnicity, and by social class—and to determine whether different groups tend to die earlier than others or whether different groups tend to die of different causes. Mortality statistics also show us how health changes over time. In 1900, the three leading causes of death were influenza/pneumonia, tuberculosis, and diarrhea/enteritis. In the year 2002, heart diseases, cancer, and stroke were the top three. Chronic diseases are now the leading cause of death (Gorina et al., 2006). When we look across different racial and ethnic groups, there is both significant overlap and differences in leading causes of death (Figure 5.4). As an example of the overlap, among people aged 65 years and older, heart disease and cancer were the top two causes of death for all racial and ethnic groups. We can begin to see differences when we note that stroke was the third leading cause for all but American Indians, and chronic lower respiratory diseases were the fourth leading cause of death only for Whites. Diabetes mortality illustrates additional differences as it was the third leading cause of death for American Indians, the fourth leading cause of death for

Cause of Death	All		White		Black		American Indian		Asian and Pacific Islander		Hispanic	
	Percent all deaths	Rank	Percent all deaths	Rank	Percent all deaths	Rank	Percent all deaths	Rank	Percent all deaths	Rank	Percent all deaths	Rank
Heart Disease	31.8	1	31.8	1	32.0	1	27.4	1	30.7	1	32.4	1
Cancer	21.6	2	21.5	2	22.7	2	20.6	2	22.9	2	21.0	2
Stroke	7.9	3	7.8	3	8.3	3	6.7	3	10.9	3	7.4	3
Chronic lower respiratory diseases	6.0	4	6.3	4	3.4	4	5.8	5	3.9	6	3.9	5
Influenza and pneumonia	3.2	5	3.3	6	2.7	6	3.6	7	4.1	5	3.5	6
Alzheimer's disease	3.2	6	3.4	5	2.0	5	1.9	9	1.3	10	2.2	7
Diabetes	3.0	7	2.8	7	5.0	7	7.3	4	4.1	4	6.3	4
Nephritis, nephrotic syndrome, and nephrosis	1.9	8	1.8	9	3.1	9	2.2	6	2.0	8	2.0	8
Accidents	1.9	9	1.9	8	*	8	2.8	*	2.3	7	1.9	9
Septicemia	1.5	10	1.4	10	2.5	10	1.9	8	*	10	*	*

Figure 5.4 Leading causes of death for persons ages 65 years and older by race—Hispanic origin, 2002. (Gorina, Hoyert, Lentzner, & Goulding, (2006). *Note:* ° indicates not in top 10 for that group.

Blacks, Asian and Pacific Islanders, and Hispanic or Latino elders, but only the seventh leading cause of death for Whites.

Race/Ethnicity and Mortality

As you can see from Table 5.1, mortality rates do differ by ethnicity, but focusing on an overall age-adjusted mortality rate can ignore striking disparities that occur between different ethnic groups across the lifespan. For example, consider Black mortality rates. Blacks have an overall mortality rate from birth to 84 years of age that is higher than all other ethnic groups. But after age 84, their mortality rate is actually lower than Whites (Table 5.1). This change from having a higher death rate than Whites to having a lower one has been called a *crossover effect*. Although there is some debate about whether crossover effects reflect actual group differences or are merely statistical artifacts due to data error, these effects are often found in the data. For example, in Table 5.1 American Indians show higher mortality rates than whites until the age of 74, and then they have lower mortality rates than Whites. Why might these crossover effects occur? Some researchers suggest that higher mortality at younger ages results in a survival of only the very fittest such that the people from minority groups who manage to live to an advanced age are hardier than mainstream group members and thus live longer.

Mortality rates for Asian Americans and Pacific Islanders help make the argument that it is inappropriate to report all of these groups as one large group. As an aggregate, Asian Americans have higher life expectancy and lower rates of mortality from most causes of death than do other racial and ethnic groups. But if one

TABLE 5.1   Overall Age-Adjusted Mortality Rates for 1998–2000[a] and Age-Specific Death Rates for 2000[b] for Whites and Minority/White Rates

Age (years)	Non-Hispanic White Rate	Black/White Ratio	AmInd/White Ratio	API/White Ratio	Hispanic/White Ratio
All Ages	85.5	1.3	0.9	0.6	0.8
1–4	2.79	2.0	2.0	0.7	1.0
5–14	1.72	1.5	1.0	0.5	1.0
15–24	7.21	1.9	1.7	0.6	1.3
25–34	9.26	2.2	1.8	0.6	1.1
35–44	17.97	2.1	1.7	0.5	0.9
45–54	39.31	2.1	1.3	0.5	0.8
55–64	96.00	1.8	1.2	0.6	0.8
65–74	240.94	1.4	1.0	0.6	0.7
75–84	572.87	1.2	0.7	0.6	0.6
85+	1582.64	0.9	0.4	0.6	0.6

Notes: Rates per 10,000 population. (AmInd–American Indian. API–Asian and Pacific Islander.)
[a] National Center for Health Statistics (2003).
[b] National Center for Health Statistics (2004).
Source: From Williams (2004).

considers Pacific Islanders alone, then they have a lower life expectancy and higher rates of mortality from most causes of death.

American Indians have higher rates of death for 6 of the 10 leading causes of death in the United States. There are especially high rates of death from diabetes (2.9 times higher rate than Whites), chronic liver disease and cirrhosis (2.4 times higher rate), and nephritis, nephritic syndrome, and nephrosis (1.6 times higher rate), which are terms used to describe diseases of the kidney that can be caused by kidney disease or as a complication from another disorder like diabetes. Mortality data for Native Americans are especially suspect due to problems in mortality data. Mortality data are collected from death certificates, and often the person filling out the death certificate may not know the person's ethnic background or age or may not have a good understanding of the person's medical history. This can result in misclassification of cause of death, misidentifying race of person, and inaccurate age of death reports. These errors are especially prevalent for American Indians. After the age of 75, American Indians have a somewhat better life expectancy than White Americans, with American Indian women living longer than American Indian men. Thus, there is some evidence of a mortality crossover effect, but there is also concern that this is simply an artificial data artifact due to small numbers of the population and errors in data reporting (John, 2004).

Mortality and Socioeconomic Status

Mortality rates differ not only by ethnicity but also by SES. People who have lower levels of education, lower income, and fewer resources tend to die younger than people with more education, income, and resources. But both ethnicity and SES are independently related to longevity. Given that Whites tend to have higher socioeconomic levels than Blacks, one might think that this SES difference is what causes the racial difference in mortality. But Table 5.1 shows that when we compare Blacks and Whites who have the same education level, at almost every level of education Whites have a longer life expectancy than Blacks. Thus, mortality is not simply affected by one's social class; race matters as well (Williams, 2004).

Gender and Mortality

It is a well-known finding that women tend to live longer than men. Once people have reached 65, women have 19.2 years on average longer to live, whereas men have 16.3 years on average (Merck Institute of Aging and Health & Gerontological Society of America, 2002). But mortality rates are declining, in particular for men. For example, between 1990 and 2002 for people 85 and older, the "all cause" death rate declined 9% for men and increased 1% for women (Gorina et al., 2006).

CHAPTER SUMMARY

In this chapter, we focused on health inequalities for older adults from diverse backgrounds. We began by defining acute and chronic conditions and described several common chronic conditions for older adults including diabetes, dementia, and Alzheimer's disease. Mental illness is often separated from physical illness in Western cultures, and we followed this tradition when describing rates of mental illness in older adults and then focused on depression as an important mental illness for which many treatments exist and that can go untreated in older adults.

To facilitate understanding of the social inequalities of health outcomes, we presented a conceptual model. Working with this model, we described how the health outcome of diabetes might be affected by various elements of diversity. Given the prevalence of dementia in older people, we then presented a detailed case analysis of how race or ethnic background might affect many aspects of dementia from beliefs about dementia to services for elders with dementia. Socioeconomic status, gender, race/ethnicity, rural/urban community location, and sexual orientation are also related to health inequalities, and we discussed the research findings, albeit very limited for some groups. The data on mental health inequalities in older adults are even more limited. However, we have reviewed important trends. Finally, we turned to examine mortality. Mortality rates refer to the percentage of people who die from a given disease. Comparing mortality rates by gender, socioeconomic status, and race/ethnicity completed this presentation of health inequalities.

ACTIVE LEARNING EXPERIENCE: CHAPTER 5 QUIZ

The purpose of this experience is to gauge your present knowledge of issues related to health inequalities for elders from diverse groups. Upon completion of this activity, you will be able to:

1. Assess your knowledge of health inequalities.
2. Gain feedback on your knowledge of important issues related to illness and diversity.

This activity should take 30 minutes (10 minutes to complete the quiz and 20 minutes to discuss your answers with another person or in a classroom setting).

Instructions:

Complete the following quiz. Your instructor may lead an in-class review of the answers to the quiz. Check the appropriate column to indicate whether each of the following statements is true or false.

Quiz Items	True	False
1. Chronic illnesses are of short duration.	_____	_____
2. Rates of dementia vary by ethnicity.	_____	_____
3. All neuropsychological assessments of dementia are not affected by language differences.	_____	_____
4. There is a high prevalence of Alzheimer's disease in people over the age of 85.	_____	_____
5. Women's longer lives are healthier than men's lives.	_____	_____
6. Health inequalities refer to the difference in the rate of morbidity (illness) and mortality between different social groups in the United States.	_____	_____
7. Asian Americans experience few health inequalities as their health status is better than that of White Americans.	_____	_____
8. IHS stands for individualized health systems, which are designed to provide culturally competent care.	_____	_____
9. The prevalence of schizophrenia varies widely across different cultural groups.	_____	_____
10. Depression may be influenced by culture.	_____	_____

GLOSSARY

acute conditions: Illnesses that occur over a short duration and have severe symptoms. Pneumonia is an example of an acute condition.

Alzheimer's disease (AD): A common, chronic, disabling disease of the brain characterized by the loss of communication and eventual destruction of nerve cell centers. People with AD may begin showing symptoms of mild memory impairment that then progresses to extreme difficulties with cognitive function. AD is a fatal disease.

chronic conditions: Illnesses that occur over a relatively long period of time and are more difficult to resolve than acute conditions. Arthritis is an example of a chronic condition.

compression of morbidity: Refers to the delay of the onset of illness to the very end of life such that old age is characterized by good health with a precipitous decline in health immediately prior to death.

crossover effect: Occurs when minority group members who reach the oldest age have better health outcomes and live longer than the dominant group.

dementia: A condition characterized by a loss of cognitive function, particularly memory function.

health inequalities: Refer to the difference in the rate of morbidity (illness) and mortality between different social groups in the United States. These inequalities are also often called *health disparities*.

morbidity: Illness or disease; morbidity rates refer to the proportion of people who have a particular illness or disease.

mortality: Death; mortality rates represent the proportion of deaths due to a particular cause.

prevalence: The number of people or proportion of the population who have a specific illness at a given point in time.

socioeconomic status (SES): The level of economic privilege or status that one has. SES is often measured by educational attainment, income, and occupation.

somaticization: The presentation of physical bodily symptoms (e.g., headache, backache) in response to psychological distress.

SUGGESTED READINGS

Alvord, L. A. & Van Pelt, E. (1999). *The scalpel and the silver bear: The first Navajo woman surgeon combines Western medicine and traditional healing.* New York: Bantam Books.

This book, cowritten with journalist Van Pelt, describes Lori Alvord's journey from her birth to a White mother and a Navajo father living on the edge of a Navajo reservation in New Mexico through medical school at Stanford University. When she returned to practice medicine on the reservation, she discovered that she needed to combine her new medical skills with her traditional culture.

Butcher, H. K. & McGonigal-Kenney, M. (2005). Depression & dispiritedness in later life: A "gray drizzle of horror" isn't inevitable. *American Journal of Nursing, 105*(12), 52–61.

This article delivers a very important message: Depression in later life is not inevitable, and there are many things that can and should be done to address depression in older people. The article reviews the different causes of depression in older people and the corresponding treatments.

Grossman, A. H. (2006). Physical and mental health of older lesbian, gay, and bisexual adults. In D. Kimmel, T. Rose, & S. David (Eds.), *Lesbian, gay, bisexual, and transgender aging: Research and clinical perspectives* (pp. 54–69). New York: Columbia University Press.

This book chapter gives a clear description of the research on the physical and mental health of older LGBT persons.

Iwamasa, G. Y. & Sorocco, K. H. (2007). The psychology of Asian American older adults. In F. T. L. Leong, A. G. Inman, A. Ebreo, L. H. Yang, L. Kinoshita, & M. Fu (Eds.), *Handbook of Asian American psychology*. Thousand Oaks, CA: Sage.

This handbook chapter provides a very accessible and informative overview of psychological issues facing Asian American older adults.

Knight, B. G., Kaskie, B., Shurgot, G. R., & Dave, J. (2006). Improving the mental health of older adults. In J. E. Birren & K. W. Schaie (Eds.), *Handbook of the psychology of aging* (6th ed., pp. 407–424). Burlington, MA: Elsevier Academic Press.

This handbook chapter summarizes the primary psychological issues that face older adults and then discusses how the treatment of these issues interfaces with our health-care system. It also contains a brief section examining how ethnic diversity relates to these issues.

Land, K. C. & Yang, Y. (2006). Morbidity, disability and mortality. In R. H. Binstock & L. K. George (Eds.), *Handbook of aging and the social sciences* (6th ed., pp. 41–58). Burlington, MA: Elsevier Academic Press.

This handbook chapter provides a comprehensive overview of the research on morbidity, disability, and mortality in the United States. This discussion includes how demographic variables such as gender, race, and ethnicity are related to morbidity, disability, and mortality.

Miles, T. P. (Ed.) (1999). *Full color aging: Facts, goals, and recommendations for America's diverse elders.* Washington, DC: Gerontological Society of America.

Prepared by the Gerontological Society of America Task Force on minority issues in gerontology, this publication includes an excellent collection of articles that is thought provoking as well as informative. Topics include demography, racial disparity in retirement income security, Alzheimer's disease in minority populations, living with chronic diseases, aging among American Indians, and critical issues in understanding family support. Also includes an annotated bibliography of articles on or about minority research that appeared in the *Journal of Gerontology* and the *Gerontologist* from 1989 to 1998.

Myers, H. F., Lewis, T. T., & Parker-Dominguez, T. (2003). Stress, coping, and minority health: Biopsychsocial perspective on ethnic health disparities. In G. Bernal, J. E. Trimble, A. K. Burlew, & F. T. L. Leong (Eds.), *Handbook of racial & ethnic minority psychology* (pp. 377–400). Thousand Oaks, CA: Sage.

This book chapter presents a model of stress and coping that may help explain the ethnic health disparities that we discuss in this chapter. In doing so, they also provide a compelling description of the stress and coping that ethnic minority group members face.

Whitfield, K. E. (Ed.) (2004). *Closing the gap: Improving the health of minority elders in the new millennium.* Washington, DC: Gerontological Society of America.

This edited volume builds on a 1999 publication, *Full color aging* (Miles, 1999) noted earlier in this section. It focuses on health disparities experienced by minority populations. In addition, the publication includes a highly useful chapter on population aging describing the stunning increase in the minority elderly population projected by the middle of this century. Includes an annotated bibliography of articles on or about minority aging that appeared in the *Journal of Gerontology* and the *Gerontologist* from 1989 to 2003.

Yeo, G. & Gallagher-Thompson, D. (Eds.). (2006). *Ethnicity and the dementias* (2nd ed.). New York: Routledge.

This book provides an excellent resource for service providers working with people suffering from dementia. In contains contributions from researchers and practitioners who have considerable experience working with individuals from diverse groups.

Journal Special Issues

Special issues of journals often focus around a particular topic. Examples include the two special issues described herein. Although due to space limitations we cannot list all of the articles in each special issue, we highlight the ones we find particularly relevant. Interested readers should see the full issue for additional articles.

Journals of Gerontology, October 2005 Series B: Psychological Sciences and Social Sciences. This special issue focuses on health inequalities across many different groups. The following suggested readings focus on health inequalities due to SES, due to race or ethnicity, and due to gender, respectively.

House, J. S., Lantz, P. M., & Herd, P. (2005). Continuity and change in the social stratification of aging and health over the life course: Evidence from a nationally representative longitudinal study from 1986 to 2001/2002 (Americans' changing lives study). *Journals of Gerontology: Series B: Psychological Sciences and Social Sciences,* 60(Special Issue 2), 15–26.

Moen, P., Moen, P., & Chermack, K. (2005). Gender disparities in health: Strategic selection, careers, and cycles of control. *Journals of Gerontology: Series B: Psychological Sciences and Social Sciences,* 60(Special Issue 2), 99–108.

Williams, D. R. (2005). The health of U.S. Racial and ethnic populations. *Journals of Gerontology: Series B: Psychological Sciences and Social Sciences,* 60(Special Issue 2), 53–62.

Journal of Applied Gerontology, 2006 This special issue focuses on American Indian and Alaska Natives and the striking health disparities that they experience.

Goins, R. T. & Manson, S. M. (2006). Introduction to a supplemental issue of the Journal of Applied Gerontology: Research on American Indian and Alaska Native aging. *Journal of Applied Gerontology,* 25(1), 5S.

Rhoades, D. A. (2006). National health data and older American Indians and Alaska Natives. *Journal of Applied Gerontology,* 25(1), 9S.

Pamphlets

Federal agencies often work together to publish resources. The following pamphlets are examples of such collaborative resources. Additional resources may be found on the agency websites. These pamphlets provide accurate, accessible information about these conditions. Although they are not extremely detailed, they are an excellent starting point for understanding these conditions and for obtaining resources for additional information.

Understanding Alzheimer's disease. (2006). (NIH Publication No. 06-5441): U.S. Department of Health & Human Services, Public Health Service, National Institutes of Health, National Institute on Aging.

Understanding memory loss. (2006). (NIH Publication No. 06-5442): U.S. Department of Health & Human Services, Public Health Service, National Institutes of Health, National Institute on Aging.

AUDIOVISUAL RESOURCES

The Checker King. This film focuses on the life of an older man, Harold, who comes out of his depression after his wife's death and reclaims his life. He asks his nephew to join him on a road trip to Newton, Iowa, to prepare for the National Checker Tournament. There are some health and disability elements as Harold had Bell's Palsy at a young age and still has some paralysis. 39 minutes. Available from http://www.fanlight.com.

Away from Her. This major cinema film gives a moving portrayal of issues that can occur with long-term care, Alzheimer's Disease, and caregiving. Julie Christie received an Oscar nomination for her portrayal of a woman with AD. 110 minutes. Available from http://www.imdb.com/title/tt0491747/#comment

A Quick Look at Alzheimer's. These four very short films from the MetLife Foundation and the Alliance for Aging research are designed to increase understanding of AD. They are free for noncommercial use. 2–3 minutes each. Available from www.aboutalz.org

Everyday Choices. Ethics and decision-making in home care and community nursing. This discusses the choices that a young nurse must make when working with Gerardo, a 75-year-old Cuban man. It looks at how much the decisions that she makes affects his life as his health and mental state deteriorate. During her time working with him, he loses much of his independence and must be placed in a nursing home. The movie looks at her commitment and dedication to Gerardo, despite many difficulties. It is an especially good movie for health-care providers. There is a great deal of focus on the emotional nature of working in this field as well as "cultural realism" in terms of Gerardo's background. 28 minutes. Available from http://www.terranova.org.

Li Biyiin (Horse Song). This film is a dramatization about a Navajo man who finds out he has diabetes. 57 minutes. Available from Four Directions Health Communications, Northern Navajo Medical Center, P.O. Box 160, Shiprock, NM 87420. Phone: (505) 368-6499.

KEY: CHAPTER 5 QUIZ

1. False. Chronic conditions occur over a relatively long period of time and can be very difficult to resolve. Often they start with mild symptoms and are usually not an immediate threat to one's life, although they do impact the quality of life and can ultimately decrease longevity.
2. True. Even though there are biological bases for dementia, rates of dementia do vary by gender, ethnicity, and race (Yeo & Gallagher-Thompson, 1996).
3. False. Some neuropsychological assessments are affected by language. To the extent that an assessment relies on written or spoken instructions or questions, then it will be affected by language differences. Some neuropsychological assessments like functional magnetic resonance imaging (fMRI) discussed in chapter 2 do not depend on words and so are not affected by language differences.
4. True. Researchers estimate that 1 in 2 people over the age of 85 have Alzheimer's disease (Allery et al., 2004).
5. False. Although women do live longer on average than men, in their older years, women have higher rates of chronic illnesses than do men (Rieker & Bird, 2005).
6. True. Health inequalities are also often called health disparities.
7. False. Although some ethnic groups within the Asian American category do experience many positive health outcomes, recent Asian immigrants (e.g., from Southeast Asia) have higher morbidity and mortality rates than White Americans.
8. False. IHS stands for Indian Health Service, an agency within the federal government that provides health-care services for American Indian and Alaska Native people.
9. False. Rates of schizophrenia are approximately 1% worldwide. This suggests that this mental disorder has a strong biological basis.
10. True. The prevalence of depression ranges from 2% to 19% between different cultures, suggesting that depression may have a cultural or social context component (Weissman et al., 1996).

REFERENCES

Allery, A. J., Aranda, M. P., Dilworth-Anderson, P. D., Guerrero, M., Haan, M. N., Hendrie, H., et al. (2004). Alzheimer's disease and communities of color. In K. E. Whitfield (Ed.), *Closing the gap: Improving the health of minority elders in the new millennium* (pp. 81–86). Washington, DC: Gerontological Society of America.

Angel, J. L., & Hogan, D. P. (2004). Population aging and diversity in a new era. In K. E. Whitfield (Ed.), *Closing the gap: Improving the health of minority elders in the new millennium* (pp. 1–12). Washington, DC: Gerontological Society of America.

Ardila, A. (1995). Directions of research in cross-cultural neuropsychology. *Journal of Clinical and Experimental Neuropsychology, 17,* 143–150.

Baker, F. M. (1994). Suicide among ethnic minority elderly: A statistical and psychosocial perspective. *Journal of Geriatric Psychiatry, 27,* 241–264.

Baker, F. M., & Espino, D. V. (1997). A Spanish version of the geriatric depression scale in Mexican-American elders. *International Journal of Geriatric Psychiatry, 12*(21), 21–25.

Bell, R. A., Smith, S. L., Arcury, T. A., Snively, B. M., Stafford, J. M., & Quandt, S. A. (2005). Prevalence and correlates of depressive symptoms among rural older African Americans, Native Americans, and whites with diabetes. *Diabetes Care, 28*(4), 823–829.

Black, B. S., Rabins, P. V., German, P., Roca, R., McGuire, M., & Brant, L. J. (1998). Use of formal and informal sources of mental health care among older African-American public-housing residents. *Psychological Medicine, 28*(3), 519–530.

Blow, F. C., Zeber, J. E., McCarthy, J. F., Valenstein, M., Gillon, L., & Bingham, C. R. (2004). Ethnicity and diagnostic patterns in veterans with psychoses. *Social Psychiatry and Psychiatric Epidemiology, 39*(10), 841–851.

Braun, K. L., Yee, B. W. K., Browne, C. V., & Mokuau, N. (2004). Native Hawaiian and Pacific Islander elders. In K. E. Whitfield (Ed.), *Closing the gap: Improving the health of minority elders in the new millennium* (pp. 55–67). Washington, DC: Gerontological Society of America.

Bulatao, R. A., & Anderson, N. B. (Eds.). (2004). *Understanding racial and ethnic differences in health in late life: A research agenda.* Washington, DC: National Academies Press.

Butcher, H. K., & McGonigal-Kenney, M. (2005). Depression & dispiritedness in later life: A "gray drizzle of horror" isn't inevitable. *American Journal of Nursing, 105*(12), 52–61.

Claes, J., & Moore, W. R. (2001). Caring for gay and lesbian elderly. In L. K. Olson (Ed.), *Age through ethnic lenses: Caring for the elderly in a multicultural society* (pp. 217–229). Lanham, MD: Rowman & Littlefield.

Conwell, Y. (1994). Suicide in elderly patients. In L. S. Schneider, C. F. I. Reynolds, B. D. Lebowitz, & A. J. Friedhoff (Eds.), *Diagnosis and treatment of depression in late life* (pp. 397–418). Washington, DC: American Psychiatric Press.

Du Bois, B. C., Yavno, C. H., & Stanford, E. P. (2001). Care options for older Mexican Americans: Issues affecting health and long-term care service needs. In L. K. Olson (Ed.), *Age through ethnic lenses: Caring for the elderly in a multicultural society* (pp. 71–85). Lanham, MD: Rowman & Littlefield.

Dwyer, K. (2000). Culturally appropriate consumer-directed care: The American Indian choices project. *Generations, 24*(3), 91–93.

Elliot, K. S., Di Minno, M., Lam, D., & Tu, A. M. (1996). Working with Chinese families in the context of dementia. In G. Yeo & D. Gallagher-Thompson (Eds.), *Ethnicity and the dementias* (pp. 89–108). Bristol, PA: Taylor & Francis.

Federal Interagency Forum on Aging-Related Statistics. (2006). *Older Americans update 2006: Key indicators of well-being.* Washington, DC: U.S. Government Printing Office.

Gorina, Y., Hoyert, D., Lentzner, H., & Goulding, M. (2006). *Trends in causes of death among older persons in the United States. Aging trends, No. 6.* Hyattsville, MD: National Center for Health Statistics.

Gurland, B., Wilder, D., Lantigua, R., Mayeux, R., Stern, Y., Chen, J., et al. (1997). Differences in rates of dementia between ethno-racial groups. In L. Martin & B. Soldo (Eds.), *Racial and ethnic differences in the health of older Americans.* Washington, DC: National Academies Press.

Heurtin-Roberts, S. (1993). "High-pertension"—the uses of a chronic folk illness for personal adaptation. *Social Science & Medicine, 37*(3), 285–294.

Hooyman, N., & Kiyak, H. A. (2008). *Social gerontology: A multidisciplinary perspective* (8th ed.). Boston, MA: Allyn and Bacon.

House, J. S. (2002). Understanding social factors and inequalities in health: 20th century progress and 21st century prospects. *Journal of Health and Social Behavior, 43*(2), 125–142.

House, J. S., Lantz, P. M., & Herd, P. (2005). Continuity and change in the social stratification of aging and health over the life course: Evidence from a nationally representative longitudinal study from 1986 to 2001/2002 (Americans' changing lives study). *Journals of Gerontology: Series B: Psychological Sciences and Social Sciences, 60*(Special Issue 2), 15–26.

House, J. S., Lepkowski, J. M., Kinney, A. M., Mero, R. P., Kessler, R. C., & Herzog, A. R. (1994). The social stratification of aging and health. *Journal of Health and Social Behavior, 35*(3), 213–234.

Hunter, S. (2005). *Midlife and older LGBT adults: Knowledge and affirmative practice for the social services.* New York: Haworth Press.

John, R. (2004). Health status and health disparities among American Indian elders. In K. E. Whitfield (Ed.), *Closing the gap: Improving the health of minority elders in the new millennium* (pp. 27–44). Washington, DC: Gerontological Society of America.

Kemp, B. J., Staples, F., & Lopez-Aqueres, W. (1987). Epidemiology of depression and dysphoria in an elderly Hispanic population: Prevalence and correlates. *Journal of the American Geriatrics Society, 35,* 920–926.

Kessler, R. C., Barker, P. R., Colpe, L. J., Epstein, J. F., Gfroerer, J. C., Hiripi, E., et al. (2003). Screening for serious mental illness in the general population. *Archives of General Psychiatry, 60*(2), 184-189.

Kessler, R. C., Berglund, P., Demler, O., Jin, R., Koretz, D., Merikangas, K. R., et al. (2003). The epidemiology of major depressive disorder: Results from the national comorbidity survey replication (NCS-R). *Journal of the American Medical Association, 289*(23), 3095–3105.

Land, K. C., & Yang, Y. (2006). Morbidity, disability and mortality. In R. H. Binstock & L. K. George (Eds.), *Handbook of aging and the social sciences* (6th ed., pp. 41–58). Burlington, MA: Elsevier Academic Press.

Larson, E. B., & Imai, Y. (1996). An overview of dementia and ethnicity with special emphasis on the epidemiology of dementia. In G. Yeo & D. Gallagher-Thompson (Eds.), *Ethnicity and the dementias* (pp. 9–20). Washington, DC: Taylor and Francis.

Lebowitz, B. D., Pearson, J. L., Schneider, L. S., Reynolds, C. F., III, Alexopoulos, G. S., Bruce, M. L., et al. (1997). Diagnosis and treatment of depression in late life: Consensus statement update. *Journal of the American Medical Association, 278,* 1186–1190.

Longobardi, P. G., Cummings, J. L., & Anderson-Hanley, C. (2000). Multicultural perspectives on the neuropsychological and neuropsychiatric assessment and treatment of the elderly. In E. Fletcher-Janzen, T. L. Strickland, & C. R. Reynolds (Eds.), *Handbook of cross-cultural neuropsychology* (pp. 123–144). New York: Kluwer Academic/Plenum Publishers.

Merck Institute of Aging and Health, Centers for Disease Control and Prevention, & Gerontological Society of America. (2004). *The State of Aging and Health in America*. Retrieved July 29, 2006 from http://www.cdc.gov/aging/pdf/State_of_Aging_and_Health_in_America_2004.pdf

Merck Institute of Aging and Health & Gerontological Society of America. (2002). *The State of Aging and Health in America*. Retrieved July 29, 2006 from http://www.agingsociety.org/agingsociety/pdf/state_of_aging_report.pdf

National Advisory Committee on Rural Health and Human Services. (2006). *The 2006 Report to the Secretary: Rural Health and Human Service Issues*. Hyattsville, MD: U.S. Department of Health & Human Services.

Polacca, M. (2001). American Indian and Alaska Native elderly. In L. K. Olson (Ed.), *Age through ethnic lenses: Caring for the elderly in a multicultural society* (pp. 113–122). Lanham, MD: Rowman & Littlefield.

Rieker, P. P., & Bird, C. E. (2005). Rethinking gender differences in health: Why we need to integrate social and biological perspectives. *Journals of Gerontology: Series B: Psychological Sciences and Social Sciences, 60B*(Special Issue 2), 40–47.

Rooks, R. N., & Whitfield, K. E. (2004). Health disparities among older African Americans: Past, present and future perspectives. In K. E. Whitfield (Ed.), *Closing the gap: Improving the health of minority elders in the new millennium* (pp. 45–54). Washington, DC: Gerontological Society of America.

Schaie, K. W., & Willis, S. L. (2002). *Adult development and aging* (5th ed.). New York: Prentice-Hall.

Scott, J. P. (2001). Long-term care: The case of the rural elderly. In L. K. Olson (Ed.), *Age through ethnic lenses: Caring for the elderly in a multicultural society* (pp. 242–250). Lanham, MD: Rowman & Littlefield.

Shibusawa, T., Lubben, J., & Kitano, H. H. L. (2001). Japanese American elderly. In L. K. Olson (Ed.), *Age through ethnic lenses: Caring for the elderly in a multicultural society* (pp. 33–44). Lanham, MD: Rowman & Littlefield.

Silver, B., Poland, R. E., & Lin, K.-M. (1993). Ethnicity and the pharmacology of tricyclic antidepressants. In K.-M. Lin, R. E. Pland, & G. Nakasaki (Eds.), *Psychopharmacology and psychobiology of ethnicity* (pp. 61–89). Washington, DC: American Psychiatric Press.

Stoller, E. P., & Gibson, R. C. (2000). *Worlds of difference: Inequality in the aging experience* (3rd ed.). Thousand Oaks, CA: Pine Forge Press.

Teresi, J. A., Holmes, D., Ramirez, M., Gurland, B. J., & Lantigua, R. (2002). Performance of cognitive tests among different racial/ethnic and education groups: Findings of differential item functioning and possible item bias. In J. H. Skinner, J. A. Teresi, D. Holmes, S. M. Stahl, & A. L. Stewart (Eds.), *Multicultural measurement in older populations* (pp. 85–95). New York: Springer Publishing Company.

Thorson, J. A., & Powell, F. C. (1993). The rural aged, social value, and health care. In C. N. Bull (Ed.), *Aging in rural America* (pp. 134–145). Newbury Park, CA: Sage.

U.S. Department of Health and Human Services. (2001). *Mental health: Culture, race and ethnicity—a supplement to mental health: A report of the surgeon general*. Rockville, MD: U.S. Department of Health & Human Services, Substance Abuse and Mental Health Services Administration, Center for Mental Health Services.

Vedantam, S. (2005a, June 26). Patients' diversity is often discounted; alternatives to mainstream medical treatment call for recognizing ethnic, social differences; final edition. *Washington Post*.

Vedantam, S. (2005b, June 27). Social network's healing power is borne out in poorer nations; final edition. *Washington Post*.

Weissman, M. M., Bland, R. C., Canino, G. J., Faravelli, C., Greenwald, S., Hwu, H. G., et al. (1996). Cross-national epidemiology of major depression and bipolar disorder. *Journal of the American Medical Association, 276*(4), 293–299.

Williams, D. R. (2004). Racism and health. In K. E. Whitfield (Ed.), *Closing the gap: Improving the health of minority elders in the new millennium* (pp. 69–80). Washington, DC: Gerontological Society of America.

Williams, D. R. (2005). The health of U.S. racial and ethnic populations. *Journals of Gerontology: Series B: Psychological Sciences and Social Sciences, 60B*(Special Issue 2), 53–62.

Wong, M. G. (2001). The Chinese elderly: Values and issues in receiving adequate care. In L. K. Olson (Ed.), *Age through ethnic lenses: Caring for the elderly in a multicultural society* (pp. 17–32). Lanham, MD: Rowman & Littlefield Publishers.

Yau, E., & Yeo, G. (2007). *How dementia impacts caregiving in diverse ethnic and racial communities.* Paper presented at the Institute on Aging Professional Educational Program: Alzheimer's Disease and other Dementias: Advances and Issues, San Francisco, CA.

Yeo, G. (2006). Prevalence of dementia among different ethnic populations. In G. Yeo & D. Gallagher-Thompson (Eds.), *Ethnicity and the dementias* (2nd ed.). New York: Routledge.

Yeo, G., & Gallagher-Thompson, D. (Eds.). (1996). *Ethnicity and the dementias.* Washington, DC: Taylor and Francis.

Yeo, G., & Gallagher-Thompson, D. (Eds.). (2006). *Ethnicity and the dementias* (2nd ed. pp. 3–9). New York: Routledge.

Zhang, A. Y., Snowden, L. R., & Sue, S. (1998). Differences between Asian and White Americans' help seeking and utilization patterns in the Los Angeles area. *Journal of Community Psychology, 26,* 317–316.

6

Informal and Formal Care
for Older Persons

- How does informal caregiving vary across ethnic and cultural groups?
- Who does most of the caregiving: men or women?
- What options are available for formal care? To what extent is each of these options used by different ethnic groups?
- What barriers hinder the use of available programs and services by ethnic elders? How does research contribute to help overcome these barriers?

As you may recall from Chapter 1, the percentage of racial and ethnic minority elders will increase at a much higher rate than that of non-Hispanic White elders over the next 50 years. Similarly, the population of elders representing other elements of diversity (i.e., gender, socioeconomic status, sexual orientation, community size, and religious background) will also increase substantially. Unfortunately, elders must often pay a price for their long lives: it comes in the form of a greater need to rely on others for things they could once do for themselves. The dependence on others for assistance sharply escalates with age, as health problems that limit functional autonomy also increase with age. As discussed in Chapter 5, "Health Inequalities," prevalence of these functional limitations is significantly higher among minority elders than their White counterparts (U.S. Department of Health & Human Services, 1991). This may lead one to conclude that a relatively large proportion of minority elders live in long-term care facilities. This is, however, not true for all minority populations. In fact, there are important differences across racial and ethnic groups. While African Americans enter nursing homes at a higher rate than other racial and ethnic groups, nursing home use by Hispanic and Asian elders is substantially lower than that for other groups (Angel & Hogan, 2004). This portends a continuing need for care provided by relatives, friends, and informal caregivers (National Academy on an Aging Society, 2000). These categories of people assist older people with personal care, household chores, and transportation and by managing finances and performing other tasks associated with daily living.

Before we examine caregiving in detail, let us first look at the living arrangements of diverse elders. In many cases, these living arrangements are interrelated with the type of caregiving that an elder receives.

LIVING ARRANGEMENTS

The term *living arrangements* refers to household composition—the people who live in a single dwelling unit. The U.S. Census Bureau provides valuable information about the percentage of older people who live with their spouse, with other relatives, with nonrelatives, and alone. Why should we learn about living arrangements? The occupants of an elder's household represent part of his or her personal environment. The nature of this environment affects the way the older person's day is spent, his or her behavior and activities, and the care and support available to him or her. Living arrangements depend on a number of factors: What is the elder's health status? What are his or her financial resources? What is the elder's marital status? What are his or her cultural values? Where are family members located? What is the nature of these family ties? Consider an example case of Ms. Williams (an African American, aged 65). She lives alone because she lost her spouse recently, is in good health, and has adequate income to make ends meet. Though she does not have any relatives living nearby, she has a number of friends with whom she maintains ongoing contact. In a way they are like members of her extended family who are always there to help her in times of need. They go to the same church and celebrate holidays together. How long would Ms. Williams stay alone in her home? What factors would affect her living arrangements? Perhaps the most important factors in this regard would be her health, financial resources, and social support.

Examine the data from the U.S. Census Bureau presented in Figure 6.1. These data focus on living arrangements of the population aged 65 and over by sex, race, and Hispanic origin. What do these data reveal? Some key points include:

- In the total population, older men are more likely to live with their spouses than are older women.
- In the total population, older women are twice as likely as older men to live alone.
- Living arrangements differ by race and Hispanic origin.
- Older Asian women are far more likely than women of other races to live with relatives other than a spouse.
- When compared with men from other ethnic groups, older Black men have the highest rate of living alone.

Now that you have examined these data, we invite you to complete an active learning experience, which will give you an opportunity to identify additional factors regarding living arrangements of older men and women from different ethnic groups.

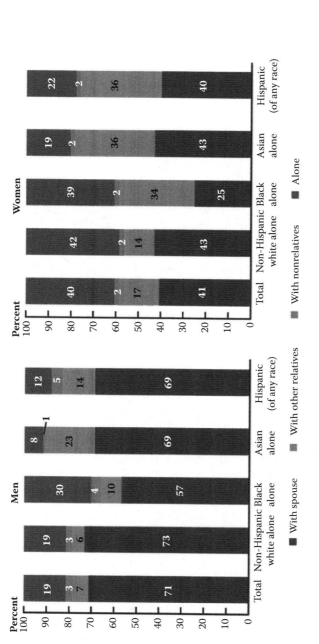

Figure 6.1   Living arrangements of the population age 65 and over, by sex and race and Hispanic origin, 2003. *Source:* Federal Interagency on Aging-Related Statistics (2004).

TABLE 6.1   Population Aged 65 and Over Living Alone, by Age Groups and Sex, Selected Years 1970–2003

	Men		Women	
Year	65–74 (%)	75 and over (%)	65–74 (%)	75 and over (%)
1970	11.3	19.1	31.7	37.0
1980	11.6	21.6	35.6	49.4
1990	13.0	20.9	33.2	54.0
2000	13.8	21.4	30.6	49.5
2003	15.6	22.9	29.6	49.8

Source: Federal Interagency Forum on Aging-Related Statistics (2004).

ACTIVE LEARNING EXPERIENCE: LIVING ARRANGEMENTS

The purpose of this experience is to provide you with an opportunity to examine how the living arrangements of the older population are linked to factors such as gender, race, and age group. Upon completion of this activity you will be able to:

1. Describe gender differences in the living arrangements for the older population as a whole as well as for Non-Hispanic Whites, Blacks, Asians, and Hispanics.
2. Describe how the percentage of older men and older women living alone varies with age and how this relationship has changed during the past 30 years.

Time required is 45 minutes (30 minutes to prepare answers to the questions and 15 minutes to discuss the answers with another person).

Instructions:

1. Complete the questions included in this activity either as a homework assignment or in a class setting.
2. Discuss your responses with another person.
3. Participate in a class discussion of student responses to this activity.

Examine the data on living arrangements provided in Figure 6.1 and Table 6.1. Prepare written responses to the questions given in the following section, and discuss these responses with another person.

Discussion Questions:

1. In the data for 2003, for which ethnic group was (a) the percent of older men living alone the highest? and (b) the percent of older men living with other relatives the highest? What are the implications of these data for those who provide health care services to these segments of the population?
2. In the data for 2003, (a) what percent of Non-Hispanic White women over the age of 65 were living alone and (b) what percent of Black women over the age of 65 were living alone? Why were they living alone? (c) What percent of Black men were living alone? What factors may have contributed to these findings? (d) What are the implications of these data for both informal care and formal care?
3. In which ethnic group were the highest percent of women living with other relatives in 2003? What are some possible reasons for such living arrangements? What are the implications of these arrangements for informal care? For providers of formal care?
4. Table 6.1 presents data for older people living alone by age group and sex for selected years from 1970 to 2003. What do these data tell us about the percent of men living alone? How does this percentage differ for the two age groups?
5. What do these data in Table 6.1 tell us about the percentage of women from each of the two groups living alone? How have these percentages changed since 1970? What factors may have contributed to the increase in the number of older people living alone?

INFORMAL CARE

In this section, we first describe informal caregiving and then discuss gender differences among providers of informal care. We then devote our attention to informal caregiving among Blacks, Hispanics, Asian/Pacific Islanders, Native Americans, and lesbians, gay men, and bisexuals. To introduce our discussion of informal caregiving and diversity, we invite you to consider the following vignettes.

Vignette 1

Andy Johnson, a 35-year-old African American teacher in an elementary school, is the only surviving son in his family. His mother had given birth to four other sons, all of whom were stillborn or died shortly after birth. At this point, Andy is providing care for his 75-year-old father, who recently suffered a heart attack, and his sister, who has four children and whose husband died 2 years ago. When asked about his family caregiving, he indicated, "I was asked by my family to provide care to all members of my family. My duties include (a) You will never get married; (b) You will continue to work full time; (c) You will take care of your parents in their old age; (d) You will take care of your sisters and their children; and (e) You will enjoy performing these tasks." Indeed, he has done nothing else with his life other than working and providing care for the members of his family. The decisions he has made about his life have always been influenced by his caregiving responsibilities. He says he feels good about what he has done to date and how he has faithfully met the expectations of his family.

Vignette 2

Irshad Khan, now 68, came to the United States from Bangladesh when she was 40. Her son, Aziz, is now 42 and has started his own software business 200 miles away from home. Her 35-year-old daughter, Shaila, lived with her mother when she was a student at a local university. Upon graduation, she left her hometown to take up a position in the governor's office at the state capital 150 miles away from her mother. Two years after the move, she learned that her mother had developed cancer. She is now back living with her mother and devotes almost all of her time providing the care her mother needs. While Aziz comes to see his mother at least once a month, Shaila serves as the primary caregiver. She cooks meals for the family, takes her mother to the clinic almost every week, manages all of the financial affairs, and keeps all of the relatives in Bangladesh, Canada, and England informed about her mother's changing health condition. The only people she sees are those who come to visit her mother. Irshad continues to do her prayers five times a day according to Islamic religious tradition, shares the teachings of Islam with her two children, and maintains contact with the religious leader, who lives in a neighboring community. In addition, she provides consultation to both Shaila and Aziz in matters related to employment, religious traditions, and social obligations. For their part, both adult children display a great deal of respect and affection for their ailing mother and do their best to provide the highest quality of care that is humanly possible.

What is the nature of support that informal caregivers provide to older adults? Caregivers may be assisting with personal care functions (activities of daily living [ADLs]), such as dressing, feeding, or bathing, or with instrumental activities of daily living (IADLs), such as managing finances, assisting with shopping or housework, or administering medications. In addition to these caregiving behaviors they may also be engaged in expressive caregiving behaviors, which include sharing in social activities, providing emotional support, and "being there" when the older adult needs someone. Note that informal caregivers often work with formal caregiving sources such as physicians, hospitals, paid home care, adult day care, community long-term care services, and nursing homes. In other words, informal and formal care systems do not exist side by side as separate or independent processes. Instead, they are usually brought together through the efforts of the informal caregivers. How the two systems are integrated varies according to factors such as the gender of the caregiver, socioeconomic status of the caregiving unit, size of the community, and racial/ethnic group membership of the families.

Gender of Caregivers

Providers of informal care are overwhelmingly women: mostly wives, daughters, and daughters-in-law. However, husbands, sons-in-law, brothers, and other men also take care of frail elderly family members. Although still a minority, men constitute up to a third of primary caregivers (Kaye & Applegate, 1990). As families continue to change and conceptions of gender roles broaden, the number of male caregivers is likely to grow.

Research comparing male and female caregivers appears to confirm some stereotypes regarding gender roles. A traditional division of labor is particularly true of sons and daughters caring for their parents. Rathbone-McCuan and Coward (1985) found that daughters were eight times more involved in household chores and three times more likely to give personal care to their parents than sons. Sons, in turn, were nine times more likely than daughters to provide home repairs and maintenance. In their research with Puerto Rican caregivers, Delgado and Tennstedt (1997) found that sons often provided financial management and transportation, whereas daughters provided more personal care (e.g., bathing, dressing). In addition, these investigators discovered that Puerto Rican sons provided similar amounts of informal care as the daughters although the daughters were more likely to have someone to turn to for assistance and emotional support than the sons. In their research with African Americans and White caregivers, Haley et al. (1995) also found that male caregivers were likely to have fewer social supports than female caregivers. They added that women received more visits from relatives and friends than did men.

While caregiving can provide substantial personal satisfaction, it can also be a tremendous burden. Caregivers are left with less time for themselves and less privacy. This is especially true for women between the ages of 35 and 55, who experience pressure from two potentially competing values: (1) the traditional value that care of older adults is a family responsibility; and (2) the newer value that women should be free to work outside the home if they wish and the expectation that women will take outside employment if the family needs financial assistance. Elaine Brody (1981) termed this group *women in the middle.* As the phrase implies, such women are in middle age, in the middle from a generational standpoint, and in the middle in that the demands of their various roles compete for their time and energy. In short, the roles of paid workers and caregivers have been added to women's traditional roles of wives, homemakers, mothers, and grandmothers. As Moen, Robison, and Fields (2000) found, when women who are employed take on caregiving tasks they are unlikely to leave the labor force as a result despite any possible strains they may experience. Moen and her colleagues also found that (1) more recent cohorts of American women take on the caregiving role despite their increased involvement in the paid labor force and the societal revolution in gender expectations; and (2) level of education also affects the likelihood of working and caregiving. During the later years of adulthood, highly educated women are less likely to be providing care to their ailing relatives than those with a high school education or less (Moen, Robison, and Fields, 2000).

Women in minority families face additional difficulties as caregivers. Since many minority elders experience chronic diseases and higher levels of disability at younger ages (Cox, 2005), they need care and assistance early in the family's life cycle when the women are still engaged in addressing the needs of younger members. On the other hand, there is a lower rate of nursing home use among minority groups than in the general population (Gaugler, Kane, Kane, Clay, & Newcomer, 2003; Wallace, Levy-Storms, Kington, & Anderson, 1998), indicating that a greater proportion of older persons in minority families are cared for at home. It follows that minority women are more likely to have competing responsibilities such as working outside the home, raising children, and providing care to older family members.

While caregiving can be stressful for both men and women, each may express the effects in different ways (Aneshensel, Rutter, & Lackenbruch, 1991). Female caregivers tend to report more symptoms of stress, are more likely to take antidepressants, and participate in fewer recreational and social activities than do male caregivers (George, 1984). They also report lower morale (Gilhooly, 1984) and higher levels of burden (Barusch & Spaid, 1989; Young & Kahana, 1989). In contrast, male caregivers are more likely to report physical health symptoms and loss of financial resources. To some extent these gender differences may be due to the higher caregiving expectation for women than for men. There is a universal cultural expectation that women will provide care for family members regardless of their employment status or other demands on their time. Men's "getting-the-job-done" approach may help them keep greater emotional distance from their caregiving tasks and thus may shield them from some of the guilt, depression, and feelings of burden experienced by female caregivers. It is also possible that male caregivers may have learned to mask their feelings more effectively, living out the prevailing stereotype that they should "bear up" and suppress indications of personal vulnerability. Indeed, a number of studies suggest that, in contrast to women, men tend not to use caregiver support groups (Hlavaty, 1986; Snyder & Keefe, 1985). Those who do attend support groups welcome information and appear more concerned with the specific issues of care provision than with discussing their feelings (Davies, Priddy, & Tinklenberg, 1986). The following activity addresses differences in caregiving perceptions and responsibilities between men and women.

ACTIVE LEARNING EXPERIENCE: GENDER DIFFERENCES IN CAREGIVING

The purpose of this experience is to provide you with an opportunity to examine how gender influences the caregiving experience. Upon completion of this activity, you will be able to:

1. Describe gender differences in the experiences of caregiving spouses.
2. Explain how caregiving responsibilities may affect men and women differently.

Time Required: 45 minutes (30 minutes to complete the questions and 15 minutes to discuss the answers with another person).

Instructions:

1. Read the following case study, either as a homework assignment or in a class setting.
2. Prepare written responses to the questions at the end of the case study on your own or as a part of the class discussion designed for this activity.
3. Discuss your responses with another person.

Case Study

Dr. Craig Gordon is a physician in private practice. He has been providing in-home care to his wife, an Alzheimer's patient, for more than 8 years. As a result of the ongoing demands of caregiving, he has gradually reduced his professional practice but has continued to participate in professional and civic organizations. He has three sons and a daughter. All of them are married and live within a 2-hour drive of their parents' rural home. Dr. Gordon's daughter, Karen, who works full time and has her own three young children, plays an active role in the care of her mother. She knows what her father expects of her and does her best to meet these expectations. While the sons have more resources, they feel less distressed and are less involved in their mother's daily care. Occasionally they provide transportation for their mother, and they come to see her whenever they can. In contrast, their wives participate actively in providing care and support to Mrs. Gordon. They call her three or four times a day, take her out three times a week, call professionals for consultation, and attend support group meetings.

Dr. Gordon approaches care for his wife as he has done for his patients. It appears that he views caregiving as problem solving that needs to be handled in a scientific manner. He manages his wife's money, medicines, and symptoms. The unfair division of responsibility among the various members of the family is of no importance to him. While he has adequate income, he has not hired in-home help because his daughter and three daughters-in-law are always available in that capacity.

Through the support group meetings, Karen recently learned about a day care program available for elderly people with Alzheimer's disease. With the assistance of a county social worker, she has now been able to persuade her father to enroll Mrs. Gordon in this program. The day care provides much-needed respite to the family caregivers and provides a social environment for Mrs. Gordon. However, gradually she has become too impaired to attend day care. As in the past, Dr. Gordon expects that Karen and her three sisters-in-law will take on all caregiving responsibilities. However, these female caregivers feel physically and emotionally drained and are thinking of placing Mrs. Gordon in a nursing home. While they have done their best, they feel guilty and ineffective. On the other hand, Dr. Gordon and his sons feel no guilt or remorse. They believe that they have done their part as best they could.

Discussion Questions:

1. Who are the caregivers in the Gordon family?
2. How does Dr. Gordon approach the tasks associated with providing care to his wife? What caregiving tasks does he perform?
3. What care-related tasks are performed by female caregivers?
4. How do the caregiving responsibilities affect these women?
5. What gender differences do you observe in this case study?
6. What are some possible consequences of the caregiving role for Dr. Gordon's daughter, Karen?
7. What sources of support are used by Dr. Gordon?
8. What sources of support are used by his daughter and daughters-in-law?
9. How might this situation be different if they had limited finances?

Informal Caregiving Among Blacks

Grace Clay is a 45-year-old, recently remarried, African American woman. She has always been very close to her neighbor, Ms. Joan, the 80-year-old African American mother of her friend Chuck. When Chuck was recently transferred to Atlanta, about 500 miles away from his mother, Grace told him not to worry about his mother and promised she would take care of her. She would take her shopping every week, would provide transportation to the doctor's office as needed, and would maintain regular telephone contact with her. Chuck said that he would also call his mother regularly and would come home to be with her during the holidays. Last year, however, Ms. Joan had a heart attack; though she recuperated well, she now finds that many of the day-to-day tasks are beyond her ability. This means that she has to depend on Grace and other neighbors for a number of chores. As always, Grace continues to do as she had promised Chuck when he was leaving for Atlanta. For her, providing care to a friend's mother with whom she has always been so close is a part of her life, not a disruption.

As this vignette shows, many African American elders rely heavily on informal helpers for assistance (Chatters, Taylor, & Jackson, 1986; National Alliance for Caregiving & American Association of Retired Persons, 1997). The major sources of caregiving for elderly Blacks are their kin and fictive kin networks (informal support systems). Kin support includes members of immediate family; fictive kin include non-blood-related individuals such as friends, neighbors, and church members who provide significant caregiving support to older adults. In one national survey, 45% of African Americans had fictive kin with whom they maintained close relationships (Chatters, Taylor, & Jayakody, 1994). In another study, Johnson (1999) found that African Americans over the age of 85 utilized fictive kin for social support. This research shows that members of these fictive kin networks are often viewed as part of the extended family. The use of statements such as, "They are my family," "She is a daughter who is always there to help me," and "He is like a son to me" are all indicators of such fictive kin relationships.

The Black church also plays a special role in the support network of many African American elders, especially in rural communities. It remains a significant provider of tangible services (e.g., assistance with shopping or housework and administering of medications) as well as emotional and social support to Black elders (Kunjufu, 1994). In addition to such assistance, African American churches often (1) serve as conveyers of health-related information about formal organizations that assist elderly people and those who care for them (Levin, 1986; Wood & Parham, 1990); and (2) function with formal and informal support systems to act as bridges, linking older individuals and their family caregivers to formal services.

Note that the prevalence of informal caregiving among African American families is not simply a result of their economic status. In fact, there is a pervasive cultural tradition of providing care to parents, siblings, and other relatives (MaloneBeach & Cook, 2001). Research shows that African American daughters have a strong sense of filial responsibility, making them less receptive to the use of formal services (Price, 1994). However, the continuing increase in single mothers living in poverty means less capability to provide the needed support to their older parents. To what extent fictive kin will be able to compensate for these changes remains to be seen.

African American caregivers for elders with dementia cling to values of responsibilities to family, the extended family network, and in-home care for as long as possible. A particularly important aspect of informal caregiving in these situations is caregiver stress. What strategies are most often used to cope with caregiving stress? While a review of the literature does not indicate any clear-cut patterns, some investigators have reported that African Americans are more likely to use prayer than their nonminority counterparts (Wood & Parham, 1990; Wykle & Segall, 1991). In addition, these caregivers report deriving a higher level of day-to-day satisfaction and spiritual meaning from caregiving (Farran, Miller, Kaufman, & Davis, 1997). In general, the literature suggests that African Americans may show considerable resilience and adaptability when required to assume the role of caregiver. As compared with their nonminority counterparts, they find caregiving tasks less stressful and report higher self-efficacy in coping with caregiving problems. Perhaps previous experience with adversity helps many African Americans to reframe difficult life circumstances that cannot be readily changed.

Despite their resilience and coping strategies, many African Americans providing care to older adults with dementia do experience burden from this role and find that at times the caregiving tasks become difficult and overwhelming. They report that they would benefit from education and support aimed at helping them overcome these challenges. Learning how to manage problem behavior of the care recipients and to minimize these behaviors would help reduce their stress. This is indeed the focus of Resources for Enhancing Alzheimer Caregivers' Health (REACH), which we present in the concluding section of this chapter. In addition to interventions like REACH, the Internet offers a large number of valuable resources for all caregivers, including those who provide care to elders with dementia. We present a number of caregiving resources in the following Aging and Diversity Online section.

Aging and Diversity Online: Caregiving Resources

Children of Aging Parents. This nonprofit group provides information and materials for adult children and their older parents. Caregivers of people with Alzheimer's disease also may find this information helpful http://www.caps-4caregivers.org

Eldercare Locator. The Eldercare Locator is a nationwide, directory assistance service helping older people and their caregivers locate local support and resources for older Americans. Funded by the Administration on Aging (AoA), it also provides a caregiver resource called *Because We Care—A Guide for People Who Care* http://www.eldercare.gov

Family Caregiver Alliance. This community-based nonprofit organization offers support services and publications for those caring for adults with Alzheimer's disease, stroke, traumatic brain injuries, and other cognitive disorders http://www.caregiver.org

National Family Caregiver Support Program. The AoA, in an attempt to centralize information, runs this website, which primarily provides links to a vast array of other helpful websites http://www.aoa.gov/prof/aoaprog/caregiver/caregiver.asp

Well Spouse Foundation. The foundation offers support to people caring for a sick spouse who need a little emotional care themselves. Members are directed to support groups, can be assigned pen pals if desired, and receive a newsletter http://www.wellspouse.org

National Family Caregivers Association. Caregivers get free membership that entitles them to a newsletter and a pamphlet on caregiving. Other materials are available for a fee http://www.nfcacares.org

---

Informal Caregiving Among Hispanics

Juanita Fernandez is a 40-year-old Cuban American who has a 12-year-old daughter and 10-year-old son. She lives 2,000 miles away from where she was raised. She works full time in a neighborhood bakery, and her husband is employed in a paper mill 25 miles away from their home. Her brother Roberto lives within 15 miles of their parents' home. Over the years Juanita has maintained contact with her parents through telephone calls, letters, and occasional visits. Yesterday her brother called to discuss his concerns regarding their father's failing health. He also said that their mother finds it overwhelming to provide the care her husband needs. She is worried about her own health. She prays daily for strength to keep her going and to do the best she can for her husband. While Juanita would very much like to go stay with her parents and help them in any way she can, she does not know what to do. On the one hand, she loves her parents and would very much like to help them in their time of need, but, on the other hand, she is concerned about her children and her husband. She is also thinking about her job at the bakery and the income she needs to support her family. It really is difficult being so far away from home.

Although Hispanic elders report a higher level of impairment and a greater need for services than the mainstream population, they underutilize community-based long-term care services (Markides & Wallace, 1996). Instead they expect the members of their family (nuclear and extended) and their community (friends and neighbors) to provide the needed support (Gallagher-Thompson, Talamantes, Ramirez, & Valverde, 1996). In fact, Hispanic elders rank second only to Asian/Pacific Islanders in living with relatives (Federal Interagency Forum on Aging-Related Statistics, 2006). Why do they prefer these living arrangements? Some authors indicate that these arrangements are a result of health or economic necessity. Others say this is because of the value of familism, which can be defined as a strong feeling of reciprocity and solidarity among family members (Ayalon, Lopez, Huyck, & Yoder, 2001). Thus, caregiving between generations has been the basis for a natural helping network as well as for providing links with the formal system.

The level of family support available for Hispanic elders in urban communities differs significantly from that available in rural areas. In urban barrios, older people may have a substantial number of friends and nonrelatives who provide assistance. In rural areas, the family may be even more important as a source of support. A study of assistance patterns in rural Colorado indicated extensive linkages between Mexican elders and their family (Magilvy, Congdon, Martinez, Davis, & Averill, 2000). Family members maintain daily contact with one another via telephone or in person. This high level of contact may, to some extent, explain why decisions about appropriate care for an older person are made by the family unit rather than by the individual caregiver (Ayalon et al., 2001).

In the Hispanic community, elders are viewed as wise, knowledgeable, and deserving of respect. They continue to expect, receive, and be satisfied with the help their children provide and feel that their support needs are being met adequately. In a study of four generations of Hispanic women, Garcia, Kosberg, Mangum, Henderson, and Henderson (1992) found that (1) very high percentages of all four generations of Hispanic women believed that adult children—not formal services—should care for them; (2) children should share their homes with their older parents; and (3) no matter how inconvenient, contact should be maintained between children and their older parents. It is difficult to predict the degree to which such support will persist in light of the increasing participation of adult children in the labor force and in light of their geographic mobility.

As noted earlier, providing care to people with dementia can impose substantial burdens and demands on caregivers' emotional and physical resources. As a result of these demands, Hispanic caregivers show a higher sense of burden and appear to be more depressed than their non-Hispanic counterparts (Aranda & Knight, 1997; Phillips, Torres de Ardon, Komnenich, Killeen, & Rusinak, 2000). This is especially true for caregivers adhering to norms of filial support, according to which children should care for their parents and not use professional help. However, as the care recipients' physical condition deteriorates, caregivers tend to make more use of formal assistance. This decision to use formal services occurs only when the family is overwhelmed. Research shows that for Mexican American elders who live in nursing homes, levels of impairment both cognitively and functionally are greater than for non-Hispanic Whites (Chiodo, Kanten, Gerety, Mulrow, & Cornell, 1994). A South Texas study also showed that Mexican American elders in nursing homes had significantly worse ADL scores and were more dependent than their non-Hispanic White counterparts. Although this sample of Mexican Americans was younger, its members had a greater number of impairments than the non-Hispanic residents (Mulrow et al., 1996). Prior to admission to the nursing home, these Mexican American elders were not living alone; rather, they were living with family members. In other words, Hispanic family members care for their frail elders with significant ailments as long as they can (perhaps longer than their counterparts from the mainstream population), turning to nursing home placement as a last resort. Since the use of formal services contradicts cultural norms of responsibility, it is not surprising that such use is associated with depression among many caregivers, who view it as a failure to live up to their expected role.

Service providers should be aware that reaching out for assistance may be traumatic for persons who have been raised to view caregiving as a family responsibility. Counseling and reassurance to relieve caregivers' guilt should be incorporated into service programs, and counselors should be sensitive to the cultural experiences, norms, and values of the caregivers and have an understanding of the conflicts that may relate to the use of the formal system. In addition, churches should be encouraged to organize volunteer and support groups for providing caregivers with periodic relief or respite. Programs such as those offered through county social services, area agencies on aging, hospitals, and nursing homes could play very meaningful roles in terms of caregiver support.

Informal Caregiving Among Asian/Pacific Islanders

Sarla Devi is a single 48-year-old computer programmer from India. She has been working for a consultant firm since she obtained her master's degree in computer science. About 5 years ago she was transferred to Ohio, and she has lived there since then. At that time her mother in India died. Since she has no brothers or sisters, she sponsored her 70-year-old father from India to come to the United States to live with her. During the past year her father began to show problem behaviors related to dementia, and his physical care needs increased beyond what Sarla was able to manage. Though Sarla considered placing him in a nursing home, she was not able to find a facility that would work for her father, who does not speak English and has been a vegetarian all his life. She did not know what to do. Finally she found a home in India and with great reluctance decided to send him there. It was not an easy decision, but she did not have any other choice.

As you may recall from Chapter 1, Asian/Pacific Islanders include residents of the United States from Chinese, Japanese, Asian Indian, Pakistani, Korean, Vietnamese, Hmong, Laotian, Thai, Filipino, Samoan, Native Hawaiian and other Pacific Islanders, and other backgrounds. The vast cultural variation among these subgroups makes aggregating them for scientific purposes even more inappropriate than aggregating the various Hispanic groups, who at least share a common language. In addition, generalizations about Asian elders are difficult because of not only their cultural diversity but also the different patterns of immigration among these groups. While more than

80% of Asian elders (except Japanese) are foreign born, the percent of foreign born elders among Native Hawaiians, Samoans, Guamanians, and other Pacific Islanders is substantially lower. An important correlate of these differences is the proportion of elders in these subgroups who have limited contact with mainstream populations due to language difficulties. More than 40% of these linguistically isolated elders are from Chinese, Korean, Vietnamese, Cambodian, and Hmong populations. This, in turn, has important implications for providing informal and formal care that is culturally appropriate. Although there is a concentration of these elders in the Western United States as well as in New York, New Jersey, Virginia, Massachusetts, Texas, and Florida, the Midwest has also experienced significant increases in recent years. Minnesota, for example, has a sizable population of elders with Hmong, Vietnamese, and Korean backgrounds.

Recent data on living arrangements indicate that in comparison with non-Hispanic Whites, African Americans, and Hispanics, a significantly smaller proportion of Asian older men and women live alone. In fact, older Asian men and Asian women are far more likely than their counterparts of other races to live with relatives other than a spouse (Federal Interagency Forum on Aging-Related Statistics, 2006). These living arrangements may, to a great extent, be indicative of the cultural traditions and values common in many of the Asian groups. In these cultures filial piety continues to be an important norm in caring for aging parents; this norm includes issues of respect, responsibility, family harmony, and sacrifice (Sung, 1990). However, there are indications that these traditional norms may be beginning to decline both in the United States and Asia. The factors producing this change are the same on both continents: the movement of children and family away from each other, large numbers of women in the workforce, and the lack of availability of housing units that allow for intergenerational living. Furthermore, a strain faced by many Asian families in the United States is the duality of cultures within families and the inevitable clashes that result when different generations have different languages and values.

In brief, Asians who came to the United States in their youth or during early middle age have become acculturated to less traditional family relationships. However, in contrast to White families, the needs of their elders still take precedence for them. Given the variability among the various subgroups within this population, service providers should resist the temptation to treat Asian elders as if these subgroups were all alike.

Informal Caregiving Among Native Americans

Eddie Banton is a 70-year-old Native American (Ojibwa) male who lives on the White Earth Reservation with the family of his son, Christopher. Although he was deeply saddened by his wife's death 5 years ago, he adjusted well. Christopher's wife, Diane, and his two teenage daughters enjoy the stories Eddie tells about his childhood, his experiences in a Bureau of Indian Affairs boarding school and a Catholic mission school, and his work in high steel construction. Eddie believes it is essential to share his knowledge with his children and grandchildren: "If we educate them right, our children tomorrow will be wiser than we are today." On their part, the children provide the care and support Eddie needs. Since he is not able to drive, they very often take him to the community meetings or take him to see the doctor, about 40 miles away. They also do most of the cooking and enjoy preparing his favorite foods.

Native Americans have traditionally placed a high value on the extended family (Lockery, 1991). This holds true even more for families living in rural America, where the elders are more likely to live with close relatives. In addition to cultural traditions, poverty may be another determinant of extended families. A large number of older Indians in rural communities live with their children and grandchildren not only because of cultural norms but also to share and exchange limited resources. These living arrangements also allow them to transmit cultural lore across generations, thus ensuring the cultural integrity of the group.

In addition, Native American families are more interdependent than White families (Yee, 1990). Caregiving is thus regarded as a reflection of the cultural ethos of interdependency (Red Horse, 1980), and a high value is placed on providing care for older family members. Female relatives often assume the role of primary caregiver, with many of them dividing their time between elder care and taking care of their own children or grandchildren. This situation parallels findings reported for caregivers in the general population. However, in contrast to caregivers in the mainstream population, Native American caregivers attribute the burden they experience with caregiving to having outside responsibilities rather than to caregiving interfering with outside responsibilities (Hennessy & John, 1996).

Based on a series of focus groups with Native American caregivers, Hennessy & John (1996) reported that these caregivers find it very satisfying to fulfill the cultural prescription to provide care for a frail family member. However, many of them experience substantial burdens in providing care. This is mainly due to holding a full-time job while at the same time taking care of a homebound person. The focus group participants identified four major sources of burden related to caregiving responsibilities:

1. Anxiety about managing severe disease conditions in the home.
2. Problems with difficult psychosocial aspects of care such as care recipients' noncompliance and mental health problems.
3. Strains on family relations.
4. Negative affects on personal health and well-being.

In addition, the focus group participants also described the circumstances that contributed to their sense of efficacy and their ability to persevere in their efforts. These sources of satisfaction included (1) achieving control over caregiving by developing fixed routines for managing the medical and nonmedical aspects of care; (2) creating family consensus about the caregiving situation and its demands, including mobilizing family assistance; and (3) obtaining periodic respite from caregiving (Hennessy & John, 1996).

While rural elders living on reservations depend mainly on family caregivers, urban elders augment their informal support through formal sources (Shomaker, 1990). Research indicates that urban Native Americans use long-term care facilities at twice the rate of those who live in rural communities (Manson, 1993). However, this may be due to the availability of such facilities in urban areas. With the recent advent of nursing home construction in Native American communities, it will be important to monitor the use of these facilities and its impact on the tradition of informal caregiving.

In summary, the extended family continues to be the norm in Native American communities. All members of the household influence each other directly, with the older members providing leadership. In addition, awareness of service needs, knowledge of service agencies, and use of agency services are higher for those living in extended family settings than for those living alone. Thus, family structure contributes not only to providing care and sharing resources but also to an increased awareness and accessibility of services available for older adults.

Informal Caregiving Among Elders Who Are Lesbian, Gay, and Bisexual

---

Donna Lund is a 60-year-old White lesbian who lives with her partner, Sarah, aged 72. They both have lived together in a small Midwestern community for more than 25 years. Though Donna provides Sarah informal care and assistance with transportation to appointments, shopping, and managing finances, she is worried as Sarah has begun to show signs of dementia and may have to be placed in a nursing home. She is aware of the prejudice and misinformation health-care staff can have, especially in smaller communities, but does not know what to do. She has now started exploring various options through the Internet and is considering moving to San Francisco with Sarah to place her in a nursing home that welcomes people with different sexual orientations and provides the care they need.

Lesbian, gay, bisexual, and transgender (LGBT) elders often receive informal care from biological children, grandchildren, or stepchildren from past heterosexual unions as well as from other biological family members (Coon, 2003). In addition, many LGBT seniors have expanded multigenerational social and professional networks that can help them contend with discrimination and adjust more easily with growing older (Grossman, D'Augelli, & Hershberger, 2000; Kimmel, 1978). However, for one reason or another, in recent years these networks have been somewhat truncated (Shippy, Brennan, & Cantor, 2002), and social losses due to the AIDS epidemic have severely reduced the networks of many gay male cohorts (Coon, 2003). This means that many LGBT elders may have to modify their expectations that blood relatives or friends will provide them the needed care beyond a certain point (Kimmel, 1978; Quam & Whitford, 1992).

In a society with few legal protections for LGBT people, fear of discrimination and intolerance—including fears of hate crimes, loss of employment, and social stigma—stops many LGBT caregivers and care recipients from seeking or acquiring the care they need. Many service agencies and organizations discourage LGBT outness, which, in turn, can create particularly sticky situations in smaller communities. In addition, when health and social service professionals have limited information for these care recipients and caregivers, it can lead to misdiagnosis and can obstruct effective treatment and care management.

LGBT persons of color seeking refuge in LGBT communities may experience both overt discrimination similar to that found in larger societies and subtler forms of discrimination due to absence of leaders of color in LGBT community organizations (Gock, 1992; Greene, 1994). As a result, LGBT caregivers of color may be reluctant to use formal programs offered by LGBT communities. Thus, they often struggle with caregiver duties and stress more than the caregivers from the general population. It is essential to foster the development of effective services for all LGBT caregivers, including those from communities of color. We return to a discussion of these services and interventions in another section of the chapter.

Aging and Diversity Online: Caregiving in LGBT Communities

Family Caregiver Alliance. This website includes a monograph on caregiving in LGBT communities. In addition to a large number of references, the monograph also includes a list of readings and websites as well as mailing addresses for relevant organizations http://www.caregiver.org

---

The next section focuses on formal care. We first discuss formal assistance available to older people who live at home, and then we turn our attention to institutional care. Next we outline the barriers that hinder the use of available services and suggest strategies to help overcome these obstacles. The concluding section of the chapter is devoted to programs and services that have been successful in meeting health and social service needs of ethnically diverse elders and their caregivers.

FORMAL CARE

As we noted earlier, placing their elders in nursing homes continues to be the last resort for all ethnic groups. Over the decades, federal, state, and local services have become available to help older people remain in their homes. Why? Using these services allows them to maintain their independence as long as possible. Also, in-home services are often less expensive than nursing home care. What do these services include? These services may be classified into two major groups:

1. Services brought to the older people in their own homes: for example, home health services, home delivered meals, and home improvement.
2. Community-based services that require the older person to leave home to receive them: for example, adult day care centers, assisted living facilities (ALFs), and nursing homes.

Medicare reimburses home health care services, defined as skilled nursing or rehabilitation benefits that are provided to older persons in their home as prescribed by a physician. The three most widely used home health care services include skilled nursing, home health aides, and physical therapy. Research reveals that home health care is substantially less expensive than hospital care and nursing home care (Hughes et al., 1997).

ACTIVE LEARNING EXPERIENCE: HOW THE FORMAL AND INFORMAL CARE SYSTEMS WORK TOGETHER

The purpose of this experience is to provide you with an opportunity to examine a variety of ways formal and informal systems work together to provide care to older adults. Upon completion of this activity, you will be able to:

1. Describe various ways formal and informal systems may work together in providing care to older adults.
2. Outline factors that affect how caregiving tasks are shared between a family member and a paid care provider.

Time required: 45 minutes (30 minutes to complete the questions and 15 minutes to discuss the answers with another person).

Instructions:

1. Complete the questions included in this activity either as a homework assignment or in a class setting.
2. Discuss your responses with another person.
3. Participate in a class discussion of student responses to the activity.

Vignettes

Vignette 1

David Peterson, 82, lives in a one-room apartment in a large metropolitan area. He requires assistance to move from his bed to a wheelchair or from his chair to the toilet. He receives both personal care and homemaking services for a few hours every day. His 58-year-old daughter lives about a mile away from him and comes regularly to provide informal care. However, she is not able to lift her father or to provide hands-on care.

Vignette 2

Rosanne Sanchez is a 76-year-old widow who is both physically and mentally incapacitated from a recent stroke. She lives in a rural community of 5,000 people. Her son lives about 500 miles away. A paid caregiver, Andrea, was legally appointed as her guardian to manage her affairs. As a result of their ongoing association, Rosanne has developed a strong emotional attachment to and dependence on Andrea.

Vignette 3

Meg Rosenberg, an 85-year-old widow, lives alone in an apartment about 5 miles away from a comprehensive medical center. Her son lives about

1,500 miles away and maintains ongoing contact with her. He calls her on a regular basis and visits her three or four times a year. Meg subscribes to Lifeline, an emergency response system for summoning help in times of need. Recently, she made use of this system when she suffered a mild stroke. Her son came the day she was admitted to the local hospital.

Discussion Questions:

1. In the first vignette, how do the "formal" and "informal" systems of care work together to address David's needs?
2. What conditions lead to cooperation between family caregivers and paid home care workers? What conditions may produce conflict among them?
3. In the second vignette, how would you describe Rosanne's relationship with the paid caregiver? How does this relationship compare with that between David and his daughter in the first vignette?
4. In the third vignette, how is the coordination between "formal" and "informal" systems of care different from what you observed in the first two cases?

Before we proceed to discuss formal care options, it would be beneficial to outline the Person–Environment Congruence Model (Lawton & Nahemow, 1973). According to this model, an important factor in the living arrangements for older people is the extent to which there is congruence between their competence and the environmental press. Competence is defined as the theoretical upper limit of an individual's abilities to function in the areas of health, social behavior, and cognition. Thus, a person with multiple physical disabilities and chronic illnesses has reduced physical competence, which then limits the level of social and physical demands with which he or she can cope. Environmental press refers to the potential of the environment to influence behavior (e.g., the level of stimulation, physical barrier, lack of privacy). Individuals perform at their maximum level when the environmental press slightly exceeds the level at which they adapt. In other words, the living arrangements (e.g., one's home, ALFs, a nursing home) should challenge the residents but not overwhelm them.

Adult Day Care

Adult day care involves long-term care support to older adults who live in the community. As a structured, comprehensive program, it provides older adults with a variety of health, social, and related support services in a protective setting during any part of a day but less than 24-hour care (National Institute on Adult Daycare, 1984). The program assists participants in remaining in the community and in enabling informal caregivers to continue caring for impaired elders at home.

Although a 1990 U.S. Census identified more than 2,100 adult day care centers nationwide, 40% of them were established after 1984 (Zawadski & Stuart, 1990).

Despite the continuing increase in the number of day care centers, fewer than half of Americans know what an adult day care center is (Yu, Kim, Liu, & Wong, 1993). This is especially true for many Asian Americans and other recent immigrants. In a survey of Chinese and Korean elders from four congregate housing units in Chicago, interviewers had to explain what an adult day care center was before the respondents could give their answers on using these services. Only 37% of the Chinese and 23% of the Koreans indicated their willingness to use the services of an adult day care center. However, research with participants from day care centers in Missouri shows that African American elders are more likely than older Whites to use these services and that they use them more frequently. They are substantially less likely to be married than Whites, have nonspousal caregivers who work outside the home, have limited economic resources, and use Medicaid funding to pay for their day care (Wallace, Snyder, Walker, & Ingman, 1992). Since a companion survey of the general population is not available, it is not clear why day care use rates are higher for older African Americans than Whites. Other data show that African American elders are more likely to have functional disabilities, to live in poverty, and to live with nonspousal family. Each of these characteristics could increase the need for day care and contribute to increased use by this population.

Assisted Living Facilities

Given the continuing need to explore cost-effective alternatives to nursing homes, a large number of community residential care options have become available. These new models provide group housing with services such as meals, basic health care, and some personal assistance. While a variety of options are available, space limitations do not allow us to include all of them in our discussion. We, therefore, devote our attention to the option that has gained popularity not only with the mainstream population but also with ethnic minorities: assisted living facilities (ALFs).

An ALF is a congregate setting that provides or coordinates personal services, 24-hour supervision and assistance (scheduled and unscheduled), activities, and health-related services. It is designed to minimize the need to move; to accommodate individual's changing needs and preferences; to maximize residents' dignity, autonomy, privacy, independence, and safety; and to encourage family and community involvement (Assisted Living Quality Coalition, 1998). As this definition suggests, the key elements of assisted living include the following (Hawes, Phillips, Rose, Holan, & Sherman, 2003):

1. Services and oversight available 24 hours a day.
2. Services to address scheduled and unscheduled needs.
3. Care and services aimed at promoting independence.
4. An emphasis on consumer privacy, dignity, autonomy, and choice.
5. An emphasis on a home-like environment.

Although there has been general agreement on the key principles or elements of assisted living, this does not mean that all ALFs embody these principles. A national survey conducted by Hawes and colleagues found that ALFs differ widely in ownership, size, philosophy, and population served.

Overall, residents of ALFs are still quite healthy but require assistance with personal and household care. They often get prepared meals, housekeeping services, assistance with medication and transportation, and help with bathing, dressing, and personal care needs. While most facilities indicate a willingness to admit residents with moderate physical limitations, fewer than half would admit residents with moderate to severe cognitive impairments (Hawes et al., 2003). In terms of cost, assisted living is much less expensive than nursing home care. However, most residents pay for their own housing costs, as assisted living is generally not covered by Medicare or Medicaid. Thus, people with limited finances may not have access to assisted living and end up going to nursing homes where they are covered by Medicaid.

Do ethnic minorities use ALFs? While we do not have adequate information for all ethnic minorities, Ball et al. (2005) provide a rich description of six ALFs that are home to African American elders. Each of these facilities is unique—in size, appearance, and neighborhood, types of residents who live there, and care provided. Of the six facilities, five are owned and operated by African Americans and more than half of the residents and their caregivers are poor. The sixth is a large, corporately owned home that serves the more affluent African American community. As these authors indicate, these facilities provide a good solution for African Americans when the family members are not able to take care of these elders. It is important to note that in most states, support for assisted living from the Medicaid program and other sources is extremely limited or nonexistent. Under these circumstances many poor elders, regardless of their ethnic background, cannot afford assisted living facilities and end up going to nursing homes where Medicaid covers the cost of care.

Nursing Homes

Nursing homes—or nursing facilities, as Medicaid and Medicare refer to them—are the institutional setting for long-term care. In 2002, there were approximately 16,491 nursing homes in the United States (Cowles, 2003), and the average annual cost of nursing home care was $52,000 for a semiprivate room and $61,000 for a private room (MetLife Mature Market Institute, 2002). Public funds, primarily Medicaid and Medicare, account for approximately 60% of national long-term care spending on older adults.

The distinctive feature of nursing homes is their potential for meeting all of the residents' needs within the institution itself. Residents may be admitted to a facility during their process of recovery after a surgery and return to their community residences once the desired level of functioning is achieved. Data from the National Center for Health Statistics (2003) indicate that, since the mid-1970s, nursing home utilization rates for older adults, including those for the oldest old, have decreased. This decline in the use of nursing home care may be due to the increase in the availability of long-term care alternatives such as assisted living facilities, adult day care, and in-home health care. It is estimated that almost three of four people 65 or older are likely to use some type of in-home care services over their lifetime (Alexcih, 1997). In other words, while traditional nursing homes will continue to be a component of care for the oldest and frailest member of society, other creative approaches to providing formal and informal care will continue to be developed (Gallagher, 2000).

Nursing Home Residence by Race and Ethnicity

As we have noted in earlier sections of this chapter, older African Americans, Latinos, and Asian Americans, like older non-Hispanic White individuals, remain in their own homes even after their spouse has died (Burr, 1990). Nursing homes are indeed the last resort for all groups. However, African Americans enter nursing homes at a higher rate than other racial and ethnic groups (Angel & Hogan, 2004). Additional research needs to be conducted to examine factors that contribute to variability in use of nursing home care across ethnic groups. Hispanic elders are far less likely than other racial and ethnic groups to use nursing home care (Angel & Hogan, 2004). Why? This underutilization by Hispanic elders may reflect cultural traditions and values, but it may also be due to several other factors. Many Spanish-speaking elders may experience difficulty filling out forms that are written in English, may not like food they are unaccustomed to eating, and may feel isolated from friends and family. In addition, inability to pay for nursing home care may also play a key role in their decision about living arrangements (Himes, Hogan, & Eggebeen, 1996).

To some extent, similar factors may help explain limited use of nursing home care by Asian Americans, especially those who immigrated to the United States later in life. Many of them have different religious backgrounds, have limited English language skills, and are not accustomed to the food served in the nursing home. In the coming decades this may change when the Asian Americans currently in the workforce reach old age, develop disabilities, and need long-term care. They are likely to explore long-term care options that are culturally sensitive. Given the continuing increase in the diversity of the older population, it is reasonable to expect that culturally competent care will become increasingly available, thereby providing a range of long-term care options to members of different ethnic and racial groups. These all-inclusive services would, in turn, enhance the quality of life for diverse segments of the older population. We provide one example of such culturally sensitive care in a later section of the chapter.

Nursing Home Residence by Sex

The majority of older people residing in nursing homes are women. In 1999, oldest-old women, aged 85 or older, accounted for 42% of all older nursing home residents. In comparison with women, male nursing home residents tend to be younger. This difference may be due to longer life expectancies and longer disability-free lifetimes that women experience. In addition, it may also be due to the serious and permanent injuries men experience at younger ages (National Center for Injury Prevention and Control, 2001). After women enter nursing homes in old age, they tend to stay longer, thereby further extending the average age of female residents. Research indicates that after the age of 65, the average stay in a nursing home is 26 months for women and 19 months for men (Freedman, 1993). Another study reported that at 85 years of age, women can expect to spend about 30% of their remaining life in nursing homes compared with about 10% for men (Laditka, 1998).

Nursing Home Use in Rural Communities

Older people living in rural areas have an adequate supply of nursing home beds available to them: There are 62 nursing home beds per 1,000 older adults in nonmetropolitan counties compared with 45 in metropolitan areas (Shaughnessy, 1994). Coward, Netzer, and Mullens (1996) also reported a high rate of nursing home admissions among older populations in rural areas. One possible explanation may be the limited availability of other long-term alternatives such as in-home care and community-based services in rural communities (Ricketts, Hart, & Pirani, 2000; Rogers, 2002; Stearns, Slifkin, & Edin, 2000). It is also possible that in some rural areas older people may not be aware of the available options or may not have the transportation they need to use these services. Another explanation may be that residents of rural communities may have positive attitudes regarding nursing home care (Rowles, Beaulieu, & Myers, 1997; Schoenberg & Coward, 1997).

In summary, traditional nursing homes will continue to be a component of care for the oldest and frailest members of society. The challenge will be how to reclaim the term *home* and to create resident-centered living spaces where demands, preferences, and lifestyles are addressed for all ethnic and racial groups. It will remain essential to acknowledge the centrality of the consumer (the resident) and to recognize that the nursing home is the home to given individuals regardless of their ethnic and cultural background, place of residence, and sexual orientation. Fortunately, a range of initiatives are currently under way to improve the quality of care nursing homes provide to older people (see, e.g., Fagan, 2003; Weiner & Ronch, 2003).

Barriers Hindering the Use of Formal Care

In this section, we present four groups of obstacles that may hinder the use of available services by ethnic elders, women, and residents from rural communities. We also suggest strategies to help overcome these problems and to promote the use of available services.

Lack of Knowledge and Information

People are not able to use services if they do not know about them. Research reveals that elders' degree of knowledge regarding medical and social services varies considerably from study to study and from service to service. For ethnic elders, this awareness also depends on factors such as the length of time they have lived in the United States, the type of community or neighborhood in which they now live, their mastery of English, and their use of media (Krout, 1983).

In total, 98% of documents regarding essential services such as Medicare, Medicaid, Social Security, food stamps, public assistance, and Supplemental Security Income require a reading level of ninth grade or higher (Walmsley & Allington, 1982). This makes it difficult for many ethnic elders to read and understand the documents and to gain access to the services. This is especially true for recent immigrants and refugees, who may have a limited knowledge of English.

However, merely knowing about these services is not enough. They have to be perceived as culturally relevant and accessible. People become discouraged when they are "ping-ponged" from agency to agency and when they are asked to complete long, complicated forms in an unfamiliar language with technical jargon. Hayes and Guttmann (1986) found that 60% of the people who seek social services are turned away from agencies. With the goal of increasing service use by diverse elders and their caregivers, researchers have been exploring a range of approaches and assessing their effectiveness. Following are some examples of approaches that have been effective in overcoming these obstacles.

Using Church and Neighborhood Networks Geriatric professionals have been successful in reaching ethnic and minority elders, both in rural and urban areas, through informal networks such as families, friends, neighbors, and churches. Members of these networks can be helpful in communicating essential information about available services and in providing links to service providers.

Using Ethnic Newspapers, Radio, and Television Wide use of media and non-English printed materials has been successful in targeting information about programs and services to various ethnic groups. In a study of Hispanic caregivers of people with dementia in New York City, researchers found that Spanish radio and television stations successfully reached and informed them about formal services (Cox & Monk, 1993).

Using Outreach Workers Elders in rural communities and ethnic neighborhoods feel isolated and lack knowledge about essential programs and services. Outreach workers with background concerning the special needs of ethnic elders can play an important role in making the needed services accessible to the target population.

Location of Service
The physical location of the service affects the extent to which it is used (Cox, 2005). Traveling to an unfamiliar area outside an ethnic neighborhood means not only venturing into strange surroundings but also negotiating new and often complex environments. Transportation difficulties are a consideration for recent immigrants, low-income elders, and residents of rural communities. If an adult day care center is out of the immediate neighborhood and away from a mass transportation line, it may be available but not accessible.

The location of the nursing home plays an important role in making it possible for families to be closely involved in maintaining ongoing contact with residents. Research with nursing homes for Native Americans indicates that those built on reservations by tribal entities are defined as extensions of family care, demonstrating the continued value and esteem with which elders are treated (Manson, 1989; Shomaker, 1981). Fandetti and Gelfand (1976) report similar findings with Italian and Polish respondents. Whereas most of these respondents preferred to care for their elderly family members in their own homes, there was a surprising willingness to consider placement in an institution connected with their respective ethnic communities. Merely locating health and social services in the racial or ethnic community may not necessarily solve the problem. Trust and faith in the efficacy of service providers also need to be developed.

Language Issues   Two particular obstacles to the use of formal programs by older adults are language barriers and lack of sensitivity to cultural traditions and beliefs (Harbert & Ginsberg, 1979). The greater the language barrier, the more isolated the group and the more unable its members are to participate in services provided in the wider society. This is especially true for elders who are recent immigrants. They differ markedly from the foreign-born individuals who have lived in the United States for many decades. These recent immigrants are less likely to speak English and are more likely to trace their origin to Asia and Latin America than to Europe. While they may be able to get along in day-to-day life in the United States, they are more likely to experience difficulties in communicating personal problems involving the expression of feelings and emotions (Westermeyer, 1987). Furthermore, under severe stress or physical illness, they may lose the secondary language but still retain their native language (Marcos & Alpert, 1976).

Communication problems present obstacles not only for recent immigrants but also for native-born, low-income, minority, and rural elders (Hollis & Woods, 1981; Wallace, Campbell, & Lew-Ting, 1994). Many service providers use unnecessary jargon, do not understand clients' dialect, or are unfamiliar with the expressions used by members of a particular ethnic group. It is also possible that clients may "choose not to understand" when understanding is anxiety provoking or demands activities that are viewed as difficult or unnecessary (Arroyo & Lopez, 1984). Furthermore, many elders have difficulty in understanding the technical language used by service providers.

What steps can be taken to overcome the communication barrier?

- Health and social service agencies should continue their efforts to diversify their workforce. Having bilingual-bicultural workers on their staff is helpful in providing services to non-English-speaking elders.
- Given the shortage of professionally trained ethnic workers, interpreters are necessary. It is essential to develop a pool of carefully selected and trained interpreters to ensure sensitivity, accuracy, confidentiality, and the ability to interpret cultural content.
- Communicating in a "user-friendly" language makes a difference. When documents use an abundance of technical jargon, clients appreciate an explanation in an easy-to-understand language. Service providers should consider their clients' educational level, socioeconomic status, and cultural background. They should remember that communication problems extend beyond older persons who speak a foreign language and also include those who are illiterate. Providing services to these elders will continue to present a challenge.

Social Psychological Barriers   Even when formal services are available in the broader community, social psychological as well as bureaucratic and physical barriers may prevent their use by ethnic and low-income elders. Many older Blacks are reluctant to seek help from a formal service agency. They may view the use of such services as a reflection of defeat or powerlessness. Others may have a mistrust of helping professionals (Corbie-Smith, Thomas, & St. George, 2002). One study notes that Blacks drop out of treatment earlier and more frequently than Whites as a result of negative experiences with helping professionals (Sue, McKinney, Allen, & Hall, 1974). In addition, historical cohort experiences may play a role in shaping an older person's view of help taking. If in the past, members of certain ethnic groups have experienced discrimination from service providers, they may continue to avoid using these services.

It is important to note that, within the same ethnic group, use levels may differ from one service to another. For example, Hispanic elders make frequent visits to their physician's office but do not typically use social services such as transportation, senior centers, meals-on-wheels, homemaker assistance, routine telephone checks, and church-based assistance. It is not clear whether the low rates of use actually represent unmet needs for this population or whether the members of this group do not need more social services than what they use currently. Another possibility is that the design of these services does not take into account the cultural uniqueness of the older groups they are meant to serve. This problem can be addressed by involving ethnic elders in designing programs that are culturally sensitive. Research indicates that involving ethnic elders in designing programs makes services more culturally meaningful and promotes use (Chen & Soto, 1979). In addition, use is further increased by involving members of ethnic communities in the delivery of services for their elders.

In summary, use of many programs and services can be substantially increased if program design takes into account cultural values and practices of potential users. It is important that services be delivered in such a way that the dignity, pride, and respect for recipients are preserved. Use is also increased by involving leaders and members of ethnic communities as full partners with professionals in all phases of the planning and delivery of services. This approach empowers communities and neighborhoods, connects the formal system with informal sources of support, increases elders' knowledge of available services, and promotes acceptance of services by ethnic elders and their families. Regardless of the model or approach used, it is essential to incorporate cultural practices in all programs and services aimed at meeting the needs of ethnic elders. Violating cultural norms shows disrespect to elders, their families, and their cultures.

In the following section we present examples of programs and services that have been specifically designed for diverse elders or their informal caregivers. In addition, we include references to resources you may use to learn about a variety of other programs and interventions, their distinctive features, the population they aim to serve, and the outcomes they expect to achieve.

PROGRAMS AND SERVICES

Culturally Sensitive Care

As we have noted earlier, service utilization is increased when the services are congruent with both the values and needs of the target population. In addition, using staff members from the same ethnic group as the intended client population also helps increase the effectiveness of the services. One excellent example of how community care services can incorporate these features to serve diverse elders is provided by On Lok Senior Health Services, now called On Lok Lifeways, in the San

Francisco Bay Area. On Lok provides community-based comprehensive medical, social, and rehabilitation services to frail elders integrating acute care and long-term care under one health-care delivery system. Thus, the program prevents institutionalization of frail elders who are certified as needing a nursing home level of care. On Lok receives a flat amount for each person served, similar to the way that health-care maintenance organizations (HMOs) are paid. A comprehensive day health program is integrated with home care including nursing, social work, meals, transportation, personal care, homemaker, and respite care (see Figure 6.2).

Begun in 1972 as a social model and adult day health-care program, On Lok serves frail elders at eight sites in the San Francisco Bay Area from the following ethnicities: Caucasian, African American, Hispanic, Asian Pacific Islander, and American Indian and Alaska Native. It is important to note that the staff members share the ethnic diversity represented among program enrollees. Furthermore, given the program's commitment to provide quality and compassionate care to ethnic elders, continued attention is given to increasing staff's knowledge about cultural similarities and differences (Kornblatt, Eng, & Hansen, 2003).

Unlike traditional programs, On Lok consolidates the delivery of various services. Its extensive multidisciplinary team assesses participants' needs, develops care plans, delivers most services, manages the care given by contracted providers, monitors treatment results, and adjusts the care plans as needed. Six principles underlie the On Lok model (Van Steenberg, Ansak, & Chin-Hansen, 1993):

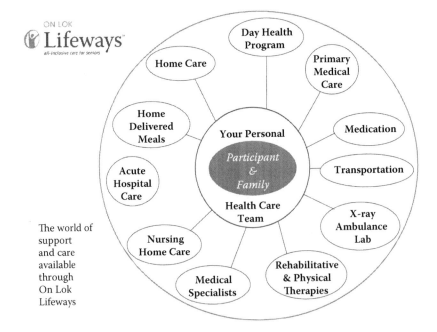

Figure 6.2   Circle of Care: the world of support and care available through On Lok Lifeways. (Source: On Lok Lifeways.)

1. It serves impaired and frail elders who need ongoing care for the rest of their lives. Participants have an average of more than seven medical diagnoses each. These diagnoses include dementia, hypertension, cerebral vascular disease, and arthritis.
2. Participants' continued residence in the community and the community's ongoing participation in the program are emphasized. Respect for the cultural preferences of the participants is given a high priority.
3. Comprehensive medical, social, and supportive services are included. All services are available on a 24-hour basis. In-home care includes personal as well as skilled care.
4. Service interpretation through consideration and team control is the fourth principle. On Lok's multidisciplinary team determines service needs and mobilizes the service required since fee-for-service restrictions do not apply. The team imposes no limitations a priori for any service.
5. Resources from Medicare, Medicaid, and private individuals are pooled to provide needed services, including preventive care.
6. The provider organization must be able to manage risk—that is, monitor clients, services, and costs, and readily adapt to change. This assumption provides an incentive to increase the service system's efficiency and effectiveness.

In summary, the On Lok model is effective in serving low-income elders of diverse ethnicities in their communities and has been widely replicated to varying degrees nationwide, often through the Program for the All-inclusive Care for the Elderly (PACE).

Interventions for Enhancing Alzheimer's Caregiver Health

The majority of persons with AD are cared for at home by a family member such as a spouse or daughter. Providing care to these persons places enormous demands on the informal caregivers. As a consequence, many caregivers experience considerable burden and stress, resulting in compromised physical and mental health. Clearly, there is a need for efficacious interventions that would help reduce the burden and stress experienced by family caregivers of older persons with AD. Since ethnicity affects how families approach the demanding task of caring for a relative with AD, a successful intervention must address culturally specific elements and individual needs. A recently completed REACH study attempted to create intervention models capable of addressing both of these criteria (cultural specificity and individual variability). This multisite research project, sponsored by the National Institute on Aging (NIA) and the National Institute of Nursing Research, was designed to evaluate the efficacy of a variety of behavioral, social, and environmental interventions to relieve and support family caregivers.

As Table 6.2 indicates, REACH included nine well-defined interventions that were implemented at six sites across the country. These interventions consisted of psychosocial-psychoeducational services, behavioral interventions, environmental modifications, and technology interventions. Please note that not all interventions were implemented at each site. Three sites included a minimal support telephone contact control group, and three sites included a usual care control condition. The

TABLE 6.2   REACH Interventions by Site

Site	Participants' Ethnicity (%)	Interventions
Birmingham, Alabama	White, 57.1 Black, 42.9	*Skill Training Condition*: Problem-solving training designed to increase caregivers' ability to manage care recipients' behavioral excess and deficits and to increase caregivers' ability to cope with these and other daily stressors.
Boston, Massachusetts	White, 79 Black, 16 Hispanic/Other, 2	*REACH for Telephone-Linked Computer (TLC) System*: Telephone-based intervention designed to reduce caregiver stress. The system provides automated monitoring of caregiver stress levels, a voicemail caregiver bulletin board, an ask-the-expert call option, and care recipient behavioral distraction to reduce disruptive behaviors.
Memphis, Tennessee	White, 58.6 Black, 39.8	*Behavior Care*: Caregivers receive written information plus skills training and materials in patient behavior management (periodic consultations and phone calls with behavior management interventionist to manage care recipients' behaviors). *Enhanced Care*: Caregivers receive written information and skills training plus behavioral modification strategies to decrease stress for the caregiver (relaxation training, coping strategies).
Miami, Florida	White, 49.8 Hispanic, 50.2	*Family-Based Structural Multisystem In-Home Intervention (FSMII)*: In-home family system therapy designed to reduce caregiver's distress of managing and living with care recipient and to enhance family functioning. *FSMII + Computer Telephone Integration System (CTIS)*: Designed to augment FSMII with a computerized telephone system. The CTIS system is used to facilitate communication among the therapist, caregiver, family, and other support systems by providing messaging, conferencing, access to prestored information, and respite functions.
Palo Alto, California	White, 57.2 Hispanic, 42.8	*Coping with Caregiving Class*: Psychoeducational class designed to teach caregivers coping and mood management skills. *Enhanced Support Group*: Support group patterned after local community support groups (standardized meeting frequency, duration, length of time in group, and educational materials).
Philadelphia, Pennsylvania	White, 48.2 Black, 47.8	*Environmental Skill-Building Program*: Home-based intervention that provides caregivers with skills and technical support to modify the home to manage excess care recipient behaviors. Problem areas addressed may include managing activities of daily living (ADLs), excess agitation, wandering or incontinence, and caregiver need for respite.

Source: Adapted from Shulz et al. (2003).

participants included African American, Cuban American, Mexican American, and White American family caregivers of older people with AD and related disorders. With the goal of assessing the effectiveness of the intervention, the investigators used several measures at a number of points in time. These measures included indications of caregiver well-being and depression; social support; caregiver burden; religiosity; service utilization; caregiver and care recipients' physical health and medication usage; and care recipients' behavior and cognition (see Wisniewski et al., 2003 for detailed information regarding intervention, sample, design, and measures.)

Did these interventions make a difference? Key findings include (Schulz et al., 2003):

- Among all caregivers combined, active interventions were superior to control conditions in reducing caregiver burden.
- Among all caregivers combined, active interventions that emphasize active engagement of caregivers had the greatest impact in reducing caregiver depression.
- Women and those with high school or lower education who were in active interventions reported reduced burden compared with similar individuals in control conditions.
- Caregivers in active interventions who were Hispanic, those who were nonspouses, and those who had less than a high school education reported lower depression scores than those with the same characteristics who were in control conditions.

What we have outlined is a very brief summary of the overall findings. Details regarding the impact of individual interventions, the range of outcomes examined, and the depth of analyses carried out at each site are available in a special section of the journal *The Gerontologist* (2003, Volume 43, No. 4). Clearly, these studies provide a rich array of effective intervention strategies that can be used to enhance different outcomes of persons with dementia. In addition, they also provide important leads regarding which types of intervention approaches work with which types of caregivers. Given the outcomes achieved in this project, a follow-up study (REACH II) is currently under way. The primary goal of REACH II is to test a single intervention at multiple sites with an ethnically diverse population of caregivers. It is too early to report findings for this follow-up. Interested readers should monitor the publication of these findings in journals such as the *Gerontologist, Psychology of Aging,* and *Annals of Internal Medicine.*

Technology to Help Older Persons and Their Family Caregivers

The past 10 years have witnessed dramatic development and deployment of computer technology. Many older people now have access to computers, have learned how to use them, and can navigate the Internet. A number of educational programs have also become available for those interested in learning how to use a computer. A successful example of these programs is Senior-Net, which provides older people with computer education and access to computers and the Internet to enrich their lives. In addition, the American Association of Retired Persons (AARP) provides online basic how-to programs, and many health organizations offer training programs on how to gain access to health information via computers.

Although there are substantial differences across cohorts and across different segments of the older population, there is evidence that many middle-aged and older adults are quite receptive to some form of modern technology (Czaja, 1997; Kelly, 1997; Wagner & Wagner, 2003; Zimmer & Chappell, 1999). Research indicates that older people are willing to use technologies if (1) benefits are clear to them; (2) they receive adequate instructions on how to use a system; and (3) the system itself is easy to use (Fiske, Rogers, Charness, Czaja, & Sharit, 2004). Research on interest in the use of technology by middle-aged and older adults has led to the new field of gerontechnology defined as the study of technology and aging for the improvement of daily functioning of older people (Bouma, 1993). In addition to enhancing the quality of life of older people, information technology has also been used to provide support to family caregivers, especially those who provide support to adults with dementia. We begin this section by presenting some examples of how technology has been used to help older persons remain independent and then discuss the use of telecommunication technology as an aid to family caregivers of persons with dementia.

Technology to Help Older Persons Remain Independent

Consider the following examples of how older persons use technology for a range of purposes.

Vignette 1

Chuck Dietrich, 78, found and joined SeniorNet, an organization for computer-using older people. This membership provided him with unlimited access to specialized chatrooms and discussion areas. He made new friends from different parts of the country. One lady heard him say in the chatroom that he was deaf and was having difficulty with the telephone. She provided him the telephone number of the local Deaf Resources. She also got someone to install a special telephone with a voice clarifier, free of charge, without going to the agency.

Vignette 2

Wilma Temple, 70, lives in a small rural community in Wisconsin. Her son, John, lives in Oakland, California, with his wife and two children. Two years ago he got a computer for his mother and taught her how to use email and the Internet. Wilma now maintains ongoing contact with John and his family via email. John often sends her photos of her grandchildren through email. She always looks forward to hearing from her son and the grandchildren. It makes her feel connected with her son and his family even though they are so far away.

Vignette 3

Irma Smith, 76, has been using her computer for the past 4 years. However, she has been experiencing difficulty with reading the text on the computer screen.

She saw her eye doctor last month. The doctor suggested that she should use software that enlarges the text on the screen or add a function on her computer so that it can "speak" the text aloud.

Vignette 4

About 10 years ago, a Comprehensive Health Enhancement Support System (CHESS) was developed at the University of Wisconsin. Using a personal computer placed at homes, users can obtain answers to many standard health questions as well as detailed articles and description of services they may need. They can also anonymously ask questions of experts and communicate with and read personal stories about people with similar problems. CHESS computerized systems help users monitor their health status, make important health decisions, and plan how to implement those decisions. Research with AIDS patients found significant increases in the quality of life. In addition, CHESS significantly reduced the probability of their hospital admission and length of stay. Given the effectiveness of CHESS with AIDS and breast cancer patients, a prototype module has also been developed for caregivers of patients with Alzheimer's disease (Gustafson, Gustafson, & Wackerbarth, 1997).

Vignette 5

John Burton, a 75-year-old African American, lives alone in a small rural community in Mississippi. Because he takes multiple medications throughout the day, his computer has been programmed to remind him when to take what specific drug and to provide him information about drug interactions. He very much appreciates these reminders. He knows that when medication adherence falters, catastrophic consequences often result.

As these vignettes indicate, older people now have increased access to resources such as libraries, service providers, support groups, health-care information, and even distant family members through email, the Web, and stand-alone computer systems. For people with sensory impairments, computer software is available to enlarge text on the screen or to speak the text aloud. Computers can also be helpful to older people who take multiple medications throughout the day. They can be programmed to remind the person when to take the specific medicine. In addition to computers, personal digital assistants (PDAs) also have the potential to greatly benefit older adults as a memory aid and organizer. PDAs can remind the individual about appointments and medications and track health-relevant information such as exercise or glucose levels. Recently an NIA-supported project has brought together a hybrid PDA cell phone with a patented integrated pill box attachment and a software program called Rx Reminder (Sterns, 2005). Since this portable package has been designed for older people, all the buttons and text are oversized. As we have seen with computers, success of a given technology depends on factors such as ease of use, understandability, and the availability of training that helps older adults overcome the barriers of using the technology (Sterns, 2005).

Telephone equipment has also become more user-friendly. Phones with large buttons, larger text, and automatic dialing capacity are all available. In addition, voice-activated phones are available. These phones can be dialed by voice commands and answered from across the room, thereby making it convenient for older people who have problems pressing buttons or rushing to answer the incoming call.

In addition to the "high-tech" devices, a number of other products and services have become available to assist older people in emergency situations, especially those who live alone. Examples include pull cords in the bathroom or bedroom that are connected to a hospital or to the local emergency medical service and life safety systems and Lifeline Service, which use a portable medical alert device on a necklace or watchband to transmit signals for a fire or medical emergency through telephone lines or computers. These technologies have been found to be cost-effective in enhancing the older person's sense of security about living alone (Hooyman & Kiyak, 2008).

Aging and Diversity Online: Technology and Disabilities

Alliance for Technology Access. Provides highly useful information regarding Alliance for Technology Access, a network of community-based technology centers. The alliance is dedicated to making technology a regular part of the lives of people with disabilities, thereby helping them to unlock the enormous potential of technology, and it includes a number of useful resources. http://www.ataccess.org

---

Technology to Help Family Caregivers of Persons With Dementia

Many family caregivers find it difficult to participate in the traditional approach to support services where they have to be physically present to obtain information, to consult with professionals, or to attend a support group. This is especially true for families living in rural areas where many of them lack transportation and easy access to respite care. Another large group of caregivers are those who are juggling demands at work and in the home. Given the barriers faced by many family caregivers in participating in on-site programs, a number of technology-based programs and services have been designed in recent years. You may recall that in our discussion of interventions we listed telephone-linked care (TLC) as a component of the REACH program at its Boston site (Table 6.2). We begin with a brief description of TLC and then present the key features of the Link 2 Care program.

REACH for Telephone-Linked Care (TLC)   The TLC system is a telephone-linked computerized system that provides caregivers access to a four-part intervention through their regular home telephone. According to Steffen, Mahoney, and Kelly (2003), the four modules are as follows:

1. Caregiver monitoring and counseling module. Once a week participating caregivers call into REACH for TLC. Upon receipt of the call the caregiver is asked about problematic behaviors exhibited by the care recipient. This allows the system to offer strategies to reduce the problematic behaviors. If the situation continues, the nurse is alerted to make a follow-up call.

2. Caregiver voicemail bulletin board. Any participating caregiver can anonymously ask other caregivers a question about caregiving issues or offer advice to other caregivers. Participants can also send and receive personal messages to others on the system through their individual mailbox.

3. Ask-the-expert module. Caregivers can call into the nurse's voicemail with a question for the nurse or the experts. The nurse specialist monitors the line and either responds directly or forwards the call to the appropriate expert from the advisory board. She ensures that the questions are answered in a timely manner.

4. Activity distraction module. This is an 18-minute conversation intended to engage the care recipient in a simple nondemanding conversation designed to distract the person from disruptive behavior. This conversation is individualized and uses the person's name and facilitates the recollection of favorite memories. It is designed to proceed even if the recipient does not verbalize any responses.

The investigators found strong support for their hypothesis that there would be differential adoption of these components according to user preference and needs. They also found that caregiver monitoring and care recipient distraction telephone conversations were most utilized. It is important to note that prior technology experience, caregiver relationship, perceived stress, and sources and type of counseling exerted no influence on usage (Mahoney, Tarlow, & Jones, 2001). Also note that the pilot testing for TLC and other computer telephone integration systems have included African American and Hispanic caregivers (Table 6.2).

In introducing the section on technology we suggested that despite the differences across cohorts, many middle-aged and older adults are users of technology, including computer-based services. This population is likely to expand dramatically during the next 10 to 20 years. As the next cohorts of caregivers age, advanced telephone and computer technologies will be increasingly viewed as assets. Service providers in the future will also be more open to using technology as a convenient tool to enhance the lives of the caregivers and the care recipients. Furthermore, access to the Internet will continue to become easier and affordable. This, in turn, will further increase the use of technology by ethnic minorities and-low income caregivers who were underserved in the past.

It is important to point out that the technologies discussed in this section do not completely eliminate the interaction of the caregivers with the service providers. Instead, they contribute to enhancing the effectiveness and efficiency of the available services, make the resources available at all times, and link the caregivers with others engaged in performing similar tasks. The question is not whether the health-care and social service agencies should encourage caregivers to choose between using technology or the service providers. Instead, the question is how these agencies can optimize the use of these resources to address the needs of diverse caregivers effectively and efficiently.

SUMMARY

Both informal caregivers and formal service providers work together to care for older adults. In what ways and how much each contributes varies with factors such as gender of the caregiver, socioeconomic status of the caregiving unit, size of the community, and racial/ethnic group membership of the families. Research reveals important gender differences in the provision of care. Women are much more likely than men to attend to the personal hygiene needs of the care recipients and to engage in household tasks and meal preparation. In contrast, male caregivers typically provide transportation and help the older person with home repair and financial management. While caregiving can provide substantial personal satisfaction, it can also be a tremendous burden.

Informal caregiving for older adults is the predominant type of caregiving among all racial/ethnic groups. However, older Blacks rely far more heavily on informal care than their White counterparts. Within Hispanic cultures, adult children have traditionally served as the main providers of assistance. Although there is considerable variation among the major Asian American groups, values supporting the care of older adults appear to be strong, and rates of co-residence are higher than those found in the general population. The evidence on Native American groups also suggests high rates of co-residence and strong family support systems. However, ethnic families are changing with increased acculturation and assimilation into the larger society.

Formal care includes not only nursing home care but also a number of alternatives such as assisted living facilities, adult day care, and home health care. In recent years the nursing home occupancy rates have been falling, and the characteristics of the residents have also been changing. These changes are probably a function of the shifting configuration of available services, including (1) a move toward short-term post-acute care being provided in nursing homes; (2) an increase in home care use; and (3) the increased use of assisted living facilities. Currently Hispanic elders are far less likely than other racial and ethnic groups to use nursing home care. In addition, they also underutilize in-home services such as visiting nurse, home health aide, and homemaker.

Having services available does not mean that they are easily accessible to all members of the older population. Barriers that hinder their use by ethnic elders, women, and residents of rural communities include lack of knowledge, location of services, communication problems, and insensitivity to cultural traditions and beliefs. We have presented some strategies that may be helpful in overcoming these barriers.

Many older persons and their informal caregivers now have access to computers, have learned how to use them, and can navigate the Internet. They use the Internet for social interaction, self-enhancement, and information gathering. Online support groups provide caregivers the flexibility to overcome constraints imposed by time and distance. We have described in some detail a telephone-linked computerized system that provides caregivers access to continuing support through their home telephone.

ACTIVE LEARNING EXPERIENCE: CHAPTER 6 QUIZ

The purpose of this experience is to gauge your present knowledge of issues related to caregiving for elders from diverse groups. Upon completion of this experience, you will be able to:

1. Assess your knowledge of informal and formal care, and
2. Gain feedback on your knowledge of important issues related to caregiving for elders from diverse groups.

Instructions:

Complete the quiz below. Your instructor may lead an in-class review of the answers to the quiz. This activity should take 30 minutes (10 minutes to complete the quiz and 20 minutes to discuss your answers with another person or in a classroom setting).

Indicate whether each of the following statements is true or false.

	Quiz Items	True	False
1.	The majority of older people are socially isolated.	_____	_____
2.	Older Blacks rely far more heavily on informal care than do older Whites.	_____	_____
3.	Native Americans have traditionally placed a high value on the extended family.	_____	_____
4.	Older parents expect their sons to provide more personal care than their daughters.	_____	_____
5.	Elderly women are more likely than elderly men to live alone.	_____	_____
6.	In Asian/Pacific Islander families, adult children are expected to provide ongoing assistance to their parents.	_____	_____
7.	Older Whites are more likely than older African Americans to use adult day care services.	_____	_____
8.	The rate of nursing home use among Hispanics is significantly higher than the rate in non-Hispanic Whites.	_____	_____
9.	Technology-based interventions for caregivers have eliminated their contact with service providers.	_____	_____
10.	The use of nursing home care has continued to increase in recent years.	_____	_____

GLOSSARY

adult day care: A community facility that frail older adults living at home can attend several hours each day. Facilities based on a health rehabilitation model provide individualized therapy plans; those based on a social model engage the participants in social and psychotherapeutic activities.

assisted living facilities: These facilities serve elders who need assistance with personal care (e.g., bathing, taking medications) but who are not so physically or cognitively impaired that they need 24-hour care.

caregiving: Assisting people with personal care, household chores, managing finances, providing transportation, and performing other tasks associated with daily living; provided either by family members or by professionals.

competence: In the person–environment interaction model, competence is defined as the theoretical upper limit of an individual's capacity to function.

culturally sensitive care: Care that acknowledges and understands cultural diversity, considers cultural needs of the recipients, and respects their health beliefs and practices.

environmental press: Refers to the varying demands placed on the person by social, interpersonal, and physical features of the environment.

fictive kin: This term is used to describe non-blood-related individuals such as friends, neighbors, and church members in African American communities who provide significant caregiving support to older people.

filial piety: Love and respect toward parents. Three important conditions for filial piety are respecting parents, bringing no dishonor to them, and taking care of them.

long-term care: Includes a broad range of services designed to help frail older people. Examples include nursing homes, assisted living facilities, adult day care, and home health services.

SUGGESTED READINGS

Allen, J. & Pifer, A. (Eds.). (1993). *Women on the front lines: Meeting the challenge of an aging America.* Washington, DC: Urban Institute Press.

This book covers a wide range of issues, including high rates of poverty among older persons who live alone, middle-aged women's struggles to combine family care with paid work outside the home, women's prospects in the growing health-care occupations, and older women's status in the labor force. The theme of care-giving and social values permeates the book and is the major focus of Chapter 3, "Caring Too Much? American Women and the Nation's Caregiving Crisis."

Alliance for Technology Access (2004). *Computer resources for people with disabilities* (4th ed.). San Rafael, CA: Author.

This highly useful publication brings together user-friendly support, information, and up-to-date answers to questions. Included are ways to make use of conventional, assistive, and information technologies; real-life stories about people of all ages with disabilities who are using technology successfully; a toolbox section with practical information about the latest computer technology, including screen enhancements, speech synthesizers, and customized keyboards; and a full set of organizations, vendors, publications, and online resources to contact for additional information.

Ball, M. M., Perkins, M. M., Whittington, F. J., Hollingsworth, C., King, S. V., & Combs, B. L. (2005). *Communities of care: Assisted living for African American elders*. Baltimore, MD: Johns Hopkins University Press.

This book examines the daily lives of the people who live, work, and visit in six assisted living facilities for African American elders. Provides a detailed profile of each of the six facilities, examines the components of care provided in these communities, and recounts the journey of becoming a resident. Includes a discussion of the facility care providers, the "kin-work" in residents' day-to-day lives, and the role of a wider community. Outlines public policy implications of the findings for residents, providers, and family members.

Barresi, C. & Stull, D. (Eds.). (1993). *Ethnic elderly and long-term care*. New York: Springer.

Barresi and Stull provide a rich survey of health-care issues in a variety of ethnic communities. Chapters focus on factors related to caregiver burden, documentation of long-term care practices in different ethnic communities, and discussion of how ethnicity may influence the delivery of care and individual adaptation. Directly related to the focus of this chapter is Part 2 of the volume, which deals with caregiver issues in home-based long-term care, particularly informal care provided to rural elders and those suffering from dementia.

Cox, C. B. (2005). *Community care for an aging society: Issues, policies, and services*. New York: Springer.

Cox presents an overview of the current array of community-based services for older adults. She provides brief assessments of the strengths and weaknesses of these services, identifies service gaps, and offers policy recommendations.

Kaye, L. W. & Applegate, J. S. (1990). *Men as caregivers to the elderly: Understanding and aiding unrecognized family support*. Lexington, MA: Lexington Books.

This book reports the findings of a much-needed study addressing questions such as the following: What do male caregivers do? What are the attitudes, expectations, and needs of men acting as caregivers? What are the distinctive characteristics and coping strategies of men performing this role? What are the factors that instigate the allocation of caregiving to men in families? What are the incentives and disincentives for successful male caregiving performance? To what extent have support groups responded to the unique needs of male caregivers?

Kolb, P. J. (2003). *Caring for our elders: Multicultural experiences with nursing home placement*. New York: Columbia University Press.

This book is distinctive in its focus on listening to and learning from culturally diverse, often low-income nursing home residents and their family members. Another important feature is its examination of how some relatives and friends assume new and additional responsibilities after placing their elders in a nursing facility. In addition, the author identifies several concepts and principles related to race and ethnicity that would be of interest to those who provide nursing home care to culturally diverse residents.

Kramer, B. J. & Thompson, E. M. (Eds.). (2002). *Men as caregivers*. New York: Springer.

This edited volume presents theories and research about the growing male sub-population of caregivers. The authors identify the serious limitations that result from viewing men caregivers through the lens of women's experiences. Special consideration is given to men who care for a family member with dementia, fathers of adult children with mental retardation, gay male caregivers for partners with AIDS, and sons and parent care.

Newhouse, J. K. (1995). *Rural and urban patterns: An exploration of how older adults use in-house care*. New York: Garland.

This book surveys a large, representative, statewide sample of Virginians who live in both rural and urban communities and explores how older adults use in-home services and what factors predict the use of such services. Although both rural and urban residents are included, the examination emphasizes the rural population.

AUDIOVISUAL RESOURCES

Sunset Pink Villa: A Home for Gay and Lesbian Elders. This video portrays the creation of an apartment community dedicated to gay and lesbian elders in Holland. It introduces the viewers to residents who have chosen this new housing option and provides insights into intolerance and persecution that gay men and lesbians have experienced. Incorporating the metaphor of home, it suggests a sense of belonging, a place of sanctuary, and a center for familial care, love, and affection. Sharing the home with people who have an understanding of what others have experienced makes it all the more significant for everyone. 50 minutes. Available from Filmakers Library.

When Help Was There: Four Stories of Elder Abuse. This award-winning video presents four victims of domestic elder abuse who have all found help within the local community or agencies available to them. The stories look at a Latino mother, a recently emigrated Chinese couple, an African American woman, and a White male. It looks directly at the emotional toll the abuse on the individuals involved, the varying kinds of loss they experienced, and the types of services they were able to receive. Some of the abuse was physical but more often came in the form of loss of dignity or control. 19 minutes. Available from Terra Nova Films.

Everyday Choices: Ethics and Decision-Making in Home Care and Community Nursing. Discusses the choices that a young nurse must make when working with Gerardo, a 75-year-old Cuban man. It looks at how much the decisions that she make affect his life as his health and mental state deteriorate. During her time working with him, he loses much of his independence and must be placed in a nursing home. The movie looks at her commitment and dedication to Gerardo, despite many difficulties. It is an especially appropriate movie for health-care providers. There is a great deal of focus on the emotional nature of working in this field as well as "cultural realism" in terms of Gerardo's background. 28 minutes. Available from Terra Nova Films.

Almost Home. A documentary set in retirement residence with multiple forms of assisted living in downtown Milwaukee. It relates the interactions and relationships among residents, staff, and management without narration. A wide variety of issues related to assisted living care are addressed, primarily the idea that they are striving to create a home and family in this assisted residence environment but that it can never be completely realized because of the type of system that we have in our society. The film also addresses social class in that the residents are mainly middle- and upper-class Whites. On the other hand, the staff is ethnically diverse and will never have access to the type of care the residents are receiving. 84 minutes. Available from the Center on Age and Community, University of Wisconsin, Milwaukee.

Long Shadows: Stories from a Jewish Home. Set in a Jewish nursing home in Melbourne, Australia, the film primarily focuses on the types of unique issues the Jewish older population faces and the way assisted living facilities address them. Although the film is centered mainly on a few selected residents, it also discusses the idea that all of the residents are connected by "their religious beliefs and their refugee experiences," as many of the residents are Holocaust survivors. Their past is extremely relevant to the type of care they need because the memories are still a part of their lives, especially now that they are once again in a position with little control over the pain they experience. 52 minutes. Available from Filmakers Library.

KEY: CHAPTER 6 QUIZ

1. False. The majority of older people are not socially isolated. As shown in Figure 6.1, about 81% of men and 61% of women aged 65 or over live with their spouse or with other relatives or nonrelatives. In addition, most elders have close relatives within easy visiting distance, and contacts between them are relatively frequent.

2. True. Numerous authors have indicated that older Blacks have more powerful kinship networks than do Whites and tend to rely far more heavily on informal care than do older Whites (Dilworth-Anderson, Williams, & Gibson, 2002).

3. True. Native Americans have traditionally placed a high value on the extended family (Lockery, 1991). The exact form of the extended family is influenced by place of residence (urban or reservation), socioeconomic issues, and acculturation factors (John, 1991).

4. False. Older parents expect their daughters to provide more personal care than their sons (Horowitz, 1985; Zarit, Todd, & Zarit, 1986). Women are much more likely than men to take care of the personal hygiene needs of care recipients, including bathing, dressing, toileting, and cleaning and cooking (Senate Select Committee on Aging, U.S. House of Representatives, 1988). In contrast, sons typically assist parents with transportation needs, home repairs, and financial management and devote fewer hours to caregiving commitments over shorter periods of time.

5. True. As Figure 6.1 indicates, in 2003 older women were more twice as likely as older men to live alone (40% and 19%, respectively). Furthermore, women aged 65–74 were less likely to live alone than women aged 75 and over (30% and 50%, respectively). As age increases and widowhood rates rise, the percentage of women living alone increases accordingly.

6. True. Many Asian cultures are influenced by Confucian ideology emphasizing filial piety and children's moral obligation for the care of family elders. In a study of older ethnic groups in San Diego (Weeks & Cuellar, 1981), high percentages of Filipino, Samoan, Guamanian, Japanese, Chinese, and Korean elders reported that they would turn to family members for help.

7. False. Wallace et al. (1992) examined a representative sample of 317 adult day care participants from most of the ADC centers in Missouri and found that African American elders used ADC at twice the rate of older Whites. No racial differences were found in the functional or cognitive need levels of participants, but African American participants were more likely than Whites to depend on their children as primary caregivers and to rely on Medicaid.

8. False. Research indicates that Hispanic elders are far less likely than other racial and ethnic groups to use nursing homes (Angel &

Hogan, 2004). On the other hand, frail and functionally impaired African American older adults are the most likely racial group to use nursing facilities. Today, a greater proportion of non-Hispanic whites with compromised functioning use assisted living facilities as an alternative to nursing homes.

9. False. As we noted in our discussion of REACH, technologies do not completely eliminate the interaction of the caregivers with the service providers. Instead, technologies help make resources available at all times, link the caregivers with others who perform similar tasks, and allow the caregivers to ask specific questions they may have for the nurses, other service providers, and experts.

10. False. NCHS (2003) data indicate that the number of people 65 and older who reside in a nursing home has continued to decrease since 1970. This decline may be due to improved health or the substitution of other kinds of formal care such as assisted living, in-home care, and adult day care.

REFERENCES

Alexcih, M.B. (1997). What it is, who needs it, and who provides it. In B. L. Boyd (Ed.), *Long-term care: Knowing the risk, paying the price* (pp. 1–17). Washington, DC: Health Insurance Association of America.

Aneshensel, C. S., Rutter, C. M., & Lackenbruch, P.A. (1991). Social structure, stress, and mental health. *American Sociological Review, 56*, 167–178.

Angel, J. L., & Hogan, D. P. (2004). Population aging and diversity in a new era. In K. E. Whitfield (Ed.), *Closing the gap: Improving the health of minority elders in the new millennium*. Washington, DC: Gerontological Society of America.

Aranda, M. P., & Knight, B. G. (1997). The influences of ethnicity and culture on the caregiver stress and coping process: A sociocultural review and analysis. *Gerontologist, 37*, 342–354.

Arroyo, R., & Lopez, S. A. (1984). Being responsive to the Chicano community: A model for service delivery. In B. W. White (Ed.), *Color in White society* (pp. 63–73). Silver Spring, MD: National Association of Social Workers.

Assisted Living Quality Coalition. (1998). *Assisted living quality initiative: Building a structure that promotes quality*. Washington, DC: Author.

Ayalon, L., Lopez, G., Huyck, M., & Yoder, J. (2001, November). *Providing informal care to an elderly family member: The Latino perspective*. Paper presented at the annual meeting of the Gerontological Society of America, Chicago.

Barusch, A. S., & Spaid, W. M. (1989). Gender differences in caregiving: Why do wives report greater burden? *Gerontologist, 29*, 667–676.

Ball, M. M., Perkins, M. M., Whittington, F. J., Hollingsworth, C., King, S. V., & Combs, B. L. (2005). *Communities of care: Assisted living for African American elders*. Baltimore, MD: Johns Hopkins University Press.

Bouma, H. (1993). Gerontechnology: A framework on technology and aging. In H. Bouma & J. A. Graafmans (Eds.), *Gerontechnology* (pp. 1–6). Amsterdam: ISO Press.

Brody, E. M. (1981). Parent care as a normative family stress. *Gerontologist, 25*, 19–28.

Burr, J. A. (1990). Race/sex comparisons of elderly living arrangements: Factors influencing institutionalization of the unmarried. *Research on Aging, 12*, 507–530.

Chatters, L., Taylor, R., & Jayakody, R. (1994). Fictive kinship relationships in black extended families. *Journal of Comparative Family Studies, 25,* 297–312.

Chatters, L. M., Taylor, R. J., & Jackson, J. S. (1986). Aged Blacks' choice for an informal helper network. *Journal of Gerontology, 41,* 94–100.

Chen, J. N., & Soto, D. (1979). *Service delivery to aged minorities: Techniques of successful programs.* Sacramento, CA: Sacramento State University, School of Social Work.

Chiodo, L. K., Kanten, D. N., Gerety, M. B., Mulrow, C. D., & Cornell, J. E. (1994). Functional status of Mexican American nursing home residents. *Journal of the Geriatric Society, 42,* 293–296.

Coon, D. W. (2003). *Lesbian, gay, bisexual and transgender (LGBT) issues and family caregiving.* Family Caregiver Alliance, National Center on Caregiving.

Corbie-Smith, G., Thomas, S. B., & St. George, D. M. M. (2002). Distrust, race, and research. *Archives of Internal Medicine, 162,* 2458–2463.

Coward, R. T., Netzer, J. K., Mullens, R. A. (1996). Residential differences in the incidence of nursing home admissions across a six-year period. *Journal of Gerontology Series B: Psychological Sciences and Social Sciences, 51*(5), S258–S267.

Cowles, M. K. (2003). *Nursing home statistical yearbook, 2002.* Gaithersburg, MD: Cowles Research Group.

Cox, C. B. (2005). *Community care for an aging society: Issues, policies, and services.* New York: Springer.

Cox, C., & Monk, A. (1993). Black and Hispanic caregivers of dementia victims: Their needs and implications for services. In C. M. Barresi & D. E. Stull (Eds.), *Ethnic elderly & long-term care* (pp. 57–67). New York: Springer.

Czaja, S. J. (1997). Using technologies to aid the performance of home tasks. In A. D. Fisk & W. A. Rogers (Eds.), *Handbook of human factors and the older adult.* San Diego, CA: Academic Press.

Davies, H., Priddy, J. M., & Tinklenberg, J. R. (1986). Support groups for male caregivers of Alzheimer's patients. *Clinical Gerontologist, 5,* 385–395.

Delgado, M., & Tennstedt, S. (1997). Making the case for culturally appropriate community services: Puerto Rican elders and their caregivers. *Health & Social Work, 22,* 246–255.

Dilworth-Anderson, P., Williams, I. C., & Gibson, B. E. (2002. Issues of race, ethnicity, and culture in caregiving research: A 20-year review (1980–2000). *Gerontologist, 42*(2), 237–272.

Fagan, R. M. (2003). Pioneer network: Changing the culture of aging in America. In A. S. Weiner & J. L. Ronch (Eds.), *Culture change in long-term care,* (pp. 125–140). Binghamton, NY: Haworth Press.

Fandetti, D. V., & Gelfand, D. E. (1976). Care of the aged: Attitudes of White ethnic families. *Gerontologist, 16,* 544–549.

Farran, C. J., Miller, B. H., Kaufman, J. E., & Davis, L. (1997). Race, finding meaning, and caregiver distress. *Journal of Aging and Health, 9*(3), 316–333.

Federal Interagency Forum on Aging-Related Statistics. (2006, May). *Older Americans update 2006: Key indicators of well-being.* Washington, DC: U.S. Government Printing Office.

Fiske, A. D., Rogers, W. A., Charness, N., Czaja, S. J., & Sharit, J. (2004). *Designing for older adults: Principles and creative human factors approaches.* Boca Raton, FL: CRC Press.

Freedman, V. A. (1993). Kin and nursing home lengths of stay: A backward recurrence time approach. *Journal of Health and Social Behavior, 34,* 138–152.

Gallagher-Thompson, D., Talamantes, M., Ramirez, R., & Valverde, R. (1996). Services delivery issues and recommendations for working with Mexican American family caregivers. In G. Yeo & D. Gallagher-Thompson (Eds.), *Ethnicity and the dementias* (pp. 137–152). Washington, DC: Taylor & Frances.

Gallagher, R. M. (2000). How long-term care is changing. *American Journal of Nursing, 100*, 65–67.

Garcia, J., Kosberg, J., Mangum, W., Henderson, J., & Henderson, C. (1992, November). *Caregiving for and by Hispanic elders: Perceptions of four generations of women.* Paper presented at the annual meeting of the Gerontological Society of America, Washington, DC.

Gaugler, J., Kane, R. L., Kane, R. A., Clay, T., & Newcomer, R. (2003). Caregiving and institutionalization of cognitively impaired older people: Utilizing dynamic predictors of change. *Gerontologist, 43*(2), 219–229.

George, L. K. (1984). The burden of caregiving: How much? What kinds? For whom? *Center Reports on Advances in Caregiving, 8*, 1–8.

Gilhooly, M. L. M. (1984). The impact of care-giving on care-givers: Factors associated with the psychological well-being of people supporting a demented relative in the community. *British Journal of Medical Psychology, 57*, 35–44.

Gock, T. (1992). The challenges of being gay, Asian, and proud. In B. Berzon (Ed.), *Positively gay* (pp. 247–252). Millbrae, CA: Celestial Arts.

Greene, B. (1994). Ethnic minority lesbians and gay men: Mental health and treatment issues. *Journal of Consulting and Clinical Psychology, 62*, 243–251.

Grossman, A. H., D'Augelli, A. R., & Hershberger, S. L. (2000). Social support networks of lesbian, gay, and bisexual adults 60 years of age and older. *Journal of Gerontology, 55B*, 171–179.

Gustafson, D. H., Gustafson, R. C., & Wackerbarth, S. (1997). CHESS: Health information and decision support for patients and families. *Generations, 21*(3), 56.

Haley, W. E., West, C. A., Wadley, V. G., Ford, G. R., White, F. A., Barrett, J. J., et al. (1995). Psychological, social, and health impact of caregiving: A comparison of Black and White dementia caregivers and noncaregivers. *Psychology and Aging, 10*, 540–552.

Harbert, A. S., & Ginsberg, L. H. (1979). *Human services for older adults.* Belmont, CA: Wadsworth.

Hawes, C., Phillips, C. D., Rose, M., Holan, S., & Sherman, M. (2003). A national survey of assisted living facilities. *Gerontologist, 43*(6), 875–882.

Hayes, C. L., & Guttmann, D. L. (1986). The need for collaboration among religious, ethnic, and public-service institutions. In C. L. Hayes, R. A. Kalish, & D. L. Guttmann (Eds.), *European-American elderly* (pp. 198–211). New York: Springer.

Hennessy, C. H., & John, R. (1996). American Indian family caregivers' perceptions of burden and needed support services. *Journal of Applied Gerontology, 15*(3), 275–293.

Himes, C. L., Hogan, D. P., & Eggebeen, D. J. (1996) Living arrangements among minority elders. *Journal of Gerontology: Social Sciences, 51B*, 542–548.

Hlavaty, J. P. (1986, April). *Alzheimer's disease and the male spouse caregiver.* Paper presented at the 10th Annual Ohio Conference on Aging, Columbus.

Hollis, F., & Woods, M. E. (1981). *Casework: A psychosocial therapy* (3rd ed.). New York: Random House.

Hooyman. N. R., & Kiyak, H. A. (2008). *Social Gerontology: A multidisciplinary perspective* (8th ed.). Boston, MA: Allyn and Bacon.

Horowitz, A. (1985). Sons and daughters as caregivers to older parents: Differences in role performance and consequences. *Gerontologist, 25*, 612–617.

Hughes, S. L., Ulasevich, A., Weaver, F. M., Henderson, W., Manheim, L., Kubal, J. D., et al. (1997). Impact of home care of hospital days: A meta-analysis. *Heath Services Research, 32*, 415–432.

John, R. (1991). The state of research on American Indian elders' health, income security, and social support networks. In U.S. Department of Health and Human Services (Ed.), *Minority elders: Longevity, economics, and health, building a public policy base* (pp. 38–50). Washington, DC: Gerontological Society of America.

Johnson, C. (1999). Fictive kin among oldest old African Americans in the San Francisco Bay area. *Journal of Gerontology: Social Sciences, 54B,* S368–375.

Kaye, L. W., & Applegate, J. S. (1990). *Men as caregivers to the elderly: Understanding and aiding unrecognized family support.* Lexington, MA: Lexington Books.

Kelly, K. (1997). Building aging programs with online information technology. *Generations, 21,* 15–18.

Kimmel, D. C. (1978). Adult development and aging: A gay perspective. *Journal of Social Issues, 43,* 113–120.

Kornblatt, S., Eng, C., & Hansen, J. (2003). Cultural awareness in health and social services: The experience of On Lok. *Generations, 26,* 46–53.

Krout, J. A. (1983). Knowledge and use of services by the elderly: A critical review of the literature. *International Journal of Aging and Human Development, 17,* 153–167.

Kunjufu, J. (1994). *Adam! Where are you?* Chicago: African American Images.

Laditka, S. B. (1998). Modeling lifetime nursing home use under assumptions of better health. *Journal of Gerontology: Social Sciences, 53B*(4), S177-S187.

Lawton, M. P., & Nahemow, L. (1973). Ecology and the aging process. In E. Eisdorfer & M. P. Lawton (Eds.), *Psychology of adult development and aging.* Washington, DC: American Psychological Association.

Levin, J. S. (1986). Roles for the Black pastor in preventive medicine. *Pastoral Psychology, 35*(2), 94–103.

Lockery, S. (1991). Family and social supports: Caregiving among racial and ethnic minority elders. *Generations, 15*(4), 58–62.

Magilvy, J., Congdon, J., Martinez, R., Davis, J., & Averill, D. (2000). Caring for our own: Experiences of rural Hispanic elders. *Journal of Aging Studies, 14,* 171–190.

Mahoney, D. F., Tarlow, B., & Jones, R. N. (2001). Factors affecting the use of a telephone-based intervention for caregivers of people with Alzheimer's disease. *Journal of Telemedicine and Telecare, 7,* 139–148.

MaloneBeach, E., & Cook, T. (2001). *African American women: A legacy of caregiving?* Paper presented at the annual meeting of the Gerontological Society of America, Chicago.

Manson, S. M. (1989). Long-term care in American Indian communities: Issues for planning and research. *Gerontologist, 29,* 38–44.

Manson, S. M. (1993). Long-term care of older American Indians: Challenges in the development of institutional services. In C. M. Barresi & D. E. Stull (Eds.), *Ethnic elderly & long-term care* (pp. 130–143). New York: Springer.

Marcos, L. R., & Alpert, M. (1976). Strategies and risks in psychotherapy with bilingual patients: The phenomenon of language independence. *American Journal of Psychiatry, 133,* 1275–1278.

Markides, K. S., & Wallace, S. P. (1996). Health and long-term care needs of ethnic minority elders. In J. C. Romeis, R. M. Coe, and J. E. Morley (Eds.), *Applying health services research to long-term care* (pp. 23–42). New York: Springer Publishing.

MetLife Mature Market Institute. (2002). *MetLife market survey on nursing home and home care costs.* Westport, CT: MetLife.

Moen, P., Robison, J., & Fields, W. (2000). Women's work and caregiving roles: A life course approach. In E. P. Stoller & R. C. Gibson (Eds.), *Worlds of difference: Inequality in the aging experience* (3rd ed., pp. 165–175). Thousand Oaks, CA: Pine Forge Press.

Mulrow, C. D., Chiodo, L. K., Gerety, M. B., Lee, S., Basu, D. S., & Nelson, D. (1996). Function and medical comorbidity in South Texas nursing home residents: Variations by ethnic group. *Journal of American Geriatric Society, 44,* 279–284.

National Academy on an Aging Society. (2000, May). *Caregiving.* Washington, DC: Author.

National Alliance for Caregiving & American Association of Retired Persons. (1997). *Family caregiving in the U.S.: Findings from a national survey.* Bethesda, MD: Author.

National Center for Health Statistics. (2003). *Health, United States, 2002, Special Excerpt: Trend Tables on 65 and older population*. Centers for Disease Control and Prevention/ National Center for Health Statistics, Department of Health and Human Services Publication No.03-1030.

National Center for Injury Prevention and Control. (2001). *Injury fact book 2000–2001*. Atlanta, GA: Centers for Disease Control and Prevention.

National Institute on Adult Daycare. (1984). *Standards for adult day care*. Washington, DC: National Council on Aging.

Phillips, L. R., Torres de Ardon, E., Komnenich, P., Killeen, M., & Rusinak, R. (2000). The Mexican American caregiving experiences. *Hispanic Journal of Behavioral Science, 22*(3), 296–313.

Price, M. (1994). African American daughters' attitudes about caregiving to frail, elderly parents. *ABNF Journal, 5*(4), 112–116.

Quam, J. K., & Whitford, G. S. (1992). Adaptation and age-related expectations of older gay and lesbian adults. *Gerontologist, 32*, 367–374.

Rathbone-McCuan, E., & Coward, R. T. (1985, November). *Male helpers: Unrecognized informal supports*. Paper presented at the 38th Annual Scientific Meeting of the Gerontological Society of America, New Orleans, LA.

Red Horse, J. G. (1980). American Indian elders: Unifiers of Indian families. *Social Casework, 61*, 490–493.

Ricketts, T. C., Hart, L. G., & Pirani, M. (2000). How many rural doctors do we have? *Journal of Rural Health, 16*(3), 198–207.

Rogers, C. C. (2002). Rural health issues for the older population. *Rural America, 17*(2), 30–36.

Rowles, G. D., Beaulieu, J. E., & Myers, W. W. (1997). *Long term care for the rural elderly*. New York: Springer.

Schulz, R., Burgio, L., Burns, R., Eisdorfer, C., Gallagher-Thompson, D., Gitlin, L. N., et al. (2003). Resources for Enhancing Alzheimer's Caregiver Health (REACH): Overview, site-specific outcomes, and future directions. *Gerontologist, 43*(4), 514–520.

Schoenberg, N. E., & Coward, R. T. (1997). Attitudes about entering a nursing home: Comparisons of older rural and urban African American women. *Journal of Aging Studies, 11*, 27–47.

Senate Select Committee on Aging, U.S. House of Representatives. (1988). *Exploding the myths: Caregiving in America*. Washington, DC: U.S. Government Printing Office.

Shaughnessy, P. W. (1994). Changing institutional long-term care to improve rural health care. In R. T. Coward, C. N. Bull, G. Kukulka, & J. M. Galliher, (Eds.), *Health services for rural elders*. New York: Springer.

Shippy, R. A., Brennan, M., & Cantor, M. H. (2002, November). *Caregiving experiences of older gay and lesbian individuals*. Paper presented at the Annual Scientific Meeting of the Gerontological Society of America, Boston, MA.

Shomaker, D. (1981). Navajo nursing homes: Conflicts of philosophies. *Journal of Gerontological Nursing, 7*, 531–536.

Shomaker, D. (1990). Health care, cultural expectations, and frail elderly Navajo grandmothers. *Journal of Cross-Cultural Gerontology, 5*, 21–34.

Snyder, B., & Keefe, K. (1985). The unmet needs of family caregivers for frail and disabled adults. *Social Work in Health Care, 10*, 1–14.

Steffen, A., Mahoney, D. F., & Kelly, K. (2003). Capitalizing on technological advances. In D. W. Coon, D. Gallagher-Thompson, & L. W. Thompson, (Eds.), *Innovative interventions to reduce dementia caregiver distress*. New York: Springer.

Sterns, A. A. (2005). Curriculum design and program to train older adults to use personal digital assistants. *Gerontologist, 45*, 828–834.

Stearns, S. C., Slifkin, R. T., & Edin, H. M. (2000). Access to care for rural Medicare beneficiaries. *Journal of Rural Health, 16*(1), 31–42.

Sue, S., McKinney, H., Allen, D., & Hall, J. (1974). Delivery of community mental health services to Black and White clients. *Journal of Consulting and Clinical Psychology, 42*, 794–801.

Sung, K. (1990). A new look at filial piety. *Gerontologist, 30*, 610–617.

Taylor, R. J. (1985). The extended family as a source of support to elderly Blacks. *Gerontologist, 25*, 488–495.

U.S. Department of Health and Human Services. (1991). *Health status of minorities and low-income groups: Third edition* (DHHS Pub. No. 271-848/40085). Washington, DC: U.S. Government Printing Office.

Van Steenberg, C., Ansak, M. L., & Chin-Hansen, J. (1993). On Lok's model: Managed long-term care. In C. M. Barresi & D. E. Stull (Eds.), *Ethnic elderly & long-term care* (pp. 178–190). New York: Springer.

Wagner, L. S., & Wagner, T. H. (2003). The effect of age on the use of health and self-care information: Confronting the stereotype. *Gerontologist. 43*, 318–324.

Wallace, S. P. (1990). The political economy of health care for elderly Blacks. *International Journal of Health Services, 20*, 665–680.

Wallace, S. P., Campbell, K. L. & Lew-Ting, C. (1994). Structural barriers to the use of formal in-home services by elderly Latinos. *Journal of Gerontology: Social Sciences, 49*(5), 5254–5263.

Wallace, S. P., Snyder, J. L., Walker, G. K., & Ingman, S. R. (1992). Racial differences among users of long-term care: The case of adult day care. *Research on Aging, 14*, 471–495.

Wallace, S., Levy-Storms, L., Kington, R., & Anderson, R. (1998). The persistence of race and ethnicity in the use of long-term care. *Journal of Gerontology: Social Sciences, 53B*, S104–112.

Walmsley, S. A., & Allington, R. L. (1982). Reading abilities of elderly persons in relation to the difficulty of essential documents. *Gerontologist, 22*, 36–38.

Westermeyer, J. (1987). Clinical considerations in cross-cultural diagnosis. *Hospital and Community Psychiatry, 38*, 160–164.

Weeks, J. R., & Cuellar, J. B. (1981). The role of family members in the helping networks of older people. *Gerontologist, 21*, 388–394.

Weiner, A. S., & Ronch, J. L. (Eds.). (2003). *Culture change in long-term care*. New York: Haworth Press, Inc.

Wisniewski, S., Belle, S. H., Coon, D., Marcus, S., Ory, M., Burgio, L., et al. (2003). The Resources for Enhancing Alzheimer's Caregiver Health (REACH) project design and baseline characteristics. *Psychology and Aging, 18*(3), 375–384.

Wood, J. B., & Parham, I. A. (1990). Coping with perceived burden: Ethnic and cultural issues in Alzheimer's family caregiving. *Journal of Applied Gerontology, 9*, 345–355.

Wykle, M., & Segall, M. (1991). A comparison of Black and White family caregivers' experience with dementia. *Journal of the National Black Nurses' Association, 5*, 29–41.

Yee, B. W. K. (1990). Gender and family issues in minority groups. *Generations, 14*, 30–42.

Young, R. F., & Kahana, E. (1989). Specifying caregiver outcomes: Gender and relationship aspects of caregiving strain. *Gerontologist, 29*, 660–666.

Yu, E. S. H., Kim, K., Liu, W. T., & Wong, S. C. (1993). Functional abilities of Chinese and Korean elders in congregate housing. In C. M. Barresi & D. E. Stull (Eds.), *Ethnic elderly and long-term care* (pp. 87–100). New York: Springer.

Zarit, S. H., Todd, P. A., & Zarit, J. M. (1986). Subjective burden of husbands and wives as caregivers: A longitudinal study. *Gerontologist, 26*, 260–266.

Zawadski, R., & Stuart, M. (1990). ADC growth uneven, but impressive. *NCOA Networks, 2*(9).

Zimmer, Z., & Chappell, N. L. (1999). Receptivity to new technology among older adults. *Disability and Rehabilitation, 21*, 222–230.

7

Work, Retirement, and Leisure

- What are the trends in employment for older workers? How have these trends changed over time and why?
- Why is it important to create new opportunities for older persons to work?
- How is retirement viewed by members of diverse groups?
- How can retirement preparation programs take elements of diversity into consideration?

Members of the baby boom generation (persons born between 1946 and 1964) will soon begin moving from the traditional working ages to the ages when many people begin to retire. In fact, the first cohorts of the baby boomers will start to turn 65 in 2011, and the last of the boomers will be 65 in 2029. This development will significantly change the ratio of the working age population (defined as aged 20 to 64) to the population aged 65 or older. This ratio, called *dependency ratio,* indicates how many workers are available to support each retiree. This ratio was 21% in 2000, indicating that there were five working age individuals for every person over the age of 65. With the aging of the baby boom generation, the aged dependency ratio will continue to rise. By 2030, it will reach 35%. What does this trend tell us? It indicates that there will be fewer than three persons of traditional working age for every person aged 65 or over (U.S. General Accounting Office, 2001). Note that this increase in the aged dependency ratio is occurring for two reasons: (1) continuing increase in the numbers of older persons; and (2) slowing growth of younger workers in the labor force. These continuing trends have raised concerns such as whether sufficient numbers of appropriately trained workers will remain available to maintain economic productivity and whether the existing retirement and pension programs will be able to support the growing number of retirees. In addition, given the increase in longevity, older people will need resources to support themselves during a longer period of retirement. There is, therefore, increased interest in older workers as well as in issues related to retirement.

In the first part of this chapter, we discuss the employment status of older adults in the context of their gender, racial/ethnic group membership, socioeconomic status (SES), and sexual orientation. We then review the barriers to their employment and explore new models and approaches that may be fruitful in extending the periods of labor force participation. The second part of the chapter focuses on retirement and diversity, including topics such as retirement planning, the decision to retire, adjustment to retirement, and leisure activities. As an introduction to our discussion of work and retirement, consider the following vignettes.

Vignette 1

Sarah Martin, a 58-year-old Black woman, works in a sales position at Anderson's Department Store. She enjoys working with the customers as well as with other employees. In recent years, the turnover at Anderson's has been quite high, especially in the women's division, where Sarah works. In less than 2 years, she has worked under the supervision of three division managers. Every time there is an opening, a salesperson from the women's division or from another division within the store is brought in to manage the division. All of them tend to be under the age of 40. Last month, Sarah requested that she be considered the next time there was an opening for the division manager's position. She knows that the position involves more responsibility than her current position. However, a higher salary, a commission on total sales within the division, and the availability of stock options make the position financially attractive for her. She feels that her 5 years of experience at Anderson's, together with her previous experience in similar companies, have prepared her well for the position.

During the past 8 months, she has been passed over for promotion on two occasions. At first she informally expressed her disappointment to Ronald Johnson, the store manager. On the second occasion, she demanded an explanation from him. Ronald finally agreed to meet with Sarah. He began by reviewing Sarah's work record. Although the company did not have a formal employee review policy, Ronald referred to handwritten notes from Sarah's personnel file. He pointed out that her record was only average. While he acknowledged that she was a dependable worker with a good attendance record, he said that these qualities alone do not make her a first-rate candidate for the division manager's position.

Although Sarah is still working at Anderson's, she is disheartened by the lack of opportunities to handle new challenges and responsibilities. Some of her associates think that this may be a case of age discrimination and have encouraged her to discuss the situation with an attorney. She is hesitating to lodge an age discrimination complaint, because such an action may create additional difficulties for her in the company and may lead to harassment by management.

Vignette 2

Claude Atwood, a 68-year-old Native American, retired from his position with the U.S. Forest Service about 3 years ago. At the same time his wife, Jean, also retired from her position with the Minnesota Department of Natural Resources. Upon retirement, the Atwoods decided to maintain their residence in Minneapolis, where they have lived for the past 10 years. They now spend about 5 hours a day in a Minneapolis high school that serves a large number of Native American students. In their role as teachers' aides, they work closely with the teachers, especially those responsible for classes in science and mathematics. Students appreciate the help they receive from Claude and Jean in understanding difficult concepts. It appears that the Atwoods have a knack for explaining complex ideas and principles in an easy-to-understand manner. Their examples from many years of work experience make abstract concepts concrete and meaningful for their students. In addition, their use of hands-on instruction seems to be highly effective with Native American students.

In addition to tutoring, the Atwoods have also been able to offer some invaluable career advice to a large number of students. Jean's ability to provide informal counseling to women and her sound knowledge of Indian traditions and culture have been much appreciated by the young Native American women who attend the high school. Both Claude and Jean have also brought to students' attention summer work opportunities available in state and federal agencies.

Students also enjoy the stories the Atwoods tell them about what life was like when they were teenagers 50 years ago: no indoor plumbing, central heat, TV, VCRs, or computers. The couple often shares work-related experiences, stories from their travels, and the lessons they have learned in life. The principal and the teachers from the school appreciate the perspectives the Atwoods bring to the school, the ongoing support they provide to students, and the interaction they promote between the school and the American Indian community. At a recent school board meeting, the principal reported that since the Atwoods' arrival at her school she has observed a significant increase in the participation of Native American parents in parent–teacher conferences and a variety of other school activities.

Vignette 3

This September, Diane Garcia, a 74-year-old widow from Willmar, Minnesota, did something unusual for a woman her age: She went back to work. Why? Though she retired about 10 years ago, Diane found that she needed more money for living expenses and also wanted more opportunities for mental stimulation and social contacts. So she started working 4 days a week for an elementary school about 2 miles from the apartment where she lives. She found the job through a training program offered by Experience Works, an advocacy group for older workers. She does secretarial work and acts as a translator when Spanish-speaking parents contact the school. Until she started working again, her only income came from Social Security, which covered her rent and utilities but little else. Now she has some extra income, which allows her to go out occasionally and to buy things when she wants them. In addition, she remains mentally active and enjoys the interaction with children and their parents. Since Willmar has a large number of immigrant farm workers from Mexico, working at the school allows her to talk to them and their children in Spanish.

GENDER AND ETHNIC DIFFERENCES IN THE OLDER WORKFORCE

Increase in Labor Force Participation

To set the stage for examining gender and ethnic differences in the older labor force, we begin by presenting data regarding the continuing increase in the number of older workers and then discuss why many older adults continue working at least part time as they move into what has traditionally been thought of as retirement years.

Over the next two decades, the number of older workers will grow substantially, and they will become an increasingly significant proportion of the workforce. In 2000, 18.4 million persons over the age of 55 were in the labor force (Figure 7.1). Estimates indicate that by 2015, the number of workers over 55 will be about 31.8 million, a 77% increase since 2000, and by 2025, this number will increase to approximately 33 million (U.S. General Accounting Office, 2001).

The increase shown in Figure 7.1 is not simply due to the growth of the older population. It is also due to the continuing increase in the labor force participation rates for older men and women. The trend of increased participation is significantly different from what was observed in the preceding decades when the typical retirement age had declined from 70 in 1940 to 62 in 1985. This downward trend in labor force participation of older workers has been attributed to increased personal wealth, growth in employer-sponsored pension plans (called defined benefit plans), and Social Security benefits, which allowed a large proportion of American workers to have financial resources available during retirement years. Why did the downward trend in labor force participation rates end in the mid 1980s? This change in the trend is due to the following factors.

Social Security Benefits   Historically, public policy had encouraged those aged 65 and over not to work, thereby making room for younger workers. Social Security benefits were weighted to provide incentives for early retirement. For example, workers who were between the ages of 62 and 64 and who earned more than

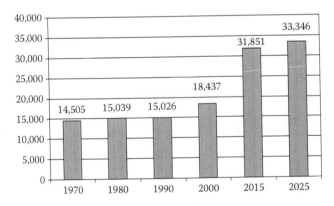

Figure 7.1   Past and projected number of workers over the age of 55, 1970–2025 (in thousands). *Source*: U.S. General Accounting Office (2001).

$10,800 a year used to lose $1 in benefits for every $2 in earnings they received in excess of $10,800. Until recently, workers between the ages of 65 and 69 lost $1 in benefits for every $3 in earnings in excess of $17,000. At one time the earning limits were even lower. For the most part, these incentives have now been removed. The practice of reducing Social Security benefits when a person has earnings and has reached the normal retirement age has been eliminated, and those who work past the normal retirement age receive increased amounts of Social Security benefits upon retirement. These additional benefits, called delayed retirement credits, are steadily being increased to encourage older workers to delay their retirement. In addition, major Social Security reforms in 1983 increased the age of eligibility for full retirement benefits from the age of 65 to 67. Furthermore, the Age Discrimination in Employment Act (ADEA) was amended in 1986 to eliminate a mandatory retirement age for most occupational groups.

Rising Importance of Health Insurance Most working-age Americans receive health insurance coverage as part of an employer's compensation package. Since they are most likely to lose the health insurance coverage if they retire and because health insurance costs continue to increase, they have an incentive to remain in the job, at least until the age of 65 when they become eligible for Medicare. Even after they become eligible for Medicare, they need to pay additional out-of-pocket premiums to fill the gap between what is provided by Medicare and what they received when they had full-time employment. In sum, the rising importance of health insurance coverage to older workers may have a sizable impact on retirement patterns.

Concerns about Available Resources With the increase in longevity and rising cost of living, many older adults are concerned that they may not have adequate income to support their needs during retirement years. The U.S. General Accounting Office (2001) reports that only about 52% of retirees receive pension income. Thus, millions of workers are not covered by private pensions; they rely on Social Security as their sole source of income. This group is at the risk of having inadequate income during their retirement years. Note that this group includes a large number of women and minorities. A 2003 Minority Retirement Confidence Survey found that Hispanic workers tend to be the least confident about various financial aspects of retirement. While Black workers are more confident than Hispanic workers, they are less confident than workers in general about having enough money for retirement (EBRI, 2003). A 2006 survey of older workers aged 55–59 found that those working but having no expectations of retirement benefits are more likely to be women (40%) than men (27%) (MetLife Mature Market Institute, 2006). This study also found that among 50- to 59-year-old workers the most frequently mentioned reason for continuing to work was "need income to live on" (72%). The same reason was most frequently noted by 60- to 65-year-olds as well (60%). In sum, a relatively large proportion of older workers above the age of 50 plan to continue working because they don't have enough money for retirement.

Cohort Differences and Attitudes toward Working and Leisure In national surveys, baby boomers report that they want to work after traditional retirement age.

Although many workers indicate the need for income as one of the reasons for which they want to continue working, a substantial proportion of those expressing little or no concern about retirement finances say they will work in retirement. Why? In the MetLife study mentioned earlier (MetLife Mature Market Institute, 2006), workers aged 60–65 indicated reasons such as "a desire to stay active and engaged" (45%) and "do meaningful work" (43%). In the 66- to 70-year-old age group, 72% of the respondents reported "staying active and engaged" as a primary reason to continue to work. Their second choice was "want the opportunity to do meaningful work" (47%) and third choice was "the social interaction with colleagues."

Health of the Older Population   On a number of indices, today's older adults are healthier than previous generations. The numbers of people aged 65 and over reporting very good health and experiencing good physical functioning, such as ability to walk a mile or climb stairs, has increased in recent years. Disability rates among older people are also declining (Federal Interagency Forum on Aging-Related Statistics, 2006). Researchers have also found significant improvements in the ability to work for men and women in their 60s (Crimmins, Reynolds, & Saito, 1999). While the likelihood of developing a disability increases with age, most older individuals around age 65 are active and capable of full-time work (National Research Council, 2004). Of course, within every generation there will be workers who are in poor health and who work in physically demanding jobs. These workers will be among the first to retire. Overall, the aging workforce appears to be healthy enough to handle the physical demands of work.

Shift in Labor Force from Industrial Sector to Service Sector   Though America was an industrial giant in the first half of the twentieth century, American strength now lies in the service sector. In providing services, older workers are competitive with their younger counterparts. Note that service industries such as educational services, social services, and medical services employ the greatest number of female older workers from diverse ethnic and racial groups. Physical demands in these jobs are relatively easier to meet. Overall, a much smaller proportion of jobs now requires strenuous physical effort, and a larger percentage requires only moderate or light physical exertion (Manton & Stallard, 1994), thereby allowing older adults to continue working.

Potential Labor Shortages   Labor shortages are cyclical and are influenced by the overall economy. In times of economic expansion, given the smaller cohorts of younger workers, employers look for retired workers who are often considered reliable and conscientious employees. Even in times of recession, there may be sectors with labor shortages such as nursing and teaching that employ the greatest number of female workers.

Educational Background   Younger cohorts of aging adults, especially women, reflect higher educational attainment. This greater level of educational attainment among the baby boomers may lead to more employment opportunities as they age. They may have a broader diversification of jobs available to them compared with the current generation of older workers (U.S. General Accounting Office, 2001). These trends are already seen in the data currently available. Data from 1991 to 1999 shows that on the average, labor force participation rates for people aged 50 and older were 23% for high school dropouts and 62% for those with more than a college level education (Haider & Loughran, 2001).

Aging and Diversity Online: Research and Dissemination

The Center on Aging and Work/Workplace Flexibility. The center, located at Boston College, conducts research aimed at providing important insights into employers' adoption and implementation of flexible options, as well as older workers' use of these options. http://www.bc.edu/agingandwork

---

Gender Differences

As shown in Table 7.1, labor force participation rates of women between the ages of 55 and 61 have increased from 47% in the mid 1980s to 63% in 2005. Similar increases are also seen in the data for women aged 62 and higher. Note that (1) men still participate at a higher rate than women in each of the four age groups; and (2) the participation rates for men aged 62 and over have also increased. However, as Table 7.1 indicates, the increase has been significantly greater for older women than for older men.

Given this increase, older men's and women's labor force participation rates have converged over the past decades. Figure 7.2 demonstrates the percent differences between men and women for those aged 55–64 and those 65 and over. In 1950, the participation rate of men aged 55 to 64 was 59.9% higher than that of women in the same age group. Thirty years later, the gap had narrowed by about half, to a 30.8% difference. By 2003, the gap was 12.1%. The gender gap

TABLE 7.1 Labor Force Participation Rates of People Aged 55 and Older by Age Group and Sex, Annual Averages, 1970–2005 (in percent)

	Men				Women			
Year	55–61	62–64	65–69	70 and Over	55–61	62–64	65–69	70 and Over
1965	88.8	73.2	43.0	19.1	45.3	29.5	17.4	6.1
1970	87.7	69.4	41.6	17.6	47.0	32.3	17.3	5.7
1975	81.9	58.6	31.7	15.0	45.6	28.9	14.5	4.8
1980	79.1	52.6	28.5	13.1	46.1	28.5	15.1	4.5
1985	76.6	46.1	24.4	10.5	47.4	28.7	13.5	4.3
1990	76.7	46.5	26.0	10.7	51.7	30.7	17.0	4.7
1995	74.3	45.0	27.0	11.6	55.9	32.5	17.5	5.3
2000	74.3	47.0	30.3	12.0	58.3	34.1	19.5	5.8
2005	74.7	52.5	33.6	13.5	62.7	40.0	23.7	7.1

Source: Adapted from Federal Interagency Forum on Aging-Related Statistics, (2006).

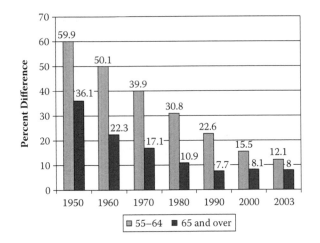

Figure 7.2 Gender gap in labor force participation rates by age, 1950–2003 (in percentage points). *Source*: He, Sengupta, Velkoff & Debarros (2005).

for workers 65 and over also narrowed from 1950 to 1990, with the 1990 gender difference being one fifth of the 1950 difference. However, the gender gap did not change from 1990 to 2003. Why? While the participation rates for men have increased during this period, the rates for women have increased as well.

Although on the surface women's participation rate by age continues to parallel that of men, deeper examination of the structure of their labor force participation (i.e., race, education, occupation, patterns of work, earnings) reveals that their employment is actually more dissimilar than similar to men. Some examples are as follows:

- Women on average earn less in wage and salary compensation than men, which accounts for at least part of the reason that women receive lower benefit payments from Social Security and employment-based pension plans. In 2000, median weekly earnings for women were $491 compared with $646 for men (EBRI, 2001).
- The majority of working women (70% in 2000) are concentrated in two industries: services (49.0%) and wholesale/retail trade (20.9%). By comparison, men are not heavily concentrated in one or two industries. In 2000, 26% of working men were in service industries, 20% were in wholesale/retail trade, and 19% were in manufacturing (EBRI, 2001).
- Women caregivers often need to decrease their work hours or have flexible work schedules to meet their caregiving responsibilities. The Cornell Retirement and Well-Being Study (Dentiger & Clarkberg, 2002) found that women caring for their husbands were five times more likely to retire than those without such care responsibilities.
- While the proportion of older adults that works part time increases with age for both men and women, the percent of older women working part time is significantly greater than for their male counterparts. Women are more likely to move into part-time work as a bridge job between career

employment and complete retirement (Quinn & Kozy, 1996). Using data from the Health and Retirement Survey these researchers found that bridge jobs are less common among Black women than either White or Hispanic women. For men, bridge jobs are more common among Hispanic men than among White or Black men.

Ethnicity and Labor Force Participation

In the preceding section we discussed gender differences in the labor force participation of older adults and reviewed the employment status of older women. We now turn our attention to the growing diversity of the workforce and examine the labor force participation rates for older Whites, Blacks, Asian Americans, and Hispanics. (Note that data for Native Americans are not available at this time.) Table 7.2 presents cross-sectional data for the population aged 55 and over by age, sex, race, and Hispanic origin for 1980 to 2003. What do these data reveal? Some key points are as follows:

1. Regardless of their race/ethnicity, the percentage of women who participate in the labor force has been increasing in the age groups 55 and over.
2. The percentage of older men participating in the labor force is higher than that of women in each ethnic group and in each age group.
3. For both men and women in each ethnic group the labor force participation rates decline with age.
4. In comparison with other ethnic groups, the participation rate for Asian women is significantly lower than for their male counterparts.
5. In the 65–69 age group, labor force participation of men and women has been steadily increasing in each ethnic group. The only exception has been Hispanic males, who experienced a decline rather than an increase in the labor force participation. For each ethnic group, the participation rates of males 70 and older has held steady at about 20% since 1980.
6. In 2003, Asian men aged 55–59, 60–64, and 65–69 had the highest rate of participation in the workforce.
7. In 2000 and 2003 Black men aged 55–59 and 60–64 had the lowest rate of labor force participation.

While there has been a steady increase in the labor force participation of older men and women from different ethnic and racial groups, it is important to note that continued employment of workers, especially older workers, depends not only on the events in their lives but also on external conditions beyond their control. Examples of these conditions include labor markets, financial markets, employment policies, tax structures, and retirement policies. In addition, as we have seen in recent years, the process of globalization continues to have a profound impact on the nature and intensity of competition among workers, employers, and national economies.

Labor force participation rates are commonly used because of the measurement ease, simplicity of interpretation, and their historical longevity as part of federal, state, and local population statistics. They provide information convenient for examining similarities and differences among diverse groups across time.

TABLE 7.2   Labor Force Participation Rates of the Population Aged 55 and Over by Age, Sex, Race, and Hispanic Origin, 1980 to 2003 (in percent)

Age Group	Men				Women			
	1980	1990	2000	2003	1980	1990	2000	2003
Non-Hispanic White								
55–59	82.8	80.9	80.2	78.7	48.4	56.4	62.9	67.4
60–64	61.7	56.5	56.0	58.0	33.1	36.1	41.8	46.9
65–69	28.6	26.8	30.6	33.4	14.9	17.2	20.0	23.6
70–74	18.2	15.8	18.2	19.5	7.5	8.0	10.4	12.0
75 and over	8.8	7.4	8.4	8.4	2.5	2.6	3.5	4.2
Black								
55–59	70.2	67.2	67.2	67.5	52.5	51.7	59.7	59.8
60–64	51.2	47.4	44.2	46.7	35.6	34.3	34.6	41.8
65–69	25.3	19.1	21.5	28.1	18.7	17.7	19.0	21.2
70–74	16.2	14.2	14.1	16.2	7.9	9.8	7.5	8.3
75 and over	6.7	4.9	6.7	7.4	2.5	3.2	4.2	4.3
Asian and Others								
55–59	77.8	80.6	77.5	83.2	50.0	56.5	58.4	64.0
60–64	71.0	62.8	60.7	70.4	31.8	30.3	39.0	41.5
65–69	30.2	25.0	35.9	37.6	17.0	14.6	13.7	19.0
70–74	26.5	11.1	17.4	13.1	2.5	7.6	7.4	5.3
75 and over	9.5	6.3	4.9	8.8	4.1	2.9	4.4	3.0
Hispanic (Any Race)								
55–59	84.0	78.0	79.3	77.1	39.6	46.3	48.6	55.8
60–64	57.7	52.8	56.6	57.5	28.0	31.1	32.2	35.6
65–69	33.1	22.4	31.6	27.7	9.9	12.1	16.2	18.1
70–74	16.3	9.6	18.8	15.4	4.9	8.5	8.5	8.8
75 and over	7.4	5.6	8.3	9.1	0.7	1.3	3.0	2.8

Source:: Adapted from He, Sengupta, Velkoff, & DeBarros (2005).

However, simply knowing these rates is not enough to answer questions such as the following:

- What is the nature of work performed by older workers from different ethnic and racial groups?
- Why do they continue to participate in the workforce?
- What factors lead them to withdraw from the workforce?
- What difficulties do they experience in reentering the labor force?
- How does their health affect their participation in the labor force?

In other words, the participation rates may mask significant variations across different segments of the workforce. Having this information along with the participation rates would help promote a better understanding of employment-related experiences of older workers from diverse groups. We now turn to a discussion of these underlying factors for Blacks, Hispanics, Asian Americans, and American Indian and Alaska Natives.

Blacks

Many Blacks have more varied work histories than Whites. More often than not, these differences in work histories can be attributed to education and occupational status. The Census Bureau (2000) reports that in the population 65 and over, 53% of Blacks had completed a high school education or more and only 11% had obtained a bachelor's degree or more. Although the high school completion rate for the Black population as a whole is reported to be 72%, only 14% of Blacks have a college degree or more education, a proportion substantially lower than that for Asians and Whites. Given these lower levels of educational attainment, it is not surprising to note that Blacks have poverty rates that are considerably higher than those of Whites and Asians (Bishaw & Iceland, 2003). Census data also reveal that Blacks are prominent in service occupations as well as in production, transportation, and material moving occupations. The probability of being employed in upper-class white-collar jobs (professionals, executives, and managers) is much lower for Blacks than for Whites and Asians (Fronczek & Johnson, 2003).

These demographic and socioeconomic characteristics are also related to their health status. As demonstrated in Chapter 5, the health status of African Americans is worse than that of their White counterparts. Data from the Health and Retirement Study indicate that Black people aged 51 to 59 who are retired are less physically healthy than their White counterparts who are also retired. Among young retirees, more than one third of the Whites report they are in excellent to very good health compared with 13% of Blacks. Since Blacks with lower levels of education are concentrated in physically strenuous jobs, any deterioration in health has a greater impact on their capacity to continue to work than on those employed in less strenuous jobs. Thus, Blacks' higher rates of disability at older ages and higher disability rates of younger Blacks carried forward contribute to the race differences in labor force participation rates for men 55 and over (Hayward, Friedman, & Chen, 1996). In other words, Blacks with lower education levels are likely to have impairments affecting their employment and thus to spend a greater portion of their lives disabled. However, those with higher educational attainment are both less likely to need to leave a job due to impairment and more likely to regain employment after losing it because of disability.

Among White workers aged 60 and over there are minimal differences between men and women with respect to health status. However, among older Black workers men are generally in better physical health than women. For example, more than one third of working Black men report that they are in excellent to very good physical health compared with less than one quarter of working Black women (National Academy on an Aging Society, 2000). However, the health status of Black men and women who are retired is similar.

Hispanics

As discussed in earlier chapters, this population in the United States is composed of subgroups such as Mexicans, Cubans, Puerto Ricans, and Hispanics from Central and South America, other Spanish-speaking countries, and the Dominican Republic. Each of these subgroups immigrated under different political circumstances and settled in different parts of the country that offered varying occupational opportunities. Now each of these subgroups includes both foreign-born and U.S.-born Hispanics. Another key feature of this population is the undocumented status of a substantial population of immigrants who are therefore not included in research based on data from decennial census and current population surveys. We begin with a discussion of educational attainment, the key determinant of employment and earnings.

Educational Attainment   For Hispanics aged 25–59, immigrants average less than 10 years of schooling, but mean educational attainment rises sharply to more than 12 years for U.S.-born Hispanics. Despite this sizable improvement associated with nativity, U.S.-born Hispanics trail the average educational attainment of Whites by more than a year, and as Table 7.3 shows, they even trail the educational attainment of Blacks considerably. Note that Cubans stand out from the other subgroups of Hispanics with markedly high levels of educational attainment. In terms of average schooling, Cuban immigrants exceed U.S.-born Mexicans and approach the level of U.S.-born Puerto Ricans; in addition, U.S.-born Cubans equal or surpass the educational attainment of Whites (Duncan, Hotz, & Trejo, 2006).

Educational attainment of Hispanics aged 65 and over is the lowest among all racial and ethnic groups. As Table 7.4 indicates, almost half of Hispanic men and women have completed less than a 9th-grade education, and only 22% have completed high school. In addition, a much lower proportion of older Hispanics (aged 65 and above) have completed a college degree or more. Furthermore, the proportion of women with a college degree or higher is significantly lower than the proportion for men. Although comparable data for this age group are not available for the U.S.-born versus foreign-born Hispanics, it is likely that the older population includes a large proportion of foreign-born Hispanics for whom the education deficits are more pronounced. In addition, for many Hispanic immigrants, foreign schooling and work experience transfer imperfectly into the U.S. labor market. Many U.S. employers typically place a lower value on education and professional

TABLE 7.3   Average Years of Schooling by Gender, Ethnicity, and Nativity (in percent

	Men by Nativity			Women by Nativity		
Ethnicity	All	Foreign Born	U.S. Born	All	Foreign Born	U.S. Born
Whites	–	–	13.6	–	–	13.6
Blacks	–	–	12.4	–	–	12.8
All Hispanics	10.5	9.5	12.2	10.8	9.8	12.4
Mexicans	9.8	8.5	12.1	10.1	8.6	12.2
Puerto Ricans	11.7	11.2	12.4	12.0	11.4	12.7
Cubans	12.7	12.4	13.6	12.9	12.5	14.2

Note: Samples include individual ages 25–59.
Source: U.S. Census Bureau (2000).

TABLE 7.4   Educational Attainment of the Hispanic (of Any Race) Population Aged 65 and Over by Sex

Educational Level	Men (%)	Women (%)
Less than 9th grade	43.23	50.20
9th to 12th grade	13.55	12.67
High school graduate or general equivalency diploma (GED)	20.43	21.54
Some college or associate's degree	12.26	8.63
Bachelor's degree or higher	10.54	6.97

Source: U.S. Census Bureau (2005).

training acquired abroad than on that acquired in the United States (Schoeni, 1997). These differences play a key role in shaping the labor market success of middle-age and older immigrants. Closely related to nativity is English language proficiency. English deficiencies can explain a substantial portion of Hispanic employment and earning deficits, especially for immigrants. In addition, undocumented status of immigrants also affects the kind of jobs they are able to secure, the salary levels they are able to negotiate, and retirement benefits they are able to receive. In short, low levels of educational attainment, limited English proficiency, and foreign work experience play a key role in explaining their lower rate of labor force participation and earnings deficits.

Employment   Hispanic workers on the whole are younger than their counterparts from other ethnic and racial groups. In 2000 their median age was 34.9 compared with a median age of 39.7 for Whites, 37.3 for Blacks, and 37.8 for Asians (Fullerton & Toossi, 2001; Toossi, 2002).

From 1998 to 2000 nearly one half of all Hispanic men (aged 16 and over) were employed in blue-collar jobs in occupational groups "precision production, craft, and repair workers" and "operators, fabricators, and laborers" (Duncan, Holtz, & Trejo, 2006). In contrast, nearly 64% of Hispanic women were in "technician, sales, or administrative support" jobs (mostly administrative support) or in service occupations.

Hispanic men and women were more likely than White workers to be employed in higher-risk blue-collar and service occupations. Hispanic men accounted for 25% of male employment in farming, forestry, and fishing jobs; 17% of male employment in service occupations; and 16% of the occupational group "operators, fabricators, and laborers." In the latter group, Hispanic men were especially numerous in the occupational group "handlers, equipment cleaners, helpers, and laborers." This group includes occupations requiring less skill and involves higher job risk (Duncan, Holtz, & Trejo, 2006).

As noted previously, Hispanic women were also more frequently employed in blue-collar and service jobs. They accounted for about 18% of female employment in the occupational group "operators, fabricators, and laborers." In addition, they accounted for 15% of female employment in farming, forestry, and fishing occupations and 14% in service occupations. Further, 31% of female employment in the relatively small private household occupational group was composed of Hispanics.

Given their lower levels of educational attainment and limited English proficiency, it is not surprising to see that the occupations that stand out for Hispanic men require physical labor and low skill levels: farm workers, janitors and cleaners, groundskeepers and gardeners, and construction and nonconstruction laborers. Similarly, the occupations where Hispanic women are most frequently found include cleaning: janitors and cleaners, private household cleaners, and maids. Hispanic women are also found in such traditional and lower-skilled "female" jobs as cooks, cashiers, and secretaries.

Fatal Work Injuries   From 1995 through 2000, 4,167 Hispanic workers died as a result of fatal injury on the job, accounting for about 11% of the total number of fatal work injuries that occurred during this period. While the rates for workplace fatalities fell among Whites, Blacks, Asians, and Native Americans, the fatality rate for Hispanics increased during this time period. The most frequent types of events in fatal injuries were transportation incidents followed by assaults and violent acts, contact with objects or equipment, and falls. The percentage of falls and homicides for Hispanics represented a higher proportion of total fatalities than for all workers. Construction laborers and truck drivers accounted for more than 20% all fatal work injuries among Hispanic workers. Foreign-born workers appear to bear a disproportionate share of the fatal work injury burden among Hispanic workers. Many of them do not speak English, and their supervisors do not speak Spanish, which makes safety training harder. Translating training materials into Spanish does not always help because many immigrants do not read Spanish. In addition, a very large number of construction workers are illegal immigrants who do not complain about unsafe work because they fear deportation.

Nonfatal Injuries and Illnesses   Data from the National Institute for Occupational Safety and Health Study (2004) reveal that the median of days away from work due to injury or illness was the highest for Hispanic workers (7 days compared with 6 days for Whites and Blacks.) Topping the nonfatal list of injuries are laborers (both construction and nonconstruction) and truck drivers. Farm workers and groundskeepers and gardeners also appear in the nonfatal list. For Hispanic women the occupations with the most nonfatal injuries and illnesses are nursing aides, orderlies, and attendants. Cleaning jobs such as maids, janitors, and cleaners rank second on this list.

Labor Force Participation Rates   As Table 7.2 shows, the participation rates for Hispanic men declined from 1980 to 2003 whereas the rates for their counterparts from other ethnic and racial groups increased. What are some possible explanations for this decline? One possibility has to do with the physical demands of the jobs they hold. Since a relatively large population of Hispanic men have limited educational attainment, they work as laborers (construction and nonconstruction), truck drivers, farm workers, groundskeepers, equipment cleaners, operators, and fabricators. These occupations are not only physically strenuous but are also riskier than occupations such as management, professionals, and related occupations where the proportion of Hispanics is the lowest among all ethnic groups. In fact, research indicates that Hispanic men have a higher risk of nonfatal workplace injury or illness than any other gender, race, or ethnicity group (National Academy of Sciences, 2003). While data are currently not available for injuries and illnesses among Hispanic men aged 55 and over, we do know that they are more likely to report poor physical health than their counterparts from other ethnic groups. Moreover, they receive benefits from the Social Security Disability Insurance program at an earlier age (National Committee to Preserve Social Security and Medicare, 2004). As you may recall from Chapter 5 on health inequalities, Hispanics have higher life expectancies at the age of 65 than other ethnic and racial groups. Thus, although they have a higher-than-average life expectancy, their rates of participation in the workforce at 55 and above are not proportionately higher. Further, many of them may not be eligible to receive Social Security benefits upon retirement. Why? Since 16% of Hispanic immigrant workers in 1997–2001 came to the United States after they were 30 years old, they will not have time to accumulate a full 35 years of earnings required to receive full Social Security benefits. Moreover, they are more likely to work in jobs not covered by Social Security or to have employers who do not report their earnings such as domestics, agricultural workers, or in the informal economy (Kijakazi, 2002). In addition, as noted earlier, undocumented workers do not get Social Security credit for their earnings while in that status.

The labor force participation rates for Hispanic women in all age groups above 55 have increased consistently across the four periods in Table 7.2. However, in comparison with White, Black, and Asian women, their rates are the lowest except for the 70–74 age group. As we have seen already for Hispanic men, these relatively lower rates may be due to the physically demanding jobs they hold. In addition, many of these occupations have relatively high rates of injuries and illnesses, thereby making it difficult for women to continue working.

Asian Americans   More than 1.1 million Asian American elders 65 and over live and work in the United States. This population is expected to grow faster than any other minority group over the next decade. As discussed in earlier chapters, this group is highly diverse in terms of population characteristics such as immigration history, languages, nationalities, English proficiency, and life span experiences. Of particular relevance to our focus in this chapter is the fact that since 1970, Asians have comprised the largest percentage (43.5%) of the elderly immigrant population (He, 2002). Except for doctors, scientists, and other highly trained professionals, older immigrants arrive in the United States with few high-demand skills, and if they find work at all, it is often in services or manual labor (DeFrietas, 1991). With low incomes and relatively few years to work, they are simply unable to save much for retirement or to obtain retirement benefits. Note that 80% of Asian elders speak a language other than English and that one third live in a household where no adult speaks English. According to the U.S. Census Bureau (2004), 60% of all Asian elders are limited English proficient. This percentage is even higher for certain ethnic groups, especially Southeast Asians and Koreans. Thus, language barriers rank highest among many unmet needs of Asian elders in the United States. We begin this section with a discussion of educational attainment and then focus on their participation in the workforce.

TABLE 7.5 Educational Attainment of the Population Aged 65 and Over by Race and Hispanic Origin, 2004

Race and Hispanic Origin	High School Graduate or More	Bachelor's Degree or More
	Percent	
Total	73.1	18.7
Non-Hispanic White	78.0	19.8
Black alone	52.5	10.7
Asian alone	64.8	29.8
Hispanic (of any race)	37.6	8.3

Source: Federal Interagency Forum on Aging-Related Statistics (2006).

Educational Attainment   As discussed in Chapter 1, the percentage of Asians who have completed a bachelor's degree or more is higher than each of the four ethnic and racial groups included in Table 7.5. However, a closer look at the data for this population tells a different story. Table 7.6 presents a further analysis of these data in terms of the proportion of men and women who have completed each level of education. What conclusions do you draw from the data presented this way?

There are substantial gender differences in the educational attainment for Asians aged 65 and over. For Asians, 40% of women and 26% of men have not completed high school. On the other end of the distribution are 23% of women and 38% of men who have completed a bachelor's degree or more. In other words, how you look at the educational attainment of Asian Americans depends on whether you are focusing on the high end or the low end of the bimodal distribution. It is likely that the high end of the distribution includes physicians, scientists, professors, and other professionals and that the low end includes a sizable population of refugees from Southeast Asia for whom migration has created the loss of high-status work and community roles. Many of them have limited proficiency in English and may have arrived with job skills not transferable to the United States. In other words,

TABLE 7.6 Educational Attainment of the Asian American Population Aged 65 and Over by Sex

Educational Level	Men	Women
	Percent	
Less than 9th grade	17.05	32.41
9th to 12th grade	8.84	7.62
HS graduate or general equivalency diploma (GED)	24.21	25.61
Some college or associate's degree	12.63	12.15
Bachelor's degree	20.42	17.67
Master's degree	8.84	3.57
Professional degree	3.58	0.65
Ph.D.	4.42	0.32

Source: U.S. Census Bureau (2005).

the widely held perception that Asian Americans are better educated and better off financially than other minority groups overlooks the wide range of individual differences among them and ignores the problems faced by the recent refugees. Note that foreign-born Asians have brought a wide range of immigration experiences to their new homes. Some fled from war as refugees, others were granted political asylum from oppressive governments, and many more relocated to be with their family members. Some arrived as children; others arrived already matured. It is also important to remember that the age at which an individual immigrates makes a substantial difference in the extent and success of his or her material and psychological incorporation in the host society (Angel, Buckley, & Sakamoto, 2001).

Occupations and Type of Employment U.S. Census Bureau (2000) reports that in the Asian population as a whole, the percentage of workers employed in management, professional, and related occupations was higher (44.6%) than for other ethnic and racial groups. The second ranking occupational group for this population was sales and office work followed by service and the occupational group "production, transportation, and material moving." The proportion of Asians employed in construction, extraction, and maintenance was the lowest among all groups. Similarly, a very small proportion of Asians worked in farming, fishing, and forestry. As you can see, the employment pattern is consistent with the distribution of their educational attainment. The highly educated segment of the population is employed in management, professional, and related occupations. Those who are high school graduates or have completed some college are either employed in sales and office work or are working in service-related jobs.

Workforce Participation Rates Data presented in Table 7.2 show that in 2003, Asian men aged 55–59, 60–64, and 65–69 participated in the workforce at a rate higher than other ethnic and racial groups. This level of participation may, to some extent, be due to the high level of educational attainment and to the nature of the jobs they hold. Table 7.2 also shows a steady increase in the workforce participation of older women from 1980 to 2003. However, their participation rate remains lower than that of their male counterparts. Furthermore, there are pronounced gender differences in the participation rates for groups aged 65–69, 70–74, and 75 and over. The lower rates of women's participation in the workforce may be due to factors such as declining health, relatively low levels of educational attainment, the nature of jobs they hold, retirement benefits available to them, and the amount of financial support they receive from their spouses or adult children. Since most of Asian workers in higher age groups may be foreign born, it is possible that religious and cultural values may also be contributing to lower levels of workforce participation for both men and women. This is perhaps why Asian men aged 70–74 and 75 and over also participate in the workforce at rates lower than the other three groups included in Table 7.2. Since these are cross-sectional data, it is not possible to make any projections regarding the extent to which men and women currently in the 55–59 and 60–64 age groups would participate in the workforce after they become eligible to receive full retirement benefits. Longitudinal studies would need to be conducted to track the participation rates for different cohorts of older adults. In addition, such studies would also need to examine the patterns of workforce participation of the U.S.-born versus foreign-born Asians.

In concluding this section on the employment of older Asians, it is essential to emphasize again that the image of "model minority" ignores variation both among Asian American nationality groups and between generations within groups, thus obscuring the economic hardships and cultural isolation experienced by many older members of this population. As we have indicated by presenting the distribution of educational attainment levels and by examining the data on type of employment, there is a substantial population of elderly households that have low incomes. Also note that statistical data do not provide any indication of the isolation experienced by many elderly immigrants who feel isolated not only by different language, customs, and way of life in the host country but also by the acculturation of their own children and grandchildren.

American Indians and Alaska Natives   While discussing the workforce participation rate for diverse ethnic and racial groups, we had noted that the available data do not include any information about American Indians and Alaska Natives. The same is true for other data related to work and retirement. However, this population was included in the 2000 U.S. Census, and some valuable information is available for the Native American population as a whole (U.S. Census Bureau, 2000). We have therefore drawn upon the 2000 U.S. Census report in examining their participation in the workforce.

As noted in earlier chapters, the American Indians and Alaska Native population is younger than the total population. Its median age of 29 years is about 6 years less than the national median of 35 years. In the 2000 Census only 5.6% of the American Indians were 65 and older as compared with 12.4% in the total population. Some important characteristics relevant to their workforce participation include the following:

- Most American Indians spoke only English at home; 18% spoke a language other than English at home yet spoke English very well; 10% spoke a language other than English at home and spoke English less than "very well."
- The educational levels of American Indians were below those of the total population in 2000: 71% of this population aged 25 and older had at least a high school education compared with 80% of the total population, and 11% had at least a bachelor's degree compared with 26% of all people.
- The workforce participation rate of American Indian men (66%) was lower than that of all men (71%), whereas the rate for American Indian women (57%) was just slightly lower than for all women (58%).
- In comparison with the total population, high proportions of American Indians were employed in occupational groups such as service; construction, extraction, and maintenance; production, transportation, and material moving; and farming, fishing, and forestry jobs. Lower proportions were employed in management, professional, and related jobs and in sales and office jobs.

- The median income of American Indian men ($28,900) and women ($22,800) who worked full time and year-round were substantially below those of all men ($37,000) and women ($27,200).
- While the prominent image of American Indians depicts people living on remote Indian reservations, about 60% of them live in urban areas where more educational and employment opportunities are available than on reservations.

It is important to emphasize that the U.S. Census (2000) reports significant differences in the educational attainment, workforce participation rates, and the types of jobs held across tribal groupings. In addition, differences were also noted between American Indians and Alaska Natives. Furthermore, among the Alaska Native tribal groupings there were substantial differences as well. Details about the American Indians and Alaska Native population are available on the U.S. Census Bureau website in the following Aging and Diversity Online section.

Aging and Diversity Online: U.S. Census Bureau

American Indian and Alaska Native Census Information. This website includes the publication *We the People: American Indians and Alaska Natives in the United States.* http://www.census.gov/population/www/cen2000/briefs.html

---

Gaming Casinos   The Indian Gaming Regulatory Act passed by the U.S. Congress in 1988 has had a major impact on the economy of Indian tribes across the United States. The economic benefits of gambling for the tribes are most evident in the labor market. Casinos have hired large numbers of resident and nonresident Indians for both skilled and nonskilled jobs, thus lowering the tribal unemployment and welfare rates. For example, in Minnesota there are 17 Indian gaming operations that currently employ approximately 14,000 people. However, 78% of these employees are non-Indians. (No information is currently available for the age distribution of casino workers.) With the millions of dollars that the tribes are receiving in profits, they are building schools and community centers, setting up education trust funds, underwriting the cost of tribal government, financing new business enterprises, and putting in water and sewer systems on the reservations. In short, gambling and gaming present the opportunity for many tribes to develop an industry that has the potential of solving their economic problems in the short run and of supporting tribal government. However, the outlook in the long run is not clear. The greater the number of tribes that enter the market, the smaller will be their share of economic benefits. In addition, Indian gaming has led to pressures on lawmakers to open gambling to all. If this happens and additional casinos are opened within major population centers, there will be no reason for gamblers to travel to distant reservations. If the market becomes oversupplied, the tribes may be left with empty casinos and high unemployment rates again (McCulloch, 1994).

Unpaid Work   Despite considerable changes in recent years, Native American elders, especially those who live on reservations, continue to perform meaningful functions in the family and the community (Williams, 1980). However, as suggested by Stoller and Gibson (2000), using paid work as the only measure of Native Americans' contribution does not provide a complete picture of their productivity. Their contributions to society are underestimated when unpaid work is not considered. An excellent example of such contribution is provided by the work of Native American women artists. As you may know, many Native women create objects (especially beadwork, ribbon-work, weaving, pottery, and basketry) that carry messages about their community and cultures. In addition to these fiber and ceramic arts, Native artists use photography to carry messages about their culture and community. As noted by Jensen (1998), adding camera to fiber and clay allows Native women to explore creative ways to combine a search for personal and public identity. Often these photographers portray their cultures as a part of a lively, assertive group of people confident about the importance of their cultures in the past, their importance to the present, and their influence on the future. As women artists, their photographs tell stories that relate to women's history and may have messages about gender relations, differences among Indian cultures, or commentary about Indian-Euro-American history.

Older Workers in Rural Communities

The preceding section discussed how ethnicity influences the employment-related experiences of older workers. We now turn our attention to experiences of older workers who live in rural communities. In 2004, the population aged 65 and older living in nonmetropolitan areas numbered just under 7.5 million. Two processes contributing to nonmetropolitan aging will accelerate over the next several years:

- Aging in place: Growth rates from aging in place alone will triple among the nonmetropolitan older populations—from 6% in this decade to 18% in the 2010s.
- Net migration: The propensity to migrate to rural settings increases among empty nesters and retirees, and their numbers are rising as the baby boom generation enters this life cycle stage.

In other words, the percentage of older people in rural counties is higher than in urban counties, and this trend is projected to continue. Note that their educational attainment is significantly lower than that of their metropolitan counterparts. Given their limited educational attainment, a large proportion of workers are employed in low-skill jobs. However, these low-skill jobs have continuously been declining as a share of U.S. jobs. In 1900, two thirds of all workers were employed in agriculture and manufacturing, mostly holding manual or routine jobs in the field or factory. By 2000, less than 40% of the U.S. workforce was employed in low-skill occupations. Today, most rural low-skill workers are employed in the growing service sector, in which a typical job demands higher skills than a typical job in goods-sector industries such as manufacturing, mining, and agriculture. In addition, new production methods in many industries are raising occupational skills demands and are thereby contributing to the decline in the low-skills share of rural employment. The implications of these trends are as follows:

1. Encouraging new technology that creates high-skills jobs would make rural communities less vulnerable to international competition.
2. Rural communities would benefit by choosing effective development strategies.
3. Since many seniors are eager to work to support themselves financially, there is a need to develop workforce training programs to help those who want to work.

The Graying of Farmers   In 1998 the average age of the civilian labor force was 38, whereas that of full-time farmers was 57. Although 13% of the population was 65 and older, about 35% of the farmers were in this age group. However, structural changes currently under way may alter the demographic profile of farming. The average size of holdings is increasing as producers attempt to capture economies of scale so that they can compete in the market-driven global economy. It may be that a large number of farms operated by families will give way to agro-industrial enterprises managed by professional managers. If this happens, the number of full-time farmers will continue to diminish, and the average age of farmers may decline.

Aging and Diversity Online: Rural America

U.S. Department of Agriculture. This website provides a large number of reports prepared by the Economic Research Service. Report No. 10 focuses on the low-skill employment and the changing economy of rural America. http://www.ers.usda.gov

---

BARRIERS TO EMPLOYMENT

As earlier sections of this chapter have shown, since the mid 1980s the United States has witnessed a continuing increase in the labor force participation rates for men and women over the age of 55. While this trend may give the impression that it has become easier for older persons to continue in their current position or to find new employment, this is not generally true. In fact, older persons, especially members of minority ethnic and cultural groups, continue to face a variety of obstacles in their search for employment. In this section, we outline major barriers to employment and explore some possible strategies to overcome these obstacles.

Age Discrimination

Age prejudice (ageism) is one of the most socially accepted forms of prejudice in the United States today. Older workers continue to face ageist attitudes and age discrimination (McCann & Giles, 2002). Many employers engage in a variety of personnel practices that differentiate among employees or applicants based on their age. Removing older employees from the workforce through negative performance evaluations or through encouraging their retirement, refusing to hire or promote older persons, and limiting older workers' access to job-related education are examples of these common practices. To prohibit these age/work practices, Congress enacted the ADEA in 1967. This act aims to achieve age-neutral decisions in ensuring that hiring, promoting, training, education, and other personnel actions are not influenced by a person's age. This act was amended in 1978 to prohibit the use of pension plans as justification for not hiring older workers and to raise the mandatory retirement age to 70. In 1986, the mandatory retirement age was eliminated for businesses with more than 20 employees.

The ADEA has three purposes: (1) to promote the employment of older persons based on their ability rather than on their age; (2) to prohibit arbitrary age discrimination in employment; and (3) to help employers and workers to overcome problems arising from the impact of age on employment. It protects individuals 40 years of age and older and is enforced by the Equal Employment Opportunity Commission (EEOC), a federal agency. Despite such legislation, age discrimination alleged as the basis for loss of employment is the fastest growing form of unfair dismissal litigation. According to the federal government, age discrimination complaints filed with the EEOC rose more than 24% between 2000 and 2002. In addition, an average of 16,500 age discrimination cases per year have been filed with the EEOC since 1995, a figure that amounts to roughly 20% of all cases filed with the agency (McCann & Giles, 2002). Thus, although many older workers may view themselves as healthy and productive, their employers may be guided by age stereotypes and may ignore individual differences in skills, abilities, and motivation.

Aging and Diversity Online: Good Practices

European Foundation for the Improvement of Living and Working Conditions. This website includes a report titled *Combating Age Barriers in Employment: A European Portfolio of Good Practices* http://www.eurofund. europa.eu

ACTIVE LEARNING EXPERIENCE: BARRIERS TO EMPLOYMENT FOR MINORITY ELDERS

The purpose of this experience is to engage you in thinking about the difficulties faced by older adults representing ethnic minority immigrants. Upon completion of this activity, you will be able to:

1. Understand the obstacles many older immigrants face in finding employment that is consistent with their educational preparation and experience.
2. Identify some possible strategies that can be used by this population to overcome barriers to finding adequate employment.
3. Outline the losses experienced by older immigrants upon arrival in the United States.
4. Describe why some older adults prefer to continue working.

This activity will take 1 hour (30 minutes to read the case and answer the questions and 30 minutes to discuss responses in class).

Instructions:

1. Prepare written responses to the questions following the case as a homework assignment.
2. Your instructor will ask you to discuss your responses with a classmate during the class session in which this assignment is due.
3. Your instructor will lead a discussion of the losses experienced by older immigrants, the barriers they face in finding adequate employment, and the approaches that may be helpful to them in overcoming the barriers.

With your group, read and analyze the case and answer the questions that follow it.

Case Study

Jose Cerventes is a 55-year-old Hispanic man who lives with his son in Evanston, Illinois, a Chicago suburb. He is originally from Colombia and first came to the United States at the age of 53. His wife died of cancer before he immigrated to the United States. He has since moved from New York to Florida, back to Colombia, to California, and then to Illinois. Most of his moves have been precipitated by job searches. When he first came to the United States, he had a Colombian license as a civil engineer but quickly learned that his educational credentials were not recognized in the United States. Although this had a serious effect on his potential for employment, he accepted the reality and decided to take any job he could find. This led to a varied work history for Jose. For example, he has made blueprints and cables for microwaves, has worked in gas stations, has distributed telephone books, has supervised construction for swimming pools, has served as an interpreter for a travel agency, and has worked in warehouses and factories. While living in Florida, he worked for a consulting firm that moved him back to Colombia, but the firm had financial difficulties, which forced him to move back to the United States.

He has now resumed his search for employment. He says that work is important for him to maintain his mental health. It makes him feel good, provides him opportunities for social interaction with a variety of interesting people, and allows him to maintain financial independence. Though his son is always willing to support him, he prefers not to ask him for money. In fact, Jose would rather give his son the money, as he would have done if they had continued to live in Colombia. He feels strongly that older adults should be able to find employment regardless of their chronological age, and that the most important criteria for employment should be applicants' health and their ability to do quality work.

Discussion Questions:

1. Why did Jose face difficulties in finding employment consistent with his educational preparation and experience?
2. What losses did he experience upon arrival in the United States?
3. Why does he consider it important to continue working?
4. What strategies can he use to make himself more marketable in the world of work?

Discrimination Against Individuals with Disabilities

In addition to discrimination based on age, race, gender, and sexual orientation, older persons with disabilities also face discrimination in aspects of employment such as job application procedures, hiring, firing, advancement, compensation, job training, and other terms, conditions, and privileges. An individual with a disability is a person who has a physical or mental impairment that substantially limits one or more major life activities. Title I of the Americans with Disabilities Act (ADA) of 1990, which took effect in July 1992, prohibits private employers, state and local governments, employment agencies, and labor unions from discriminating against qualified individuals with disabilities. This law may also be used by older persons to challenge discrimination in seeking or retaining employment. The law requires that employers make "reasonable accommodations" to the known physical or mental limitations of an otherwise qualified individual with a disability, unless doing so would impose an "undue hardship" on the operations of their business. Reasonable accommodations may include, but are not limited to, the following:

- Making existing facilities readily accessible to and available for use by persons with disabilities.
- Restructuring, modifying work schedules, reassignment to a different work position.
- Acquiring or modifying equipment or devices; adjusting or modifying examinations, training materials, or policies; and providing qualified readers or interpreters.

The law prohibits the use of employment tests, qualification standards, or other selection criteria that disproportionately screen out individuals with disabilities unless they can be shown to be job related. While the ADA encourages persons with disabilities to stay at work or to return to work by promoting the "carrot" of increased accommodation, it also includes the "stick" of strict criteria used to be eligible for receiving Social Security disability benefits.

The employment provisions of the ADA are enforced under the same procedures now applicable to race, color, gender, national origin, and religious discrimination. Complaints in this regard may be filed with the EEOC or designated state human rights agencies. Available remedies include their reinstatement, promotion, back pay, restored benefits, reasonable accommodation, attorneys' fees, expert witness fees, and court costs. Compensatory and punitive damages may also be available in cases of intentional discrimination or where an employer fails to make a good faith effort to provide a reasonable accommodation. Given the continuing increase in the number of older workers with disabilities, it will be important to track the extent to which the employers make the reasonable accommodations needed by these workers.

ACTIVE LEARNING EXPERIENCE: OLDER WORKERS WITH DISABILITIES AND THE WORKPLACE

The purpose of this experience is to acquaint you with some of the obstacles confronting older employees with disabilities. Upon completion of this activity, you will be able to:

1. List several types of problems in the workplace facing elders with disabilities.
2. Analyze case material relevant to the ADA.

This activity will require 40 minutes (20 minutes to read the cases and answer the questions and 20 minutes for class discussion).

Instructions:

1. Read the cases and answer the questions following them.
2. Discuss your responses with another person.
3. Your instructor will lead a discussion of student responses.

After reading each case, prepare written responses to the accompanying questions, and discuss them with another person.

Case 1

For 22 years, Ruby Kelso has worked as a cashier at the cafeteria operated for the students and staff of Wordsworth College. She has been a good employee, witnessed by the fact that, several times, she has been named College Employee of the Year. Although 67 years old, Ruby wants to continue to work—she needs to work. Ruby's husband died of cancer last year. She misses him and finds that most of her social interaction involves her job. She also needs the money. Her salary is small, but it is better than for her to try to scrape by on Social Security. As a result of arthritis and back pain, Ruby performs her job at a slower pace than she used to. She could really use a more comfortable chair that would give her back more support. She has mentioned this to her supervisor, Sara Kennon, who told Ruby that the college couldn't afford to buy the chair, and she has made veiled threats that if Ruby doesn't get faster at her job, she could be let go.

Discussion Questions:

1. What options does Ruby have?
2. Under the ADA, what is Wordsworth College required to do in terms of accommodating her disabilities?
3. What rights does Ruby have under the ADA?
4. How could Sara have better handled the situation?

Case 2

Sam Nkrumah works in the office of the regional telephone company. A 58-year-old manager, Sam is in charge of a staff of 30. As a result of a motorcycle accident at the age of 19, Sam is confined to a wheelchair. After receiving a master's degree in business administration at the age of 24, Sam went to work for the phone company, and he has been there ever since. He has received numerous promotions and is eligible to be named as general manager. However, he has been told by his boss, Russ Merdly, a company vice president, that he would not present the kind of image the company wants. His boss makes overtures suggesting that Sam consider taking retirement. Sam is furious and feels betrayed by the company to which he has given so much.

Discussion Questions:

1. What are Sam's options?
2. Under the ADA and other civil rights legislation, what obligations does Sam's employer have regarding Sam's employment?
3. If you were Sam, what would you do?

Discrimination Based on Sexual Orientation

Three federal statutes—Title VII of the Civil Rights Act of 1964, the Americans with Disabilities Act, and the Age Discrimination in Employment Act—together make it unlawful for the employer to discriminate against an employee on the basis of characteristics such as race, color, religion, sex, national origin, disability, and age. Note that these characteristics do not include sexual orientation. However, in recent years there have been a number of new developments in this regard, including the following:

- In 1998, President Bill Clinton signed an executive order that prohibits discrimination based on sexual orientation within executive branch civilian employment. The executive order states this policy uniformly by adding sexual orientation to the list of categories for which discrimination is prohibited. As the nation's largest employer, the federal government provided an example for other employers that employment discrimination based on sexual orientation is not acceptable.

- The cabinet-level agencies also have issued policy statements prohibiting discrimination based on sexual orientation. In addition, some agencies have developed complaint procedures allowing employees to file equal employment opportunity complaints based on sexual orientation within their agencies.

- Seventeen states have enacted laws that prohibit discrimination in employment on the basis of sexual orientation. The data from these states show that relatively few complaints of discrimination on the basis of sexual orientation were filed, whether measured in absolute numbers or as a percentage of all employment discrimination complaints under state law. In addition, many city and local ordinances prohibit such discrimination.

- Exactly 49 of the Fortune 50 Companies now include sexual orientation in their nondiscrimination policies. In addition, 431 Companies in the Fortune 500—or 86%—include sexual orientation in their nondiscrimination policies.

In short, considerable progress has been made to ensure fairness in the workplace for lesbian, gay, bisexual, and transgender (LGBT) workers who have often been denied the right to perform their jobs and to contribute to society without facing unfair discrimination. The Human Rights Campaign, an advocacy group, is currently working with U.S. Congress to introduce federal legislation that would prohibit discrimination based on sexual orientation and gender identity.

Aging and Diversity Online: Laws Regarding Discrimination in the Workplace

Equal Employment Opportunity Commission (EEOC). This website presents laws, regulations, and guidance related to discrimination in the workplace. In addition to English and Spanish websites, some information about the EEOC and the laws it enforces is also available in Arabic, Chinese, Haitian, Creole, Korean, Russian, and Vietnamese. http://www.eeoc.gov/index.html

Negative Stereotypes

Although full- and part-time work among older persons has increased significantly since the mid-1980s, employers' views of older workers remain mixed. Positive traits associated with older workers include loyalty, dependability, good work attitudes, low absenteeism, low turnover, and strong motivation (Rix, 2001). Unfortunately, many employers are influenced by the stereotypical view that older workers increase health costs, resist new assignments, lack technological competence, and are unsuited to retraining. Thus, although employers give older workers high marks on certain characteristics, negative stereotypes of older workers persist among American employers. In addition, other stereotypes persist about the work behavior of older persons from different ethnic and cultural groups. Research on Asian Americans has uncovered stereotypes comprising excessive competence (too ambitious, too hardworking) and deficient sociability. Blind people are perceived as socially sensitive (intuitive and friendly) but otherwise incompetent (helpless, dependent, incapable) (Cuddy & Fiske, 2002). African American and Hispanic workers are perceived as physically strong but lazy; Native Americans are viewed as if they are only interested in hunting and fishing. Whether these stereotypes are accurate or not, they guide the behavior of employers and often influence what information they seek, heed, and remember. Thus, stereotypes can have a profound impact on decision making in areas such as hiring, training allocation, and performance management. Indeed, negative stereotypes can become self-fulfilling prophecies. For example, the stereotype of older workers as resistant to learning and change often results in denying them training opportunities and placing them in jobs that may not be meaningful or cognitively challenging for them. As their skills become obsolete and their motivation declines, the stereotype is reinforced (Mauer, 2001).

In work settings, two closely related types of stereotyping behaviors operate. One is age stereotypes per se, which refers to implicit ideas employers have about the relationship between age and worker characteristics. The other is *age norming* of jobs, which occurs when implicit correlations are made between certain jobs and the typical age of persons in those jobs. For example, some jobs are seen as "older person" jobs and some as "younger person" jobs (Finkelstein, Burke, & Raju, 1995). In addition, age norms can develop around organizational issues such as pay levels and duty assignments (Doeringer & Terkla, 1990). These age norms are generalizations that may bias decisions without considering a given individual. In other words, age stereotyping and age norming distort evaluations of older workers and the decisions based on those evaluations. It is, therefore, essential to combat these distorting forces.

What steps can be taken to change long-held stereotypes that persist in organizations? A useful first step may be to conduct an age audit (Sterns & Doverspike, 1988), where organizations examine the distribution of age across jobs and how personnel decisions differentially affect persons of different ages. Although this approach may be useful, it should be emphasized that not all age differences may be the result of stereotypes. Certainly, genuine differences in values and preferences for various jobs exist among different age groups. In addition to conducting age audits, steps need to be taken to ensure that older persons from diverse groups are represented throughout the organization. This goal can be achieved through targeted recruitment of job applicants from diverse groups. Furthermore, we suggest that steps be taken to make the contributions of older workers more visible and prominent on a regular basis.

Individual and Job Obsolescence

When employees fall behind in understanding how to use new tools and techniques or fail to recognize how the application of new knowledge can improve their performance, they become vulnerable to obsolescence. In addition, jobs themselves may become obsolete or disappear when demands for certain products or services decline or new manufacturing techniques replace older, less efficient processes. Older workers are particularly vulnerable to both job obsolescence and individual obsolescence. The greater vulnerability of older women and minorities to job obsolescence is reflected in the longer period of unemployment that they typically experience. Other factors responsible for these difficulties include limited educational preparation, reluctance to admit that certain essential skills have become rusty, and fear of learning the use of new technology. These problems may be exacerbated by reluctance on the part of employers to invest in upgrading the skills of older workers. Furthermore, research indicates that when older workers are provided with training, inappropriate methods are often used, thereby perpetuating the myth that older workers cannot be trained as successfully as their younger counterparts (Warr, 1998). These difficulties can be addressed if the older workers are allowed to learn new skills in appropriate training situations. In other words, employers need to structure training programs that are appropriate for older workers.

In summary, despite the projected decrease in the number of new entrants in the workforce and the increased interest of many older workers in full-time or part-time employment, a number of businesses prohibit their participation in the workforce. It is, therefore, essential to reeducate employers about the strengths and weaknesses of older workers from diverse ethnic and cultural backgrounds, to draw their attention to the increased individual differences in this population, and to emphasize the need to make decisions based on records of performance appraisal rather than age. Involving employees in the design of the appraisal system, evaluating their performance on a regular schedule, and making decisions based on performance would be helpful in drawing upon the untapped potential of older workers. Note that the records of employees' performance appraisals play the most critical role in defense against the charge of age discrimination (Mehrotra, 1984).

CREATING NEW OPPORTUNITIES FOR WORK

As noted in earlier sections, many Americans aged 55–70 are continuing to work (either full time or part time) after retirement. These aging workers remain in the workforce for two primary reasons: (1) financial necessity; and (2) the desire to remain active or to try something new. Financial necessity is a driving factor for many older women and minority seniors to work—whether on a part-time, full-time, or on a self-employed basis. Some of them may have no access to retirement benefits when they stop working and may not have been able to save enough for retirement. A MetLife study (MetLife Mature Market Institute, 2006) reported that older women are more likely than men to work because they need income to live on. This is also true for single and divorced employees as well as for immigrant seniors. What are the implications of these findings? Some examples include the following:

- Given the widespread use of technology in most occupations, technology access and training programs need to be targeted for older women and minority populations. Participating in such programs can play a key role in increasing job opportunities and in reducing the time out of work for displaced workers. Although there is widespread stereotypical thinking about the trainability of older workers, most of them are quite capable of learning new skills (Charness, Kelley, Bosman, & Mottram, 2001). Training programs, which provide ongoing development of new skills and knowledge (e.g., information technology classes), will be an important investment to help ensure that older workers feel a sense of challenge and meaning in their jobs.

- Employers need to evaluate how jobs are designed for older workers and to make accommodations for physical limitations that may increase with age. Examples of these adaptations include changing work environments to limit unnecessary physical strain, paying attention to lighting, reducing lifting requirements, and minimizing the need to stand for long periods of time. Technology may also be used to reduce physical demands of work, thereby increasing employment opportunities for older adults. In addition, computer technology also makes working at home a more likely option and allows for more flexible work schedules. Finally, advances in technology may also help older adults with disabilities function in the workplace. Examples include portable Braille computers, speech synthesizers, screen enlargement software, and video (closed-circuit TV) magnifiers.

- There is a need to design employment programs that assist low-income older adults—including immigrant seniors—to join or reenter the workforce, an excellent example of which is the Senior Community Service Employment Program (SCSEP). First established more than 40 years ago, SCSEP (pronounced SEE-sep) is one of the major programs funded under Title V of the Older Americans Act as well as through state and local grants to help low-income individuals aged 55 and older throughout the United States. Through this program, seniors benefit from training, counseling, and community service assignments at faith-based and community organizations in their communities prior to transitioning into the workforce. About 18,000 participants have gained regular employment through this program (Senior Service America, 2006). Details regarding eligibility criteria, training design, instructional approaches, and outcomes are available on the websites included in the Aging and Diversity online section.

In addition to the federally funded employment programs like SCSEP, a number of other organizations and agencies help provide training, employment, and community service opportunities to seniors. Their websites are also included in the Aging and Diversity online section. Note that there are important differences in the missions of the organizations and the populations they serve.

Aging and Diversity Online: Employment Programs

The U.S. Department of Labor Employment and Training Administration (DOLETA). This site offers useful information regarding programs aimed at providing employment opportunities to older people. DOELTA funds SCSEP, administered by Senior Service America. http://www.doleta.gov/seniors

Senior Service America. A nonprofit organization that provides community service and employment opportunities for low-income older adults who wish to reenter the workforce. It administers SCSEP grants to nonprofit agencies throughout the country. www.seniorserviceamerica.org

---

In summary, many older people desire or need to work for financial or social reasons. On the other hand, over the next few years the number of workers aged 25–54 is expected to decrease. Clearly there will be a continuing need to develop strategies to prepare for and accommodate an aging workforce. This will require understanding the characteristics of older workers representing diverse populations and the potential implications of aging for work and work environments. This will also require retraining older adults, strengthening their technological skills, and redesigning existing jobs and work options. In addition, there will continue to be a need to create new opportunities for work that draw upon the background and experience of older adults from diverse populations.

RETIREMENT

So far our discussion has focused on work. We have discussed ethnic and gender differences in the older workforce, have outlined factors affecting the participation of older women and minorities in the workforce, and have reviewed barriers to their employment. We have also presented examples of programs that have been designed specifically for older adults from economically disadvantaged populations. Our discussion now shifts to retirement. This discussion includes issues such as how retirement is viewed by women and minorities, what factors influence their decision to retire, what should be included in retirement preparation programs for diverse populations, and how elements of diversity influence adjustment to retirement.

What is retirement? Does it have a definition that is universally accepted? There are many retirements, or at least many forms of retirement. Theory and research have provided us with concepts such as *phased* or *partial retirement, voluntary retirement, social security* (or *pension*) *eligibility* or *receipt, perceived retirement,* and *early retirement.* We could continue and list a number of other forms of retirement, but by now our point should be clear. There are many forms of retirement, and new variations continue to emerge. In addition, there are considerable variations in how retirement is viewed by women, low-income workers, and ethnic and cultural minorities and what factors influence their decision to retire.

Diversity and Retirement

Theories and research on retirement focusing primarily on White men may not generalize to women and minorities. The traditional retirement criteria (e.g., being aged 65, a clear line between working and not working, income primarily from retirement sources, viewing oneself as retired) do not apply to a large proportion of women or to ethnic and cultural minorities. Why? Consider the following elements of diversity as they influence how retirement is viewed.

Gender   Researchers have documented differences in the paid work patterns of men and women and changes that have occurred in the pattern of these differences over time. In addition, within given cohorts, women's participation in paid employment has varied by social class and by ethnicity. It is clear that the continuing wage gap between men and women will contribute to a future gap in retirement benefits and accumulated assets, especially for single, divorced, or widowed women who cannot pool their resources with a second wage earner. Research indicates that the proportion of men aged 65 and older receiving pension income is significantly higher than women in the same age group (Purcell, 2000). This is mainly because many women move in and out of the workforce, in and out of part-time jobs in tandem with shifting family responsibilities. They are thus less likely to be covered by pensions than are men, and those with pensions have incomes lower than men's. For couples who have favored traditional gender roles, retirement often means that the man stops doing his paid work but that the woman continues her unpaid work in the home managing the household. However, given the increased participation of women in the workforce, there will be increased participation of women in the retirement transition as well. This means that in the future a larger proportion of women will retire from their own career jobs, and couples will increasingly face the reality of two retirement exits, "his" and "hers" (Han & Moen, 1999). Retirement will no longer be an almost exclusively male status passage.

Ethnicity   As with the work patterns of women, many minority workers also have experienced intermittent employment that undermines their ability to accumulate financial resources to support their retirement. Their checkered work lives often continue into old age, and many of them continue their lifelong pattern of sporadic work in low-paying jobs. The continuation of this employment pattern seems to blur the line between work and nonwork to the degree that these older workers do not always consider themselves retired even though they are not employed on a continuing basis. Many of them who are eligible for disability pay call themselves disabled rather than retired, because disability benefits are often higher than retirement benefits based on a lifetime of low-wage work (Zsembik & Singer, 1990).

There is a widespread expectation that retirees sustain themselves on Social Security benefits, private pensions, savings, and investment income. These sources of income are often referred to as the *three-legged stool* of retirement. However, for many minority elders, especially Latino and Black retirees, because of their labor market status during the working years, Social Security is the only leg on which they can rely. As a result, poverty among these two groups remains disproportionately high. For example, in 2005, 20% of older Hispanics and 23% of older African Americans were poor. Meanwhile, only 8% of older Whites and 13% of older Asians were poor. The highest poverty rates were experienced among older Hispanic women (46%) and older Black women (37%). Given these high rates of poverty among Hispanic and Black women, it is not surprising to note that they often do not anticipate retiring.

Retirement in Rural Communities   With respect to work and retirement in rural communities, the greatest disadvantages are observed among nonfarm

elders, older women, and single elders, who are more likely to depend on Social Security and need help from Supplemental Security Income. For rural elders, income from continuing labor force participation tends to be low. As a result, poverty rates are high among nonmetropolitan elders compared with their metropolitan counterparts. For example, in 1999, 50% of rural elders were considered low income compared with 38% of metropolitan dwellers (Coburn & Bolda, 1999). This income disadvantage is mainly due to the lifelong employment trajectories of many rural adults. They have experienced limited access to well-paying jobs and have seen a gradual decline in choice of occupations during their working years. In short, chronic unemployment and underemployment have made them vulnerable to entering old age with much diminished resources.

Social Class People with limited education and from working-class backgrounds have a lifetime of lower wages, less job security, fewer pensions and other benefits, and greater risk of occupational injury than their counterparts from middle- and upper-class backgrounds. They are unable to save for retirement, and their employers rarely provide them with health or retirement benefits (Crystal & Shea, 2003). With minimum Social Security and Medicare, they are at serious risk of poverty and inadequate medical care when they retire.

The factors that make a difference in the economics of retirement among minority elders include the sector—public or private—in which a person worked, the occupational category of the job held, and the length of time the person worked at a particular job. Many minorities are at a disadvantage, since fewer work in the public sector (with its better pension coverage) than Whites. Also, they are often in lower occupational categories and therefore have lower incomes and may have a more unstable work tenure. They are thus less likely to accumulate vesting rights and wage provisions necessary for receiving the maximum postretirement incomes from pensions and Social Security. Although more established Asian Americans have worked in professional and managerial positions and are likely to have adequate income during their retirement years, many recent immigrants (e.g., newly arrived Vietnamese and Hmong elders) have not worked long enough to be eligible for pension and Social Security benefits.

As noted earlier, the concept of retirement continues to evolve. Although traditionally retirement has been considered synonymous with the absence of paid employment among older adults, today many retirees (particularly in their 50s, 60s, and early 70s) engage in some forms of paid employment. What options are available for such employment? The following section presents two options used widely by older workers.

Variations of Retirement

Phased Retirement In the traditional view of retirement, a worker moves from full-time employment to complete withdrawal from the labor force in a single step. In fact, however, some workers choose to continue working after they have retired from their "career" jobs. They view retirement as an opportunity for a "whole new chapter." For them, the process of retiring occurs gradually over a number of years, with many workers retiring from year-round full-time employment and moving to part-time or part-year work at the same or another organization. This process is sometimes referred to as phased retirement and is often viewed as a transition into full retirement. Research indicates that almost 11% of men and 7% of women aged 65 and older who received income from private pension plans in 1999 were also employed in 2000.

Bridge Employment

As the term implies, bridge employment provides older workers a "bridge" between their career jobs and complete withdrawal from the workforce. Thus, such employment is often used by older workers as a part of the transition process from full-time work to retirement. The evidence is quite strong that bridge employment does facilitate adjustment to retirement by providing older adults with some structure for their time, supplemental income, and opportunities to develop new routines and interests before leaving work behind for good (Weckerle & Schultz, 1999). In view of such evidence, it is not surprising to note that a majority of workers now retire from bridge jobs rather than their career jobs. Although bridge jobs quite often involve changes in occupation and industry, with significant loss of occupational status and pay, this is not true for all bridge jobs (Schultz, 2003). Often bridge jobs are customized to the needs of individual workers. They provide flexibility, economic benefits, and status that make them an attractive option for older workers. These arrangements are created not out of social consciousness but due to the needs of the employers. As the workforce ages, such needs are likely to grow, and organizations will be forced to create bridge employment opportunities with flexible arrangements to attract older workers out of retirement. It is important to note that access to bridge employment tends to be available mainly to older workers who live in metropolitan areas. Rural older adults have limited opportunities for such employment. Furthermore, bridge jobs are less common among Black women than either White or Hispanic women. If public policy initiatives are pursued to assist older adults in obtaining bridge employment, it would be beneficial to target them at disadvantaged groups who do not have easy access to such opportunities.

As the previous discussion indicates, growing numbers of older workers are not simply selecting between continued employment and retirement. Instead, they are choosing to pursue a variety of options in between. These choices are influenced by their health status, their cognitive functioning, their evolving fit in the workplace, and social and economic factors. Thus, there is an increasing tendency toward "blurred" rather than "crisp" exits from the workforce.

Regardless of whether you view retirement as a single step from full-time work to complete withdrawal or prefer to facilitate the transition to retirement through part-time employment, advance planning plays a pivotal role in adjustment to retirement. Research shows that retirement planning can be linked to lower anxiety and depression, a better attitude toward retirement, and better postretirement adjustment. Perhaps these outcomes are primarily related to the formation of realistic expectations about the social and financial aspects of retirement (Taylor & Doverspike, 2003). Furthermore, the planning process engages the participant in setting goals for financial, physical, and social well-being after retirement. The following segment begins with a discussion of the need for retirement planning and then focuses on retirement planning programs, what they aim to achieve, and what they generally include.

Need for Retirement Planning

Numerous studies document that the current generation of aging workers are woefully uninformed about the options and decisions that they will confront on retirement and are unprepared for the realities that await them. This is especially true for a large proportion of women and ethnic and cultural minorities. Consider a sample of findings from recent studies:

1. Most minorities (and most workers overall) do not try to figure out their retirement needs. Only one quarter of African Americans and Hispanics have tried to calculate how much money they need to save for a comfortable retirement—a significant decline from recent years. Among workers overall, less than half (43%) say they have tried to do a calculation (EBRI, 2007).
2. Many African Americans and Hispanics are counting on employer-provided retirement benefits (e.g., pensions, retiree health insurance, and long-term care) even though such benefits are increasingly unlikely to be offered to future retirees.
3. Less than half of African American workers say they (or their spouse) have personally saved or are currently saving for retirement. The likelihood of saving for retirement increases sharply as household incomes rise.
4. Four in ten Hispanic workers report that they (or their spouse) have personally saved money for retirement. However, only one third indicate they are currently saving for retirement. As noted for African Americans, the likelihood of saving for retirement increases sharply as household income rises. Furthermore, native-born Hispanics are at least twice as likely as their foreign-born counterparts (62% vs. 31%) to have saved for retirement and to be currently saving for retirement (53% vs. 25%) (EBRI, 2007).
5. Only about half of Hispanic and African American workers compared with 6 in 10 workers overall say they consider the number of years they (and their spouse) might spend in retirement when doing their planning.
6. Overall, minority workers tend to think they will spend somewhat less time in retirement than do workers overall. They are also more likely to say they do not know how long their retirement will last (EBRI, 2007).
7. Minority workers are less likely to cite the correct eligibility age of unreduced Social Security benefits than workers overall. This lack of knowledge may be due to the fact that only 60% of African Americans and half of Hispanic workers remember receiving a statement from the Social Security Administration in the past year.
8. The vast majority of men and women in their 50s and 60s engage in at least some retirement planning, but men are significantly more likely than women to have actually planned (94% compared with 85%) (Quick & Moen, 1998).
9. Men (43%) are more likely than women (32%) to plan to retire before the age of 65, whereas women are more likely than men to retire at 65.

10. Men are more likely than women to say that they are very confident about having enough money to live comfortably throughout retirement, about having money to pay for long-term care, and that the Medicare system will continue to provide benefits equal to those received by retirees today (EBRI, 2007).

11. Research from a sample of same-sex relationships indicates that women plan less than men. When they plan, they are most likely to describe their plans as interdependent, whereas men were most likely to characterize their retirement plans as unilateral (Mock, Taylor, & Savin-Williams, 2006).

Retirement Planning Programs

Frequent advertisements in the newspapers and on radio and television, unsolicited email messages, and a large number of attractive websites may give you the impression that retirement planning is synonymous with making appropriate financial investments. However, the fact is that retirement planning programs (also called *preretirement education programs*) are becoming more encompassing in scope, moving from primarily financial to covering more of social and psychological issues of retirement. Key objectives of retirement planning programs include the following:

- To provide general financial, psychological, and health information to participants.
- To help them understand the value of retirement benefits (i.e., pension, Individual Retirement Accounts [IRAs], 401(k) plans, and Social Security benefits) to determine if there is a need for continuing employment or additional savings.
- To motivate participants to plan for retirement.
- To reduce anxiety before retirement.
- To enhance adjustment to retirement.
- To help individuals identify their desired lifestyle in retirement.

Given these objectives, a typical program may include topics listed in Table 7.7.

Pension Plans   Although financial health is an important component of retirement planning, many workers do not have adequate knowledge and understanding of pension plans and how they are changing. Most of these plans fall into the category of either a defined benefit (DB) plan or a defined contribution (DC) plan. A DB plan generally provides pensions that are based on a percentage of one's final pay, prior earnings, years of service, and age at retirement. These benefits are typically paid as an annuity (Campbell & Munnell, 2002). The number of these plans in private sectors has decreased substantially in recent years.

In contrast, the number of DC plans has been increasing. DC pension plans give participants flexibility and portability and provide generally lower co-pays and investment risks for employers (Campbell & Munnell, 2002). These pension plans involve a specific payment out of each paycheck into an employee-specific account, to which an employer often adds a partially or fully matched contribution.

TABLE 7.7   Topics in a Typical Pre-Retirement Education Program

Topic	Subtopics
Deciding when to retire	When is the right time?
Variations of retirement	Phased retirement
	Bridge employment
Psychological aspects of aging	Work roles and retirement
	Personal identity issues
	Retirement as a process
	Effects on relationship with family and friends
Finances and insurance	Social security
	Pension
	Insurance
Legal aspects	Wills
	Personal rights as a senior citizen
Health-related issues	Health promotion, wellness, and prevention
	Health insurance issues
	Medicare and Medicaid programs
Where to live	Moving: its advantages and disadvantages
Leisure activities	Travel
	Hobbies
	Clubs and organizations
	Volunteering
	Lifelong learning

Source: Adapted from Cavanaugh & Blanchard-Fields (2006).

Examples of such plans include 401(k), profit sharing, 403(b), and 457. The exact amount of pension a worker receives is not predetermined. Instead, it depends on many factors, including the amount contributed by the employer and the employee and the rate of return on the investment of the pension funds. The accrued amount is available in a lump-sum payment at the time of retirement or may be taken as an annuity.

As noted earlier, today DC plans have replaced the traditional DB plans as the primary retirement vehicle for a significant and increasing number of employees. What are the implications of this shift for women, low SES, and minority workers? First, the decision of whether to participate in the plan and the decision regarding how much to contribute to the plan are made by the employee. Workers with lower incomes may feel that current demands on their income must take precedence over long-term investment. The result is that many workers do not participate at all and that many do not contribute the maximum amount permitted by the plan. In addition, many minorities and recent immigrants begin contributing when they are significantly older than their mainstream counterparts. Since compounding returns make a substantial impact on retirement income, those who do not begin saving early in life are severely penalized.

A second major problem is that DC plans place investment risk on the shoulders of the participants. Many of the participants have limited knowledge and understanding of financial concepts, investment options, and their long-term implications. Research shows that the financial and investment knowledge of women, low-income workers, and recent immigrants tends to be less sophisticated than workers overall. Thus, the problems of poor investment decisions are often not an issue of volition but rather a lack of knowledge and understanding of financial concepts and available instruments.

A third problem is that, under DC plans, workers are permitted to borrow on their retirement investment accounts or to receive a lump-sum payout when they change jobs. There is a tax penalty for early withdrawal. However, families without resources for unexpected expenses may see no alternative. As a result, when these workers grow old they will have little or no pension income from their DC plans. In sum, defined DC pension plans are unreliable vehicles to achieve the goal of retirement income security. It is not realistic to assume that all participants have the ability to invest their own pension assets wisely. Many of them may not realize that the funds invested in the stock market do not always grow. The market moves in both directions.

Engaging Diverse Populations in Retirement Planning

Given the critical role played by financial stability in adjustment to retirement, a discussion of financial considerations is incorporated in almost all retirement planning seminars. However, those who most need this planning—women, ethnic and cultural minorities, and those in lower-paying lower-skilled jobs—are also the least likely to engage in formal planning programs. Why? Many of them feel that the available programs are not offered at the level appropriate for their needs. It is essential, therefore, to consider participants' characteristics such as income levels, work history, language skills, health status, and family circumstances in designing and offering a retirement education program. A one-size fits all approach to planning does not serve the purpose. What steps can be taken to engage diverse populations in retirement planning? The following suggestions may be helpful to those involved in designing and offering such programs:

1. Know your target audience. Start by preparing an accurate profile of the demographic, social, economic, and cultural characteristics of the group you plan to serve. If the profile is developed accurately, it will allow you to understand the level of assimilation and acculturation in the group and thus will enable you to determine the extent to which cultural factors must be taken into account.

2. Seek active consultation with representatives of the population you plan to serve. These representatives may be consulted on program content, format, and instructional methods. Remember that communicating with minority participants requires more than speaking their language; it involves being sensitive to their history, traditions, and situations. It may be useful to establish advisory committees to ensure ongoing dialogue with community representatives.

3. Obtain assistance from employers, union representatives, and company officials. Collaboration with these groups plays a major role in encouraging minority and low-income workers to take advantage of retirement preparation programs. Such partnerships also make the program an integral

part of other services that are provided to members of the population you aim to reach.

4. Make effective use of radio and television. In every community with large numbers of ethnic and cultural minorities, radio, television, and print media exist that cater to these groups. Identify these media, and use them frequently and effectively to make potential participants aware of the program you plan to offer. Many effective programs are not used because there is a lack of knowledge regarding their availability.

5. Conduct the program in minority neighborhoods. Many communities have gathering places for members of ethnic populations. Using these locations creates a comfortable surrounding and shows a serious intent to reach out to these groups.

6. Examine the educational program and materials in terms of cultural bias. It is important that they be changed to account for variations in realities, perceptions, and conditions faced by participants who may not be the so-called typical retiree. Determine how handouts and instructional materials can be adapted to match participants' level of educational attainment. Including factual data and information about the retirement experience of the group you plan to serve is also important.

7. Include a discussion of informal and natural support networks. Informal networks that provide information, services, and support have existed in many ethnic communities for many years. It would be beneficial for educational programs to identify and discuss these networks in reference to their utility in planning for retirement. In addition, it would be good to emphasize the vital role played by social networks and social interaction in facilitating adjustment to retirement. Planning should incorporate strategies for enhancing this dimension of life as well.

8. Increase participants' awareness of planning resources available through the Internet. To help address the concern regarding limited participation in retirement planning, a large number of useful resources have been made available through the Internet. These resources have been developed by (a) federal agencies such as the U.S. Department of the Treasury and U.S. Department of Labor; (b) advocacy groups such as American Association of Retired Persons and Consumer Federation of America; (c) professional associations such as the Actuarial Foundation, American Savings Education Council, and Certified Financial Planners Board of Standards; and (d) investment companies such as Vanguard and Fidelity. Fortunately some of these resources are also available in Spanish. In addition, a number of them are designed specifically for women. Participants in retirement planning will appreciate knowing about these practical resources. (See examples of useful websites about retirement in the Aging and Diversity Online section.)

<hr/>

Aging and Diversity Online: Retirement Planning Resources

The Retirement Savings Education Campaign. Offers useful information about saving for retirement and the tools to get started. Its publications are available in Spanish. https://www.dol.gov/ebsa/savingmatters.html

Wise Up. Designed for women, this e-mentoring project aims to promote financial security by encouraging responsible savings habits for future retirement. Participants can interact with mentors through a listserv maintained by the University of Texas at Dallas. http://wiseupwomen.tamu.edu

Preparing Financially for Retirement. This website is designed by U.S. Department of Agriculture Cooperative Extension Service to give you the skills, confidence, and motivation to build financial security for you and your family. It includes a useful consumer guide to help older adults prepare financially for retirement. http://www.csrees.usda.gov/nea/economics/fsll/cons_intro.html

<hr/>

Adjustment to Retirement

Retirement, like other critical transitions, often affects one or more of the basic elements of an individual's life, including self-identity, self-worth, relationships with others, financial status, and daily activities. Since American society values youth and productivity, men and women who retire may lose status, income, and personal and social worth. As a new, untried experience, retirement engenders anxiety, but, as we have discussed, advance planning helps in facilitating one's adjustment to retirement. The importance of retirement planning on postretirement adjustment cannot be overstated. Having discussed planning in the preceding section, we now proceed to examine how elements of diversity influence adjustment to retirement.

Two main attributes associated with adjustment to retirement are financial status and health (Schultz, Morton, & Weckerle, 1998). Those in better health show higher levels of adjustment and satisfaction with retirement and are also more likely to seek part-time work. On the other hand, there are workers who encounter health problems and take early retirement. This means that they may not be eligible to receive full Social Security benefits. However, since they have limited financial resources, they opt to receive benefits at a reduced level. They may not realize that although people become eligible for Social Security at the age of 62, benefits are reduced from 5.5% to 6.5% per year prior to full retirement age—which is now between 65 and 67, depending on date of birth.

Research suggests that the self-reported health of older Black men is worse than for White males and that permanent workforce withdrawal occurs at an earlier age (Hayward, Friedman, & Chen, 1996; National Academy on an Aging Society, 2000). For example, the percentage of young retirees (aged 51–59) indicating that their health was "fair" to "poor" was 65% for Black males and 51% for White males. For Black women, 67% reported fair to poor health compared with only 35% of White women. In addition to poor health, disability rates also tend to be elevated for Blacks (Brown, Fukunaga, Umemoto, & Wicker, 1996). Since the overall educational attainment for Blacks is lower than the mainstream population, they are often overrepresented in physically demanding jobs where compensation levels are low, retirement benefits are few, and disability rates are high.

These characteristics (i.e., poor health, higher disability rates, and limited financial resources) may lead to a significantly more negative experience for this population (Hayward, Friedman, & Chen, 1996). Long-term financial and health-oriented planning is, therefore, critical to facilitate their adjustment to retirement.

Limited research on adjustment to retirement is currently available for older Hispanics. It is, however, reasonable to assume that as long as they are concentrated in occupations that require manual, back-breaking, physical work (e.g., agriculture, warehouse, assembly line), they will continue to experience low job satisfaction, increased physical impairment, and early retirement. Thus, poor health and limited financial resources will also affect their adjustment to retirement. Such difficulties with adjustment to retirement were substantiated by Markides and Mindel (1987). These investigators reported that their Mexican American subjects, in comparison with socially advantaged Anglo elders, adjusted more poorly to retirement. Since many Mexican Americans drop out of the labor force after being unsuccessful in their job-seeking efforts, these findings corroborate previous studies documenting greater adjustment problems among involuntary retirees. It is also believed that many Hispanic retirees do not apply for Social Security benefits because they are unsure of their legal status in the United States, are afraid of dealing with government agencies as a result of past negative experiences, or simply do not know how to apply for benefits (Garcia, 1993). For some, ineligibility for benefits may result from intermittent work patterns, late-in-life migration to the United States, work in uncovered employment, and unscrupulous employers who do not report employee contributions to Social Security. Consequently, many older Mexican American immigrants and other Hispanics often remain dependent on their families because they do not qualify for government programs.

While the critical importance of financial support and positive levels of health is clear, it is essential to note the pervasive influence of social networks and social support in postretirement satisfaction and adjustment for all retirees, especially those from ethnic and cultural minorities and those who live in rural communities. Research on social support has focused on two different dimensions: sources of support and types of interactions that occur. Studies on Black, Hispanic, and Asian communities reveal that extended family, community groups, and religious organizations (e.g., churches, mosques, temples) continue to play a major role as members age (Weeks & Cuellar, 1981). The family, in particular, is important. As noted earlier, many minority retirees depend on the family for financial, emotional, and physical support, and their major activities center around the family. This continuing support is a central factor in postretirement affect and adjustment of many retirees from ethnic and cultural populations. In addition, quality of relationships and the frequency of aid from friends and relatives have also been found to be consistent predictors of retirement satisfaction among rural men and women retirees (Dorfman, Kohout, & Heckert, 1985).

In addition to sources of social support, it is also important to consider the types of interaction that occur during the retirement years. Interactions can take different forms. Social support may take the form of receiving concrete, necessary resources such as transportation (tangible support) or receiving information needed to solve problems (informative support). A third form of social support involves receiving affection from family, friends, and the community. As noted earlier, extended family, church, and neighborhood groups in many ethnic communities provide older adults with the kind of support they need during different phases of their retirement period. Since informal networks that provide information, services, and support have existed in many minority communities and rural areas for years, retirement planning programs need to identify and discuss these networks with reference to their usefulness during retirement years. In addition, these programs should also emphasize the changes in the family and social relationships that may occur over a lifetime. These changes may create culture shock to those who find that those traditional patterns no longer exist. Educating the participants to these upcoming changes and how to cope with cultural transitions may help facilitate their cultural and psychological adjustment to retirement in the new environment. It is also important to emphasize that while social support plays a significant role in facilitating adjustment, it does not in any way minimize the critical influence of financial support and positive levels of adjustment. In addition, religious organizations and neighborhood groups outside the work setting can help educate members on the essentials of retirement planning and can then provide follow-up support to facilitate transition from work to retirement.

Gender Differences   As noted by many researchers, we know little about women's retirement as compared with men's. However, we do know that retirement models based on men may not be appropriate for understanding women's retirement. Separate models may be more appropriate. Consider, for example, the following factors:

1. Men and women have different work histories. For most men, work has been continuous; for many women work has been discontinuous. Women move in and out of the workforce more frequently than men due to family caregiving responsibilities. These interrupted work histories have significant implications for Social Security and pension benefits during retirement years. This, in turn, affects women's adjustment to retirement.

2. Women tend to be segregated in a limited range of occupations and industries. Many of these occupations are characterized by relatively low wages and a decreased likelihood of pension coverage. Thus, women who have worked in such jobs have limited financial resources and may face a difficult economic transition at retirement. Furthermore, they may not have access to retirement preparation programs. On the other hand, there are women who are more educated and have been employed in higher-paying jobs. They are more likely to receive a pension and to be financially secure.

3. Many women retire suddenly because their husband or an aging parent unexpectedly falls ill. Traditional roles dictate that wife/daughter provide care for the ailing relative. Other women are forced to retire simply because their husband has retired. Some retired husbands decide to relocate despite the likelihood that the working wife may have difficulty obtaining employment after a move. Women who retire suddenly because of family obligations do not have adequate time to formulate a strategy for successful adjustment to retirement. Since they had not foreseen

retirement occurring for several years, they may experience difficulty in adjusting to retirement, especially during the initial phase.

Clearly, retirement models based solely on a male sample may overestimate the financial security of women in general. More importantly, there may be qualitative differences in the predictors of adjustment for men and women. If you are asked to design a retirement planning program for women, be sure to engage them in economic planning. Note that men begin planning for retirement earlier than women and that men generally give attention to financial planning and discuss retirement more frequently than women (Moen, Erickson, Agarwal, Fields, & Todd, 2000).

In sum, we need models of retirement based on a diverse sample of individuals. These models would provide a more accurate reflection of the workforce and would take into account the fact that not all gender and racial groups may have similar retirement experiences. While retirement planning enhances adjustment, it does not mean that the same program works well with all populations. It is essential to take into consideration characteristics of the target population. This would ensure that the educational program would provide the participants with information that is most relevant and helpful for them. This, in turn, would enhance their adjustment to retirement.

LEISURE PURSUITS

Leisure has been defined as an inherently satisfying activity that is characterized by the absence of obligation. Free time alone is not necessarily leisure. Instead, the key variable is how a person defines tasks and situations to create intrinsic meaning. Thus, leisure implies feeling free and satisfied. There are important differences in how men and women, as well as people in different ethnic/racial groups, view leisure. For example, one study of Black women reported that they view leisure as both freedom from the constraint of needing to work and as a form of self-expression (Allen & Chin-Sang, 1990). What do people do with their time when they retire? Studies reveal that they engage in many more activities with an increase in free time. The most common leisure activities chosen by retirees are reading or writing, watching television, listening to music, visiting family and friends, exercising, traveling, shopping, engaging in personal hobbies, and participating in religious and spiritual activities (Wink, 2007). Contrary to the popular notion of disengagement, the image of "active old" continues to be more accurate than that of voids of time and commitment. Furthermore, the activity patterns of retirees are characterized by considerable continuity with the activities and relationships that were meaningful to them in their preretirement years. This engagement in productive activities is presumed to ease adjustment to retirement and to provide new sources of personal meaning and competence.

Cutler and Hendricks (1990) identified gender differences with regard to leisure activities. Women tend to engage in sociocultural and home-centered activities, whereas men seem to prefer outdoor activities (e.g., fishing, hunting), sports (both playing and observing), and travel. Type of residence also makes a difference. People who live in retirement housing participate more frequently in leisure activities than people living in traditional neighborhoods (Moss & Lawton, 1982).

This may be due to the fact that retirement communities often provide structured activities for their residents whereas many age-integrated neighborhoods and communities do not.

Older adults' leisure activities also vary by SES. Not surprisingly, those with high incomes tend to be more active in leisure pursuits than low-income elders (Riddick & Stewart, 1994). These differences may be due to the costs of pursuing leisure activities rather than to inherent differences in people with low and high income levels. Older men tend to do more household maintenance and paid work outside the home; older women perform more housework, child care, and volunteer work, and participate in more voluntary associations (Hooyman & Kiyak, 2002). Older adults, especially women, rural elders, and low-income minorities, may face barriers to leisure participation such as health problems and lack of transportation. These barriers are especially important for understanding the participation patterns of these populations. Indeed, health problems are the primary reason given when older adults explain their lack of participation in leisure activities. A challenge for service providers is to create leisure opportunities that are both meaningful and accessible to this segment of the population. Participation in such activities is especially important for single elders who lack daily companionship.

Senior Centers

Senior centers are one mechanism providing such opportunities to older adults. Although there are variations in the services offered by senior centers across the country, core services recommended in one study (Gelfand, Bechill, & Chester, 1991) include congregate meals, home-delivered meals, exercise, information and assistance, socializing, and transportation. Despite this large variety of services offered by the senior centers, they have had limited success in attracting older people. This may be due to reasons such as the following:

- Individuals may be busy elsewhere.
- They may not be interested in the activities offered by the center.
- They may be in poor health.
- They may not have necessary transportation.
- They may not want to be with only older people.
- A lower proportion of men in many centers may discourage other men from taking part.

Given the relatively low rate of utilization and improved health and educational attainment of older people, marketing firms, social workers, and others who work with older adults have been pondering how to attract and meet the needs of an active generation of older adults who prefer not to call themselves senior citizens. In fact, some of the centers have now changed their names to "community centers." They welcome anyone older than 18 and create the perception that the centers are designed for adults with similar interests rather than as a place for adults who might share little else than an age range. Some of them remain open until 10:00 p.m. to allow working adults to participate in their programs and services. In addition, they have added fitness classes, yoga, salsa dancing, martial arts, and van trips to a variety of concerts and plays to the mix of standard offerings like billiards, cards, and crafts. Moreover, some of the centers also provide a wide range of health, legal, and financial services, a nutritional lunch 5 days a week, and deliver meals-on-wheels to the homebound. The underlying assumption is that offering a wide range of activities and services and remaining open late in the evenings will attract a good mix of people who will then continue to participate as they age.

In addition, many communities with ethnic minority populations have established multipurpose senior centers that are the primary source of assistance for diverse elders and their families. As suggested by Gelfand (2003), multipurpose centers may find a number of supplementary programs and services worth hosting. They may offer classes in English, which may be useful for recent immigrants negotiating the American service-delivery system. Facility in English would also make it possible for Latino or Asian elders to shop, to use public transportation, or to develop friendships with individuals outside their own ethnic group. The centers may also design programs that may foster intergroup cohesion as well as intragroup understanding. An excellent example is provided by a senior center in Rhode Island that sponsors an ethnic day focused around the Easter holidays. This allows the participants from different ethnic groups to discuss how they celebrate Easter. Similarities are sometimes the basis for discussions, but differences provide participants an opportunity to share the distinctiveness of their holiday celebrations in the context of their culture and traditions (ibid.).

Volunteering

One of the most popular forms of leisure involvement among retirees is volunteering. The reasons for volunteering vary. Some retirees engage in voluntary activities to meet people, and some do so to keep active. Most of them volunteer because it provides a sense of satisfaction. An excellent example of a volunteer service program is provided by the Experience Corps, which has been expanded from 2 schools in 1996 to more than 40 schools, 7 retirement facilities, and 14 summer or after-school settings on more than 60 sites. The impact of Experience Corps members has been dramatic in improving the learning environment of schools and in increasing reading levels of students. In addition, participation in the program has been found to yield health-related improvements for the volunteers, including those from ethnically diverse populations (Fried et al., 2004). Additional evidence of the beneficial effects of volunteering is provided by Omoto and Aldrich (2006), who found that residents of retirement communities who actively participated in volunteer work were happier and healthier than those who were less involved in such activities.

However, having more free time does not mean that the rate of volunteerism increases with age. Rather, the percentage of Americans who engage in volunteer work remains stable at just under 30% from middle adulthood onward (Grafova, McGonagle, & Stafford, 2006). What increases with age is the average number of hours devoted to volunteering by those who undertake such activities. In fact, individuals 65 and over spend more than twice as much time than do persons under the age of 50. The best predictor of volunteering in old age is participation in such activities during earlier time periods. Further, volunteering is strongly affected by physical health status, with more than twice as many individuals in excellent health engaging in volunteer work than do their counterparts in fair or poor health (Grafova et al., 2006).

Differences in volunteering have also been observed among minorities. Volunteering as a way to help others through informal social networks is common in minority communities. Black community churches are extensively involved in providing support to their members. This may represent a history of self-reliance and indicate the tradition of incorporating hard work into leisure experiences and service to others (Allen & Chin-Sang, 1990). Providing mutual assistance (e.g., food and lodging to older adults) is also a common practice in American Indian communities. Volunteer activities among Asian/Pacific Islanders tend to be ethnically specific and to reinforce the continuation of their value systems. Some Asian Indian elders volunteer through temples or mosques that have now become available in their communities. These activities provide them with new opportunities for intergenerational interaction. Hispanic communities tend to emphasize self-help, mutual aid, neighborhood assistance, and advocacy for older members. Although different ethnic groups often have different ways elders volunteer their time, they all share the fact that they are giving back to the community through their service to others.

Valuable contributions are also made by volunteers in rural communities where volunteer seniors perform home repairs and modifications such as fixing a leaking roof, adding a ramp, and repairing kitchen appliances. An evaluation of this program in Wisconsin indicated that making such services available helped older adults remain in their own homes and communities. In addition, it allowed volunteer seniors to develop and sustain social relationships with each other as well as with the residents they served, thereby helping them maintain a quality of life they value (Mehrotra, 2003).

Religious Participation

As we have noted, in many ethnic communities members of churches, temples, and mosques have taken the role of caregiver for needy parishioners as well as for people who are not members of their congregations, identifying such efforts as part of their main missions to uplift the community and to ameliorate hard conditions of the unfortunate. Thus, religious affiliation provides older people with valuable opportunities to engage in a range of volunteer activities. For many elders, much of their leisure time is spent in performing religious and spiritual activities. A discussion regarding the nature of such participation and its impact on the well-being of older adults is provided in Chapter 8.

Lifelong Learning

Respondents to an American Association of Retired Persons (AARP) survey in 2004 indicated that they expect to spend time in lifelong learning and personal development. A number of other investigators (see, e.g., Wilson & Simson, 2006) also report high levels of interest in lifelong learning and personal development. These findings are corroborated by the continuing increase in the number of older adults enrolled in the courses, seminars, and workshops offered at more than 300 colleges and universities across the country. In addition, the Elderhostel Institute network (see the website included in the list provided at the end of this section) offers a variety of learning opportunities using a number of formats aimed at addressing the wide range of needs, preferences, and styles of older learners. Why do older adults engage in lifelong learning? Participation in educational programs allows older learners to attend to the deeper search for understanding, meaning, and purpose stimulated by advancing years. It facilitates late adulthood transitions and helps them in coping with challenges posed by developmental tasks such as adjusting to retirement, death of a spouse, and declining health and strength. It allows them to explore new areas of interest, to meet people they find interesting, to contribute to society, and to improve their social life. In addition, continued use of the mind through engagement in challenging activities helps them to maintain their cognitive abilities (Mehrotra, 2003).

Note that the concept of lifelong learning has itself been changing. Highly educated baby boomers are seeking additional formal education that will prepare them to make a career change into more meaningful and rewarding work. Globally, lifelong learning has been viewed as a way for governments to achieve their social objectives by improving the overall welfare and earning ability of constituents, thus reducing poverty and inequality (Kroukamp, 2004). Concurrently, the pace of technological change has made lifelong learning, whether formal or informal, critical for career progress. As we have indicated already, a variety of formats is used to address the educational needs of older learners. Provided next are examples of formats that have worked well for this population of learners.

Example 1

On a college campus, older adults take courses along with traditional students. These courses may represent areas such as psychology of learning, introduction to computers, American history, health and wellness, and algebra. The instructors for these courses may be full-time faculty or a team of two faculty members with varied experiences. Older learners may take the course for credit or may simply enroll on an audit basis. In addition to taking courses, they may also attend concerts, see films and plays, and participate in recreational activities. Some campuses also have designed housing facilities to allow older learners to stay on campus. See the LaSell College website (http://www.lasell.edu/path/village.asp) for an example of housing facilities designed for older adults on a college campus.

Example 2

The College of St. Scholastica offers "Emeritus College," a program designed especially for older learners with limited resources. Funding from private foundations, endowments, and other sources makes it possible to offer these courses at a reduced cost to the participants, thereby making them accessible to low-income learners both on campus and in rural communities throughout the region. Emeritus College begins each fall with a daylong program called "A

Day at the College," which offers 1-hour courses to give the participants a taste of what will be offered in the upcoming semester. Participants then sign up for 6-week courses that match their interests and backgrounds. The instructors for the courses are college teachers or retired professionals from the community. Each course meets once a week for 2 hours. Participants read the assigned material and come prepared for in-class discussion. This emphasis on exchange of ideas rather than lectures engages the participants in active learning and creates a community of learners. In an Emeritus College course on learning and memory, taught by one of the authors of this book, the participants formed a group of active learners. After each session, the group met at a restaurant to socialize and discuss what was covered in the class. Such active participation has been shown to be more effective than mere attendance.

Example 3

Imagine a college student stumbling into a large classroom and finding it filled with more than 400 older adult students. Since 1976, the Fromm Institute for Lifelong Learning at the University of San Francisco has offered college-level courses for older people taught by retired faculty from around the country. Currently, almost 1,000 elders enroll in one of their 8-week sessions. The Bernard Osher Foundation has been funding similar institutes that follow this peer-taught model (called Osher Lifelong Learning Institutes) around the country since 1997.

Although there has been an overall increase in educational attainment among older Americans, substantive individual differences exist in this population. Those with higher levels of educational attainment and more recent learning experiences are often "savvy" learners. They need little encouragement to participate, and for them any instructional approach would work. But there are others who have lower levels of formal education (e.g., ethnic minorities and recent immigrants). They are far less likely to participate in educational programs, and many need individualized guidance, encouragement, and support when they do participate. The challenge is how to reach these subgroups that are presently underserved but are likely to benefit. Unless we take steps in this regard, the educational gap between the highest socioeconomic level and the lowest will widen, and educational programs for older people will serve only a limited segment of the population.

SUMMARY

The American workforce is aging. Over the next two decades, the numbers of older workers will grow substantially, and they will become an increasingly significant proportion of the workforce. This increase in the number of older workers is not simply due to the growth of the older population; it is also due to the continuing increase in the participation rate of older men and women in the workforce. Why do they continue working after traditional retirement age? Besides the need for income and health insurance coverage, they cite reasons such as "a desire to stay active and engaged," "to perform meaningful work," and "to interact socially with colleagues." Another contributing factor may be the changing nature of work. Given the growth of the service economy, work relies increasingly on computer and people skills, and fewer and fewer jobs require considerable physical strength. With the smaller cohort of younger workers and projected labor shortages in a number of sectors (e.g., nursing, teaching), many employers welcome continuing participation of older workers.

Regardless of their race/ethnicity, the percentage of older women (aged 55 and over) who participate in the workforce has also been increasing. However, the participation rates for older men remain higher than those for women in each ethnic group and in each age group. In comparison with other ethnic groups, Asian men aged 55–69 have the highest rate of participation in the workforce. Data from the Health and Retirement Study indicate that older Black men are less likely to participate in the workforce than similarly aged White men. In addition, among persons out of the labor force, Blacks are more likely to report that they are disabled compared with Whites. For older women, there are relatively small differences between Blacks and Whites. Although Hispanics have a higher than average life expectancy, their rates of participation in the workforce at 55 and over are not proportionately higher than other ethnic groups. This may be due to some extent to their employment in occupations that are more physically strenuous and riskier than management and professional occupations. Very limited information is available about participation of older American Indians in the workforce. However, data from the 2000 U.S. Census indicate that a high proportion of American Indians are employed in occupational groups such as service, construction, farming, and fishing. A large proportion of American Indian elders, especially those who live on reservations, continue to perform meaningful functions in the family and in the community.

Although the United States has witnessed a continuing increase in the older workforce, this does not mean that it has become easier for older persons to continue in their current positions or to find new employment. In fact, older persons, especially members of minority ethnic and cultural groups, continue to face a variety of obstacles in their search for employment. These obstacles include age discrimination, discrimination against individuals with disabilities, discrimination based on sexual orientation, negative stereotypes, and individual and job obsolescence. We have suggested some steps that may be helpful in removing these barriers.

Women and ethnic and cultural minorities view retirement differently from the dominant culture, experience retirement differently, have access to fewer retirement benefits, and may face problems in adjusting to retirement. In addition to the critical importance of health and financial resources, social networks and social support have a significant impact on their retirement satisfaction and adjustment. Retirement planning, both formal and informal, can make a difference in their adjustment to retirement. However, the effectiveness of retirement planning programs depends on the extent to which they take into account the characteristics of the population they aim to serve. A one-size-fits-all approach is not very effective. This chapter has included suggestions that may be useful to those involved in designing and offering such programs.

Many retirees engage in leisure pursuits, lifelong learning, and volunteer work. However, there are important differences in how men and women as well as members of different ethnic and cultural minorities view leisure and what they do with their time when they retire. Continuing attention needs to be devoted to making senior centers, volunteering opportunities, and educational programs accessible to all segments of the older population, especially those who have had limited access in the past.

ACTIVE LEARNING EXPERIENCE: CHAPTER 7 QUIZ

The purpose of this experience is to gauge your present knowledge of issues related to diversity in work, retirement, and leisure. Upon completion of this activity, you will be able to:

1. Assess your knowledge of diversity in work and retirement.
2. Gain feedback on your knowledge of important issues related to diversity in work and retirement.

This activity will require about 30 minutes (10 minutes to complete the quiz and 20 minutes to discuss your answers with another person or in a classroom setting).

Instructions:

1. Complete the quiz.
2. Your instructor will lead an in-class review of the answers to the quiz.

Quiz Items	True	False
1. The participation of older adults in the workforce has declined in recent years.	_____	_____
2. A major impetus for legislation against age discrimination was the need for more workers.	_____	_____
3. Mandatory retirement age is now 65.	_____	_____
4. The Americans with Disabilities Act (ADA) of 1990 is targeted to the older population.	_____	_____
5. Retirement for health reasons is much more common among Blacks than among Whites.	_____	_____
6. Older Black women return to work more often than do any other group.	_____	_____
7. Members of minority groups prepare for retirement as efficiently as the White majority.	_____	_____
8. Financial planning dominates retirement planning programs in many organizations.	_____	_____

9. Defined contribution pension plans promise that employees will receive a specific benefit in their retirement years. _____ _____

10. Compared with Blacks, Asians, and Whites, a higher proportion of Hispanic men and women qualify for Social Security benefits. _____ _____

11. Many older adults continue working not because of financial need but because of opportunity for social connection, daily routine, and personal meaning. _____ _____

12. In same-sex relationships, men's degree of retirement planning is lower than that of women. _____ _____

13. Middle-age and older workers are aware of the age at which they can receive full Social Security benefits without a reduction for early retirement. _____ _____

14. Most older adults in the United States do volunteer work after they retire. _____ _____

15. Social networks and social participation contribute to retirement satisfaction among rural elders. _____ _____

16. Relative to men, women are less likely to experience financial difficulties in retirement. _____ _____

17. Bridge employment is more prevalent among low-income workers than among high-income workers. _____ _____

18. Phased retirement has now been made available by almost all employers. _____ _____

19. There is a positive correlation between annual earnings totals and participation in retirement plans. _____ _____

20. For the current cohort of older women returning to work, the need for computer training may be somewhat greater than for older males. _____ _____

GLOSSARY

Age Discrimination in Employment Act (ADEA): Legislation enacted to protect individuals aged 40 and older from employment discrimination on the basis of age and to promote job opportunities for older workers on the basis of their ability rather than age.

Americans with Disabilities Act (ADA) of 1990: Legislation enacted to prohibit discrimination in employment against individuals with disabilities.

bridge employment: An increasingly prevalent transition employment status that allows older workers' employment in a new line of work, typically part-time wage, salary jobs, self-employment, full-time work of relatively short duration.

defined benefit pension plan: A type of pension program where employees who retire are guaranteed an annual pension, generally calculated on the basis of salary and years of service. Usually employees have to be vested (i.e., have worked for the same company) for 5 years to be eligible for pension benefits. Often there are penalties associated with early retirement.

defined contribution pension plan: A type of pension program in which employees' contributions are deducted from their paychecks prior to taxes and employers match a part or the entire amount of employees' contributions. Under these plans, the organization delegates control for management of retirement funds to individual employees themselves. Thus, the defined contribution plans shift the investment risk to the worker, a fact that becomes all too clear during market declines. Examples of defined contribution plans include 401(k) and 403(b).

dependency ratio: Refers to the proportion of the population that is employed and the proportion that is not in the workforce (and is thus viewed as dependent or as requiring support). This ratio has increased steadily, such that proportionately fewer employed persons appear to support retired older persons today.

individual obsolescence: Refers to a gradual reduction in workers' effectiveness. When they fall behind in understanding how to use new tools, techniques, and technology or fail to recognize how the application of new knowledge can enhance their performance, they become vulnerable to obsolescence.

job obsolescence: Jobs become obsolete and gradually disappear when demands for certain products or services decline or new techniques replace older processes that are comparatively less efficient.

leisure: An inherently satisfying activity characterized by the absence of obligation.

phased retirement: Refers to the gradual reduction of work hours and responsibilities, until the point of full retirement. This approach to retirement allows for a gradual exit from full participation in the workforce.

senior center: A community facility in which older people come together to fulfill many of their social, physical, and intellectual needs. The Older Americans Act identifies senior centers as preferred focal points for comprehensive, coordinated delivery of services.

Senior Community Service Employment Program (SCSEP): A federal program designed to assist low-income older adults—including immigrant seniors—to join or reenter the workforce.

SUGGESTED READINGS

Adams, G. A. & Beehr, T. A. (Eds.) (2003). *Retirement: Reasons, processes, and results.* New York: Springer.

This book provides a detailed discussion of topics we have covered, including retirement planning and preparation, extending work lives, self-management of career and retirement, and bridge employment. If you are interested in learning about work and retirement in other countries, you will find a chapter on early retirement systems and behavior with an international perspective.

Beatty, P. T. & Visser, R. M. S. (Eds.) (2005). *Thriving in an aging workforce: Strategies for organizational and systemic change*. Malabar, FL: Krieger.

This volume is organized around seven critical issues: recruiting and retaining older workers, training older workers, career development for older workers, enhancing intergenerational relations, health and older workers, pensions and older workers, and redefining retirement. In addition, the book includes two very useful chapters on the workforce and workplace of tomorrow.

Dorfman, L.T. (1998). Economic status, work, and retirement among the rural elderly. In R. T. Coward & J. A. Krout (Eds.), *Aging in rural settings: Life circumstances and distinctive features*. New York: Springer.

This chapter provides a synthesis of research on the economic status, work, and retirement patterns of rural elders. Particular attention is given to the role of social networks in facilitating adjustment to retirement of rural elders.

Generations: Civic engagement in later life. (4), Vol. XXX, Winter, 2006–2007.

This special issue of the *Generations* journal includes papers on different types of civic engagement, such as volunteering, civic service, and political participation. Also included is a paper on civic engagement and lifelong learning.

Growing older in America: The health and retirement study. Washington DC: The National Institute on Aging.

Sponsored by the National Institute on Aging under a cooperative agreement with the University of Michigan, the Health and Retirement Study (HRS) follows more than 20,000 men and women over 50, offering insights into the changing lives of the older U.S. population. This report described the HRS's development and offers a snapshot of research findings. Sections of the report look at older adults' health, work and retirement, income and wealth, family characteristics, and intergenerational transfers.

James, J. B. & Wink, P. (Eds). (2006). *Annual review of gerontology and geriatrics, The crown of life: Dynamics of the early postretirement period* (Vol. 26). New York: Springer.

This edited volume is organized around four sections: (1) demographic characteristics of Third Age individuals; (2) anticipation of Third Age during the Second Age; (3) change over time during the Third Age; and (4) life in the Third Age. It includes a number of readings directly related to what we have covered in this chapter, including the work and retirement experiences of aging Black Americans, satisfaction with retirement in men's lives, and gay men's lives in the Third age.

Koenig, H. A. (2002). *Purpose and power in retirement: New opportunities for meaning and significance.* Philadelphia: Templeton Foundation Press.

This highly readable book includes an excellent chapter on volunteerism, reviews common myths about retirement, and outlines concrete steps that, if taken seriously, will help achieve a purpose-filled retirement.

Mock, S. E., Taylor, C. G., & Savin-Williams, R. C. (2006). Aging together: The retirement plans of same-sex couples. In D. Kimmel, T. Rose, & S. David (Eds.), *Lesbian, gay, bisexual, and transgender aging: Research and clinical perspectives.* New York: Columbia University Press.

This chapter examines retirement planning of same-sex couples and how their patterns of retirement planning converge with and diverge from those of cohabiting and married heterosexual couples.

Schlossberg, N. K. (2004). *Retire smart, retire happy: Finding your true path in life.* Washington, DC: American Psychological Association.

This thought-provoking book provides guidance on the psychological and emotional adjustment people make in retirement. It offers tips on coping with ups and downs and reassures readers that retirement can be a fulfilling time of their lives. It contains dozens of examples of situations experienced by men and women retirees and includes short self-assessment quizzes.

AUDIOVISUAL RESOURCES

Age No Problem. Vita Needle, a company based in Needham, Massachusetts, has a remarkable and successful employment policy: It hires only older persons. The average age of its staff of 35 is 73, and the company has no fixed retirement age. The unique people in the film talk about the joy of learning new things, about solidarity, and about their ability to give meaning to the last phase of life. Most of them work 20 to 25 hours per week and schedule their workweek themselves. No one has ever been fired, and all employees share in the profits. This heartwarming video affirms the potential of older adults to continue to be productive. 50 minutes. Available from Filmakers Library.

A Place of Our Own. This video is about Native American elders living in Los Angeles who have developed an outreach program to help them with financial health and transportation needs and to identify any other needs. The title refers to their efforts to establish a community center where they can gather for programs and meetings. 13 minutes. Available from Upstream Productions.

A Tale of Nisei Retirement, Japanese American Citizens League. In an effort to stimulate Nisei (second-generation Japanese Americans) to think about and plan for retirement and to confront those cultural and historical factors that impact satisfaction with retirement, this video presents a Nisei family's struggle to cope with passage to retirement. 29 minutes. Available from Japanese American Citizens League.

Busy Forever: The Golden Years in Japan. Aging in Japan is occurring at a much faster rate than anticipated. By the year 2025 there will be only two working people for every retired person, and within the next 50 years one of every three Japanese will be over the age of 65. Many Japanese respond to this phenomenon by staying in the workforce long after the normal retirement age. Today, more and more Japanese continue to work into their 70s. Employment agencies specialize in finding work for older Japanese who are determined to remain busy forever. This video shows us some of the older workers in their 70s and 80s: a physician who expects to continue his practice until the age of 80; an 83-year-old vegetable seller; an 80-year-old taxi driver; and an engineer who is passionate for karate yet finds time to work as an engineer. 52 minutes. Available from Filmakers Library.

Mission Retirement: A Retirement Planning Video. This 5-part video series is designed to help you in building your financial future. It emphasizes personal responsibility to plan and save for retirement, the benefits of tax-advantaged savings opportunities, the importance of making the right decisions, and managing your assets in retirement. 25 minutes. Available free from AARP.

Some Ground to Stand On. This compelling documentary tells the life story of Blue Lunden, now in her 60s, a working-class lesbian activist whose personal life chronicles 40 years of changes in lesbian identity and consciousness. 35 minutes. Available from Women Make Movies at http://wmm.com.

The SCSEP Story. This engaging DVD presents stories of older adults who were seeking a new start in life through the Senior Community Service Employment Program (SCSEP). Their poignant stories demonstrate that SCSEP is not only a job-training program; it is also a life-changing experience that brings participants hope and a renewed sense of purpose; 20 minutes. Available free from SCSEP (brendab@ssa_i.org) or by mail from SCSEP, 8403 Colesville Rd., #1200, Silver, MD 20910-3314.

KEY: CHAPTER 7 QUIZ

1. False. As shown in Table 7.1, workforce participation rates for men aged 55 to 61 years old appear to have stabilized at about 75% (as of 2005); the rates for women 55 to 61 years old have risen since 1965, reaching about 63% by 2005. Employment among men and women 62 to 64 years old actually increased between 1995 and 2005, from 45% to 53% for men, and from 33% to almost 40% for women.

2. False. The major impetus for the Age Discrimination in Employment Act of 1967 was the perception that older workers were unfairly stereotyped. When older workers became unemployed for some reason, they had a difficult time finding alternative employment and their periods of unemployment were longer.

3. False. In 1986 the upper age limit was removed, thereby prohibiting mandatory retirement at any age, except in jobs for which age is considered a bona fide criterion of ability (e.g., piloting an airplane or working in public safety).

4. False. The ADA is targeted not to the older population but to persons with disabilities. However, its coverage enables many older persons to benefit from its antidiscrimination and reasonable accommodations provisions. For example, the ADA has given a major boost to the development of home- and community-based alternatives to nursing home placement.

5. True. In retirement decisions, although health is important for both Blacks and Whites, it seems to play a more central role for Blacks. Blacks in poor health are more likely to leave the workforce than are Whites in poor health. This may be due to the fact that many of them are employed in blue-collar positions that require rigorous physical labor or toiling in hazardous working environments.

6. True. Older Black women are the poorest in the older population, having the lowest net worth, widowed or divorced, and having to return to work because of lack of retirement benefits more often than do any other groups. Although they had worked for more years and longer hours than older White women, Black women report lower Social Security benefits and meager, if any, other income assets.

7. False. Many members of minority populations do not participate in retirement planning programs. Factors contributing to this limited participation include lack of access to retirement planning programs, the level at which these programs are offered, and the language used in explaining key principles and concepts. This does not imply that all White people plan for retirement efficiently, and this is especially the case for low-income Whites. We have suggested a number of strategies that may be useful to those involved in designing effective programs.

8. True. Although financial planning is emphasized in most of these programs, providing practical tips on health-related issues, social networking, and leisure pursuits may help older adults anticipate and plan for change, thereby leading to a more positive retirement experience.

9. False. DC plans promise not a certain level of benefit but rather periodic contributions at a certain level into an employee's pension account. The ultimate benefit one will receive is unknown because it is dependent on contributions, management fees, and investment returns.

10. False. In comparison with Blacks, Asians, and Whites, a significantly smaller proportion of Hispanic men and women qualify for Social Security benefits. Furthermore, many Hispanic retirees do not apply for Social Security benefits because they are unsure of their legal status in the United States, are afraid of dealing with government agencies, or do not know how to apply for benefits.

11. True. Many economically well-off workers continue working not because of the need for more income but rather because of the opportunity for social connection, daily routine, and personal meaning. Vaillant and DiRago (2006) reported that socially and economically privileged graduates of Harvard University retired on the average 5 years later than more economically challenged inner-city men. It is much more tempting to continue working if one has a profession or is self-employed and therefore exercises relative autonomy over one's working circumstances or is engaged in work that is personally stimulating, is meaningful, and plays a central role in one's identity.

12. False. Although some women prepare thorough financial and lifestyle retirement plans, in general women's degree of planning is lower than that of men. Women should, therefore, be encouraged to seek out retirement planning information and assistance.

13. False. Only 18% of workers are able to give the correct age at which they can receive full Social Security retirement benefits without a reduction for early retirement. The percentage responding correctly is unchanged since the question was first asked in an EBRI survey in 2000. Another consistent finding is that knowledge about the correct age for eligibility increases sharply among workers 55 and older who are more than twice as likely as younger workers to respond correctly.

14. False. Most of the older adults do no volunteer work at all. Even after controlling for health and socioeconomic status, increasing age is not associated with increased volunteering (Koenig, 2002). If people do not engage in volunteering before retirement, they are unlikely to begin doing so after retirement. Only a small percentage of retired persons who are not already volunteering say that they would consider volunteering if the opportunity arose.

15. True. Research with rural men and women indicates that a social network of friends, neighbors, family members, and formal social participation in clubs, organizations, and volunteer work play a particularly important role in adjustment to retirement (Dorfman, 1998).

16. False. Despite their growing participation in the workforce and increased access to a range of choices and opportunities, the typical work patterns for women still differ from those of men. Compared with men, women are more likely to work part time to accommodate family demands, to change jobs more frequently, and to work in small businesses. For many women, these factors may lead to retirement benefits that are substantially inferior to those for men.

17. False. Data from the HRS indicates that older workers at both ends of the wage distribution have higher rates of bridge employment than those in the middle. A similar U-shaped pattern existed by job type, with those at the ends (low-skilled blue-collar and high-skilled white-collar) more likely than others to have moved to bridge employment after leaving career jobs. These relationships highlight the difference between those who chose bridge jobs voluntarily (i.e., those who want to work) and those who did so out of financial necessity (i.e., those who have to work).

18. False. Although in principle a majority of businesses appear to be confident that some type of phased retirement could be worked out for some of their employees, few employers have developed any formal phased retirement policies. Prevalence of phased retirement varies by industry sector, with this option being most common in the health-care/social assistance, education, and manufacturing industries.

19. True. In general, the greater the annual salary workers earn, the more likely they are to participate in employment-based retirement plans. Low-income workers are less likely to participate in any kind of retirement plan. In 2004, less than one third of those who earned $15,000–$19,999 annually participated in a retirement plan, whereas this number increased to 73.2% of those earning $50,000 or more (Copeland, 2005). Although the government offers many tax breaks to encourage savings, many low-income individuals either are not eligible or have limited incentives to participate in these tax breaks.

20. True. Because of occupational differences, the use of computers at work is greater among females than among males. This difference is consistent across all ages. Furthermore, there are gender differences in computer use. Women aged 60+ are less likely than men to use computers (U.S. Department of Commerce, 2002). Thus, for the current cohort of older women returning to work, the need for computer training may be somewhat greater than for older men.

REFERENCES

Allen, K. R., & Chin-Sang, V. (1990). The lifetime of work: The context and meanings of leisure for aging Black women. *Gerontologist, 30,* 734–740.

American Association of Retired Persons (AARP). (2004). *Baby boomers envision retirement II: Survey of baby boomers' expectations for retirement.* Retrieved from: http://www.aarp.org

Angel, J. L., Buckley, C. J., & Sakamoto, A. (2001). Duration or disadvantage? Exploring nativity, ethnicity, and health in midlife. *Journals of Gerontology, Series B: Psychological Sciences and Social Sciences, 56B*(5), S275–S284.

Bishaw, A., & Iceland, J. (2003). *Poverty :1999. Census 2000 Brief Series,* C2KBR-19. Washington, DC: U.S. Census Bureau.

Brown, M. T., Fukunaga, C., Umemoto, D., & Wicker, L. (1996). Annual review; 1990–1996: Social class, work and retirement behavior. *Journal of Vocational Behavior, 49,* 159–189.

Campbell, S., & Munnell, A.H., (2002, May). Sex and 401(k) plans. *Just the Facts on Retirement Issues, 4.* Boston, MA: Center for Retirement Research at Boston College.

Cavanaugh, J. C., & Blanchard-Fields, F. (Eds.). (2006). *Adult development and aging.* Belmont, CA: Thomson Wadsworth.

Charness, N., Kelley, D. L., Bosman, E. A., & Mottram, M. (2001). Word processing training and retraining: Effects of adult age, experience, and interface. *Psychology and Aging, 16,* 110–127.

Coburn, A. F., & Bolda, E. J. (1999). The rural elderly and long-term care. In T. C. Ricketts (Ed.), *Rural health in the United States* (pp. 179–189). New York: Oxford University Press.

Copeland, C. (2005, October). *Employment-based retirement plan participation: geographic differences and trends, 2004.* EBRI Issue Brief 286. Retrieved from: http://www.ebri.org

Crimmins, E. M., Reynolds, S. L., & Saito, Y. (1999). Trends in health and ability to work among the older working-age population. *Journals of Gerontology Series B-Psychological Sciences and Social Sciences, 54*(1), S31–S40.

Crystal, S., & Shea, D. G. (2003). Prospects for retirement resources in an aging society. In S. Crystal & D. G. Shea (Eds.), *Focus on economic outcomes in later life: Public policy, health, and cumulative advantage* (pp. 271–281). New York: Springer.

Cuddy, A. J. C., & Fiske, S. T. (2002). Doddering but dear: Process, content and function in stereotyping of older persons. In T. Nelson (Ed.), *Ageism: Stereotyping and prejudice against older persons* (pp. 3–26). Cambridge, MA: MIT Press.

Cutler, S. J., & Hendricks, J. (1990). *Leisure time use across the life course.* In R. H. Binstock & L. K. George (Eds.), *Handbook of aging and social sciences* (3rd ed., pp. 169–185). New York: Academic Press.

DeFreitas, G. (1991). *Inequality at work: Hispanics in the U.S. labor force.* New York: Oxford University Press.

Dentiger, E., & Clarkberg, M. (2002). Informal caregiving and retirement timing among men and women: Gender and caregiving relationships in late midlife. [Special Issue: Care and Kinship]. *Journal of Family Issues, 23*(7), 857–879.

Doeringer, P. B., & Terkla, D. G. (1990). Business necessity, bridge jobs, and the nonbureaucratic firm. In P. B. Doeringer (Ed.), *Bridges to retirement: Older workers in a changing labor market* (pp. 146–171). Ithaca, NY: ILR Press.

Dorfman, L. T. (1998). Economic status, work, and retirement among the rural elderly. In R. T. Coward & J. A. Krout (Eds.), *Aging in rural settings: Life circumstances and distinctive features* (pp. 47–66). New York: Springer.

Dorfman, L. T., Kohout, F. J., & Heckert, D. A. (1985). Retirement satisfaction in the rural elderly. *Research on Aging, 7,* 577–599.

Duncan, B., Hotz, V. J., & Trejo, S. (2006). Hispanics in the U.S. labor market. In M. Tienda & F. Mitchell (Eds.), *Hispanics and the future of America* (pp. 228–290). Washington, DC: National Academies Press.

Employee Benefit Research Institute (EBRI). (2001). *Facts from EBRI: Women in retirement.* Washington, DC: Author. Retrieved from: http://www.ebri.org/pdf/publications/facts/1101fact.pdf

Employee Benefit Research Institute (EBRI). (2003). *The 2003 Minority Retirement Confidence Survey Summary of Findings.* Washington, DC: Author. Retrieved from: http://www.ebri.org/pdf/surveys/rcs/2003/03mrcssf.pdf

Employee Benefit Research Institute (EBRI) (2007, June). *Minority workers remain confident about retirement, despite lagging preparations and false expectations.* Washington, DC: Author. Issue Brief 306. Retrieved from: http://www.ebri.org/pdf/publications/facts/ 1101fact.pdf

Federal Interagency Forum on Aging-Related Statistics. (2006, May). *Older Americans update 2006: Key indicators of well-being.* Washington, DC: U.S. Government Printing Office.

Finkelstein, L. M., Burke, M. J., & Raju, N. S. (1995). Age discrimination in simulated employment contexts: An integrative analysis. *Journal of Applied Psychology, 80,* 652–663.

Fried, L. P., Carlson, M. C., Freedman, M., Frick, K. D., Glass, T. A., Hill, J., et al. (2004, March). A social model for health promotion for an aging population: initial evidence on the Experience Corps model. *Journal of Urban Health, 81*(1), 64–78.

Fronczek, P., & Johnson, P. (2003). *Census 2000 Brief. Occupations: 2000.* Washington, DC: U.S. Government Printing Office.

Fullerton, H. N., & Toossi, M. (2001). Labor force projections to 2010: Steady growth and changing composition. *Monthly Labor Review, 124*(11), 21–38.

Garcia, A. (1993). Income security and elderly Latinos. In M. Sotomayor & A. Garcia (Eds.), *Elderly Latinos: Issues and solution for the 21st century* (pp. 17–28). Washington, DC: National Hispanic Council on Aging.

Gelfand, D., Bechill, W., & Chester, R. (1991). Core programs and services at senior centers. *Journal of Gerontological Social Work, 17,* 145–161.

Gelfand, D. E. (2003). *Aging and ethnicity.* New York: Springer.

Grafova, I., McGonagle, K., & Stafford, F. P. (2006). Functioning and well-being in the Third Age: 1986–2001. In K. W. Schaie (Series Ed.), J. B. James, & P. Wink (Vol. Eds.), *Annual review of gerontology and geriatrics: "The crown of life: Dynamics of the early postretirement period* (Vol. 26, pp. 19–38). New York: Springer.

Haider, S., & Loughran, D. (2001, September). *Elderly labor supply: Work or play?* Boston College CRR Working Paper 2001-04. (DOI: 10.2139/ssrn.285981).

Han, S.-K., & Moen, P. (1999). Work and family over time: A life course approach. *Annals of the American Academy of Political and Social Science, 562,* 98–110.

Hayward, M. D., Friedman, S., & Chen, H. (1996). Race inequities in men's retirement. *Journal of Gerontology: Social Sciences, 51B,* S1–S10.

He, W. (2002, September). *The older foreign-born population in the United States: 2000* (P23-211). Washington, DC: U.S. Government Printing Office.

He, W., Sengupta, M., Velkoff, V. A., & DeBarros, K. A. (2005, December). *65+ in the United States: 2005* (P23-209). Washington, DC: U.S. Government Printing Office.

Hooyman, N. R., & Kiyak, H. A. (2002), *Social gerontology: A multidisciplinary approach.* Boston, MA: Allyn and Bacon.

Jensen, J. M. (1998). *Native American women photographers as storytellers.* Retrieved from: http://www.cla.purdue.edu/waaw/Jensen/NAW.html

Kijakazi, K. (2002). Impact of unreported Social Security earnings on people of color and women. National Academy on an Aging Society, Gerontological Society of America. *Public Policy and Aging Report, 12*(3), 9–12.

Koenig, H. A. (2002). *Purpose and power in retirement: New opportunities for meaning and significance.* Philadelphia: Templeton Foundation Press.

Kroukamp, H. (2004). Life-long learning: A tool to combat poverty and inequality in South Africa. *Politeia 23*(2), 23–35.

Manton, K. G., & Stallard, E. (1994). Medical demography: Interaction of disability dynamics and mortality. In L. G. Martin & S. H. Preston (Eds.), *Demography of aging* (pp. 217–278). Washington, DC: National Academy Press.

Markides, K. S., & Mindel, C. H. (1987). *Aging & ethnicity.* Newbury Park, CA: Sage.

Mauer, T. J. (2001). Career-relevant learning and development, worker age, and beliefs about self-efficacy for development. *Journal of Management, 27,* 123–140.

McCann, R., & Giles, H. (2002). Ageism in the workplace: A communication perspective. In T. Nelson (Ed.), *Ageism: Stereotyping and prejudice against older persons* (pp. 163–199). Cambridge, MA: Bradford.

McCulloch, A. M. (1994, Summer). The politics of gaming: Tribe/state relations and American federalism. *Publius, 24*(3), 99–112.

Mehrotra, C. M. (1984). Performance appraisal of older workers. In P. K. Robinson, J. Livingston, & J. E. Birren (Eds.), *Aging and technological advances* (pp. 353–355). New York: Plenum Press.

Mehrotra, C. M. (2003). In defense of offering educational programs for older adults. *Educational Gerontology, 29*(8), 645–655.

MetLife Mature Market Institute. (2006). *Living longer, working longer: The changing landscape of the aging workforce—A MetLife study.* New York: Metropolitan Life Insurance Company.

Mock, S. E., Taylor, C. G., & Savin-Williams, R. C. (2006). Aging together: The retirement plans of same-sex couples. In D. Kimmel, T. Rose, & S. David (Eds.), *Lesbian, gay, bisexual, and transgender aging: Research and clinical perspectives.* New York: Columbia University Press.

Moen, P., Erickson, W. A., Agarwal, M., Fields, V., & Todd, L. (2000). *The Cornell Retirement and Well-Being Study: Final report.* Cornell: Brofenbrenner Life Course Center.

Moss, M. S., & Lawton, M. P. (1982). Time budgets of older people: A window on four lifestyles. *Journal of Gerontology, 37,* 115–123.

National Academy of Sciences. (2003). *Safety is seguridad: A workshop summary.* Washington, DC: National Academies Press.

National Academy on an Aging Society. (2000, December). *Do young retirees and older workers differ by race? (Data Profiles: Young Retirees & Older Workers).* Washington, DC: Author.

National Committee to Preserve Social Security and Medicare. (2004, October). *Why social security is important to Hispanic and Latino Americas.* (NCPSSM Policy & Research). Washington, DC: Author.

National Institute for Occupational Safety & Health (2004). *Worker Health Chartbook (2004).* Department of Health and Human Services and NIOSH (Publication 2004-146). Retrieved March 2008 from: http://www.cdc.gov/niosh/docs/chartbook/pdfs/Chartbook_2004_NIOSH.pdf

National Research Council. (2004). Technology for Adaptive Aging. Steering Committee for the Workshop on Technology for Adaptive Aging. In R. W. Pew & S. B. Van Hemel (Eds.), *Board on behavioral, cognitive, and sensory sciences, division of behavioral and social sciences and education.* Washington, DC: National Academies Press.

Omoto, A. M., & Aldrich, C. D. (2006). Retirement community life: Issues, challenges, and opportunities. In K. W. Schaie (Series Ed.), J. B. James, & P. Wink (Vol. Eds.), *Annual review of gerontology and geriatrics: The crown of life: Dynamics of the early postretirement period* (Vol. 26, pp. 283–304). New York: Springer.

Purcell, P. J. (2000, October). Older workers: Employment and retirement trends. *Monthly Labor Review,* 19–30.

Quick, H., & Moen, P. (1998). Gender, employment, and retirement quality: A life course approach to the differential experiences of men and women. *Journal of Occupational Health Psychology, 3*, 44–64.

Quinn, J. F., & Kozy, M. (1996). The role of bridge jobs in the retirement transition: Gender, race, and ethnicity. *Gerontologist, 36*(3), 363–372.

Riddick, C. C., & Stewart, D. G. (1994). An examination of the life satisfaction and importance of leisure in the lives of older female retirees: A comparison of Blacks to Whites. *Journal of Leisure Research, 26*, 75–87.

Rix, S. E. (2001, November). *Toward active ageing in the 21st century: Working longer in the United States.* Paper prepared for the Japanese Institute of Labour Millennium Project, Tokyo, Japan. Retrieved April 4, 2007 from: http://www.jil.go.jp/jil/ seika/us2.pdf

Schoeni, R. F. (1997, Fall). New evidence on the economic progress of foreign-born men in the 1970s and 1980s. *Journal of Human Resources, 32*(4), 683–740.

Schultz, K. S. (2001). The new contingent workforce: Examining the bridge employment options of mature workers. *International Journal of Organizational Theory and Behavior, 4*, 247–258.

Schultz, K. S. (2003). Bridge employment: Work after retirement. In G. Adams & T. Beehr (Eds.), *Retirement: Reasons, processes, and results* (pp. 214–241). New York: Springer.

Schultz, K. S., Morton, K. R., & Weckerle, J. R. (1998). The influence of push and pull factors in distinguishing voluntary and involuntary early retirees' retirement decision and adjustment. *Journal of Vocational Behavior, 53*, 45–57.

Senior Service America. (2006). *A guide for providers: Engaging immigrant seniors in community service and employment programs.* Silver Spring, MD.

Sterns, H. L., & Doverspike, D. (1988). Training and developing the older worker: Implications for human resource management. In H. Dennis (Ed.), *Fourteen steps in managing an aging work force* (pp. 97–110). Lexington, MA: Lexington Books.

Stoller, E. P., & Gibson, R. C. (Eds.). (2000). *Worlds of difference: Inequality in the aging experience.* Thousand Oaks: Pine Forge Press.

Taylor, M. A., & Doverspike, D. (2003). In G. Adams & T. Beehr (Eds.), *Retirement: Reasons, processes, and results* (pp. 53–82). New York: Springer.

Toossi, M. (2002). A century of change: The U.S. labor force, 1950–2050. *Monthly Labor Review, 125*(5), 15–28.

U.S. Census Bureau. (2000). *Public use microdata sample (PUMS) files.* Washington, DC: Author.

U.S. Census Bureau. (2004). *Educational attainment—People 25 years old and over, by total money earnings in 2004, work experience in 2004, age, race, Hispanic origin, and sex* (Current Population Survey Annual Social and Economic Supplement PINC-03). Washington, DC: Author. Retrieved October 17, 2006 from: http://pubdb3.census. gov/macro/ 032005/ perinc/ toc.htm

U.S. Census Bureau. (2005). *Current population survey: 2005 annual social and economic supplement.* Washington, DC: Author.

U.S. Department of Commerce (2002). *A nation online: How Americans are expanding their use of the Internet.* Economics and Statistics Administration. National Telecommunications and Information Administration. Washington, DC: U.S. Department of Commerce.

U.S. General Accounting Office (2001). *Older workers: Demographic trends pose challenges for employers and workers.* (Report GAO-02-85). Washington, DC: U.S. General Accounting Office.

Vaillant, G. E., & DiRago, A. C. (2006). Satisfaction with retirement in men's lives. . In K. W. Schaie (Series Ed.), J. B. James, & P. Wink (Vol. Eds.), *Annual review of gerontology and geriatrics: The crown of life: Dynamics of the early postretirement period* (Vol. 26, pp. 227–242). New York, Springer.

Warr, P. (1998). Age, work, and mental health. In K. W. Schaie & C. Schooler (Eds.), *Impact of work on older adults* (pp. 252–296). New York: Springer.

Weckerle, J. R., & Shultz, K. S. (1999). Influences on the bridge employment decision among older U.S.A. workers. *Journal of Occupational and Organizational Psychology, 72,* 317–300.

Weeks, J. R., & Cuellar, J. B. (1981). The role of family members in the helping networks of older people. *Gerontologist, 21,* 388–394.

Williams, G. C. (1980). Warrior no more. In C. L. Fry (Ed.), *Aging in culture and society* (pp. 101–111). New York: Bergen.

Wilson, L. B. and Simson, S. P. (Eds.). (2006). *Civic engagement and the baby boomer generation.* New York: Haworth Press.

Wink, P. (2007). Everyday life in the third age. In K. W. Schaie (Series Ed.), J. B. James, & P. Wink (Vol. Eds.), *Annual review of gerontology and geriatrics: The crown of life: Dynamics of the early postretirement period* (Vol. 26, pp. 243–261). New York: Springer.

Zsembik, B. A., & Singer, A. (1990). The problem of defining retirement among minorities: The Mexican Americans. *Gerontologist, 30*(6), 749–757.

8

Religious Affiliation and Spirituality

- What is the difference between religion and spirituality?
- What is the impact of religious activities on the mental and physical health of older African Americans?
- What is the concept of *fe*? What purposes does it serve for Hispanic elders?
- How are Native American elders viewed in their communities?
- What are some similarities and differences in the religious traditions of Asian Americans?

In this chapter, we examine religion and spirituality among Black Americans, Hispanics, and American Indians. In addition, we provide an introduction to Hinduism, Buddhism, and Islam, the three major religions represented among the older population of Asian Americans. In each case, we outline the distinctive characteristics of the religion, its views on aging and family life, and implications for its followers as well as for those who provide them with health and social services. Consider the following vignettes as an introduction to our discussion of spirituality and aging.

Vignette 1

Lester Dale, a 67-year-old African American accountant, has been active in his Baptist church for more than 40 years. He has been a deacon, has taught Sunday school, has served as treasurer, and has provided a variety of services to fellow members. The church has always been an important part of his life; after his recent retirement, however, he has begun to spend even more time there. He helps members who need assistance in filing their income tax, in preparing paperwork for Social Security benefits, and in selecting adequate health insurance for their older relatives. For the last 2 months, he has also been providing transportation for Chuck Johnson, a senior member of his church who needs to see his physician at a local clinic almost every week. As a result of this experience, Lester is now developing a pool of volunteers to make transportation available for other elders who are unable to drive.

When asked why he continues to do so many things at the church, he says that he is performing God's work. He feels that God has truly blessed him. His energy to do all that he does comes from his faith in God, and the work that he does helps him in developing new relationships. Lester often says that the role of the church is not only to offer Sunday services but to provide social support to Black individuals and their families.

Vignette 2

Rama Sharma, 63, is a physician at University Hospital in Minneapolis. Born and raised in India, he came to the United States after obtaining his medical degree in New Delhi. He completed his residency in pediatrics at University Hospital and decided to stay in America to engage in research and to open a medical practice. For the past 10 years, he and his wife have taken leadership roles in the Hindu temple that they helped to establish in an old church building. The temple does not have a priest. Instead, Rama and other senior members of the community take turns in leading a discussion on teachings of Bhagavad Gita and Ramayana. Every Sunday, one or two families bring vegetarian food that is served after the worship service. During the summer months Rama and his colleagues organize a summer camp for Hindu children from Minneapolis and neighboring communities with the goal of enhancing their awareness of culture and religion. This allows the children to interact with their counterparts from other communities, to learn about their cultural heritage, and to develop relationships with older adults who bring wisdom and insights from their experiences. In addition, the children learn to respect all religions when they attend festivities associated with the birthdays of leaders representing a full range of religions. This makes them aware that all religions aim toward the same goals and differ only in rituals and other day-to-day practices.

DEFINING SPIRITUALITY AND RELIGION

It is important to distinguish *spirituality* from *religion*. Although these two terms are related, they are not synonymous. Religion is generally defined as a formal system of belief in God or another supernatural being and refers to efforts aimed at relating the human to the divine. Thus, religiousness has specific behavioral, social, doctrinal, and denominational characteristics because it involves a system of worship and doctrine that is shared within a group.

The term *spirituality* pertains to (1) one's inner resources, especially one's ultimate concern; (2) the basic values around which all other values are focused; (3) the central philosophy of life—religious, nonreligious, or antireligious—that guides day-to-day living; and (4) the supernatural and nonmaterial dimensions of human nature. This generic nonreligious spirit, then, is the energy that enables one to reach out and embrace one's basic life-enhancing value, ethic, and ultimate concern, however those concepts are defined. Thus, the term *spirituality* refers to the way the person seeks, finds, creates, uses, and expands personal meaning in the context of the entire universe (Ellor, Netting, & Thibault, 1999). In other words, spirituality is the human drive for meaning and purpose. This definition implies that spiritual activities and perspectives are interwoven with all other aspects of life and, hence, are found in a wide range of contexts, not simply those related to organized religion.

Whereas religiousness includes personal beliefs (as in God) and organizational practices like church activities and commitment to the belief system of a religion, spirituality is concerned with the transcendent, addressing ultimate questions about life's meaning with the assumption that there is more to life than what we see or fully understand. Spirituality can call us beyond self to concern and compassion for others. Although religions aim to foster and nourish spiritual life, it is possible to adopt the outward forms of religious worship and doctrine without having a strong relationship to the transcendent. On the other hand, a person may be spiritual without being affiliated with a religion.

In recent years the subject of religion and aging appears to have captured the interest of scholars from a broad array of disciplinary backgrounds, works that include perspectives from the behavioral and social sciences. And like most research in gerontology, the quality has improved dramatically with the public availability of large, longitudinal data archives including measures of religious attitudes and behaviors and with increasing methodological training and sophistication on the part of the researchers. In light of these improvements, mainstream journals such as the *Journals of Gerontology* and the *Gerontologist* now regularly publish research articles on this topic.

Why has gerontology witnessed increased interest in religion and spirituality? To a great extent, this interest is fueled primarily by research on religion and health. As a large number of studies suggest, older people who are more deeply involved in religion tend to enjoy better physical and mental health than older adults who are not religious (Koenig, McCullough, & Larson, 2001). Review of research indicates that empirical studies on religion and aging have emphasized use of racial or ethnic minority samples, have used multiple measures of religiousness, and have focused on analysis of religious effects on a variety of outcomes related to life satisfaction, health, and well-being (Levin, 1997). Although this is an excellent record, continuing attention needs to be devoted to focus on patterns of involvement across religions and their impact on health and well-being.

CONCEPTUALIZATION AND MEASUREMENT OF RELIGIOUSNESS AND SPIRITUALITY

Quantitative Methods

Health researchers who seek to include religiousness and spirituality in their studies need a measure that adequately represents these constructs. However, currently no single index or scale is recognized as the gold standard representing these constructs. Furthermore, given the variety of religious and spiritual phenomena and the recognized complexity of their diverse relationships to physical and mental health outcomes, a single scale is simply not feasible (Fetzer Institute/NIA Working Group, 1999). Fortunately, several programs of research on religiousness and spirituality are currently under way. These efforts are resulting in a greater clarity in defining the nature and boundaries of relevant content areas (e.g., conceptual definitions, multiple dimensions) and careful consideration of research methodologies

TABLE 8.1   Dimensions of Religiousness/Spirituality

Number	Dimension
1.	Religious meaning
2.	Religion values
3.	Religious beliefs
4.	Forgiveness
5.	Private religious practices
6.	Religious coping
7.	Religious support
8.	Religious history
9.	Religious commitment
10.	Organizational religiousness
11.	Religious preference
12.	Daily spiritual experiences

Source: Fetzer Institute/National Institute on Aging Working Group (1999).

and procedures. One such program of developing measurement instruments has been undertaken by the Fetzer Institute/NIA Working Group (1999). This group identified 12 key dimensions of religiousness/spirituality that were thought to be significant for health outcomes. Measures of these dimensions were then developed and published in a monograph. The dimensions of religion identified by this panel are presented in Table 8.1.

Since health studies are often faced with space and time constraints, the Fetzer Institute/NIA Working Group (1999) also developed a brief measure titled the "Brief Multidimensional Measure of Religiousness/Spirituality (BMMRS): 1999." This measure is based substantially on selected items from each of the 12 domains. The BMMRS was included in the 1998 General Social Survey, a national survey conducted annually by the National Opinion Research Center at the University of Chicago. Its initial report on the psychometric properties of the measure confirms the value of the multidimensional approach. The report also indicates that the items form reliable indices that are only moderately correlated with one another (Idler et al., 2003). In short, the BMMRS holds promise for generating valuable information on religion–health relationships in diverse populations.

Aging and Diversity Online: Measurement

Measurement of Religiousness/Spirituality. This website includes a copy of the document titled *A Multidimensional Measurement of Religiousness/Spirituality for Use in Health Research: A Report of the Fetzer Institute/NIA Working Group (1999).* The report also includes "Brief Multidimensional Measures of Religiousness/Spirituality: 1999." In addition, the website offers a list of articles that cite the report and a new preface added in October 2003. http://www.fetzer.org

Qualitative Methods

As you may recall from Chapter 2, both quantitative and qualitative data are used in behavioral and social science research related to different aspects of aging. The same is true for the study of religion in the lives of older people. The measures designed by the Fetzer Institute/NIA Working Group (1999) are designed to provide quantitative data on 12 dimensions of religiousness and spirituality. But what methods have been used to collect qualitative data regarding the nature and meaning of religious participation and its impact on older people? How do these methods enhance our understanding about the role of religion in late life? Rather than defining the questions and circumscribing the answers, qualitative methods give voice to participants' understanding of religion and how it fits into their world as their life draws to a close. In addition, these methods of inquiry open up discussion about religious matters in late life (Eisenhandler, 2003). Focus groups and one-on-one interviews have been used by a number of investigators to obtain qualitative data on religious behavior and beliefs of older adults. Note that these methods are particularly appropriate for many older adults who may not be able to respond to self-administered questionnaires because of vision, other health problems, and reading difficulties. We next provide two examples to illustrate the use of these methods.

Focus Groups   Focus groups may be conducted as the sole method of collecting data or to complement quantitative data the investigators may have obtained. Taylor, Chatters, and Levin (2004) conducted a focus group study titled "Appraisals of Religiosity, Coping and Church Support." The primary purpose of this research was to explore the relationship between religion and mental health among African Americans. The study protocol covered the following content areas:

- Religious activities
- Prayer
- The use of prayer as a form of coping with serious life problems
- The use of church members as a source of informal social support
- Negative social interactions among church members
- The use of pastors and ministers for help when dealing with a serious personal problem

The focus group narratives reveal a number of themes that speak to both prominence and patterns of particular forms of religious activities and their functional significance in the lives of individual participants. For example, among focus group participants one of the most frequently noted religious activities was prayer. Reading the Bible and other religious and devotional materials was also frequently mentioned by the participants. Their comments suggested that they consider reading religious materials to be an integral part of their daily lives and view it as being critical to their religious and spiritual development. Consistent with the survey data, watching religious television programs and listening to religious music were also reported as an important component of daily religious activities. In addition, the participants commented that their fellow church members were emotionally warm, compassionate, and caring and provided concrete and tangible assistance on an ongoing basis as well as during critical times of need.

Face-to-Face Interviews

Eisenhandler (2003) provided an instructive example of conducting face-to-face interviews with older people living independently in the community and in long-term care facilities. With the goal of understanding the ways aging and faith are connected to the individual's sense of self-identity, the researcher examined participants' personal engagement with religion, the role of socialization in retaining faith in late life, and the extent to which older people participate in religious behavior and find religious beliefs relevant to their present life. The study addressed questions such as:

- What role does faith play in coming to terms with the many changes faced in late life?
- How does the place of residence, living independently in the community as contrasted with living in a long-term care facility, influence the practice of faith?
- Is religion an anchor for the self-identity of older adults?
- What happens when attendance and participation are no longer viable routes for religious practice?

After completing the interviews, the researcher synthesized material from questions that were asked of everyone and from questions that arose from unique characteristics of the participants and from their thoughts, musings, and doubts about religion and the folkways of faith. In the final analysis, the content of the report was shaped as much by the participants and dynamic processes that underlie qualitative research as by theoretical concepts and the interview guide that directed the investigation. This is indeed a key strength of qualitative methodology that works well when the aim is not to test a specific theory or to collect data for statistical extrapolations but to draw together responses of people living and aging in the social context of interest and to place these understandings in a broader framework.

You have now seen examples of both quantitative and qualitative methods used in the study of religion in late life. Which of these methods should you use? Our response to this question is simply this: The method you select should depend on the purpose of the study, the nature of questions you aim to answer, the characteristics of the population you plan to study, and the level of preparation you have in each of the available methods. As noted earlier, many researchers have used a combination of methods, thereby balancing the strengths and limitations of each method.

ACTIVE LEARNING EXPERIENCE: PERSONAL BELIEFS ABOUT AGING AND THE MEANING OF LIFE

The purpose of this experience is to engage you in an analysis of your beliefs concerning aging and the meaning of life. Upon completion of this activity, you will be able to:

1. Describe personal beliefs about aging and the meaning of life.
2. Appreciate the diversity of personal belief systems.

Time required: 40 minutes (20 minutes to answer the questions and 20 minutes to discuss responses in class or with another individual).

Instructions:

1. Answer the following questions as a homework assignment.
2. Discuss responses in class or with another person.

Discussion Questions:

a. When you were a child, what religion(s) did your parent(s) or guardian(s) consider themselves to be?
b. Were you raised in a particular religion? If yes, what was the religion?
c. With what religion or philosophy of life do you identify?
d. In what ways does your religion or philosophy of life help you in coping with disappointments, sadness, and loss?
e. What does your religion or philosophy of life have to say about the meaning of life?
f. How does your religion or philosophy of life view aging and the value of elders?

RELIGIOUS PARTICIPATION AMONG AFRICAN AMERICANS

Religion and churches occupy an important position in the lives of Black Americans in general and older Blacks in particular. Black churches are a unique social entity. Historically their mission has been enacted within a societal and cultural environment characterized by social oppression and discrimination. Given this environment, the churches have played a key role in safeguarding the health and well-being of its members. A survey of African American congregations in the northern United States found that churches offer a variety of services including the following (Billingsley, 1999):

- Basic needs assistance (e.g., food and clothing distribution, home care)
- Income maintenance programs (e.g., financial services and low-income housing)
- Counseling and intervention (e.g., family counseling, parenting/sexuality seminars)
- Educational and awareness programs (e.g., child care, life skills, and academic tutoring)
- Health-related activities (e.g., HIV/AIDS care, substance abuse counseling)
- Recreation and fellowship for families or individuals

Clearly, these efforts draw on the tradition of mutual assistance and self-reliance within Black churches to improve the health and well-being of both congregation and community members. In addition, Black congregations constitute an important social network for their members that involves the exchange of various forms of social support (Krause, 2002).

Organizational activities (e.g., attending church services) and nonorganizational activities (e.g., watching or listening to religious programs) are two key domains of religious behavior among older Blacks. We next examine their participation in each of these domains and then discuss its effect on their mental and physical health.

Organizational Religious Participation

This domain refers to behaviors that occur within the context of a church, mosque, or other religious setting (e.g., church attendance, membership, participation in auxiliary groups). Data from a variety of surveys indicate that Black Americans demonstrate a high degree of religious involvement. Analysis using data from the National Survey of Black Americans reveals that less than 10% of Black Americans have not attended religious services as an adult except for weddings and funerals. Of the respondents who have attended, 70% state that they attended religious services at least a few times a month, and two thirds report that they are church members. As compared with Whites, Black elders demonstrate higher levels of attending religious services. Even though older Blacks show overall elevated rates of church attendance, church membership, and identifying themselves as religious, there are significant differences within this group (Taylor, 1986), including the following:

- The oldest of the older group of Blacks are more likely than their younger counterparts to describe themselves as "religious."
- Compared with men, women exhibit higher levels of religious involvement on measures of attendance and membership in the church.
- Persons who are divorced from their spouses have lower levels of religious involvement compared with married persons.
- Widows attend church less frequently than married persons.
- Although health problems may lead to a decrease in service attendance, frequency of watching or listening to religious programs remains unaffected.

What is their religious affiliation? African Americans report more than 40 different religious affiliations; half identify with the Baptist tradition, about 1 of 10 report being Methodist, and 6% to 8% state they are Catholics. Religious affiliation among Black Americans is relatively stable over time (Ellison & Sherkat, 1990). In terms of rural–urban differences, a number of studies report that African Americans who resided in rural communities were more likely to be church members and be involved in organizational religious activities (Ellison & Sherkat, 1995). In other words, rural residents attend church services more frequently than their urban counterparts. In addition, Southern Blacks have higher levels of service attendance than Blacks from other regions of the country.

For older Blacks, fellow church members are an important source of informal assistance. Persons who are official church members, attend services more frequently, and indicate that religion is important are more likely to receive support from church members. These findings suggest that current assistance from church members is contingent on one's level of tangible investment in the life of church and past record of participation (Taylor & Chatters, 1988). Further, dynamics of support from church members also depends on one's age. Among older adults of very advanced years, those who have children are more likely than their childless counterparts to receive assistance from church members. Why? Perhaps because adult children may act on behalf of their parents to facilitate support exchanges from church members.

What is the nature of assistance provided by church members? Information from the focus group study described earlier (Taylor, Chatters, & Levin, 2004) indicates that church members provided tangible forms of assistance (e.g., money, food) and services (transportation), emotional aid, companionship and fellowship, and spiritual support. Many members underscored the importance of church members providing supportive encouragement and fostering a sense of belonging in the church. This support is ongoing and is offered on a regular basis. However, it becomes especially important during times of illness, bereavement, and financial difficulties. Many participants emphasized the similarity between church members and family members with regard to the conditions and circumstances of giving and receiving assistance. Although the participants were positive in their comments, they did not idealize their relations with church members. When asked about potential problems and negative social interactions, they candidly discussed the problems associated with the development of cliques and factions and often disruptive interpersonal disagreements and interactions among church members. However, data from two national surveys reveal that negative interaction among church members is a relatively rare event for Black Americans. In fact, Black adults receive emotional support from church members more frequently than they experience negative interaction. Furthermore, older Blacks are significantly more likely than older Whites to report receiving emotional support and spiritual support from members of their church (Krause, 2002).

Nonorganizational Religious Involvement

This domain includes private religious behaviors that can be conducted outside the context of an organization, such as reading religious materials, watching television programs, listening to religious music, engaging in private prayer, and requesting prayer. Nonorganizational religious participation is a critical dimension of religious involvement because it indicates the degree to which religiosity is an integral component of daily activities. In addition, persons with functional limitations can still undertake these activities.

The focus group study with African Americans (Taylor, Chatters, & Levin, 2004) devoted a portion of the protocol to the investigation of nonorganizational forms of religious involvement. Among the participants in this study, one of the most frequently noted religious activities was prayer. They reported making use of prayer as a daily religious activity, and many of them emphasized the importance of starting their day with prayer. These focus group findings are similar to the findings from an analysis of survey data conducted by Levin and Taylor (1997). This analysis revealed that prayer is practiced at all ages but is more frequent among older people, women, and Black Americans than among their counterparts (i.e., young adults, men, and Whites). Among Black Americans, age and gender are particularly strong correlates of prayer (Chatters & Taylor, 1989; Chatters, Taylor, & Lincoln, 1999). Successively older age groups report a higher frequency of prayer, with the oldest age group (75 years and older) praying most frequently. Women also pray more frequently than men, although both groups report higher levels of prayer. In addition, Catholics report praying more frequently than Baptists. Engagement in prayer is not limited only to those who attend church. In fact, 4 out of 10 Blacks who are not affiliated with a religious denomination and almost half of Blacks who have not attended church since the age of 18 report that they pray nearly every day.

Reading the Bible and other devotional materials represents another nonorganizational religious activity undertaken by many African Americans. The participants in the focus group study reported that reading religious materials is an integral part of their daily lives and is critical to their religious and spiritual development. In addition, data from the National Survey of Black Americans and the American Changing Lives Survey reveal that more than half of the Black population watch or listen to religious programming at least once a week (Taylor, Chatters, & Levin, 2004). These findings were confirmed by the participants in the focus group study.

Spending quiet time in reflection is also an important religious activity for a large proportion of African Americans. Data from the 1998 General Social Survey reveal that two of three Black Americans engage in meditation (Taylor, Chatters, & Levin, 2004). Slightly more than half of all Black Americans meditate at least once a week, and one out of three meditate at least once a day. These survey findings are consistent with what was reported by many participants in the focus group study. "Being still" and "going inside" are important aspects of their religious experience. These moments of reflection provide opportunities not only for talking with God and listening to and discerning God's will but also for regulating emotions and relieving stress.

After examining the participation of older African Americans in religious activities we now turn our attention to tangible impacts of religiousness on their mental and physical health. We then review some explanations that have been proposed to help understand the ways religiousness makes a difference in participants' health.

Impact of Religion on Mental Health and Well-Being

There is a growing body of research investigating the effects of religious factors on mental health and psychological well-being in the Black population. This research has focused on beneficial effects of religious participation on depression and other psychiatric outcomes, indicators of positive well-being (i.e., life satisfaction and happiness), and other psychological constructs. Here we present key findings from this research. Religiosity is significantly associated with life satisfaction among older African Americans. Religion may influence well-being in this population in multifaceted ways and not just as a result of the positive effect on satisfaction resulting from a perception that one is personally religious (Walls & Zarit, 1991). In addition, studies of religion and depression indicate protective effects of religiosity and denominational affiliation. Further, given the strong significant effect of religiosity on self-esteem, it is likely that self-esteem, in turn, strongly protects against depression (Krause, 1992). In other words, religiousness provides participants with personal resources useful in coping with life stress. It is not clear whether religion is a more salient preventive resource among African Americans than among Whites. However, we do know that religiousness is a protective factor for psychological distress and well-being among African Americans, especially older adults.

Impact of Religion on Physical Health

Participation in organizational religious activities is associated with better health. This is true for White Americans as well as for Black Americans (Levin & Chatters, 1998a). Does religious participation serve to protect against premature mortality and to increase longevity? A longitudinal study with African Americans aged 70 and older found that respondents who did not attend church services or church-based meetings had 1.77 times the odds of dying within the 4-year follow-up period than church attendees (Bryant & Rakowski, 1992). This research underscores the advantage attributable to church attendance in older African Americans in as brief an interval as 4 years. Other studies conducted with national samples of African Americans confirm a "strong effect of nonattendance on mortality risk that is robust, pervasive and remarkably strong across all subgroups of the population" (Ellison, Hummer, Cormier, & Rogers, 2000, p. 630).

In sum, religiousness is significantly associated with physical health outcomes. This is true for both morbidity and mortality—for indicators of health and illness and for rates of death or survival. Evidence for racial differences in religion–health relationships is mixed: some studies show Black–White differences, and others do not. However, among older people, religion's salutary effect is most observed for African Americans. Given these observed effects of religious involvement on health and well-being you may be wondering how we can explain these effects. In recent years scientists have proposed a number of explanations regarding these effects. We present some of these explanations in the following section.

One possible explanation for the significant association between religion and health is that strong commitment to a religious system of beliefs may lead people to adopt healthy behaviors that are known to reduce the risk of morbidity due to chronic illness. Religions typically prescribe and proscribe certain behaviors such as those related to smoking, drinking, substance abuse, diet, sexuality, and hygiene (Spector, 1979). This correspondence between behaviors most discouraged by religions and those identified as risk factors may be the underlying factor in the impact of religion on health.

A second explanation is that regular participation in organizational religious activities may serve to strengthen connections to supportive resources in most African American communities. As noted earlier, strong social ties lower the risk of morbidity and mortality in both Blacks and Whites (House, Landis, & Umberson, 1988). Thus, in addition to spiritual sustenance, active participation in church provides African Americans access to personal and social resources. These resources provide churchgoers with help in coping during times of need, moderate the effect of chronic life stressors, reduce the risk of depressive symptoms, and cultivate healthy relationships (Ellison, 1994). Furthermore, regular participation in devotional activities may serve to buffer the stress of daily life, provide a sense of purpose and meaning to life, discourage hopelessness and the belief that things happen only by chance, engender the expectation of good health, and provide a framework for recontextualizing disability and suffering (Koenig, 1994).

A third explanation is that religious worship may engender positive feelings that influence the susceptibility to, course of, or recovery from illness. Prayer can be motivated by and can instill feelings of gratitude, forgiveness, comfort, peace, joy, trust, and love. In addition, it can relieve the weight of accumulated stressors and can provide an opportunity for renewal of mind, body, and spirit. Furthermore, positive psychological events may have an immune-modulating effect that can mitigate pathophysiological responses (Maier, Watkins, & Fleshner, 1994). Research by Steffen, Hinderliter, Blumenthal, and Sherwood (2001) revealed that religious coping is associated with lower ambulatory and clinic blood pressure among African Americans but not among Whites. The investigators suggest that this may be one of the pathways through which religiosity and cardiovascular health are related.

In sum, religious participation of African Americans may influence their self-perceptions of health and may also affect the actual biological parameters or markers of physical health by way of the complex pathways believed to link beliefs and behaviors with neurological, endocrine, and immune systems. Studying the connection between religion and health in all segments of the population is exciting because it cuts right to the heart of age-old questions about the interface between mind and body.

Aging and Diversity Online: Spiritual Dimensions of Health

Spirituality and health. The George Washington University Center on Spirituality and Health works toward a more compassionate health-care system by recognizing spiritual dimensions of health and educating clinicians about the role of spirituality in medicine, http://www.gwish.org

ACTIVE LEARNING EXPERIENCE: THE CASE OF THE MARSHALL SISTERS AND THEIR CHURCH

The purpose of this experience is to help you learn about the role of church in the lives of older African Americans. Upon completion of this activity, you will be able to:

1. Understand the important role religious institutions play in the lives of some African American elders.
2. Describe spiritual, social, and psychological needs met by an elder's affiliation with an organized religion.

Time required: 30 minutes (15 minutes to read the case and answer the questions and 15 minutes to discuss the case in class or with another person).

Instructions:

1. Read the following case and prepare answers to the accompanying questions.
2. If the activity is part of a class, the instructor divides students into groups of four or five.
3. In groups, students discuss the case and answer the questions that follow it.
4. The instructor leads a discussion of group responses.
5. If the students are completing the activity for self-development, they prepare written responses to the questions and discuss their responses with another person.

Case Study

The Marshall Sisters view the Baptist church as the center of their lives. Ella, 74, Wanda, 70, and Dorothy, 67, attend services almost every Sunday morning as well as Sunday and Wednesday evenings. In addition, Dorothy teaches a scripture class for adult Sunday School, and the Marshall home is the site of another weekly Bible study class. The church has been of great importance to them since their childhood as the daughters of sharecroppers in Alabama. Ella is a widow, Wanda never married, and Dorothy is divorced. Ella has three children, one of whom lives just across town. Dorothy has two children, who live in their birthplace some 100 miles away. Between them, Ella and Dorothy have nine grandchildren and seven great-grandchildren. Some of the children and their families are very active in their churches, while the others attend church only a few times a year, including Easter.

The Marshall sisters consider the members of their congregation to be family as well. When church members are sick, the sisters visit them in the hospital or take them food if they are at home, and when members die, the sisters grieve with the family members of the deceased. Even though they live on Dorothy's meager pension and Social Security, the Marshall sisters have been known to quietly donate money to other church members they believe to be in need. All of their close friends either belong to the church or are members of their family.

Discussion Questions:

1. By the sisters being so active in their church, what personal psychological needs are met?
2. The church occupies a central place in the sisters' social life. Explain.
3. The sisters not only believe in the religious doctrine of Christianity, but they also try to live their religion. Explain.
4. What do religious institutions, such as a Baptist church, have to offer to older adults?

Before we proceed to discuss religious behavior of other ethnic and cultural groups, we should note that, to date, the amount of research conducted with these groups has been significantly smaller than that conducted with mainstream and African American populations. This is especially the case with Native Americans as well as with Muslims, Hindus, and Buddhists. We have very limited information about their participation in religious activities and its impact on their health and well-being. In addition, it should be underscored that religion is not one thing but many. Indeed, complex and distinct belief systems make different religions what they are. Thus, when we say *religious participation* for one ethnic group, it may not refer to the same beliefs and behaviors that you have learned for other groups. For example, some religions have placed much less emphasis on veneration of old age as a time for the contemplative, spiritual life and have given much more emphasis to youth, activity, change, and control over the environment. Then there are other traditions that place comparatively less emphasis on teachings regarding the old. With this introduction we now proceed to examine religious behavior and traditions in the Hispanic population.

RELIGIOUS PARTICIPATION AMONG HISPANICS

Organizational Religious Practices

Attending religious services appears to be a weekly activity among a high percentage of older Hispanics (Stevens-Arroyo & Díaz-Stevens, 1998). The participation rate for women tends to be higher than that for men. Although most studies show that functional limitations tend to discourage religious attendance, functional limitations in late life may also explain why some people attend church more than once per week (Hill, Angel, Ellison, & Angel, 2005). It allows them to remain integrated in a value system, family, neighborhood, religious community, and the larger society. In addition, they are able to use religious organizations as a source of assistance.

Nonorganizational Religious Practices

As is true for older Blacks, private prayer devotion is the most commonly used religious practice among older Hispanics. The second most commonly used practice among this population is that of meditation. A majority of both men and the women in the San Antonio survey reported that they meditate daily, although it is not clear how they define meditation. It is noteworthy that a majority of older Hispanics view themselves as religious, with women reporting higher levels of self-perceived religiosity (Maldonado, 1995). Moreover, religious involvement (i.e., church attendance, private prayer, and self-rated religiosity) remains stable over time (Markides, Levin, & Ray, 1987).

Faith

Faith represents a way of being, living, and imagining and is considered a prerequisite for spiritual growth. Whereas some people believe that faith is a gift from a supreme being, others think that it can be developed in response to life events (Carson, 1989). The concept of *fe* incorporates varying degrees of faith, spirituality, hope, cultural values, and beliefs. *Fe* can be conceptualized as a continuum of behaviors and beliefs that begin with conception and include the baptismal ceremony, the birthday, and the last rites and continue in the remembrance of the departed loved one throughout the year and especially on the death anniversary (Villa & Jaime, 1993). *Fe* includes sharing food and drink to celebrate a birth as well as a death. It is also used in involving divine will in curing the sick.

The concept of *fe* embodies a way of life as well as the culture in which it is lived; out of this life experience has developed a unique worldview that is both Indian and Spanish (Villa & Jaime, 1993). The symbolic embellishment of these two influences is found in *la fe de la gente:* the faith of the people. Note that *fe* is defined by each person in a way that makes the most sense to that individual. To understand how a person copes with the negative effects of social forces, one must understand his or her unique *fe*. In other words, *fe* serves as a coping mechanism and helps people maintain a positive attitude when dealing with the harsh realities of life. It is a method of coping with poor health, poverty, and death.

Impact of Religiousness on Health and Well-Being

Given the importance of religion in the lives of Hispanics in the United States, particularly older Hispanics, research has begun to focus on examining the impact of religiousness on their health, well-being, and mortality. Key findings from this research include:

- Rich religious traditions combined with routine religious activities and a strong religious identity benefit the health of older Hispanics (Stolley & Koenig, 1997). However, there may be important within group differences associated with gender and generational status.
- The more private aspects of religiosity, including personal prayer, Bible reading, meditation, self-expressions of spirituality, and the use of faith as a healing strategy, also help older Hispanics to cope effectively with illness (Maldonado, 1995).
- There is an inverse association between religious attendance and depression (Levin, Markides, & Ray, 1996). Religious involvement is correlated with greater hope and optimism, a greater sense of meaning and purpose, and greater social support, and each of these mechanisms is thought to benefit mental health.
- Church attendance is a unique form of social engagement that may influence cognitive functioning over and above other types of social engagement. Older Mexican Americans who attend church monthly, weekly, or more than weekly tend to exhibit slower rates of cognitive decline than those who do not attend church (Hill, Burdette, Angel, & Angel, 2006).
- Cognitive function serves as a significant mediator of the effect of religious attendance on mortality (Hill, Angel, Ellison, & Angel, 2005)

As this summary indicates, progress has been made in understanding the relationship between religion and health in this population. However, much remains to be investigated. Continuing research needs to be conducted to examine how the relationship between religion and health is affected by social demographic characteristics (i.e., gender, social class, region of the country), nativity status (i.e., native-born or immigrant), family structure, level of assimilation, and religious denomination. Further, research on the relationship between religiousness and health also needs to focus on within group variability in terms of racial status (e.g., Black Hispanic, White Hispanic) and country of origin (e.g., Mexico, Puerto Rico, Cuba, Dominican Republic).

RELIGIOUS PARTICIPATION AMONG NATIVE AMERICANS

Although we often refer to Native American religion as spirituality in the singular, there is a fundamental diversity regarding religious traditions in this population. In the United States there are more than 500 recognized tribes that speak more than 200 different indigenous languages and have been courted by missionaries of each branch of Christianity. Despite centuries of horrible assimilative policies often aimed at dismantling structures of indigenous communities, language, and belief systems, recent years have witnessed remarkable revitalization and renewal of Native traditions. Throughout the country Native communities have vigorously pressed their claims to religious self-determination. This, in turn, has contributed to significant differences in religious practices across communities. However, people from different Native nations remind us that their respective languages have no word for *religion*. They emphasize ways of life in which, for example, economy, medicine, art, and agriculture are ideally integrated into a spiritually informed whole. It has, however, not been easy for them to achieve this kind of integration (McNally, 2005).

Another feature that cuts across the diversity of Native Americans is the primacy of oral tradition. They have maintained their culture and traditions with remarkable care through orality. In fact, orality has proved to be a valuable resource to Native elders and their communities, especially with regard to maintaining proper protocols around sacred knowledge. "Religious" regard for land represents another feature that remains consistent across their fundamental diversity. Native religious traditions are oriented fundamentally in space rather than in time-oriented traditions of Christianity and Judaism. For Native people, living in balance with particular landscapes has been the fruit of hard work, a matter of ethical living in worlds where nonhuman life has moral standing and disciplined attention to ritual protocol. Many places on the landscape have been sacred and have been sources of material and spiritual sustenance. This is also true for sacred practices of living on landscapes. These practices include harvesting wild rice, spearing fish, and hunting certain animals. In short, many places and practices have often had both sacred and instrumental value.

The elderly have had a special place in the cultures and religions of the American Indian population. They are honored and respected and serve as elders of the tribe and the clan. In Indian communities, older adults are the "wisdom-keepers," the repositories of the sacred ways and natural world philosophies that extend indefinitely back in time (Arden & Wall, 1990). Older Indians serve the larger world not from mystic sentimentalism but from a felt experience, and they provide spiritual direction to the members of their community. The wisdom of thousands of years flows through their lips. Many Indians view the world as one family connected through bonds of love. Their deepened sense of time, along with their sense of responsibility, heightens the intimate care they extend to all creation. Thus, they serve as sacred ecologists who protect all of their "relatives," including human, animal, and plant life. The next active learning experience will help you develop a deeper understanding of a religion different from your own as well as how that religious system operates in the life of a particular older adult.

ACTIVE LEARNING EXPERIENCE: INTERVIEW WITH AN ELDER FROM A DIFFERENT RELIGIOUS TRADITION

The purpose of this experience is to provide an opportunity for you to develop an appreciation and a better understanding of a religion different from your own and of how the system functions in the life of a diverse elder. Upon completion of this activity, you will be able to:

1. Describe several aspects of a religion that differs from yours.
2. Understand the role of a particular religion in the life of a diverse elder.
3. Discuss differences between your own religion and another one.

Time required: 90 minutes (40 minutes to conduct the interview, 20 minutes to write up the results, and 30 minutes to discuss the results in class or with another individual).*

Instructions:

1. Interview an older adult from a religious or other spiritual tradition that differs from yours.
2. Use the questions listed below to structure your interview.
3. After completing the interview, prepare written responses to the questions.
4. Discuss your responses in class or with another individual.

Use the following questions to guide your interview. Following the interview, prepare written responses to each of the interview questions.

1. Do you have a religious affiliation?
2. In what ways does your religion influence the way you live?
3. What does your religion have to say about the role of the family and respect for elders?
4. Does your religion or philosophy of life include a belief in an afterlife (life after death), heaven, or hell?
5. Do you attend religious services? If yes, how often do you attend?
6. Do you consider yourself to be more or less religious than you were when you were growing up? Explain.

Following the interview, write down responses to the above questions as well as to those listed below.

1. In what ways are the elder's spiritual/religious beliefs and practices similar to your own?
2. In what ways do the elder's religious beliefs and practices differ from yours?
3. How does the elder's religion affect his or her adjustment in the dominant society?
4. Why is it essential for service providers to have some knowledge regarding the religious beliefs and practices of the elders they serve?

---

* Instructors should be sensitive to students' feelings and experiences with religious traditions. Some students may have difficulties with this activity. Instructors should provide a classroom climate in which students are comfortable in sharing experiences or are free not to share.

RELIGIOUS TRADITIONS AMONG ASIAN AMERICANS

As noted in earlier chapters, Asian Americans represent an example of combining diverse groups under one label. This group is composed of 26 census-defined subethnic groups. While some segments of the Asian American population have been in the United States for many generations, others have arrived only recently. They have come from more than two dozen different countries. They do not share a common language, a common religion, or a common cultural background. As Diana Eck (2001) of the Harvard Pluralism Project noted, the United States has become the most religiously diverse nation in the world. Muslims, Buddhists, Hindus, and many others have arrived here from every part of the globe, radically altering the religious landscape of the United States. But what does all of this have to do with the study of aging? Religious traditions and beliefs, by definition, focus on views about birth, life, and death. These views influence the rituals and rights of passage from one phase of the life course into the next. These traditions and beliefs also influence how older people contribute to society, how they create personalized meaning for their lives, how they are treated by the young, and how they approach death. Space limitations in this text do not allow us to cover all religious traditions represented in the United States. Our focus is limited to a discussion of Islamic, Hindu, and Buddhist traditions.

Why did we select these religious traditions? As noted in Chapter 1, the United States has witnessed a continuing growth in the Asian population, which includes a large number of Muslims, Buddhists, and Hindus. For example, during the past decade, the Asian Indian population has grown more than two fold from 815,447 in 1990 to 1.9 million in 2000 (Barnes & Bennett, 2002). This population is composed of Muslims and Hindus, with a majority being Hindus. In addition, the number of Muslims has increased dramatically in recent years. Ignoring the influence of religion from the discussion of these populations would omit a major component of their ethnic identity. A related reason for including a discussion of these traditions has to do with the differences in their beliefs about life and death from those of the mainstream population. Furthermore, if we take a global point of view, then Islam, Hinduism, and Buddhism are three of the world's largest religious traditions. Together these three religions represent about 2 billion followers, or nearly 40% of all human beings now living (Thursby, 2000). Despite the continuing increase in these populations and their commitment to maintaining their ethnic identity, traditions, values, and beliefs about life and death, they have received limited attention in the study of aging. In fact, what we know about the impact of participation in religious activities on health and well-being has been based mainly on Judeo-Christian traditions (Schaie, Krause, & Booth, 2004). We do not know the extent to which results generated in Western settings can be generalized to other traditions. Our hope is that including a discussion of these traditions will introduce you to beliefs, values, and expectations of these populations, will stimulate new research, and will be helpful in addressing their needs in culturally appropriate ways.

Aging and Diversity Online: New Religious Diversity

The Pluralism Project. This website is designed to engage learners in studying the new religious diversity in the United States. It explores particularly the communities and religious traditions of Asia and the Middle East that have been woven into the religious fabric of the United States in the past 25 years. For each major religion, it offers statistical information, bibliographies, syllabi, and audiovisual resources. http://www.pluralism.org

Islamic or Muslim Tradition

Muslims in the United States   Though the U.S. Census does not collect data on religious affiliation of the population, estimates indicate that there are 2.35 million Muslims in the United States (Pew Research Center, 2007). Many of them are immigrants who have come from countries such as Egypt, Iraq, Iran, Saudi Arabia, Kuwait, Jordan, Afghanistan, Pakistan, Bangladesh, Nigeria, Malaysia, and Indonesia. More than 25% of Muslims are Black African Americans who converted. In addition, there are more than 8,000 White converts. Of these White converts, 80% are women who converted to Islam after marrying Muslims (Goodwin, 1994). Like any other religious group, Muslims have different divisions and sects with differing beliefs and levels of activism. The major divisions are Sunni and Shiite, and there are various sects within these larger divisions.

According to Harvard University's Pluralism Project (Eck, 2001), there are 1,583 Muslim Centers in the United States. Although there is some variability in the number of centers located in a given state, such centers can be found in each state. Research by the Pew Research Center (2007) indicated that Muslim Americans continue to participate in a number of religious observances. Friday prayers represent one such observance. In addition to congregational prayers on Fridays, it is stipulated that all Muslims pray at home five times each day: on arising, when the sun reaches its zenith, when the sun reaches its mid-decline, sunset, and before retiring. Regardless of where they live, Muslims read the Qur'an on a regular basis.

What Is Islam?   The word *Islam* is closely related to *salam,* which means peace or salvation. Thus, its full connotation is "the peace that comes when one's life is surrendered to God" (Smith, 1991). In other words, Islam seeks to cultivate the attribute that life is total surrender to God. Those who adhere to Islam, known as Muslims, are literally those who have been reconciled or have surrendered to God. They believe that Islam reached its definitive form through the prophet Mohammed. While there had been authentic prophets of God before Mohammed, he was their culmination; hence, he is called "The Seal of Prophets." No valid Islamic prophets will follow him.

The language of scripture and divine revelation in Islam is Arabic, and nearly all of the key terms and concepts of religious life are derived from that language. Allah is the Arabic name of God. This revered name refers to the sole divine creator, of incomparable majesty, who is to be supremely praised and respected. In the Qur'an, the holy scripture that was transmitted through Mohammed, Allah is believed to have revealed perfectly how he intends people to live. Because translations cannot possibly convey the emotions, the fervor, and the mystery that the Qur'an holds in the original, Muslims have preferred to teach others the language in which they believe Allah spoke with incomparable force and directness.

Language, however, is not the only barrier the Qur'an presents to outsiders. In its content, it is like no other religious text. It does not ground its theology in dramatic narratives, as do the Indian epics of Ramayana and Mahabharata, or in historical ones, as do the Hebrew scriptures, nor is God revealed in human form as in the Gospels and Bhagavad Gita. Whereas the Old and New Testaments are directly historical and indirectly doctrinal, the Qur'an is directly doctrinal and indirectly historical. In the Qur'an, God speaks in the first person. Allah describes himself and makes known his laws. The Muslims consider each sentence as a separate revelation and experience the words themselves as a means of grace. As pointed out by Cragg (1988), the Qur'an is not about the truth; it is the truth.

In addition to the Qur'an there is the Tradition or Hadith, the sayings and doings of the Prophet Mohammad. The Hadith is the body of traditions on which much of the life and traditions of the Muslim community is based. After belief in God there is belief in angels, Satan, spirits (jinn), the Day of Reckoning, Heaven and Hell, and the Prophets and Messengers (including Abraham, Moses, Joseph, and Jesus). As noted earlier, Mohammad is considered to be God's final Prophet and Messenger. There are also five pillars of faith in Islam:

1. Faith in one God, explicated by daily recitation of the testimony or Shahada: There is no God but Allah, and Mohammad is His Prophet.
2. Daily prayer at least five times daily.
3. Alms giving.
4. Fasting (sunrise through sundown), principally during Ramadan.
5. Pilgrimage to Mecca, if possible.

Women in Islam   In the United States, the common picture of a Muslim woman is the stereotype of a woman hidden behind a veil, a voiceless, silent figure, bereft of rights. It is a picture familiar to all of us, to a great extent because of how the Western media portrays women in Islam. However, the fact is that Islam covers many lands with many diverse cultures. Each Islamic nation has its own distinct culture. As we have emphasized throughout the book, there is a great diversity of cultures within each ethnic group. This is especially true for Islam. Islam is practiced in each country according to that country's characteristics. In the United States a very small proportion of older Muslim women cover their head with a scarf; however, most of the Muslim women do not use the veil. These women decide not to wear the veil for various reasons. Wearing the veil in the United States can draw undue attention to a woman, which would negate the modesty intent of wearing it; it can also draw unnecessary attention to their religious background when some of them may desire to become a part of the host society. To understand the role of women in Islam and to learn how the rules of Islam apply to them, it is essential to become familiar with Islam, apart from politics practiced in Muslim countries. We next outline some key areas related to women in Islam.

The Spiritual Aspect   The Qur'an provides clear evidence that woman is completely equated with man in the sight of God in terms of her rights and responsibilities. The Qur'an states, "Whoever works righteousness, man or woman, and has faith, verily to him will We give a new life that is good and pure, and We will bestow on such persons their reward according to their actions" (Qur'an 16:97).

Respect for Women   A famous saying of the Prophet is, "Paradise lies under the feet of mothers." It is therefore a religious responsibility, a praiseworthy act, to respect and honor women. Among the praiseworthy acts is to treat your mother with honor and respect. When a man asked Prophet Mohammad, "Who among the people is the most worthy of his good company?" The Prophet said, "Your mother." The man then asked, "Who else?" the Prophet replied, "Your mother." When the man again asked the same question, only then did the Prophet answer, "Your father." It should be noted that the right of women to seek knowledge is not different from that of men. Prophet Mohammad said that seeking knowledge is mandatory for all Muslims—males and females. It is the religious duty for every Muslim to treat sons and daughters justly and for men to provide support, not obstacles, for women and their achievements.

Employment   With regard to a woman's right to seek employment, it should be stated first that Muslim women regard their role in society as a mother and a wife as the most sacred and essential one. Neither maids nor babysitters can possibly take the mother's place as the educator of carefully reared children. Such a noble and vital role, which largely shapes their lives and the future of nations, cannot be regarded simply as "idleness." However, there is no decree in Islam that forbids women from seeking employment whenever there is a need, especially in positions that fit her nature and in which the society needs her most.

In sum, Islam does not include any decree that justifies mistreatment of women, nor does it allow for the distortion, reduction, or cancellation of women's clear-cut legal rights. Throughout history, the reputation, chastity, and maternal role of women were objects of admiration by impartial observers.

Vision for Human Life   Human life is relatively weak and limited in contrast to the absolute power and majesty of Allah. The Qur'an tends to regard the loss of capacities that typically are suffered in old age to be only the most obvious evidence of the universal frailty and dependence that is the inevitable condition of all human beings. It is the nature of ordinary human life to be limited and to undergo eventual destruction. The Qur'an teaches that old age will "overtake and destroy a person in the same way that even a flourishing and well-watered orchard will be burned up by a scorching whirlwind" (Thursby, 2000, p. 159). Everything that lives has its "stated term" and so has human life.

The Qur'an does not dwell on the linear stages of life. It sees all created things as caught up in a vast cosmic cycle, proceeding from their origin in God and bound finally to return again to Him. It is human beings' illusion to imagine themselves as self-sufficient or independent. Aged Muslims are expected to contribute to society as long as physically possible; there is no expectation of or allowance for withdrawal and contemplation.

It is assumed that age brings with it wisdom and maturity, which can be drawn on even when the individual is not able to perform physically demanding tasks. Regardless of their physical and mental state, older people should be treated with honor and respect and cared for when in need. Special respect is reserved for parents, especially the mother. However, even parents can be mistaken, and if one has to choose between obedience to God and to parents, God must come first but the offspring should continue to treat them with kindness and respect. As we noted earlier, the pillars of faith includes giving alms. Simply stated, this means that those who have been blessed by sufficient resources should provide support to those who are less fortunate, less able, and weaker members of society, particularly orphans, elders, and women. In short, the whole of human life is considered to be a trial, and at the precise time determined by Allah, death brings life to a close. In the hereafter, Allah will judge and punish or reward each soul.

Aging and Diversity Online: Arab World

Culture and Civilization in the Arab World. Developed by the National Institute on Technology and Liberal Education, this site focuses on culture and civilization of the Arab world and includes 10 modules that can be used by independent learners. Each module, including the one on Islam, contains a set of readings, audiovideo resources, and relevant images. http://arabworld. nitle.org

---

Hindu Tradition

There are about 1.5 million Hindus in the United States, and they are evenly spread across the country. Most of them live in urban areas, especially in large metropolitan areas. Despite their ongoing assimilation into schools, the workplace, and the community, members of this population continue to maintain their ethnic identity. Given the continuing growth of the Hindu population in recent years, a large number of Hindu temples have been constructed in different parts of the country. Harvard University's Pluralism Project Directory (Eck, 2001) lists 714 Hindu temples and centers in the United States. These temples provide a range of opportunities for teaching and learning about Hinduism (Prentiss, 2006). Examples of these opportunities include the following:

1. Allowing people to ask constructive questions about their tradition and thus to develop new ways of thinking about it; providing clear explanations of practices, beliefs, and traditions, often directed toward young people in special youth programs but also present in adult programs (e.g., study groups, language classes).
2. Applying Hindu ideals to the American context to understand that while the problems encountered may be American, solutions can be developed that are consistent with Hindu values.
3. Extending the teaching to a dialogue with other faith groups.

Hinduism emphasizes that various religions are alternate paths to the same goal. To claim salvation as the monopoly of any one religion is like claiming that God can be found in this room but not in the next, in this attire but not in another. In other words, according to Hinduism, various religions are simply different languages through which God speaks to the human heart. Truth is one; people simply call it different names. This acceptance of other religions and receptivity to other beliefs and practices makes it easier for members of the Hindu population to accept the cultural traditions of their host country while maintaining some core beliefs of their own heritage.

The Stages of Life Model   Hindus have an explicit set of beliefs regarding the four stages of life (*Ashramas*) that start around age 8 and continue through one's life. The Sanskrit word *Ashrama* refers to a religious retreat or commune. Individuals move through different stages, each of which calls for its own appropriate conduct. As each day passes from morning through noon and afternoon into evening, so every life likewise passes through four stages. Each stage requires distinct modes of response. In response to the question of how we should live, Hinduism answers that it depends on what stage of life you are in. As we discuss next, the framework provides ethical and behavioral expectations at different points in one's life.

1. Student stage (*Brahamacharya Ashrama*). Traditionally, this stage begins after the rite of initiation, between the ages of 8 and 12. It lasts for 12 years. A student's primary responsibility at this stage is to learn, to offer a receptive mind to all that the teacher transmits. The goal is to acquire knowledge and skills essential to meet the demands of life. In addition, habits are to be cultivated and character to be acquired. The liberally educated student is expected to emerge equipped to turn out a good and effective life.

2. Householder stage (*Grihastha Ashrama*). This stage begins with the sacrament of the tying of the husband's body to the wife—that is, getting married. In this stage, the person is fully engaged in the pleasure, duties, and success of raising a family, working at a vocation, and serving the surrounding community. Normally, attention is divided between the family, vocation, and the community to which one belongs. This is the time for satisfying the first three human wants: pleasure, primarily through marriage and family; success through vocation; and duty through civic participation. It should be noted that even the life of a householder is considered *ashrama*, thereby placing it on par with the other stages. Furthermore, ancient Hindu writings emphasize that the householder is the source of support for members at other stages, feeding and sustaining them all. If worldly achievement and the exercise of power are best, then middle age (i.e., the stage of the householder) will be considered life's apex. But if vision and self-understanding carry rewards equal to or surpassing these others, old age has its own opportunities, as we discuss next.

3. Retirement stage (*Vanaprastha Ashrama*). The third stage may be entered following the birth of a grandchild. At this stage the individual makes a

transition from the household duties to a more retiring and contemplative mode of life. Thus far, the society has required the individual to specialize, leaving little time to read, to think, to ponder life's meaning without interruption. The time has arrived to begin one's true adult education with the goal of discovering who one is and what life is about. What is the secret of "I" with which one has been on such intimate terms all these years yet that remains a stranger, full of inexplicable quirks and irrational impulses? Why are we born to work and struggle each with a portion of happiness and sorrow, only to die too soon? In other words, the challenge is to find meaning in the mystery of existence. It is the time to work out a philosophy and then to work that philosophy into a way of life, a time for transcending the senses to find and dwell with the reality that underlies this natural world (Smith, 1991).

4. Renunciation stage (*Sannyasa Ashrama*). This is the stage when, as Bhagavad Gita says, "one neither loves nor hates anything." Indifferent to everything, firm of purpose, one concentrates and meditates for the sake of realizing the supreme reality (*Brahman*). By not injuring any creatures, by detaching the senses from the objects of enjoyment, by performing the rites prescribed in the Veda, and by rigorously practicing austerities, the state of the ultimate reality (*Brahman*) is reached even in this world. In short, life is seen as a pursuit of the path leading up to this stage of serenity—not unlike the Western concept of *wisdom* (Baltes & Staudinger, 1993).

Analysis of the Model   Only in the second half of life do followers of the Hindu view develop cognitions that meaningfully relate tasks accomplished in the early years of life to those to be accomplished in the later half (Tilak, 1989). The cognitive shift during the midpoint in the lifespan facilitates true understanding and the ability to make the transition from the householder stage, bound to deeds, to the hermit or wanderer phase, bound to knowledge. As stated earlier, the stages-of-life model sees the later years as a time for integration. While this period is a continuation of early years in some ways, it is distinct from them in other ways. The key task during the last two stages is to meaningfully integrate and relate one's life as it has been lived and to accept one's own death. This task is essentially different from the task of earlier stages where the concern is with fulfilling the worldly ends in life. These have been called *ordinary norms* in contrast to *extraordinary norms* of spiritual liberation (*moksha*) to be attained in the final years of life.

Clearly, the norms of liberation make relatively higher demands of metaphysical and ethical nature on older adults in stages 3 and 4. Although the philosophy and practice of abandonment implicit in spiritual norms of *moksha* may appear negative or disengaging compared with the usual worldly norms, it is a direct consequence of a metaphysical understanding realized in later years (Herman, 1976). What is learned in the course of the final stage of life is to draw the existential consequences ensuring from this deepened understanding. In short, the stages-of-life model prescribes with equal care and consideration the tasks to be accomplished in one's early years as well as in later years. This approach is also harmonized with the view that psychodynamic unfolding of the potential of the mind is a function of advancing age. The focus, therefore, must not be on vain and futile attempts to deny or avoid aging but rather on the growing awareness of the widening opportunities for self-realization offered by the aging process. Anticipating the position taken by humanistic psychologists (e.g., Abraham Maslow), the stages-of-life model states that desire and motivation for attaining liberation will only be felt after the basic needs for psychological well-being, love, and belongingness have been met. Thus, the earlier stages are prerequisites to the later and the last. To be sure, Hindu texts discuss disengagement and retreat in the last stage of life, but this disengagement from the active role of householder is for the sake of reengagement in the tasks of self-realization in old age. As such, this approach seems to provide meaningful ways of coping with the stress of old age and of maintaining high morale and life satisfaction in aging (Tilak, 1989). It should also be noted that the model implies planning for an active late life as a career and learning the appropriate mechanisms of coping with old age starting early in life.

Reincarnation   The stages of life outlined in the preceding section are lived out in the repetitive cycle of birth and death and rebirth. This, in both Hinduism and Buddhism life, is seen as a perpetual cycle (see Figure 3.2 in Chapter 3). The fate of all beings, as determined by their own *Karma* or modes of action over successive lifetimes, is to suffer a ceaseless rebound of rebirths into various bodies until they are able to discover and dedicate themselves to an effective method for attaining release. Thus, death is seen not as the end of life but as the beginning of the next one. From this point of view, life is seen as a brief visit from the more fundamental process of the universe. Reincarnation, then, is not only a real possibility, but, in fact, life after death may be where we mortals truly belong; it is where one can have full freedom from a series of worldly toils, responsibilities, duties, and obligations (Kitayama, 2000). An Indian verse captures the idea this way:

> Do you remember that when you were born,
> You were crying and everyone else was rejoicing.
> Do you also remember that when you died,
> You were smiling and everyone else was crying.

Consider the following Hindu prayer, which captures the same idea:

> From the unreal lead me to the Real,
> From the darkness lead me to light,
> From ignorance lead me to knowledge,
> From death lead me to immortality.

Note that these ideas are in stark contrast with the mainstream views that regard birth as the beginning and death as the end, at which point one is destined to enter heaven or hell. It is important to emphasize that beliefs about life and death go beyond the imagination of world-renouncing monks, philosophers, and historians of ideas. These beliefs organize life, in part because people necessarily live life not purely as a biologically prescribed event but as a personally meaningful sequence of social and individual experiences. Cultural worldviews provide a system of meanings that are then used by the members to create personalized meanings for their lives. In addition, these views also lead to collective practices and conventions, thereby providing an overarching framework for activities. Thus, socially shared *ideas* about aging can cause changes in psychological *realities* of aging. In short, social beliefs about aging and old age have a causal impact on cognitive functioning, practices and behavior in old age (Kitayama, 2000).

Thus, in Hindu texts, the notion of aging emerges as a variety of images of the upward and downward as well as the forward march of life through time and space:

- Aging as a marker of life's journey. This sense is suggested in a number of texts by the institution of age-specific rites of passage that effectively distinguish one period of life from another by reason of privilege or duty.
- Aging as growth and maturity. The individual's growth and development with age are conceptualized positively in physical, psychological, and spiritual terms.
- Aging as decline and loss. The later phases of life and the associated meanings are presented negatively as physical losses and finitude.
- Aging as an accomplice of death. The meaning of aging as a handmaiden of death is presented in striking similes and metaphors in many texts (Tilak, 1989).

As we have noted, Hindu culture provides for knowing one's place in the universe (reincarnation); its stages-of-life model provides normative guidelines for navigating the life course. While every individual may not reach the final stage of renunciation, the ideal provides agreed on guidelines to aid individuals in their later years. Perhaps the main contribution of the stages-of-life (*Ashramas*) model to the aging Hindu is the sanction to engage in reflection and contemplation. In other words, the aging individuals are freed from trying to live in the second half of the life cycle by the agendas of the first half. Members from other stages provide them with support they may need to engage in reflection and contemplation in old age.

Aging and Diversity Online: Hinduism

The Heart of Hinduism. This site presents an overview of Hinduism in clear terms. Produced by practitioners of the tradition, it is meant for users who wish to broaden their knowledge of Hindu traditions. Includes key concepts, core values, rites of passage, lifestyles, and historical perspectives. Also provides a comprehensive index and glossary. http://www.hinduism.iskcon.com

We now proceed to discuss Buddhists' views of aging and their implications.

Buddhist Tradition

Buddhists in the United States   Similar to the increase in the Muslim and the Hindu population, the United States has witnessed a dramatic increase in the Buddhist population. Estimates indicate that there are 3 to 4 million Buddhists in the United States, the most in any Western country (Seager, 1999). These estimates include 800,000 converts and between 2.2 and 3.2 million Buddhists in immigrant communities. Buddhist immigrants have come from countries such as Cambodia, Laos, Thailand, Burma, Sri Lanka, Vietnam, China, and Japan. Thus, in a particular location there may be one or more of each of a Laotian Buddhist temple, a Cambodian Buddhist temple, a Japanese Buddhist temple, a Chinese Buddhist temple, and so on. One estimate indicates that there are more than 2,000 Buddhist temples and centers in the United States (Eck, 2001).

What Is Buddhism?

The term *Buddha* literally means "enlightened" or "mentally awakened." According to Buddhism, one becomes a great or a liberated person when one's mind (by the power that is within it) becomes enlightened enough to look at life realistically. Buddhism began with a man who shook off the daze, the doze, and the dream-like vagaries of ordinary awareness. It began with a man who woke up. This man was Siddhartha Gautama. According to Buddhist tradition, Gautama is said to have set out on the search for realization that led him to become the Buddha, the Enlightened One, after seeing four disturbing sights. The first of them was an old man who had experienced a large number of aging-related problems. This sight, which revealed to innocent Gautama the consequences of aging, played a key role in the development of Buddhism and its views about life. The next two, of a sick man and a dead man, further increased the awareness of suffering that had been created by the first sight. Then the fourth sight was of a monk, a recluse with a calm and serene face. This sight represented to the receptive Gautama an alternative way to engage the limited resources and possibilities available to humans during their lifetime.

Distinctive Characteristics

The essence of Buddhism is found in the Four Noble Truths, the realization of which resulted in Gautama becoming the Buddha:

1. All human beings suffer. Birth, illness, death, and other separations are inescapable part of life.
2. The cause of suffering is desire. Desire is manifested by attachment to life, to security, to others—most specifically the desire "to be."
3. The way to end suffering is to cease to desire.
4. The way to cease to desire is to follow the Eightfold Path: right belief, right intent, right speech, right conduct or action, right endeavor or livelihood, right effort, right mindfulness, and right meditation.

Following the Eightfold Path leads to cessation of desire and to Nirvana. Rather than denying the certainty of aging and death of the embodied self, the Buddhist method of meditation or mindfulness opens with a preparatory level of practice in which one is required to look closely and repeatedly at all conditions of life until no longer perturbed by them. Then at a second level of practice, the goal in meditation is to settle into calm, clear insight. As support for practice of meditation, Buddhism recommends study of method and teaching of Buddha and life of the monastic order. Together they create a path of spiritual development that is directed toward the cessation of a desire-driven separate identity and leads one toward release, toward Nirvana (Thursby, 2000). What is Nirvana? The Buddha is quoted describing what it is not rather than what it is. Nirvana is something "unborn, unbecome, unmade, unconditioned." It is compared to coolness after a fever, and Buddhists have called it the cool cave, the harbor of refuge, the holy city, the further shore. It is a condition in which the individual personality is snuffed out, as it were, and thereby experiences perfect peace. Its nearest parallel is a state sometimes reached in travel, of total absorption in which the external world ceases to impinge on the mind and in which there is a sense of freedom and tranquility.

In summary, for both Buddhism and Hinduism, life is conceptualized as a perpetual cycle. Death is not the end of life but the beginning of the next one. Fate of all human beings, as determined by their own Karma or modes of action over successive lifetimes, is to suffer a ceaseless round of rebirths into various bodies until they are able to discover and dedicate themselves to an effective method for attaining release. Thus, life after death may be where one truly belongs; it is where one can have full freedom from worldly toils, responsibilities, duties, and obligations.

Aging and Diversity on line: Resources on Buddhism

Buddhist Studies Virtual Library. This virtual library includes leading information sources in the area of Buddhism and Buddhist studies. All links are inspected and evaluated before being added to the virtual library. http://www.ciolek.com/wwwvl-Buddhism.html

---

In the next learning activity, you will become familiar with how some Japanese Americans use customs from other religious traditions.

ACTIVE LEARNING EXPERIENCE: MULTIRELIGIOUS CUSTOMS AMONG JAPANESE AMERICANS

The purpose of this experience is to provide an opportunity for you to examine multireligious customs of Japanese Americans and to analyze how some Buddhists remain open to customs, traditions, and values from a variety of other religions. Upon completion of this activity, you will be able to:

1. Outline benefits of accepting and respecting others' religions in a spirit of mutual give and take.
2. Share examples of how some other groups in the United States take an active part in learning from other religions.
3. Discuss how such interactions among members of different religious groups affect the quality of life for older adults.

Time required: 30 minutes (15 minutes to read the case and prepare group answers to the questions and 15 minutes for a general class discussion).

Instructions:

1. The instructor divides the class into groups of five to seven students.
2. Each group selects a member who is responsible for writing down the group's answers and for reporting them to the class.
3. Groups answer the questions that follow the case.
4. Group recorders report their group's answers to the class.
5. The instructor leads a discussion reflecting group responses.

Case Study

Buddhism and Shintoism are two major religions of Japanese Americans. A family uses both Buddhist and Shinto customs in daily life. Some Christian customs are also used in annual life events. This is a case of a family that uses Buddhism, Shintoism, and Christianity in their life events.

Fumi Ito is a 70-year-old widow who lives with her first daughter's family. Since Fumi and her husband did not have a son, their first daughter, Akiko, has taken a role to keep their last name, and Akiko's husband, Nobuo, accepted changing his last name Yamaguchi to Ito when they married. Fumi's husband, Akio, died 2 years ago. His funeral was observed with the traditional Buddhist custom. The third anniversary of his death was observed last month. Fumi visits his grave once a week. She pours water over the gravestone, makes floral offerings, lights incense, and prays for him. Fumi's family also visits the grave at least once a month (usually on the date of his death). When they visit the grave, they offer rice cakes or Akio's favorite things and pray.

Akiko and Nobuo have a son, Koichi, and a daughter, Mika, so Mika does not need to keep their last name. When Koichi married, Koichi and his wife, Sachiko, had a wedding ceremony at a Shinto shrine. For marriage, Shinto is the most common religion. Many wedding ceremonial halls in Japan have a room for Shinto wedding ceremonies. Only the closest family can attend the ceremony. During the ceremony, a Shinto priest prays for the new couple, and the bride and groom exchange nuptial cups for their marriage pledge and then exchange their rings. The ceremony is about 30 minutes long, and the reception follows the ceremony in another hall.

Mika married last month. She and her husband, Takayuki, had their wedding ceremony at church. Mika's favorite singer had a wedding ceremony at this church, and she longed to have one at the same church. Neither Mika nor Takayuki are Christians. However, the pastor allowed them to be married at the church. Both of them had to go to church at least four times to learn about Christianity and marriage before their ceremony. Some Christian churches allow any couple to have a wedding ceremony with some conditions.

All of the Ito family members attended these events. They used Buddhism, Shintoism, and Christianity each time. Many Japanese people use Shintoism, Buddhism, and Christianity in their lives. Christmas is an annual event for many Japanese people, even if they are not Christians. Social interaction among members of different religious groups provides them with ongoing opportunities to see important similarities in different faiths, promotes acceptance and respect for each other, and allows them to live together in a spirit of mutual give and take.

Discussion Questions:

1. What aspects of Japanese multireligious customs did you find unique? Why?
2. Why has intercommunication between religions become important in Japan?
3. Given the large number of Buddhist immigrants in the United States, what are the benefits of their accepting and respecting other religions?
4. Give examples of creative approaches that may be useful in promoting interaction among older adults representing different religious traditions in the United States.
5. What other religious traditions that you have studied in this chapter view all religions as having the same goal?

SUMMARY

This chapter was devoted to an examination of religion and spirituality among Black Americans, Hispanics, American Indians, and Asian Americans. In the first section of the chapter, we distinguished between *religion* and *spirituality*, outlined procedures used to assess these constructs, and stressed the importance of including religion in the study of aging. In the next section, we focused on religious behaviors of elderly Blacks. While religious involvement is high among Black Americans of all ages, this is especially true for the oldest age cohorts. They participate in both organizational and nonorganizational activities at a very high rate. In addition to attending church, a majority of them engage in daily prayer, read religious materials, watch or listen to religious programs, and request prayer. Their participation in religious activities is associated with better health.

After reviewing the religious behaviors of Blacks, we examined the practices of Hispanics. We noted that, in the everyday life of older Hispanics, both Aztec and European influences are still in place today. Out of this mixture of Indian and European ideologies evolved the unique concept of *fe*, which incorporates varying degrees of faith, spirituality, hope, cultural values, and beliefs. Attending religious services and engaging in private prayer are also common in this population. Regular participation in religious activities benefits their mental and physical health. The next section focused on religious practices among American Indians. As noted for Hispanics, religion is not a "pure" concept for American Indians. They consider it essential that Christianity be rooted in Indian culture and practices. Traditionally, elders have a special place in the culture and religions of the American Indian population. They are the wisdomkeepers—the repositories of the sacred ways and natural world philosophies that extend indefinitely back in time.

The concluding section of the chapter was devoted to an examination of Islamic, Hindu, and Buddhist conceptions of aging. Islam views old age as a natural part of the human cycle. It does not focus on the detailed stages of the life course but on the human being's origin and final end. Hinduism readily accepts other religions and views them as simply different languages through which God speaks to the human heart. Hindus have an explicit set of beliefs regarding the four stages of life: student, householder, retirement, and renunciation. Withdrawing from activities and pleasures in old age allows the older person to concentrate on the spiritual life and to approach death without anxiety as it is viewed merely as a passage into the next life. Both Buddhism and Hinduism share the view that the fate of all beings is to suffer a ceaseless round of rebirths until they are able to discover and dedicate themselves to an effective method for attaining release.

As a means of reviewing some key concepts presented in this chapter, complete the following quiz.

ACTIVE LEARNING EXPERIENCE: CHAPTER 8 QUIZ

The purpose of this experience is to assess your knowledge of variations in religion and spirituality among older Black Americans, Hispanics, American Indians, and Asian/Pacific Islanders. Upon completion of this activity, you will be able to:

1. Assess your knowledge of diversity issues in religion, spirituality, and aging.
2. Gain feedback regarding your knowledge of these issues.

Time required: 30 minutes (10 minutes to complete the quiz and 20 minutes to discuss your answers in class).

Instructions:

1. Complete the quiz.
2. Your instructor will lead a review of the answers to the quiz in class.

Quiz Items	True	False
1. Older White adults demonstrate significantly higher levels of religious participation than do older Black adults.	___	___
2. Participation in nonorganizational religious activities among elderly Blacks tends to be very low.	___	___
3. Self-administered questionnaires work well for assessing religiousness in all segments of older population.	___	___
4. Religious involvement of older Blacks has no effect in reducing the negative impact of life stressors.	___	___
5. Participation in religious activities is associated with better health.	___	___
6. For older persons of Mexican heritage, *fe* always implies identification with a specific religious community.	___	___
7. The place of spiritual leaders in American Indian tribes is similar to that of religious leaders in the dominant society.	___	___
8. Older Black women are as active in religious organizations as older Black men.	___	___
9. Among American Indians, orthodox religious beliefs and practices are often combined with indigenous ones.	___	___
10. According to Islam, aging is a sign of God's mercy, justice, and power.	___	___
11. Islam encourages an ascetic lifestyle and a detachment from family life.	___	___
12. For Asian Indian Hindus, old age is the time to obtain spiritual self-realization.	___	___
13. Buddhism promotes family life.	___	___
14. The majority of Asian refugees follow Islam.	___	___
15. For immigrant elders, the local church may play a unique role in resettlement and acculturation activities.	___	___

GLOSSARY

Aztecs: A pre-Colombian group that ruled much of what is now modern Mexico.

Bhagavad Gita: Refers to a very famous poem that is the spiritual textbook of almost all educated Hindus. Its first six chapters deal mainly with the psychology of the human spiritual life, the second six with devotion and the nature of God, and the third six with practical applications.

***fe*:** For older adults of Mexican heritage, the concept of *fe* incorporates varying degrees of faith, spirituality, hope, culture, values, and beliefs.

karma: Associated with Hinduism, this Sanskrit term refers to action or deed. The concept of karma is the driving force behind the cycles of reincarnation in Hinduism and many other Asian religions. Karma is a law of consequences for one's actions, which will come to bear upon the individual in this life or a future life. In essence, morally good actions will produce positive consequences whereas morally reprehensible deeds will produce negative results.

Lakota: This is the second largest American Indian tribe. Whites often call this tribe by the name of Sioux.

moksha: In Hinduism this term refers to the spiritual liberation to be attained in the final years of life. The stages-of-life model focuses on the innate need as well as desire on the part of the individual to fulfill his or her potential through striving for liberation (*moksha*).

Nirvana: A term usually associated with Buddhism. It refers to the extinction of all worldly desires and effects for a given person. Nirvana is also referred to as the "state of illumination."

nonorganizational religious participation: Refers to religious activities that can be undertaken outside the context of an organization such as reading religious books, engaging in private prayer, requesting prayer, and listening to religious music.

organizational religious participation: Refers to behaviors that occur within the context of a church, mosque, synagogue, temple, or other religious settings. Examples include church attendance, church membership, and participation in auxiliary groups.

Qur'an: The sacred text of Islam, considered by Muslims to contain the revelations of God through their prophet Mohammed. It is a manual of definitions and guarantees, and it provides Muslims a collection of maxims on which to meditate.

SUGGESTED READINGS

Arden, H., & Wall, S., (1990). *Wisdomkeepers: Meetings with Native American spiritual elders.* Hillsboro, OR: Beyond Words.

This book describes interviews with 17 spiritual or political leaders representing a full range of American Indian communities. The authors learned a different way of thinking that affected their views about the earth, sovereignty, family, community, and the future. Included are a large number of excellent photographs.

Cole, T. R., Kastenbaum. R., & Ray, R.E.(Eds.). (2000). *Handbook of the humanities and aging.* (2nd ed.) New York: Springer.

The authors cover aging through history, world religions, arts and literature, and contemporary topics in humanistic gerontology. It includes chapters on aging in eastern religious, traditions, aging in the Christian tradition, and aging in Judaism. In addition, it includes a chapter devoted to spirituality.

Eisenhandler, S.A., (2003). *Keeping the faith in late life*. New York: Springer.

This highly readable book reports the findings of face-to-face interviews the author conducted with older people living independently in the community and in long-term care facilities. Provides valuable insights into the folkways of prayer and faith in late life.

Koenig, H.G., McCullough, M.E., & Larson, D.B., (2001). *Handbook of religion and health*. New York: Oxford University Press.

Presents a comprehensive and thorough review of existing research on religion and health, examines the clinical implications of this research, makes recommendations for future research, and offers suggestions on how to design and conduct research that avoids the flaws and weaknesses of previous work.

Schachter-Shalomi, Z., & Miller, R. S., (1995). *From age-ing to sage-ing: A profound new vision of growing older*. New York: Warner Books.

This book proposes a new model of late-life development called sage-ing, a process that enables older people to become spiritually radiant, physically vital, and socially responsible "elders of the tribe." The three sections of the book focus on (a) the theory of spiritual "eldering," (b) spiritual eldering and personal transformation, and (c) spiritual eldering and social transformation. The appendix includes 11 exercises for sages in training.

Schaie, K.W., Krause, N., & Booth, A. (Eds.). (2004). *Religious influences on health and well-being in the elderly*. New York: Springer.

Focuses on the impact of religious institutions, religious practices, and religious organizations upon the health and well-being of older persons. Includes a chapter on how religious influences might work among older African Americans, older Whites, and older Hispanics.

Taylor, R. J., Chatters, L. M., & Levin, J. (2004). Religion in the lives of African Americans: Social, psychological and health perspectives. Thousand Oaks, CA: Sage.

This book examines many broad issues concerning religion and African Americans, including the relationship between religion and physical and mental health and well-being and the role of religion within women and older people.

Thomas, L. E., (1994). The way of the religious renouncer: Power through nothingness. In L. E. Thomas & S. Eisenhandler (Eds.), *Aging and the religious dimension* (pp. 51-64). Westport, CT: Auburn House.

Thomas explores the issues of aging and religion by means of a case study of an elderly religious renunciate from India, along with a comparison of Gandhi's life in his later years. Using a cross-cultural perspective, the author examines these two instances in which aging has not led to a loss of prestige and personal authority. This analysis provides an in-depth look at the factors contributing to this phenomenon, and it explores the implications they might have for aging in Western society.

KEY: CHAPTER 8 QUIZ

1. False. Race comparative analyses among older adults (Levin, Chatters, & Taylor, 1994) and adults (Taylor, Chatters, Jayakody, & Levin, 1996) indicate that African Americans are more religious than Whites from comparable social backgrounds, for both organizational and nonorganizational activities.
2. False. Taylor, Chatters, and Levin (2004) report that the prevalence of private religious activities among older Blacks tends to be very high. Examples of these activities include reading religious materials, listening to religious programs, engagement in prayer, and requests for prayer.
3. False. While self-administered questionnaires work well for collecting data on religiousness and spirituality in some segments of older populations, such measures may be problematic for use with older people who may suffer from vision and other serious health problems or may experience reading difficulties.
4. False. Organizational religiosity is associated with better health. This is true for White Americans as well as for Black Americans. (Levin, Chatters & Taylor, 1995; Levin & Chatters, 1998a).
5. True. Church attendance is associated with a wide range of physical health outcomes, including lower blood pressure, boosted immune function, and enhanced physical functioning (Koenig, McCullough, & Larson, 2001).
6. False. *Fe* does not necessarily imply identification with a specific religious community. Instead, it incorporates varying degrees of faith, spirituality, hope, cultural values, and beliefs. It embodies a way of life as well as the culture in which it is lived.
7. False. Among American Indian tribes, spiritual elders are the wisdomkeepers, the repositories of the sacred ways, and natural world philosophies that extend indefinitely back in time (Arden & Wall, 1990). Their place is much more central than that of religious leaders in the dominant Western society. They share dreams and visions with members of their tribe, perform healing ceremonies, and may make apocalyptic prophecies.
8. False. Older Black women are more active in religious organizations than their male counterparts (Levin & Taylor, 1993). This

involvement in church social events helps them maintain an informal support network that extends beyond family members.

9. True. Many American Indians prefer to merge Christian and indigenous beliefs. They consider it essential that Indian Christianity be rooted in their culture and practices. It is not surprising to find the sacred pipe, the drum, sweat lodges, native prayers, and eagle feathers in Indian churches (Weaver, 1993).

10. True. According to the Qur'an, aging is a sign and reminder of the overwhelming mercy, justice, and power of Allah (Thursby, 2000).

11. False. Islam discourages ascetic lifestyles and emphasizes the family. It expects adult children to show kindness and respect to their aged parents (Thursby, 2000).

12. True. For Hindus, old age is the time to obtain spiritual self-realization through renunciation and contemplation (Idler, 2006). The signs of old age are not symbolic of physical and mental decline; rather, they are indications for beginning a new life task.

13. False. Buddhism values giving up attachment to the seemingly enduring personal identity that is created by interaction with family, friends, and institutions. It values detachment from family life. Its determining orientation is toward the celibate, homeless, wandering world renouncer (Thursby, 2000).

14. False. The vast majority of Asian refugees are Buddhists. They have come from Cambodia, Laos, and Vietnam, where more than 80% of the population follows Buddhism (Kitano & Daniels, 1995).

15. True. For immigrant elders and their families, churches provide a place for meeting people, learning the language and culture of the United States, and obtaining social services (Kitano & Daniels, 1995).

REFERENCES

Arden, H., & Wall, S. (1990). *Wisdomkeepers: Meetings with Native American spiritual elders.* Hillsboro, OR: Beyond Words.

Baltes, P.B., & Staudinger, U. M. (1993). The search for a psychology of wisdom. *Current Directions in Psychological Science, 2,* 75–80.

Barnes, J. S. & Bennett, C. E. (2002) *U.S. Census Bureau, the Asian Population: 2000.* Washington, DC: U.S. Government Printing Office.

Billingsley, A. (1999). *Mighty like a river: The Black church and social reform.* New York: Oxford University Press.

Bryant, S. & Rakowski, W. (1992). Predictors of mortality among elderly African Americans. *Research on Aging, 14,* 50-63.

Carson, V. B. (Ed.). (1989). *Spiritual dimensions of nursing practice.* Philadelphia: W.B. Saunders.

Chatters, L. M., & Taylor, R.J. (1989). Age differences in religious participation among Black adults. *Journals of Gerontology: Social Sciences, 44,* S183–S189.

Chatters, L. M., Taylor, R. J., & Lincoln, K. D. (1999). African American religious participation: A multi-sample comparison. *Journal for the Scientific Study of Religion, 38,* 132–145.

Cragg, K. (1988). *Readings in the Qur'an.* London: Collins.

Eck, D. L. (2001). *A new religious America.* New York: Harper Collins.

Eisenhandler, S. A. (2003). *Keeping the faith in late life.* New York: Springer.

Ellison, C. G. (1994). Religion, the life-stress paradigm, and the study of depression. In J. S. Levin (Ed.), *Religion in aging and health: Theoretical foundations and methodological frontiers* (pp. 78–121). Thousand Oaks, CA: Sage.

Ellison, C. G., Hummer, R. A., Cormier, S., & Rogers, R. G. (2000). Religious involvement and mortality risk among African American adults. *Research on Aging, 22,* 630–667.

Ellison, C. G., & Sherkat, D. E. (1990). Patterns of religious mobility among Black Americans. *Sociological Quarterly, 31,* 551–568.

Ellison, C. G., & Sherkat, D. E. (1995). The "semi-involuntary institution" revisited: Regional variations in church participation among Black Americans. *Social Forces, 73,* 1415–1437.

Ellor, J. W., Netting, F. E., & Thibault, J. M. (1999). *Understanding religious and spiritual aspects of human service practice.* Columbia: University of South Carolina Press.

Fetzer Institute/National Institute on Aging (NIA) Working Group (1999). *Multidimensional measurement of religiousness, spirituality for use in health research: A report of a national working group* (supported by the Fetzer Institute in collaboration with the National Institute on Aging). Kalamazoo, MI: Fetzer Institute.

Goodwin, J. (1994). *Price of honor.* Boston: Little, Brown.

Herman, A. L. (1976). *Introduction to Indian thought.* Englewood Cliffs, NJ: Prentice Hall.

Hill, T. D., Angel, J. L., Ellison, C. G., & Angel, R. J. (2005). Religious Attendance and mortality: An 8-year follow-up of older Mexican Americans. *Journal of Gerontology, Social Sciences, 60B*(2), S102–S109.

Hill, T. D., Burdette, A. M., Angel, J. L., & Angel, R. J. (2006). Religious attendance and cognitive functioning among older Mexican Americans. *Journal of Gerontology, Psychological Sciences, 61B*(1), P3–P9.

House, J. S., Landis, K. R., & Umberson, D. (1988). Social relationships and health. *Science, 241,* 540–545.

Idler, E. L. (2006). Religion and aging. In R. H. Binstock & L. K. George (Eds.), *Handbook of aging and the social sciences,* (6th ed., pp. 277–300). New York: Academic Press.

Idler, E. L., Musick, M. A., Ellison, C. G., George, L. K., Krause, N., Ory, M. G., et al. (2003). Measuring multiple dimensions of religion and spirituality for health research. *Research on Aging, 25*(4), 327–365.

Kitano, H. H., & Daniels, R. (1995). *Asian Americans: Emerging minorities* (2nd ed.). Englewood Cliffs, NJ: Prentice Hall.

Kitayama, S. (2000). Cultural variations in cognition: Implications for aging research. In P. C. Sterns & L. L. Carstensen (Eds.), *The aging mind: Opportunities in cognitive research. Committee on Future Directions for Cognitive Research on Aging* (pp. 218–237). Washington, DC: Commission on Behavioral and Social Sciences and Education. National Research Council, National Academy Press.

Koenig, H. G. (1994). Religion and hope for the disabled elder. In J. S. Levin (Ed.), *Religion in aging and health: Theoretical foundations and methodological frontiers* (pp. 18–51). Thousand Oaks, CA: Sage.

Koenig, H. G., McCullough, M. E., & Larson, D. B. (2001). *Handbook of religion and health.* New York: Oxford University Press.

Krause, N. (1992). Stress, religiosity, and psychological well-being among older Blacks. *Journal of Aging and Health, 4,* 412–439.

Krause, N. (2002). Church-based social support and health in old age: Variations by race. *Journal of Gerontology: Social Sciences, 57B,* S332–S347.

Levin, J. S. (1997). Religious research in gerontology, 1980–1994: A systematic review. *Journal of Religious Gerontology, 10*(3), 3–31.

Levin, J. S., & Chatters, L. M. (1998a). Religion, health, and psychological well-being in older adults: Findings from three national surveys. *Journal of Aging and Health, 10,* 504–531.

Levin, J. S., Chatters, L. M., & Taylor, R. J. (1994). Race and gender differences in religiosity among older adults: Findings from four national surveys. *Journal of Gerontology, 49,* S137–S145.

Levin, J. S., Chatters, L. M., & Taylor, R. J. (1995a). A multidimensional measure of religious involvement for African Americans. *Sociological Quarterly, 36,* 157–173.

Levin, J. S., Chatters, L. M., & Taylor, R. J. (1995b). Religious effects on health status and life satisfaction among Black Americans. *Journal of Gerontology: Social Sciences, 50B,* S154–S163.

Levin, J. S., Markides, K., & Ray, L. A. (1996). Religious attendance and psychological well-being in Mexican Americans: A panel analysis of three-generation data. *Gerontologist, 36*(4), 454–463.

Levin, J. S., & Taylor, R. J. (1993). Gender and age differences in religiosity among Black Americans. *Gerontologist, 33*(1), 16–23.

Levin, J. S., & Taylor, R. J. (1997). Age differences in patterns and correlates of the frequency of prayer. *Gerontologist, 37*(1), 75–88.

Maier, S. F., Watkins, L. R., & Fleshner, M. (1994). Psychoneuroimmunology: The interface between behavior, brain, and immunity. *American Psychologist, 49,* 1004–1017.

Maldonado, D. (1995). Religion and persons of color. In M. A. Kimble, S. H. McFadden, J. W. Ellor, & J. J. Seeber (Eds.), *Aging, spirituality, and religion: A handbook* (pp. 119–128). Minneapolis, MN: Fortress Press.

Markides, K. S., Levin, J. S., & Ray, L. A. (1987). Religion, aging and life satisfaction: An eight-year, three-wave longitudinal study. *Gerontologist, 27,* 660–665.

McNally, M. D. (2005). *Native American religions and cultural freedom: An introductory essay.* Retrieved July 3, 2006 from: http://www.pluralism.org/research/profiles/display.php?profile=73332

Pew Research Center (2007). *Muslim Americans: Middle class and mostly mainstream.* Washington, DC: Author.

Prentiss, K. P. (2006). *The pattern of Hinduism and Hindu temple building in the U.S.* Retrieved July 3, 2006 from: http://www.pluralism.org/research/articles/pp_hinduism_article.php?from=articles_index

Schaie, K. W., Krause, N., & Booth, A. (Eds.). (2004). *Religious influences on health and well-being in the elderly.* New York: Springer.

Seager, R. H. (1999). *Buddhism in America.* New York: Columbia University Press.

Smith, H. (1991). *The world's religions* (2nd ed.). New York: Harper Collins.

Spector, R. E. (1979). *Cultural diversity in health and illness.* New York: Appleton-Century-Crofts.

Steffen. P. R., Hinderliter, A. L., Blumenthal, J. A., & Sherwood, A. (2001). Religious coping, ethnicity, and ambulatory blood pressure. *Psychosomatic Medicine, 63*(4, special issue), 523–530.

Stevens-Arroyo, A., & Díaz-Stevens, A. (1998). *The Emmaus paradigm: The Latino religious resurgence.* Boulder, CO: Westview Press.

Stolley, J., & Koenig, H. (1997). Religion/spirituality and health among elderly African Americans and Hispanics. *Journal of Psychosocial Nursing, 35,* 32–38.

Taylor, R. J. (1986). Religious participation among elderly Blacks. *Gerontologist, 26,* 630–636.

Taylor, R. J., & Chatters, L. M. (1988). Church members as a source of informal social support. *Review of Religious Research, 30,* 193–203.

Taylor, R. J., Chatters, L. M., Jayakody, R., & Levin, J. S. (1996). Black and White differences in religious participation: A multi-sample comparison. *Journal for the Scientific Study of Religion, 35*, 403–410.

Taylor, R. J., Chatters, L. M., & Levin, J. (2004). *Religion in the lives of African Americans.* Thousand Oaks, CA: Sage.

Thursby, G. R. (2000). Aging in Eastern religious traditions. In T. Cole, R. Kastenbaum, & R.E. Ray (Eds.), *Handbook of the humanities and aging* (2nd ed., pp. 155–180). New York: Springer.

Tilak, S. (1989). *Religion and aging in the Indian tradition.* Albany: State University of New York Press.

Villa, R. F., & Jaime, A. (1993). La fe de la gente. In M. Sotomayor & A. Garcia (Eds.), *Elderly Latinos: Issues and solutions for the 21st century* (pp. 129–142). Washington, DC: National Hispanic Council on Aging.

Walls, C. T. & Zarit, S. H. (1991). Informal support from Black churches and the well-being of elderly Blacks. *Gerontologist, 31*, 490–495.

Weaver, J. (1993). Native reformation in Indian country: Forging a relevant spiritual identity among Indian Christians. *Christianity and Crisis, 53*(2), 39–41.

9

Death, Dying, and Bereavement

- How does the mainstream population approach end-of-life care?
- What services are available to provide support to families and friends before, during, and after the death of a loved one?
- How do beliefs about life after death vary across different ethnic and religious groups?
- What similarities and differences are observed in the funeral practices followed by different groups?

In this chapter, we examine beliefs about life and death, how we care for people who are dying, the practices that occur around the end of life, and how people cope with the loss of a loved one. We first examine these concepts in the mainstream U.S. population and then see how they differ according to key elements of diversity with a particular focus on minority ethnic groups. The following vignettes illustrate some of the issues we address in this chapter.

Vignette 1

Maria del Carmen Perez was born and raised in Mexico but now lives in the United States. A coworker's grandmother just died and Maria del Carmen was surprised at how different her old age and death were from what she was familiar with in Mexico. When Maria del Carmen was a child, her grandmother lived with them. As her grandmother became ill, her parents took care of her in their home. One night Maria del Carmen remembers being awakened to the voices of her parents immediately after her grandmother died. The next morning, people from the funeral home came and took her grandmother's body. After the funeral home had cleaned and prepared the body, Maria del Carmen's parents went to dress her grandmother in her final clothes. The funeral was at the local Catholic church, and her grandmother was buried in the village cemetery. After hearing about her coworker's grandmother's death in a hospital, Maria del Carmen is resolved that it won't be that way for her parents. Although Maria del Carmen lives and works in the United States, she is confident that her sisters will be able to take care of her parents as they become more dependent and that they will be able to die a peaceful death at home.

Vignette 2

At 68 years of age, Binh Nguyen was too busy enjoying life and his grandchildren to give any thought to preparations for the end of his life. But his 3-year-old grandson recently died of cancer, and he is now thinking a lot about the end of life. Binh was born in Vietnam and came to the United States with his wife and two children after the Vietnam War. In Vietnam, his family followed Buddhist traditions, but these were difficult to continue when they were fleeing Vietnam; after they came to the United States, they were focused on helping the children adapt to U.S. culture. As a result, his children had limited exposure to formal Buddhist rituals and no exposure to any rituals around death. So, when it became clear that his grandchild was going to die, his children were at a real loss as to what to do; they had no experience with death, and they were devastated at the thought of losing their son. The doctors recommended hospice care to manage his pain, so they arranged for hospice workers to come to their house and help keep the child as comfortable as possible. When he died, the entire extended family was there with him. They then took his body to be cremated and returned with his ashes to their home. Binh's children's friends helped them prepare a memorial service for his grandchild, and Binh thought it was very moving, but foreign. He wonders if his children would have had access to their Buddhist heritage and rituals, and whether it would have brought them any comfort at such a difficult time. Binh is not sure what he wants when he dies.

Vignette 3

Linda Johnson has just returned from her partner Elizabeth Allen's funeral, and she feels both relieved and terribly bereft. Her relief comes from the knowledge that Elizabeth did not appear to suffer as she died and that she is no longer experiencing the debilitating weakness that congestive heart failure had brought. Linda had been worried that the health-care professionals might ignore Elizabeth's wishes to die without intervention or that Linda's position as partner rather than spouse might give her difficulties in being with Elizabeth in the end. But Elizabeth and Linda had prepared well for the legal issues at the end of life, and the health-care professionals and hospice workers had accepted Linda's role in Elizabeth's life and had not questioned her presence or Elizabeth's requests. But Linda is now alone and very sad. Elizabeth had been her best friend in childhood and adolescence. Linda's mother had been uncomfortable with their close friendship and discouraged correspondence when Elizabeth's family moved away when they were both 15. Elizabeth and Linda married men in college and raised families, but after a 25-year separation, they renewed their relationship in midlife when they found out that they were both divorced. They have been together every day for the past 30 years, and Linda doesn't know what she will do without Elizabeth. She feels like crawling into bed and sleeping forever.

U.S. "MAINSTREAM" APPROACH TO LIFE AND DEATH

What Do We Mean by Mainstream Group?

As you may have noticed throughout this book, we have often referred to the *main-stream* U.S. culture as a comparison with groups from key elements of diversity. This mainstream group is a bit tricky, in part because it changes as we switch elements of diversity: from being White when discussing race, to being male when discussing gender, to being middle class when discussing socioeconomic status (SES), to being heterosexual when discussing sexual orientation, to being urban when discussing rural issues, and to being Christian when discussing religion and spirituality. This comparison group is also tricky because the differences within the group are so large. Nowhere does this become more apparent than when we try to discuss mainstream beliefs and behaviors related to death, dying, and bereavement.

One may ask why an attempt should be made to define a mainstream group at all, if it is indeed so heterogeneous? Perhaps understanding each group from within is a better approach instead of constantly comparing different groups? Indeed, there are advantages to allowing each culture to be defined in its own right without comparison with a mainstream or a standard. But, as we discussed with health inequalities, comparisons are sometimes necessary, as when we want to determine whether there are inequities that occur across social groups. With issues of death and dying, it is also important to try to describe some kind of mainstream, because it is from that mainstream that our institutional systems around death and dying were created. Given that we consider it important to describe a mainstream group, who should our comparison group be? As we said earlier, here is where the differences within a group make it difficult to describe one mainstream group. If we determine "White" as our mainstream comparison group, then we include beliefs and rituals from both the Christian and Jewish traditions. If our comparison group should be White and Christian, where do the Jewish beliefs belong? With the differences discussed in ethnic minority sections? And if we keep this White and Christian mainstream, where do we put Catholics, who, although sometimes will refer to themselves as Christians, have been separated from Protestants both by choice and sometimes by antipathy? We present this difficulty of defining a mainstream group neither as a pessimistic note nor with a perfect solution in mind but rather as a reminder that within-group differences for any one of the key elements of diversity can be quite significant. Please keep these within-group differences in mind as we examine death, dying, and bereavement in both mainstream and minority groups.

Beliefs About Life and Death

Attitudes and practices surrounding dying, death, and bereavement vary from culture to culture and from subculture to subculture. Philosophical and psychological issues concerning mortality, the meaning of life and death, and the losses associated with the death of a loved one appear to be universal concerns. As a means of coping with these concerns, people have developed beliefs, rituals, and norms for managing anxieties associated with death, the possibility of an afterlife, burials, and expectations regarding grieving practices (Markides & Mindel, 1987). Current Western conceptions of death can be traced back to early Semitic people in what is now considered the Middle East: "Their beliefs and practices evolved into the Judaic, Christian, and Islamic religions of today" (Spector, 1991, p. 120). These early Semitic people perceived evil spirits to surround the dying and the dead, and they developed rituals aimed at protecting those who were in the process of dying, the dead, and their families and communities. Numerous rites, including washing of the body, sending the dead off with food for the coming journey, and the development of prayers and incantations to protect survivors from the evil spirits, evolved into contemporary practices (Spector, 1991).

Many American death and bereavement attitudes are rooted in 17th- and 18th-century Puritan New England (Eisenbruch, 1984; Stannard, 1977). Believing in predestination, Puritans viewed the afterlife as already fixed, so there was no necessity for an elaborate funeral ceremony. The Puritan system of bereavement reflected the following elements:

- No embalming
- A simple funeral
- No eulogy
- A minimum of outward expression of grief

Apparently, the Puritans also attempted to get nearby Indians to engage in similar bereavement and funeral practices, which were contrary to their own religious practices (Eisenbruch, 1984).

David Stannard (1977), a social historian, offered an explanation as to why many American funerals have become demonstrably more elaborate than those of Pilgrim forebears. He contended that funerals in New England (the home of the Puritans) became much more extravagant during the middle of the 17th century with the death of many of the Puritan leaders and the growth of religious tolerance in England, their country of origin. These changes presented a threat to the Puritan community's survival, and perhaps more extravagant funerals and more open expressions of grief were efforts at maintaining the community's existence and importance (Eisenbruch, 1984; Stannard, 1977).

Although religious freedom is a strong value in the United States, Christianity is the mainstream religious perspective that forms the underpinnings of U.S. culture. One needs only to note the fact that Christmas is a federal holiday to see just one small example of the impact that Christianity has on U.S. culture. For people who consider themselves Christian or who were raised in a Christian background, seeing the influence of this religion on their culture is difficult. For people who do not have any Christian roots, it is much easier to see the religious influences of Christianity and the ways other religious beliefs are excluded from mainstream society. Of course, Christianity does not contain just one religious group, and thus there is a tremendous diversity of religious beliefs, values, and practices from different Protestant (e.g., Baptists, United Methodists) and Catholic groups. Even within specific religious groups, there are regional and ethnic differences in beliefs and practices. Nevertheless, these religious groups share in the belief that after death there is an afterlife in heaven or hell. Although many refer to this as *life after death,* it is clear that this afterlife is different from life as we know it on Earth. Death brings the end of the physical body and the afterlife is often referred to as a spiritual life. This continuation of life after death is also very different from the cyclical nature of life after death in reincarnation discussed in Chapter 8 on religious affiliation and spirituality. Thus, although people in the United States often believe in some kind of life after death, death brings an end to life on earth, and thus death is often viewed with fear and anxiety as something to be avoided at all costs. This avoidance occurs even at the level of language as people are often very reluctant to say that someone has *died,* preferring to use euphemisms such as *passed away, went to sleep,* or *passed on.*

This avoidance of death fits well within the biomedical model of health discussed in Chapter 4 on health beliefs. If health has been historically defined as the absence of disease, then death is the failure to cure or rid the body of that disease. Within this biomedical view of health, the focus of health-care professionals is to cure disease and to keep their patients from death. Thus, death is something that is to be avoided—it is not a natural ending to life. In this context, it is perhaps not surprising that many health-care professionals do not receive much training and do not feel comfortable in dealing with issues of death. In this light, death could be viewed as the failure of the medical system. Of course, these views of life and death cannot be taken out of the cultural context of aging discussed in Chapter 3 on psychology and aging. In the United States, speed and youth are valued, "anti-aging" labels are pinned on numerous health products to increase their sales, and the avoidance of the appearance of aging is heavily valued. In this context, death could be viewed as the ultimate failure of avoiding aging.

As discussed in Chapter 5 on health inequalities, the common causes of death in the United States have shifted from acute, brief illnesses to long-term, chronic conditions. At the beginning of the 20th century, death rates were higher in infancy and then very similar across the lifespan (child, middle-aged adult, older adult). In the past 50 years, death has now become the purview of old age (Lynn, 2000). At the same time as this shift from acute to chronic conditions, there was also a shift from family members caring for dying relatives to health-care professionals caring for the dying with the result that most people die in institutions (hospitals or nursing homes) rather than at home (Ferrell & Coyle, 2002). Thus, there has been increased separation between people and the actual processes of death and dying. Given that the majority of people die in hospitals and nursing homes away from their families, most people from mainstream groups in the United States (especially children) do not have much contact with death. Even as a favorite grandparent is dying, White children are often not taken to the hospital to visit for fear of germs (either for the child or for the elder) or because parents think the child is too young to understand. Similarly, young children are often absent from funerals. People have concerns that the hospital visit or funeral will be so striking and foreign that children will only remember their elder as ill or dead instead of remembering the more lively times that they shared. As we discuss later in the chapter, familiarity with death varies by ethnic group and by community location. For example, in rural areas where animals are raised, the natural cycle of birth and death in animals is visible, and thus death may be seen as part of the life cycle. Similarly, in cultures with higher infant and child mortality rates, seeing and knowing someone who has died is more common. This increased familiarity with death may facilitate acceptance of death as a natural ending to life rather than as something to be avoided.

End-of-Life Practices

Caring for the Dying Person

As we mentioned previously, the biomedical view has resulted in the health profession's focus on avoiding death at all costs. Historically, this death-avoiding focus involved invasive treatments even when likely outcomes were poor. For example, 30 years ago, at the time of death almost every hospitalized patient experienced an effort at resuscitation regardless of prognosis (Lynn, 2000). Although this is no longer routine, the roots of that behavior (i.e., trying to keep people alive at all costs) are still present in our system. Yet this invasive intervention is not what most people want at the end of life. Approximately 90% of people want to die a "good death," by which they mean a short, pain-free death at home and surrounded by family. However, very few people in the United States experience this so-called good death, with 60% of people dying in hospitals and 20% in nursing homes (Hooyman & Kiyak, 2008). This strong disconnect between the vast majority of people wanting to die at home and the vast majority dying in institutions where aggressive interventions are common has driven many people to pursue changes in the care of people who are dying. This "end-of-life care," if provided by people with expertise around the physical, psychological, and spiritual aspects of dying, can facilitate the good death that many people want.

Hospice and Palliative Care   Hospice care is one example of the changes being made to end-of-life care. Hospice "refers to a program of care that supports the patient and family through the dying process and the surviving family members through bereavement" (Ferrell & Coyle, 2002, p. 27). Hospice programs are designed to have specially trained professionals who have expertise in the end of life around issues of pain management, death and dying, and spiritual and psychological issues. Hospice programs are sometimes housed in a particular location or in a special unit of the hospital, but most hospice care is provided to people in their homes or nursing homes. Thus, hospice care often comes to where the ill person is—in his or her own home or in a nursing home. A person is eligible for hospice care after being diagnosed with a terminal illness, being given a prognosis of less than 6 months to live, and deciding not to pursue curative treatment. A growth in hospice care occurred when Medicare began paying for a hospice benefit in 1982, thus providing a source of funding for this kind of care. Other insurance providers also often provide a hospice benefit, as hospice care can be much more affordable than hospital care. Individual hospice programs can differ from one another as they can be created by different groups for different purposes. Some hospice programs are offered by nonprofit organizations that may have been created by a particular religious group (e.g., Catholic Social Services), whereas other hospice programs may have been created by an individual as a for-profit enterprise. In some larger communities, an individual may have an option to choose between different hospice programs to find a program that fits his or her beliefs toward death and dying, but in smaller communities or in certain insurance settings, one's choices for hospice programs may be limited. Thus, one may be faced with a hospice program that promotes spiritual assistance based on specific religious beliefs with little to no attention to one's culture.

Palliative care refers to the total care provided to an individual whose disease does not respond to curative treatment (Ferrell & Coyle, 2002). Although some people assume that palliative care (or comfort care) is only given at the end of life, this definition could encompass a much longer period and could significantly improve the quality of life for people who are dying. Instead of being treated as someone for whom death is imminent, providing palliative care over a longer period of time could facilitate psychological and spiritual acceptance at the end of life. Unfortunately, unlike hospice programs, palliative care provided outside of a 6-month prognosis is not necessarily covered by Medicare or other insurance programs and thus is often only available to people with considerable financial resources.

Aging and Diversity Online: Palliative Care

End-of-Life Issues. This Center for Disease Control and Prevention (CDC) website provides basic information and links to end-of-life issues including palliative and hospice care. http://www.cdc.gov/aging/EOL.htm

Education in Palliative and End-of-Life Care (EPEC) Project. Providing education in palliative and end-of-life care, this group provides training (both online and at conferences) in palliative and end-of-life care. http://www.epec.net/EPEC/Webpages/index.cfm

Hospice Foundation of America. Provides resources for those who are personally or professionally coping with terminal illness or death. http://www.hospicefoundation.org

---

Choices One Can Make about End-of-Life Care

As we noted earlier, most people in the United States want to have a "good death." One fear shared by many is to end up in a hospital, incapacitated and unable to express one's wishes, kept alive by machines with life-sustaining yet invasive procedures being performed. Yet relatively few people plan ahead to help ensure that their feared end is avoided and that their preferred end happens. The primary way that people can help control the care that they receive at the end of life is through advance care directives. These are instructions prepared in advance to direct medical care in the event that one cannot communicate one's wishes. *Advance care directive* is a term used to describe a full range of different types of instructions for future care. Advance care directives can include simple verbal instructions or more complex legal documents. Verbal instructions are one example of an advance care directive that can be given to a close family member or to a more officially designated health-care advocate. Family members and health-care advocates (also called health-care proxies) can aid health professionals in deciding what procedures a person may want to avoid (or want to have conducted) if the person cannot speak for themselves. Health-care advocates can also help a person ask pertinent questions of health professionals when the seriously ill person may not have the physical, cognitive, or emotional resources to have such conversations. Some people go beyond verbal instructions given to family members or advocates and designate a person to have medical power of attorney (another example of an advance care directive) for them. In some states this is called a durable power of attorney for health decisions. A person who is given the medical power of attorney has the legal right to make health-care decisions for that person in the event that they become unable to make or communicate those decisions themselves (e.g., due to advanced stages of dementia or due to being unconscious). The *medical* power of attorney does not give the power to make other legal or financial decisions; it is restricted to health-care decisions. Yet another example of an advance care directive is a living will, which is a written, legal document containing health-care instructions in the event of a terminal illness or other life-threatening condition. Living wills should not be confused with a last will and testament, which is a legal document that specifies how one's financial assets should be distributed after one's death. Living wills may include directions concerning certain procedures that a person does not want performed under specific circumstances.

The medical and legal systems in the United States convey certain privileges upon married couples. These can include the right to direct a spouse's medical care in situations where the spouse cannot speak for himself or herself. A parent directs the care of a child, but when the child becomes an adult and marries, the spouse becomes next-of-kin and can direct care and has access to the married spouse at times that friends may not. These same privileges are often not given to lesbian, gay, bisexual, and transgender (LGBT) couples. In many parts of the country where partner rights have not been legalized (and where marriage is not allowed), LGBT partners may find that they are treated as a friend rather than as a family member to their partner. This means that their access to their partner may be limited to restrictive visiting hours and that the blood relatives of their partner may have more say over their partner's care than they do (even though the family members may have been estranged for years). Advance care directives can help LGBT couples protect their decision-making power up to a point but may not override a hospital and nursing home's regulations regarding patient access.

Many health professionals and other legal experts argue that every person over the age of 18 should have advance care directives. Consider for a moment whether you have completed advance care directives for yourself. Do your loved ones have advance care directives? If your response is "no," then consider why you (or your loved ones) have not taken such basic steps. Too often, we fail to realize that in the case of serious illness or other life-threatening condition, we will not have the mental faculties available to us that we do now. For example, we may be dealing with intense pain and not be able to fully master the complexities of a situation. Completing advance care directives is an important step toward ensuring that we obtain the kind of care that we would want. Helping everyone in the United States, both people from mainstream and minority groups, realize the importance of these advance care directives is one of the important challenges for service providers.

The Patient Self-Determination Act (PSDA) is a federal law that requires many Medicare and Medicaid providers (e.g., hospitals, nursing homes, home health agencies) to give patients information about advance care directives upon enrollment in a plan or admission to a facility (Kornblatt, Eng, & Hansen, 2002). As a part of this act, health-care providers must ask a patient whether he or she has an advance care directive and, if the patient does not, the provider must provide information about advance care directives. Although some patients may not fill out formal advance directives such as a living will, many will discuss with a trusted health-care professional their wishes should they become ill in the future and be unable to communicate at that time. Notes about a patient's wishes can be written into the patient file, and, if there is continuity of care with the same provider and the medical records are easily accessible, these notes may be referred to if the patient becomes unable to communicate, if a written advance care directive has not been made, and if family members are unaware of the patient's wishes. There is some evidence that the PSDA has increased the use of advance care directives but that use of these directives differs significantly by ethnic group. In one study, White elders were the most likely to have a durable power of attorney, Asian elders were most likely to designate a health-care proxy, African American elders were unlikely to have written advance directives due to distrust of the health institution, and Hispanic elders were least likely to have indicated any advance directives, formal or informal (Eleazer et al., 1996). Informing people about advance care directives and promoting their use are challenges made much more complex by the diversity within the U.S. population.

Aging and Diversity Online: Preparing for the End of Life

American Bar Association's Commission on Law and Aging. This website provides many excellent resources regarding legal concerns around the end-of-life care, including the Consumer's Toolkit for Healthcare Advance Planning. http://www.abanet.org/aging

End-of-Life Decisions. This section on the Alzheimer's Association's website provides information about end-of-life decisions for people who have Alzheimer's disease. http://www.alz.org/professionals_and_researchers_end_of_life.asp

American Association of Retired Persons (AARP) End of Life. This section of the AARP website provides detailed information on preparing for the end of life, including estate planning, hospice care, and recommendations for living life to its fullest. http://www.aarp.org/families/end_life

---

On Lok, a health-care provider known for its focus on providing care in culturally appropriate ways for patients from diverse backgrounds (and discussed in detail in Chapter 6 on caregiving), has developed an approach to determining what kinds of care a patient would like at the end of his or her life (Kornblatt et al., 2002). With the diversity of their client groups, On Lok cannot create one set strategy for all of their patients. Some of their African American patients, for example, may distrust institutions and may be uncomfortable limiting future care options in a written living will. For other patient groups, talking about death in explicit terms may be seen as taboo and with the possibility of bringing misfortune. The result is that at On Lok, all care providers are given culturally based training to facilitate an understanding of different cultural perspectives on these issues (Kornblatt et al., 2002). Strategies to work within each cultural group's beliefs are provided. For example, although talking explicitly about one's own death might be taboo in some cultures, when patients are healthy (e.g., at a routine doctor visit), they are often willing to engage in a discussion about the kind of care they would like if they happen to become ill. Through these discussions, a health-care proxy (in many cultures, an adult child or spouse) can be named and notes can be made in the patient file and referred to at a future date, if needed. Although these notes do not serve as a formal advance care directive, they can give family members some direction and peace of mind as they make difficult choices for their dying loved one. Family members will be more likely to trust a health-care provider's information if he or she has been caring for the patient for a long time and knows the family as well. To help you develop better understanding of advance care directives, online resources for advance care directives are provided in the aging and diversity online section.

ACTIVE LEARNING EXPERIENCE: OSCAR THE CAT PREDICTS DEATH

The purpose of this experience is to provide you with an opportunity to consider the end of life and ways that we might determine that the end of life is near. Upon completion of this activity, you will be able to:

1. Describe Oscar's behavior.
2. Provide possible explanations for this phenomenon.

Time required: 30 minutes (15 minutes to read the case study and answer the questions and 15 minutes to discuss responses with another person).

Instructions:

1. Read the case study, either as a homework assignment or in a class setting.
2. Prepare written responses to the questions at the end of the case study either on your own or as a part of a small-group discussion.
3. Discuss your responses with another person.

Case Study

Oscar the cat lives in the advanced-dementia unit of a nursing home. Since being adopted by the staff as a kitten, Oscar has demonstrated an uncanny ability to predict when residents on the unit are about to die. He has been present at the deaths of more than 25 residents, and the physicians and nursing staff regard his presence as a strong predictor of impending death. This allows them to notify families so that they can be with their loved ones when they die. For residents who might have died alone, Oscar is there with them to provide companionship. The following excerpt from the *New England Journal of Medicine* describes Oscar's behavior (Dosa, 2007, pp. 328–329):

Making his way back up the hallway, Oscar arrives at Room 313. The door is open, and he proceeds inside. Mrs. K. is resting peacefully in her bed, her breathing steady but shallow. She is surrounded by photographs of her grandchildren and one from her wedding day. Despite these keepsakes, she is alone. Oscar jumps onto her bed and again sniffs the air. He pauses to consider the situation, and then turns around twice before curling up beside Mrs. K.

One hour passes. Oscar waits. A nurse walks into the room to check on her patient. She pauses to note Oscar's presence. Concerned, she hurriedly leaves the room and returns to her desk. She grabs Mrs. K.'s chart off the medical-records rack and begins to make phone calls.

Within a half hour the family starts to arrive. Chairs are brought into the room, where the relatives begin their vigil. The priest is called to deliver last rites. And still, Oscar has not budged, instead purring and gently nuzzling Mrs. K. A young grandson asks his mother, "What is the cat doing here?" The mother, fighting back tears, tells him, "He is here to help Grandma get to heaven." Thirty minutes later, Mrs. K. takes her last earthly breath. With this, Oscar sits up, looks around, then departs the room so quietly that the grieving family barely notices.

Discussion Questions:

1. Do you think that Oscar actually predicts death? If so, how do you think he is doing it?
2. What alternative explanations for his behavior can you come up with?
3. What other roles are played by cats and dogs in the lives of older people?
4. What other stories do you know that demonstrate the unique abilities of animals?

Rituals Around Death   Despite dramatic advances in health care, it can be very difficult to predict exactly when a person is going to die (unless you are Oscar the cat!). Of course, there are sudden, unexpected deaths due to accident or heart attack that are unpredictable, but even predicting the death of a terminally ill person can be difficult. There is some evidence that people themselves have some control over their death as there are increases in death immediately following a person's birthday or other major holiday as if the person were holding on for that event (Hooyman & Kiyak, 2008). But as it becomes clear that a person is dying, close family members and loved ones are often called to be with the person. Throughout this time period that is sometimes called the vigil or "keeping vigil," an effort is made to always keep someone with the person who is dying as there is the strong belief that people should not die alone. Some hospice programs have "vigil volunteers." They have received hospice training and remain available to be with a person who is dying. Sometimes they may be there with family members, providing information and support if needed, but primarily their role is to be there with the dying person. Given that families are often spread out across the country and even the world, vigil volunteers may be the only person with the person as he or she dies. The vigil volunteer can call a hospice nurse if any medical issues arise, and, upon death, the volunteer calls the hospice nurse to come and certify that the person has died. This certification is important in the United States, as it provides an official judgment that the person has died. A death certificate indicating cause of death and ethnic background of the deceased is filed with the government. Much like a birth certificate is needed to prove that a person was born, a death certificate is needed to be able to handle the myriad details from the deceased person's life, ranging from handling of the person's remains to distributing the person's assets. If surviving family or friends want to move the body to another location (perhaps returning the person to his or her ancestral home), then a death certificate is often needed to transport the body. In later sections of the chapter, we discuss religious traditions related to requirements for the final resting place for the deceased.

After medical professionals have certified that a person has died, often a funeral home or mortuary is called to take the body to the mortuary. There, the body is prepared for the funeral as specified by the family's wishes. If the family wishes include preservation of the body, then embalming will occur. This involves injecting chemicals into the body to preserve the body and to prevent decay and decomposition. Preservation of the body may be important for practical, personal, or religious reasons. If the body is going to be put on display, called a viewing, then embalming may be a practical matter. But some religious groups believe that the physical body will be used in the afterlife and that it is important for this body to be intact; thus, embalming may be done for religious reasons as well. The body is dressed in clothing provided by the family (sometimes a favorite or memorable outfit from the person who died or other times a specially chosen formal dress just for the funeral), makeup is applied to the person's face, and the person's hair is styled to make him or her look as "natural" as possible. Depending on the person's preferences, a funeral may be conducted. This can occur in the mortuary chapel or in a local church and typically happens within one week of the death. Depending on religious custom, a wake may be held. Wakes are a time for family and friends to gather and console the surviving family members, and for some religious and cultural groups, this ceremony may involve solemn ritual (e.g., saying the rosary). Sometimes the wake is held in the funeral chapel, at a religious location, or at the home of the person who has died. Similarly, a funeral can be held in a religious location or in a mortuary chapel, and the nature of ceremony conducted depends on the religious affiliation of the person who died. In the United States, burial is the most common final resting place for the body, although cremation is becoming increasingly common.

ACTIVE LEARNING EXPERIENCE: END-OF-LIFE CARE AND RITUALS AROUND DEATH

The purpose of this experience is to provide an opportunity to consider mainstream approaches to end-of-life care and rituals around the end of life. Upon completion of this activity, you will be able to:

1. Describe examples of end-of-life care and rituals.
2. Explain how culture may affect these rituals.

Time required: 45 minutes (30 minutes to complete the questions and 15 minutes to discuss the answers with another person).

Instructions:

1. Read the following case study, either as a homework assignment or in a class setting.
2. Prepare written responses to the questions at the end of the case study on your own or as a part of the class discussion designed for this activity.
3. Discuss your responses with another person.

Case Study

After his grandfather died, Michael's grandmother, Anne Ring, remained in the house where she and her husband had raised their children. She was adamant that she remain in her own home, by herself, until she died. When she started to become more frail, her children, who lived more than 200 miles away, asked her to move in with one of them or to at least move into housing designed for seniors. But Anne wanted to remain in her home and in the community where she had lived for 60 years, so her children arranged for a medical monitoring system. If she needed assistance, she would press a button on the pendant she wore around her neck, alerting emergency personnel. Eventually, Anne needed assistance 24 hours a day and was moved to a nursing home nearby. The staff there cared for her, and when she came very close to death, Anne was moved to the hospice wing of the nursing home. The hospice staff took care of her health needs and helped the family prepare for her approaching death. When she died, Michael's mom was with her. After his grandmother's death, the hospice staff prepared the appropriate paperwork and, with the direction of Michael's mom, arranged for the mortuary to come and take her body.

At the mortuary, Anne's body was injected with chemicals (or embalmed) to preserve it and was dressed in fine clothes, and makeup was applied to her face. When Michael came to the rosary service and viewing at the mortuary two nights later, his grandmother's body was at the front of the small chapel in a fancy casket lined with satin; she was wearing her favorite church outfit. Michael thought she looked as if she were asleep. Everyone knelt in their pews, and the prayers began. As the rosary was said, Michael fumbled with the beaded rosary his mother had given him and tried to remember which prayer went with which bead. He was impressed that his cousins seemed to know the prayers so well.

The next day, the funeral was held, and people from all over town came to the Catholic Mass. Michael thought that his grandmother would have liked her "good seat" at the funeral as her casket was at the head of the church, in front of the altar. Afterward, the people got into their cars, and all followed in procession with their headlights on to the cemetery. In this small community, cars pulled over to let the funeral procession pass. After a short ceremony conducted by the parish priest, Michael's grandmother was buried next to his grandfather. Pink roses, Anne's favorite, were dropped into the grave by family members. Finally, everyone returned to the church communal hall where the Daughters of Isabella, a women's group within the church, had prepared a lunch for the mourners. Although Michael was sad at his grandmother's death, he felt worse for his mom as he saw her sadness. And, although it felt a bit strange, he was glad to be able to see all of his cousins at the lunch and talk together outside as the adults chatted over their food.

Discussion Questions:

1. Where did Anne want to spend her last days? Where did she end up dying?
2. What end-of-life practices were used with Anne?
3. What rituals were performed around Anne's death?
4. How were these rituals affected by cultural influences?
5. In what ways would these rituals have changed if Anne had been from a different ethnic or religious group?

Bereavement and Coping

The loss of a loved one can produce bereavement, a state of sadness, grief, and loneliness over the loss of a loved one. Researchers and mental health professionals have tried to understand the grief process to help those grieving. Elizabeth Kubler-Ross's (1969) classic work initially identified five stages of coping with the dying process:

1. Shock and denial
2. Anger, resentment, and guilt
3. Bargaining, such as trying to make a deal with God

4. Depression and withdrawal from others
5. Adjustment/acceptance

The publication of these stages spurred people in the United States to talk more about death and loss and gave a common language with which to recognize and describe different reactions to death. There was also criticism of these stages as people recognized that the grief process could not be defined by a step-by-step process that each individual experiences in a certain order and in a certain time frame. More recently, people have recognized that grief is a very individualized process with large differences between what is considered normal grieving both between and within different cultural groups (Kalish & Reynolds, 1976). In contrast with Kubler-Ross's (1969) orderly progression of stages, Hooyman and Kiyak (2008) describe the grief process as a roller coaster with individual variability in the highs and lows and with individual differences in the time in between them: "There can even be mixed reactions within the same person, who may simultaneously experience within a matter of hours anger, guilt, helplessness, loneliness, and uncontrolled crying—along with personal strength and pride in their coping" (p. 570). Determining how best to help people when they are grieving is a difficult yet important challenge for service providers and for those who support loved ones who are grieving.

The death of a spouse or partner is considered to be one of the most difficult events for older people. This death has ramifications beyond the loss of the important person and includes a change in status for the surviving spouse as he or she leaves the status of being a "couple" to being single in widowhood. In a world designed for married couples, this can be a tremendous identity shift. Not only must an older person cope with the physical and emotional loss of his or her life partner, but he or she also may need to assume the roles that person played (e.g., cook, bill payer, driver) while simultaneously mourning the loss of his or her friend and companion. The loss of a spouse can take a toll on health, with older widows and widowers being more likely than younger adults to become sick and die within the first 6 months following the death. Chronic conditions and disabilities can become worse, visits to the doctor may increase, and hospitalizations or moving to a nursing home are more likely to occur. Gender also plays a role in widowhood. For women, becoming a widow is almost a normative life role because it occurs to so many of them. For women who are 65 and older, almost 70% are widowed, more than three times the rate of their male peers (Federal Interagency Forum on Aging-Related Statistics, 2006). In addition to losing one's spouse or partner, older people are also at risk for multiple losses as lifelong friends and family members die. U.S. society does not recognize the difficulties of these multiple losses, nor does it have systems in place to help people experiencing them. Although the funeral is considered the societal event that provides a ritual for recognizing a person's life and death and for the spouse, family members, and friends to grieve and say goodbye, the grieving process extends beyond this ceremony. For people who are significantly impacted by the loss as spouses and partners are, there are almost no societal structures in place to facilitate the transition from married person to widow or widower.

The Widowed Persons Service (WPS) is one exception to this lack of services. Founded by the AARP, the WPS provides a model for promoting peer support among widowed persons. People who have previously been widowed volunteer to help newly widowed persons. These volunteers are trained to conduct outreach visiting the newly widowed and to discuss problems that the newly widowed might face. Individual communities sponsor local WPS, so each community has slightly different programs, but most include the following services:

- Outreach
- Telephone service
- Mutual help group sessions
- Referral service

See the aging and diversity online section for additional information about the WPS.

Most health-care professionals (e.g., physicians, nurses, social workers, psychologists) receive almost no formal training around end-of-life issues. This leaves them with limited knowledge and few resources to aid their clients at the end of life. Given the importance of end-of-life issues, there has been a call to provide more end-of-life training. One way to provide such training would be through online courses. The National Institute on Mental Health (NIMH) has funded the development and testing of an online end-of-life training program. Developed by the American Psychological Association Office on AIDS in collaboration with a small business partner, eNursing IIc, this end-of-life training program provides training in 10 areas including diagnosis and treatment of cognitive changes, understanding and supporting family caregivers, spirituality issues, legal, and ethical issues. Where relevant, each module also addresses cultural diversity. To find additional information about this end-of-life training program, see the following aging and diversity online section.

Aging and Diversity Online: Bereavement and End-of-Life Assistance

AARP Grief and Loss. This section of the AARP website provides detailed information on many different areas ranging from legal issues to adjustment to being alone. http://www.aarp.org/families/grief_loss

Widowed Persons Service (WPS). Established by the AARP, the WPS provides outreach, telephone service, mutual help group sessions, and referrals. The website listed here describes the program, but individual communities develop their own WPS and may include contact details on their own organization's websites. http://seniors-site.com/widowm/wps.html

End-of-Life Training. APA has developed this end-of-life training program, funded by NIMH. http://enursingllc.com/apa/main_page.htm

ACTIVE LEARNING EXPERIENCE: FAMILY CUSTOMS AROUND DYING AND BEREAVEMENT

The purpose of this experience is to provide an opportunity to examine your family's practices around death, dying, and bereavement. Upon completion of this activity, you will be able to:

1. Describe practices common in your family.
2. Compare these practices with those of another student's family.

Time required: 60 minutes (40 minutes to prepare responses to the questions and 20 minutes to discuss the responses with another person).

Instructions:

1. Prepare written responses to the following questions. If you are unable to answer these questions on your own, please contact a family member (e.g., a parent or grandparent) for assistance.
   a. What does the religious or spiritual belief system in your family have to say about death? Does this system include a belief in an afterlife? Explain.
   b. Suppose that an elder relative dies. What end-of-life care practices might that relative have experienced?
   c. Describe what the typical funeral of an elder family member might be like. Include a description of any family, ethnic, or religious customs that the funeral might reflect.
   d. How might your family grieve for this elder? Would there be a proscribed period of mourning? If yes, how long would this last, and what types of behaviors would mourners do?
   e. What assistance might you be able to provide to a family member who is experiencing a loss? How long after the death would you plan to provide that assistance?
2. Discuss your responses with another person.

APPROACHES TO LIFE AND DEATH FROM DIVERSE CULTURAL GROUPS IN THE UNITED STATES

We now turn to consider beliefs and behaviors around life and death for groups that are not considered mainstream in the United States. In many respects, religious affiliation may be the primary determinant of behaviors related to death. Religion often determines rituals that are appropriate when a person dies. For example, religion affects one's belief in an afterlife, the characteristics of that afterlife, and the behaviors that should be performed to attain that afterlife. So an examination of end-of-life behaviors by religion would seem appropriate. But, as noted in

Chapter 8 on religious affiliation and spirituality, the U.S. Census does not collect data on religion; thus, a definitive determination of the demographics of different religious groups is difficult. Also, even within a religion (e.g., Catholicism), there are sometimes different rituals performed depending on the ethnic background of the people (e.g., Hispanic versus Caucasian). Because other chapters have presented information separately by ethnic background, we continue that organizational strategy here even though it does not fit as well here as in other chapters. Thus, we examine how ethnicity relates to different beliefs and behaviors around death, focusing on the major religions for each ethnic group. Again, it is necessary to remember the importance of the diversity within each group as the end-of-life behaviors for different religions within an ethnic group will likely differ; for example, rituals for Protestant Hispanics may be very different from rituals for Catholic Hispanics.

African Americans

Beliefs about Life and Death African American beliefs about life and death, like many ethnic groups, are rooted in their religious belief systems. Contrary to the simplistic media portrayals of African Americans and religion, many argue that African American religious life is multifaceted, complex, and diverse (Taylor, Chatters, & Levin, 2004). Although we do not want to stereotype all African Americans as religious, indeed often the strength of their religious beliefs and their ties to community religious groups are what differentiate African Americans from others. The three religious denominations with which African Americans are most likely to be affiliated are Baptist, Methodist, and Catholic. Summarizing data from six different national surveys, Taylor and colleagues estimated that approximately half of all Blacks report being Baptist, approximately 10% report being Methodist, and 5% to 6% report being Catholic. An additional 10% report no current religious denomination, and less than 1% indicate that they are agnostic or atheist (Taylor, Chatters, & Levin, 2004). Beliefs about life and death and the appropriate care to provide a person who is dying can differ according to the person's religious affiliation. Yet, in sharing a common belief in God, many African Americans' beliefs are similar. When discussing issues around the end of life, African Americans typically describe death as "passing over," reflecting a belief in the afterlife similar to African religions' discussion of death as "returning home, going away, being called away, becoming God's property" (Mbiti, 1991, p. 119).

In their classic study comparing beliefs about death among four different ethnic groups from the Los Angeles area (Black Americans, Japanese Americans, Mexican Americans, and Anglo Americans), Kalish and Reynolds (1976) found interesting ethnic differences in beliefs about life after death. Although most Black Americans believed in some kind of life after death (including heaven and hell), only about one third believed that "those in heaven, watch over those on earth" (p. 108). This was considerably different from the other ethnic groups in which the majority of people who believed in some life after death believed that those in heaven watch over those on Earth (100% of Japanese, 82% of Mexican, and 83% of Anglos) (Kalish & Reynolds, 1976). This may suggest that, for Black Americans, death is a significant break between the living and the dead compared, for example, with the Japanese perspective of one's ancestors watching what one does. Black American respondents also indicated that they experience more contact with death than the other ethnic groups. This increased contact with death has certainly not changed in the past 30 years as the death of African American children, adolescents, and younger adults continues at a much higher rate than for other ethnic groups. Within this context of death, hope, supported by prayer and belief in God, still reigns as people express certainty that their loved ones are in a better place.

End-of-Life Practices

African Americans are more likely than other ethnic groups to turn to friends, church members, neighbors, and other nonrelated folks in times of need (Dilworth-Anderson, Gibson, & Burke, 2006) and this does not change for end-of-life caregiving. Both family and non-kin community members provide support for African Americans at the end of life. Although in general, older people choose quality of life when considering the care that they want at the end of life, African Americans are less likely to have advance care directives that limit procedures and are more likely to request aggressive, invasive interventions that prolong life, even when death is imminent (Hooyman & Kiyak, 2008). Some believe that this reflects their psychological disposition to continue to work through difficulties in the face of overwhelming adversity (e.g., John Henryism), whereas others suggest that a lifetime of experiencing racism in institutional settings may make African Americans unlikely to trust physicians and other healthcare providers when they suggest that palliative or hospice care is indeed the best care for themselves or their loved ones: "In contrast to a peaceful death, aggressive medical treatment ('fighting while going down' as an expected part of life's ongoing struggle) is often viewed as a sign of respect among African Americans, even if it means feeding tubes, pain, and loss of life savings" (Hooyman & Kiyak, 2008, p. 553). Others point to religious beliefs that God is the ultimate decider of life and death and to religious prohibitions against anything that might be seen as hastening death. Thus, although the causes for these differences are complex, African Americans are less likely to have advance care directives like living wills and are less likely to enter hospice programs than White Americans. As most African Americans have passed through the hospital immediately prior to death or actually die in the hospital, Perry (1993) reported that "going to the hospital" has come to mean dying for many African Americans.

Rituals around Death Given their support networks and the importance of the church community, it should not be surprising that African Americans turn to their religious community when death is imminent. A clergy member will come to the hospital to be with the person who is dying, and other church members may go to the home to help support the family both emotionally and practically (e.g., with food). After the person has died, employees from the mortuary or the funeral home come to pick up the body. Mortuaries owned and run by African Americans have a long-standing presence in the African American community.

Many experts ground African Americans' funeral practices in their African roots, in their experience of slavery practices, and in their lifelong experience of racism. Funeral services are very important for African Americans. In addition to providing a place for the community to gather, mourn, and grieve together (common characteristics of funerals across different ethnic groups), there is some discussion that African American funerals are also important for extolling the worth of the person, perhaps recapturing the self-esteem that a lifetime of being oppressed due to the color of one's skin has diminished. Funerals are a place to notice that a person of worth has died. As such, the funeral is traditionally the focal point in African Americans' external expression of grief. Expectations are extremely high that all family members, loved ones, and even acquaintances do everything possible to attend.

Several unique customs are a part of African American funerals, especially in the South (Perry, 1993, pp. 63–64):

> "Flower girls"—the female counterparts of pallbearers—give special attention to the closest family members. "Nurses" in white dresses care for those who may be overcome by emotion. The reader of the obituary generally is chosen from within the same "social class" or as a member of the school class of the deceased adult, adolescent, or child. Solos, choir renditions, or other musical offerings are important. Flowers add significantly to the ambience.

For African Americans who are Protestant (e.g., Baptist, Methodist), there is no specific denominational procedure to follow in a funeral; thus, without religious restriction the family can select the music, participants, and place of service. Typically, the minister leads the procession from the church to the hearse and from the hearse to the gravesite. A viewing of the body often occurs at the close of the church service, prior to the procession to the cemetery. For Catholic African Americans, the religious ceremony is much more restricted, with even choices of music likely to be determined by the priest who conducts the service.

As in any community, the cost of these funeral services can be quite prohibitive, requiring the purchase of a coffin and the service fees for embalming, transport of the body (from the hospital and to the cemetery), burial, and the purchase of a burial plot. The average funeral costs approximately $5,000, although extras like flowers, service costs, and upgrades to the casket can easily result in a $10,000 funeral. The fact that many in the African American community cannot afford these costs has not escaped notice. Many feel that ostentatious funerals are not appropriate, but the costs of even relatively simple funerals can be steep, especially if advanced planning has not been done. When a loved one who has been important to us (e.g., a parent, a child, a grandparent) has just died, wishes to provide "the best" for this person can override our rational knowledge of affordability. As we mentioned earlier, African Americans experience death more frequently than other ethnic groups and also have fewer economic resources at their disposal. Thus, the cost of funerals to the community is significant. Sometimes financial collections are taken at the viewing to help the family pay these expenses. Families will go into considerable debt to honor their deceased loved ones.

Bereavement and Coping   There is considerable diversity within the African American community regarding the bereavement expressed at funerals and following the loss of a loved one. African American funerals are often portrayed as events where grief emotions are strongly and freely expressed to the extent that close family members may collapse upon viewing the body. This level of emotional expression is not typical of all African American religious groups. Some groups within the African American community disdain this emotional display and value a more restrained public expression of emotion (Nelsen, 1993). Others find that the public expression of emotions is expected, with funeral attenders commenting that the surviving family members must not have cared much for their deceased relative because they did not wail and mourn publicly (Perry, 1993).

In addition to the substantial difficulties that all widows face, African American women face further stressors. African American women are typically widowed earlier than White women, and the ratio of widows to widowers is significantly higher among African American women (Hooyman & Kiyak, 2008). Given the decrease in income and access to resources that occurs when a spouse dies, African American women are likely to experience more financial difficulties than White women and will have to face these difficulties over a longer period of time. Combined with the high cost of a funeral, death can be a time of considerable financial difficulties for some African Americans.

Aging and Diversity Online: African American Communities and End of Life

Key Topics on End-of-Life Care for African Americans. Derived from "The Last Miles of the Way Home 2004 National Conference to Improve End-of-Life Care for African Americans," this electronically published document gives information about providing end-of-life care for African Americans. http://www.iceol.duke.edu/resources/lastmiles/index.html

Seattle African American Comfort Program (SAACP). The mission of SAACP is to advocate for, create, and coordinate culturally appropriate end-of-life services for African Americans. http://www.saacp.org

ACTIVE LEARNING EXPERIENCE: AFRICAN AMERICAN END-OF-LIFE CARE

The purpose of this experience is to provide an opportunity to consider African American approaches to end-of-life care and rituals around the end of life. Upon completion of this activity, you will be able to:

1. Give examples of end-of-life care and rituals among African Americans.
2. Explain how culture may affect these rituals.

Time required: 45 minutes (30 minutes to complete the questions and 15 minutes to discuss the answers with another person).

Instructions:

1. Read the following case study, either as a homework assignment or in a class setting.
2. Prepare written responses to the questions at the end of the case study on your own or as a part of the class discussion designed for this activity.
3. Discuss your responses with another person.

Case Study

As a 65-year-old African American man, James Taylor has had many life struggles that he has simply had to push through. He now says that he is facing his biggest struggle yet. In the advanced stages of kidney failure, he has politely rejected any suggestions of comfort care from health-care professionals. Even though the doctors say his prognosis is not good and there is very little chance that interventions will sustain his life—let alone give him a good quality of life—he has requested every possible intervention. He has told the hospital staff that he wants to "go down fighting" and that he has struggled throughout life so he does not expect that death should be any different. Reverend Thomas from James's church visits him twice each week and they pray together. James's lifelong faith in God gives him strength, and he knows that God would not give him more than he can handle.

Discussion Questions:

1. Why is James refusing palliative care?
2. Should health-care professionals try to encourage him to use hospice care?
3. How might culture be affecting his decisions?
4. If you were in his situation, would you make similar decisions?
5. If your loved ones were in his situation, would you recommend that they take a different course of action?

Hispanic Americans

Beliefs About Life and Death

Que triste seria la vida si no existeria la muerte (How sad life would be if there were no death).

Kalish and Reynolds (1976, p. 158)

In contrast to the Anglo American culture that, at the very least, tries to avoid all aspects of death, the Hispanic culture acknowledges and recognizes death. Predominantly Catholic, Latin American culture contains a unique mix of Indian and Catholic ritual, both of which recognize the importance of death and their belief in life after death. For example, the Mexican holiday *Dia de los Muertos* (Day of the Dead) has Aztec roots. Combined with the Catholic "All Saints Day" and "All Souls Day," Dia de los Muertos is celebrated on November 1 and 2. Although individual villages may have unique rituals associated with this holiday, the celebration revolves around the spirits of the dead and honoring one's deceased relatives. During this time, the spirits of the dead are expected to visit and families should be prepared to make them comfortable. In each home, an altar is made with offerings for the spirits that include their favorite food and drinks, toys for children who have died, and bottles of beer or tequila for adults. Special sweet breads, called *pan de muerto,* are made. For families who have experienced a death in the past year, the holiday takes on particular importance as a time to honor and remember that person. The gravesites of family members and ancestors are cleaned and decorated, often with orange-yellow marigolds, the family member's favorite foods, and other offerings. Skulls, skeletons, and other symbols of death are commonly used as decorations, as are more traditional religious symbols such as crucifixes or statues of the Virgin Mary. On November 2, family members visit the gravesites, sometimes bringing guitars or radios to play favorite music and to share memories of the person. Viewed from outside of the cultural context, picnicking in the cemetery may seem strange to some, but understood within a cultural background it is a ritual celebration.

What does *Dia de los Muertos* have to do with Hispanic American beliefs about life and death? This holiday provides a concrete example of the large presence and role that death is given in the Hispanic or Latino community. Although the death of a loved one is still met with sorrow and grief, death is viewed as a natural part of life, as suggested by the quote at the beginning of this section. Of course, acculturation to the United States can result in changes to traditional rituals. During their study, Kalish and Reynolds could not find any evidence of the unique Day of the Dead rituals practiced in their sample. These holidays were treated as all Catholics in the United States do (i.e., attending a special mass to honor the dead) but without the unique cultural additions from Mexico. But in the past 20 years, Dia de los Muertos celebrations have cropped up in Mexican American communities around the country and even all over the world. Although in this chapter we focus primarily on Mexican Americans (the largest Hispanic group in the United States), other Hispanic groups (e.g., Cuban Americans, Puerto Ricans) share the strong influence of the Catholic religion with a unique blending of indigenous rituals that include the belief in life after death.

End-of-Life Practices   As with other aspects of life, family is the centerpiece around Latino end-of-life care, together with religion and the expression of emotions. The family is the locus of emotional support, warmth, and shared activity, so the family typically plays an integral role in all end-of-life care. Mexican Americans were less likely (than Blacks, Japanese Americans, or Anglo Americans) to think that a terminally ill person should be told that their condition was fatal, and they were less likely to want to know themselves if they had a fatal condition (Kalish & Reynolds, 1976). They thought that knowing of one's impending death makes it harder for the person and harder for those close to them. This may relate to the concept of fatalism discussed earlier in the chapters on health. If death is indeed a natural part of life, then we all are going to die, and there is no point in giving people extra stress in knowing that they will die from their condition.

End-of-life care decisions also must reflect the religious beliefs of Latinos, and although some are Protestant or not religiously affiliated, most are Catholic. As such, they have strong prohibitions against doing anything that may be seen as hastening the end of life. With the availability of medical technology in the United States, it can be difficult to convey the complexities of end-of-life care options as some may view ending intravenous feeding or fluids as hastening death, and others may view it as providing comfort to a body that can no longer process these nutrients. Thus, it is essential that health-care providers who serve Latino communities, at the very least, have interpreters who can explain these options. Promoting stronger ties with the religious community that might allow accurate conveyance of religious prohibitions on end-of-life care prior to hospital admission (rather than relying on family members' perceptions of religious doctrine at a very emotional time) is important.

Rituals Around Death   When a person is very ill, both family members and the priest are called to be with the person. Depending on the family's background, a *santero* or a *curandero* may also be called to help dispel bad spirits from the individual (Younoszai, 1993). If in a hospital, often the family will "camp in" to make sure that a family member is always with the loved one. From the Catholic perspective, it is considered very important that a dying individual receive a special sacrament for healing provided by a priest prior to death. A sacrament can be defined as a religious ceremony that gives a particular grace to the person. Baptism is one example of a sacrament. Commonly known as *last rites*, the Anointing of the Sick is a sacrament for those who are ill, including physical and mental illnesses, and it is meant to provide both spiritual and physical healing. Considered extremely important for admission into heaven, this ritual provides an opportunity for the person to ask for forgiveness for the sins he or she has committed and helps prepare the person to enter heaven.

After the person has died, the body is usually taken to a mortuary or funeral home for funeral preparation. Traditionally, after the body has been cleaned, the family would return to dress the body in funeral clothes. As with other religious and ethnic groups, a wake is often held prior to the funeral. In Puerto Rico and Cuba, long wakes of at least 48 hours are common. For Puerto Rican wakes, the family may abstain from food or beverages to show respect for the dead. Typically, the rosary is said as part of the wake, and the casket is open during the wake.

The funeral is also an important community event, with people coming from far away to attend funerals, especially for elders who have died. Usually a funeral includes a full Catholic funeral mass and burial in Catholic cemetery, all of which is conducted by a Catholic priest. Some groups have wakes that continue (in the cemetery or at the family's home) for 24 hours after the deceased has been buried. At Latino Catholic wakes and funerals, emotional expressions of grief are common and accepted (Younoszai, 1993). For Latino Protestants, controlling one's emotions is valued. Although Kalish and Reynolds (1976) reported that many Mexican Americans were concerned about exposing children under the age of 10 to emotion-filled death scenes, others reported seeing young children frequently at funerals (Younoszai, 1993). Thus, there is evidence that children are included and brought to funerals and that the culturally important reverence for the dead may be taught from generation to generation in this way. Taking photographs of the deceased is another way to honor and remember the person who died. Given the expense of funerals and the low income of many Latino Americans, relatives and other community members may donate money to make sure that a "proper" burial occurs. Proper remembrance and honoring of the dead is also important for many Latino Americans. This may be done by attending mass on All Saints Day and All Souls Day, by dedicating a mass to loved ones on the anniversary of their death, and by visiting their gravesites.

Aging and Diversity Online: Latino Communities and End of Life

Hispanic Diversity Notes. The National Resource Center on Diversity in End-of-life Care, originally funded by the Robert Wood Johnson Foundation, created this document to help service providers understand culturally appropriate end-of-life care for Hispanic people. http://nrcd.com/HispanicDiversityNotes.doc

Spanish Language Resources on End-of-Life Care. Also created by the National Resource Center on Diversity in End-of-life Care, this document provides Spanish language resources around end-of-life care. http://www.nrcd.com/DiversityNotes-SpanishLanguageResources.pdf

---

American Indians and Alaska Natives

Beliefs About Life and Death When considering beliefs about life and death, treating people who are of American Indian or Alaska Native heritage as if they are from one group is inappropriate. Each tribe or nation has its distinct values and beliefs about life and death. For example, the Apache believe that a dead person's body is an empty shell, whereas the Lakota still value the body. They "speak to the body, visit it, and understand it to be sacred" (Brokenleg & Middleton, 1993, p. 103). Whereas most American Indian or Alaska Native groups believe in an afterlife, the Navajo do not. While the Chiricahua, Lipan, Mescalero, and Jicarilla Apache tribes express little anxiety concerning their own death, many Navajos and Pueblos demonstrate a great deal of fear regarding death. Fearing ghosts, traditional Navajos are quick to bury the dead, since they believe the dead may have negative effects on the living. Such fears also extend to the terminally ill, who may spend the final few days of their lives in hospitals or shelters away from home. Pueblo Indians demonstrate a fear of dying, death, and the dead as well, but not to the extent of Navajos (Markides & Mindel, 1987). In addition, individuals may have also assimilated to the mainstream culture in varying degrees, so it can be difficult to determine whether someone still holds traditional beliefs and cultural values.

To describe each tribal group's end-of-life attitudes and behaviors is beyond the scope of this chapter. Instead, we describe one group, the Lakota (also known as the Sioux), with the acknowledgement of the diversity present both between and within tribal groups. For people who provide services to American Indian or Alaska Native groups, it is important to understand the beliefs and practices of the group in their region of the country. For the Lakota, death is viewed as a natural aspect of the human experience, part of the balanced cycle of nature. For all who die, both animal and human, there is an automatic afterlife not tied to one's performance in this life.

End-of-Life Practices

When death appears imminent, terminally ill Lakota distribute valuables to family members and friends to show acceptance of upcoming death and to demonstrate appreciation to those with whom there has been a significant relationship. As the time of death approaches, family and friends gather with the person who is dying. This gathering is very important yet may not be understood by hospital staff. Understanding the cultural importance of this ritual is important, as there may be 20 or more family and friends present. If a Lakota were to die alone, the family would suffer tremendous grief as a result. Upon the death of a loved one, the extended Lakota family members gather for the wake and funeral. Even very young children attend wakes and funerals and thus are exposed to the rituals and learn appropriate behavior at a young age. The Lakota family includes all to whom one is related, including second and third cousins, and every family member makes a sincere effort to come to the funeral. Some even travel from different continents. Perhaps 500 to 1,000 mourners attend ceremonies, and the family is responsible for feeding those in attendance. Flowers are typically not a part of the ritual, though it is common for friends to donate money to help the family with the various costs of the funeral. Ceremonies take place at the home reservation, even if the family of the departed has lived away for several generations (Brokenleg & Middleton, 1993).

Christian clergy are more likely than medicine men to be involved substantially in various death rituals, with most Lakota families practicing a blend of tribal and Christian beliefs. Tribal customs do not allow for cremation, since the body is sacred and is the home of the deceased. Mourning is believed to be natural, and unrestrained expressions of grief can be seen by both men and women (Brokenleg & Middleton, 1993).

Traditionally, there is a 3-day-long wake, which is typically not held at a funeral home due to the number of people in attendance. Tribal songs and Christian hymns are sung, prayers are offered, and fond memories of the deceased are shared. A meal is served, along with cigarettes (tobacco use belongs to a centuries-old tradition). Because the spirits of dead family members may be in attendance at the wake, portions of food to feed them are placed outside the building where the wake is held. Mourners view the body and are permitted to touch, kiss, and embrace it. Important objects such as jewelry or locks of a mourner's hair may be placed in the casket. Brokenleg and Middleton (1993, p. 108) described several Lakota grieving customs in the following passage:

As each person greets the family mourners, the mourners' expression of grief is renewed in intensity. Cutting the hair, cutting or scratching the forearms and face, tearing clothing, and wearing black are common and appropriate outward displays of grief. These are not empty displays, but rather the ritualized expressions of deep grief.

At the funeral, grief is generally subdued except for during the final hymn, when wailing may return. Friends and relatives assist at the gravesite by helping to fill in the grave and do not leave until the burial is complete. At the gravesite, both men and women mourn and express their emotions freely and grieve the loss of their loved one.

Aging and Diversity Online: Native Americans and End-of-Life Care

Native American Palliative Care and End-of-Life Curriculum. Available from the Native American Cancer Research site, this curriculum evolved from the End-of-Life Nursing Education Consortium (ELNEC). It covers many end-of-life issues for Native Americans, including culturally appropriate ways to talk about the end of life. http://natamcancer.org/ap/EOL_intro_10-18-04_ FAC/slides.html

Bristol Bay Helping Hands Program. Sponsored by the Bristol Bay Area Health Corporation, also called *Ikayurtem Unatai* (Helping hands in Yup'ik), this project responded to the needs of people who were dying in the rural villages of Southwest Alaska to find ways to allow people to remain in their homes and communities instead of in the hospital in larger cities. http://www.promotingexcellence.org/i4a/pages/Index.cfm?pageID=3593

Asian Americans

The way older people and others handle the prospect of death varies from culture to culture, depending on their worldview, religious orientation, and metaphysical conceptions regarding this world and the next world. As discussed in Chapter 8 on religious affiliation and spirituality, a large proportion of Asian immigrants and refugees from countries such as India, Nepal, Pakistan, Bangladesh, Vietnam, Cambodia, and Japan are Hindus, Buddhists, and Muslims. Note that Asian immigrants from the Philippines are predominantly Catholic (Becker, 2002); they are not included in the discussion that follows. As growing numbers of these immigrants and refugees become frail and their awareness of death gradually becomes ever present, it becomes increasingly important to understand their views about the approach of death and associated rituals. Before we examine death-related attitudes, beliefs, and rituals for each of these groups, it is important to draw your attention to the following questions, which are highly relevant in this regard.

- At what age did a given individual from this population come to the United States?
- Was this move voluntary or involuntary?
- What do we know about the socioeconomic status of the person?

- To what degree is the individual able to maintain ongoing contact with other members of his or her population, thereby sustaining a sense of self and ethnic identity?
- Does the individual have an extended family in the United States that may symbolize place, tradition, and continuity?
- What is known about the availability of traditional ritual practices and services in the United States and in the community where the individual resides?

We begin with a discussion of the Hindu tradition and then focus on the Buddhist view of life and death before proceeding to review Islamic perspectives. Please note that what we present in the following sections are generalized viewpoints and practices from the three groups. This does not mean that each member of a given group follows these practices in the same way; there are substantial differences within each of these groups.

Hindu Tradition

Beliefs about Life and Death   In the Hindu tradition, old age is seen as a period of preparation for death and as such a propitious time for planning, reflecting, reviewing, and summing up. Although death may occur at any stage of life, there is a natural tendency to associate old age with death and dying. In fact, an old Hindu text features the image of old age as a ferryman carrying individuals to the other shore to death. The ferryman is not a person but a personification; he or she is old age incarnate, and it is old age that carries us to death. Note that this imagery depicts a positive appreciation of the role of old age.

If old age is the final act of the human drama, then death is the final curtain (Tilak, 1989). Accordingly, death is viewed as a form of erosion whereby life and the body are gradually worn away. Thus, death is the inevitable end product of the aging process. As you may recall from Chapter 8, Hindus believe in reincarnation. For them death represents a transition from one life to another. When a person dies, the body dissolves into its constituent parts, only to rejoin their cosmic counterparts. In the next birth, these same elements are drawn out of the cosmos and recombined into a new living organism; thus, every birth is a rebirth. Conversely, death is never final but repeated. Cremation of a dead person is, therefore, seen as a form of sacrifice. A person performs this final sacrifice to ensure the continued existence of the universe. Viewing death as sacrifice also helps Hindus in allaying the fear of death while they are still alive. In other words, they view death as some sort of transition from one mode of life to another. This, in turn, contributes to increased acceptance of death. As discussed in Chapter 8, Hindus have an explicit set of beliefs regarding the four stages of life:

1. Student stage: Here the goal is to acquire knowledge and skills to meet the demands of life.
2. Householder stage: The person is fully engaged in the pleasure, duties, and success of raising a family, working at a vocation, and serving the community.

3. Retirement stage: Here the person makes a transition from the household duties to a more retiring and contemplative mode of life.

4. Renunciation stage: At this stage, the emphasis is on withdrawing from activities and pleasures. This withdrawal allows older persons to concentrate on the spiritual life, fix their mind on God, and approach death without anxiety, as it is simply a passage into the next life. (See the active learning exercise at the end of the following section.)

End-of-Life Practices   Many Hindus prefer to die at home rather than in a hospital, nursing home, or a hospice. Some prefer to go back to India, especially to the sacred city of Varanasi, to die. Often elders and others who are terminally ill may put significant effort into restoring any relationships or other personal matters. This allows them to die full of love and acceptance rather than full of anger or fear. As noted earlier, the belief that they have already been born and have died many times in the past contributes to increased acceptance. A good death is a conscious death entered willingly, after having dealt with unfinished business and saying goodbyes to relatives and friends. In the Bhagavad Gita, Krishna says, "And whoever, at the time of death, gives up his body and departs, thinking of me alone he comes to my status of being; of that there is no doubt (Firth, 1999, p. 161)." Traditionally, a person near death is placed with her or his head facing east and a lamp placed near the head. Family members are generally present as death nears. Often family members help the dying person keep God in mind by chanting, singing hymns, or reading from a favorite text, especially Bhagavad Gita (Firth, 1999). They perform rituals such as placing water from the sacred Ganges River in the dying person's mouth and applying sandalwood paste or sacred ash to the forehead. Traditionally, the person who is dying will chant his or her own *mantra* (a personal, sacred phrase). If this is not possible, a family member may softly chant the mantra in his or her right ear (Kemp & Bhungalia, 2002).

After death, the family members should be the only persons to touch the body. Ideally, a family member of the same sex cleans the body, dresses it according to the wishes of the person, wraps it in a red cloth, and places it with the head facing up. If the person dies in a hospital, the family members obtain the death certificate as soon as possible and bring the body home rather than to a funeral home. The ceremony at home includes prayers, incense, chanting, and singing sacred songs. In the Hindu tradition, the preference is for cremation and for spreading the ashes over the holy river Ganges in India. Often the men and the boys of the family shave their hair as a symbol of mourning for the deceased person. The mourning family generally invites a *Brahmán* (Hindu priest) to perform prayers and a blessing (Kemp & Bhungalia, 2002). This is then followed by preparing a meal and inviting friends and relatives to eat together. Many families also celebrate the 1-year anniversary of the death of their elders by providing food and clothing to *Brahmáns* and those less fortunate.

ACTIVE LEARNING EXPERIENCE: ACCEPTANCE OF DEATH BY HINDU ELDERS

The purpose of this experience is to enhance your understanding of how Hindu elders in the renunciation stage accept death as a part of life by withdrawing from activities and pleasures and meditating for the sake of realizing the supreme reality. Upon completion of this learning activity, you will be able to:

1. Describe the attitudes, behaviors, and practices of Hindus during the renunciation stage.
2. Explain their views regarding death.
3. Outline how Hindu views regarding death differ from those of the mainstream population.

Time required: 30 minutes (15 minutes to answer the questions in groups and 15 minutes to discuss the answers with another person).

Instructions:

1. Read the following case study, either as a homework assignment or in a class setting.
2. Prepare written responses to the questions at the end of the case study on your own or as a part of the class discussion designed for this activity.
3. Discuss your responses with another person.

Case Study

Mrs. Kapoor, aged 70, is a Hindu widow who came from India to the United States to live with her son in Washington, D.C., when her husband died. She devotes most of her time to reading religious books and doing prayers at home. She goes to the Hindu temple in a neighboring community when she has transportation. She believes that God gives us a body and *atma* (soul) and that when the body is dead and burned the atma remains eternal. If you are too attached to people and material things, death is very painful because you know you have to leave everybody and everything behind. On the other hand, if you start giving up things, you feel a different kind of happiness—the stronger the attachment, the more intense the pain. Mrs. Kapoor appears content and believes that, if death is in God's hands, why fight it? When her time comes and she dies, she would like her son to take her body to India for cremation in the holy city of Varanasi and spread her ashes over the river Ganges (*Ganga Ma*). She has instructed her son accordingly. He has graciously agreed to follow her wishes.

Discussion Questions:

1. How does Mrs. Kapoor spend her time at this stage of life?
2. What are her attitudes toward life and death?
3. In what ways do Hindu views regarding death differ from views of the mainstream population?

Buddhist Tradition   As you may recall from Chapter 8, Buddhists in the United States have come from countries such as Sri Lanka, Myanmar (formerly Burma), Tibet, Nepal, India, Thailand, Cambodia, Laos, Vietnam, Korea, China, and Japan. Although they are all Buddhists, there are within-group differences in their beliefs and traditions. However, all of them share the central focus of attaining a clear, calm mind that is undisturbed by worldly events and full of compassion. The underlying belief is that skillful actions that do not cause further suffering for the practitioners and other living beings will naturally result from this state rather than from an agitated or unclear mind.

Buddhists believe in the impermanence of all forms, feelings, and mental constraints. During his lifetime, the Buddha also instructed his followers to embrace suffering as the true meaning of existence and to contemplate death as a means of understanding impermanence. Dying and death thus become the only real purpose of the birth and life process. In the moment of death, all is achieved, for which the whole course of life was only the preparation and introduction. Disease, old age, and death are the résumé of life. Buddhist literature provides a poignant story (Narada, 1973, p. 657):

> A young widow lost her only infant. In her grief she approached Buddha and asked him for a remedy. He said to her "Well, sister, can you bring some mustard seed?" She replied "Certainly, Lord." He then added "But, sister, it should be from a house where no one has died." She, of course, found mustard seeds but not from a place where death had not visited. She understood the nature of life: death is part of the life cycle.

As the story illustrates, Buddhist teachings on death are derived from an understanding of impermanence and reject all cosmetic masks for the realities of death and decay. It is emphasized that ultimately enlightenment can be gained from a proper orientation to this universal experience. In other words, we must look death in the face, recognize it, and accept it, just as we accept life. As we had noted for Hindus, Karma is the most central belief for Buddhists as well. According to this belief, individuals' actions in previous lives and the resulting store of merit that they have accumulated determine their current life situation. In other words, individuals' actions in a previous life inform the next life. In addition, the state of mind of the dying person at the moment of death is also thought to influence the rebirth process—thus, the better the state of mind, the better the chances of a favorable rebirth. To produce a calming effect on the dying person's mind, monks, relatives, and friends chant certain *sutras* (recorded teachings of the Buddha). These *sutras* are also expected to protect the listener by driving away evil influences and directing the mind to Buddha's teachings. Often this preparation serves as an initiation of the dying person to the transition from birth to rebirth. Instructions are read to help guide the person through the transitional state between life forms. The goal of the instructions is to initiate the consciousness of the dying person to the great opportunity of a favorable rebirth that lies ahead. Given this focus on rebirth, elaborations of this ceremony continue for 49 days until rebirth is assured. In a sense, death becomes the highlight of life, a great opportunity for realizing pure enlightenment through attainment of the Buddha mind.

As we noted in earlier sections of this chapter, people's views of death are shaped by culture and religious affiliation Through in-depth interviews with a sample of Cambodian American Buddhists over a 1-year period, Becker (2002) found that they appear to view death as a form of continuity rather than as a discontinuity. Not only do they emphasize the continuous aspects of life rather than the finality of death through their religious belief in reincarnation; they also anticipate a better life next time. In a way, they attempt to cope with the problem of death by linking existence to something that transcends it. Furthermore, members of the ethnic community play a critical role in people's anticipation of death. They evoke powerful images of continuity through a variety of rituals when the person is dying as well as after his or her death. In Becker's study, many Cambodian Americans expressed a desire to die in their home country. Whether or not they desired to return to the homeland to die was mediated by the presence or absence of the extended family, members of the homeland, and the availability of traditional ritual practices in the United States. This preoccupation with where to die apparently reflects the desire to create continuity in their lives. It also appeared to reflect a desire to bring closure to unresolved conflicts in their lifetime.

Like Cambodian Americans, Vietnamese Americans Buddhists also see death as a fortunate and fitting natural phase of the life cycle. It should be noted that many Vietnamese Catholics also endorse Buddhist concepts as well as practices. Buddhist concepts such as reincarnation, Karma, and enduring suffering all play important roles in how they view life and death. In a study conducted in Hawaii by Braun and Nichols (1996), both Catholic and Buddhist Vietnamese elders said that preparation for death included praying and preparing wills for distribution of property. The act of making concrete preparation for one's own death is viewed as a common responsibility that elders carry out for themselves as well as for their children. Although they may prepare for rituals of death, active end-of-life care planning is a foreign and unfamiliar undertaking for most Vietnamese families. Braun and Nichols found that few Vietnamese elders were aware of their options with regard to advance directives. This may be attributable to a great extent to reliance on their children for interpretation and the possibility that their children may be uncomfortable with the subject matter.

End-of-Life Practices   A key issue in dying for many Buddhists is to maintain consciousness. They believe that this will allow them to go through the process of dying with equanimity and "wholesome thoughts." Such thoughts include awareness of the transient nature of existence, reflection on past good efforts, and letting go of life "without clinging and grasping." Everything is done to ensure a calm and peaceful environment of the dying person. Caregivers are concerned about the comfort and state of mind of the one being cared for. A noted monk or lay religious leader may chant or lead chants to help promote a peaceful or insightful state of mind at the time of death. Many families burn incense in the room and place images of Buddha near the dying person. Upon death, people other than Buddhists may also touch the body, and there is no definitive belief about how the body should be treated (except, of course, with respect) and when it should be buried or cremated. The question of burial or cremation is more cultural than religious. For example, Becker (2002) found cremation to be the general practice in her sample of Buddhist Cambodian Americans in California. To help you develop an understanding of the death ritual among Buddhist Cambodian Americans, we next present an example of such a ritual adapted from Becker (2002).

> Following a person's death, a monk from the temple visits the family daily until the following Saturday when the funeral takes place. Also, when a person dies, a son, grandson, or a nephew becomes a monk for a day to help the deceased go to heaven. Early on the day of the funeral, that person has his head shaved, is then dressed in a Buddhist robe, and prays with two monks at the temple. Such prayers are followed by a ceremonial feast at the home. At that time, more prayers are offered on behalf of the deceased. Another service is held at the funeral home where the family prays over the casket and says goodbye to the deceased. The visitors place a flower inside the coffin and offer a prayer for the deceased before the lid is closed. They give monetary offerings to the immediate family to help provide food for the family members and the visitors. The adult child then accompanies the deceased to the crematorium where he is responsible for pushing the casket into the flames. A full 100 days after the death, the monk comes to the family home for prayer. He again returns for a 2-hour ceremony on Sunday morning to pray, speak, and sprinkle holy water on everyone who is present and also on the outside of the house. He then eats a bite of the food that has been prepared for the family members and the guests.

When people were cremated in Cambodia, their ashes were kept at the temple. In the United States, the temples are not available in many communities, and, when available, these temples have limited space. Many families in the United States, therefore, keep ashes at home and create a shrine by placing Buddha and flowers around the container. Eventually, the families try to take the ashes to Cambodia to store them at the temple in the family's village.

As you can see from the previous description, Buddhist Cambodians in the United States try to maintain their traditions and at the same time make necessary adaptations in the given circumstances. A number of authors have described similar rituals for Japanese Americans (e.g., Kalish & Reynolds, 1976) and Vietnamese Americans (e.g., Crawford, 1961) who are Buddhists. A review of these descriptions provides a clear indication of how the ritual practices from the homeland have been modified in light of the availability of the temples, monks, and crematoriums in the community of residence. In this regard, it is also important to note the influence of non-Buddhist customs (e.g., processions, formal dinners, anniversary ceremonies) in the rituals practiced by Japanese Americans, Vietnamese Americans, and Cambodian Americans who are Buddhists. Furthermore, there is considerable variability regarding the extent to which these influences are seen in Buddhist families. For example, Kalish and Reynolds (1976) reported substantial differences across four generations of Buddhist Japanese Americans. Similarly, Truitner and Truitner (1993) reported that a large number of customs practiced in Vietnam, such as processions and anniversary ceremonies, had non-Buddhist origins. In addition, many Vietnamese Americans often carry out funeral and anniversary observances without the monks' presence. While funeral practices vary significantly from family to family for Buddhists in the United Sates, the importance of anniversary services is maintained consistently. Most Buddhist Americans feel a need to maintain these customs that reflect both their cultural and religious identities.

ACTIVE LEARNING EXPERIENCE: A JAPANESE AMERICAN BUDDHIST FUNERAL*

The purpose of this experience is to provide you with an opportunity to analyze a case regarding the Buddhist funeral of a Japanese American. Upon completion of this activity, you will be able to:

1. Describe Buddhist burial customs common to many Japanese Americans.
2. Compare these customs with those practiced by your family or religion.

Time required: 30 minutes (20 minutes to read the case and prepare group answers to the questions and 10 minutes for a general class discussion).

Instructions:

1. The instructor divides the class into groups of three to five.
2. Each group selects a member who is to be responsible for writing down the group's answers and for reporting them to the class.
3. Groups answer the questions following the case.
4. Group recorders report their group's answers to the class.
5. The instructor leads a discussion reflecting group responses.

Case Study

Kiyoshi Yamada has died of liver cancer. Kiyoshi emigrated 10 years ago at 63 years of age from a small town on the main island of Japan to

---

* Megumi Kondo designed this learning activity.

New York City to be with his eldest son and a number of other family members.

After Kiyoshi's death at home, all of his New York relatives have come to his home to maintain a vigil over his dead body. A Buddhist priest comes and chants a *sutra*, and some of Kiyoshi's family members and friends join in the chanting. Kiyoshi's oldest son, Kazuo, notifies the head of the community of his father's death.

Kazuo calls the crematorium to schedule the cremation. Kiyoshi's body is wrapped in a white kimono, with a white cloth for the forehead, white wrist wrappers, and white leggings. These clothes indicate that the soul will travel into the next world. The clothed body is then placed in a coffin located on an altar with the head of the body facing north.

Female relatives and community members have cooked meals to give to those who come by the home to express their goodbyes to Kiyoshi. Only vegetarian meals are served. Family and friends are responsible for making sure that candles and incense are kept burning for 100 days following Kiyoshi's death. The light from the candles serves as a guide to the next world.

Usually, the funeral is held the day after an individual dies. At Kiyoshi's funeral, a black-and-white photograph of him, with black and white ribbon attached, is placed on the altar. His relatives provide white chrysanthemums and pale-colored flowers. A candle and incense are burned, and the priest chants the *sutra* with a wooden gong and a bell. The female relatives wear mourning dresses or kimonos, and the male family members wear black or other dark-colored suits with black mourning bands. Family members burn powdered incense and, using strings of beads, pray for Kiyoshi while the priest chants the *sutra*. Next, Kazuo, the head mourner and Kiyoshi's eldest son, gives a brief eulogy and thanks those present who have come to send his father off to the next world. Then family members place flowers, a few of Kiyoshi's favorite things, and some money into his coffin.

After the funeral service, Kazuo, as the head mourner, carries Kiyoshi's black-and-white photograph to the crematorium. Relatives follow the hearse to the crematorium, and they wait for Kiyoshi's body to be incinerated. After his bones and ashes come out of the incinerator, relatives pray with a string of beads. They pick up some of the remains with very long chopsticks and place them in an urn that is put into a wooden box and wrapped with a white cloth. The family members take it back to their home to be placed in front of the family Buddhist altar.

Discussion Questions:

1. In what ways is Kiyoshi's funeral similar to ones that you have attended?

2. What are some ways this funeral differs from the ones with which you are familiar?
3. Cremation is a central element of Kiyoshi's funeral. Why is cremation a practical choice for disposing of the dead in Japan?

Islamic Tradition   Islam is the second largest religion in the world (after Christianity) and will soon be the second largest religion in America (Esposito, 2002). Approximately two thirds (65%) of adult Muslims living in the United States were born elsewhere, and 39% have come to the United States since 1990. Although a relatively large proportion of Muslim immigrants are from Arab countries, many have also come from Pakistan and other South Asian countries. Among native-born Muslims, slightly more than half are African American (20% of Muslims overall), many of whom are converts to Islam (Pew Research Center, 2007). Since Muslims are and will increasingly be our neighbors, colleagues at work, and fellow citizens, it is important to include a discussion of their beliefs and practices related to death, dying, and bereavement.

Death is frequently discussed within the Islamic tradition; sometimes it appears that a Muslim is taught more about life after death than about life itself. In the Islamic conception, God is the creator and originator of all things. He has not only ultimate authority but also the authority over the beginning, duration, and the final dispensation of all things. The questions related to nature and purpose of life must be framed within this divine perspective. Life has a purpose: the events of human history, both individual and communal, are in the hands of a just and merciful God; death is not the end but the passage into a new and eternal existence. Note that in Islam the emphasis is not on impersonal determinism but on divine prerogative; God ascertains the lifespan of persons and of communities, and it is in His hands where lies the fate of all that He has brought into being.

According to the Qur'an, while life in this world (*dunya'*) provides the first and necessary arena for carrying out the divine will, one's vision should focus on the things to come. The world per se is not to be rejected—the reward of the hereafter (*akhira*) is for those who do not neglect their duties in the world—but one's vision should focus on the joy of the hereafter. Thus, like the concept of Karma in Hinduism, Islam states that as people choose in the *dunya'*, so they will be rewarded both in the *dunya'* and, in greater magnitude, in the *akhira*. In other words, Islamic thinkers emphasize the need to understand the significance of the next life in providing a contract and a sanction for the moral imperative in this life (Smith & Haddad, 1981). However, there is one important difference between Hindu and the Islamic perspectives. According to Islam, we have only one opportunity—that of this world—to earn the recompense that will determine our eternal existence. Thus, Islam has rejected completely the suggestion that human souls will or could be reincarnated in different bodies for the purpose of improving their previous records of performance. Since one gets only one life, it needs to be lived in faith, obedience, and submission. The entire message of the Qur'an supports the idea that we have only one life on Earth and that our assessment will be of the ways

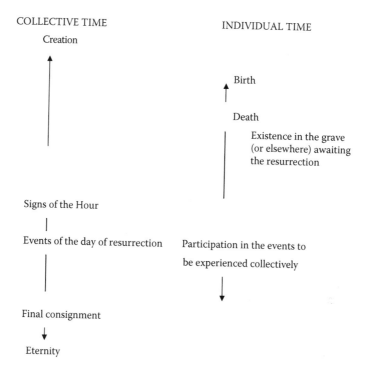

COLLECTIVE TIME

INDIVIDUAL TIME

Creation

Birth

Death

Existence in the grave
(or elsewhere) awaiting
the resurrection

Signs of the Hour

Events of the day of resurrection

Participation in the events to
be experienced collectively

Final consignment

Eternity

Figure 9.1 The Islamic understanding of death and resurrection. Adapted from Smith & Haddad (1981).

we have chosen to live in terms of God's specifications. What happens after death? As the time chart in Figure 9.1 indicates, each individual span includes a period between death and resurrection in which one waits the coming of the hour of resurrection. If we look structurally at the overall conception of time in the Islamic understanding, we see one pattern juxtaposed over another—individual time set within the context of collective time.

In one sense the death of the body, by definition, means a cessation of involvement with *dunya'* and, thus, a necessary entry into the sphere of *akhira*. In another sense, the circumstance of the deceased awaiting resurrection forms another possibility. This circumstance, called *barzakh*, expresses the inability of the departed to return to Earth. The term *barzakh* also refers to the time every person must wait between death and resurrection. In addition, it also includes the concept of place or abode of that waiting. In this regard, a number of modern Muslim authors have stated that *barzakh* is only a prelude to the common resurrection and that both are beyond human comprehension. These authors also understand that some kind of punishment or reward takes place in the grave and the nature of this retribution results directly from the quality of one's' life on earth (Smith & Haddad, 1981). In other words, they emphasize the Quar'anic theme of continuity between this life and the next. Instead of articulating many details of the life after death, modern Islamic writers and theologians are generally more interested in discussing the nature of human responsibility and accountability. Thus, faith in afterlife is essential to being a Muslim and is the incentive for acting responsibly in this life. Drawing on the work of Smith and Haddad (1981), we next outline some key points about Islamic conception of life and death:

1. Human beings have a conscience and inherent sense of justice but need the awareness of the hereafter to maintain high ethical standards. Constant sensitivity to the imminence of the Day of Judgment is essential.
2. They are responsible and intellectually capable of understanding their responsibility. A purposeless life is unimaginable.
3. Human beings are essentially free but not independent. Despite the innate freedom of choice, it is an error to suppose that we are independent creatures fully capable of determining our own affairs. One must act according to the plan and divine rules of conduct laid down for him or her. A failure to recognize God's sovereignty leads to defeat and destruction.
4. Individuals operate in their ethical life from inside the community. As we are not independent from the divine will, neither are we independent from our fellow community members.
5. Human beings are capable of continuing progress toward perfection. This progress is conditioned by faith in the last day and in the possibility of eternal bliss in which perfection can be realized.

End-of-Life Practices In the Islamic tradition, death is viewed merely a transitional stage in a continuous and flowing process. Up to a point the soul and the body together constitute a unit and are indissoluble; then dissolution comes, and that is the end of the life on Earth. But this does not mean that it is the end of life itself. Death is, in fact, a rest from the troubles of life. Thinking about death should bring calmness to the soul because it is merely a journey to another life, a change in the order of life, and a single step on the road to eternity (Smith & Haddad, 1981). In other words, Islam insists on the belief that there is life after death. This belief is concomitant with the belief in the existence of God. It also implies that the soul does not disintegrate at death but is characterized by continuity and awareness. While the brain cells die and disintegrate, the memory continues. It remains alive and constantly reminds us of every deed we have done. Will the soul be sent to heaven or hell? The answer to this question depends on a person's actions and intentions during the lifetime (Smith & Haddad, 1981). It is said that human beings are aware of their death at the time of departure from this world. Those who are afraid of death are those who panic when they are aware of entering the afterworld and the hell it probably holds for them.

As we noted previously, concepts of death and dying, the soul or spirit, and the Day of Judgment are emphasized in the Islamic tradition. The purpose of the funeral ceremony, therefore, is to make the dead person ready for the Day of Judgment. This is, indeed, a matter of very serious concern for every Muslim, especially for Muslim immigrants who live where Islam is not the dominant religion. During their last dying moments, Muslims are to be in the company of a close relative. At that time, the relative prays for God's blessing and reads the Qur'an to remind the dying person about the unity of God and the Prophet Muhammad.

Immediately following the family member's death, the relative performs the following duties (Gilanshah, 1993):

- Turns the body to face toward Mecca.
- Has someone sitting near the body read the Qur'an.
- Closes the body's mouth and eyes and covers the eyes and the face.
- Straightens both legs and stretches both hands by the sides.
- Announces death immediately to all friends and relatives.
- Hastens to bathe the body and cover it with white cotton (*kafan*).

Farah Gilanshah (1993, p. 14) wrote of the importance of ritual bathing of the recently deceased:

> Before the bathing, the relative should have an assurance from the doctor that the person is not alive. There are always two people who wash the dead body. Males always bathe a male and female always bathe a female. It is a sin if females wash a male's body or vice versa. Three kinds of water are used: water with leaves of plum tree; camphorated water; and pure water. If only one kind of water is available, the caretakers are allowed to wash the body three times in the water that is available.

Funeral Ceremonies   Generally, four individuals place the four corners of a bier on their shoulders. No one should walk in front of the bier; while changing shoulders one should therefore walk behind the bier. While carrying the body, all of the carriers repeat *Allah Akbar* (God is great) and pray for his blessing. It is common practice to show the face of the deceased to some close relatives before burial. However, since death is most tragic for those closest to the deceased, spouses, daughters, and sons are not shown the face.

The man who buries the body should be able to stand or sit between the body and the side of the grave. He should not wear shoes at that time. The grave should face Mecca, and the burial should take place between sunrise and sunset on the day of the death or the following day. At the time of the burial, friends and members of the family gather with a religious person, pray, and ask God for forgiveness. Loud lamenting is forbidden, but it is acceptable to cry because it is believed that it allows them to release their sadness. Excessive lamentation is forbidden because it seems to imply that an injustice has been done in taking the life. This, of course, cannot be the case since every death is decreed by God. Other reasons include that it is simply a waste of time to lament the inevitable and that weeping actually worsens the condition of the dead. Thus, instead of excessive lamenting, family members and friends are expected to pray for the deceased and give alms on his or her behalf.

Following the funeral ceremony, all friends and relatives go to the home of the deceased's family. There a meal is prepared for them, and they stay for the whole day or night. Often, close relatives stay with the family for the entire week. This helps the family members in adapting to their new situation.

On the third day after the burial, a ceremony is held at the mosque or the Islamic center where friends and relatives gather to pray. A religious leader reads from the Qur'an and prays for blessing the deceased. It is believed that these prayers help the departed person in the afterworld. Given this belief regarding the life in the afterworld, prayers continue for the first 7 days, after which time a prepared stone is placed to cover the grave and fresh flowers are put on the grave. It is customary for close relatives to wear black clothing for 40 days. After 40 days, they again gather in the cemetery or at the house of the departed to pray from the Qur'an and ask for God's blessings. Thereafter, all except close relatives change their clothes to a color other than black. However, widows often wear black for a year. One year after the person's death, another ceremony is conducted to pray for and remember the departed person. All through the year, it is recommended that friends and relatives pray for the deceased, give money to the poor, and ask for God's blessing. In short, Islamic traditions indicate that family members pray for the deceased and give alms on his or her behalf. (See the active learning experience at the end of this section.)

ACTIVE LEARNING EXPERIENCE: TEACHING CHILDREN TO PRAY FOR THEIR DECEASED PARENTS

The purpose of this experience is to enhance your understanding of the Islamic tradition concerning the duty of a son to pray for his dead father as well as to give alms on his behalf. Upon completion of this activity, you will be able to:

1. Describe the role of community experience in the Islamic tradition.
2. Explain what is expected of adult children after the death of their parents.

Time required: 30 minutes (15 minutes to answer the questions in groups and 15 minutes to discuss the answers with another person).

Instructions:

1. Read the following case study, either as a homework assignment or in a class setting.
2. Prepare written responses to the questions at the end of the case study on your own or as a part of the class discussion designed for this activity.
3. Discuss your responses with another person.

Case Study

Dr. Raza Khan, a wise man, saw in a dream a cemetery where suddenly the graves opened, and the dead men from his community came out of them. They sat on the edges of their graves, and each one of them had before them a light. Raza saw among them one of his neighbors, who was deceased, with no light in front of him. He asked the neighbor, "Why do I not see any light in front of you?" The neighbor said, "These others have children and friends who pray for them and give alms on their behalf, and their light is produced by that. I have only one son and he is no good; he does not pray for me and does not give alms on my behalf. I have, therefore, no light in front of me, which makes me ashamed in front of my neighbors." When Raza woke up, he called the man's son and told him what he had seen in the dream. The son promptly said, "I will mend my ways and will not continue doing what I have been doing." He then became obedient and started praying for his father and giving alms on his behalf. Sometime later Raza again saw the same graveyard in his dream. This time he saw the same man with a light brighter than the sun and greater than the light of his companions. And the man said, "Oh, Raza, may God reward you well for me. Because of what you said to my son, I am saved from the shame in front of my neighbors" (based on a story provided by Smith & Haddad, 1981.)

Discussion Questions:

1. What is the duty of the son for his deceased parents? How does this duty in the Islamic tradition differ from the practices followed by the mainstream population?
2. What does this story tell you about the role of the community?
3. In what ways does the story use a common sequence of successive dreams showing a situation before and after the event?
4. What themes stayed with you after reading the story?

SUMMARY

In this chapter we focused on the end of life. We examined beliefs about life and death, discussed how care is provided to those who are dying, outlined practices and rituals associated with end of life, and described how friends and family members cope with the loss of a loved one. To help you develop an understanding of the similarities and differences in attitudes, beliefs, and practices observed across different ethnic and religious groups, we began by focusing on the mainstream U.S. population. This chapter examined the roots of contemporary American death customs, discussed beliefs about life and death, presented services provided by hospice and palliative care programs, and discussed how individuals indicate their choice about end-of-life care through advance care directives. We concluded this section by summarizing research on coping with the loss of a loved one and underscored the limited availability of programs and services designed to provide support to those affected by the loss of a spouse, partner or a friend.

We then turned our attention to beliefs, attitudes, practices, and rituals among diverse cultural groups in the United States. As in the previous chapters, we first focused on African Americans, Hispanic Americans, and American Indian and Alaska Natives. We then proceeded to discuss three major Asian American groups: Hindu Americans, Buddhist Americans, and Muslim Americans. For each group we examined beliefs about life and death, end-of-life practices and rituals around death, and ways of bereavement and coping. Note that what we presented are generalized viewpoints and practices for each group. It does not mean that each member of the group follows the same practices. Examples of factors influencing the practices for a given person include his or her religious background, socioeconomic status, the level of acculturation, community location (rural vs. urban), and access to culturally specific programs and services.

ACTIVE LEARNING EXPERIENCE: CHAPTER 9 QUIZ

The purpose of this experience is to help you gauge your present knowledge of issues related to death, dying, and bereavement. Upon completion of this activity, you will be able to:

1. Assess your knowledge of beliefs and behaviors related to the end of life.
2. Gain feedback on your knowledge of important end-of-life issues.

Time required: 30 minutes (10 minutes to complete the quiz and 20 minutes to discuss your answers in class).

Instructions:

1. Complete the quiz.
2. Your instructor will lead a review of the answers to the quiz in class.

Quiz Items	True	False
1. Wakes can occur before or after burial.	____	____
2. The last will and testament is an example of an advance care directive.	____	____
3. Hospice care is the same as palliative care.	____	____
4. African Americans use hospice care more than other ethnic groups.	____	____
5. The Catholic religion is the primary determinant of Latino end-of-life rituals.	____	____

6. Not all American Indian tribes believe in an afterlife. ____ ____

7. For Muslims, it is essential to have faith in afterlife. ____ ____

8. In the Islamic faith, Day of Judgment refers to the day the person dies. ____ ____

9. In the Hindu and Buddhist traditions, death is viewed as a transition from one mode of life to another. ____ ____

10. Buddhist Vietnamese elders in the United States give considerable thought to end-of-life care. ____ ____

11. According to the Islamic faith, the dead are to be turned to face in the direction of Mecca immediately after death occurs. ____ ____

12. Compared with the White population, the ratio of widows to widowers is significantly lower among Black Americans. ____ ____

13. Fear of death varies among tribes of American Indians. ____ ____

14. The ancestral shrine in the homes of many Japanese families fosters communication with deceased family members. ____ ____

15. Islamic texts provide limited discussion regarding death. ____ ____

GLOSSARY

advance care directives: Instructions to direct medical care in the event that one cannot communicate one's wishes. Advance care directives can include verbal instructions given to a health-care proxy or family members, a medical power of attorney (also called a durable power of attorney for health care), or a living will.

akhira: An Arabic word used in Islam to refer to the next world; hereafter.

death certificate: A legal document signed by a coroner or health professional that certifies the death of a person. This document is needed for many legal processes ranging from the handling of the remains (e.g., burial) to settling the deceased person's assets. The U.S. government uses the information gathered from death certificates to determine vital statistics on cause of death and to examine gender and ethnic disparities in cause of death.

dunya': An Arabic word for life in this world.

hospice: A program providing palliative care and supportive services aimed at addressing the emotional, social, financial, and legal needs of terminally ill patients and their family members.

last will and testament: This legal document specifies how one's assets (e.g., one's property, financial holdings) should be distributed upon one's death.

living will: An example of an advance care directive. A living will is a written, legal document containing health-care instructions in the event of a terminal illness or other life-threatening condition. Living wills may include directions concerning certain procedures that a person does not want performed under specific circumstances. The laws for living wills may vary from state to state.

palliative care program: A program providing specialized medical care, drugs, or therapies to manage acute or chronic pain and to control other systems. The program is run by specially trained physicians and other clinicians. It also offers services such as counseling about advance directives, spiritual care, and social services to seriously ill patients and their family members.

viewing: Often held the day before the funeral, the viewing allows family and friends to see the deceased person. Sometimes this is also called a wake.

vigil: Being with the person who is dying.

wake: The time for family and friends to gather and console the surviving family members. This ceremony differs depending on the culture. For some cultures, this ceremony happens prior to funeral services and may involve solemn ritual (e.g., saying the rosary) or dancing and having alcoholic drinks. In other cultures, it occurs after the funeral service.

SUGGESTED READINGS

Becker, G. (2002). Dying away from home: Quandaries of migration for elders in two ethnic groups. *Journal of Gerontology: Social Sciences, 57B*(2), S79–S95.

This easy-to-read paper by an anthropologist describes how Cambodian Americans and Filipino Americans view their homeland in old age and how these views affect the contemplation of death. The author found that (1) many members of the two groups have a desire to die in their homeland; and (2) whether they desire to return to the homeland to die was mediated by the presence or absence of the extended family, memories of the homeland, and the availability of ritual practices in the United States.

Blevins, D., & Werth Jr., J. L. (2006). End-of-life issues for LGBT older adults. In D. Kimmel, T. Rose, & S. David (Eds.), *Lesbian, gay, bisexual and transgender aging: Research and clinical perspectives* (pp. 206–226). New York: Columbia University Press.

This chapter examines the issues faced by LGBT older adults at the end of life. It includes a discussion of issues of stigma, discrimination, and prejudice and legal issues that can affect the end-of-life care for LGBT elders.

Chatterjee, S. C., Patnaik, P., and Chariar, V. M. (Eds.) (2008). *Discourses on aging and dying.* New Delhi, India: SAGE.

This valuable volume from India is divided into three sections. The first provides a rich spectrum of cosmologies and religious beliefs—Hindu, Buddhist, and Islamic—that interpret the place of death in our lives. The second section presents information about current conditions and problems of older people in India. The third section deals with critical issues in end-of-life care for the elders, including ethical issues on dignity and end-of-life decisions for the dying.

DeCourtney, C. A., Jones, K., Merriman, M. P., Heavener, N., & Branch, P. K. (2003). Establishing a culturally sensitive palliative care program in rural Alaska Native American communities. *Journal of Palliative Medicine, 6*(3), 501–510.

This journal article describes a program developed by the Bristol Bay Health Corporation to allow Native Alaskan elders the ability to die at home rather than in hospitals and nursing homes far from their communities.

Institute of Medicine. (2000). *Working together: We can help people get good care when they are dying.* Retrieved from: http://www.nap.edu/catalog.php?record_id=9798

"This 16-page booklet summarizes the findings from the 1997 report, *Approaching Death: Improving Care at the End of Life,* for the lay reader. Approaching Death reflects a wide-ranging effort to understand what we know about care at the end of life, what we have yet to learn, and what we know but do not adequately apply. It seeks to build understanding of what constitutes good care for the dying and offers recommendations to decision makers that address specific barriers to achieving good care."

Irish, D. P., Lundquist, K. F., & Nelsen, V. J. (Eds.). (1993). *Ethnic variations in dying, death and grief: Diversity in universality.* Philadelphia, PA: Taylor & Francis.

An excellent resource on diversity, death, and grief, this book includes a chapter on cross-cultural variation in grief as well as separate chapters on African American, Mexican American, Hmong, Native American, Jewish, Buddhist, Islamic, Quaker, and Unitarian death customs. A chapter on personal reflections on grief, death, and diversity includes a variety of learning activities.

Kalish, R. A., & Reynolds, D. K. (1976). *Death and ethnicity: A psychocultural study.* Los Angeles: University of Southern California Press. Andrus Gerontology Center.

Subsequently reprinted in 1981 by Baywood Publisher, this classic study focuses on the topic of death and ethnicity. Kalish and Reynolds completed an exhaustive analysis of African American, Japanese American, Mexican American, and Anglo subjects on numerous death-related topics. They also included observations, interviews with professionals in death-related fields, and content analyses of newspapers.

Smith, J. I., & Haddad, Y. Y. (1981). *The Islamic understanding of death and resurrection.* Albany: State University of New York Press.

This authoritative text familiarizes Westerners with Islamic teachings on death and resurrection through the use of religious and philosophical sources. The book is written in such a way that the reader does not need to have prior knowledge of Islam and Islamic cultures.

Wilkinson, A. M., & Lynn, J. (2001). The end of life. In R. H. Binstock & L. K. George (Eds.), *Handbook of aging and the social sciences* (5th ed., pp. 444–461). San Diego: Academic Press.

This handbook chapter presents a detailed summary of end-of-life issues for elders from mainstream populations in the United States. It includes information about how the experience of death has changed historically, summarizes research about patients' and families' experience of the end of life, and addresses areas in which the health-care system is failing to meet the needs of people at the end of life.

AUDIOVISUAL RESOURCES

203 Days   This film looks at the day-to-day interactions between terminal patients and caregivers, in this case an 89-year-old woman who is living with her daughter. 27 minutes. Available from http://fitsweb.uchc.edu/days/days.html.

On Our Own Terms   This television series hosted by Bill Moyers examines important topics around death, dying, and bereavement. This 4-part, 6-hour series includes personal stories and information about end-of-life care and end-of-life decisions. It features programs such as the Balm of Gilead Center, which promotes palliative care in Alabama African American communities. 6 hours. Available from http://www.pbs.org/wnet/onourownterms.

KEY: CHAPTER 9 QUIZ

1. True. Although traditionally a wake occurs prior to the funeral and burial, the traditions around wakes vary by ethnicity and religious background. For Lakota American Indians, wakes are a 3-day event that encompasses the funeral and burial (Brokenleg & Middleton, 1993). Similarly, for some Latin American groups, the wake may extend after the burial as family and friends gather (Younoszai, 1993). In England, wakes occur after the burial when friends and family gather to support the family and to share companionship and food.

2. False. The last will and testament includes instructions for the distribution of one's worldly goods (e.g., property, financial holdings) and is not a type of advance care directive. This should be distinguished from a living will, which is a legal document containing instructions for the kinds of health-care procedures that an individual would like to have (or does not want to have performed) if the person becomes incapacitated and cannot speak for himself or herself. A living will is an example of an advance care directive.

3. False. Hospice care refers to care provided to an individual who has received a prognosis from a physician that he or she has a terminal condition, is not expected to live more than 6 months, and who agrees to forgo any curative treatments (e.g., chemotherapy) for his or her condition. Because hospice care is often covered by Medicare or other insurance, restrictions apply to who can receive the care and to the type of care that they can receive. Palliative care refers to the total care provided to an individual whose disease does not respond to treatment (Ferrell & Coyle, 2002). Hospice care is an example of palliative care, but because palliative care can be provided outside of the 6-month prognosis, hospice care is not the same as palliative care.

4. False. African Americans are less likely than White Americans to use hospice care. Choosing hospice care also means forgoing curative treatment for one's condition, and African Americans are more likely to request interventions to prolong life, even when death appears to be very near (Hooyman & Kiyak, 2008).

5. False. Latino American end-of-life rituals are a complex blend of influences from the Catholic Church, from different American Indian tribes, and from the Caribbean. This blend differs depending on the ethnic background and national origin of the person— Puerto Ricans have rituals that differ from Cuban Americans who have rituals that differ from Mexican Americans—although all of these groups are influenced in some degree by the Catholic Church (Younoszai, 1993).

6. True. Although most American Indian and Alaska Native groups do believe in an afterlife, the Navajo do not (Brokenleg & Middleton, 1993).

7. True. Faith in afterlife is essential to being Muslim. This belief provides the incentive for acting responsibly in this life—for growing, developing, and improving (Smith & Haddad, 1981).

8. False. The Day of Judgment refers to the day when all bodies will be resurrected and all persons called to account for their deeds and for the measure of their faith (see Figure 9.1).

9. True. Since Hindus and Buddhists believe in reincarnation, they view death as a transition from one life to another. They, therefore, approach death without anxiety; it is simply a passage into the next life.

10. False. While Buddhist Vietnamese elders may prepare for rituals of death, they do not carry out active end-of-life care planning. Braun and Nichols (1996) found that few Vietnamese elders were familiar with the options regarding advance directives. They believe that their children will take the necessary steps.

11. True. It is imperative that a close relative turn the body to face Mecca immediately after death occurs (Gilanshah, 1993).

12. False. Since Black men have lower life expectancy compared with Black women and White men, Black women are typically widowed earlier than White women. This means that the ratio of widows to widowers is significantly higher among Black women than among White women.

13. True. Attitudes concerning death vary dramatically from tribe to tribe. Many Pueblos and Navajos express intense anxiety concerning death while Chiricahua, Lipan, Mescalero, and Jicarilla Apache demonstrate little fear of their own demise (Brokenleg & Middleton, 1993; Markides & Mindel, 1987).

14. True. In a sample of Buddhist and Christian Japanese American widows, 65% of the respondents said that having a shrine in their home helped them to sense the presence of their dead husbands (Kalish & Reynolds, 1976).

15. False. In the Islamic texts death is discussed so frequently that it appears as if a Muslim is taught more about life after death than about the life itself.

REFERENCES

Becker, G. (2002). Dying away from home: Quandaries of migration for elders in two ethnic groups. *Journal of Gerontology: Social Sciences, 57B*(2), S79–S95.

Braun, K. L., & Nichols, R. (1996). Cultural issues in death and dying. *Hawaii Medical Journal, 55*(12), 260–264.

Brokenleg, M., & Middleton, D. (1993). Native Americans: Adapting, yet retaining. In D. P. Irish, K. F. Lundquist, & V. J. Nelsen (Eds.), *Ethnic variations in dying, death and grief: Diversity in universality* (pp. 101–112). Philadelphia, PA: Taylor & Francis.

Crawford, A. (1961). *Customs and culture in Vietnam*. Tokyo, Japan: Charles E. Tuttle.

Dilworth-Anderson, P. D., Gibson, B. E., & Burke, J. D. (2006). Working with African American families. In G. Yeo & D. Gallagher-Thompson (Eds.), *Ethnicity and the dementias* (pp. 127–145). New York: Routledge Taylor & Francis Group.

Dosa, D. M. (2007). A day in the life of Oscar the cat. *New England Journal of Medicine, 357*, 328–329.

Eisenbruch, M. (1984). Cross-cultural aspects of bereavement:II: Ethnic and cultural variations in the development of bereavement practices. *Culture, Medicine and Psychiatry, 8*(4), 315–347.

Eleazer, G. P., Hornung, C. A., Egbert, C. B., Egbert, J. R., Eng, C., Hedgepeth, J., et al. (1996). The relationship between ethnicity and advance directives in a frail older population. *Journal of the American Geriatrics Society, 44*(8), 938–943.

Esposito, J. L. (2002). *What everyone needs to know about Islam*. New York: Oxford University Press.

Federal Interagency Forum on Aging-Related Statistics. (2006). *Older Americans update 2006: Key indicators of well-being*. Washington, DC: U.S. Government Printing Office.

Ferrell, B. R., & Coyle, N. (2002). An overview of palliative nursing care. *American Journal of Nursing, 102*(5), 26–31.

Firth, S. (1999). Spirituality and ageing in British Hindus, Sikhs and Muslims. In A. Jewell (Ed.), *Spirituality and ageing* (pp. 158–174). London: Jessica Kingsley Publishers.

Gilanshah, F. (1993). Islamic customs regarding death. In D. P. Irish, K. F. Lundquist, & V. J. Nelsen (Eds.), *Ethnic variations in dying, death and grief: Diversity in universality* (pp. 137–145). Philadelphia, PA: Taylor & Francis.

Hooyman, N., & Kiyak, H. A. (2008). *Social gerontology: A multidisciplinary perspective* (8th ed.). Boston, MA: Allyn and Bacon.

Kalish, R. A., & Reynolds, D. K. (1976). *Death and ethnicity: A psychocultural study*. Los Angeles: University of Southern California Press.

Kemp, C., & Bhungalia, S. (2002). Culture and the end of life: A review of major world religions. *Journal of Hospice & Palliative Nursing, 4*(4), 235–242.

Kornblatt, S., Eng, C., & Hansen, J. C. (2002, Fall). Cultural awareness in health and social services: The experience of On Lok. *Generations*, 46–53.

Kubler-Ross, E. (1969). *On death and dying*. New York: Macmillan.

Lynn, J. (2000). Learning to care for people with chronic illness facing the end of life. *Journal of the American Medical Association, 284*(19), 2508–2511.

Markides, K. S., & Mindel, C. H. (1987). *Aging & ethnicity*. Newbury Park, CA: Sage.

Mbiti, J. S. (1991). *Introduction to African religion* (2nd ed.). Oxford, England: Heinemann Educational Publishers.

Narada. (1973). *The Buddha and his teachings*. Colombo, Sri Lanka: Vajirarama.

Nelsen, V. J. (1993). One woman's interracial journey. In D. P. Irish, K. F. Lundquist, & V. J. Nelsen (Eds.), *Ethnic variations in dying, death, and grief: Diversity in universality* (pp. 21–27). Philadelphia, PA: Taylor & Francis.

Perry, H. L. (1993). Mourning and funeral customs of African Americans. In D. P. Irish, K. F. Lundquist, & V. J. Nelsen (Eds.), *Ethnic variations in dying, death and grief: Diversity in universality* (pp. 51–65). Philadelphia, PA: Taylor & Francis.

Pew Research Center. (2007). *Muslim Americans: Middle class and mostly mainstream*. Retrieved March 18, 2008 from: http://pewresearch.org/assets/pdf/muslim-americans.pdf

Smith, J. I., & Haddad, Y. Y. (1981). *The Islamic understanding of death and resurrection*. Albany: State University of New York Press.

Spector, R. E. (1991). *Cultural diversity in health and illness* (3rd ed.). Norwalk, CT: Appleton & Lange.

Stannard, D. E. (1977). *The puritan way of death: A study in religion, culture, and social change.* New York: Oxford University Press.

Taylor, R. J., Chatters, L. M., & Levin, J. (2004). *Religion in the lives of African Americans: Social, psychological and health perspectives.* Thousand Oaks, CA: Sage.

Tilak, S. (1989). *Religion and aging in the Indian tradition.* Albany: State University of New York Press.

Truitner, K., & Truitner, N. (1993). Death and dying in Buddhism. In D. P. Irish, K. F. Lundquist, & V. J. Nelsen (Eds.), *Ethnic variations in dying, death and grief: Diversity in universality* (pp. 125–136). Philadelphia, PA: Taylor & Francis.

Younoszai, B. (1993). Mexican American perspectives related to death. In D. P. Irish, K. F. Lundquist, & V. J. Nelsen (Eds.), *Ethnic variations in dying, death and grief: Diversity in universality* (pp. 67–78). Philadelphia, PA: Taylor & Francis.

Epilogue

BRINGING IT ALL TOGETHER

The whole purpose of this text has been to engage you with the study of aging and diversity through active participation in the learning process. Drawing on theory, research, and practice, we have presented what is important and useful in making a difference in the lives of older adults from diverse ethnic and cultural groups. Throughout the text we have tried to maximize your responsibility for your own learning and have encouraged you to obtain hands-on experience using your newly acquired knowledge, your powers of observation, and your interpersonal skills. We have provided learning experiences that involve discussion with peers and opportunities for mutual support and interaction. Our aim throughout has been to provide you with opportunities for elaboration—putting material into your own words—as well as a chance to begin interpreting the observations in light of research we have presented. We have also invited you to share your responses to the questions from the exercises interspersed throughout the text.

Our experience indicates that such discussions stimulate learners to explain concepts and principles, to express opinions, to admit confusion, and to reveal misconceptions; at the same time, these interactions give learners a chance to listen to their peers, to respond to their questions, to question their opinion, and to provide information to clear up confusion. This, in turn, contributes to changing attitudes, to the development of problem solving abilities, and to enhancing interpersonal skills. In addition to completing learning exercises that require discussions with peers, you have also completed questions for chapter quizzes and have compared your answers with those we have provided. Our hope is that this feedback was helpful and allowed you to identify what you have learned well and what not so well.

Continuing this active learning approach, we have designed the following exercise to foster the integration of the concepts, principles, and assumptions with the concreteness of day-to-day life. We believe that integrative learning experiences take on new meaning and vitality when they are directly connected with integrative challenges of working with older adults and their families. As noted earlier, we also believe that a rich source of integrative development lies in the dialogue with peers and those from other age groups. We hope that completing this exercise will allow you to synthesize what you have learned in different chapters, will provide you an opportunity to reflect on the importance of what you have learned, and will satisfy your own yearning for relevance and immediacy.

ACTIVE LEARNING EXPERIENCE: INTEGRATIVE FINAL PROJECT

The purpose of this experience is to provide you with an opportunity to integrate the topics addressed in each chapter into a coherent understanding of a given person's experience with aging in the United States. Upon completion of this activity, you will be able to:

1. Describe the primary strengths and challenges that this person will have, and
2. Compare them with the information about different people presented by your fellow students.

Time required: Variable depending upon instructor's wishes and adaptations.

Instructions:

1. Choose a fictional person as the focus of your project. Your instructor may assign the characteristics of this person to you (e.g., by drawing from a hat), or you may select the person's characteristics yourself. In either case, the person should be a member of one of the ethnic minority groups we have covered in this book (African American, Latino American, Asian American, American Indian or Alaska Native). The person's sex, sexual orientation, socioeconomic status, religious affiliation, and rural or urban location should also be specified. Finally, the person must be over the age of 65 with one or more health-related concerns.
2. Review each book chapter to consider the concepts presented in each and how they relate to your person. For example, from Chapter 1, you may want to determine the demographics of your person's cultural groups and how this relates to his or her experience of aging. In Chapter 2, you may want to consider the experience that this person may have had with research and researchers and what steps researchers may need to take to include this person in research. With each chapter, you are likely to need to conduct additional reading about your particular person's groups. Feel free to use the aging and diversity online sections and the suggested readings at the end of each chapter as starting points for that reading. Additional readings may be found on scholarly databases such as Pubmed and Psychinfo.
3. Compile the information that you have gained (from the textbook, online, and more scholarly resources) into a coherent description of the strengths that this person brings to aging and the challenges

that this person may face while aging. Define and apply relevant concepts from this book throughout your description.

4. Prepare a 20-minute presentation that conveys the most important information from item 3.

5. Write a 10- to 15-page term paper that conveys this person's experience with aging.

Note to Instructors

This learning exercise can be adapted to suit your individual needs and your students' abilities and interests. For example, in many college settings, PowerPoint presentations by all students can provide a good opportunity for integration of the textbook material while simultaneously exposing the students to the different characteristics that each student investigated. Similarities and differences across groups can be seen easily. By necessity, presentations like these need to be fairly short, so a more detailed term paper (with appropriate citation of all sources) can aid assessment of an individual student's true understanding of important course concepts. For courses in which the instructor is more flexible with writing style, students could write magazine-style articles (complete with photographs) in which they tell the story of their fictional person. Additional adaptations can be made to make this a group project with each group focused on one primary ethnic group (for example) and then each group member taking different characteristics within that group. The project is limited only by your imagination and course requirements, but our intention is to provide a sample assignment that would promote integration and reflection on aging and diversity.

Index

F